Reprint of document originally issued
by the U. S. Government Printing Office
entitled TOWARD ECONOMIC DEVELOPMENT FOR NATIVE AMERICAN COMMUNITIES

AMERICAN INDIANS:
FACTS AND FUTURE

TOWARD ECONOMIC DEVELOPMENT
FOR NATIVE AMERICAN COMMUNITIES

AMERICAN INDIANS:

FACTS AND FUTURE

TOWARD ECONOMIC DEVELOPMENT
FOR NATIVE AMERICAN COMMUNITIES

Joint Economic Committee   ☆   Congress of the United States

ARNO PRESS

A Publishing and Library Service of The New York Times

Reprint Edition 1970 by Arno Press Inc.
Library of Congress Card No.   76-128179
ISBN   0-405-02561-0
Manufactured in the United States of America

91st Congress }   JOINT COMMITTEE PRINT
1st Session }

TOWARD ECONOMIC DEVELOPMENT
FOR NATIVE AMERICAN COMMUNITIES

A COMPENDIUM OF PAPERS

SUBMITTED TO THE

SUBCOMMITTEE ON ECONOMY IN GOVERNMENT

OF THE

JOINT ECONOMIC COMMITTEE
CONGRESS OF THE UNITED STATES

Part I: DEVELOPMENT PROSPECTS AND PROBLEMS
Part II: DEVELOPMENT PROGRAMS AND PLANS
Part III: THE RESOURCE BASE

Printed for the use of the Joint Economic Committee

U.S. GOVERNMENT PRINTING OFFICE
31–685   WASHINGTON : 1969

JOINT ECONOMIC COMMITTEE

[Created pursuant to sec. 5 (a) of Public Law 304, 79th Cong.]

WRIGHT PATMAN, Texas, *Chairman*
WILLIAM PROXMIRE, Wisconsin, *Vice Chairman*

HOUSE OF REPRESENTATIVES

RICHARD BOLLING, Missouri
HALE BOGGS, Louisiana
HENRY S. REUSS, Wisconsin
MARTHA W. GRIFFITHS, Michigan
WILLIAM S. MOORHEAD, Pennsylvania
WILLIAM B. WIDNALL, New Jersey
W. E. BROCK III, Tennessee
BARBER B. CONABLE, JR., New York
CLARENCE J. BROWN, Ohio

SENATE

JOHN SPARKMAN, Alabama
J. W. FULBRIGHT, Arkansas
HERMAN E. TALMADGE, Georgia
STUART SYMINGTON, Missouri
ABRAHAM RIBICOFF, Connecticut
JACOB K. JAVITS, New York
JACK MILLER, Iowa
LEN B. JORDAN, Idaho
CHARLES H. PERCY, Illinois

JOHN R. STARK, *Executive Director*
JAMES W. KNOWLES, *Director of Research*

ECONOMISTS

LOUGHLIN F. McHUGH   JOHN R. KARLIK   RICHARD F. KAUFMAN

COURTENAY M. SLATER

Minority: DOUGLAS C. FRECHTLING   GEORGE D. KRUMBHARR

SUBCOMMITTEE ON ECONOMY IN GOVERNMENT

WILLIAM PROXMIRE, Wisconsin, *Chairman*

SENATE

JOHN SPARKMAN, Alabama
STUART SYMINGTON, Missouri
LEN B. JORDAN, Idaho
CHARLES H. PERCY, Illinois

HOUSE OF REPRESENTATIVES

WRIGHT PATMAN, Texas
MARTHA W. GRIFFITHS, Michigan
WILLIAM S. MOORHEAD, Pennsylvania
BARBER B. CONABLE, JR., New York
CLARENCE J. BROWN, Ohio

FRAZIER KELLOGG, *Economist*

(II)

LETTERS OF TRANSMITTAL

DECEMBER 18, 1969.

To the Members of the Joint Economic Committee:

Transmitted herewith for the use of the members of the Joint Economic Committee and other Members of Congress is a two-volume study entitled "Toward Economic Development for Native American Communities," prepared for the Subcommittee on Economy in Government.

The views expressed in this document do not necessarily represent the views of the members of the committee or the committee staff, but are statements of issues and alternatives intended to enlarge public knowledge of the subject and to provide a focus for further discussion.

WRIGHT PATMAN.
Chairman, Joint Economic Committee.

DECEMBER 17, 1969.

Hon. WRIGHT PATMAN,
Chairman, Joint Economic Committee,
Congress of the United States,
Washington, D.C.

DEAR MR. CHAIRMAN : Transmitted herewith is a two-volume compendium of study papers entitled "Toward Economic Development for Native American Communities." The compendium is intended to serve as a resource document for members of the Joint Economic Committee, other Members of Congress, and others who are concerned with formulating and executing effective policies of economic development for American Indian and Alaskan native communities.

The papers in this compendium document the fact that, despite greatly increased levels of Federal assistance, the vast majority of native Americans continue to live in extreme poverty and deprivation. The need for a searching evaluation of Federal Indian policies is apparent. Many new types of economic assistance programs have been instituted by the Federal Government in the past 5 or 6 years. Some of these appear to hold considerable promise for the future, but the lack of adequate evaluation has made it difficult to know which policies are working and which are not. This compendium is intended to help put current policies in perspective and to suggest appropriate directions for the future.

The compendium contains contributions by a number of invited individual experts, statements by Federal agencies having responsibility for various programs to assist native Americans, and statements by organizations representing native groups. The subcommittee is indebted to the authors for their excellent contributions and to the various Federal agencies for their cooperation in this endeavor.

As the Executive Director's letter indicates, the compendium should not be interpreted as an expression of views or conclusions by the subcommittee, its individual members, or the committee staff.

WILLIAM PROXMIRE,
Chairman, Subcommittee on Economy in Government.

DECEMBER 16, 1969.

Hon. WILLIAM PROXMIRE,
*Chairman, Subcommittee on Economy in Government, Joint Economic
Committee, U.S. Congress, Washington, D.C.*

DEAR SENATOR PROXMIRE: Transmitted herewith is a two-volume
study entitled "Toward Economic Development for Native American
Communities." The study addresses itself to the serious problems of
poverty and economic insecurity found in native American communities and to the apparent inability of the Federal Government to provide effective assistance in improving the economic situations of American Indian and Alaskan native groups.

The compendium contains papers by invited individual experts,
statements by Federal agencies, and statements by native organizations. It is intended as a resource document for Members of Congress
and others concerned with achieving an effective Federal policy in this
area. By providing historical background, descriptions of new programs instituted in the 1960's, assessment of current economic and social conditions, and suggestions for future policy directions, the study
can form a basis for informed discussion and necessary action.

Frazier Kellogg had staff responsibility for compiling and editing
the compendium. He was assisted in the earlier stages by Michael J.
Duberstein, and throughout the study he had the administrative and
secretarial assistance of Mrs. Anne McAfee. The papers in the compendium represent the views of their authors, and should not be interpreted as reflecting the opinions of members of the Joint Economic
Committee or the committee staff.

JOHN R. STARK,
Executive Director, Joint Economic Committee.

CONTENTS

Part II: DEVELOPMENT PROGRAMS AND PLANS

Part III: THE RESOURCE BASE

INTRODUCTION

The Subcommittee on Economy in Government has devoted much of its activity in the past year to public expenditure policy, both in respect to (a) determination of priorities, and (b) assuring greater effectiveness of program. Examination of the effectiveness of Federal programs concentrated for the most part on defense spending and to a lesser extent on the question of public works evaluation. Obviously, there are many other public programs that warrant attention from the point of view of program effectiveness. Our Indian programs are an obvious candidate for such attention. While expenditures for this purpose constitute but a small part of the total budget, past failure to apply necessary funds effectively have incurred large costs in human terms. Now, with the renewed emphasis on economic rehabilitation that characterizes our efforts to improve the impoverished sectors of the U.S. economy, it seemed an appropriate time for the subcommittee to undertake this review of our Indian policy objectives and our programs to achieve them. This compendium is intended to aid the Congress in its consideration of means to improve the presently intolerable situation of the Indian population in the United States.

The need to preserve economic and social opportunities for native Americans—the American Indians and the Alaskan native groups—has troubled thoughtful citizens virtually ever since the arrival of the first white settlers on the American Continent. The Federal Government has now had official trust responsibilities for the American Indians for well over 100 years. A variety of different Indian policies have been tried out, ranging from efforts to completely assimilate the Indians into the dominant white culture and economy, thus causing them to disappear as a separate group, to efforts to preserve traditional Indian societies totally intact and totally divorced from the rest of the American economy. These various policy efforts would seem to have had only one thing in common: none of them worked. The American Indians continue to be the most poverty-stricken group in American society. Perhaps three-quarters of reservation Indian families have incomes below the poverty level, unemployment exceeds one-third of the reservation labor force, educational opportunity and attainment are substantially below the national average, and many Indian communities would appear to have developed attitudes of total discouragement and hopelessness.

Certainly predominant public attitudes toward the American Indians have not always been ones of concern and good intentions. But even where intentions have been of the best, remarkably little appears to have been achieved in the way of actually improving Indian living conditions. Recently there has emerged a great deal of public concern for the impoverished and disadvantaged groups in our society, and this concern has been reflected in substantially increased Federal expenditure on Indian programs. Total Federal expenditure on programs to assist the Indians and the Alaskan natives is now in the neighborhood of $500 million per year. Many new programs of economic development assistance have been introduced in the last 5 or 6 years, and a number of Government agencies have become involved in these programs. In addition, there seems to be an increased awareness of the need to have the Indians participate fully in planning their own future.

All these are hopeful signs. Good intentions, a willingness to make the necessary financial investments, and respect for the Indian's right to self-determination are fundamental to any successful program to improve economic conditions, but they are only the beginning. In order to plan and implement a successful economic development effort, it is necessary to know which specific programs will work and under what circumstances. Among the questions which need answering are:

- What are the potentials of the natural resource base found on the Indian reservations?
- How can this potential be utilized?
- What types of industry can operate with economic efficiency on the reservations?
- How can these industries be encouraged to locate there?
- How much and what kind of job training is required?
- How will development on the reservation affect the surrounding region and vice versa?
- What is the appropriate role of the Federal Government in Indian economic development and which agencies should be given which responsibilities?

These questions and many others require answers. If they are not answered, current efforts to assist the Indians will be no more successful than past efforts. Some of the answers can be found through a thorough evaluation of past and current programs, particularly the proliferation of new programs which have been instituted since about 1963. The Joint Economic Committee's compendium is addressed to the specifics of economic development, and it includes descriptions and evaluations of the new efforts of the 1960's. The compendium is thus intended to make a contribution not only to the stimulation of public concern regarding the plight of the American Indians, but also to the knowledge and understanding required to translate this concern into successful action.

The publication of this compendium follows closely upon the release of the report of the U.S. Senate's Special Subcommittee on Indian Education, a report which makes recommendations for improving not only the education but the total social and economic environment of the American Indians.[1] Education and economic development are obviously too closely interrelated to be considered in isolation from each other. Material in the Joint Economic Committee's compendium should form a useful part of the background information needed to evaluate and carry out the recommendations of the Special Subcommittee on Indian Education.

Part I of the compendium contains 16 studies by outstanding experts. These studies summarize current economic conditions among the American Indians, the frustrations and failures of earlier assistance efforts, the mixed results of the new initiatives undertaken since 1963,

---

[1] U.S. Senate, Committee on Labor and Public Welfare, Special Subcommittee on Indian Education, *Indian Education: A National Tragedy—A National Challenge*, Nov. 3, 1969.

and the history of Indians' own attitudes toward Federal assistance programs. They also contain a number of recommendations for the future direction of Federal policy. The first article in Part I describes the serious deficiencies of current statistical information. The lack of sufficient statistical data makes adequate evaluation of present Federal Indian policies almost impossible. New policy planning cannot proceed rationally until it can be learned which current policies are producing results and which are not.

Several subsequent articles describe the social and economic conditions in which Indian famililies now live. On many reservations, extreme poverty and high unemployment are coupled with dependency on Federal welfare programs and a sense of despair born out of the failure of past efforts to improve living conditions. Because long-endured poverty has led to this sense of frustration and despair as well as to serious health problems, economic development efforts will succeed only if they are accompanied by the necessary programs of social rehabilitation, including improved education and health care and the provision of adequate housing.

If economic development among the Indians is to succeed, it must be compatible with the Indians' own sense of values. It is now widely recognized, as unfortunately it often was not in the past, that the Indian does not wish to abandon his identity and his traditional cultural and social values and to become completely assimilated into an acquisitive, capitalistic society. Indian cultures place high value on preservation of the natural environment, on sharing of material goods among the extended family and the tribe, and on maintaining a life style which allows time for quiet leisure and contemplation. The Indians have no wish to abandon these values in favor of industrial society's emphasis on individual competitive achievement and frenetic activity. The problem the Indians face is to come to terms with the surrounding industrial society in a way which permits them to maintain a decent standard of living while still remaining true to their own culture. Achieving compatability between these two somewhat conflicting objectives is obviously not easily done. Failure to recognize and solve this conflict is undoubtedly a large factor in explaining the overall failure of past Federal efforts to assist the Indians.

Part I of the compendium also contains discussions of job training and industrialization efforts sponsored by the Bureau of Indian Affairs, the Labor Department, and other Federal agencies. These articles emphasize the great variety of situations found among different Indian groups. Among the specific situations discussed are the economic status of the large Navajo reservation, the adjustment problems faced by Indians who migrate to an urban environment, and the special problems faced by rural Indians who do not live on reservations.

Part II of the compendium contains statements by Federal agencies which have responsibility for programs affecting the American Indian and by native organizations. These statements not only describe present programs, but provide various views of currently unmet needs and the manner in which programs should go forward in the future. The Bureau of Indian Affairs has, of course, long been the agency primarily concerned with programs of Indian economic development. While this agency still has a major share of the responsibility for economic development programs, several other agencies have, in recent years, become involved in important ways. The Economic Development Administration and the Office of Economic Opportunity are cooperating in a program of industrial and community development on a selected group of reservations judged to have the greatest development potential. The manpower and job placement services of the Department of Labor, the rural development programs of the Department of Agriculture, and the loan and management assistance programs of the Small Business Administration are available to Indians, and these agencies are undertaking special efforts to assure that Indians have full access to these programs. The Department of Health, Education, and Welfare administers an extensive Indian health services program and has established an Office of Indian Affairs to assure that Indians are aware of and full participants in other HEW programs.

Although the situation of the reservation Indian is often described as one of frustration and despair, it would be a serious mistake to think that the Indians are making no organized effort to improve their own economic situation. A statement prepared for this compendium by the National Congress of American Indians, an organization representing over 100 tribes, outlines extensive plans for assisting Indian tribes in development planning and in making maximum use of available Federal programs. A statement by the Oklahomans for Indian Opportunity describes this relatively new organization and indicates the substantial progress which can be made when local concern and desire for self-improvement are effectively mobilized. A statement by the Alaska Federation of Natives describes their position with respect to disposition of the extensive and valuable Alaskan land areas currently under dispute. The particular problems of Alaskan natives and the importance to them of an equitable settlement to this land dispute are also discussed elsewhere in the compendium in two excerpts from the report of the Federal Field Committee for Development Planning in Alaska.

Part III of the compendium discusses the resource base available to the American Indians. The total land area set aside as Indian reservations is, of course, no longer adequate to support a traditional Indian economy based on hunting and grazing. Nor do agricultural pursuits offer much opportunity for improvement in economic conditions. For some Indian tribes, agriculture is simply not a traditional pursuit. Other tribes once had economies based on agriculture, but, like other small and poorly financed farmers, now find themselves with no place in a modern mechanized agricultural industry.

Indian lands do contain valuable forest and mineral resources. One problem which severely complicates advantageous exploitation of these resources is the complicated land ownership situation. A substantial fraction of the Indian lands has at various times been awarded to individual Indians and held in trust for them by the Bureau of Indian Affairs. Through the process of inheritance, many of these parcels of land have come into multiple ownership. The administrative problems connected with management of land held in trust for multiple owners prevent effective use of these lands. In some cases, they prevent any use whatsoever. Effective land management will require some sort of consolidation and simplification of land ownership. In the arid and semiarid areas of the Southwestern United States, adequate rights to the use of water resources are another crucial element in economic development. The protection of Indian water rights and planning for the best use of these valuable rights must be an integral part of any development program.

Perhaps one of the most encouraging aspects of the current Indian situation is that substantial funds are becoming available to many of the tribes through awards by the Indian Claims Commission and through leasing of mineral rights on Indian lands. In the past, some of these funds have been distributed on a per capita basis and the remainder have been held in trust by the Federal Government, earning, in general, below-market rates of return. Recently some of these funds have been put to use in tribal development programs, but their potential for financing development remains largely unrealized. More effective use of these funds could go a long way toward financing economic development for some tribes. It must be remembered, however, that such funds are very unevenly distributed among the tribes and can thus represent only one part of a total solution to the problem of the Indians' needs for financial resources.

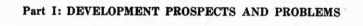

Part I: DEVELOPMENT PROSPECTS AND PROBLEMS

Toward Economic Development for Native American Communities

Part I: DEVELOPMENT PROSPECTS AND PROBLEMS

A STATISTICAL PROFILE OF THE INDIAN: THE LACK OF NUMBERS

By Stephen A. Langone*

FOREWORD

Efficient planning and execution of development programs must be based on accurate information concerning current economic and social conditions and changes in these conditions over time. Stephen A. Langone points out that such data is simply not available with respect to the American Indians. Information compiled on a reservation basis was more adequate a hundred years ago than it is at present, despite the fact that over this period Federal expenditures for Indian programs have risen from $7 million to perhaps $500 million (no one knows the exact total), and the number of Indians under Federal jurisdiction has risen from 290,000 to nearly 400,000. After describing and analyzing this current lack of information, Langone presents a detailed outline for an informational handbook on the American Indians designed to provide the economic and social data which are essential to any rational development program.

Introduction

The purpose of this paper is to point out the absence of adequate statistical information on the American Indian and the need for such information by the Federal Government, the various States, the tribes themselves and the private organizations active in the field. In the Library of Congress Main Catalog there are—under the heading *Indians of North America*—12 drawers of cards. Twelve drawers contain approximately 18,000 cards and of this number only 16 cards are under the subheading *Statistics* and 11 cards under the subheading *Census*. Yet under the subheadings *Pottery* and *Legends* there are 103 for the former and 314 for the latter. Under the subheadings *Population* and *Income* there are no cards at all. The only reason for this observation is to point out that a person with an interest in the American Indian can get much more information on subjects such as pottery and legends than he can on the income, educational attainment, land, etc., of the American Indian today.**

In any discussion concerning statistical information about the American Indian, his problems, and progress, one of the prime sources of information would seem to be the Annual Report of the Commissioner of

---

*Analyst, American Indian Affairs, Government and General Research Division, Legislative Reference Service, Library of Congress.

**Much of the material available from the Department of the Interior, Bureau of Indian Affairs on the American Indian is not available in public libraries because (1) there is no program to circulate such items to the libraries and (2) it is not combined in one publication that could be printed at the Government Printing Office and sent to depository libraries.

Indian Affairs. One hundred years ago—1869—the Annual Report of the Commissioner of Indian Affairs,[1] E. S. Parker, was published in book form and contained 619 pages of information. The report included a 42-page statement by the Commissioner concerning general problems, policy decisions during the year, and a summary of the situation at various field jurisdictions, then identified as: Washington, Oregon, California, Nevada, Arizona, Utah, New Mexico, Colorado, Wyoming, Idaho, Montana, Dakota, the Northern Superintendency (Nebraska), the Central Superintendency (Kansas, Indian Territory), the Southern Superintendency (Indian country south of Kansas and west of Arkansas), Independent Agencies, and Indians Not Embraced in Any Agency. Following the Commissioner's statement are reports from each agency, some miscellaneous reports concerning Indians, and a section on statistics (in addition to local statistics given throughout the report) 54 pages long, containing detailed tables on population, education, agriculture, trust funds, trust land sales, and liabilities of the U.S. Government.

In contrast the latest available Annual Report of the Commissioner [2]—1967 at this writing—contains 15 pages (double spaced) including approximately six pages of pictures. Statistical tables (two-thirds of one page) include (1) Awards by Indian Claims Commission; (2) Budget, Department of the Interior, Bureau of Indian Affairs; and (3) Income from Mineral and Surface Leasing of Indian Lands. Of course, the Bureau publishes separate reports that encompass other subjects, for example: *U.S. Indian Population and Land;*[3] *Statistics Concerning Indian Education,*[4] etc., but the population statistics are seven years old, those for land are six years old* and those for education are two years old.** The Bureau of Indian Affairs complies various statistical reports but they are either for administrative use only, or in some cases, not current enough for effective use. An example is the *Summary of Reservation Development Studies,*[5] a continuing study, begun "In response to a growing awareness of the need for more reliable human and natural resources data * * *." Other publications such as the *Annual Statistical Summary* [6] compiled by the Branch of Employment Assistance and the *Annual Report on Indian Lands* [7] would be of much more value to the entire Federal Government structure, the Indians and private organizations if they were (1) published together; (2) in a somewhat different from; and (3) covered the same period of time.

These observations are not intended as an indictment of the Bureau of Indian Affairs, but to illustrate that it is considerably easier for a

*There is a report with statistics up to June 30, 1968, but this is evidently for limited use since the older publication referred to is sent in answer to requests on Indian land.

**This report covers Indian students. It does not provide information on the education of the Indian labor force which would be very useful.

[1] U.S. Bureau of Indian Affairs. Report of the Commissioner of Indian Affairs made to the Secretary of the Interior for the year 1869. Washington. 1870. 619 p.
[2] U.S. Bureau of Indian Affairs. Indian Affairs 1967 ; a Progress Report from the Commissioner of Indian Affairs. Washington, 1968. 15 p.
[3] BIA. *U.S. Indian Population (1962) and Land (1963)*, 35 p.
    NOTE.—There is a later report published : *Annual Report on Indian Lands, June 30, 1968*, but evidently is only for Departmental use since the above is used for distribution.
[4] *Statistics Concerning Indian Education, Fiscal Year 1967* (latest available). 35 p.
[5] U.S. Department of the Interior. *Indians: Summary of Reservation Development Studies.* Fiscal Year 1970, September 24, 1968, 113 p.
[6] U.S. Bureau of Indian Affairs. Branch of Employment Assistance. *Annual Statistical Summary, 1968.* 123 p.
[7] U.S. Bureau of Indian Affairs. *Annual Report on Indian Lands.* June 30, 1968, 61 p.

researcher to study the conditions of the American Indian 100 years ago than it is to study conditions today. The information needed today is scattered, incomplete, and in some cases, unavailable, nonexistent, or contradictory. It is understandable that the Bureau of Indian Affairs statistical data is geared to the Bureau's own needs and limited by available funds and staff. But there is a real need for more complete and current information throughout the government.

In times past one of the finest sources of information was the annual report of each agency superintendent that appeared in the Bureau Annual Reports during the 1800's. Agency reports were a primary source providing a "bird's eye" view of the reservation, and any problems the Indians might have had, but the publication of such reports was discontinued early in this century. The absence of such reports today prevents the study of a given reservation—and the existing conditions—over a period of years. Whatever information is available, by agency, is generally found in congressional studies.

Keeping the comparative informational picture—1969 and 1869—in mind, we might point out that in 1869 the expenditure of the Bureau of Indian Affairs was $7,042,923, the agency had approximately 400 employees, and there were 289,778 Indians under the jurisdiction of the Federal Government. In fiscal year 1969, by contrast, the Bureau of Indian Affairs appropriation is approximately $250,000,000, the staff exceeds 16,000, and there are about 300,000 Indians living on trust land and 66,000 living nearby. In addition, the Department of Health Education, and Welfare spends about $150,000,000 per year and has a staff of over 6,000 people working on Indian programs. Other Government agencies such as the Office of Economic Opportunity, Economic Development Administration, Small Business Administration, Department of Housing and Urban Development, Farmers Home Administration, Rural Electrification Administration, Forest Service, Bureau of Sport Fisheries and Wildlife, Bureau of Commercial Fisheries, U.S. Geological Survey, and the Department of Labor (Manpower Development and Training Act) spend annually an additional $75,000,000 or more on Indian programs.

With all the millions spent—no one knows the total—and the thousands of Government employees working in the subject field it is literally impossible to obtain *up-to-date* and *accurate* information on such basic questions as employment and unemployment, average educational attainment, income, land ownership, reservation population, interest and vocational abilities. The Bureau of Indian Affairs does not have a research organization that can provide the Congress with such up-to-date information and Congress, as a result, has been forced to undertake much of the basic research necessary to legislative action in the field of Indian affairs. The only alternative for the Congress is to content itself with statistics that are, in many cases, five, ten, twenty, or more years old, and often incomplete and inaccurate. The result of this problem is a lack of continuity of statistical information on the conditions of the American Indian. Therefore there is no sound basis for comparison to determine the increase or decrease of given problems or indeed the improvement or lack of improvement in the economy of Indian tribes.

The Bureau of the Census publishes rather detailed information on Indians every decade, but as the Bureau of Indian Affairs points out [8]—

---

[8] BIA. *U.S. Indian Population and Land.* p. 1.

Because the enumeration districts for the Decennial Census do not generally match reservation boundaries, and trust land may be scattered in some areas, the Bureau cannot use Census data for estimating and planning for potential service requirements.

In discussing the general Census, the Bureau of Indian Affairs stated that:

The count of Indians in the 1960 Decennial Census was the most accurate since 1930, when all persons were asked if they were Indian and additional questions were asked of those who said they were Indian. In 1940 and 1950 enumerators did not ask questions about race and used their own judgment. This resulted in many undercounts, especially in large cities, and in counties and states without Federal Reservations, where the scattered Indian population was not generally recognized and recorded.

In 1960 people in postal areas received enumeration sheets by mail on which they recorded the basic information about themselves, including race. In non-postal areas enumerators were instructed to ask questions about race. The result was a higher count of Indians than ever before.

The major problem encountered in using Census Bureau statistics is that the Federal Government Indian program does not extend to all persons of Indian ancestry but only to those under the jurisdiction of the Bureau of Indian Affairs. Another related problem that has been a question for generations is "Who or what is an Indian?" Neither the Congress nor the Executive Branch has defined Indian other than for the purpose of a specific piece of legislation. An "Indian" can be a person with anywhere from a drop of Indian blood to a full-blood in the present confusion over definition. For example, there are people recognized by the Federal Government as Indians, others recognized by the various States, and others by the Census Bureau. As another example of the confusion, the Bureau of Indian Affairs publication on Indian land and population carried a covering memo stating:

Because of differences in definitions and in the wording and timing of requests for population data, there has been wide variation in statements about Indian population. This has sometimes led to misunderstandings. To prevent such misunderstanding, the data in this publication should be used throughout the Bureau for public statements and replies to information requests until later figures are available and officially distributed.

During the 85th Congress, the House Interior Committee published a study on the American Indian [9] and pointed out that during the study it had encountered the same problem of definition:

Another aspect of the committee study included an analysis of expenditures by the various state governments for assistance to Indians. In drafting the questionnaire directed to state officials, the committee again encountered one of the most perplexing questions in this field: Who is an Indian? Various Federal laws define an Indian for the purpose of the legislation itself and Federal Government agencies are not in agreement concerning the recipients of services provided by them to variously defined

---

[9] *Present Relations of the Federal Government to the American Indian.* Committee Print No. 38. 346 p.

"Indians." [Discussion of the term "Indian" follows.] This is a general racial definition of the people known as "Indians"; however, the problem at the moment is, who are "Indians" for the purpose of supplying services to these people by the Federal and State Government?

The Committee then went on to point out that the Department of Health, Education, and Welfare—

considers an individual to be an Indian "if he is regarded as an Indian by the community in which he lives as evidenced by such factors as membership in a tribe, residence on tax-exempt land, ownership of restricted property, and active participation in tribal affairs."

For the purpose of a State receiving financial assistance for Indian education, the Code of Federal Regulations required ¼ or more Indian blood. For the purpose of eligibility for cattle loans the requirement was membership in a tribe *and* ¼ or more Indian blood. However, under the regulations concerning law and order any person of Indian descent and a member of a recognized tribe was considered an Indian. The Indian Reorganization Act of 1934 (48 Stat. 984) authorizes the tribes themselves to define "Indian" for purposes of tribal membership. In contacting States with large Indian populations the Committee found that two States accepted the individual's opinion, four used the "recognition in the community" approach, Alaska required ¼ Indian blood, five accepted residence on a reservation, and one used the Census Bureau definition. The Committee concluded its discussion concerning the definition of Indian with a statement that is undoubtedly as accurate today as it was then:

The definition of "Indian" presents one of the most difficult problems in the field of Indian affairs and no doubt accounts for many of the inconsistencies in various data supplied to the committee. Although all engaged in the field use the term "Indians," by applying the many and varied definitions we perceive a kaleidoscope of ever-changing groups. This accounts for many of the frustrations and difficulties in dealing with Indian legislation.

The research done over the years, by the Congress, to obtain adequate information on areas, within the field of Indian affairs, of legislative concern, has been carried on with the committee staffs available and the assistance of Library of Congress staff, as needed. As far back as 1904 when Charles J. Kappler—a Senate Indian Affairs Committee staff member—compiled the first two volumes of his four volume publication, *Indian Laws and Treaties*, the very same informational problem existed. The introduction to Kappler's Volume I states that—

an accurate compilation of the treaties, laws, executive orders, and other matters relating to Indian affairs, from the organization of the Government to the present time, has been urgently needed for many years, and its desirability has been repeatedly emphasized by the Commissioner of Indian Affairs in his annual reports to the Congress.[10]

---

[10] Indian Affairs: Laws and Treaties. 58th Congress, 2d session. Senate Document No. 319.

6

In the 81st Congress when the "compilation" [11] was published, the
House Interior Committee pointed out that it had—
> long recognized the need for gathering into one compilation all
> available important statistical information relative to the Indians
> under the committee jurisdiction and the laws affecting such
> Indians.

In 1952 when the revised compilation [12] was published the Committee
stated that—
> Congress wants information on the history of the special legisla-
> tion affecting the several tribes, and statistical information re-
> garding the effects of this legislation and the policies pursued
> under it, on the social and economic progress and welfare of the
> tribes themselves.

During the 85th Congress (1958) there was some concern about
the diminishing Indian land base. The Senate Interior Committee
found that "detailed statistics on the extent of Indian trust land dis-
posals were not available in Washington" and undertook an extensive
research project entitled *Indian Land Transactions*.[13] The problem
was again pointed out in 1959 when the House Interior Committee
published a study [14] on Government-Indian relations and stated
that—
> In past years the Congress has been frequently handicapped by
> the lack of available up-to-date and accurate information re-
> lating to the various problems within the vast field of Indian
> Affairs.

Another extensive study was made in 1959 by the Senate Interior
Committee on the Indian heirship land problem [15] and the Chairman
stated that his—
> Intention was to make available to the members of this Com-
> mittee a detailed analysis of the problem which could be used
> in drafting corrective legislation.

The Congress has relied heavily on its own staff, with some assistance from the Library of Congress staff, to carry out extensive studies
on specific issues before the Congress. However, in each case, the staff
starts from "scratch" and must contact pertinent Government
agencies, tribes, individuals, Indian interest organizations, and, after
collecting the basic data, proceed to the analysis. This has been mostly
a "one-shot" approach since neither the congressional committees nor
the Library of Congress has the staff necessary for continuous data
collection, analysis, and publication. The following citations indicate
the depth of research and the span of subject matter that the Congress
has covered in the field of Indian affairs:

1904 58th Congress, 2d Session. Senate. Committee on Indian
      Affairs. Charles J. Kappler. *Indian Affairs: Laws and Treaties.*
      Vol. I. (Laws, 1162 p.). Vol. II. (Treaties, 1099 p.). Senate
      Document 319.

[11] House. 81st Congress, 2d session. Committee on Public Lands, Subcommittee on Indian Affairs. *Compilation of Material Relating to the Indians of the United States and the Territory of Alaska, Including Certain Laws and Treaties Affecting Such Indians.* June 13, 1950. Serial No. 30. 1110 p.
[12] House. 82d Congress, 2d Session. Committee on Interior and Insular Affairs, Subcommittee on Indian Affairs. *Report with Respect to the House Resolution Authorizing the Committee on Interior and Insular Affairs to Conduct an Investigation of the Bureau of Indian Affairs.* House Report No. 2503. 1594 p. (plus 157 maps and index).
[13] Senate. 85th Congress, 2d Session. Committee on Interior and Insular Affairs, *Indian Land Transactions.* December 1, 1958. Committee Print. 838 p.
[14] See footnote 9. p. 4.
[15] Senate. 86th Congress, 2d Session. Committee on Interior and Insular Affairs. *Indian Heirship Land Survey.* Committee Print. 2 vols. p. 1.

1913 62d Congress. 2d Session. Senate. Committee on Indian
Affairs. Charles J. Kappler. *Indian Affairs: Laws and Treaties.*
Vol. III. (Laws). Senate Document No. 719. 798 p.

1929 70th Congress, 1st Session. Senate. Committee on Indian
Affairs. Charles J. Kappler. *Indian Affairs: Laws and Treaties.*
(Laws). Senate Document No. 53. 1406 p.

1950 81st Congress, 2d Session. House. Committee on Public
Lands. Subcommittee on Indian Affairs. *Compilation of Material
Relating to the Indians of the United States and the Territory of
Alaska, Including Certain Laws and Treaties Affecting Such
Indians.* June 13, 1950. Serial No. 30. 1110 p.

1952 82d Congress, 2d Session. House. Committee on Interior and
Insular Affairs. *Report with Respect to the House Resolution
Authorizing the Committee on Interior and Insular Affairs to Con-
duct an Investigation of the Bureau of Indian Affairs.* House
Report No. 2503. 1594 p. (plus 157 maps and index).

1952 82d Congress, 2d Session. House. Committee on Interior and
Insular Affairs. *Statistical Charts Regarding the Indians of the
United States.* 45 p.

1954 83d Congress, 2d Session. House. Committee on Interior and
Insular Affairs. *Report with Respect to the House Resolution
Authorizing the Committee on Interior and Insular Affairs to
Conduct an Investigation of the Bureau of Indian Affairs.* House
Report No. 2680. 576 p.

1958 85th Congress, 2d Session. Senate. Committee on Interior and
Insular Affairs. *Indian Land Transactions: An Analysis of the
Problems and Effects of Our Diminishing Indian Land Base,
1948-1957.* Committee Print. 838 p.

1959 85th Congress, 2d Session. House. Committee on Interior and
Insular Affairs. *Present Relations of the Federal Government to
the American Indian.* Committee Print No. 38. 346 p.

1959 86th Congress, 1st Session. House. Committee on Interior and
Insular Affairs. *Indirect Services and Expenditures by the Federal Government for the American Indians.* Committee Print No.
14. 61 p.

1960 86th Congress, 2d Session. Senate. Committee on Interior and
Insular Affairs. *Indian Heirship Land Survey.* Committee Print.
2 Vols. 1186 p.

1960 86th Congress, 2d Session. House. Committee on Interior and
Insular Affairs. *Indian Heirship Land Study.* Committee Print
No. 27. 2 Vols. (Vol. I, 555 p.; Vol. II, 1010 p.).

1962 87th Congress, 2d Session. Senate. Committee on Appropriations. *Federal Facilities for Indians.* 1955-1961. 209 p.

1963 88th Congress, 1st Session. Senate. Committee on Appropriations. *Federal Facilities for Indians.* 29 p.

1964 88th Congress, 2d Session. House. Committee on Interior and
Insular Affairs. *List of Indian Treaties.* Committee Print No.
33. 45 p.

1964 88th Congress, 2d Session. Senate. Committee on Appropriations. *Federal Facilities for Indians.* 25 p.

1964 88th Congress, 2d Session. House. Committee on Interior and Insular Affairs. *Information on Removal of Restrictions on American Indians.* Committee Print No. 38. 90 p.

1965 89th Congress, 1st Session. Senate. Committee on Appropriations. *Federal Facilities for Indians.* 390 p.

1966 89th Congress, 2d Session. Senate. Committee on Appropriations. *Federal Facilities for Indians.* 856 p.

1967 90th Congress, 1st Session. Senate. Committee on Appropriations. *Federal Facilities for Indians.* 862 p.

The studies listed represent only a selection of congressional publications on the subject of Indian Affairs, but show the continuing congressional interest in the subject and the intent to pass effective legislation even though extensive research is required to establish the basic facts. While these studies have been most helpful at the time of publication, and—for lack of more recent information—still represent the latest "information" in some cases, they could be much more useful if they were current. However, with the Federal Government spending increased amounts on Indian programs and more and more agencies providing services to Indians, we seem to be in a position of having less information while programs, expenditures and staff are increasing.

Where does one go to find a complete list of all agencies and bureaus in the Federal Government operating Indian programs? How much does the Federal Government expend on Indian programs each year? Are all the programs using different definitions of "Indian"? How does an Indian or an Indian tribe find out about all the programs and how they can benefit from them? How can the Congress legislate effectively and how can the Executive Branch program effectively, if we do not have accurate and current statistics on unemployment, educational attainment, land interests, income, etc., for those Indians residing on reservations? These are some of the questions that have been brought up from time to time by the Congress and researchers in the field. There obviously is a real need for current information, published in usable form, and available throughout the country.

The experience of Representative William V. Roth in attempting to untangle the mass of all Federal assistance programs is instructive. Following an eight-month study in which some 1,091 distinct programs were identified, Representative Roth noted that "no one anywhere, knows how many programs there are; information on some programs is virtually impossible to obtain." The results of the Roth study of Federal assistance programs in general are an accurate reflection of the problem in the field of Indian programs, and there should be a similar concern to develop comprehensive and detailed information on Indian programs.

Fortunately, in this day and age, the problem could be approached through the use of computers and the centralization of source material. Once the information is fed into computers the basic task is correcting and up-dating statistics and program information. In an attempt to determine the types of information that would be most useful in such a publication careful attention was given to Congressional needs in the field of Indian affairs over the past few decades. The following outline will give the reader an indication of how valuable a "Handbook" could be.

PART I

INDIAN TREATIES, AGREEMENTS, AND EXECUTIVE ORDERS

(This part would be based on Kappler's Laws and Treaties, Royce's Indian Land Cessions, and the National Archives' List of Documents Concerning the Negotiation of Ratified Indian Treaties. The organization could place the treaties, agreements, and executive orders in chronological order with the maps and lists of related documents with the pertinent treaty.)

PART II

HISTORY, LEGISLATION, AND CURRENT CONDITIONS ON INDIAN RESERVATIONS

NOTE.—The following would be a "form" report filled out by the Federal Officer in charge each year. It is based on a "questionnaire on a reservation profile" drafted by the Bureau of Indian Affaris a few years ago. Some changes have been made.

A. *Nomenclature.*
    1. *Proper name of tribes.* If unorganized the generally accepted name.
B. *Land.*
    1. *Location.* Describe the reservation's geographic location within a State or States and county or counties. Describe the proximity of trade centers, identifying the same and giving a general statement concerning size, population, and industry.
    2. *Climate.* State the length of the growing season, the length of the tourist or recreational season, and give average temperature ranges and average annual precipitation.
    3. *Historical.* Give the initial date of establishment of the reservation and groups and/or tribes for whom established, and citations to treaties, laws, and executive orders and original and present land area of the reservation.
    4. *Ownership.* (a) Tribal (trust and fee separately), trust allotted, Government-owned (totals as of June 30, last fiscal year). (b) Characteristics of ownership. Show the pattern of ownership, whether it is checkerboarded, scattered or contiguous. Make a brief comment on the possible improvement in the characteristics of ownership by unitization, syndication, etc.
    5. *Present Land Use.* Include the major categories of land use on the reservation with an average by percentage of each type, e.g. farming, grazing, commercial, etc. The percentage of Indian and non-Indian use of Indian land should also be given. The various categories of use should include a breakdown between individual Indian trust land and tribal lands.

6. *Heirship*. Number and percentage breakdown of allotted trust tracts belonging to a single owner, 2–10 owners, over 10 owners. Number of probate cases completed during the last fiscal year and the number pending. Total acreage in heirship status. Describe the heirship problem on the reservation.

7. *Potential*. Give a brief statement on reservation land potential. Describe tribal land acquisition program, if any. Indicate income from tribal land purchases made during the last year and the purchase price.

8. *Transportation*. Describe the major highways giving access to the reservation and the intra-reservation roads. How many miles of roads are there on the reservation? How many miles of roads are Bureau maintained? What jurisdiction(s) maintain the balance? Indicate commercial airports and railroads nearest to the reservation. List by percentage use of transportation, such as truck, car, horse, public, etc. Does the present adequacy or inadequacy of the road system hinder or help economic development of the reservation or the Indian's work opportunities?

C. *Population*.

1. *Resident Total*. (a) Give the total number of Indian residents on the reservation, number of families, average number per family, average age, and other pertinent data. (b) Provide similar information for Indians residing adjacent to the reservation, i.e., service area population. (c) State briefly population trends. (d) Provide total number of adults (over 18), subdivided by sex, and the total number of minors. (e) Provide the total number of Indians residing on the reservation who are members of tribes other than those in residence.

2. *Tribal Membership*. (a) Give total membership of tribe at present time. If an estimate, indicate, (b) Date of latest tribal roll.

D. *Tribal Administration and Government*.

1. *Governing Body*. Give history of the tribal governing body, its functions, and membership.

2. *Budget*. Give income and expenditures for the last fiscal year differentiating between tribal and other funds.

3. *Member Civic Participation*. Describe the interest and activity of tribal members in tribal or social affairs and off-reservation, non-Indian affairs.

E. *Disposition of Judgment Awards*.

1. *Past*. Describe and evaluate the use of any judgment awards in the past.

2. *Current*. How does the tribe propose to use funds from the current award? (Attach any resolutions or program outlines.)

F. *Economic Activities and Potentials.*
　　1. *Reservation Development.* Indicate both resource development and industrial or commercial potential for the reservation.
　　2. *Labor Force.* (a) List the number of resident Indians employed on or near the reservation. (b) List the number of unemployed under the headings: temporary, seasonal, and permanent. A breakdown by sex should be included. Also distinguish between those residing on the reservation and those adjacent to.
　　3. *Employment Opportunities.* (a) Briefly state the livelihood source history of the Indian population. (b) Discuss the livelihood sources for non-Indians on the reservation and in adjacent areas.
　　4. *Income from Reservation Resources.* (a) List the total income from surface leases of all types, both to the Indians and non-Indians. If free use, or less than fair market value, is approved to Indian operators, calculate the rental rate on the average income from non-Indian use. (b) For grazing permits, use the same as above. (c) For timber, give the gross dollar income from stumpage sold; give estimated value of free-use forest products harvested. (d) For minerals include income from leases, bonuses, royalties, etc. (e) For commercial recreation, give the net profit from Indian and tribal recreational enterprises. (f) Under business enterprises, list the net profit from tribal enterprises other than recreation.
　　5. *Income from Employment for Reservation Residents.* (a) This should include a breakdown of those self-employed, and the Indian operator's income, less economic rent for land and operating expenses. (b) For those self-employed, other than in agricultural operations, calculate the disposable income from the business. (c) Other than self-employed should include all income from wages for Indians living on and working on, or living on and working near the reservation. This should include all types of employment (Federal Government, tribal, industrial, and private business). A breakdown of major employers by skilled, semi-skilled, or unskilled workers should be included. (d) Estimate the value of services received from the Federal Government that a non-Indian in the surrounding area would have to pay for.
　　6. *Income from Resources and Employment.* For purposes of comparison, the total income from resources and employment should be divided by the number of families on the reservation to indicate the average amount per family that can be expected from these sources.
　　7. *Median Effective Family Buying Income in Surrounding Counties.* Include a comparison of on-reservation

income per family with the income of non-Indians living in counties surrounding the reservation. This appears to be the best measure of income that should be expected for Indian reservation residents. A national or state income level is too general and has less application to the program objectives.

G. *Health.*

 1. *United States Public Health Service.* What facilities are provided by the United States Public Health Service?

 2. *Adequacy.* Are these facilities adequate to meet the health needs of Indians?

 3. *Use.* Are the facilities fully used by Indians?

 4. *Needs.* What are the major health needs of the Reservation?

 5. *Water and Sanitation.* Describe briefly the availability of water and sanitary facilities to meet normal needs for both family and community.

 6. *Comparison.* How do each of these services compare with those of non-Indian families in the surrounding areas?

H. *Welfare.*

 1. *General Assistance.* Give the BIA general assistance for the last fiscal year by number of cases, persons, and amount, and a breakdown of high and low months for such assistance.

 2. *Other Financial Assistance.* Any Federal, State, or county assistance to Indians received through county Departments of Public Welfare. Include types of cases, total cases, and total number of persons involved.

 3. *Commodity Program.* The numbers involved and the cost of any commodity program.

 4. *Summary.* Give total of tribal members receiving assistance and indicate categories.

 5. *Attitude.* What is the attitude of State and local officials regarding welfare to Indians?

I. *Education.*

 1. *Level.* Give the average educational level for the following age groups in terms of the highest grade completed.

	Male	Female
18–25 years, inclusive		
26–45 years		
46 years and over		

 2. *School Age Population.* Give the numbers of resident tribal members in the following age groups.

	Male	Female
1–5 years, inclusive		
6–13 years		
14–18 years		
19–21 years		

3. *School Facilities.* Give the following data regarding school facilities on the reservation (last fiscal year).

System	Number of schools	Capacity	Grades served	Indian enrollment Elementary	Secondary
Public schools					
BIA schools					
Mission schools					
Other schools					

4. *Special.* (a) Describe briefly participation of Indian parents in school affairs. (b) What is the attitude of tribal members toward education? (c) Special problems related to school attendance, dropouts, etc. (d) Special services such as counseling, adult education, etc., available or needed in local schools and communities. (e) Scholarship aid (if any) provided by the tribe.
5. If available, provide the same for 1, 2, 4 (a) and (c) concerning the non-Indian population in surrounding area.

J. *Housing.*
   1. *Existing Conditions.* (a) Briefly state the adequacy of existing housing. (b) Give the percent of Indian homes with electricity and telephones. (c) Briefly describe the availability of water and sanitary facilities. (d) Provide the same information for non-Indians of surrounding areas.
   2. *Housing Authority.* Has the tribe established a housing authority?
   3. What are current plans for (a) new homes, and (b) repair of homes?

K. *Relocation.*
   1. *Employment Assistance.* List the number of units and people assisted in placement in direct employment through the employment assistance programs.
   2. *Returnees.* Estimate by percentage those who have returned from relocation and the major reason for returning.

L. *Readiness of Indians to Manage Their Own Affairs.*
   1. *Problem Areas.* Evaluate the capacity of the members of this particular tribe to manage their own affairs. Discuss any major problem areas.
   2. *Cultural Isolation.* This entails an evaluation of participation by Indians on or off the reservation in what may be described as distinctly Indian culture (including language use, religious or secular ceremonies, social mores relating to an older Indian culture, etc.) The proportion of Indians (irregardless of degree of blood) contained in the "core" of cultural Indians constitutes a good measure of the degree of acculturation experiences by the tribe.
   3. *Non-Indian Community.* Evaluate the relationship of this tribe or reservation to the non-Indian community,

i.e., local, county and State. This includes not only attitudes but abilities of these governmental units to carry any economic services necessary for future development.

4. *Bureau Appropriations.* Provide breakdown of appropriations, by activity, for three fiscal years: (a) Actual expenditures last fiscal year; (b) Funds programmed current fiscal year (or expended where applicable); (c) Funds programmed next fiscal year.

M. *Other Government Programs.*

1. List all other Government programs in operation on the reservation or assisting the reservation population.
2. Briefly describe each program, the number of participants, etc.

Part III

FEDERAL GOVERNMENT INDIAN PROGRAMS, ALL AGENCIES*

This part would be based on a form annual report for all agencies, bureaus, and departments, in the Federal Government responsible for any aspect of Indian programs. The reports would contain—as indicated in the ouline below—specific information on the program and expenditures. Should the *Program Information Act* (H.R. 3860, Representative Roth) become law, Section 11 would prohibit all other compendiums of program information "in order to make the catalog the exclusive source of such program information both for the public and for the program officers." In developing a proposed catalog of Indian program information, every possible attempt could be made to incorporate the findings and recommendations of the Roth Study in determining the information to be included and the format as well. This could be expected to result in an efficiently organized and extremely useful compilation with a minimum of unnecessary duplication of effort. If H.R. 3860 is enacted, this part would simply be an extract of all Indian programs from the proposed *Catalog of Federal Assistance Programs.*

A. *Identification of Organization.*

1. Full legal name of program.
2. List each administrative level between the program and the highest agency or department.
3. Enabling legislation.

B. *Funding.*

1. Actual expenditures for the past fiscal year.
2. Appropriations for the present fiscal year.

C. *Purposes.*

1. Briefly outline the programs.

---

*The idea for this part came from the Roth Study entitled *Listing of Operating Federal Assistance Programs as Compiled During the Roth Study* by the Honorable William V. Roth (Congressional Record, June 25, 1968. pp. H5441–5585; and House Document 399, 90th Congress, 2d session). This catalog has been an extremely useful reference tool and the writer has benefited not only from the information contained but the quick reference organization and indexing of the report itself.

2. Are there any plans for expanding or reducing the programs?
3. What has been the reaction of the Indians or Tribes?
4. Are there any other Government programs closely related to this one?
5. What are the eligiblity requirements for participation in the program?

D. *Offices.*
1. List headquarters office, contact officer, and telephone number.
2. List all field offices, contact officers, and telephone numbers.

E. *Personnel.*
1. How many employees were there on the last day of the preceding fiscal year?
2. Of this number how many were full time and how many part time?
3. What were the total man-years expended in the previous fiscal year?
4. What was the total administrative overhead of supplying, equipping, and servicing those man-years?

F. *Publications.*
1. List all reports published during the past fiscal year by author, title, and pagination.
2. Provide a brief summary for each publication.

PART IV

STATISTICAL COMPILATION ON INDIANS AND INDIAN RESOURCES

A. *Population.*
1. Total Indian population in the United States (Bureau of the Census).
2. Reservation population (Bureau of Indian Affairs).
   a. Living on Reservations.
   b. Living on trust lands (not on Reservations).
   c. Living near Reservations.
3. Service population.
   a. Total "service" population and definition of same (Bureau of Indian Affairs).
   b. Total "service" population and definition of same (Division of Indian Health, Public Health Service).

B. *Health.*
1. Infant death rate compared to non-Indian.
2. Life expectancy for Indians as compared to non-Indians.
3. General statement on the Indian's health today in comparison with the non-Indian.
4. Programs.
   a. How many hospitals there are (location, number of beds, personnel service population, etc.).
   b. How many health centers (location, personnel, service population, etc.).

      c. How many health stations (location, personnel, service population, etc.).

      d. How many beds are available in community hospitals built through Public Law 85–151 (name of hospital and location).

C. *Employment and Unemployment.*

    Total population.

    1. Between the ages of 18 and 55 able to work.

      a. On the reservation, male, female.

      b. Near the reservation, male, female.

    2. Working full time.

      a. On the reservation, male, female.

      b. Near the reservation, male, female.

    3. Working part time.

      a. On the reservation, male, female.

      b. Near the reservation, male, female.

    4. Between the ages of 18 and 55, physically able and wanting to work, now unemployed.

      a. Comparison with non-Indian labor force in area.

D. *Education.*

    1. *Level.* Average educational level for the following age groups in terms of the highest grade completed:

	Male	Female
18–25 years, inclusive		
26–45 years		
46 years and over		

    2. *School Age Population.* Number of resident tribal members in the following age groups:

	Male	Female
1–5 years, inclusive		
6–13 years		
14–18 years		
19–21 years		

    3. *School Facilities.* On the reservation.

System	Number	Capacity	Enrollment Elementary	Secondary
Public				
BIA				
Mission				
Other				

E. *Land.*

    1. Total acreage of tribal land.

    2. Total acreage of tribal *fee* land.

    3. Total acreage of tribal *trust* land.

    4. Total acreage of individual trust land.

    5. Total acreage of individual trust land in heirship status.

        a. Number of tracts.
        b. Number with 2–10 owners.
        c. Number with more than 10 owners.
    6. Total acreage of Federal lands on Indian reservations.

F. *Law and Order.*
    1. Number of reservations under State law.
    2. Number of reservations having:
        a. Traditional courts.
        b. Courts of Indian Offenses.

PART V

STATE AGENCIES AND PRIVATE ORGANIZATIONS IN THE FIELD OF INDIAN AFFAIRS

A. *State Agencies.*

    NOTE.—General statement on each state agency, operation, staff, budget, programs, publications, etc.

B. *Private Organizations.*

    NOTE.—General statement on each private organization, officers, operation, budget, publications, programs, etc.

PART VI

PUBLICATIONS AND REPORTS IN THE FIELD OF INDIAN AFFAIRS

    NOTE.—Those published on a continuing basis by all levels of Government concerned with the Indian problem, the private organization publications, tribal newspapers, etc. The intent would be to annotate each publication indicating content and providing thereby a comprehensive list of publications containing current information from all over the United States.

PART VII

INDEX

A "handbook" as outlined above might well become a prime mover in the field of Indian affairs by providing a concentration of available information and by revealing the many deficiencies in our knowledge of the American Indian today. In addition, the inclusion of all programs—whether Federal, State, county or private—would, for the first time in the history of the subject, create a complete picture of the problem area and those organizations active in the field. Another positive aspect is that—with continued up-dating—the Federal Government would have a handy yardstick available to measure progress in terms of education, income, employment, and other factors.

In the author's opinion all the good intentions of the various governmental authorities—Congressional, Executive and State—are weakened by the fact that the problem itself has not been clearly delineated. An opportunity to determine rates of improvement—if any—in the American Indian's economic condition is a necessary foundation to any programs designed to solve the "Indian problem." The picture of the American Indian today is hazy and confusing and the statistical information available fails to clarify that picture. A central collection and publication point for the basic statistics necessary to adequate consideration of the subject matter and the Indian peoples concerned would, in the writer's opinion, result in more advantageous use of the monies appropriated and the creation of a specific yardstick with which to measure Indian progress.

The goal of the Federal Government, State governments, and private organizations active in the field of Indian affairs is to improve the economic conditions on Indian Reservations, and in that manner raise the Indian's standard of living to that of the non-Indian in this country. The attainment of the goal will require a vast improvement in our knowledge of Indians—and of ourselves.

AMERICAN INDIANS IN RURAL POVERTY

By HELEN W. JOHNSON [*]

FOREWORD

It is widely recognized that poverty among American Indians continues to be severe and widespread. Making use of the findings of Department of Agriculture studies of rural poverty, Helen W. Johnson details the extent of this poverty in 16 counties in which the population contains a substantial proportion of Indians. In order to illustrate the effect of severe poverty on the quality of life, some actual family situations found among the Indians in Oklahoma are described. Also described are life on a reservation in North Dakota and rural off-reservation Indian life in various parts of the country. It is pointed out that the Indian has been the object of many decades of management and that this has engendered dependence on an alien culture. Thus the Indian does have special problems. Current needs include both the provision of essentially welfare assistance for much of the adult Indian population and the provision of the educational and other services needed to make Indian young people self-sufficient either on or off the reservation.

Introduction

The American Indian population is rural, poor, and essentially outside of the mainstream of the larger society. This states the basic framework of the analysis presented in the following pages.

The problems of American Indians are not new. They stem from many roots—historic, economic, social, and cultural. Contributing to the present alienation of the American Indian has been the ambivalent U.S. policy toward this minority ethnic group, along with the deliberate separation of Indians from the dominant white society. Acculturation of a minority is never an easy process, and advanced civilizations have not been too successful in their dealings with groups at lower levels of technological development. The American experience with the Indians is only one instance of a more general problem occurring when two different societies meet.

Anyone acquainted with Indian affairs has recognized that adjustment of the Indian in the dominant white society in America would take time and present many problems. The road has been long and difficult indeed, and acculturation is still far from accomplished. As long ago as 1926, a government survey directed by Lewis Meriam found the Indians to be "extremely poor, in bad health, without education and lacking adjustment to the dominant culture around them." [1]

The poverty of rural Indians is not of resources alone—it is also of the spirit. It is not enough to raise the level of living of a deprived people; it is also necessary to give them identity and purpose. As Peter Farb has written, worse than the educational, health, and housing deficits Indians suffer is the implication that Indians are "irrelevant

---

[*] Economic Development Division, Economic Research Service, U.S. Department of Agriculture.

[1] Encyclopaedia Britannica, 1954 ed., vol. 12, p. 209.

to the American culture." He says further that, "A white education
system has turned out imitation whites who succumb to the bleakness
of reservation life and the prejudices around them." He quotes William
Byler of the Association on American Indian Affairs on the seriousness of the current alienation: "The American Indian today is about
to go over the brink—not only of poverty and prejudice, but of moral
collapse." [2]

The issue of future direction to achieve a better life, *in* the white
society or *out* of it, is particularly pressing for the young people who
are on the threshold of making that choice. Torn between the Indian
life and culture and the unfamiliar ways of the non-Indian world, they
are confused and uncertain. Poised between two worlds, sociologically
they are as much "cultural hybrids" as many second-generation immigrants of yesterday. They are in limbo, not really conditioned to be at
home in either world. As one commentator put it recently, about these
Indian youth, "They have one eye on the outside world, which means
opportunity and fears; the other eye on the reservation, which means
security and hopelessness." [3]

THE RURAL AMERICAN INDIAN IN THE 1960's

Basic data in this report concerning the rural Indian are derived
chiefly from the 1960 Census of Population, the most recent information available on a residence and county basis, supplemented by findings from a field survey conducted by the Economic Research Service,
as well as selected other materials. Economic and social characteristics
of the rural Indian population which are considered to be linked with
poverty status will be discussed.

The 1960 Census of Population reported 524,000 in the Indian population, about 87 percent of them living in 23 States. Nine out of ten
Indians in these States were on reservations. To the above number
should be added 28,000 Eskimos and Aleuts in Alaska, who will be included in this analysis of rural Indians. More than fifty percent of
the Indian population in each of 19 States was classified by the Census
as living in rural areas.

The Indian population is very young, as evidenced by the fact that
the median age of rural Indians in 1960 was 17.7 years, compared with
27.3 years for the rural population as a whole. Rural Indians are also
in poverty—62 percent of the rural Indian families had incomes of less
than $3,000 in 1959. This is of special significance in light of the large
size of their families. Two out of three rural Indian families had four
persons or more, over a fourth had seven persons or more.

Other social and economic characteristics indicate their disadvantaged position in 1960. Nearly half of the rural Indian males who were
employed were in blue-collar occupations. The unemployment rate of
18.6 for rural Indian males was more than three times the rate of
5.1 for all rural males in 1960. Twelve percent of rural Indian males,
and nearly 15 percent of the females 14 years old and over had no
schooling, compared with 2.5 and about 2 percent for males and females in the total rural population. Infant mortality, maternal and

---

[2] Farb, Peter, "The American Indian, A Portrait in Limbo," Saturday Review, Oct. 12,
1968, p. 26.
[3] Greider, William, "Wounded Knee Still Festers," Washington Post, Feb. 23, 1969,
p. B4.

other mortality rates, and morbidity rates from various causes were two to fifty times higher than U.S. rates in 1964. Life expectancy at birth for Indians was 63.5 years, whereas it was 70.2 for the United States as a whole.[4]

INDIANS IN SIXTEEN RURAL COUNTIES

In order to shed some further light on the status of the rural Indian, we have chosen for detailed examination sixteen counties in eight States, two counties in each State. These counties were selected because they were predominantly rural in 1960, Indians represented a substantial proportion of the total population of the county, and the incidence of poverty among all families in the county was high.[5] Analysis at the county level permits a closer look at areas in which rural Indians live.

To the extent that the status of the population in these rural counties represented the Indian population's position at that time, certain generalizations can be drawn about how they were faring. Rural Indians in the sixteen counties numbered 157,316, including Eskimos and Aleuts in Alaska. We will not know until 1970 Census data become available whether their situation has in fact bettered or worsened, nor even what the size of the Indian population is today.

The States and counties selected for analysis are the following: Alaska, Bethel and Wade Hampton (election districts); Arizona, Apache and Navajo; Montana, Big Horn and Glacier; New Mexico, McKinley and Sandoval; North Carolina, Hoke and Robeson; North Dakota, Rolette and Sioux; Oklahoma, Adair and McCurtain; and South Dakota, Shannon and Todd.

LOW INCOME

An important criterion in the selection of the sixteen counties was the level of family income in 1959. Poverty is obviously widespread in counties in which more than half of the families had incomes under $3,000, as was true in all of the sixteen counties. In one county in Oklahoma, the proportion was 85 percent. In all cases 80 and 90 percent of the families had less than $6,000, rising as high as 97 percent in Alaska and North Carolina. At the other end of the scale, fewer than 6 percent of the families had $10,000 income or more; in most counties, it was 4 percent or less. Even median family income reflects substantial rural poverty, ranging from a low of $955 in New Mexico to $2,778 in Montana. This analysis of family income was based on the 1959 income of some 30,000 nonwhite families.

EDUCATION

The educational level in the sixteen counties under consideration was well below the U.S. average of 10.6 in terms of median years of school completed by persons 25 years old and over in 1960. The range was from 0.9 years in Apache County, Arizona to a high of 8.8 years in Glacier

---

[4] Indian Health Highlights, Public Health Service, U.S. Department of Health, Education, and Welfare, 1966, pp. xvi and 7.

[5] Counties were 53 to 100 percent rural, Indians were 20 to 90 percent of the total county population, and 30 to 80 percent of all families had less than $3,000 income in 1959.

County, Montana. The range for the rest of the sixteen counties was from 1 to 8.5 years of school completed, close to minimum functional literacy standards.

HEALTH

One measure of health associated with poverty is available in a series of county data from the National Center for Health Statistics on infant mortality rates. These data reflect not only poverty and malnutrition, but a lack of prenatal and postnatal medical services more typical of underdeveloped than advanced industrial societies. Infant mortality rates in the sixteen selected counties in this report were, in 1961–65, in some cases two to nearly four times as high as the national average of 25.1.[6] The range was from 32.3 in Adair County, Oklahoma, to 94.2 in Bethel district in Alaska.

In some counties where the Maternal and Child Health Care project has been operative, or for other reasons, significant improvement has been achieved in lowering infant mortality rates since 1956–60. Of the sixteen counties considered here, all but three have achieved reduced rates since the 1956–60 period, some significantly. Still, the high rates in these counties of predominantly Indian population are an abysmal commentary on the availability of health and medical services as well as on the lack of dietary and child care information for this segment of our population. Infant mortality of this magnitude, not by any means restricted to the Indian population, is a matter for urgent national concern.

WELFARE

To measure objectively the welfare status of the Indian or any other population is precarious. In the broad sense of the term, welfare implies well-being, security, happiness, pride of person and race, and other intangible factors not susceptible of statistical or quantitative measurement. One might assume, however, that if substantial numbers of people in a given county are obliged to be public welfare recipients, at the least poverty conditions are also prevalent.

The level of welfare support cited here is the number of public assistance recipients in the total population of each county in 1964. This includes such programs as old age assistance, medical assistance for the aged, aid to dependent children, aid to the blind, and aid to the permanently and totally disabled, as well as some general assistance programs administered and financed by States or localities without Federal participation. Data are not available for Alaska except for the State as a whole, which reported 6,319 such recipients. Among the other 7 States, public assistance recipients in 1964 represented as high as 21 percent of the total county population in Adair and McCurtain counties in Oklahoma, 17 percent in Shannon, South Dakota, and 11 percent each in Apache County, Arizona, and Todd County, South Dakota.[7]

[6] Infant and Perinatal Mortality Rates, HEW, Jan. 1968. Infant mortality rates are deaths under 1 year per 1,000 live births.
[7] County and City Data Book, 1967, Bureau of the Census, Table 2.

OCCUPATIONAL STRUCTURE

The occupational pattern in the sixteen counties exhibited clear relationships with poverty-related factors such as low levels of income and education in terms of the relatively low proportions of nonwhite males in white-collar and service occupations. The proportion in white-collar occupations in the Alaskan districts in 1960 was about 30 percent, but in all other counties except Sioux, North Dakota, it was about 20 percent or less. Service workers did not figure prominently in any of the counties—18 percent or less of the total nonwhite males. Blue-collar workers represented the predominant occupational category in all of the States except North Carolina where farmworkers accounted for more than half of the occupations. Overall, Indian males in these counties were clearly nonfarm workers.

INDUSTRIAL STRUCTURE

Turning now to the industrial picture in these counties, the same general emphasis on nonagricultural work was found. Looking at 31,000 workers of both sexes in the nonwhite population of the sixteen counties, more than half were employed in nonagricultural industries. Six counties had 80 percent or more employed in such industries. Except in Oklahoma, the largest percentage of workers in nonagriculture were in business and other services; the lowest proportion was in finance, insurance, and real estate.

THE INDIAN SITUATION IN OKLAHOMA

We have chosen to describe the Oklahoma picture in some detail because the Economic Research Service conducted a survey in that area in 1966, which enables us to present reasonably current information on the status of some of the rural Indian families interviewed.

According to a recent Oklahoma publication, there are 67 Indian tribes in Oklahoma embracing a total population of about 65,000 or 12 percent of all U.S. Indians. Although some live and work in cities, they are mainly rural residents of little income and education and a great deal of unemployment and hardship. As the bulletin says about the Indian population, "To this day, many live in small isolated rural communities in abject poverty. A few * * * do not speak English and seem almost hopelessly alien to our society." [8] Living in a State that is 63 percent urban, 63 percent of the Indians are rural residents, more than one-half of them nonfarm. In Adair County, 23 percent of the total population was Indian in 1960, the largest proportion of any county in Oklahoma.

As in a number of States in which Indians represent a significant part of the rural population, including the seven other States previously discussed, certain poverty-related characteristics are in evidence in Oklahoma also. Nearly three-fourths of all Oklahoma Indian males had less than $3,000 income in 1959, and about 60 percent had less than $2,000 income. Limited education, both in quantity and quality, is also

---

[8] Indians in Oklahoma, Oklahoma Employment Security Commission, Oklahoma City, Okla., August 1968, p. 3.

a factor contributing to the disadvantaged position of the Indian. For example, 6 percent of Oklahoma Indians in 1960 reported no schooling, and nearly three out of five had not gone beyond the eighth grade. In terms of median years of school completed for persons 25 years old and over, however, Oklahoma Indians were one year ahead of U.S. Indians as a whole—8.3 and 7.4 respectively. Only slightly more than one-third of all persons 14 years old and over in Oklahoma were attached to the civilian labor force, and the unemployment rate was three times that of the State as a whole.

Case Studies [9]

The field research of the Economic Research Service mentioned above was directed to the discovery of rural poverty family characteristics and problems in several areas, not specifically those of the Indian population. While the number of rural Indian families surveyed in the Oklahoma counties of the Ozarks Region was too small to permit generalizations, a few case studies based on interviews will portray what may be typical rural Indian family situations in the two Oklahoma counties included in the sixteen discussed briefly above.

Certain common threads run through all these brief vignettes, even though all age groups are represented in the eight stories selected. To summarize some of the findings, in all cases education and job training were severely limited; income was low, mostly from public assistance; unemployment was almost universal for both male and female household heads; housing and plumbing facilities were both poor and inadequate; social participation went little beyond church attendance, visiting relatives and friends, listening to the radio or watching television. Most had some indebtedness outstanding, mainly for medical and dental services. Few carried either life or health insurance. While some had gardens, few produced any other food for home consumption. Attitudes concerning the present and future ran the gamut from mild optimism to deep pessimism.

Mrs. A

The youngest household head in this group of rural Indian families is a 22-year-old widow whom we shall call Mrs. A. Although she has only one child, a one-year-old son, she presides over an extended family which includes six other members—her mother, step-father, three sisters, and a brother. They share a rented two-story house, which is larger than most Indian families have (about 1,200 square feet of living space), and which has adequate plumbing facilities, also unusual—hot and cold running water, two baths, indoor toilet, public water supply and waste disposal. The house is heated with wood.

Mrs. A is not herself employed, but her mother and step-father are both working full-time and one of her sisters is employed part-time. Her brother and youngest sister are in school; the third sister is unemployed.

Mrs. A has had nine years of schooling; her mother and step-father have had none; two of her sisters have had eight and ten years. Mrs. A is interested in job training which would equip her to become a telephone switchboard operator.

[9] The information on which these case studies are based was developed by O. Wendell Holmes, Economic Development Division, Economic Research Service.

To support this family of eight, income in 1965 was $4,512, $1,152 from Mrs. A's welfare assistance and $3,360 from the combined earnings of her parents. Rent payments are $35 per month.

Mr. and Mrs. B

Mr. and Mrs. B are 29 and 27 years old, respectively. They are the parents of seven children ranging in age from one through nine, living in a small, one-story house they rent for $30 a month. Living space of about 500 square feet is something less than adequate for a family of nine; there is no basement. The house construction is poor, with outside wall covering of tarpaper-composition material, and there are no inside plumbing facilities, no public sewage disposal system nor septic tank. Their water supply must be carried from a well. The house is heated with gas.

Mr. B has been unemployed since early 1966 when he sustained an injury while working in a lumber mill. The accident required surgery, during which time the mill replaced him. He feels that he has now recovered sufficiently to work full-time and would like training, if free, to become a machinist. Mrs. B is also interested in employment and would like to be trained for a factory sewing job. Both would be willing to commute to jobs or move to another community for employment. In either case, the pay level would have to be high enough to warrant such a change—$60 a week or more if commuting, $75 a week if it entailed a move to another location.

Mr. and Mrs. B both completed nine grades of school. Three of their children are in school; the other four are pre-schoolers. Mr. B has considerable faith in the value of education for his children, at least through high school.

The sole source of income for this family was $1,924 per year from Mr. B's unemployment compensation. He did slightly better in 1965 when he earned $2,374, but far below the poverty threshold for a family of this size.

Mr. and Mrs. C

The parents in this family are 47 and 36 years old, respectively. They have eight children whose ages range from three to nineteen. The family is housed in a one-story wood dwelling which allows only about 100 square feet of living space per family member. These rented quarters contain no indoor plumbing facilities, except spring-fed cold running water, and no sewage disposal system. The house is heated with wood.

Mr. C, partially disabled by inactive TB, works only part-time, as a laborer, for his landlord. This work pays the rent. He is not interested in job training as he feels he is unable to work full-time. Mrs. C, who has been a housewife since the age of fifteen, would like to learn to be a typist. She is willing to commute to a job, but does not want to leave the community to live elsewhere. The nineteen-year-old son, who completed eight years of school, is unemployed.

Mr. C has had no formal schooling, cannot read, and can write only his name. Except for two preschool-age children and the oldest child, the rest of the children are in school. The father hopes they will all achieve at least a high school education and encourages them to do so.

This family's income is derived from welfare payments, amounting to $1,950 in 1965, plus Mr. C's earnings from part-time work for his landlord. Of the $466 he gained from this source in 1965, $360 was allocated to rent payments. Total spendable income for this family of ten in that year was, therefore, about $2,000.

Mrs. D

The head of this household is a 43-year-old divorcee, the mother of eleven children, seven of whom are still at home with her. They range in age from four to fifteen years. One of the seven, a six-year-old son, was in an Indian TB hospital at the time of the survey, but was expected to return home soon, hopefully to stay. The four who have left are employed full-time, two of them in the military service. Mrs. D and her children live in a rented one-story frame house with no basement, which gives them about 1,000 square feet of living space. Indoor plumbing facilities, drinking water, and public sewage disposal system are available. Rent is $40 per month with no utilities furnished. The house is heated with gas.

Mrs. D is not presently employed, but expressed some interest in training to become a practical nurse. She has had virtually no work experience in the past and is partially disabled, limiting the kinds of employment she might seek. She completed only five years of school and has had no job training. The oldest five of her children at home are attending school, and two of the children who have left home completed high school; the other two had eleven years of school.

Mrs. D's income is derived from welfare checks amounting to $2,964 per year, out of which she pays $40 monthly for rent.

The E Family

The father in this family is 55 years old, his wife is 47. Their six children, all living at home, range in age from twelve through twenty-four. Although this is an eight-member household, their one-story dwelling affords them less than 800 square feet of living space. The monthly rent for this small house, which has no indoor plumbing except cold piped water, is $30. Drinking water comes from a well; there is no septic tank or public sewage disposal system. The house is heated with a wood-burning stove.

Mr. E owns and operates a garage, although he has had no formal training as a mechanic. His wife works part-time, making and selling beaded purses and other items, for which she recently had some instruction. Their oldest daughter, aged 24, works part-time doing ironing, and their 22-year-old son, who had just returned from Army service at the time of the survey, was beginning full-time employment. Both of the parents are interested in receiving training, Mr. E in mechanics and Mrs. E in learning to arrange artificial flowers in a florist shop. Both, however, consider themselves partially disabled with high blood pressure, and Mrs. E also has kidney trouble.

Although Mr. and Mrs. E had limited schooling, two and five years, respectively, they value education for their children and are keeping four of them in school, including an 18-year-old son in the tenth grade and a 20-year-old son in the eleventh grade. Their oldest daughter (24) completed eight years of school and their 22-year-old son had ten years.

Total income in 1965 for this family of eight was $2,980 from all sources. Mr. E earned $1,200 in his work as a garage mechanic, his wife received $180 from the sale of her handwork, the daughter earned $480 from ironing, and two sons together earned $1,120 in an aid program at school.

Mr. F

Mr. F is the only bachelor in our series of case studies presented here. He is 56 years old and has been living rent-free in a small house owned by his sister. The house has no plumbing facilities of any kind and no sewage disposal system. Water must be carried from a spring. The heating arrangement for this dwelling consists of a metal barrel in which logs are burned. About the time of the survey, Mr. F's sister sold this house, so her brother was obliged to look for other quarters.

This man has been a laborer in the past, but has been disabled with arthritis since late 1964. He is now able to do only occasional chores, such as cutting wood or building fences. From work of this kind, he received total income in 1965 of less than $500.

Mr. F had eight years in school and lives a very quiet life. He is a World War II veteran, but does not participate in veterans' activities because their meetings are held too far away from where he lives.

Mr. and Mrs. G

This family unit is in the concluding stage of the life cycle. Mr. and Mrs. G, aged 74 and 70 are now living alone, their ten children all having left home to make their own living. Their progeny range in age from 25 to 45. The aging parents own their single-story house of wood siding. Space is ample for the two of them, some 1,000 square feet, but there is no indoor plumbing, no public sewage system, and no septic tank. Drinking water supply is from a well. The house has no basement or garage, and is heated with wood.

In 1960, Mr. G retired from forty-two years of farming. He has had no other work experience.

Education has played little part in the lives of Mr. and Mrs. G and their children. Mr. G had only one year of schooling and his wife had none. Neither can read, and Mr. G can write only his name. Their oldest son graduated from high school, but he is the only one of their ten children who completed more than six years of school; the others dropped out after six years or less.

This couple lives on a monthly check of $105 from the Veterans' Administration. In 1965, Mrs. G earned $60 picking berries, making their total income for that year $1,320.

Mr. and Mrs. H

This is an elderly retired couple whose lives have been spent in farming. Mr. H is 81 years old, his wife is 72. They live in a small, one-story house which they own. They have indoor plumbing facilities and a septic tank; drinking water comes from a well. The house is heated with gas.

Mr. H has been retired from farming since 1950 and has had no other employment experience. Mrs. H has been a full-time housewife and was recently partially disabled by a stroke. Their 43-year-old daughter, a registered nurse, has returned home to care for her parents. Their three sons are living away from home, working full-time.

This family has had little schooling, except for the daughter who is a college graduate. The father had only six years of school, the mother completed eight grades, and the sons finished only elementary school.

Total income for this couple is $984 a year, from old-age assistance. Need for cash income is reduced somewhat by the fact that their house is debt-free, and they supply some of their food needs from a garden and keeping some poultry.

All of the above families lived in either Adair or McCurtain counties, in Oklahoma. They did not live on reservations. The initials used for the various families are simply alphabetical, with no relation to their real names.

LIFE ON A RESERVATION IN NORTH DAKOTA

North Dakota is another State which has a large number of rural Indians. The following description of life on a reservation in one of our sample counties, Rolette, will yield some insight into the relatively recent situation there.

There are four Indian reservations in North Dakota which embrace, in one way or another, the full gamut of problems and issues arising from the special reservation status of the American Indian. Running through the fabric of all four North Dakota reservations are similar threads of concern about how to deal with the human problems which become special and complex because they are peculiarly Indian problems.

In a series of carefully researched articles appearing in the Fargo Forum in 1966, the writer quotes one Indian as saying that, "Being an Indian is a state of mind." [10] The Indian, who has been the object of many decades of management which has engendered dependence on an alien culture, *does* have special problems. Those who are concerned with administering reservation affairs are faced with the dual problems of essentially welfare assistance for the residual population now living on the reservation and preparing the young people through education and training, better health and employment opportunities to become self-sufficient on or off the reservation. None of the aspects of these twin problems will be solved easily or quickly.

TURTLE MOUNTAIN CHIPPEWA RESERVATION

In microcosm, the Turtle Mountain Reservation, wholly within the borders of Rolette County, offers an illustration of the ways in which these myriad problems and issues hamper efforts to alleviate poverty among rural Indians. This reservation is located in rolling hills just south of the Canadian border. Because of this geographical position, the Indians have acquired considerable French culture through intermarriage with French Canadians for many generations. Their surnames, speech, and customs evidence strong French influence.

Turtle Mountain is small in land area but large in population size compared with the other reservations in North Dakota. There are more than 7,000 Chippewa Indians on and adjacent to the reservation, in a total county population of 10,641. The principal center of activity is in Belcourt, where the Bureau of Indian Affairs (BIA) headquarters is located, as well as the Turtle Mountain Community School, the Public Health Service hospital, and St. Ann's Catholic Mission.

But most of the Indians do not live in Belcourt. Their small cabins are out in the hills, close together, off the gravel roads. Constructed

[10] Olson, Cal, "The Indian in North Dakota," The Fargo Forum and Moorhead News, January 16–20, 1966. (Five-part series)

of logs, the cabins are stuccoed with a clay-water mixture as a protection against rugged North Dakota winters. The cabins are heated mostly with oil, although a few still use wood for heating. Many of the residents have electricity and television sets. They live on the land, but most do not farm it—fewer than seventy families make all or part of their living from farming, even though agriculture is what they know and other work is scarce.

Nearly sixty percent of the Turtle Mountain Indians have incomes of less than $3,000 a year from all sources—wages or salaries, land lease fees, welfare payments. This income level reflects in part the work scarcity, but it is also related to the skill level of the population. Aside from the relatively few Indians who are employed by BIA and the U.S. Public Health Service on the reservation, the principal sources of jobs are two small local industries. One is a Bulova Watch Company jewel bearing factory located in Rolla, in which 100 Indians earned an average of $70 weekly at the time this newspaper account was written. The other enterprise is a souvenir plant called Chippewayan Authentics which employed twelve people. While Indians, noted for their manual dexterity, have been successful in this kind of work, the total number represented on these payrolls is obviously insignificant in terms of employment needs, and efforts to induce other industries to locate in the area have been so far without success.

The Work Experience Program (WEP) of the Office of Economic Opportunity fills in some of the unemployment gap for adults. This program was said to be the first Indian-oriented WEP to be funded in the United States, as of June 1965. Because 157 of the 175 men in the program were receiving BIA general assistance, BIA continued its share of their financial welfare. About three-fifths of the WEP budget was earmarked for salaries of the participants so they could maintain their families while engaged in the program. The average worker received $180 monthly.

Although most of the men were anxious to learn a trade, especially the operation of heavy road construction equipment, the WEP budget did not permit renting such equipment. The jobs they performed, therefore, consisted of working as orderlies or janitors in nearby hospitals and schools, cutting roads and fire breaks into lakes and recreation areas on the reservation, cleaning up the litter of junk automobiles and burying the debris, and renovating submarginal housing where owners would pay for the materials. The participants spent two hours two evenings each week in classes studying elementary and junior high school subjects.

Other OEO programs on the reservation were CAP-sponsored education programs, including remedial education, Head-Start and kindergartens, and guidance counseling, plus a supervised recreation program. In 1965, there were 51 CAP employees on the reservation, 41 of them Indians, mostly serving as teacher aides and aides in guidance counseling.

Educational facilities on and near the reservation appear to be fairly ample. The Turtle Mountain Community School in Belcourt operates grades one through twelve and three other day schools have grades one through six. Indian students also attend four other day schools on the perimeter of the reservation, as well as three off-reservation boarding schools. Total enrollment in these schools accounts for about 1,800 students. In addition, some thirty-six high school graduates are in college, and sixty others are taking some form of post-high school vocational and technical training. Regular school attendance is said to be a problem, made difficult by the indifference of some of the parents. Dropouts are numerous, thought to be because the educational program may be too academic for the many students who are not college-bound.[11]

Although the health of the Indians on this reservation has greatly improved and the free PHS medical facilities and services are heavily used, there remain serious health problems. Turtle Mountain has a 46-bed PHS hospital in Belcourt in which nearly all of the Indian mothers have their babies, to which admissions increase 8 percent a year and outpatient visits nearly 11 percent yearly, at the rate of 70 outpatient visits for examination or treatment daily. The hospital has four PHS doctors, two dentists, and two pharmacists to handle this heavy caseload. The facilities of the hospital are so old that only emergency surgery is performed there. Hospital care at Federal expense may be authorized by PHS at other community hospitals, mainly at Rolette, North Dakota, and at the Air Force Base hospital in Minot.[12]

The health problems which plague this reservation, as is true of many others, probably call for education as much as medicine, since they grow out of the environment. Such ills as dysentery, skin diseases, respiratory illnesses, and malnutrition are caused by such elementary defects as lack of cleanliness, poor ventilation and improper heating, inadequate or improper diet. Preventive health measures, including better information on hygiene and nutrition, are needed. A further, major cause of poor health and other problems among these Indians is alcoholism. Here again, the answer is not primarily medicine, but rather in the environment—education, regulation, better social and economic conditions.

Turtle Mountain, on the plus side, has available schools and free medical care; it has a self-governing Tribal Council of nine men headed by an elected college graduate; the BIA Superintendent is also an Indian, employed by BIA for fifteen years; it has two small industries and some OEO activities; it has BIA and State welfare assistance.

On the other side of the coin, Turtle Mountain has low income and few occupational skills; it has poor land, and there has always been too little of it for each tribal member to receive an allotment there; the steadily growing population has made land scarcity an acute problem. As elsewhere, the land has been fragmented through years of inheritance since the time of allotment, and because of its low rental value, provides the tribe with little money income. The area lacks water for improved sanitation. The reservation is confronted with complicated jurisdictional relationships at Federal, State, county, and tribal levels in the administration of justice—crime, juvenile delinquency, and disputes of all kinds. Unemployment and underemployment are widespread. Perhaps most important of all, the thoughtful Indian is uncertain about the future and confused by conflicting advice as to where and how he should find it—on or off the reservation, "Amer-

---

[11] Federal Facilities for Indians, Tribal Relations with the Federal Government. Report by Mamie L. Mizen for Committee on Appropriations, U.S. Senate, 1965–66, p. 54.
[12] Ibid., p. 53.

icanized" or as an Indian. These social and psychological problems do not yield to easy solution, but they are very real.

RURAL NONRESERVATION INDIAN GROUPS

It has been estimated in the Economic Research Service that there were scattered throughout the United States in 1960 more than 100,000 rural Indians who lived off the reservations.[13] They lived in the rural areas of some twenty States, the largest numbers in Oklahoma and North Carolina. These estimates include only those counties which had at least one hundred rural Indians. Every part of the country was represented by the twenty States, from Maine to California.

Information is limited about these Indian groups, which have no official connection with the Federal government and receive no services such as reservation Indians do. Their status and characteristics vary widely from Region to Region, and even from State to State. Four States each in the Northeast, North Central, and West Regions, and eight States in the South are included in this discussion of rural nonreservation Indian groups.

NORTHEAST REGION

In this Region, there were estimated to have been in 1960 nearly 7,000 Indians in rural communities in New York, about 1,400 in Maine, 425 in Massachusetts, and 300 in Rhode Island, a total for the Region of about 9,000.

New York State Indians are members of various Iroquois tribes located mainly in eight counties. Although they live on reservations, they receive so little Federal support that, for all practical purposes, they must be regarded as nonreservation Indians. Federal land trusteeship was terminated in 1948 and 1950. In Cattaraugus County, the tribes are composed of Senecas, who earn below-average income from a very poor land base. Senecas are also located in Chautauqua, Erie, and Genesee counties, pursuing a variety of occupations. A total of nearly 3,000 Senecas live in these four counties. About 1,700 rural Mohawks are found in Franklin County where they are mostly farmers and steel workers. In Niagara County, the Tuscarora Indians generally commute to Niagara Falls for employment, while Syracuse is the commuting center for Onondagas, Oneidas, and Cayugas in Onondaga County. There are only about two hundred rural Indians in Suffolk County, and they live on a small State reservation. The Indian population in this county is mixed, especially with the Negro population. Jobs are plentiful, but improvement of their housing by Farmers' Home Administration assistance has been hampered by their common ownership of land.

In Maine, rural nonreservation Indians were in three counties—Aroostook, Penobscot, and Washington. They were scattered in Aroostook County, the largest group being in Houlton Town, and no information is available on their situation. The Penobscot tribe in the county of that name lived mainly on a State reservation with no Federal support. They had a tribal government of their own, subject

---

[13] This portion of the report on nonreservation Indians is based almost entirely on an unpublished paper by Calvin L. Beale, entitled "Estimated Population in Rural Nonreservation Indian Groups in the United States, 1960," Economic Research Service, 1968.

to the State of Maine, and were found principally on islands in the Penobscot River. Social and economic conditions of this tribe were poor. In Washington County, about three-fifths of the Passamaquoddy tribe lived on a State reservation similar to that in Penobscot and the remainder in two settlements in unorganized territory.

In both Massachusetts counties in which rural Indians lived—Barnstable and Dukes—the Indian population is mixed, with white and Negro ancestry. In Barnstable, the Indians have customarily made their living from fishing, oystering, and cranberry picking, but with more general work in recent years, while in Dukes County, they depend on the summer resort trade on Martha's Vineyard Island. Only about three hundred Indians, mixed-blood descendants of the Narragansett tribe, live in Washington County, Rhode Island. They live in two towns—South Kingstown and Charlestown—under fairly good economic conditions.

NORTH CENTRAL REGION

This Region contains something over 5,000 rural nonreservation Indians in four States—Wisconsin, Michigan, Nebraska, and Ohio. Wisconsin has the largest number—2,400—all in Menominee County where they comprise 92 percent of the total population. This county was created in 1961 when Federal trusteeship of the Menominee tribe's land was terminated. The Menominees control the government of the county, which has the same boundaries as the former Menominee Reservation, and they are engaged in timber and sawmill operations. Farming is only a part-time, non-commercial enterprise for those classed as farmers. The area, which is wooded and has many lakes, provides good hunting and fishing for the residents. While the economic and social conditions of this tribe are better than many Indian communities, they fall far below U.S. standards. Median family income in 1959 was only $2,638, and more than two-thirds of the housing units were considered deteriorating or dilapidated.[14]

In Michigan, about four hundred Indians are scattered through the population of Allegan, Berrien, and Van Buren Counties, and something over 1,000 Ottawa and Chippewa Indians live along the northwestern coast of the Lower Peninsula in six counties, as well as in two counties in the Upper Peninsula. The largest single concentration in the Lower Peninsula is in Sutton's Bay Township of Leelanau County. Information is lacking on the current socioeconomic status of the rural Indians in Michigan.

There are about 1,000 rural Indians in northwestern Nebraska, presumably Sioux, who do not live on reservations, but are effectively adjacent to the large Pine Ridge Reservation in South Dakota. The small group of Indians in Highland County, Ohio, is not classified as Indian in the Census, but these 130 people consider themselves to be Cherokees, linked with Indian relatives in Oklahoma, and they carry on some Indian traditions. They are poor hill people who live in the hollows of the Appalachian border of Highland County, near the community of Carmel, and the settlement extends somewhat into Pike County. In the mid-1960's, they organized a development program and received an OEO grant as Indians. They are heavily dependent on welfare assistance.

---

[14] Weidemann, Wayne H. and Fuguitt, Glenn V., "Menominee : Wisconsin's 72nd County," Dept. of Sociology, College of Agriculture, Univ. of Wisconsin, Madison, Population Note No. 3, April 1963, pp. 30–31.

THE WEST

In the West, which has about 17,000 rural nonreservation Indians, the great majority lives in California—about 14,000 in some thirty-four counties. The rest are in Oregon, Nevada, and Utah. The number of rural Indians per county in this Region ranges from only 100 to about 2,000.

The rural California Indians, who were given "rancherias" or residential homesites rather than being placed on reservations, have been excluded from most Federal programs for Indians, according to a recent report of the California State Advisory Commission on Indian Affairs. By and large, their socioeconomic status is superior to that of most Indian communities.

Oregon has approximately 3,000 nonreservation Indians in eight counties. Most of the Indian reservations and special Federal services for Indians in Oregon have been terminated during the last fifteen years. Many of these Indian groups live on or near what were formerly reservation lands. In at least two counties, Klamath and Lincoln, they are said to have better than average socioeconomic status, but in Wasco County, some 440 Indians of the former Umatilla Reservation have low average income. The status of Indians in the remaining counties is not known.

There are about 100 rural Indians in Churchill County, Nevada, and a like number in Washington County, Utah. The Nevada Indians are of the Shoshone tribe who formerly lived on the Austin Reservation. In Utah, they are of the Paiute tribe, also living on a former reservation.

THE SOUTH

This Region as a whole had nearly 75,000 nonreservation rural Indians located in eight States.[15] It is estimated that there were nearly 38,000 of them in Oklahoma in 1960. Determination of their precise number is complicated in this State by several factors, most importantly the fact that their ancestry is now so mixed with white and Negro populations that Indians are often indistinguishable as Indians, even though they can trace part of their heritage back to tribal rolls. In addition, all Indian reservations, except that of the Osage tribe, have been terminated—some many years ago, others since 1959. Indians are therefore dispersed throughout the population and retain a somewhat tenuous connection with the Bureau of Indian Affairs, which still maintains agency offices in the State and "assumes some responsibility" for Indians. It is not only difficult to determine the number and location of this fractionally mixed Indian population, but it is also difficult to know the extent of their need for additional assistance *as Indians*. This kind of knowledge depends on county-by-county, tribe-by-tribe information supplied by persons who are thoroughly familiar with local conditions.

Rural nonreservation Indians were living in fifty Oklahoma counties in 1960, the largest number in Adair County. Low family income and low educational levels were widespread in many of the counties. These were also counties in which there were relatively large concentrations of rural Indians.

In North Carolina, more than 31,000 rural nonreservation Indians

---

[15] The eight States are: Oklahoma, North Carolina, Virginia, Alabama, Louisiana, Delaware, South Carolina, and Texas.

were found in twelve counties. About 29,000 Lumbee were located in Cumberland, Harnett, Hoke, Robeson, Sampson, and Scotland counties, the largest numbers in Robeson and Hoke counties. The Lumbee are of tri-racial origin, but have been enumerated in the Census as Indian since 1890 and were officially so recognized by Act of Congress in 1953, although not granted Federal services by that Act. They were mostly poor and undereducated, and are engaged in agriculture as small-scale owners, tenants, and hired workers. They have one of the highest fertility rates of any ethnic group in the nation; their rate of natural increase is therefore very high. Some have recently migrated from North Carolina, going principally to Baltimore.

Other tri-racial groups of Indians live in back-country tobacco farming sections of North Carolina in Halifax, Nash, and Warren counties. They have been officially recognized as Indians only since 1950. A tri-racial group in Person County, also tobacco farmers, has been recognized by North Carolina as Indian since 1920.

Virginia had slightly over 1,000 rural Indians who lived in seven counties in 1960. In Halifax County, there were about 120 Indians who are a part of the tri-racial group in Person County, North Carolina, mentioned above, in which many of their children have gone to school. They are mostly tobacco farmers. As in North Carolina, the Indians of Virginia are of tri-racial origin. Most of them are not officially recognized as Indians by the State, and are living under very poor socioeconomic conditions.

Indians in Alabama, numbering about 750, were found in Escambia and Washington counties. In the former, they are mixed blood descendants of the Creek Indians who did not go to Oklahoma. Poor, part-time farmers, they receive no Federal support or services, but would like assistance to make a tourist attraction of Fort Mims. They have their own churches and a segregated elementary school, and have revived some Indian dancing and handicrafts. About 280 Census Indians in Washington County are part of a larger tri-racial group in the central and southern part of the county who are known colloquially as "Cajans." Some of their descent can be traced to the Creek Indians of Escambia County, but the Cajans are a separate population. Living in rather isolated piney woods country on dirt roads, they are in very poor straits economically and socially.

In the remainder of the South, the number of rural Indians per State is rather small, ranging from 370 in Texas to 2,470 in Louisiana. Delaware had only about 540 and South Carolina, 535. In Louisiana, 180 rural Indians of the Coushatta tribe lived in Allen Parish, still speak their native language, and carry on some handicraft work. Their children have attended public schools since 1949. Their economic and social status is fair. Houma Indians live in Lafourche Parish (140) and in Terrebonne Parish (1,900). Of mixed racial origin, they speak French and live mainly along the bayous, where many engage in fishing and trapping for a livelihood. Income levels and housing conditions are poor, and only recently has a public school been available to them. Most of these Indians are landless, and were characterized in an Interior Department report as severely exploited in their fishing and trapping operations. Some 250 Indians live in Plaquemines and Rapides parishes, in the latter county being of mixed blood but claiming Choctaw ancestry. Educational opportunity has been limited until recently to a segregated elementary school; none of the residents has gone to high school. Their dependence for employment in the past has been on a large timber company, but this work is no longer available.

Delaware had 130 Indians in Kent County, a tri-racial group claiming descent from the Nanticoke tribe. They have lived for many years as a separate population group with their own elementary school. In Sussex County, the 400 Indians are also Nanticokes, but live as a separate population also, principally in an area known as Indian Hundred. They have historically maintained separate schools and have tried to preserve their Indian tradition. Their social and economic condition is intermediate between local whites and Negroes.

Lumbee Indians in Dillon and Marlboro counties in South Carolina numbered about 110 in each county. They are part of the tribe mentioned earlier as residing in Robeson County, North Carolina. They are quite poor. There were some 315 Catawba Indians in York County, South Carolina, located on a former reservation southeast of Rock Hill. Federal trusteeship of their land terminated in 1962, and they are provided no Federal services. They are mainly employed in cotton mills and other industrial enterprises.

The only rural nonreservation Indians in Texas were living in Polk County. They were residents of the former Alabama-Coushatta Reservation near Livingston. Federal land trusteeship for this group was terminated in 1955, but tribal members are still eligible for Federal education and medical aid.

Considerably more information is needed about the estimated 100,000 people in rural nonreservation Indian groups. No person or agency at the present time has the requisite knowledge to report on their current social and economic situation with precision. It is believed that many groups are in poverty, in poor health, in poor housing. Educational levels are generally low, and either unemployment or underemployment is widespread. For these Indians, there is little or no Federal support as Indians, and for some there never has been. As American citizens, they are entitled to assistance where it is needed. Detailed local knowledge about them is absolutely required in order to ensure that such assistance is given intelligently and with understanding.

CONCLUSION

While the same symptoms of rural poverty have been repeated monotonously here as everywhere, the picture is not dark for all Indians or in all places. Some tribes have demonstrated that Indians can be enterprising and successful. They have converted some of their lands into profitable uses, lured industry to their areas, supplied a stable local labor force—and prospered. Some of the thousands who have gone to large cities have made satisfactory adjustments to urban life and living.[16] But this is not the usual pattern; the majority have not prospered, especially in the rural sector where most of them are.

Hopeful signs are appearing among Indian young people who are seeking higher education as the avenue to promising employment opportunities in a modern affluent society. Some have succeeded despite the pervasive, ambivalent feeling about leaving their reservations and families behind in their search for greater opportunity in the world outside. Also, there are now in existence at least five national Indian organizations to give voice to Indian needs and to help Indians help

16 Hoffman, James W., "A Comeback for the Vanishing American?" Presbyterian Life, Jan. 15, Feb. 1 and 15, and March 1, 1969.

each other to satisfy those needs. There are many outstanding Indian leaders in all segments of American society—business, politics, the arts, the entertainment world. The great diversity of special talents the American Indian has to offer—in industry, in government, in sports, in arts and crafts—is becoming better known to society at large.[17] All these are true accomplishments and promising signs.

Unfortunately, these forward strides leave many thousands of rural Indians still in the hinterland, still looking for the economic and social opportunities that are widely available to the society around them. The predicament of thousands of rural Indians is largely untouched and unbenefited by the continuously rising standards of living of much of the rest of the American population.

What the Indian today wants is what most American citizens not only want but demand. As a recent report of a Task Force of the Chamber of Commerce of the United States put it, "Indian spokesmen have stated Indian wants. They want to retain their culture. They want to be consulted and to have a real voice in decisions relating to themselves. They want to retain their reservation lands. And Indians want to enter modern economic life and enjoy its advantages. * * *" [18]

Like other minority groups, American Indians want to control their own destinies. The way to make this a realistic goal is not at all clear. The basic issue of separatism versus integration with the larger society is crucial in America today. How to join the mainstream of the society and yet retain a separate cultural heritage has not been satisfactorily demonstrated by any substantial minority group with that posture. Barriers of economic and social status, customs, language, and traditions continually get in the way of acculturation of the minority population.

The plight of the rural Indian, on or off the reservation, is exacerbated by his isolation, his dependent status for too long, his lack of preparation for modern nonfarm society, and his uncertainty about where his future lies. He is still, today, "ill-fed, ill-clothed, and ill-housed"—in other words, in poverty.

REFERENCES

BEALE, CALVIN L. 1968. Estimated Population in Rural Nonreservation Indian Groups in the United States, 1960. Economic Research Service, U.S. Dept. Agr. Unpublished paper.

CHAMBER OF COMMERCE OF THE UNITED STATES. 1969. Rural Poverty and Regional Progress in an Urban Society. Task Force on Economic Growth and Opportunity, Fourth Report.

ENCYCLOPAEDIA BRITANNICA. 1954. Volume 12. Indian, North American..

FARB, PETER. 1968. The American Indian, A Portrait in Limbo. Saturday Review. Oct.

GREIDER, WILLIAM, 1969. Wounded Knee Still Festers. Washington Post. Feb. 23.

HOFFMAN, JAMES W. 1969. A Comeback for the Vanishing American? Presbyterian Life. Jan. 15, Feb. 1 and 15, and March 1.

HOLMES, O. WENDELL. 1969. Poverty Among the American Indians. Economic Research Service, U.S. Dept. Agr. Feb. Unpublished paper.

HUNT, ELEANOR P. 1967. Infant Mortality and Poverty Areas. Children's Bureau, U.S. Dept. of Health, Education, and Welfare. Reprint from Welfare in Review, Vol. 5, No. 7. Aug.–Sept.

NADER, RALPH. 1968. Lo, the Poor Indian. The New Republic. March 30.

---

[17] Ibid.

[18] "Rural Poverty and Regional Progress in an Urban Society," Task Force on Economic Growth and Opportunity, Fourth Report, Chamber of Commerce of the United States, 1969, pp. 63–64.

NATIONAL ADVISORY COMMISSION ON RURAL POVERTY. 1967. Rural Poverty. Hearings, Tucson, Arizona, Jan. 26 and 27.

OKLAHOMA EMPLOYMENT SECURITY COMMISSION. 1968. Indians in Oklahoma. Oklahoma State Employment Service. Oklahoma City. August.

OLSON, CAL. 1966. The Indian in North Dakota. The Fargo Forum and Moorhead News. Jan. 16–20.

U.S. BUREAU OF THE CENSUS. 1960. Census of Popultaion, PC(1), U.S. and individual States; PC(2)1C, Nonwhite Population by Race, Subject Reports.
——— 1967. County and City Data Book.

U.S. DEPARTMENT OF AGRICULTURE. 1966. Rural People in the American Economy. Agr. Econ. Rpt. 101. Oct.

U.S. DEPARTMENT OF HEALTH, EDUCATION, AND WELFARE. 1966. Indian Health Highlights. U.S. Public Health Service.
——— 1968. Infant and Perinatal Mortality Rates by Age and Color, 1956–60, 1961–65, United States, Each State and County. Social and Rehabilitation Service. Jan.

U.S. SENATE. 1966. Federal Facilities for Indians—Tribal Relations with the Federal Government, 1965–66. Report by Mamie L. Mizen for the Committee on Appropriations.
——— 1967. Ozarks-Four Corners Regional Development Commissions—Hearings before a Special Subcommittee on Economic Development of the Committee on Public Works, 90th Congress, 1st Session. Aug. 16–19.
——— 1967. Examinations of the War on Poverty, Hearings before the Subcommittee on Employment, Manpower, and Poverty of the Committee on Labor and Public Welfare. Part 3, Albuquerque, New Mexico, April 24, and Part 14, Sparta, Wis., May 26.

WEIDEMANN, WAYNE H. AND FUGUITT, GLENN V. 1963. Menominee: Wisconsin's 72nd County. Population Note No. 3, Dept. Rural Sociology, Coll. of Agr., Univ. of Wis., Madison. April.

———

APPENDIX TABLES

TABLE 1.—INDIAN POPULATION IN SELECTED STATES, RURALITY OF STATES AND INDIAN POPULATION, AND INDIANS ON RESERVATIONS, 1960

State	Indian population, number	Percent of total State population that is rural	Percent of Indians in rural residence	On reservations Number	On reservations Percent
Arizona	83, 387	25. 5	90. 0	83, 387	100. 0
California	39, 014	13. 6	47. 1	830	2. 1
Colorado	4, 288	26. 3	58. 2	1, 428	33. 3
Florida	2, 504	26. 1	59. 1	1, 183	47. 2
Idaho	5, 231	52. 5	86. 8	4, 194	80. 2
Iowa	1, 708	47. 0	16. 8	465	27. 2
Kansas	5, 069	39. 0	29. 7	729	14. 4
Michigan	9, 701	26. 6	48. 3	1, 073	11. 1
Minnesota	15, 496	37. 8	69. 0	11, 015	71. 1
Mississippi	3, 119	62. 3	94. 6	2, 617	83. 9
Montana	21, 181	49. 8	87. 9	19, 014	89. 8
Nebraska	5, 545	45. 7	64. 4	3, 168	57. 1
Nevada	6, 681	29. 6	74. 9	6, 000	89. 8
New Mexico	56, 255	34. 1	84. 1	55, 715	99. 0
North Carolina	38, 129	60. 5	95. 5	3, 310	8. 7
North Dakota	11, 736	64. 8	90. 0	10, 314	87. 9
Oklahoma [1]	64, 689	37. 1	63. 0	64, 596	99. 9
Oregon	8, 026	37. 8	67. 9	2, 560	31. 9
South Dakota	25, 794	60. 7	82. 3	23, 693	91. 8
Utah	6, 961	25. 1	76. 4	4, 676	67. 2
Washington	21, 076	31. 9	66. 6	14, 446	68. 5
Wisconsin	14, 297	36. 2	72. 0	6, 924	48. 4
Wyoming	4, 020	43. 2	89. 5	3, 464	86. 2
Total, 23 States	**453, 907**		76. 9	325, 457	71. 7

[1] All Indian reservations in Oklahoma except that of the Osage Tribe have been terminated since 1960.

Source: 1960 Census of Population PC(1)B and data from Everett E. White, IHS, HEW, dated Dec. 30, 1968.

TABLE 2.—DISTRIBUTION OF RURAL INDIANS AND OF TOTAL RURAL POPULATION, UNITED STATES, BY AGE, 1960

Age	Rural Indians Number	Rural Indians Percent	Total rural population Number	Total rural population Percent
Under 5 years	64, 340	16. 9	6, 260, 791	11. 6
5 to 9	56, 988	15. 0	6, 083, 155	11. 3
10 to 14	48, 481	12. 7	5, 725, 977	10. 6
15 to 19	37, 080	9. 8	4, 487, 549	8. 3
20 to 24	25, 934	6. 8	3, 076, 511	5. 7
25 to 29	21, 829	5. 7	3, 023, 849	5. 6
30 to 34	20, 161	5. 3	3, 306, 444	6. 1
35 to 39	18, 550	4. 9	3, 436, 986	6. 4
40 to 44	15, 825	4. 2	3, 275, 216	6. 1
45 to 49	15, 378	4. 0	3, 122, 993	5. 8
50 to 54	13, 120	3. 5	2, 754, 841	5. 1
55 to 59	15, 046	4. 0	2, 415, 273	4. 5
60 to 64	8, 500	2. 2	2, 051, 452	3. 8
65 to 69	7, 309	1. 9	1, 855, 498	3. 4
70 to 74	5, 139	1. 4	1, 424, 809	2. 6
75 years and over	6, 626	1. 7	1, 753, 081	3. 3
Total, all ages	380, 306	100. 0	54, 054, 425	100. 0
Median age	17. 7		27. 3	

Source: 1960 Census of Population, PC(2) 1C and PC(1) 1B.

TABLE 3.—SIZE OF FAMILY: RURAL INDIANS AND TOTAL RURAL POPULATION, UNITED STATES, 1960

Size of family	Rural Indians		Total rural population	
	Number	Percent	Number	Percent
2 persons	10,878	16.9	4,033,744	30.6
3 persons	10,091	15.7	2,673,386	20.3
4 persons	9,325	14.5	2,522,948	19.1
5 persons	8,915	13.8	1,757,769	13.3
6 persons	7,515	11.7	1,035,401	7.9
7 or more persons	17,637	27.4	1,165,107	8.8
All families	64,361	100.0	13,188,355	100.0

Source: 1960 Census of Population, PC(2) 1C and PC(1) 1D.

TABLE 4.—DISTRIBUTION OF FAMILY INCOME, RURAL INDIANS AND TOTAL RURAL POPULATION, UNITED STATES, 1960

Income	Rural Indians		Total rural population	
	Number	Percent	Number	Percent
Under $1,000	18,025	28.0	1,310,295	9.9
$1,000 to $2,999	22,085	34.3	3,112,294	23.6
$3,000 to $4,999	12,391	19.2	3,154,303	23.9
$5,000 to $6,999	6,557	10.2	2,670,812	20.3
$7,000 to $9,999	3,659	5.7	1,422,191	10.8
$10,000 to $14,999	1,290	2.0	1,198,998	9.1
$15,000 and over	354	.6	319,458	2.4
Total families	64,361	100.0	13,188,351	100.0

Source: 1960 Census of Population, PC(2)1C and PC(1)1C.

TABLE 5.—OCCUPATION OF EMPLOYED INDIANS AND TOTAL RURAL POPULATION, UNITED STATES, BY SEX, 1960

Occupation of employed	Rural Indians				Total rural population			
	Males		Females		Males		Females	
	Number	Percent	Number	Percent	Number	Percent	Number	Percent
Professional, technical, and kindred	1,701	3.5	1,324	7.4	760,566	6.0	572,794	12.3
Farmers and farm managers	6,067	12.6	752	4.2	2,265,808	18.0	109,498	2.4
Managers, officials, and proprietors, except farm	1,079	2.2	314	1.8	963,065	7.6	174,598	3.8
Clerical and kindred	1,015	2.1	1,527	8.5	465,488	3.7	958,857	20.6
Sales workers	465	1.0	467	2.6	512,327	4.1	344,867	7.4
Craftsmen, foremen, and kindred	5,266	11.0	115	0.6	2,249,467	17.9	49,112	1.1
Operatives and kindred workers	8,170	17.0	1,929	10.8	2,553,796	20.3	859,977	18.5
Private household workers	125	0.4	2,332	13.0	16,212	0.1	442,899	9.5
Service workers, excluding private households	1,939	4.0	3,986	22.3	431,953	3.4	675,614	14.5
Farm laborers and foremen	8,613	17.9	2,074	11.6	1,016,358	8.1	212,521	4.6
Laborers except farm and mine	9,413	19.6	348	1.9	963,524	7.6	31,359	0.7
Occupation not reported	4,199	8.7	2,740	15.3	402,050	3.2	216,147	4.6
Total employed	48,052	100.0	17,908	100.0	12,600,614	100.0	4,648,243	100.0

Source: 1960 Census of Population, PC(2) 1C and PC(1) 1C.

TABLE 6.—EMPLOYMENT STATUS OF RURAL INDIANS AND TOTAL RURAL POPULATION, UNITED STATES, BY SEX, 1960

Employment status	Rural Indians				Total rural population			
	Males		Females		Males		Females	
	Number	Percent	Number	Percent	Number	Percent	Number	Percent
Labor force	61,191	-------	20,494	-------	14,028,047	-------	4,946,572	-------
Armed Forces	2,191				751,090			
Civilian labor force	59,000	100.0	20,439	100.0	13,276,957	100.0	4,934,846	100.0
Employed	48,052	81.4	17,908	87.6	12,600,614	94.9	4,648,243	94.2
Unemployed	10,948	18.6	2,531	12.4	676,343	5.1	286,603	5.8
Not in labor force	50,280	100.0	86,940	100.0	4,807,228	100.0	13,168,374	100.0
Inmate of institution	4,009	8.0	1,178	1.4	476,758	9.9	251,482	1.9
Enrolled in school	15,737	31.3	15,042	17.3	1,644,527	34.2	1,743,148	13.2
Other, under 65 years old	22,694	45.1	62,268	71.6	1,099,553	22.9	9,020,556	68.5
With own child under 6			26,956	31.0			3,423,707	26.0
Other, 65 years and over	7,840	15.6	8,452	9.7	1,586,390	33.0	2,153,188	16.4
All persons 14 years and over	114,710	-------	107,434	-------	18,835,275	-------	18,114,946	-------
Labor force participation rate		53.3		19.1		74.5		27.3

Source: 1960 Census of Population, PC(2) 1C and PC(1) 1D.

TABLE 7.—YEARS OF SCHOOL COMPLETED BY PERSONS 14 YEARS OLD AND OLDER IN THE RURAL INDIAN AND TOTAL RURAL POPULATION, UNITED STATES, BY SEX, 1960

Years of school completed	Rural Indians				Total rural population			
	Males		Females		Males		Females	
	Number	Percent	Number	Percent	Number	Percent	Number	Percent
No school years completed	13,759	12.3	15,791	14.7	462,648	2.5	325,732	1.8
Elementary:								
1 to 4 years	16,431	14.7	12,589	11.7	1,584,075	8.4	1,041,925	5.8
5 to 6 years	15,130	13.6	14,213	13.2	1,713,055	9.1	1,410,388	7.8
7 years	10,900	9.8	10,580	9.9	1,654,407	8.8	1,372,365	7.6
8 years	17,797	16.0	16,788	15.6	3,766,743	20.0	3,398,506	18.8
High school:								
1 to 3 years	23,866	21.4	23,537	21.9	4,128,913	21.9	4,317,171	23.8
4 years	9,946	8.9	10,873	10.1	3,651,156	19.4	4,410,406	24.3
College:								
1 to 3 years	2,787	2.5	2,319	2.2	1,036,750	5.5	1,239,932	6.8
4 years or more	855	.8	744	.7	837,552	4.4	598,505	3.3
Total	111,471	100.0	107,434	100.0	18,835,299	100.0	18,114,930	100.0

Source: 1960 Census of Population, PC(2) 1C and PC(1) 1D.

TABLE 8.—SELECTED INDIAN AND UNITED STATES VITAL STATISTICS, 1954 AND 1964

Vital statistics	Indians	United States (all races)
Infant mortality (deaths per 1,000 live births):		
1964	35.9	24.8
1954	65.0	26.6
Maternal deaths per 10,000 live births:		
1964	6.3	3.4
1954	18.4	5.2
Mortality by specified cause (deaths per 100,000 population):		
Tuberculosis:		
1964	21.3	4.3
1954	54.0	10.2
Gastritis, enteritis, etc.:		
1964	19.3	4.3
1954	56.0	4.9
Morbidity by specified cause per 100,000 population (cases reported per 100,000 population):		
Tuberculosis:		
1964	184.1	26.6
1954	571.0	62.4
Dysentery:		
1964	417.5	8.5
1963	428.1	8.4
23 Federal Indian reservation States birth rate (registered live births per 1,000 population): 1964	43.1	21.0
Average age of death, 1964	43.8	63.6
Life expectancy at birth, 1964	63.5	70.2
Median age of population	17.3	29.5
Percent of population under 20 years	55.2	38.5

Source: Indian Health Highlights, 1966 edition U.S. Department of Health, Education, and Welfare, Public Health Service, pp. XVI, 7.

TABLE 9.—NUMBER AND DISTRIBUTION OF POPULATION BY RESIDENCE IN 16 COUNTIES IN WHICH AT LEAST 1,000 RURAL INDIANS LIVED IN 1960

State and county	Total population 1960	Percent rural 1960	Percent rural nonfarm	Percent rural farm	Percent rural nonwhite is of total population, 1960
Alaska:					
Bethel	5,537	100.0	100.0		90.9
Wade Hampton	3,128	100.0	99.0	1.0	94.6
Arizona:					
Apache	30,438	100.0	83.7	16.3	77.5
Navajo	37,994	67.7	58.3	9.4	48.6
Montana:					
Big Horn	10,007	72.1	39.7	32.4	33.3
Glacier	11,565	60.8	48.4	12.4	35.7
New Mexico:					
McKinley	37,209	52.5	38.6	13.9	42.2
Sandoval	14,201	81.9	77.4	4.5	42.0
North Carolina:					
Hoke	16,356	81.3	45.7	35.6	55.1
Robeson	89,102	79.7	37.2	42.5	52.9
North Dakota:					
Rolette	10,641	100.0	68.3	31.7	43.8
Sioux	3,662	100.0	63.2	36.8	45.2
Oklahoma:					
Adair	13,112	100.0	73.8	26.2	23.3
McCurtain	25,851	80.8	62.1	18.7	18.7
South Dakota:					
Shannon	6,000	100.0	85.8	14.2	84.1
Todd	4,661	100.0	69.2	30.8	58.1
Total	157,316				

Source: 1960 Census of Population, PC (1) C.

TABLE 10.—POVERTY-LINKED CHARACTERISTICS IN 16 COUNTIES IN WHICH AT LEAST 1,000 RURAL INDIANS LIVED IN 1960

State and county	Low income [1] (percent)	Education [2] (years)	Infant mortality [3] (rate)	Unemployment [4] (percent)	Fertility [5] (number)	Migration [6] (percent)
Alaska:						
Bethel	77.2	2.0	94.2	34.9	6,326	([7])
Wade Hampton	84.3	1.6	87.9	21.8	([7])	([7])
Arizona:						
Apache	64.9	.9	43.3	20.4	5,537	[8] −22.2
Navajo	71.3	4.5	54.6	20.1	5,307	[8] −8.7
Montana:						
Big Horn	52.7	8.5	59.4	28.6	([7])	−16.4
Glacier	55.0	8.8	54.5	32.5	5,238	−6.2
New Mexico:						
McKinley	63.1	1.0	42.8	15.6	5,571	[8] −11.2
Sandoval	81.4	5.8	44.7	14.5	4,977	−9.2
North Carolina:						
Hoke	82.8	5.7	56.2	7.3	5,395	[8] −19.8
Robeson	82.6	6.5	46.3	5.9	4,802	[8] −21.8
North Dakota:						
Rolette	61.5	7.5	33.9	35.9	7,276	−24.2
Sioux	64.8	8.5	71.1	28.1	([7])	−23.0
Oklahoma:						
Adair	85.2	5.8	32.3	5.2	([7])	−22.5
McCurtain	80.9	6.1	35.5	6.0	5,702	[8] −27.9
South Dakota:						
Shannon	66.7	7.9	55.9	21.3	5,502	−20.8
Todd	72.2	8.3	71.0	24.2	([7])	−21.5

[1] Low income: Percent of all nonwhite families with incomes under $3,000 in 1959.
[2] Education: Median years of school completed by nonwhite persons 25 years old and over, 1960.
[3] Infant mortality: Number of deaths under 1 year per 1,000 live births in the nonwhite population, 1961–65.
[4] Unemployment: Percent of the civilian labor force 14 years old and over unemployed in the nonwhite population 1960.
[5] Fertility: Number of children ever born per 1,000 women ever married, ages 35–44, in the nonwhite population, 1960.
[6] Migration: Net migration of the population 1950–60, all ages.
[7] Not available.
[8] Nonwhite population only.

Sources: 1960 Census of Population PC(1) C for individual States, Bureau of the Census, tables 87 and 88; "Infant and Perinatal Rates by Age and Color, Each State and County, 1956–60 and 1961–65, "U.S. Department of Health, Education, and Welfare. January 1968; Bowles, Gladys and Tarver, James, "Net Migration of the Population 1950–60 by Age, Sex, and Color," U.S. Department of Agriculture, Economic Research Service, Oklahoma State University, and U.S. Department of Commerce, November 1965.

TABLE 11.—FAMILY INCOME DISTRIBUTION IN 1959 OF THE NONWHITE POPULATION IN 16 COUNTIES IN WHICH AT LEAST 1,000 RURAL INDIANS LIVED IN 1960

State and county	Percent						Median family income
	Under $3,000	$3,000 to $5,999	$6,000 to $7,999	$8,000 to $9,999	$10,000 and over	All families	
Alaska:							
Bethel	77.2	13.8	5.2	2.4	1.4	100	$1.575
Wade Hampton	84.3	12.4	3.3			100	1.370
Arizona:							
Apache	64.9	23.0	5.2	4.4	2.5	100	1.718
Navajo	71.3	18.2	5.3	3.4	1.8	100	1.195
Montana:							
Big Horn	52.7	26.7	10.6	5.6	4.4	100	2.778
Glacier	55.0	24.8	8.3	5.7	6.2	100	2.716
New Mexico:							
McKinley	63.1	24.5	5.4	3.6	3.4	100	1.800
Sandoval	81.4	13.6	2.3	1.8	.9	100	955
North Carolina:							
Hoke	82.8	14.2	2.2	.5	.3	100	1.264
Robeson	82.6	13.8	2.1	1.1	.4	100	1.242
North Dakota:							
Rolette	64.1	27.6	5.1	2.7	.5	100	2.281
Sioux	64.8	26.5	5.9	2.8		100	2.000
Oklahoma:							
Adair	85.2	10.8	2.8		1.2	100	1.530
McCurtain	80.9	14.9	3.1	.3	.8	100	1.742
South Dakota:							
Shannon	66.7	20.9	7.8	4.0	.6	100	1.775
Todd	72.2	17.1	7.6	3.1		100	1.338

Source: 1960 Census of Population, PC(1) C for individual States, table 88.

TABLE 12.—OCCUPATIONAL STRUCTURE AMONG NONWHITE MALES IN 16 COUNTIES IN WHICH AT LEAST 1,000 RURAL INDIANS LIVED IN 1960

State and county	Percent					Total employed	Number
	White-collar [1]	Blue-collar [2]	Service workers [3]	Farm-workers [4]	Occupation not reported		
Alaska:							
Bethel	30.6	46.1	14.0		9.3	100	271
Wade Hampton	29.6	46.7	17.8		5.9	100	135
Arizona:							
Apache	12.6	69.6	4.8	5.9	7.1	100	2,446
Navajo	12.3	66.9	9.6	3.3	7.9	100	1,663
Montana:							
Big Horn	14.5	35.9	7.4	39.5	2.7	100	365
Glacier	22.2	29.0	5.0	41.1	2.7	100	441
New Mexico:							
McKinley	9.7	55.2	4.5	18.0	12.6	100	2,384
Sandoval	5.5	70.6	1.9	14.2	7.8	100	527
North Carolina:							
Hoke	4.2	34.6	7.9	51.8	1.5	100	1,436
Robeson	5.4	28.3	3.9	59.6	2.8	100	9,073
North Dakota:							
Rolette	8.8	39.7	14.7	35.4	1.4	100	285
Sioux	38.6	25.0	17.8	15.0	3.6	100	140
Oklahoma:							
Adair	9.1	39.7	5.0	38.4	7.8	100	242
McCurtain	10.4	59.4	4.7	24.1	1.4	100	831
South Dakota:							
Shannon	18.3	30.6	9.8	39.4	1.9	100	409
Todd	8.4	38.4	6.7	42.8	3.7	100	297

[1] White-collar occupations: Professional, technical, and kindred workers; managers, officials, and proprietors, except farm; clerical and kindred workers; and sales workers.
[2] Blue-collar occupations: Craftsmen, foremen, and kindred workers; operatives and kindred workers; and laborers except farm and mine.
[3] Service workers: Private household and service workers.
[4] Farmworkers: Farmers and farm managers; farm laborers, unpaid family workers; and farm laborers and farm foremen.

Source: 1960 Census of Population, PC(1) C for individual States, table 88.

TABLE 13.—INDUSTRIAL STRUCTURE IN THE NONWHITE POPULATION IN 16 COUNTIES IN WHICH AT LEAST 1,000 RURAL INDIANS LIVED IN 1960

[In percent]

State and county	Agriculture, forestry, fisheries, and mining	Construction	Manufacturing	Transportation, communication, and other utilities	Wholesale and retail trade	Finance, insurance, and real estate	Business and personal services	Entertainment and professional services	Public administration	Industry not reported	Total employed (both sexes)
Alaska:											
Bethel	8.5	---	3.1	11.3	13.9	---	14.1	23.8	15.6	9.7	100.0
Wade Hampton	24.5	---	10.6	2.7	18.5	---	2.7	22.5	10.6	7.9	100.0
Arizona:											
Apache	11.5	19.4	13.7	8.0	5.7	0.2	4.7	22.5	7.1	7.2	100.0
Navajo	6.6	18.2	9.2	11.4	9.0	---	5.7	20.5	8.9	10.5	100.0
Montana:											
Big Horn	34.8	8.2	5.9	1.9	2.5	---	5.0	26.8	13.8	1.1	100.0
Glacier	31.6	6.0	2.0	5.1	14.9	1.8	9.0	19.7	7.3	2.6	100.0
New Mexico:											
McKinley	18.4	8.4	14.0	8.6	8.5	---	4.8	14.1	8.3	14.9	100.0
Sandoval	11.5	15.8	20.1	6.9	7.6	---	6.9	10.6	6.4	14.2	100.0
North Carolina:											
Hoke	47.3	4.6	11.5	2.2	4.3	.2	16.5	10.4	1.5	1.5	100.0
Robeson	56.4	4.8	7.2	1.8	6.2	.1	12.2	7.4	1.0	2.9	100.0
North Dakota:											
Rolette	22.6	3.1	10.6	6.4	5.4		11.2	28.4	10.6	1.7	100.0
Sioux	11.1	4.0			3.6	5.8	11.1	35.1	25.3	4.0	100.0
Oklahoma:											
Adair	35.0	9.9	12.8	5.2	6.7	2.4	8.5	5.2	6.7	7.6	100.0
McCurtain	19.6	5.7	29.8	1.5	11.2	.4	15.1	11.1	3.1	2.5	100.0
South Dakota:											
Shannon	26.4	7.2	1.9	1.2	1.3	---	10.6	30.7	7.2	10.8	100.0
Todd	35.0	12.8	2.7		6.0	2.7	8.2	19.0	15.0	1.3	100.0

Source: 1960 Census of population, PC(1) C for individual States, Table 88.

TABLE 14.—ESTIMATED POPULATION OF RURAL NONRESERVATION INDIAN GROUPS IN THE UNITED STATES, 1960

State	Number	State	Number
Oklahoma	37,730	Alabama	754
North Carolina	31,345	Delaware	541
California	13,995	South Carolina	535
New York	6,950	Massachusetts	425
Oregon	2,955	Texas	370
Louisiana	2,470	Rhode Island	300
Wisconsin	2,400	Ohio	130
Michigan	1,715	Nevada	100
Maine	1,435	Utah	100
Virginia	1,131		
Nebraska	1,000	Total	106,381

Note: Excludes population of counties having fewer than 100 rural nonreservation Indians.

Source: "Rural Nonreservation Indian Groups in the United States," by Calvin L. Beale, ERS, 1968, unpublished paper.

THE AMERICAN INDIAN: NEEDS AND PROBLEMS

By Albert Jenny II*

FOREWORD

Federal efforts to provide economic assistance for the American Indians have a long but not very successful history. Albert Jenny II describes this history, going back to the Dawes Severalty Act of 1887. He argues that Federal policy has been paternalistic, inconsistent, and inadequately funded, and that even the most well-meaning formulators of policy have failed to recognize the Indians' desire to maintain their cultural autonomy. Indian distrust of Federal policy is understandable in view of this history, but it intensifies the difficulties of executing adequate policy today. Although the new Federal programs instituted since 1964 have failed as yet to show conclusive results, a new public attitude of increased concern, together with an apparent greater willingness to accept cultural pluralism in the United States, suggest that a real change for the better in Indian affairs may be underway.

Introduction

The American Indian, like other men, has two basic needs—to survive, and to control the quality of his life in accordance with his own insights and values. Well over half-a-million Indians in more than two hundred communities live in the United States at the present time. Each of these communities has had its separate history of survival efforts. Each represents a surviving distillation of values and concomitant life-styles which vary from each other, and, taken together, contrast more or less sharply with majority patterns of behavior in our society. Nearly all of these communities are very poor in terms of the material resources they would need to realize the fullness of *any* valued way of life—their own, *or* that of the majority.

For the greater part of the time since Indians have been living on reservations, rather than freely roaming or building upon their native land, they have been offered only one road out of a most unsatisfying, meager existence—that of assimilation into the majority. At least since the Dawes Severalty (or General Allotment) Act of 1887, it has been assumed by most whites that it would be a rather magnanimous gesture to offer Indians the opportunity to become part of the mainstream. Two factors were continuously ignored: (1) the pervasive sense of cultural difference from the white majority on the part of the several Indian groupings, which persists in spite of all dilutions and fragmentations of earlier Indian values, and (2) the extremely sophisticated and expensive procedures which would be required if one were to seriously undertake the acculturation of one people to another with any hope of success.

In recent years, there have been indications that some influential segments of the white community interested in Indian affairs are begin-

---

*Supervisor of Research, Montgomery County (Md.) Public Schools, formerly Research Scientist (in applied anthropology) at Human Sciences Research, Inc.

ning to think along lines of strengthening Indian communities, as such, rather than dispersing individual Indians throughout the nation to become merged in the general population. Some whites have long understood the Indian desire to remain autonomous culturally, but Federal agencies did not begin to work meaningfuly in this direction until late 1964, when a number of at least partially Indian-generated self-help programs were funded. There is no guarantee, of course, that such efforts will continue. Federal Indian policy has shifted with the winds of politics many times since the reservation system began. A very brief history of Indian affairs since the Allotment Act of 1887 will serve to set the stage for an examination of the general question of Indian needs and problems.

INDIAN AFFAIRS SINCE 1887

In the last quarter of the 19th Century, three organizations were formed to "help" the Indian: the Women's National Indian Association, the Indian Rights Association, and the Lake Mohonk Conference of Friends of the Indian. These groups were the driving force behind the Dawes Severalty (or General Allotment) Act of 1887 (Alberts, et al., 1966:9). The purpose of the Act was to divide tribal lands into parcels and assign these to individual Indians, with full title and citizenship to devolve upon them in twenty-five years. "Excess" land left after allotment was opened to homesteading by whites. The Act was implemented only on reservations where pressure for Indian lands existed, and in the course of time, Indian lands were reduced from 138 million acres to approximately 52 million acres. When President Grover Cleveland signed the Act, he stated that the "hunger and thirst of the white man for the Indian's land is almost equal to his hunger and thirst after righteousness." (Farb, 1968:256).

One might ask how this was intended to "help" the Indian. Those who, at the time, really believed they were acting on the Indians' behalf had two explanations. They felt that individual ownership of land by the Indians would place at least some limit on white depredations. Without such individual allotment, it was feared that whites would ultimately take over all Indian land. The other point was in line with the perennial feeling that Indian ways must be brought in line with the practices of the dominant society, that individual ownership of land would "civilize" the Indians, for their own good. The General Allotment Act provided for instruction in the arts of agriculture and animal husbandry. Little thought was given to any possible incompatibility between the requirements of an agricultural life and the values of many of the Indian communities involved, and, in any case, the technical assistance offered has been adjudged by later investigators to have been wholly inadequate, even if the Indians had been enthusiastic about the prospect of becoming farmers. Present problems and the possibilities for cooperative action are complicated by the fact that many Indian groups still assume that any offers of Federal assistance will similarly disregard Indian values, and, in any case, will be of insufficient strength to do any good, if and when implemented.

Between the General Allotment Act of 1887 and the second decade of the 20th Century, three changes in Indian conditions occurred: economic stabilization at a level of extreme poverty, levelling out of population decline, with strong indications of an upturn, and a growth

in public sentiment in favor of more fair treatment of the Indian
(though still very little understanding of what such fair treatment
might be from the point of view of the Indian himself). When a cadet
at West Point, the future General, George Armstrong Custer, had
written in a term paper, "The red man is alone in his misery. We
behold him now on the verge of extinction, standing on his last foot-
hold . . . and soon he will be talked of as a noble race who once
existed but have passed away." (Steiner, 1968: x). However, by 1910,
or so, the trend had reversed itself. Vine Deloria, Jr., former Director
of the National Congress of American Indians (NCAI), estimates
that there may be at least one million persons of known Indian ancestry today, while Mel Thom, Chairman of the National Indian Youth
Council, puts the figure at one and one-half million (Steiner, 1968:
324).

Fairer treatment of the Indian is in evidence in the public controversy which led to the defeat of the Bursham Lands Bill. This Bill
would have given white squatters on Indian lands title to land they
were using, which would have been exceedingly disadvantageous to
the Pueblos of the Southwest. In fact, a Committee of One Hundred,
appointed by the Secretary of the Interior to investigate the Pueblo
land case, "deplored the effort to obliterate the unique qualities of
Indian cultures," possibly the first time a government-sponsored body
had officially spoken on behalf of pluralism. This occurred in 1923.

Private organizations interested in the plight of reservation Indians
were also at work, and, in 1928, the first major advance in public
knowledge of Indian affairs, publication of the Meriam Report by the
Brookings Institution, made the formulation of enlightened policy a
distinct possibility. This report clearly stated that the multiple cor-
relates of poverty—ill health, poor housing, inadequate real or cash
income, and other factors—were all interrelated, so that "causes cannot be differentiated from effects" (Meriam et al., 1928). The report
listed the three causes of Indian poverty as: (1) the destruction of the
economic basis of "primitive Indian culture," (2) the irrelevance to
modern economic conditions of the social systems remaining from the
past, and (3) past government policies. The second of these could be
viewed in diametrically opposite ways. One might attempt to meet
this problem through modification of the economic conditions prevailing in specific Indian societies, or one might attempt to modify
the Indian social systems themselves. Even in 1928, the second ap-
roach was largely taken for granted as the appropriate solution by
most whites who hoped to alleviate or abolish Indian poverty.

Nevertheless, the Meriam Report was a step forward, and by 1934,
the Indian Reorganization Act, styled the "New Deal for American
Indians," had become law. This act—

1. Prohibited future allotment of tribal lands, permitting tribes
to assign use rights.

2. Returned to the Indians land not preempted by homesteaders.

3. Permitted tribes to adopt written constitutions and charters
of incorporation.

4. Provided funds for establishing revolving credit unions, for
aiding the tribes in forming internal organizations, for educational assistance, and for the purchase of land.

5. Permitted the various tribes to choose by referendum whether
they wished to have the act apply to them.

Most reservations today operate under constitutions set up under this act.

The balance appeared to have finally swung in the direction of Indian cultural pluralism, for, not only had the Indian Reorganization Act been signed into law, but a new Indian Commissioner had been appointed whose high regard for Indian lifeways broke sharply with the previous assimilationist approach. From 1933 to 1945, John Collier served as Indian Commissioner, and under his direction a policy was instituted based on the concept that the "beauty and wisdom of Indian traditions could enrich the totality of American culture." Solutions to specific problems were sought with this concept in mind. Extravagant praise was heaped on Collier. Oliver LaFarge wrote, "For about a hundred years the Bureau of Indian Affairs, charged with the protection and advancement of the original inhabitants of the United States, functioned hit or miss, with good intentions, sometimes, by trial and error always, with a total disregard of everything that the steady march of scientific knowledge had to offer. * * * today, under Commissioner Collier's administration, a completely changed Indian Bureau is not only calling upon science for all that it can give but is also, through its testing of science in practical application to human life, contributing to our knowledge." (LaFarge, 1942: vii–ix; Spicer, 1961: 169).

However, Collier's administration of Indian Affairs did not go unopposed: "Critics on one side called Collier a romantic and argued that he went to ridiculous lengths to reestablish long dead traditions thereby hampering the progress of groups which had made great strides toward acculturation. Other critics shared Collier's basic philosophy but pointed out that the format he developed for self-government and economic improvement was too arbitrary and no more suited to some tribes than earlier programs designed to expunge Indian distinctiveness." (Lurie, 1961: 480). The Indians themselves, by and large, ever mistrustful of the Federal government, considered Collier's approach just another temporary Washington policy, and since it was inadequately funded, its successes were comparatively few. On some reservations, however, in spite of the long history of half-finished, ill-conceived, and mis-administered programs, a certain amount of enthusiasm was generated by Collier's patent good intentions.

Upon the advent of World War II, however, Indian pessimism was newly justified. Officials entrusted with Indian administration, under the stress of wartime budgets, slipped back into 19th Century attitudes. Congress began talking about terminating both the Bureau of Indian Affairs (BIA) and the Indian Reorganization Act of 1934, with the intention of assigning responsibility for Indian reservations to the several states. This would have meant withdrawal of Federal supports, institution of state taxes, and the inevitable alienation of tribal lands, since very few Indians had been trained to compete for wages in the general economy. Only a handful of tribes were actually terminated. Indians managed to bring up difficult legal complications in most cases, halting termination procedures indefinitely. Among the tribes that were terminated were the Menominee of Wisconsin and the Klamath of Oregon, both originally holding valuable timber lands. (McNickle, 1962: 62). The Menominee reservation is now a county of the State of Wisconsin, subject to all the regulations and problems of county government, while its inhabitants have neither the means nor the know-how to cope with them properly.

In 1954, the BIA began two programs related to increasing population pressure on Indian reservations and the difficulties of reservation economic development. The first of these was initially called the Voluntary American Indian Relocation Program, later changed to the Employment Assistance Program. The aim of this Program was minimum subsidy of urban migration and employment placement of Indian families and adult individuals in industrial centers ranging from Cleveland,.Ohio, to Los Angeles, California. Upon arrival at such destinations, Indians found themselves doing the most menial jobs, if any, and living in the worst slum areas. They soon decided to return to the reservation, but since the BIA had sent them as far afield as possible, in order to discourage returning home, getting back was maximally difficult. In spite of this, it appears that a great many did return home. Those who managed to stick with their new experiences and "make good in the big city" were probably the ones who would have been most likely to solve reservation problems had they stayed home.

Various estimates exist as to the number of Indians living "off the reservation." Fred Eggan writes, "As we have seen, about one-third of the Indian population are no longer on reservations and are making their way in the white world. But some two-thirds of the Indians still prefer reservation life, despite its well-known difficulties. To the social anthropologist the reasons are clear. Man does not live by jobs alone, but in society. On the reservation the Indian is surrounded by kinsmen and friends, and patterns of sharing remove some of the hazards of existence. And there are rituals to maintain the relation between man and nature, as well as between man and man. The Indian who ventures into the white world meets with good will but also with race and class prejudice. But as Indian communities form in the cities they create again a society in which they can live." (Eggan, 1966: 166–167).

William H. Kelly, on the other hand, lists 285,600 Indians living on reservations out of a total of 550,908, as of 1960, giving the annual rate of increase as 28 per 1,000. However, when referring to the general ways Indians are making a living today, Professor Kelly writes, "The majority—perhaps three-fourths—of the Indians in the United States make their entire living through wage work on and off their reservations. Even so, Indians attach a great social and symbolic significance to their land and, almost universally choose to remain on their land as self-employed farmers or livestock growers until economic necessity forces them to abandon agriculture or supplement income from this source through seasonal or temporary wage work.

"This change toward wage work reflects a growing Indian population on a fixed land base, an abandonment of subsistence agriculture, and a desire for a higher standard of living which can only be secured, in agriculture, through an increase in size of land holdings." (Kelly, 1962; Owen et al., 1967: 612–613).

In an effort to meet the need for at least some salable skills on the part of Indians, the second BIA program was initiated. It was entitled the Vocational Training Program, and provided for short-term trade school courses. Employment placement was offered after graduation. These placements also were relatively far from home, and it had frequently been overlooked that unions almost invariably would not accept Indian members, either because their training was not up to standard, or for other less plausible reasons, so that, once again, stranded Indians had to find their way home to reservations where there were no opportunities to use their new skills.

These experiences led to BIA efforts to attract light industry plants to reservation sites, but since most reservations are far from major markets, and there is no social base for well-developed utilities and facilities, such as electric power, water, good roads, and the like, only a few small plants, attracted by an inexpensive and abundant labor supply with no union involvement have come in. These only use a fraction of the Indian population, and at a very low standard of both production and pay. Such shifting and inadequate policies, then, are the backdrop against which current Indian problems may be examined. They are among the major reasons for the prevalent attitude of pessimism regarding programs coming out of Washington that one found in conversation with most Indians until quite recently.

New Directions

In 1961, shortly after the Kennedy Administration assumed office, a Task Force was appointed to study Indian needs. The report of this Task Force stated, in part, "The experience of the past few years demonstrates that placing greater emphasis on termination than on development impairs Indian morale and produces a hostile or apathetic response which greatly limits the effectiveness of the Federal Indian program. The Task Force believes it is wiser to assist the Indians to advance socially, economically and politically to the point where special services to this group of Americans are no longer justified." (McNickle, 1962: 63).

It was also in 1961 that the American Indian Chicago Conference was held under the auspices of the University of Chicago. This event was originally conceived by Dr. Sol Tax, but emphasis throughout the Conference was on Indian initiative, with whites unobtrusively observing. There were 467 Indians in attendance from 90 bands and tribes. Out of this came a Declaration of Indian Purpose, the intended function of which was to guide the Bureau of Indian Affairs in its policy-making activities. The Declaration stated, "Our situation cannot be relieved by appropriated funds alone, though it is equally obvious that without capital investment and funded services, solutions will be delayed. * * *" (McNickle, 1962:66). Its final two paragraphs read, "What we ask of America is not charity, not paternalism, even when benevolent. We ask only that the nature of our situation be recognized and made the basis of policy and action.

"In short, the Indians ask for assistance, technical and financial, for the time needed, however long that may be, to regain in the America of the space age some measure of the adjustment they enjoyed as the original possessors of their native land." (Lurie, 1961:498).

There was a general spirit of cooperation throughout this conference. Only the outright assimilationists and their opposite numbers, the Indians who wish a return to full sovereignty as independent nations, stayed away, both being relatively small minorities within the total Indian world.

Then, in late 1964, Community Action Programs were instituted by the Office of Economic Opportunity (OEO). These led to a somewhat temporary reversal of pessimism in some Indian areas. When the OEO entered the picture, local policy administration on Federal reservations was divided mainly between the Bureau of Indian Affairs, and the Indian Health Division of the Public Health Service, which had been an independent agency since 1955 (before which time it was subordinate to the BIA). According to the 1966–67 *U.S. Government Organization Manual* (U.S. Government, Office of the Federal Register, 1966 : 256–257), the objectives of the BIA are : ". . . maximum Indian economic self-sufficiency; full participation of Indians in American life; and equal citizenship privileges and responsibilities for Indians." The same document lists principal BIA activities :

1. To act as trustee for Indian lands and moneys held in trust by the United States, and to assist the owners in making the most effective use of their lands and other resources;

2. To provide public services—such as education, welfare aid, and law and order—when these services are not available to Indians through other agencies;

3. To furnish guidance and assistance to those Indians who wish to leave reservation areas and enter normal channels of American economic and social life;

4. To collaborate with the Indian people (both tribally and individually) in the development of programs leading toward full-fledged Indian responsibility for the management of their own property and affairs and gradual transfer of public service responsibilities from the Bureau of Indian Affairs to the agencies which normally provide these services; and

5. To assist Indian tribes and groups, in cooperation with local and state agencies, in developing programs to attract industries to reservation areas.

This could have been a beneficial approach, but three main difficulties arose over the years. Programs which the BIA has carried out or attempted to carry out have tended to be conceived and administered paternalistically, creating and maintaining an attitude of dependence on the part of Indians, with attendant indifference and hostility arising at various places and times toward any thoroughgoing efforts to induce change. Secondly, incoming new administrations, or even changes of personnel within incumbent administrations have frequently caused the sudden shifts in policy alluded to earlier, so that programs which might have been making some headway were dropped, or reversed in midstream, leading to pronounced cynicism among Indians. Thirdly, there has been a tacit assumption evident in the nature of most such programs that Indians should assimilate to the American norm in behavior, attitudes and values. Obviously, this assumption has not been well received, since it runs counter to the widely cherished goal of cultural autonomy held by so many Indians. The combined effect of the indifference and hostility generated by paternalism, the cynicism rooted in inconsistent and abruptly terminated programs, and antagonism toward the assimilationist tendencies implicit in most Federal programs, plus the general lack of improvement in living conditions, has been a very deep hopelessness and lack of faith in any proposed ameliorative measures (Alberts et al., 1966 : 18).

In attempting to cope with this state of affairs, the Office of Economic Opportunity proposed three innovations:

1. Indians were to be asked to design their own programs and the funds for implementation were to be placed directly in Indian hands, thus defeating the dependency bred of paternalism;

2. community action in the development of self-sustaining programs, conceived, implemented and maintained by Indians was to be encouraged, thus defeating the insecurity and cynicism bred of vacillating and disappearing programs;

3. the flowering of Indian ways and values through fostering the economic viability of reservation communities was to be encouraged, thus defeating the antagonism bred of forced acculturation (Alberts et al., 1966 : 19).

Immediately new problems arose to impede the implementation of these well-intentioned plans. The degree of sophistication required to create workable proposals for correcting the economic and other inequities of Indian life (at least, as seen by OEO officials) was not often present on Indian reservations. As a result, tribal attorneys and other outside white assistance was brought to bear, and, in spite of the original intent, Indians found themselves receiving Community Action components designed by outsiders, though more influenced by Indian initiatives than past efforts had been. In view of past experience, however, many Indians were alienated by this turn of events, and initial enthusiasm waned.

Actually, there was even more reason for disillusionment than this brief oversimplification of events indicates. Most Indian groups had been oversold on the degree of autonomy they were going to have under OEO auspices by a Task Force sent out from Washington. The new departure from earlier paternalistic efforts to ameliorate Indian conditions was underscored by these men, a state of affairs which undoubtedly arose quite innocently from a natural desire on the part of the initial purveyors of the OEO message to arouse enthusiastic interest in their audiences. They succeeded. Informality and felt needs were assumed by the Indians to be appropriate bases for proposals. On many reservations contacted, Indians stayed up nights, debated at length, and did write their own proposals—some eminently reasonable, even if not geared strictly to 20th Century America. However, they did not meet the (heretofore unmentioned) criteria of the officials in Washington, and—this is the most incredible thing about the whole procedure—they were not informed of what, if anything, was wrong. Only much later, in haphazard fashion, did it become evident that prescribed forms and legal constraints definitely limited freedom of choice. It was then that outside help was resorted to, but this whole sequence of events obviously led to a rapid drop in the initial enthusiasm shown by many Indians. The result was that traditional Indian leadership tended to look upon the whole program as just one more dole to be exploited in customary fashion, rather than as a true invitation toward revitalization for Indian communities and individuals.

CURRENT PROBLEMS AND SOME BARRIERS TO THEIR SOLUTION

Present-day problems of Indian communities are basically economic and psychological. Put simply, they are poverty and the life-styles of economic dependency. Both of these point directly to the need for truly enlightening education and technological training for Indian men and women, geared to their own cultural constraints and values. However, these will be of no avail if they are not simultaneously accompanied by the development of resources and the creation of functioning enterprises within Indian communities, so that such education and training will not merely torment Indians, by inspiring rising expectations without any gain in material well-being or cultural independence.

There are, of course, problems within these problems. While the primary problems of Indians involve obtaining viable economic bases for their communities, obtaining employment and the training for such employment, and, in the case of those who would like to leave the reservation, acceptance by the white community, and the education that would make such acceptance more likely, there exist certain cultural characteristics within many Indian groups, which, as interpreted by whites, tend to impede programmatic solutions. Factionalism and nepotism, Indian style, are among the value-bound obstacles which stand against solving the primary economic problems. They make it very difficult for white-inspired programs to work, and, at the same time, as long as they are misunderstood by whites as infractions of the rules rather than alternative cultural patterns, which, if properly strengthened, might revive Indian societies, they discourage white funding of purely Indian programs.

The kinship orientation of many Indian groups leads to a special kind of factionalism, somewhat differently expressed among Northern Plains Indians than among Southwestern Indians. One can observe among the reservation descendants of the former a phenomenon that has been termed in other contexts, the "segmentary opposition of kindreds," where the several segments of a kin-group are suspicious and wary of each other at each level of distance in relationship, but unite against common threats or in pursuit of proffered opportunities only available through cooperation. Members of each segment appear to fear that the other segments at the same level (say several sets of brothers' descendants, each set being cousin to the other set) may overstep the bounds of self-seeking, violating the principle of the "image of limited good," which they themselves profess never to violate. (This principle, held to be true by many Indians, implies that there is only so much of any good available, and if one person or group takes more than a proper share, other persons or groups get less than their share.) Thus, one has groups of people refusing to be "aggressive" in the modern industrial sense, on the one hand, but suspicious of and hostile toward each other, on the other hand, for fear that one of the "other" groups will take advantage of some situation which may arise. The factionalism bred of this kind of social relation militates against strong policies and incisive responses to development programs.

Among Southwestern Indians, kin-based factions are also present, but perhaps because of the lesser degree of derangement of their original culture by whites, or the greater social cohesion developed through having faced an environment of scarcity from time immemorial, where subsistence agriculture forced long-term cooperation, the divisive aspects found in the Northern Plains are not present in marked degree. The factions are generally held in balance by powerful indigenous leadership. This is the true leadership, which is often covert in relation to whites, behind the ostensible leadership that holds such tribal offices as have been created by whites. It is the latter group which deals directly with whites, the true leaders being frequently unknown to outsiders. In the Southwest, factions tend either to mirror each other in cooperation with (or rejection of) outside programs, or to perform complementary roles.

Closely allied to factionalism on Indian reservations is an Indian variety of "nepotism." Among Indians, this is nothing more nor less than the honorable fulfillment of primary duties. To achieve a position of eminence or the power to dispense patronage, and not distribute this good fortune among one's kin would be a major infraction of Indian cultural imperatives.

Again, there is a difference, of marked importance, in the manner of implementation of this cultural characteristic as between the Northern Plains and the Southwest. Because of the greater structural cohesiveness and historical continuity in the Southwest, the leaders of most if not all kin-groupings are able to dispense some degree of patronage, so that the existence of kin-groupings works as a mechanism for widespread distribution of benefits throughout a given reservation. In the North, on the other hand, those few kin-groups with more acculturated, aggressive members are the chief recipients of or participants in the benefits of programs, while most other kin-groups are practically untouched. This is not to say that efforts are never made by Indian leaders in the North to involve non-kin, but they appear to be somewhat feeble, and are often politically motivated when they occur. The best jobs do often turn out to be held by members of a very few kin-groups. Many of the outsiders, while admitting this to be a natural course, given Indian concepts of kin-loyalty, nevertheless resent the prevailing state of affairs, and assist in the process by refusing to cooperate or learn about such opportunities as may in fact exist (Alberts et al., 1966:389–391).

A few cases will serve to document the role of unemployment as an Indian problem. Graham Holmes, former Bureau of Indian Affairs Area Director for the Five Civilized Tribes of Oklahoma has noted, "Of 19,000 adult Indians in Eastern Oklahoma, between the ages of eighteen and fifty-five, an estimated 10,000 or 52.6 per cent were unemployed; of the 10,000 jobless adult Indians, well over half received no unemployment insurance, or any other welfare insurance whatever." (Steiner, 1968:6). Among the Rosebud Sioux, 23.5 per cent of fully employable males were unemployed in the summer of 1956, and one-fourth of reservation families had annual incomes of less than $500. Sixty per cent of all Rosebud relocatees returned to the reservation after attempting city employment. (Eicher, 1961:192). Again, regarding Indians living in Yankton, South Dakota (most of whom are either from the nearby Yankton reservation or the Santee reservation), Wesley R. Hurt, Jr., states that their paramount problem is finding employment. "Many of the jobs available to the unskilled laborer are seasonal in nature because the cold winters force industries such as the seed company and box factory to curtail their production. However, the general lack of winter work is only one aspect of the employment problem. The Indian generally lacks training, is uninformed and non-aggressive in his search for jobs, and, in addition, many employers are reluctant to hire members of his race" (Hurt, 1961:227).

A variation on this theme is found among the Houma of Louisiana, who live out a meager existence shrimping in the bayous, and trapping. They live on top of one of the richest potential natural gas and petroleum fields in the United States, but, because of unfamiliarity with the law, and general lack of education, they have lost most of this land through tax sales and other devices of non-Indian oil prospectors. Recently, there has been some agitation on their part to reclaim this land, but lawyers tend to feel that, in spite of the value of the area, untangling the legal problems of reclamation would cost even more (Fischer, 1968:137).

There are considerable differences between the percentages by occupation of employed U.S. Indian males (14 years and older) and those of all U.S. males (same age group). Combining some of the items in a table presented by William H. Kelly, it appears that 64.38 percent of employed Indian males are engaged in farming, farm labor, and other labor (except mining), as opposed to 23.66 percent of all U.S. males. On the other hand, 31.05 percent of all U.S. males are in professional, managerial, and clerical work, as opposed to 7.65 percent of U.S. Indians (Kelly, 1962; Owen et al., 1967:615).

In May, 1967, a Research Conference on American Indian Education was held at Pennsylvania State University, in the hope of breaking through the barrier that apparently has stood between the Indian and his getting an education that he can use. As in other minority groups, Indian children do as well as any others up until they are eight or nine years of age. Then they begin to fall behind, and, before long, to drop out of school altogether. Two factors have been considered primarily responsible for this. By the time children have reached the ages noted, they become aware of the status of their group, and the unlikelihood of their having a future consonant with the goals of the education they are receiving. Consequently, they lose interest in playing the game. The other factor lies in the lack of orientation of teachers in Indian reservations, by and large, toward Indian cultural differences. Aggressiveness is expected where shyness is the Indian rule. Children are singled out for praise or blame where it is considered disgraceful to be in the limelight for any reason. In other words, Indian children are often made so uncomfortable in the school setting that they are unable to function as pupils.

The objectives of the Research Conference were:

1. To provide a forum for persons representing diverse groups, and with different kinds of experience in Indian education research, to express their viewpoints on the needs for long-range research and development in Indian education;

2. To provide guidelines, specifically, for a national status survey of Indian education which is being planned by the U.S. Office of Education;

3. To identify and to encourage competent researchers who might wish to become involved in interdisciplinary research in the field of Indian education.

Indian leaders, government officials, social scientists, and educators attended the conference, and, shortly after its conclusion, the National Indian Education Advisory Committee (NIEAC) appointed an all-Indian sub-committee to plan a national study of American Indian Education (Aurbach, ed., 1967:151).

Conclusion

The chief effect of most efforts to help Indians, as such efforts are presently constituted, if carried out in optimal fashion in terms of their stated ends, would be, under present reservation conditions, to markedly increase relocation possibilities and consequent acculturation processes. Indians generally appear to oppose such an eventuality, and would prefer programs leading ultimately to an economically viable reservation where Indians could maintain old associations and their own patterns of existence. Vine Deloria, Jr., former Director NCAI, is quoted by Steiner as having made a strong statement on behalf of the ideological basis for Indian separatism: "It isn't important that there are only 500,000 of us Indians. What is important is that we have a superior way of life. We Indians have a more human philosophy of life. We Indians will show this country how to act human. Someday, this country will revise its constitution, its laws, in terms of human beings, instead of property. If Red Power is to be a power in this country, it is because it is ideological." (Steiner, 1968: x).

Mr. John Belindo, Executive Director of NCAI, is presently directing the allocation of funds received by NCAI toward the economic development of reservations, with the ultimate hope that communities exemplifying Indian ways and values will become strong and serve as functioning enclaves of cultural pluralism within the United States. Mr. Belindo has indicated that plans have already been made for some fifty reservations. It is too early to tell how this particular effort will work out, but all the events leading up to this point, the American Indian Chicago Conference, the activities of the Office of Economic Opportunity, the National Research Conference on American Indian Education, and an apparent greater willingness to accept cultural pluralism in this nation, all point toward a real change in Indian affairs.

It may be of interest here to quote part of a resolution adopted 44 to 5, by leaders of thirty tribes, at a conference called by the U.S. Department of the Interior in February, 1967:

"We, the representatives of thirty Indian tribes from ten States:

"Economic development: We desire an American Indian Development Fund, of low interest, long-term nature, comparable to the funds committed to our South American cousins (via the Alliance for Progress) and the native peoples of Africa and Asia. Aid to these people totals in excess of $3 billion annually—more than was spent on the American Indian between 1789 and 1960.

"To provide rapid economic growth in the underdeveloped areas of our own country, the Indian reservations, we should immediately provide $500 million in loan funds in this proposed fund for economic development of the reservations. * * *

"We American Indians are tired of proposals which offer limited assistance and exact as the price, the risk of losing our traditional protection afforded by Federal trusteeship. We have increasingly good relations with the BIA and are not hampered by present laws and statutes in our community development. However, like any undeveloped area, we need the capital to develop. Trusteeship by the Federal government was the price the U.S. government paid for this continent and we do not agree to give it up now, nor in the future.

"Human and economic development is the essence of trusteeship. Poverty should no longer be its mark or result. * * *" (Steiner, 1968: 297–198).

There are at least two roads out of poverty for American Indians, one leading toward ethnically and culturally separate communities, the other toward individual assimilation into American society. There would seem to be no reason why *both* paths should not be entered, although flourishing enclaves with value structures differing from the norm have not been common in the American past (aside from the several "intentional societies" such as Brook Farm, the Oneida Community, and religious groups like the Amish). Other minorities, both ethnic and ideological, might be intrigued by a successful evolution of Indian communities along separatist lines.

Oscar Handlin, writing of our relations with non-Western peoples, is quoted by Stuart Levine, "In general, the anthropologists have been inclined to recommend that the social and cultural structure of a society, including its theology, be accepted without direct efforts toward immediate alteration.

"Such a course has obvious liabilities as far as policy is concerned. To put it most concretely and most bluntly, it surrenders the hope of transforming the basic value systems of the great masses of people who must be our allies in the near future. It involves the incalculable risk of materially strengthening groups whose ideas are fundamentally divergent from our own, and who would therefore, in the future, make unreliable partners. If it is not possible to spread the notion of democracy to men brought up in a patriarchal or traditional society, have we any assurance that the collaborators our aid now brings us will ever acquire an interest in our ultimate objectives?" (Handlin; Levine and Lurie, 1968: 4–5).

Levine replies, regarding the American Indian, as follows: "If we had within our borders a group which, in maintaining its essential cultural unity, identity and character, constituted a threat to the well-being of the nation as a whole, most Americans, I would guess, would feel that an attempt to alter its "social and cultural structure" should be made, humanely, of course, but made, nevertheless. * * *

"But such melodramatic issues are really not involved in the Indian situation. Indian people, first, in no sense threaten national well-being. Indian values and ideals are not especially incompatible with national norms. And Indian cultures have always adapted extremely well to change when they have been given anything like a fair chance to make a go of the new situation. Their societies can be altered quite radically without losing their essentially Indian structure and flavor.

"Indian values, when they are properly understood, are incompatible only with some of the less essential features of the dominant culture. Indian societies are traditional societies; most are less individualistic than the general society. Extended family or "clan" ties are strongly felt; to Indian people, the American "nuclear family" seems a lonely arrangement. But none of this differentness in any sense threatens the rest of us. Indeed, we could perhaps learn some useful psychological lessons from it." (Levine; Levine and Lurie, 1968: 5–6).

The general impression, derived both from the literature and direct interviews, remains that Indians prefer the path leading to viable cultural pluralism. They do not wish, seemingly with rare exceptions, to leave their own communities and assume the white man's ways.

There is some question as to the cause of this great affection for reservation life (entirely aside from the ordinary pull of birthplace and kin felt by many who are not Indian). One would surmise from some accounts that there is an innate compulsion among Indians to go back to the reservation. In reasonable terms, however, could it not be that the Indian returns to the reservation so faithfully because he is usually far less acquainted with the ways of the outside world than other men, and, furthermore, enters a world almost uniformly unfriendly and cold, indifferent to his wants and idiosyncracies? If Indians were invited to make a truly voluntary choice between pluralism and acculturation, and an exceedingly carefully thought-out (and well funded) effort to educate and acculturate could be envisioned, combined with an equally well implemented effort to provide a welcoming and sustaining environment in the outside world, perhaps a fair number of Indians would lose their reluctance toward taking the step of relocation and entrance into the larger society. Perhaps not. At any rate, previous efforts in this direction have not been sufficiently coordinated or intensive to produce the conditions whereby this hypothesis might be tested. Given existing conditions, Indians on reservations frequently appear to be aware of the unstated bias toward assimilation of most programs, and under these forced conditions, to reject them as anything other than a temporary source of funds or diversion. It is conceivable that fully elective programs avowedly pointed in *each* of the directions discussed, and presented to Indians, as such, for voluntary choice, might generate far more enthusiasm than the present offerings with conceptualization of ultimate cultural outcomes concealed or at least unstated.

An editorial in the NCAI Sentinel states, "We would advocate, therefore, a program of acculturation rather than a temporary patchwork of assimilationist programs. Acculturation is, we feel, a program by which tribes can be encouraged to change behavior patterns by giving them the opportunity to develop programs incorporating their present values with new opportunities for human resource advancement. Teach *HOW* credit works by allowing tribal credit unions to be developed, teach *HOW* to manage land by allowing tribes more freedom in leasing and range management and land consolidation. * * *" (NCAI Sentinel; Steiner, 1968 : 303).

To achieve success, even with such a twofold approach, would require intensive communication regarding real and immediately perceivable benefits to follow, in order to meet the tendency on the part of many Indians (which they share with other more or less alienated groups) to think in terms of immediate gains rather than long-term goals. Programs geared toward acculturation would have to be made much more powerful than they are now, in the sense noted above (effective and relevant education combined with assurance of genuine acceptance and adequate placement in the "outside" world) while those intended to create economically viable communities would require the coordination of many government agencies with private industry, in the creation of the kind of functioning economic base for each such community which could be sustained and enhanced by the Indians themselves in accordance with their own aims and values.

REFERENCES

ALBERTS, ROBERT C., FRANK R. BLACKFORD, Jr., ALBERT JENNY II, WILLIAM H. KELLY, GERALD M. SIDER, JAMES G. E. SMITH, and WILLIAM WILLARD. 1966. A Comprehensive Evaluation of OEO Community Action Programs on Six Selected American Indian Reservations, McLean, Va. Human Sciences Research, Inc.

AURBACH, HERBERT A. (ed.). 1967. Proceedings of the National Research Conference on American Indian Education. Kalamazoo, Mich. Society for the Study of Social Problems.

EGGAN, FRED. 1966. The American Indian : Perspectives for the Study of Social Change. Chicago, Ill. Aldine Publishing Co.

EICHER, CARL K. 1961. Income Improvement on the Rosebud Sioux Reservation. In Human Organization special issue 20 :191–196.

FARB, PETER 1968. Man's Rise to Civilization as Shown by the Indians of North America from Primeval Times to the Coming of the Industrial State, New York, N.Y. E. P. Dutton and Co., Inc.

FISCHER, ANN. 1968. History and Current State of the Houma Indians. In The American Indian Today, Stuart Levine and Nancy O. Lurie, eds. Deland, Fla. Everett/Edwards, Inc.

HANDLIN, OSCAR. ——. Race and Nationality in American Life. Cited in The American Indian Today, Stuart Levine and Nancy O. Lurie, eds. Deland, Fla. Everett/Edwards, Inc.

HURT, Jr., WESLEY R. 1961. The urbanization of the Yankton Indians. Human Organization special issue 20 : 226–231.

KELLY, WILLIAM H. 1962. Socioeconomic Conditions of Contemporary American Indians. Cited in The North American Indians : A Sourcebook, Roger C. Owen et al., eds. New York, N.Y. The Macmillan Company.

LAFARGE, OLIVER (ed.). 1942. The Changing Indian. Norman, Okla. Cited in Perspectives in American Indian Culture Change, Edward R. Spicer, ed. Chicago, Ill. The University of Chicago Press.

LEVINE, STUART. 1968. The Survival of Indian Identity. In The American Indian Today, Stuart Levine and Nancy O. Lurie, eds. Deland, Fla. Everett/Edwards, Inc.

LEVINE, STUART, and NANCY O. LURIE (eds.). 1968. The American Indian Today. Deland, Fla. Everett/Edwards, Inc.

LURIE, NANCY OESTREICH. 1961. The Voice of the American Indian : Report on the American Indian Chicago Conference. In Current Anthropology. Vol 2 No 5 :478–500.

MCNICKLE, D'ARCY. 1962. The Indian Tribes of the United States : Ethnic and Cultural Survival. London, Eng. Oxford University Press.

MERIAM, LEWIS, et al. 1928. The Problem of Indian Administration. Baltimore, Md. Johns Hopkins University Press.

OWEN, ROGER C., JAMES J. F. DEETZ, and ANTHONY D. FISHER (eds.). 1967. The North American Indian : A Sourcebook. New York, N.Y. The Macmillan Company.

SPICER, EDWARD H. (ed.). 1961. Perspectives in American Indian Culture Change. Chicago, Ill. The University of Chicago Press.

STEINER STAN. 1968. The New Indians. New York, N.Y. Harper and Row.

U.S. GOVERNMENT, OFFICE OF THE FEDERAL REGISTER. 1966. 1966–67 Government Organization Manual. Washington, D.C. Government Printing Office.

BARRIERS TO ECONOMIC DEVELOPMENT

By Gordon Macgregor *

FOREWORD

Confinement to reservations was, of course, an artificial arrangement imposed on the Indians by white men. Gordon MacGregor describes the failure of the plains Indians ever to adapt to the confined life of the reservation. Their history is thus a long one of continuing economic and social disintegration. If economic development on the Indian reservations is to succeed today, it must be accompanied by intensive social services designed to correct the attitudes of dependence, apathy, and hostility which have been engendered by many years of ill treatment.

Introduction

This article has been written to consider some of the reasons for the past failures and present handicaps to economic development on Indian reservations of the United States. Efforts to provide Indian tribes new economies to replace those of hunting, fishing and wild food gathering began nearly one hundred years ago. Yet many tribes live in a "culture of poverty" and have acquired no agricultural or other technology by which they can maintain an adequate level of living.

Some explanations are to be readily found in inadequate land resources, poor soils and the forced acceptance of land leasing caused by the heirship problem.

Because Indians have been unable to sell, transfer, or consolidate their inherited rights to allotted lands, except among a very few tribes, these properties have been frozen in an unusable state. The only benefit that can be derived feasibly is rental. Leasers are usually white men. Thus the limited land base for an Indian economy becomes further decreased by this leasing system.

The allotment system established by the Federal Government to provide Indian families homesteads on which they might become self-sufficient farmers, has been in itself-defeating. First, many Indians had no technological background or knowledge of the economic system on which American family agriculture is based. Second, most of the Indians who were nonagricultural in pre-reservation times felt no motivation to take up farming. It was women's work—if anyone's— and gave no prestige or acceptable occupation to men of Indian societies.

The agricultural program also became self-defeating in that at the same time that it was being encouraged, the Indian people starving on the reservations were being given rations of food. This ration system has been followed by other forms of food or cash subsidy, welfare programs, and employment programs financed by Federal appropriations. With this outside support supplemented by land rentals and more recently per capita payments for broken treaties, or taking of Indian

---

* Department of Anthropology, American University. Washington, D.C.

lands for reservoirs, and practice bombing areas, Indians have developed a dependency upon Federal financial support. This development has resulted in general disinterest in or rejection of taking up individual farming or cattle raising.

This dependency upon Federal largesse and windfalls in the form of tribal payments has contributed to the failure of any positive or constructive adaptation to the general patterns of American life. This is particularly true of those Indians who remain oriented to their traditional ways of life, and bitter toward their historic and present treatment at the white man's hands. This negative adjustment has become an entrenched culture of dependency.

The solution or reorientation toward a more constructive and viable life for Indians on reservations does not lie in a correction of the heirship problem or by a reduction or modification or by a reduction of individual and family subsidy programs. Indian populations on reservations have now gone through such a long period of attempted accommodation to the white man's life and have been so frustrated, defeated and impoverished that their problem now has deep and serious psychological dimensions.

It is assumed in this commentary that the primary interest of the Joint Economic Committee is in the economic development of these Indians who now suffer from lack of employment or some other means of gaining a livelihood. The observations of this report are addressed to these difficulties and the causative factors.

It must be emphasized in passing that not all Indians fall in this category of poverty and dependency. Many Indians have moved into American society and its economy with great success. The Bureau of Indian Affairs has unfortunately no records on this movement nor accounting for their success. Education, training in technical skills, opportunities in urban industrial centers are some of the explanations for success. But by and large it appears that intermarriage and the transmission of the ideas, values and customs by white American parents and their mixed blood descendants have accounted mainly for this process of adaptation and acculturation. It has been an informal and unconscious process of culture change.

For the Indian reservation residents who have not undergone this experience especially in the years of childhood training and those who although of racially mixed parentage, have remarried into the Indian full-blood population this process of assimilation has been eliminated. In them the process of change has taken a very different course. The nature of this process with its many variables appears to account primarily for the barriers and handicaps to achieving a viable economic or satisfying social adjustment.

The process has been one of group and personal breakdown or disintegration. The steps and manifestations briefly described reveal the basic problem of today's impoverished Indians. It will also indicate that any program of economic development must be incorporated within a broad social, psychological and educational program for change. It must also realize that Indian failures of adaptation have not been solely the result of poor and inconsistent Federal policies and programs in the past. Failures have been also due to the nature of Indian responses based on the fundamental principles of their life ways and the reactions to a highly dominating and coercive society. In this domination the Bureau of Indian Affairs has been the cultural agent of American society.

The process of Indian change and limited assimilation has also lacked the stated but infrequently practiced principle of executing program planning and administration *with* Indian understanding and participation as well as consent. Programs cannot be successful to any degree if they are planned and implemented by non-Indian outsiders *for* Indians.

If we may employ one tribe—the Sioux—as an example, the course of this disintegration can be put in specific if somewhat exaggerated terms. The Sioux and other Indians of the Plains exemplify the major difficulties of adaptation of many of today's Indians.

THE PROCESS OF TRIBAL DISINTEGRATION

The history of the Plains Indians on their reservations began with tribal disasters. They were overcome militarily and deprived of their food supply by the near extermination of the buffalo. Confinement on reservations was at first near-imprisonment. The means of maintaining personal prestige for men through skills and feats in war and hunting were closed. It is understandable that the beginning of life on the reservations created deep feelings of bitterness and hostility. Being thrust into dependency for food and protection upon the Federal Government, only deepened the tribal resentment. These attitudes have continued over time as barriers to positive adaptation. Although some acceptance has been made to the white man's way and the internal feeling of hostility has lessened, their poverty and social conditions have added to their bitterness and hostility. The lack of adequate income and economic opportunity and the ration system that provided insufficient food and a badly balanced diet led to extensive ill health and to a high rate of infant and early adult mortality. Illness and physical weakness have contributed to the unemployability of many men and women.

The most significant negative happening was the rapid destruction of their old life with little or no preparation for a new pattern of their own choosing or construction. The economic bases and natural resources were all but lost. The organization of family life, leadership and social control built on the former economy began to crumble.

The strong Federal and missionary attacks on the ancient religions, regardless of what may have seemed necessary in the late nineteenth and early twentieth centuries for suppressing pagan, obscene or torture elements of Indian customs, had a destructive effect in undermining the system of ideas and moral order that gave cohesion and stability to the tribal life. There has followed the spread of the so-called Peyote cult to replace the old religion with a new form comprised of old religious symbols and customs and directed toward the personal problems, unhappiness, and ill health of its adherents. Acceptance of this cult is far from universal but it appears to grow as it soothes present psychological anxieties and fills a need for an Indian-rooted belief system.

For the majority of Indians, secularization leading to an absence of religiously supported values or a code of moral standards is characteristic.

The deterioration of former tribal cultures has been accompanied by a growing acceptance of white or American economic and social forms as each generation becomes further removed from the old life and experiences American education, employment and rural or urban living.

But the change has not been one of direct transition or substitution of new for old customs, attitude or outlook on life.

The process with crushing of old ways, self-defeating programs of agriculture and rigid education poorly adapted to Indian needs for understanding has brought cultural confusion. Administration and school discipline was for many decades conducted in an atmosphere of oppressive domination and coercion to bring about assimilation. No mutual plan of transition or system of ordered relationship between American and Indian ways of life were established. Indian ways were seen by whites as incompatible and a life to be abandoned for adoption of their own. Languages were in conflict and Indian speech was forbidden in the schools before English could be learned. The effect was a breakdown in communication between members in the two different societies and to a lesser degree between generations of Indians.

This entire process has brought confusion to those who would adapt to a new life or lead their Indian communities into an orderly and satisfying life within the limitations of reservation environment. Young people especially are torn between the desire to have a job and earn money, rarely available on the reservation, and to remain in the Indian community and its familiar social life. The course of events during the history of reservation existence has led to a barren life devoid of the social and personal satisfactions that the former life offered and socially healthy and active communities provide. An increasing number of children grow up in unstable or broken homes. Fathers without any status in their communities or families or steady jobs seek escape in drinking and in casual marriage relationships. Outside the family and kinship group there are no special groups or associations in which to find some constructive activity. Recreation and recreational activities, except for scattered consolidated school buildings, are absent. Young adults have little healthy recreational life. Driving broken down cars and drinking are regular pastimes and escape from boredom.

Although informal leaders appear in communities who might organize a more orderly and satisfying life among their people, they receive little recognition from agency or tribal officials. Local leadership remains ineffective. Officials elected to tribal councils frequently become caught between their constituents who expect the council to manipulate the Indian Agency and Bureau for immediate services placing cash into their hands, and the Agency staff asking the council to join in long term programs of economic benefit such as, conservation, housing and education—which show little immediate results.

In these relationships councilmen are expected to act according to the consensus and concern for personal problems of tribal members in the manner of patriarchal chiefs. In relation to Agency and other officials, councilmen are expected to act with the aggressiveness and competitiveness of the white man. These expectations place great demands on personal and political skill of Indian leaders. The great failure leads to political defeat and inconsistency and strong factionalism in Indian politics.

Such weakening of the tribal structure combined with economic inactivity has brought great psychological stress and change in Indian personalities. The conditions given above have over time led to much apathy and passivity. Indians appear confused and without hope. But dissatisfaction with their low level of living, resulting from well remembered defeat, ill treatment and inconsistent and ineffective social, economic and educational programs has continued the early bitterness and open or covert hostility. Delinquency and criminal behavior have followed.

Personality maladjustment and psychological problems are now increasing in the wake of this history of social and personal deterioration. That an increasing rate of suicide and suicide attempts are now becoming a major concern of the Indian Health Service and other Plains Indian Reservations is an index of the seriousness of the Indian psychological problem.

This description of the conditions and processes that over time led to social breakdown of Indian communities which in turn have led to insecurity, deep anxiety, personal maladjustment of individuals has been entered into for one reason. It is to underscore the fact that the poverty, personal and social disintegration must receive the support of many sources and attention for dealing with the whole problem of rehabilitation. Economic development is certainly one procedure, but it cannot succeed alone.

SOME THOUGHTS ON RESERVATION ECONOMIC DEVELOPMENT

By BILL KING*

FOREWORD

New efforts to provide the Indians with economic development asssitance have proliferated within the last 5 years. Bill King points out the variety of situations found on the different reservations. He also points out that economic development affects the entire area, not just the Indian reservation, and that development planning must be carried out in this regional context. King also discusses some of the problems faced in drawing Indian men into regular industrial employment. The availability of Federal employment and welfare support, together with the extended family system, can reduce the attractiveness of lower paying industrial jobs. If industrial development on the reservation is to succeed, the Indians must participate in its planning and the type of jobs provided must be those which the Indians are willing and able to perform.

Introduction

You have asked me for comments on some of the prevailing problems on the majority of American Indian reservations which must be faced in order to bring about successful industrial development, and other sorts of viable employment activity aimed at reducing excessively high rates of unemployment in these areas. Those who undertake industrial development programs on behalf of Indians—and there are some very able persons working in this area—must face the fact that reservation communities compete directly with 18,000 American towns and cities also on the lookout for new economic opportunities. It is no wonder that program planners in the Indian field often are so attentive to landing a prospect—virtually any prospect—that they do not always anticipate in advance the full spectrum of local problems, much less always seek the involvement of Indian people.

Initially, this paper will comment briefly on the range of reservation community types, since it is most important to understand that no single or, for that matter, no several approaches to economic development can possibly apply to all. Next, some of the more obvious problems in adapting a reservation work force to compete in the off-reservation market place are reviewed. The paper then turns to some of the sociocultural factors which pertain in typical reservation communities and how these affect the development of a competitive work force. Finally, a consideration of how community development principles can be utilized to attract new economic activities and to adjust these activities into the life of an Indian community, will be presented.

As an example of how considerable effort often is rewarded with relatively meager results, I have appended to the paper a summary

*Director, Office of Community Development, Bureau of Indian Affairs.

of the major industrial developments which have been undertaken on the Rosebud Sioux Reservation in South Dakota over the past five years. The Rosebud example also illustrates some of the problems treated in the paper which are more or less inherent in many, if not most, reservation industrial development efforts.

Never before have so many agencies concentrated so much effort on reservation economic development as is true at present. In addition to the pioneering efforts of BIA, which in 1954 first seriously undertook to lure industry to reservations, both the Indian section of the Office of Economic Opportunity and the Economic Development Administration of the Department of Commerce directly employ, or indirectly finance, specialists in economic development to work on behalf of reservation Indians. Assisted by Federal funds and by grants from private foundations, the National Congress of American Indians also is attempting to better Indians' economic lot. A growing number of colleges and universities near Indian country are involved. Other Federal agencies, notably the Departments of Labor and Health, Education and Welfare, are focusing the attentions of their newly-organized "Indian Desks" on training reservation work forces for local employment. Representatives of the burgeoning national training industry increasingly are focusing on the relatively small but rewarding Indian field. Any single reservation with a minimum land base of 1,000 acres and a minimum population of 200 has no doubt had some sort of economic development efforts made on its behalf during the past four of five years.

The principal basis for this worthy concentration of effort is the obvious need: the rate of Indian unemployment is more than ten times that of the nation taken as a whole. The enormity of the Indian economic problem, however, should not cause us to overlook the fact that at least a part of this focus on bettering the Indian's economic condition results from reservation communities being, usually, far easier to relate to than are most impoverished areas of the nation. Reservations are, by definition, *administered* communities since they are conveniently directed by the agency superintendent-tribal council system. Potential investors, staffs of concerned government agencies, a host of economic consultants, and others who derive their livelihood from attempting to better the economic lot of the poor, find Indian reservations simple to contact initially and to work with subsequently. Some of the larger reservations have as many as fifty formal efforts at socio-economic betterment underway at a given time—a fact which dramatically highlights this point.

A second significant factor in gaining a quick overview of reservation economic development has to do with the relationships, between the nation's reservation areas, virtually all of which have been declared eligible for economic assistance, and nearby non-Indian communities which, in many instances, do not enjoy a similar designation. In the great majority of cases the airports, factories, feed lots, and irrigation projects which have resulted are of benefit to Indian and non-Indian alike. Sensitive observers, however, cannot help being concerned with the fact that, in some instances, the fruits of these nominally joint efforts are of only incidental benefit to the Indian community in whose name the development was initiated.

TYPES OF INDIAN COMMUNITIES

There are 270 Indian "reservations" in the lower 48 States. Another 24 trust reserves, along with 100 Federally-owned land areas, have been set aside in Alaska for Indians, Eskimos, and Aleuts. These range in size from the 14,000,000 acre Navajo Reservation, upon which 100,000 Indian people live, to single-acre California "rancherias" with no resident populations. Some, as is true of most of the Alaska areas, are located a great distance from larger communities and further cut off from them by the most tenuous systems of transportation and communication. Others, as certain of the Nevada colonies, some of the reservations in Washington, Arizona, New Mexico, Michigan, Wisconsin, New York, and the Indian areas of Western Oklahoma, are contiguous to or surrounded by urban or urbanizing areas. In the upper Midwest and in Oklahoma especially, reservation land often was parcelled out to individuals in trust allotments. This practice has resulted in a great deal of Indian land being sold to whites who, within the external boundaries of certain reservations, outnumber the former owners many times over. On the Flathead Reservation in Montana, for example, whites exceed Indians by roughly ten to one! An even greater population disparity holds true on the Sisseton Reservation in North and South Dakota where only ten percent of the old reserve remains in Indian ownership. On the South Dakota Pine Ridge and Rosebud Sioux Reservations, with aggregate Indian populations in excess of 17,000, less than 50 percent of the land remains in Indian hands; and much of the economic control is exercised by whites or by so-called "mixed bloods" who in some cases maintain only the most nominal, tenuous, and opportunistic sorts of tribal identities.

There are 129 reservations in the lower 48 States with Indian populations of at least 200 persons and at least 1,000 acres of trust land which have been the focus of recent economic development efforts. Of this number, 25 have greater non-Indian than Indian populations within their original boundaries; 45 are adjacent to, or in close proximity to, urban areas; and 38 have lost 50 percent or more of their original reservation areas to whites. These figures do not include the situation in Oklahoma where land alienation and residence in close proximity to large non-Indian populations is the rule. Clearly, simple generalizations about how to approach reservation economic development are invalid.

Also of importance in seeking a direction for reservation economic development is an awareness of the changing residence patterns of many reservation populations. More than one-third of all "reservation" Indians presently are living away from their home communities, often in the larger urban areas of the West Coast, the upper Midwest, or in the Southwest—particularly in Oklahoma and Texas. By far the largest off-reservation population is in Los Angeles County where between thirty and forty thousand Indians, especially Sioux, Navajos, and native Oklahomans, presently live. Under half of these have moved with the assistance of the BIA Vocational Training and Placement Program. The influence of these stabilizing urban Indian colonies in attracting others from the rural areas is only beginning to be appreciated; some observers expect that 1970, the decennial census year, will see, for the first time in history, more American Indians in small towns and in urban areas than on their home reservations.

The direction of this discussion is not to suggest that economic developments in reservation areas should be avoided; rather, it is apparent that isolated, all-Indian economic developments are not always consistent with the economic and demographic realities of much of so-called Indian country. Indians are less handicapped with geographic isolation than was the case even 25 or 30 years ago. Increasingly, reservations are integrating into larger communities of non-Indians. To maximize development dollars set aside for Indians and to assure meaningful and permanent economic development efforts, joint planning for the *total* community, Indian and non-Indian, often makes the greatest sense. But, in order to avoid possible exploitation of Indian interests by stronger and economically more experienced neighbors, the strongest possible advocacy must be maintained for Indians by their leaders and by those advising and assisting Indian leadership.

ECONOMIC CHARACTERISTICS OF A RESERVATION WORK FORCE

In many of the target areas of Indian economic development, typically the larger reservations upon which the BIA maintains superintendencies, a range of economic conditions exists about which too little is known and to which those undertaking economic development tend to pay too little attention. Employment by the Bureau of Indian Affairs and the Indian Health Service is the most significant source of Indian income on virtually all of the larger reservations. Not only are most permanent non-skilled or semi-skilled agency jobs filled by local Indian people (bus drivers, school and hospital support staffs, maintenance workers, road crews, and a variety of professional aides, etc.), but each year many part-time employees are hired for special construction projects, forest fire suppression, etc. Usually more than half of all Federal employees, although rarely the best paid employees, are recruited from local community members.

Indian employment has expanded dramatically since 1963, first with Area Redevelopment Administration projects and more recently through local employment opportunities funded by OEO, EDA, and other agencies. On the Navajo Reservation, for instance, more than 2,500 Indian people, mostly Navajos, work for the Bureau of Indian Affairs and another 650 are employed by the Indian Health Service. More than 2,900 jobs currently are funded by the OEO sponsored Office of Navajo Economic Opportunity and another 2,250 Navajos work in tribal jobs. Thus, a total of almost 8,000 Navajos, out of an estimated work force of 30,000 work at Federal or tribal jobs. (Not included in these figures are those Navajos employed for shorter periods in Neighborhood Youth Corps activities, work training programs under Title V, or other sorts of training activities for which subsistence is paid.)

Virtually all reservation employment of Indians by the government is more under the control of the employees than may appear on the surface. Reservation concepts of time, production standards, and absenteeism all tend to prevail. This derives partly from the fact that none of these activities involves anything like industrial production in which cost must be balanced against efficiency. Too, supervisor performance is evaluated, in large measure, by the extent to which employee satisfaction is expressed. Federal and tribal employment under these conditions represents the toughest possible competition for a struggling new industry offering its workers the minimum wage.

A second factor to consider in planning economic development derives from the *de facto* program of income maintenance which is inherent in the reservation system. The mass of unemployed or underemployed reservation Indians have minimal, nonetheless very real, income subsidies which have developed gradually and which are pretty much integrated into the cultural life of the group. Most pay no rent on their inadequate homes, nor are taxes paid on the trust land they own. Comprehensive medical services are available at no cost as are virtually free educations for Indian children. Federal boarding schools for children from the poorest reservation families, and for those from broken or disrupted homes further stretch limited cash income.

Another condition, which has an almost unknown effect on the sorts of economic reorientation which reservation industrial employment implies, results from our almost total ignorance about how incomes obtained from multiple sources are allocated and distributed to the members of a reservation family. That Indians share what they have with relatives is widely accepted; we need to know more about how. A hypothetical Indian extended family, let us say, is composed of two parents, five minor children, and several adult sons and daughters with small children of their own. Let us further suppose that this family shares among its members a BIA bus driver's salary, some income from allotted farm lands leased to non-Indians, limited income from seasonal agricultural labor, two aid-to-dependent children allotments, some limited income from the sale of cattle, and intermittent wages from a local CAP program. We have little idea how far the cash income, coupled with the income supplements mentioned, goes toward meeting the economic needs of this family. Certainly we have no objective basis for assuming, as we all too often do, that its "unemployed" members will flock to industrial jobs should these become available.

SOCIAL CHARACTERISTICS OF A RESERVATION WORK FORCE

Social disorganization, with such accompanying manifestations as drinking, broken homes, fatherless children, etc., are the rule rather than the exception in many Indian communities. In this social environment, not uncommonly, women are the active family heads and as such provide a better potential for developing a work force than do Indian men. Indian men with a long history of unemployment, or of intermittent or casual labor, seem to treat the prospects of steady employment with considerable trepidation. Typically, they privately express fear that they cannot handle a steady job and often hide their concern over failure behind a good deal of bluster and rationalization that the job is "women's work," that it lacks status, etc.

There is wide agreement that many reservation Indian men view open-air jobs in which they can work in large groups, under easygoing supervision and without too much attention paid to absenteeism or tardiness, as providing ideal working conditions. The Indian Division of the Civilian Conservation Corps provided jobs of this sort in the 1930's and early 1940's and are recalled by many as the high point in their work experience. The widespread employment of many Indians in the wartime economy in no small way resulted from the job-conditioning gained in CCC work. That this sort of activity remains popular with Indians was clearly established in the early 1960's when CCC-type activities were briefly reintroduced under the sponsorship of the Area Redevelopment Administration. On many reservations where these activities were initiated it is reported that Indian men, including some who had been employed steadily at off-reservation jobs, flocked back to join ARA labor gangs.

It is most unfortunate that many of those who work so diligently on behalf of decent and permanent jobs for reservation Indians pay so little heed to fundamental problems of reorienting the really difficult-to-work-with of the reservation unemployed. Few seem to accept the idea that there is a good deal more to moulding these economic outcasts into a competitive work force than prolonged on-the-job training in technical skills which lasts only as long as does the training subsidy or the patience of the trainee. Assisting socially and psychologically handicapped persons to join an industrial work force, whether they derive from an urban ghetto or a rural reservation, calls for exceptional skills and may prove quite costly. Commonly the enormity of the problem leads to ignoring it and concentrating on retraining again and again that portion of the work force which has least trouble finding jobs unaided. This suggests that a new approach to job development and skill training seriously needs to be explored.

There seems little doubt that most reservation men and women prefer to work than to remain idle and collect welfare. Initially, at least, the work must take an accepted "Indian" form. Gang work, of the sort outlined above often must be the starting point for economic reorientation. In this, the community development worker rather than economic development expert may prove to have the more valuable skills.

COMMUNITY DEVELOPMENT AND RESERVATION ECONOMIC DEVELOPMENT

It has become fashionable recently to "involve" local people in planning for economic development activities which will affect them. Instances of industrial development where plans made in Washington and brought to the attention of local Indian community leadership as accomplished facts are diminishing in number. Nominal involvement of local leadership, however, all too easy to achieve within the administered reservation system, does not provide the broad base of planning and community support that gives some assurance of success to a profit-oriented activity. That which passes as local involvement often is the mere presence of Indian spokesmen in a meeting of representatives of industry and one or more government agencies. The role of the community representative is at best advisory—answering asides directed to him such as, "Joe, isn't it true that your tribe always has wanted frozen food processing plants—that your people used to be good farmers and can't wait to start raising green peas again," or something of that sort. All too often the answer is a monosyllabic affirmative.

Conditions external to the Indian community, over which it has no control, are of such magnitude and complexity that one cannot carry the matter of local involvement and community control to academic extremes if jobs are too be gathered from the much competed-for national pool of job opportunities. However, these guidelines for maximum local involvement do make practical sense:

1. The broadest sort of initial expressions of interest in permanent job opportunities must be sought from Indian community membership. The community developer must be prepared to assist local people to build upon and to broaden what inevitably comes through initially as narrow and naive responses. Often he must be prepared to assist community leaders to "rough in" a range of alternative plans for achieving stated community employment objectives. If these are not practical, then he must withdraw and allow local leadership to sort out the problems and rearrange alternatives themselves. His role is primarily that of an arbitrator, a teacher, and a generalist researcher, never that of a community leader.

2. A sound rule-of-thumb is to help people build on what already exists. If the local pool of chronically unemployed works best in indulgently-led "gangs," then economic development activities which most nearly approximate these conditions must be sought.

3. Indian leadership (not mere spokesmen) must be assisted to understand that one can't always have unlimited subsidized tribal enterprises, canned CAP-like employment components, round after round of subsidized "training" activities which serve as a substitute (in the minds of many recipients, at least) for employment, along with permanent economic developments. Indian leadership and those who advise it must learn to reject forcefully some of the conflicting programs offered.

It will be recalled that, of 129 reservation areas with populations large enough to consider seriously economic development, 70 either are part of, or are in close proximity to, communities in which Indians numerically are in the minority.

4. Although work activities in an all-Indian setting are most attractive to many Indian people, employment as part of a mixed work force is sometimes more practical. A major function of the community development worker involved in economic development should be to assist in creating mixed economic opportunities when these seem to make the best sense and to help facilitate the adjustment of Indian workers into them.

5. Finally, the community developer must serve as a generalist-planner who helps Indian leadership and community members to prepare for the social and economic complexities which likely will attend economic developments. Most reservation communities have grown up around a BIA Agency complex, a mission, or some similar limited-purpose nucleus. These communities typically lack facilities to serve a sudden influx of new workers. At Shiprock, New Mexico, for example, when a large electronics plant was brought in with virtually no prior community planning, it was housed in the only building in the community devoted solely to recreation. Other service facilities for the large work force were virtually nonexistent. Fortunately these conditions are being rectified.

COMMUNITY DEVELOPMENT AND JOB TRAINING

The relatively high expenditure per capita for overall programs on at least some reservations is attracting increasing comment. The aggregate annual cost of all Federal, state, tribal, and local programs on the Pine Ridge Reservation is reported to be just under $8,000 per family. Reports of this sort lead some to favor rejecting the entire idea of programmed services to Indians in favor of diverting their costs *per capita* and allowing Indians to use a portion of this "income" to pay for municipal and other services in the manner of residents of more typical American communities. This, of course, represents an overly simple solution to very complex social and economic problems. A modified version of this plan, however, utilizing a *portion* of existing budgets for direct payment to *selected* reservation residents, opens the door to a whole new approach to job training and general economic reorientation of chronically unemployed or underemployed Indian people without appreciably raising the cost above present budgets.

I suggest that certain funds budgeted for welfare services, some vocational training activities, community action programs, public works programs, etc., be re-programmed to provide an income subsidy for the chronically unemployed of a reservation. This would provide a form of income maintenance to be exchanged for the use of certain amounts of the unemployed person's time. The purposes for which this "bought" time would be used would be subject to negotiation between program managers, hopefully made up in large part by community leaders, and individual program clients. The idea being that, if sincerely approached, an unemployed person will himself turn to that activity which he senses will best assist him to improve his chances to become a productive employee.

Initially, many participants likely will decide to undertake activities which do not seem relevant to the ultimate goal of reduced unemployment—requests for certain types of adult education, seemingly impractical sorts of locally-conducted vocational training activities, decisions to "clean up" the community with CCC-type labor gangs, etc. Others might want to spend their time getting on top of a drinking problem or undertaking other sorts of personal improvement activities.

The process of continued negotiations with local people for the use of their "bought" time would be employed as the program moves away from its initial phases and enters into direct negotiations with business and industry to locate economic developments in the community. Local persons, mainly those who have demonstrated the highest potential for steady employment, would be involved to the fullest possible extent in attracting economic developments and in selecting the most suitable from the range of possibilities. The income subsidy initially would be a potent force in attracting the interest of business and industry. The individual subsidy would be withdrawn as soon as a worker became a self-reliant member of the local work force. Subsidies likely would need to be maintained indefinitely for those members of the community providing certain service functions—day care center operation, carrying out certain forms of recreational activity, etc. And, as a practical matter, some community members, because of physical and psychological limitations, would need to have their incomes maintained permanently, just as presently they are being supported by categorical and general welfare assistance.

APPENDIX

Economic Developments on the Rosebud Reservation

The Rosebud Sioux Reservation, located in central South Dakota, has a resident Indian population of about 7,000, mainly in that portion of the reservation contained in Todd and Mellette Counties. Rosebud has been one of a limited number of reservation areas in which the Office of Economic Opportunity concentrated its efforts on behalf of Indians during the past four years.

Rosebud also has been served by a special Indian program sponsored by the Economic Development Administration of the Department of Commerce as well as by economic development activities by the National Congress of American Indians. The Rosebud Indian Agency has an industrial development staff; and two full-time tribal employees, paid with EDA and tribal funds, also direct their principal efforts to economic development.

In 1963 the first low-rent public housing built on any reservation was located at Rosebud. In 1965, 385 units of so-called transitional housing, mainly using local Indian labor, were constructed with funds jointly provided by the Public Housing Administration, OEO, and BIA. In early 1969, 400 additional housing units were completed by a private contractor using significant numbers of local Sioux men. The construction of close to 1,000 units of new housing in the past five or six years has had profound and diverse affects on the reservation economy.

Industrial development activities (that is, activities which have a profit motive) undertaken during the same period include:

1. *Sioux Dairy Co-op.*—In 1964 the Rosebud Sioux Tribal Council backed this effort financially and furnished the physical facility in which it is located. The business continues in operation, but only two of its eleven employees are Indians. It is reported that the Sioux do not find co-op activities attractive; the hours demanded are long and irregular.

2. *Rosebud Manufacturing Company.*—This activity was initiated in 1965 through the tribally-financed Rosebud Development Corporation and a private investor. The company manufactures formica-topped kitchen counters.

At one time the facility employed 47 Sioux men under a BIA-funded on-the-job training contract; the plant presently employs fewer than twenty persons. Following some serious personnel and financial problems, the activity was able to get on its feet through contracts with various reservation housing activities. Whether it can compete with the industry in the absence of continued reservation housing programs is open to serious question.

The present limited success of this activity is said to be due to new resident management which local workers like and respect. And, after a long period of labor turnover (many Indian people say that they worked for this factory only until they could find a job with OEO or with one of the reservation housing programs), a more or less stable work force has been built. It is understood, however, that this force is mainly composed of persons who have held jobs for extended periods off the reservation and not from among the many local people who were at various times on-the-job trainees in the plant.

3. *Rosebud Jewelry Company.*—Begun in the summer of 1967, this business lasted less than a year. Reasons given for its failure (in manufactured beads, etc., from dried corn kernels) were under-capitalization, lack of promotion of the product, etc. The most creditable reason for its failure seems to be that the Indians who worked in the activity were poorly paid and left it for better wages paid by the CAP or by the housing programs.

4. *Rosebud Electronics.*—This industry has been most successful in placing female workers. Started in the summer of 1967, it assembles electronic components for a major national corporation. The present work force is about 65, all but two of whom are Indians. Women outnumber men twelve to one. Men, it is reported, become bored with the routine assembly activities. A large percentage of the single women who work in the factory have children and previously drew ADC grants.

Plans for expanding the facility are under way. Its very capable manager, who is credited with its high degree of employee satisfaction, reports that he could hire 30 additional women if he had a place for them to work. It is housed in old government quarters turned over to the Rosebud tribe.

5. *Rosebud Sign Techniques.*—Under the same management as Rosebud Electronics, this small facility, employing five persons, was begun during the summer of 1968. The principal customer for the highway signs it produces is the Bureau of Indian Affairs. While efforts are being made to sell signs to other sources, it is doubtful that more employees will be hired since, with the complex equipment employed, production cannot be expanded without additional personnel.

INDIAN IDENTITY AND ECONOMIC DEVELOPMENT

By Sol Tax and Sam Stanley *

FOREWORD

An understanding of the type of economic development desired
by the Indians themselves is fundamental to the success of any
program of assistance. Sol Tax and Sam Stanley suggest that the
Indians have two goals which must be achieved simultaneously.
The first is to protect the Indian cultural identity. The second is to
make an adequate economic adjustment to the modern environment.
When Indians have been free to do so, they have been able to adapt
to changing circumstances. They have done this successfully for
25,000 years. The Indians cannot, however, be coerced into adjustment. Programs for Indian economic development must have maximum internal autonomy, and the Indian community must be allowed
to manage its own funds.

As soon as one approaches the problem of American Indian economic development, there is acute awareness of the complexities which
are concealed by this formulation of the basic problem. Instead of
taking a conventional approach to the subject, i.e. defining economic
goals in terms of resources and needs, we shall be anthropological and
try to start with the Indians themselves. This means that we must put
forth what they tell us about their problems, and we must draw on
the best efforts of our colleagues to help with the historical perspective.

In the context of economic development, the average Indian may
turn out to be an additional increment of unskilled labor. This might
be one way in which the economist would describe him—a kind of
shorthand approach, but it is not ours. We can only begin by asking,
"What does the Indian regard as most important in the world today?"
Our shorthand answer to this is (1) His identity, and (2) Making a
livelihood. Analytically, these two can be separated, but for most
Indians they are fused; and in some ways, they constantly find that
in pursuing one they are forced to give up the other. This has led to
the misconception that the Indian is lazy, incompetent, and wholly
lacking in the ability to adjust to new conditions. Mistakenly, he is
accused of wanting "to go back to the blanket," and anthropologists
are too often viewed as wanting this for Indians. Hopefully, we can
contribute something that will clarify the present situation.

In any case, we wish to emphasize and get on the record that: to
consider the economic development of American Indians, it is imperative at the outset to recognize the necessity of fulfilling two conditions
simultaneously, neither at the sacrifice of the other.

The first is the non-violation, indeed the protection, of Indian
identity and the values by which Indians live. Here it must be understood that for Indians this involves tribal identification, not individual
or "Indian", but, for example, Hopi.

* Dr. Tax is affiliated with the Department of Anthropology, University of
Chicago.
Dr. Stanley is with the Center for the Study of Man, Smithsonian Institute.

The second condition necessary for fulfillment is that, without threatening Indian identity or violating Indian values, we must assist Indians in making a better economic adjustment to what can be considered a new environment by making relevant resources available to them.

From every point of view, the American Indian is the most unique of all of our citizens. He entered the New World over 25,000 years ago. There is a good deal of evidence which vividly speaks of his many accomplishments. Looking at the Western Hemisphere as a whole, we should note that he had reached the southern extremes (from a presumed northernmost starting point—the Bering Sea) by at least 10,000 years ago. He may have arrived at Tierra del Fuego earlier, but this is all we know at present in the broadest sense about his earliest movements in the New World. His successful adaptation to the New World is parallel to what we know of the early post-glacial adaptation of the ancestors of the present European populations to the prevailing conditions of their Eastern Hemispheric environment. From the very day that he entered the New World, he was confronted with the problem of making a livelihood. How could he survive over time in this new environment? This historical question is more relevant to our present day than most people imagine. A .brief systematic survey of the American Indian adaptation to his environment will demonstrate this.

One anthropologist who has tried to focus on the overall adjustment of American Indians throughout the New World is the late Clark Wissler. Though much of his work is not now fashionable, he is owed a debt of gratitude by all who would look at the early people of the Western hemisphere as a whole. Wissler is relevant also because he was one of the first who focused on some classification of Indians in terms of broad regional groupings based on the notion of major subsistence pattern. If we look at these groupings, we may better grasp the essential characteristics of each major adjustment.

Taking the continent as a whole, Wissler identifies eight separate areas: Caribous Area, Salmon Area, Bison Area, Eastern Maize Area, Wild Seeds Area, Area of Intensive Agriculture, Manioc Area, and the Guanaco Area. (1938) These eight in turn can be grouped: three of them being the homes of hunting peoples, three of agriculturalists, one of fishers, and one of gatherers of wild seeds (p. 3). Here is the way in which he describes each of the eight within the context of its grouping:

HUNTING AREAS

In the caribou area live two groups of tribes generally recognized as having little in common, the Eskimo and the Canadian Indians. As we shall see later, this view as to their diversity is in a large measure justifiable, but with respect to food they have close similarities. It is customary to characterize the Eskimo as a people living upon sea mammals, particularly the seal; but we must not overlook the fact that their winter clothing is of caribou skin and that the flesh of that animal is an important part of their diet. However, the severe winters of their extreme northern range drive the caribous southward and leave the seal the only recourse during the period of prolonged darkness. Yet whenever the caribou are in reach the Eskimo places his chief dependence upon them. Thus, while our classification should not be permitted to obscure the large part that sea mammals play in the domestic economy of the Eskimo, the caribou is absolutely indispensable to his existence, not so much for food as for winter clothing. Hence, we see that Eskimo culture must be considered as a modified form of caribou culture.

The Indians of this area, chiefly the Déné and Northern Algonquin tribes, are an inland people occupying the sub-Arctic tundra and the sparse forest belt below it, which gradually shades off into the denser forests of southern Canada. Among these tribes we find the typical caribou culture. Vivid pictures of the prehistoric caribou hunting life have been penned by Hearne [1] and its surviving form by Warburton Pike. [2] In southern Canada the moose and other deer were also available and in the far north the musk-ox; wood bison were also found in a few localities, and hares and other small animals were eaten when needed. Though not reaching the seacoast at any place, these inland tribes had within their range lakes and rivers well stocked with fish, and in season frequented by water fowl. As with the Eskimo, these sources of supply were drawn upon in season. Yet all these foods were merely supplementary, for the people pinned their faith to the caribou and developed their whole feeding and clothing complex around this animal. Consequently, the failure of the caribou in any locality for even one season alone would spell disaster.

The methods of hunting are fully described in the descriptive literature of the several tribes, but, as always, such methods are largely dictated by the habits of the animals themselves. Among both the Eskimo and the Indians, the method of killing caribou is to drive or stampede them into artificial or natural lanes or defiles where the hunters are concealed. A variant of this is to run them into deep water, where they are at the mercy of swift canoe men. Snaring is also highly developed, even the largest game being caught in this way. Fishing of whatever kind is with three forms of appliances: the harpoon, the hook and line, and the net. These methods were both known to the Eskimo and to the Indian, though not used by both to the same relative degrees.

The cache is an important invention of this area and has found its way into our own culture. The name is usually applied to an elevated or a subterranean enclosure for storing dried or frozen meat. The caribou, living in great herds, must move forward as they graze over the almost barren tundra and the hunters must follow with equal speed. So the cache method was devised to solve the problem. The kill of the day is dressed as quickly as possible and then cached, after which the pursuit is again taken up. Thus, each family group will have a number of stores in various accessible places upon which they may draw in case of need.

The bison area is contiguous to the caribou area, but is of far less extent. It is also entirely inland, and like the upper portion of the caribou area, is comparatively treeless, except along the water courses and upon the higher ridges. The tribes formerly residing here are known to us as Buffalo Indians, and no characterization could be more exact. Along the foothills of the mountains, elk were formerly abundant and also mountain sheep, and out on the plain antelope were to be met, but these were obscured by the seething masses of bison, or buffalo encountered everywhere, summer or winter. Edible fish were not abundant, and some of the tribes observed a taboo against them as well as all water animals.

The methods of hunting bison bear certain analogies to those employed in the caribou area. Before horses were introduced, small herds were enticed or stampeded into enclosures where they were shot down at will; at other times they were rounded up by systematic grass firing and while in compact formation attacked at close range by foot men. [3] In favorable times, the surplus meat was dried and packed in bags.

This is a convenient place to note the manufacture of pemmican, a process which appears in some parts of the caribou area, but which seems to be more characteristic of this area. To make pemmican, the dried meat of the buffalo was pounded fine with stone hammers and packed in bags which were then sealed with melted fat. A special variety of pemmican was prepared by pulverizing wild cherries, pits and all, and mixing with the pounded meat. This is known in the literature as berry pemmican. There was also a variety in eastern Canada and New England made of deer and moose meat. When properly protected, pemmican will keep for many months and being compact and easily transported forms an exceedingly valuable food. From the very first it was adopted by Canadian and Arctic explorers among whom it is still the chief dependence.

In pemmican we have our first good example of the many ingenious processes by which the various groups of mankind have converted raw foods into more serviceable and conservable forms. In all cases, the chief consideration seems to have been its preservation and availability for transport.

The next great hunting area is in South America. From the interior of Argentine to the Horn we have in the main an open country, suggesting the central portion of the United States. There are few trees and in some parts, as the celebrated Pampas, there are rich, grassy plains. At the time of discovery (1492), the fauna here was not so rich as that of the northern continent. Yet the guanaco was abundant. This is considered to be the wild llama. a ruminant having close similarities to the camels of the Old World, but much smaller. Another animal of economic importance was the rhea, or American ostrich. The early accounts suggest that the original human inhabitants of this area were a nomadic hunting people, primarily dependent upon the guanaco, which they pursued with the bola and the bow. For this reason we shall speak of the region as the guanaco area. In the extreme southern part of the area, or lower Patagonia. we find a condition somewhat like that of the Eskimo, the tribes tending to live more on fish and seals, until we reach the Fuegians, who were almost entirely dependent upon marine fauna.

Spanish colonization soon made great changes in the guanaco area proper by the introduction of horses and cattle.* The latter soon ran wild in great herds like the buffalo of the northern

---

*Col. Church [6] states that horses were purposely turned into the Pampas in 1535.

continent, and the former not only ran wild, but were domesticated by the natives. Dobrizhoffer [4] has given us most readable accounts of how completely these natives assimilated horse culture. Some of the Patagonians are still famous for their horsemanship.

Though it is true that in these three great hunting areas the main food was flesh, many vegetable products were used. Even in the Arctic the Eskimo gather berries and edible roots in summer. Throughout the caribou area proper, the berry crop is considerable, and judging from Morice's [5] account of the Carrier some tribes dried and pressed them into cakes for storage. Edible roots also played an important part. As we come southward into the bison area, the flora grows somewhat richer in wild fruits, such as the cherry, plum, strawberry, etc., while in the more arid portions, the prickly pear is abundant. Of roots there were several species, but particularly the prairie turnip (*tipsina*, in Dakota). Even in the guanaco area we find the *Aucaria imbricata*, a kind of pine tree growing along the eastern border of the Andes, bearing abundant nuts, not unlike chestnuts, which are eaten raw, boiled, or roasted. Here also the *algarrabo*, or mesquite tree, abounds and from its seeds a food is prepared. In the treeless parts of Patagonia are the prickly pear and a few other scant food plants, while the pampas proper is devoid of all except a few edible grasses. On the other hand, the territory of the Fuegians is fairly well provided with berries which they use, but also produces wild celery and scurvy-grass, of which they make no use.

THE SALMON AREA

All the streams between San Francisco Bay, California, and Bering Straits, Alaska, draining into the Pacific, are visited by salmon. These ascend from the sea en masse to spawn, constituting a "run," in local speech. As they reach the very headwaters, they are available to all the tribes of this drainage, even those far inland. The run for each species of salmon occurs but once a year and this developed periodic seasonal practices not unlike those of agricultural peoples. As the time for the run approaches, the tribes gather upon the banks of the streams, equipped with fishing appliances, dip nets, harpoons, and weirs, as the local conditions may require. Then when the salmon pass, they are taken out in great numbers, to be dried and smoked. In the interior of the Columbia Basin, the dried fish are afterwards pounded fine in mortars, thus being reduced to a state not unlike pemmican. This pulverized food is carefully stored in baskets as the chief reserve food supply of the year. The tribes on the coast and outlying islands engage in sea fishing all the year and are almost entirely dependent upon the marine fauna, but those of the interior hunt deer and other game to complete their diet.

Of vegetable foods there are several varieties. Inland, several species of roots are gathered, dried and pounded fine in the same manner as dried fish. The chief root is camas but there are several other species in general use. In their proper season, berries are also very numerous in certain localities.

One striking peculiarity of these inland people is the extent to which they pounded or pulverized dried flesh and vegetables quite like agricultural peoples treat forms of grain. The trait seems to be almost a conventionality and leads one to suspect that the idea was borrowed from their southern neighbors who, as we shall see, were in contact with grain grinders. The tribes of the coast, particularly the indented island-studded part north of Puget Sound, did not have this pulverizing habit, nor did they make very extensive use of roots. Dried fish and berries were their staples. Where available, a kind of clover was eaten green and the inner bark of the hemlock worked up into a kind of bread-like food.

While in this area the tribes of the coast maintained fairly permanent villages; those of the interior were rather nomadic, or more correctly, moved in an annual cycle, according to their food habits. Thus at the salmon run each group took its accustomed place on a river bank; then as berries ripened, they shifted to the localities where they were abundant; later they moved again for the gathering of roots; again for hunting deer, and so on in one ceaseless round. To a less extent this seasonal shifting prevailed among the coast tribes, for by the use of canoes they could readily reach the places sought and return again to their villages.

This correlation between the use of wild foods and instability of residence is perhaps more striking in this area than in the others but, nevertheless, holds for all. The Eskimo regularly shifted from sea to inland and back again as winter set in, likewise, the caribou, bison, and guanaco hunters, each in their respective habitats, shifted according to seasonal requirements. The more extended and definite annual cycle of the salmon area seems to be due to the fact that each of their staple foods was available for but single short periods of the year, not unlike so many successive harvests of an agricultural people whose fields were far apart.

THE AREA OF WILD SEEDS

The area of wild seeds is often spoken of as the "acorn area," and will frequently be so designated in this work. However, it should be borne in mind that in southern California acorns are found only on the uplands and mountains and that in the surrounding parts and eastward over the Great Basin wild seeds take their place. Yet, since the most typical culture is found in central and southern California, we may consider the acorn the most characteristic food.

At the proper time acorns are stored in large basketry bins to protect them against thieving rodents. The raw acorns are not palatable, for they contain a large amount of tannic acid; however, this objection is eliminated by pounding the kernels into flour and then leeching with hot water. Good descriptions of this ingenious process may be read in the publications of the University of California. From this substance, a kind of bread or cake is made, which proves to be a very satisfactory food, but even here this is supplemented by foods from several varieties of wild seeds, roots, herbs, and grasses. [7] The tribes on the eastern side of the mountains out on the arid plateaus are forced to get along without the acorn and in consequence eke out their living from but a scant flora. One peculiarity of the area is the rarity of berries and fruits, which is in contrast to the interior of the salmon area. The term "digger," generally applied to the natives of this area, was suggested by their persistent gathering of roots and plants. It was also an expression of contempt due to the contrast between the scanty diet of these Indians and those of the bison area with whom travelers were more familiar. Likewise, the fauna was not particularly favorable. Deer were to be found in the mountains, but rarely in large numbers, and small game animals were not numerous. In the eastern part, the rabbit was an important item, and as noted above, salmon were caught wherever they made "runs," and other fish were used when available. Likewise, the coast people depended to some extent upon the marine fauna. Thus, notwithstanding the popular idea of modern California as an ideal habitat for us modern Americans, it must be regarded as rather unfavorable to the development of primitive tribes, for while enough food could be found, the daily routine of gathering it in small bits was time-consuming in the extreme. Moreover, in parts of Nevada, Utah, and Idaho the margin of even this sort of food was so narrow that many species of insects were eaten.

THE AGRICULTURAL AREAS

There are just two cultivated native food plants, maize and manioc (cassava), that rise to the level of chief staples. Both take the highest rank in excellence among the world's foods, and after the epoch-making discovery of Columbus were quickly spread to other parts of the world. [8] The uniqueness of these plants and the sharp contrast they make when compared with the cultivated staples of the Old World, is the strongest possible argument for the independent development of American culture.

In the first place, we have a distinct agricultural area in the eastern half of the United States, including a very small section of Canada. The chief crop was maize, on which account we speak of this division as the eastern maize area. Although its contact with the great agricultural area of Mexico and the south is slightly broken in Texas, we have no reason to doubt a historical connection between the two areas, and consequently we may consider them as parts of the same whole. The remaining inland boundaries of this eastern maize area mark the approximate climatic limits to its growth. These limits also define the distribution of agriculture, from which we have reason to infer that the introduction of that art did not precede the introduction of maize culture. However, this is a problem to be discussed later. We see, then, that the Indian tribes had extended agriculture in the east to its physical limits. The stretch of country from Louisiana to Maine presents considerable climatic variety which is reflected in the aboriginal crop lists, for though maize was grown throughout, it seems to have been more exclusively toward the north. Roughly considered, in the northern half of the area, the crops were squash, beans, and maize, all planted in the same field, while in the southern half, maize was supplemented by a kind of millet, and squashes gave way to melons, sweet potatoes, and gourds.

Tobacco, though not strictly a food, may be noted here. It was extensively grown in the south, and its cultivation carried as far north as the climate permitted.

Wild plants were also abundant and many species were used. Parker's [9] exhaustive study of Iroquois foods shows how completely that people drew upon the contiguous flora. From the data at hand, we have reason to believe that in the south a still greater number of species were eaten. In the far north wild rice became almost a staple; but while, as Jenks [10] has shown in his laudable investigation of this food, it was sometimes planted by the natives, it was not truly domesticated as was rice in the Old World.

Of manufactured foods, other than those made of maize, maple sugar takes first place. Practically every essential detail of the process now in use was developed by the Indians of this area before 1492. The sugar maple being a northern tree, the trait is almost peculiar to the northern half of the area, though the box elder and a few other trees have, in later times at least, permitted a makeshift extension of the art. That any kind of sugar was made in the south is doubtful.

Another food deserving mention is oil derived from hickory and walnuts. This oil was highly characteristic of the south and added a valuable element to the otherwise starchy diet. In early days the natives did a good business in supplying this oil to the colonists. In some parts of the Atlantic coast plain tuckahoe (a fungus) bread was made, and in the south, persimmon bread.

Of foods and dishes made with maize there is a long list, which is in the main the same as we ourselves use. Two noteworthy studies of this aspect of maize culture by Carr [11] and Parker [12] show how completely the white colonists absorbed the maize complex of the Indians.

One important characteristic of agriculture in this area is that it was woman's work, the man being a hunter. This sexual division of labor tended to give a well-balanced diet, but was not constant throughout, for in the far north where agriculture dwindled out into the caribou area, vegetable foods were decidedly in the minority, while in the extreme south, where agriculture was rather intense and the flora rich, the fruits of the chase were in the minority. The chief game was the deer. The bison of the prairies found its way as far east as the Alleghanies, but except in the open country was not an important item. The wild turkey and various small game were also abundant. Fish were taken where found by the usual methods, but in the south the use of poisons was general.

Next we turn to the great area of intensive agriculture, the only one in the New World, where work in the fields is not regarded as woman's work exclusively, and in which hunting ceases to be an occupation. As may be anticipated, it is also the home of the most advanced Indian cultures. We see from the map that it extends to about 35° on either side of the equator and is thus almost entirely within the torrid zone. On the other hand, all of this surface, except a narrow coast belt and a few intervening valleys, is the most elevated land in the New World. It is upon these highlands exclusively that maize was grown. Furthermore, there is a general tendency to aridity throughout, which, combined with the elevation, gives a very favorable climate. It is just the region where the most intensive cultures would be anticipated. As we proceed with the later sections of this book, the reader may be appalled at the complexity and variety of peoples in this area; hence it is fortunate that at the outset we are able to see one element of unity in the whole.

Beginning with the north, we have the pueblo-dwelling peoples of southwestern United States and northern Mexico. Besides maize, beans, melons, squashes and sunflower seed were the chief crops. In historic times, at least, onions and chili peppers were favorite garden plants; and according to local conditions, the following wild plants were largely used; piñon nut, mesquite, bean and saguaro. Tobacco and cotton were cultivated. Fish as food was not an important factor, in fact, it was under the ban of some tribes. Game was rather scarce, rabbits being the most numberous. Turkeys were domesticated. Of prepared foods, the most unique is the *piki* maize bread, made in thin, paper-like sheets.

For the remainder of the North American part of the area the Nahua and Maya may be taken as the types. Here agriculture was more highly organized than in any of the areas we have discussed. With the former, maize is made into peculiar cakes called "tortillas," which, with beans and the inevitable chili pepper, constitutes the usual menu. If we add to this cacao we have the list for the Maya also. In the lower parts, especially in Central America, there were many fruits, many of which are now cultivated by Europeans, as the mammae apple, the alligator pear, the cashew nut, together with the fleshy stalk of its tree, the tomato, pineapple, etc.

The Andean region of South America is peculiar in that at almost any point one may shift from high to low valleys, thus quickly passing through several varieties of climate. Likewise, one may, by lateral shifting, encounter deserts and the most wellwatered stretches in succession. All this tends to nullify the effects of changing latitude, so that the aggregate agricultural conditions in Colombia, Ecuador and Peru can be made the same. Still we find some cultural differences.

The Chibcha peoples of Colombia in the highlands raised maize, potatoes, sweet potatoes, manioc, beans, tobacco, coca, and cotton. They did not have the llama, and game was scarce, but carefully protected and conserved. The other peoples of Colombia did more hunting but in addition still cultivated maize. Salt was manufactured in favorable localities and formed an important article of trade.

The adjoining highlands of Venezuela formerly had a hunting and maize-growing population which was exterminated by the Spaniards.

Ecuador was partly under the control of the Inca at the Spanish conquest but, no doubt, still retained its former food habits. Its population was almost exclusively agricultural. Maize was the staple except on the highest levels, where quinoa was substituted. Potatoes were universal, and coca, peppers, and other plants in the lowest valleys. On the coast there was fishing.

To the south was the Inca empire with its highly organized agriculture. Here the crops were about the same as for Ecuador, but in favorable places manioc, ground nuts, beans, gourds, tomatoes, guava, and fiber plants were raised. Hunting was carried on in an organized manner, large drives being made over great areas. The game animals were chiefly the guanaco and vicuña, of which the flesh was often dried and stored for the use of the army. The familiar term "jerked meat" is believed to have come from the *charqui*, as this dried meat was called in Peru. Birds were taken in nets, and on the coast there was some fishing.

The great basin of the Amazon with the adjoining coast is one of the world's most typical tropical areas, but almost everywhere throughout there was some native agriculture. As a whole, the area presents some geographical variety, for the eastern part of South America also has its highlands, though far less pretentious than those of the west. Here, however, the elevation was much less; consequently, maize did not become the chief cultivated food, manioc or cassava, taking its place. Otherwise, the range of plants was about the same as in the Andean region. Tobacco, potatoes, and cotton were common. The celebrated maté, or Paraguay tea, and the edible clay of the Botocudo peoples are the principal unique features. Yet, in no case were the tribes of these highlands so dependent upon agriculture as were those of the west coast. In this respect they present a close analogy to the eastern maize users of North America, with whom they are geographically connected by the West Indies. Further, the almost complete delegation of agricultural responsibilities to the women is in itself an indication of the large part hunting played in their sustenance.

Finally, we come to the interior of the continent where high temperature, low elevation, and abundant moisture combine to produce rank flora. Our knowledge of this area is still rather scant, but what information we have indicates that the whole interior Amazon Basin with the contiguous east coast noted above should be considered as one distinct food area. That the art of agriculture is now absolutely unknown to any of the Amazon tribes is doubtful, because far into the interior we find manioc, tobacco, coca, pumpkins, sweet potatoes, etc., growing in the village fields. Also, maize has been reported from a number of localities, though the climate is unfavorable to it. The blowgun with poisoned darts is used in hunting, the game consisting largely of birds and small tree-climbing animals. No living thing is so abundant as to offer opportunity for food specialization, and the native must make use of everything he can lay hands upon. On the upper Amazon and elsewhere the taking of fish by poisoning the water is common. A very characteristic dish of this whole area is the "pepper-pot." Small game of whatever kind is cast into a pot and boiled into a thick broth made hot with peppers. The pot is emptied, but the contents continually augmented (Wissler, 1938: 3–19).*

We have included this extensive survey of the Indian adjustment to the New World environment in order to clarify for the reader once

* See Appendices:
    I. Bibliographic Citations for the Wissler Text.
   II. Map of Food Areas.
   III. List of Plants Domesticated in the New World.

and for all the fact that American Indians were completely capable of undertaking their own economic development from the moment that they entered this hemisphere over 25,000 years ago. They have never lost this *ability*, but they have been seriously hampered in trying to exercise it while maintaining their historic identity at the same time. Where they have been free to adapt, they have displayed a remarkable ability to take all kinds of rapid changes in stride. This has been true even after the arrival of the White Man. In fact, our point is that, in the absence of coercion, the Indian adapted healthily at a dazzling rate of speed.

The best example of this is the manner in which the Indian took to the horse. The adoption of this animal into their way of life was perhaps the most radical and rapid of all American Indian adjustments.

Within a few generations, the use of the horse spread from Spanish settlements of New Mexico throughout the central plains states and attracted Indians from all directions. When Indians first acquired horses, they used them as food; but gradually they found that, if the horse were used for hunting buffalo, it could supply many times its weight in meat. Hunting buffalo on foot had not been productive, but with the horse, the plains' way of life changed a great deal. "From all over, other Indian groups converged on the plains and quickly adapted themselves to an economy based on the bison * * * and the plains became a maelstrom of varied and often conflicting cultures." (Farb 1968: 115).

Many groups of great diversity came together and changed their ways due to the new circumstances. Cultures borrowed from each other and fit the new into their old ways. Although differences continued to exist, within a few generations, major cultural differences all but disappeared and similarities arose; for example, the Sun Dance ceremony was eventually observed by nearly every tribe.

"Even more remarkable, this homogeneity was achieved with great speed, was not imposed on unwilling people by a more powerful group, and was done in the absence of a common tongue—save for 'sign language,' the lingua franca of the Plains tribes." (p. 117)

With this "new tool" to kill greater numbers of buffalo than ever before, many of these Indians became extremely wealthy in material goods; but all this ended with the wars of the plains during which "the millions of bison very nearly vanished without leaving any survivors, the plains were turned into a dust bowl, and the once-proud Indian horsemen were broken in body and spirit." (p. 113)

It is not difficult to argue that the subsequent adaptation of Plains tribes has been difficult and tenuous. This, of course, is the reason for the whole Indian "problem." Wounded Knee and other similar events are markers for the time when Indians were no longer free to adapt to changing circumstances.

Lest we be accused of maintaining that no Indian group is able to adopt healthily to 20th Century America, we should like to briefly describe the Caughnawaga Mohawk.

These Mohawks have carried their social patterns and attendant values, developed long before Europeans invaded their land, into the modern world. They depended largely on vegetable foods produced for the most part from domesticated plants. Unlike farmers, they did not grow their crops in permanent fields, but wherever they made camp. Precise details as to how they did their farming are lacking, but all accounts agree that women bore the largest share of responsibility.

Hunting and war were the most highly valued male activities. War tended to be a small group enterprise, and followed the pattern of fighting in all other American Indian tribes. Usually, a man seeking glory or perhaps vengeance would solicit support from a few close friends. If they agreed to participate, a general call for volunteers would be issued. Men were free to join or not, and there was no stigma attached to nonparticipation. The notion of authority, characteristic of Western civilization, was quite foreign to the Mohawks, as it was to all other tribes in the league of the Iroquois to which the Mohawks belonged. In fact, almost all American Indian tribes considered the acceptance of a directive from any leader a matter of choice.

By the end of the 18th century, most of the Iroquois had been placed on reservations. The Caughnawaga Mohawks were settled on the reservation of that name about 10 miles south of Montreal, Canada. For a time they were under the protection of the Jesuits, and the reservation also served as a refuge for Christian Indians from other tribes.

From about 1800 to 1886, the Caughnawaga Mohawks were typical of most reservation Indians. They engaged in a variety of enterprises including lumbering, timber rafting, and dock and circus work. But 1886 was a significant year. Some of the Mohawks were hired as unskilled laborers on the Victoria Tubelor Bridge, which abutted on reservation land. This work opened up new opportunities for the tribe. Since the first contact with structural steel, the vast majority of Mohawk men between the ages of 18 and 60 have become noted for their ability to work at great heights on skyscrapers.

Mohawks today work in the larger cities of eastern North America, but they regard the reservation as their home. As we have noted elsewhere (Tax and Stanley 1968: 146), "For many, the reservation is where their wives, children, and mothers are, and their seasonal homecoming is reminiscent of the return from war or the hunt of bygone days. The patterns for selecting crews to work on the high steel are similar to those that produced war or hunting parties in the past. Authority is still lightly regarded; bosses have no moral basis for expecting their orders to be obeyed."

Even as many Indians eagerly accepted the horse and the Mohawk took to high steel, there was sharp rejection of other Western cultural items. In particular, this was true of the plow. The reasons for not accepting this implement and its attendant complex are varied, but the combination of Indian apprehensiveness and White force would seem to summarize them. We need to look at this combination in perspective in order to better understand the present day Indian "problem."

During the 19th century, the assumption that the "human" (civilized?) existence required every man to farm his own piece of land dominated the thinking of all who wielded power over Indians. A corollary assumption was that each family derives its subsistence solely and independently from its farm. They "knew what was best" for Indians, and they possessed the power to bring it about. The attempts to force the Indian to become a farmer probably reached their most ludicrous form in the case of the Makah Indians who live around the tip of the Olympic Peninsula in the northwesternest part of the United

States. These Indians who, for perhaps thousands of years, had successfully developed an economy based on exploitation of their abundant
sea resources were given plows and plots of rocky, forested land to till!
(Colson 1953: 3–24). Eventually good sense prevailed and the project
was abandoned; but, in addition to causing unnecessary waste and
human suffering, this experience underscores the importance of letting
Indians make their own adjustment in the absence of coercion.

We all know that there are many whites who never had any intention
of letting Indians remain Indians. This view is held by many "well-
intentioned" people who assume that Indians, like all the rest of us
want to change, want to assimilate. They assume that everyone, given
the free choice, would want to be civilized just like us. These people
have very definite ideas of right and wrong, and one of their ideas
of right is that Indians should be civilized, should become like the
white man.

What they fail to realize and understand is that perhaps Indians
prefer their own way of life and have no desire to change it. In fact,
Indians have had many opportunities to change and it should be clear
to those who make the above assumptions that those Indians who
wanted to change have done so and those who have not changed have
not because they do not want to. Furthermore, those who have not and
do not want to change resent the further assumption that assimilation
is inevitable—which in effect means that all will eventually change
even those who do not want to.

In our opinion, no white man has the right to decide what an Indian
should be; each man has the right to choose which way he wants to go.
Only two solutions have been offered the American Indian by the
white man: work hard and assimilate or stay out of sight, out of mind;
in other words, get lost in the city or starve on the reservation.

The sheer exercise of power, too often informed by ignorance, by
Whites over Indians is not sufficient to account for the tenacious resistance on the part of the latter over such a long period of time. In resist-
ing the pressure to become farmers or what-have-you, the Indians are
affirming positively their faith in their own values. However they
adapt to the changing environment, these are the trusted guidelines to
which they constantly return. It is important for all of us to understand some of the very basic differences in outlook which exist between
Western values and North American Indian values.

The distinction can best be understood if we begin by acknowledg-
ing that as people engage in activities which permit them to survive
and reproduce in a particular environment, they develop a set of beliefs and values. Anthropologists call these their "ethos." The term
has a unique reference to the character of a society, particularly in its
moral, ethical, and social outlook.

When man discovered how to domesticate plants and animals, he
arrived at a new way of adjusting to his environment. The result was
a corresponding change in ethos. The hunter ethos gave way to the
peasant ethos. Man "discovered" property and began to use concepts
of saving, land ownership, and inheritance. He developed a new way
of ordering his time—since crops had to be planted, weeded, and harvested, and animals had to be fed regularly. It has even been said that
domestication of plants and animals made man a slave to property and
time. Finally, the new ethos put an emphasis on individualism and

competition. The idea that one man could command another may have originated with domestication. Thus, what we commonly term a civilized society today is in reality a group of people living within a peasant ethos. The term peasant ethos is used here in its broadest sense, encompassing all societies with rigid class structures or hierarchies of social relationships. It is not applied strictly to farmers, since even some hunting groups have practiced some amount of farming of a rudimentary sort.

The hunter ethos stands in direct contrast to the major elements of a peasant society. The hunter considers himself a part of the land and what it bears. He feels imbedded in it. He is a natural conservationist, taking only what he needs for sustenance. He never sees himself as a lord or master, and he does not recognize any moral obligation for one man to obey the orders of another. For the hunter, time and work have not been invented, and if the choice arises he will almost certainly choose the community decision over his own individual self-interest. As might be expected, hunters and peasants have a difficult time communicating with one another because of the extreme contrasts in their patterns of living and outlook.

At the time of Columbus' discovery, most of the lush areas of North America were still inhabited by hunting peoples. This is curious since these tribes had been exposed to peasant cultures, such as the Aztec, for thousands of years. The hunters of North America—the Indians—all knew something about farming, but they apparently decided to remain hunters. Indeed, the American Indian not only failed to become a farmer-peasant before Columbus arrived, but has persistently refused to become one despite the pressures of Europeans and their descendants in North America.

It appears, therefore, that the North American Indian refused to adjust to a farming economy because to do so would have threatened all the values of his hunting ethos, and he chose to live by them as an outsider rather than to give them up. The whole history of the relationships between the Indians and the white newcomers seems to bear this out. Few American Indian groups have chosen even to make a pretense of moving into the mainstream of American life.

Now we are in a better position to understand the success of the Mohawks. High steel work has permitted these Indians to maintain their hunting ethos; they are more fortunate than most American Indian tribes who, despite immense pressures to take on new activities and a new ethos, are willing to suffer poverty and deprivation rather than compromise their ethos. Furthermore, they have not been given the chance to change by choice, despite their demonstrated ingenuity to develop a wide variety of adjustments in the past and present.

The intertwining of the desire to maintain a decent living and one's identity is the crux of the problem as we see it. The question is, "what can concerned persons who have positions of power do about it?" The answer lies partly in examining our own frame of mind, or as one of us put it:

> The conclusion I draw is not that we cannot help other communities of people, but only that we must help them pretty largely on their own terms. To do this we must be prepared to learn at least as much from them as we bring to them. More than that, we must come to them in the frame of mind that admits it can never

understand all the factors important in the situation, and so offers the widest variety of alternatives to see which might actually be suitable. I think of this analogy: I stand on a mountaintop and am about to empty a bucket of water over the edge, from where eventually it would reach the river below. I could now call in all sorts of wise men with their measuring instruments and their calculators and expect them to predict the exact course the bucket of water will take. Perhaps they would do fairly well; they might theoretically make a perfect prediction if they took as much time about it as would a monkey at the typewriter writing all the plays of Shakespeare. But if they were indeed wise men, I should expect at least one of them to suggest that we empty the bucket and let the water show the path, and then use our ingenuity to explain it. (Tax 1955: 236–237)

But in addition, we can offer assistance in the form of material resources and money. In fact, we have a moral obligation to do so, and in practical terms, it will be to the benefit of all. Surely we now know enough to begin to offer this assistance on the most open and healthy terms possible. If we consider for a minute the two important variables: Material Inputs and Locus of Decision Making, we will be able to chart the consequences of their relationship to each other.

LOCUS OF DECISION-MAKING

		In Agency	In Community
		Type A	**Type B**
	Low Emphasis and Amount	Utilize superior knowledge or expertise of experts; accept new teachings; change habits.	Develop leadership; identity problems; formulate goals through democratic means. Use "self-help" with community resources to solve problems.
MATERIAL INPUTS			
		Type C	**Type D**
	High Emphasis and Amount	"Engineering-Physical Infrastructure" Build new facilities needed for development; allow local people to figure out how to use them.	"Comilla Approach" Local group defines own problems; sets own goals. Outside organization helps it achieve goals.

(Choldin, Harvey M., "Urban Cooperatives at Comilla, Pakistan: A Case Study of Local-Level Development")

In this chart, material inputs can be high or low in emphasis and amount while the locus of decision making can be in the agency or in the community. Let us look at the four possible outcomes.

Type A is heavy on power from above, but puts very little in the way of money and material into the solution. It corresponds most closely to what is generally referred to as colonialism.

Type B seeks to develop leadership at the local level, but is accompanied by low material inputs. This comes closest to what happens (ideally) when you introduce the Peace Corps.

Type C occurs when something like a soap plant, running water, a highway, and electricity are all introduced into a community. The material inputs are large, but the agency decides what they will be and where they will go.

Type D is the kind of situation which we would recommend for assisting American Indians. Its major points are that it allows the community to define its own goals (which will surely reflect the group ethos), and features both a high emphasis on and a large amount of material input.

If we want to adopt the Comilla approach to American Indian economic development, then there are some important things that must be understood.

The basic law concerning American Indians requires that we return to the original definition of a special relation between the United States government and Indian communities. American Indians have never lost this conception because unlike most Americans, Indians do not conceive of themselves except *first* as members of communities. American Indians live in "kinship societies." As in any healthy ongoing society, a person is part of a family and its economy and is not expected to be forcibly separated from it, so American Indians are part of extended family groups which form their communities. Even when they move to cities, they form family-type communities. It is "unnatural," perhaps impossible, for Indians to be isolated from their communities. Traditionally the communities banded into larger political units called "tribes" or nations which were recognized by European nations as sovereign. But the smaller communities, whether "sovereign" or not, were indispensable and valid units. These "communities," recognized by their Indian members, must also be recognized as the units with which governmental Indian policy must deal. Individual families and persons have rights guaranteed to every citizen; and legislation need not concern them. Indian *communities* are recipients of what special rights, tradition, treaties, and the needs of Indians require.

American law recognizes corporate groups of many kinds, and provides mechanisms whereby such a group can receive and expend funds under rules established within itself. American Indian communities are not all the same. In one, the authority might be priestly and hereditary; in another secular and elected. The organization of most contains elements of both the sacred and the secular, and generally the spirit is (in great contrast to our own) non-hierarchial, non-authoritarian, stressing the agreement of all (in town-hall fashion) rather than rule by "representatives."

Legislation for American Indians has in the past been unsuccessful both because communities have been forced to operate in terms of our culture rather than their own and because they had no ultimate authority over internal management, being subject to veto power—hence constant surveillance—from outside. What is required, therefore, is a legislative program which provides maximum internal autonomy and authority for Indian communities.

American Indian communities require funds for education, health, welfare, and economic development. The general society provides such funds to replace the resource base which—if restored—would provide independence. Since the resource base (the Continent which Europeans occupied) cannot be restored to Indian communities, money must be substituted. Just as Indian communities managed their resources independently before, for the money to be useful, they must manage it independently now.

The legislation required must, therefore, be drafted in such a way that each of the many hundreds of American Indian communities, however they are defined and bounded by Indians—from the small bands and subtribes to recreated urban "Indian Center" communities—can each in its own way autonomously manage the resources that must be provided.

It would be indeed a strange procedure to try to draft such legislation without full participation of the Indian communities. What is clearly required is Indian-community self-determination for developing the conditions of their self-determination.

In 1961 there was a great conference in Chicago which for the first time brought Indian individuals together from all over the nation, where—entirely on their own—they developed a "Declaration of Indian Purpose." What would be needed now is to invite and make possible participation by every identifiable Indian community—the local Navaho, Cherokee, Iroquois, Salish, Dakotan, etc., etc., groups as well as those in Los Angeles, Minneapolis, etc., etc.—who could themselves make the necessary decision. These are the implications of adopting a "Comilla Project" approach to assisting American Indians to a healthy, viable economic development of their communities.

Before concluding this report, we think it is important to try to give an historical overview of the character of federal-Indian relationships and some suggestions for change. The viewpoint which we are setting forth is not new—in fact, it was advanced in this form as early as 1956 by Dr. Tax. Despite this fact, it applies as forcefully now to the problem as it did then. This, in itself, is some measure of the depth of the problem, especially if we measure the amount of money which has been spent in the last 13 years to "solve" the problem. In order to begin to change the hopeless policies which have been pursued in the past, the American people are going to have to internalize the major points of this overview. Failure to take our recommendations seriously will, at the very least, mean more of the same—poverty, degradation, and defensive adaptation by the Indians—and these are the very problems all of us are trying to solve!

Through all of our history, States as well as the Federal Government have been frustrated with respect to solving the problems of the American Indians. We have vacillated between (1) a policy of starving the Indians into throwing in the sponge and "getting lost" in the general population, and (2) a kinder policy of helping them to get themselves ready to leave Indian ways and get lost in the general population. In either case, they would then be off our consciences, and finally out of our pocketbooks. Both policies have failed.

When we have followed the first policy, and thrown them into the water to "sink or swim," we have found that the Indians neither sink nor swim; they just float, and remain the same problem. When we have followed the second, kinder policy, we have found that Indians do not, in fact, do the things that will lead to their disappearance. They do not want to get lost. The "kind" policy will only work if we have the patience to continue to use our resources to help Indian communities to adjust to the national economy freely and in their own way. But their own way might not be to get lost at all.

Every man and woman has the personal problem of deciding what sort of person he wants to be. Some Indians may want to become white men in their allegiance and their ways; this ought to be their right. But many Indians want to maintain their Indian values and allegiance, and many Indian communities want to maintain for their posterity and identity and heritage that were given to them. They too have this right. It is not for any white man, or Congress, or the Indian Service bureaucracy to demand that Indians stop being Indians.

It is a challenge which has never been met in the United States to help the Indians to adjust economically and socially to American life, so that they actually become financially independent. We cannot begin to solve the problem unless we first recognize that Indians have a right to make this adjustment *as* Indians.

Leaving them free to make their own choices removes the great block to constructive change. What folly it has been to demand that Indians cooperate in plans for making them something other than they want to be! What an interesting experiment, on the other hand, once the block is removed, to develop with them ways toward that greatest freedom which comes with economic independence!

The Indian policy that has most recently been with us has been the sink or swim policy, the less moral way that has never worked and never can. It does not get Indians out of our pocketbooks—indeed, this unchristian policy (as Eisenhower once called it) requires more money rather than less—and it certainly does not get them off the conscience of the nation.

The present policy, aimed at the disappearance of the Indians, is a double-edged sword. On the one side there is a nauseating paternalism. Indians get help from the government because, since we destroyed their means of livelihood, they need it; and it is our moral obligation to continue this help until we and they are wise enough to make them once again independent. But meanwhile the Indian Bureau, like any overprotective parent, demands that the Indians manage their own affairs; but, on the grounds that they do not know how, never lets them try, and become sure, more than ever, that they are incompetent to do so. They say, in effect, that as long as we pay the bills, we shall manage your communities. If you think you are competent to manage your own affairs, then cut yourselves off from the financial assistance as well. Money to live on, or freedom; you cannot have both, so take your choice.

But the Indians have not the resources for the medical, educational, and developmental needs of their communities. So they must choose the continued interference in their local affairs. This satisfies nobody, and gets nowhere. Congress, frustrated, then attempts to use force or bribery to induce Indian communities to make the other choice.

We need an entirely new approach. We need to separate the two problems of *the money which the Indians need for their community services* from *the way the money is used*.

Nobody should ever again interpret our policy as one which is importantly influenced by a desire to save money to the detriment of Indians and in violation of our traditional and moral obligations. It has been and should be our policy to *make it unnecessary to provide special services*, hence to make Indians independent. But until this is accomplished, the money should be provided because it is needed and because it is right. Therefore, the first plank of our policy is to assure Indians that we shall continue to provide in the federal budget the money needed to continue Indian services. For the time being, we suggest that the same budget now provided be continued.

But this money should be spent by the Indians, for themselves, rather than *for* the Indians by bureaucrats. Just as a government might provide a subsidy to a hospital or a university without taking over the functions of administering the hospital or university, so the funds available to Indians should be looked upon as subsidies to assist them to provide their own community services—health, welfare, public order. education, development.

But whatever changes occur from one system of administration to another or from one allocation to another, they should be entirely voluntary on the part of the Indians who are now recipients of the services for which the funds are provided. If Indians prefer to have the federal government agencies continue to administer their services, no change need be made. Whenever, however, an Indian community, or the recipients of services, wish to seek changes in administration, these changes should be provided at once.

The money in the budget is divisible into funds (a) for services: money to pay teachers and build schools; or pay doctors and nurses, and build hospitals, etc., and (b) money for general administration to pay administrative officials in Washington, in area offices, and on reservations.

Funds for services should be continued for the same services. Funds for administration should be made flexible so that as much as necessary can be used by tribes with which to hire non-governmental help for administration of their affairs, when they wish to make a change; and to pay the expenses of a panel of volunteer advisers set up independent of the Department of Interior from which Indian communities may obtain general advice in planning changes in how their affairs may be administered.

If the Bureau of Indian Affairs withers away, it will be because Indians will find other ways, which they prefer, to have their funds administered. There will be no "termination" with respect to provision of services as long as they are needed by Indians. "Withdrawal" will occur not as the government withdraws from its obligations, but as the Indians withdraw from government interference in the administration of their services.

REFERENCES

CHOLDIN, HARVEY M. n.d. Urban cooperatives at Comilla, Pakistan: a case study of local-level development.

COLSON, ELIZABETH. 1953. The Makah Indians. University of Minnesota Press. Minneapolis.

FARB, PETER. 1968. Man's rise to civilization as shown by the Indians of North America from primeval times to the coming of the industrial state. E. P. Dutton & Co. Inc. New York.

TAX, SOL. 1955. Changing consumption in Indian Guatemala. In Consumer Behavior.

TAX, SOL AND SAM STANLEY. 1967. Vanishing hunters in Science Year. Field Enterprises Educational Corporation, Chicago.

WISSLER, CLARK. 1938. The American Indian. Oxford University Press. New York.

APPENDIX I

Bibliographic Citations for the Wissler Text

1. HEARNE, SAMUEL A. 1795. I. Journey from Prince of Wales' Fort in Hudson's Bay, to the Northern Ocean. London, 1795.
2. PIKE, WARBURTON. 1892. I. Primitive Methods of Working Stone Based on Experiments of Halvor L. Skavlem (Logan Museum Bulletin, vol. 2, no. 1, Beloit, 1930).
3. ALLEN, J. A. 1876. I. The American Bisons, Living and Extinct (Memoirs, Geological Survey, Kentucky, vol. I, part 2, Cambridge, 1876).
4. DOBRIZHOFFER, MARTIN. 1822. An Account of the Abipones, an Equestrian People of Paraguay. 3 vols. London, 1822.
5. MORICE, A. G. 1906. I. The Canadian Dénés (Annual Archaeological Report, 1905, Appendic, Report, Minister of Education, pp. 187–219, Toronto, 1906).
6. CHURCH. COL. G. E. 1912. I. Aborigines of South America. London, 1912.
7. MERRIAM, C. HART. 1905. I. The Indian Population of California (American Anthropologist, N.S. vol. 7, pp. 594–606, Lancaster, 1905).
8. LAUFER, BERTHOLD. 1907. I. The introduction of Maize into Eastern Asia (Congrès International des Américanistes, XVᵉ Session, tenué à Québec en 1906, part 1, pp. 223–257, Québec, 1907).
   SPINDEN, HERBERT J. 1917. I. The Origin and Distribution of Agriculture in America (Proceedings, Nineteenth International Congress of Americanists, 1915, pp. 269–276, Washington, 1917).
   SAUER, CARL. 1936. I. American Agricultural Origins: A Consideration of Nature and Culture (Essays in Anthropology, Presented to A. L. Kroeber in Celebration of his Sixtieth Birthday, June 11, 1936, pp. 279–297, Berkeley, 1936).
9. PARKER, ARTHUR C. 1910. I. Iroquois Uses of Maize and other Food Plants (Bulletin 144, New York State Museum, Albany, 1910).
   WAUGH, F. W. 1916. I. Iroquois Foods and Food Preparation (Memoir 86, Geological Survey of Canada, No. 12, Anthropological Series, Ottawa, 1916).
10. JENKS, A. E. 1900. I. The Wild Rice Gatherers of the Upper Lakes. A Study in American Primitive Economics (Nineteenth Annual Report, Bureau of American Ethnology, part 2, Washington, 1900).
    DENSMORE, FRANCES. 1928. I. Uses of Plants by the Chippewa Indians (Forty-fourth Annual Report, Bureau of American Ethnology, Washington, 1928).
11. CARR, LUCIEN. 1896. I. The Food of Certain American Indians and their Methods of Preparing It (Proceedings, American Antiquarian Society, N.S. vol. 10, pp. 155–190, Worcester, 1896).
12. PARKER, ARTHUR C. 1910. *op. cit.*

(94)

95

APPENDIX II

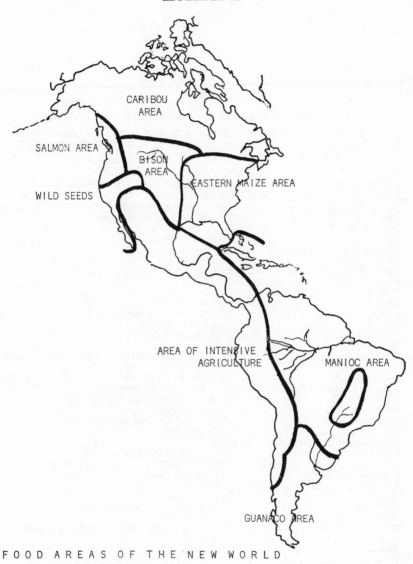

FOOD AREAS OF THE NEW WORLD

APPENDIX III

Plants Cultivated by the Natives of the New World Before 1492

The following list [1] enumerates the most important plants originally cultivated by the several Indian tribes before the discovery of the New World in 1492.

Name [2]	Area of cultivation
Agave, or aloe	Mexico to Chile.
Alligator pear	Central America and West Indies.
Arrowroot	Tropical America.
Barnyard grass	Mexico and southern United States.
Bean, kidney	Distribution same as maize.
Bean, Lima	Brazil and Peru.
Cacao	Tropical America.
Capsicum or Chili pepper	Do.
Cashew nut	Do.
Coca, or cocaine	Peru and Bolivia.
Corn. (See maize.)	
Cotton	Tropical America.
Cherimoya	Peru and Brazil.
Gourd	Distribution same as maize.
Guava	Tropical America.
Jerusalem artichoke	Mississippi Valley.
Madia	Chile.
Maize	Eastern North America, Meso-America, South American highlands.
Manioc	Amazon Basin to east coast of South America.
Maté or Paraguay tea	Paraguay and western Brazil.
Papaw	West Indies and Central America.
Peanut	Peru and Brazil.
Pineapple	Mexico and Central America.
Potato	Chile and Peru.
Prickly pear or Indian fig	Mexico.
Pumpkin	Temperate North America.
Oca	Chile and Bolivia.
Quinine, and others	Bolivia and Peru.
Quinoa	Colombia and Peru.
Squash	Tropical America.
Star apple	West Indies and Panama.
Sweet potato	Temperate America.
Tobacco and other species	Hemisphere wide except northern and southern extremities.
Tomato	Peru.

[1] Wissler, Clark, The American Indian, Oxford University Press, New York, 1938.
[2] Latin names omitted.

READJUSTMENT WITH SECURITY FOR THE AMERICAN INDIAN

By GLENN L. EMMONS*

FOREWORD

The Federal Government has always had special treaty relationships with the American Indians. Glenn L. Emmons, a former Commissioner of Indian Affairs, summarizes this history, beginning with the First Continental Congress in 1775. Mr. Emmons then outlines his own view that the present trust relationships must be gradually brought to the end and the Bureau of Indian Affairs abolished. In place of current Bureau of Indian Affairs' programs, individual Indians carried on the tribal rolls at the moment of enactment of new legislation should be accorded regular monthly income support payments. Indian families would thus be given financial security together with the freedom to manage their own affairs.

In the first place, I certainly agree with the Indians in their objection to the word "termination" when referring to the ending of the trusteeship of the Federal Government over the Indian people. To them, "termination" has a connotation of "doom" or "destruction." Many generations of Indians have lived under the paternalism of this trusteeship and therefore have an inborn feeling of dependency on the agency of Government established many years ago to manage their affairs and provide them with special services. Therefore, in abolishing this special relationship between the Government and the Indian, we must be humane as well as practical in the process. We must express to the Indians a new hope and confidence in their future by what I prefer to name, "readjustment with security." We must assure them of the retention of their Indian identification, preservation of their cultures, and the protection of their present homelands.

By terms of treaties, our Government's relation to the Indians is quite different from that with any other minority group. That relationship goes back to the First Continental Congress in 1775 when it established three Departments of Indian Affairs—the Northern, Central, and Southern—each headed by a Commissioner. In September 1824 the Congress established the Bureau of Indian Affairs under one Commissioner and placed it in the War Department, where it remained until it was transferred to the newly created Department of the Interior in 1849.

During all of this period and up to 1879 a great number of treaties were signed with various tribes and bands, and these Indians were located on areas of land called reservations. The lands in these reservations were held in trust for the Indians by the U.S. Government and the responsibility for their management rested with the Secretary of the Interior. This trusteeship extends to this time and of course, under the trust, the Indian owners have never been given the opportunity to manage these properties themselves.

---

*Commissioner of Indian Affairs, 1953–1961.

Under this paternalistic system, the increase of dependency on the Government for services from one generation to the next is only natural. The populations have grown and so have the management problems. Congress has passed over 4,000 laws relative to the Indians and over 9,000 regulations have been promulgated for the operations of the Bureau of Indian Affairs.

In August 1953, the Congress unanimously passed Joint Resolution 108, which declared:

It is the sense of Congress that the Trusteeship over all Indian tribes shall be ended as rapidly as possible.

The terms of the resolution are somewhat ambiguous. How soon is it possible to end the trusteeship and under what conditions? If it means when the majority of the tribal members have reached such a stage of well-being as their non-Indian neighbors, then what about the minority group that has not or could not attain that degree of self-sufficiency?

The Congress has been very generous in its appropriations for the operations of the Bureau of Indian Affairs for the past 15 years. These moneys are for carrying on the many responsibilities of the Bureau established by law, such as education, land management, welfare, law and order, administrative costs of the Bureau and many others.

In spite of the generosity of Congress over the years, we still find living conditions on many of the reservations on the level of direst rural slums.

With the Indian population increasing every year, the lands will simply not support the Indians living on them. It should be understood by everyone interested in the Indian problem that most of the Indian people are not interested in being agriculturists even if land was available.

In 1958 we established the Branch of Industrial Development in the Bureau to bring plants on or near reservations for Indian employment. Even if industries are continually induced to the reservations, it is hardly reasonable to assume that every employable Indian will be provided with a job in one of these plants. Also, there will be those who are not employable under any circumstances and also those with families who desire employment but are fearful of leaving the security of the reservation to seek jobs elsewhere.

With the reservation population increasing each year, additional congressional appropriations are requested for the Indian Bureau's operations and the so-called Indian problem grows bigger and bigger and costlier and costlier.

The Government has spent over a billion dollars over the past 4 years on the Indian and yet unemployment on the reservations is still several times higher than the national level.

After 145 years of Government trusteeship, is it not about time to set a definite date for ending this situation, and during that interim to concentrate on programs of education and training for the Indians to enable them to fend for themselves when that time arrives?

Three factors must be taken into consideration in ending the Indian trusteeship:

First, the welfare of the Indian people themselves;
Second, the personnel of the Bureau of Indian Affairs;

Third, the impact on the non-Indian communities near reservations whose economy is tied to the Federal expenditures in those areas through the Indian Bureau.

The legislation suggested below is designed to protect the interests of those elements involved.

It will preserve by law the tribal lands for the tribal members through tax exemptions and a restriction on the sale of these lands for a period of time. This would preserve their homeland, not only for those tribal members who cared to remain on these lands, but for those living elsewhere who would desire to return there in the future.

The tribal members would be given the opportunity to seek a higher standard of living elsewhere with financial security, thus making the tribal lands available for the use of those members who desired that type of occupation.

A great majority of the personnel of the Bureau of Indian Affairs are capable, conscientious, and dedicated public servants, and it is only right and just for their welfare, also to be considered. They are the people to carry out the congressional mandate under this act to abolish their jobs. Therefore, the Bureau employee will have priority rights for employmeent in other Government agencies when his services in the Bureau are terminated by developments created by this act.

The moneys paid the Indians on the ending of the trusteeship would doubtless all be spent for goods or needs for their families in the areas of their domicile. This cash output would far offset the loss of the Federal Bureau payroll.

The sum presently appropriated for fiscal year 1970 for the Bureau of Indian Affairs is $311,010,000 and for the Division of Indian Health, including health facility construction, $118,481,000. Several additional millions of dollars will be spent by other governmental agencies on Indian assistance programs.

Under the law, the Bureau can give its services only to those of one-quarter degree or more of Indian blood and to those who are considered residents on trust lands. It is estimated there are about 325,000 Indians in this status and eligible for the benefits provided under these appropriations.

The suggested legislation includes all Indians of tribes affected by this act who are one-quarter degree or more of Indian blood regardless of their place of residence, with the exception of the natives of Alaska. This group in Alaska, totaling about 40,000 persons, is comprised of Aleuts, Eskimos, and several Indian tribes, and is under the supervision of the Bureau of Indian Affairs. As their situation is entirely different from the other groups covered by this bill, it is recommended that their affairs be transferred to the Department of Health, Education, and Welfare within 2 years of the passage of this act.

Under these provisions there would be approximately 450,000 Indians eligible for inclusion on the rolls of this act. The essentials to carry out these purposes are proposed as follows:

"The Congress enacts legislation ending the Federal trusteeship over all Indian tribes within 8 years of the date of passage of the act.

"At midnight on the date of the passage of this Act, the rolls of every tribe will be closed for the purposes of this act. Each roll shall consist of all persons of one-quarter or more degree of Indian blood who are members of tribes under Government trusteeship, regardless of their place of residence and only such Indians living at midnight on the date of the passage of this act will be entitled to any of the benefits of this act. The natives of Alaska are excepted from the provisions of this act, but the responsibility for them shall be transferred from the Bureau of Indian Affairs to the Department of Health, Education, and Welfare within 2 years of the date of the passage of this act.

"When the trusteeship over a tribe is ended, the U.S. Government, through the Department of Health, Education, and Welfare, shall pay to each individual Indian on this tribal roll prepared beforehand by the Bureau of Indian Affairs, the sum of $60 per month. Payment to a minor child shall be made direct to the head of the family until the child leaves his parental care or until he reaches his age of majority. It is intended that the parent shall use these funds for the support of his family. In case the parents are found using these funds for other than the purposes intended, authority is given the local welfare officials to receive and administer the moneys for the use and benefit of the family.

"Prior to the proclamation of the Secretary of the Interior ending the trusteeship over any tribe, it will be the responsibility of the Commissioner of Indian Affairs to have the tribe properly and legally incorporated and the Secretary of the Interior will transfer any and all tribal property to the tribal corporation and every qualified member of the tribe will be a stockholder in such corporation.

"As additional compensation to the Indians for relinquishing all the special services now given them by the Federal Government, all the real property of the tribe and all lands individually owned by tribal members held in trusteeship by the Government on the date of the proclamation ending the said trusteeship, shall be exempt from taxation for a minimum period of 20 years from the date of termination of the trusteeship The Federal Government shall pay to the various States in which these properties are located, the taxes assessed on these lands.

"The Federal Government will continue to provide health services for those Indians covered in this legislation by the present administration of the Division of Indian Health, Public Health Service, or some group health insurance plan.

"Any Bureau of Indian Affairs employee who has served 5 consecutive years in the employment of the Bureau shall have preference rights for employment in another Government agency. Any Bureau employee whose job is abolished because of this act and who is short 5 years for qualification for full retirement benefits can elect to retire for the full benefits as though he had served his full time for qualifying for full retirement.

"All the aforesaid money payments to the Indian beneficiaries are exempt from any taxation whatever and will not be considered in determining any benefits under retirement or social security payments."

Under this plan, the Bureau of Indian Affairs, the middleman, is eliminated entirely over an 8-year period and the money now used for its operations would go directly to the Indians.

The Indian family averages about five members and would receive $300 per month, which would assist the family head in supporting his family and give him financial security when he goes to a strange community to obtain employment. He would not feel compelled to return to the reservation for Bureau services if he became unemployed. This plan would assure him of the permanency of his homeland if, later in life, he elects to return there.

By this legislation, a substitute economy is created for those states and communities that are more or less dependent on the Indian Bureau's expenditures in their areas. It would also eliminate the fear that an impossible welfare load would fall on them if the Government withdrew its services to the Indians.

The Government will, with this legislation, provide the Indian with the tools for self-adjustment with security, and will have completed its debt to him with honor and justice.

ECONOMIC DEVELOPMENT AS A MEANS OF OVERCOMING INDIAN POVERTY

By ROBERT L. BENNETT*

FOREWORD

Respect for Indian culture and values is a vital part of any assistance effort, but some conflict between traditional Indian values and successful economic development is inevitable. Saving, investment, and the profit motive are not a part of many traditional Indian cultures. Nor does individual financial success carry the status that it does in industrial society. Thus some compromises between traditional values and the prevalant economic system are essential if Indian poverty and dependency are to be overcome. Progress can be made both through identifying job opportunities near the reservation and through bringing industry onto the reservation.

Introduction

Poverty is not a new experience for Indian people; it has been with them for many years. With recent national attention being given to the general problem of poverty, poverty among Indian people has been highlighted in many statements by public officials, private organizations and individuals, and by the Indian people themselves. It is an accepted fact that poverty exists in such proportion among Indian people as to make them one of the most poverty-stricken groups in the country. Poverty has been a persistent partner of Indian people and no one knows, but we can hope, that present efforts will do much to erase this blight.

A clear distinction should be made between those poor in America who are outside the productive life of the economy, and those who are poor despite their ability to participate in the labor force. These are different aspects of the problem and require different treatment.

The attack on poverty must focus upon the special conditions and characteristics of the Indian population. There is no simple solution to the problem. Indian people are caught in the backwash of economic development. If we are to overcome poverty, then we need to identify and eliminate the negative forces which are repressing Indian people and to identify and strengthen the positive forces which bring about economic change.

Even when the Indian people accept the objectives of (1) maximum Indian economic self-sufficiency, (2) full participation of Indians in American life, and (3) equal citizenship privileges and responsibilities for Indians, their attainment is still fraught with many obstacles. These arise from the native culture, to which must be added the depressing effects of a poverty culture so interwoven with the native cultures that the two almost become one and inseparable. These cul-

---

*Commissioner of Indian Affairs, 1966–1969.

tures have many traits inimical to the objectives which the Bureau has adopted for Indian people in their best interests. Each of these cultures in itself poses serious barriers to economic self-sufficiency, and together they have withstood the onslaught of program after program, so that today we say most Indians are poor—desperately poor—as poor as any group we know of in this rich country of ours.

Indian people have lived primarily on a subsistence economy, characterized by low capital investment, do-it-yourself methods, and low levels of productivity. A money economy, however, puts a high premium on managerial skill, proficiency in using capital and labor, and ambition to get ahead. People who must shift from one economy to another must go through a marked change in values. Here one must grasp the significance of the poverty and native cultures, interwoven as they are, as they affect any attempt made by Indian people to change values. I am not concerned with any hypothesis as to whether it is good or bad that these values change. What I am saying is that, to escape poverty, some of the values will have to change. This places the Indian people on the horns of a dilemma—either to change their values or to cling to values which result in poverty as a way of life amidst new and challenging opportunities for economic betterment.

Although we have referred to many Indian people as trying to wrest a living from the land as farmers or ranchers, their basic motivation is not economic but rather an effort to maintain the bases for their way of life. Their efforts are not geared to commercial markets but to subsistence, and they operate in a functional rather than a commercial manner. Their lack of interest in the accumulation of business profits and their lack of desire to ascertain the most profitable use of their own land and labor fit into production for their own use but not for commercial use. Their values can be equated as "an intense attachment to native soil, a reverent disposition toward habitat and ancestral ways, and a restraint on individual self-seekings in favor of family and community."

Indian people lack experience in the use of money and they are at a loss as to how to handle large sums of money wisely. One of the contemporary Indian leaders listed, as priority number one of the basic needs of his people, help in managing money. For the child's education in a money world, it is the principle of saving that is of importance; that is, to postpone immediate pleasure in order to gain future satisfaction. The amount of family income and the way it is earned or acquired has a profound influence on the psychological development of the individual in the family and in the patterns of family life. The social and cultural norms of the family contribute to the choice of vocation and, to a large extent, determine values and managerial practice.

Generations of living outside of a money world and commercial activity has developed an attitude in which satisfaction with simple living is a chief element. Low levels of economic aspiration are essential to the contentment they feel and they may be more completely adjusted in their life than we are in ours.

So the major constraints on economic progress of·Indian people have been summarized as:

1. The value orientations and institutions of the tribal leaders, the people, and members of the Bureau of Indian Affairs have not changed in proportion to the sweeping changes in the economy since 1930.

2. Noneconomic factors of the lingering culture which retard economic progress.

3. Inefficient functioning of the capital market.

4. Imperfections in the functioning of the labor market.

One of our contemporary Indian leaders has said that the basic needs of his people include (1) help in managing money, (2) help in facing the reality that the way to achieve economic and social stability is to find the kind of work they can do, either for themselves or in earning wages working for someone else, (3) help in becoming responsible for the health, education, livelihood, and well-being of their families, and (4) help in learning fundamental knowledge of becoming responsible people.

It has been reported that compared with children from more privileged environments, children from lower-class, socially impoverished circumstances tend to enter school with a qualitatively different preparation for the demands of the learning process and the behavioral requirements of the classroom. Among these children there is a high proportion of school failures, school dropouts, and reading and learning disabilities, as well as life-adjustment problems.

Where all of the education and training takes place in the family circle, parents are unable to transmit values, skills, and understandings they do not have. Their way of looking at life puts a rather indifferent value on formal education. In fact, the ideas, facts, and habits learned in school may be regarded as detrimental to the values of the family.

The youth who knows too much may no longer be satisfied to live meagerly, and the school system is a way out of the subsistence way of life. The parents may either accept this or block it.

Many students in our schools are confused about what is expected of them in learning situations, as their parents do not put these expectations upon them. Their confusion produces anxieties. This is another threat to the self-image, which in many is delicate and needs reinforcement. We cannot destroy their self-assertion, but we still need to help them behave in ways appropriate to the society in which they will live. To change some of their inappropriate responses in social situations we need to offer them new experiences in learning and understanding human behavior.

The young people in our schools are feeling the impact of transition within themselves and their environment. There is a degree of conflict produced by this transition which is manifested in many ways, such as agitation by the fact that the student wants to sever his ties to his village situation but is afraid his parents will see this as a rejection of them.

The focus and intent should be to work with the whole person, and every phase of his experience should be evaluated in terms of helping him make a satisfactory and productive adjustment in school and in preparation for his future life.

You do no service to an Indian community by asking an Indian who is in conflict to come back and serve his own people, since he comes back to something he has struggled to leave. We make this mistake many times. This is no service to an Indian community. He should not come back until he is a whole individual and is over his conflict.

Now may be the time when a question should be raised as to whether or not a third dimension exists to the dilemma faced by Indian people in trying to break out of the encirclement of their interwoven native and poverty cultures. This dimension could be identified as the reservation culture which, together with the native and poverty cultures, might provide an almost impregnable barrier to the elimination of poverty. The atmosphere of the reservation culture may create attitudes which breed and insure the continued existence of poverty.

In speaking of the reservation culture, I am not referring to the ownership of property by individuals or the tribe. The ownership and reservation cultures are not synonymous. These are two distinct matters: One, the property, is an asset which with proper utilization and management can contribute to economic sufficiency. The other, the reservation culture, may negate efforts at economic sufficiency.

The reservation system, artificially created because of military and political necessity and maintained for administrative expediency, may be tolerated by Indian people for still other reasons.

Recent experiences in economic development, where efforts have been made to make work available locally as distinguished from transporting Indians far from their home communities to large urban areas for employment opportunities, give us reason for optimism. The two methods used to provide local employment opportunities are in the location of jobs already available in the area and the development of non-agricultural industries in or near Indian communities.

As a result of the first effort, over one-half of the Indian job placements have been in States of the applicants' residence, which in most cases allows either for daily or weekend commuting. This effort has proven very popular with Indians. This effort grew out of the fact that while we had our sights on the large urban centers and a huge volume of job opportunities, yet there were many local job opportunities overlooked.

In connection with the second effort, this has been accomplished through capital investment in businesses using the local resources of Indian communities, such as timber and recreational opportunities, rather than the leasing of these natural resources to outside investors. As a consequence of this effort, the Indian owners of these resources not only are able to provide employment opportunities, but manage, operate, and enjoy the profits of these kinds of commercial enterprises. The additional effort consists of bringing industries into the Indian community where a substantial labor force exists in place. While this labor force may be inexperienced, yet it is highly trainable. Tests have shown that this Indian labor force outranks the general population in the areas of hand and eye coordination, manual dexterity, and patient tolerance of repetitive operations. With the need for this kind of hand work, long an outstanding characteristic of the Indian labor force, the electronics industry in particular has had major successes with Indian employment. Because of the high value and low bulk of its products, this particular industry also is able to overcome the transportation problem, which had hampered industrial development of the isolated Indian areas.

One of the motivations for Indian participation in economic development is the high rate of population growth. Indian leadership is recognizing more and more that strenuous efforts will have to be made to provide employment for the new and increasing Indian population. There is reason for optimism because in this particular area of economic development there has at long last developed a working partnership arrangement by the Indian leaders, private industry, and government, whose combined efforts offer promise of having a major impact on unemployment and its lingering social effects.

Will the Indian people find their way out of this multidimensional dilemma which keeps them victims of poverty?

They will—when the kind of communication is established with them by which they acquire those cultural concepts necessary for their cultural and economic growth and development. They will—when we no longer provide them with the answers, make their decisions, and concern ourselves only with results. They will—when they realize that in order to be happy a person must have a sense of conviction about his own worth and dignity, and that the individual's sense of worth receives major nourishment from work and the rewards it brings.

TRENDS IN EMPLOYMENT AND EARNINGS OF AMERICAN INDIANS

By ALAN L. SORKIN *

FOREWORD

Unemployment and underemployment are fundamental causes of Indian poverty. Alan Sorkin has assembled and analyzed the available statistics on Indian employment and earnings. Declining opportunities for agricultural employment have been an important cause of high and rising Indian unemployment during a period of general prosperity. Although there has been an acceleration of reservation industrial development since 1963, such industries still employ only about 3 percent of the reservation labor force. In 1967, unemployment among reservation Indians remained about 37 percent of the labor force. Because the labor force participation rate is low, this statistic understates the real extent of Indian unemployment.

Introduction

There are an estimated 550,000 American Indians living in the United States, with approximately 380,000 residing on or adjacent to reservations.[1] The remainder have been assimilated, to varying degrees, into the dominant society. Although the vast majority of Indians reside west of the Mississippi River, there are sizeable numbers of Indians as far east as Maine and North Carolina. The Navajo Reservation, in parts of Arizona, New Mexico, and Utah, is the largest in the country, with 120,000 Indians occupying an area the size of West Virginia.

This paper will indicate recent trends in the economic position of the American Indian. Whenever possible, distinction will be made between data relating to reservation Indians and that concerning non-reservation Indians. In order to place this information in proper perspective, the economic progress of American Indians will be compared with that of non-Indians.

It should be noted that the statistics maintained by the Bureau of Indian Affairs regarding the socio-economic conditions of Indians are inadequate, not only from the point of view of the research specialist, but with regard to informing the general public about the standard of living of the first Americans.

The information which is available is often not as current as it should be, nor is it tabulated with the same degree of statistical precision which characterizes the work of other government agencies. For this reason the data to be presented below should be interpreted cautiously.

* The author is a Research Associate at The Brookings Institution, Washington, D.C.

[1] There is no official definition which can be applied to distinguish an American Indian from a non-Indian. The 1960 Census takers were instructed to let the respondent indicate his racial identity. The Bureau of Indian Affairs generally restricts services to those one-quarter or more Indian blood.

OCCUPATION CHANGES

Table I compares the occupational distribution of American Indians with that of non-Indians for 1940, 1950, and 1960.

TABLE I.—*Employed males, Indian and non-Indian, by occupational category, 1940, 1950, and 1960 (percent distribution)*

Major occupation group	Indian			Non-Indian		
	1940	1950	1960	1940	1950	1960
White-collar workers:						
Professional and technical workers_____	3.2	2.6	4.9	6.1	7.8	12.5
Managers, officials, and proprietors, except farmers_____	1.4	2.0	2.8	9.7	10.6	11.1
Clerical and sales workers_____	2.0	3.3	5.6	12.2	12.7	13.2
Blue-collar workers:						
Craftsmen and foremen_____	5.7	11.0	15.5	14.8	18.4	20.3
Operatives_____	6.2	13.1	21.6	18.3	20.1	19.9
Laborers, except farm and mine_____	11.4	17.8	20.2	9.3	8.3	7.0
Service workers:						
Private household workers_____	.2	.3	.3	.3	.2	.2
Other service workers_____	2.5	3.6	5.6	5.9	6.0	6.8
Farmworkers:						
Farmers and managers_____	45.6	24.0	9.5	14.9	10.8	6.1
Laborers and foremen_____	21.8	22.3	14.0	8.5	5.1	2.9

Source: U.S. Bureau of the Census. *U.S. Census of Population: 1940, special reports,* "Characteristics of the Nonwhite Population by Race," table 26, p. 83, Washington, D.C., 1943; *U.S. Census of Population, 1940,* vol. III, "The Labor Force," table 66, p. 104, Washington, D.C., 1943; *U.S. Census of Population: 1950, special reports,* "Characteristics of the Nonwhite Population by Race," table 10, p. 32, Washington, D.C.: 1953; *U.S. Census of Population: 1950, special report,* P-E No. 3B, "Occupational Characteristics," table 1, p. 15, Washington, D.C.̊, 1953; *U.S. Census of Population: 1960, subject reports.* "Nonwhite Population by Race." Final report PC(2)-1C, table 33, p. 104, Washington, D.C., 1963; *U.S. Census of Population: 1960 subject reports.* "Occupational Characteristics," final report PC(2)-7A, table 1, p. 1, Washington, D.C.

As the data in table I indicate, there has been a rapid decline in Indian employment in agriculture. While nearly one-half of all employed Indian males were classified as farmers or farm managers in 1940, less than 10 percent were so classified in 1960. The principal reason for the rapid decline in Indian participation in agriculture was the pressure of competition from non-Indian farmers whose greater capital resources and technical skill made farming unprofitable for many Indians.

The above table indicates that there has been a rapid expansion of employed Indians in blue collar occupations. The percentage of Indian craftsmen nearly tripled between 1940 and 1960, while the percentage of non-Indian craftsmen rose by less than two-fifths. The percentage of Indians classified as operatives increased three and one-half times, while the percentage of non-Indian operatives was relatively stable. Interestingly enough, the percentage of Indians in the nonfarm laborer classification nearly doubled between 1940 and 1960, in contrast to a decline over that time period in the percentage of non-Indian laborers. This is because with the decline in agriculture many Indian agricultural laborers simply became laborers in the nonfarm sector of the reservation economy.

Although the percentage of Indians employed in white collar occupations has increased in recent years, it still lags far behind the percentage of non-Indians involved in white collar employment. For example, in 1960 only 4.9 percent of all Indian males were employed in a professional capacity. This was approximately the same percentage of non-Indians employed in a professional capacity in 1930. Moreover, only 2.8 percent of all Indians in 1960 were classified as managers or proprietors, compared to 11.1 percent for non-Indians in 1960.

One of the primary reasons for the great disparity between Indians and non-Indians, as far as the proportion in white collar employment is concerned, is the relative lack of education of the farmer. This is discussed below in some detail.

EDUCATIONAL ATTAINMENT

Although the educational attainment of Indian males has increased substantially in recent years, there is still a substantial gap in the median educational attainment of Indian as compared to non-Indian males. This is illustrated in Table II.

TABLE II.—*Years of schooling, Indian and non-Indian males, 1940, 1950, 1960*

[Percent distribution]

Years of school	Indian			Non-Indian		
	1940 [1]	1950 [2]	1960 [2]	1940 [3]	1950 [2]	1960 [2]
0	23.8	15.5	9.6	2.1	2.1	2.1
1 to 4	19.9	15.9	12.7	9.0	8.4	6.0
5 to 8	39.0	40.9	37.8	46.2	36.7	31.5
9 to 11	9.7	16.2	22.8	16.7	20.5	21.6
12	4.9	8.1	11.6	14.0	18.8	21.5
13 to 15	2.0	2.4	3.9	5.8	7.4	9.0
16 or more	.7	1.0	1.6	6.2	6.1	8.3
Median	5.5	7.3	8.4	8.4	9.4	10.5

[1] Males 25 years and over.
[2] Males 14 years and over.
[3] Males 25 to 64 years.

Source: U.S. Bureau of the Census. *U.S. Census of Population: 1940. Special Reports*, "Characteristics of the Nonwhite Population By Race." Table 24, p. 80, Washington, D.C., 1943; *U.S. Census of Population: 1940. Special Reports*, "Educational Attainment," Table 17, p. 75, and table 18, p. 82, Washington, D.C., 1943; *U.S. Census of Population: 1950.* Vol. IV, *Special Reports*, pt. 3, ch. B, "Characteristics of the Nonwhite Population By Race." Table 10, p. 32, Washington, D.C.; *U.S. Census of Population: 1950. Special Reports*, pt. 5, ch. B, "Educational Characteristics." Table 9, p. 73, Washington, D.C., 1953; *U.S. Census of Population: 1960. Special reports, "Characteristics of the Nonwhite Population By Race."* Table 10, p. 12, Washington, D.C., 1963; *U.S. Census of Population: 1960*. Final reports. "Educational Attainment," table 4, p. 54, Washington, D.C., 1963.

The median level of schooling of the Indian male in 1960, as indicated in Table II, is equal to the median level of schooling of the non-Indian in 1940. Though the median level of schooling of Indian males has increased nearly three years since 1940, only 5.5 percent of Indian males in 1960 had any college training. This compares to 17.3 percent of non-Indian males in 1960 who had received some college training. Moreover, in 1960, better than one out of five Indian males (22.3 percent) had less than five years of schooling. This contrasts with only 8.1 percent of non-Indian males with less than five years of schooling in 1960. Not only has the relative lack of schooling contributed directly to the relatively high unemployment rates and low incomes of Indian males (to be discussed below), but it has probably reenforced the desire of many Indians to remain on the reservation. This seems likely because many less educated Indians may not feel they would be able to compete effectively in the labor market with more highly educated non-Indians in an off-reservation setting.

In 1967, 60 percent of American Indian youngsters between 6–18 years of age were being educated in public schools, another 5 percent were being educated in mission schools, and 35 percent were being educated in schools operated by the Bureau of Indian Affairs.[2]

There are two divergent trends taking place in Indian education. First there is a substantial increase in the number of Indian high school graduates furthering their education. On the other hand, the high school dropout rate remains alarmingly high. Each of these aspects of Indian education will be discussed in turn.

In 1967, nearly 30 percent of all Indian high school graduates went to college—almost double the rate of ten years ago. Furthermore, in 1967, another 25 percent of Indian high school graduates attended institutions providing advanced vocational training. Moreover, in 1966 (the most recent year for which statistics are available) there were 120 American Indian graduates from four year colleges and universities. This was an increase of 100 percent over the number five years ago.[3]

However, it appears that at most only one-half of all Indian students finish high school. Apker in his survey estimates that less than 40 percent of Indian high school entrants graduate as compared to 60 percent of all American students.[4] Spilka and Bryde state that on a national level in 1963, 77 percent of non-Indian students were graduating from high school as compared to 40 percent for reservation Indians.[5] A recent study by the Northwest Regional Educational Laboratory of the U.S. Office of Education, on the magnitude of the dropout problem on reservations in six Northwestern states, found that 50 percent of the students who were eighth graders in 1962 had graduated in 1967. A few were still in school but virtually all the rest had dropped out before graduation.[6]

MANPOWER UTILIZATION

For the period under consideration, the unemployment rates of Indians have been several times those of non-Indians. Furthermore, although data are only available for recent years, regarding the unemployment rates of reservation Indians, the statistics indicate that the unemployment rates for these Indians are much higher than those for non-reservation Indians. These points are illustrated in Table III.

Comparing first the data for all Indians with that for non-Indians, it is evident that while the unemployment rate for non-Indians fell 67 percent between 1940 and 1959, the unemployment rate for all Indians *rose* 24 percent.

[2] Bureau of Indian Affairs, *Statistics Concerning Indian Education,* Washington, D.C., 1967. Approximately one-half of the children attending Bureau of Indian Affairs educational institutions are enrolled in boarding schools located on or off the reservation.

[3] B. Spilka and J. Bryde, "Alienation and Achievement among Ogala Sioux Secondary Report from the Commissioner of Indian Affairs," issues of 1966 and 1967.

[4] Wesley Apker, "A Survey of the Literature Related to Indian Pupil Dropout," unpublished M.Ed. thesis, Washington State University, 1962.

[5]. B. Spilka and J. Bryde, "Alienation and Achievement among Ogala Sioux Secondary Studeni " unpublished, 1965.

[6] Alphonse D. Selinger, *The American Indian High School Dropout: The Magnitude of the Problem.* Northwest Regional Educational Laboratory, U.S. Office of Education, September 1968.

TABLE III.—*Male unemployment rates, Indians and non-Indians, selected years, 1940–67*

		Unemployment rates		
	All Indians	Non-reservation Indians	Reservation Indians	Non-Indians
Year:				
1940	28.2			14.6
1949		13.0		5.4
1958			43.5	6.2
1959	37.2	15.4	48.2	4.7
1960			51.3	4.7
1961			49.5	5.7
1962			43.4	4.6
1965			41.9	3.2
1966			41.9	2.5
1967			37.3	2.3

Sources: U.S. Bureau of the Census. *U.S. Census of Population: 1940, special reports,* "Characteristics of the Nonwhite Population by Race" table 25, p. 82, Washington, D.C., 1943; *U.S.Census of Population: 1950,* vol. IV, *special reports,* pt. 3, ch. B, "Nonwhite Population by Race," table 10, p. 32, Washington, D.C. 1953; *U.S. Census of Population: 1960. subject reports,* "Nonwhite Population by Race," final report PC(2)-1C, table 33, p. 104, Washington, D.C., 1963; *Indian Unemployment Survey,* U.S. House of Representatives, Committee on Interior and Insular Affairs, 88th Cong., 1st sess., 1963; unpublished tabulations, Bureau of Indian Affairs, Washington, D.C., December 1966 and December 1967; *Economic Report of the President, 1968,* Washington, D.C. p. 237.

Note: Data for Indians includes males, 14 years and over; data for non-Indians includes males, 20 years and over. Data for reservation Indians is seasonally adjusted, using as a basis the monthly fluctuations contained in the Indian Unemployment Survey:

This increase in the unemployment rate for all Indians is, primarily, a consequence of the great exodus from agriculture in search of more remunerative employment. Since, in most cases, these individuals are limited by lack of training and education, they are restricted to unskilled occupations. Such occupations have relatively high rates of unemployment particularly on reservations where there has been only token industrialization.

The data in Table III demonstrate the extremely high unemployment rates for reservation males. To place these data in proper perspective, one should consider the fact that during the great depression of the 1930's, the unemployment rate for males reached a level of about 25 percent in 1933. In the early 1960's, the male unemployment rate on reservations was almost double the unemployment rate for all workers in the depths of the depression. Another discouraging aspect of the data on unemployment among reservation Indians, is that the unemployment rates seem quite insensitive to the movements of the business cycle. This is exemplified by a decrease of 60 percent in the overall unemployment rate between 1961 and 1967—a period of increasing prosperity. However, the unemployment rate for male reservation Indians declined by only 25 percent.

On some reservations more than half of all males in the labor force are unemployed. This is illustrated in Table IV which presents data on the unemployment rates for selected reservations in 1966. Thus of the reservations included in the table, unemployment ranged from a low of 20 percent on the Colville Reservation in Washington to 79 percent on the Fort Berthold Reservation in North Dakota.

TABLE IV.—*Unemployment rates, selected reservations in Indian land areas, 1966*

Indian land areas	Unemployment rate
Reservation:	
Fort Apache, Ariz	50
Gila River, Ariz	55
Navajo, Ariz., N. Mex., Utah	39
San Carlos, Ariz	74
Fort Hall, Idaho	56
Leech Lake, Minn	31
Blackfeet, Mont	39
Northern Cheyenne, Mont	24
Pyramid Lake, Nev	23
Fort Berthold, N. Dak	79
Turtle Mountain, N. Dak	65
Pine Ridge, S. Dak	32
Cheyenne River, S. Dak	40
Colville, Wash	20

Source: U.S. Bureau of Indian Affairs, "Selected Data on Indian Reservations Eligible for Designation under Public Works and Economic Development Act," unpublished tabulation, December 1966.

In addition the unemployment problem is aggravated by a birth rate which is two to two and a half times that of the national average. This high birth rate coupled with a swiftly declining death rate has brought intensifying population pressure to the already overburdened reservation economy.[7]

On the majority of Indian reservations, the chief employer is the Bureau of Indian Affairs. On the Papago Reservation, for instance, 30 percent of all permanently employed Indians work for the Bureau of Indian Affairs.[8] An additional 17 percent are employed by the U.S. Public Health Service in the Indian hospital located on the reservation.[9]

In past years one of the leading factors responsible for the high unemployment rates among reservation Indians was the sparsity of industry located on the reservations. However, recently there has been an industrialization movement in the Indian land area which appears to be accelerating. The pertinent data are presented in Table V.

TABLE V.—*Number of plants, and labor force, factories located on Indian Reservations*

	Number of plants established	Number closed down	Total number in operation (end of year)	Labor force	
				Indian	Non-Indian
1957–60	4	1	3	391	171
1960	3	0	6	525	246
1961	4	0	10	702	505
1962	5	1	14	887	600
1963	6	2	18	1,395	1,719
1964	14	7	25	1,668	2,286
1965	21	6	40	2,011	2,479
1966	21	4	57	3,044	3,224
1967	23	3	77	3,730	3,666
1968	36	1	114	4,112	4,775
Total	137	23			

Source: U.S. Bureau of Indian Affairs, Branch of Industrial Development, "Summary of Plants Established as a Result of Indian Industrial Development Program," unpublished tabulation, "Summary of Plant Closings," unpublished tabulation; data on labor force from unpublished graph provided by Branch of Industrial Development.

[7] U.S. Public Health Service, *Indian Health Highlights, 1966*, p. 6. A 1966 task force report on Indian Housing indicates that 10,000 Indians leave the reservations each year (net migration). Many migrate under the auspices of the Bureau's relocation or adult vocational training programs. However, even with this migration there is still an increase in the reservation population of .9 percent per year.

[8] Bureau of Indian Affairs, *Survey of Income and Employment*, Papago Reservation, 1966, p. 9 (mimeographed).

[9] *Ibid.* The Indian Hospital, operated by the Public Health Service, is usually the second largest employer of reservation Indians.

The data indicate the acceleration in reservation industrial development in the 1963–68 period as compared with the slower growth in the 1957–62 period. This parallels the high rate of economic growth in the nation as a whole in the more recent period as compared to the slower pace in the 1957–62 period.[10] In addition the military needs of the Vietnam War have aided reservation development. About a dozen electronics plants have been established, partly to meet defense needs.

The growth of industry on the reservations has also been aided by the Bureau of Indian Affairs on-the-job training program. Under this program employers receive a subsidy of up to one-half the minimum wage established under the Fair Labor Standards Act while the employee is in training. Thus, with the minimum wage of $1.60 an hour, most employers are receiving subsidies of 80 cents per hour for each trainee. The length of training is determined by the Department of Labor. It should be noted that in spite of the recent acceleration in reservation industrialization, only 4,100 Indians out of a reservation labor force of 130,000, or 3 percent, have industrial employment.

SEASONAL UNEMPLOYMENT

Because a relatively high proportion of reservation Indians are still engaged in agriculture or other outside work, there is a profound fluctuation in unemployment during the year. The sole source of data concerning the fluctuations in seasonal unemployment is the 1963 Survey prepared at the request of the House Committee on Interior and Insular Affairs. In this survey, Bureau officials were asked to provide data on monthly fluctuations in unemployment. A good percentage of reservations containing 60 percent of the reservation labor force responded. The data provided are for the 1962 fiscal year and are presented in Table VI.

TABLE VI.—*Fluctuations in reservation unemployment, by month, 1962*

Month	Total unemployment	Percent of annual average	Month	Total unemployment	Percent of annual average
January	21,236	127	August	12,430	74
February	20,856	124	September	13,530	81
March	20,114	120	October	16,667	99
April	17,158	102	November	19,046	113
May	14,362	86	December	20,957	124
June	12,887	77			
July	12,458	74	Annual average	16,809	100

Source: Computed from data contained in *Indian Unemployment Survey*, U.S. House of Representatives, Committee on Interior and Insular Affairs, 88th Cong., 1st sess., 1963.

The data indicate that January is the peak unemployment month on Indian reservations. Unemployment is 59 percent higher than in August, which is the month when reservation unemployment is lowest. Moreover, in the two month period, March–May, a 30 percent decline in total unemployment is realized while the September–November period brings an increase in total unemployment of over 40 percent.

It is likely that as agriculture continues to decline and industrialization increases, fluctuations in unemployment on a seasonal basis will become smaller.

---

[10] For example, unemployment averaged 5.5 percent of the labor force in the 1957–62 period compared with 3.8 percent in the 1963–68 period.

Labor Force Participation

Manpower utilization is measured not only by the unemployment rate but by the rate of labor force participation. Table VII compares the labor force participation rates for Indian and non-Indian males, 14 and over. The data in Table VII indicate that on a cross section basis the labor force participation rates for Indian males are much lower than for non-Indian males. There are two factors responsible for this. First, the high rate of unemployment among American Indians has discouraged many potential workers from actively searching for jobs, and thus being classified as members of the labor force. There is, in addition, a significant number of Indians who have leased their allotted lands to non-Indians and are living on the property income derived thereby. Moreover, the fact that many Indian children start school at 8 or 9 years and do not leave until the ages of 18–20 has created a greater disparity between Indian and non-Indian 14–24 year old labor participation rates than would be the case if Indians began school at age 6 and graduated high school at age 17.[11]

TABLE VII.—*Labor force participation rates, Indian and non-Indian males, by age, 1940, 1950, 1960*

Age	Indian			Non-Indian		
	1940	1950	1960	1940	1950	1960
14 to 24		41.5	40.9		59.2	57.1
25 to 44		80.7	78.0		93.3	93.0
45 and over		69.8	57.8		75.5	72.4
Total	64.6	63.5	60.0	79.0	78.8	77.3

Source: U.S. Bureau of the Census. *U.S. Census of Population: 1940, special reports,* "Characteristics of the Nonwhite Population by Race," table 25, p. 82, Washington, D.C., 1943; *U.S. Census of Population: 1940,* vol. III, *special reports,* "The Labor Force," table 1, p. 15, Washington, D.C., 1954; *U.S. Census of Population, 1950, special reports,* "Characteristics of the Non-white Population by Race," table 10, p. 32, Washington, D.C., 1953; *U.S. Census of Population: 1950,* vol. IV, *special reports,* pt. 5, ch. B, education, table 9, p. 73, Washington, D.C., 1953; *U.S. Census of Population: 1960, subject reports,* "Characteristics of the Nonwhite Population by Race," final report PC(2)-1C, table 33, p. 104, Washington, D.C., 1963; *U.S. Census of Population: 1960, subject reports.* "*Educational Attainment,*" final report PC(2)-5B, table 4, p. 54, Washington, D.C., 1963.

Part of the disparity in labor force participation rates between Indians and non-Indians stems from the relatively poor health of the former. In 1966, for example, a reservation Indian was seven times as likely to contract tuberculosis, eight times as likely to be afflicted with hepatitis, and three times as likely to die of influenza and pneumonia as a non-Indian.[12]

Perhaps the most discouraging aspect of the data in Table VII is that only 78 percent of the Indian males 25–44 years were in the labor force in 1960. This age span is generally considered representative of the prime working ages. However, in the case of non-Indians, 93 percent of males 25–44 years were in the labor force in 1960.

Income

The vast majority of reservation Indians are living in poverty. According to a recent estimate, 76 percent of reservation Indian fam-

[11] On most Indian reservations, school attendance is compulsory until either the age of 18 or graduation from high school. Also, as an increasing number of Indian children attend college, the labor force participation rate of the 14–24 year old groups should continue to decline.

[12] For further information see U.S. Public Health Service, Division of Indian Health, *Indian Health Highlights, 1966.*

ilies earn less than $3,000 a year.[13] Table VIII presents income data for Indian and non-Indian males during the 1939–64 time period.

TABLE VIII.—*Median income for male Indians and non-Indians, selected years, 1939–64*

[1964 dollars]

	Income			
Year	All Indians	Nonreservation Indians	Reservation Indians	Non-Indians
1939			460	[1] 2,300
1944			670	2,940
1949	870	940	825	3,750
1959	1,910	2,570	1,550	5,030
1964			1,800	5,710
Percent increase 1939–64			290	148

[1] Wages and salaries only.

Source: *Reservation Income*, 1939, unpublished tabulation, Bureau of Indian Affairs, table IV, p. 2, Washington, D.C. 1942; U.S. Bureau of the Census. *U.S. Census of Population: 1940*. Vol. III, The Labor Force; Table 71, p. 116, Washington D.C., 1943; *U.S. Census of Population: 1950. Special Reports*, Characteristics of the Nonwhite Population By Race. Table 10, p. 32, and table 21, p. 72, Washington, D.C., 1953; *U.S. Census of Population: 1950. Special Report*, P–E No. 3B, Occupational Characteristics. Table 19, p. 183, Washington, D.C., 1953; *U.S. Census of Population: 1960. Subject Reports. Nonwhite Population By Race*. Final Report PC(2)-1C, table 33, p. 104, and table 56, p. 234, Washington, D.C., 1963; "Selected Reservations Eligible for Designation Under Public Works and Economic Development Act," unpublished tabulation, Bureau of Indian Affairs, Washington, D.C., December 1966.

The data contained in Table VIII reveal that, on a cross-section basis, Indian income is far below that of non-Indians. Although the income of reservation Indians rose nearly twice as fast from 1939–64 than for non-Indians (290 percent compared to 148 percent), income of reservation Indians was only 32 percent of that of non-Indians in 1964. This compared to a reservation Indian income of 20 percent of non-Indian income in 1939.

The high unemployment rates of Indians are a major factor in explaining their relatively low incomes. Moreover, as indicated above, because of a relative lack of education and training few Indians are able to qualify for the more lucrative white collar positions.

It is interesting to note the widening income gap between reservation and non-reservation Indians. In 1949 the median reservation Indian income was 88 percent of that of non-reservation Indians. In 1959, however, the median income of reservation Indians had declined to 60 percent of the income of non-reservation Indians. The principal reason for the widening income gap between the two groups of Indians is the migration, during the 1950's, of many of the more highly educated and skilled Indians from the reservation to the major urban centers of the United States. In these urban centers, better paying jobs, more commensurate with their level of skill, were available.

However, the standard of living for non-reservation Indians may not differ as much from that of reservation Indians as income levels would indicate. First, reservation Indians are entitled to comprehensive free medical care (provided by the Public Health Service, Division of Indian Health) if they are one-fourth or more Indian blood. Non-reservation Indians are not entitled to such care. Second, reser-

[13] U.S. Bureau of Indian Affairs, Task Force, entitled, "Indian Housing Needs, Priorities, Alternatives," unpublished manuscript, October 1966.

vation Indians often reside rent free on allotted or tribal land, but non-reservation Indians must usually pay rent for housing. Third, the cost of goods and services is likely higher in the urban areas where non-reservation Indians reside (such as Los Angeles, Denver or Chicago) than on many reservations. Thus, since the cost of living is higher for non-reservation as compared to reservation Indians, the *real income differential* between the two groups of Indians is lower than the data in Table VIII would indicate.

Moreover, a recent study by the Branch of Employment Assistance indicated that about 50 percent of a sample of Indians relocated to urban areas in 1963 were living in poverty at the time of the survey (1966).[14]

Finally, it should be noted that approximately 50 percent of those Indians relocated under the Bureau of Indian Affairs' direct employment program (a relocation program) eventually return to the reservations.[15]

Although data are not available for non-reservation Indians, there has been fundamental change in the sources of income for reservation Indians. In 1939, only 38 percent of reservation income was derived from wages, 26 percent from agriculture, 8 percent from arts and crafts, and 28 percent from various sources of unearned income.[16] In 1964, an estimated 75 percent of total income was derived from wages, with 10 percent from agriculture, 5 percent from arts and crafts, and 10 percent from various sources of unearned income.[17]

There is great variation in income between reservations. Table IX presents information on median family income for selected reservations for 1964.

TABLE IX.—*Median family income, selected reservations, 1964*

Reservation	State	Median family income
Fort Apache	Arizona	$1,310
Hopi	do	1,140
Papago	do	900
Salt River	do	2,325
Fort Hall	Idaho	2,235
Leech Lake	Minnesota	2,039
Choctaw	Mississippi	900
Crow	Montana	1,100
Northern Cheyenne	do	3,600
Zuni	New Mexico	2,126
Fort Berthold	North Dakota	1,544
Turtle Mountain	do	2,228
Pine Ridge	South Dakota	1,335
Rosebud	do	900

Source: U.S. Bureau of Indian Affairs, "Selected Data on Indian Reservations Eligible for Designation Under Public Works and Economic Development Act," unpublished tabulation, December 1966.

As the data indicate, median family income varied from a low of $900 on the Rosebud, Papago, and Choctaw reservations to $3,600 on the Northern Cheyenne Reservation. It is interesting to observe the

[14] Bureau of Indian Affairs, Branch of Employment Assistance, "A Followup Study of 1963 Recipients of the Services of the Employment Assistance Program," July 1968 (revised version).

[15] Joan Ablon, "American Indian Relocation, Problems of Dependency and Management in the City," Phylon, vol. 26, Winter, 1965, p. 365.

[16] *Reservation Income, 1939,* unpublished tabulation, Bureau of Indian Affairs, table 2, p. 1.

[17] This estimate is based on unpublished income and employment surveys conducted by the Bureau of Indian Affairs on the Navajo, Papago, Crow, Standing Rock, Pine Ridge, and Rosebud Indian reservations.

variations of income within the same state. For example, median family income on the Crow Reservation in Montana was only $1,100 compared to $3,600 on the Northern Cheyenne Reservation. Moreover, median family income on the Papago Reservation in Arizona was only $900 compared to $2,325 on the Salt River Reservation.

STATE INCOME CHANGES

It is interesting to compare the changes in median incomes for Indians from 1950 to 1960 on a state by state basis. This is presented in Table X.

TABLE X.—*Indian median income (males) levels, by State, 1950 and 1960*

State	Income		Absolute increase	Percentage increase
	1950	1960		
Arizona	$539	$1,358	$819	152
California	996	2,694	1,698	170
Idaho	500	1,304	804	161
Michigan	866	2,076	1,210	140
Minnesota	619	1,398	779	126
Mississippi	341	650	309	91
Montana	681	1,368	687	101
Nebraska	746	1,589	843	113
Nevada	865	1,748	883	102
New Mexico	661	1,703	1,042	157
New York	1,401	3,497	2,096	149
North Carolina	628	950	322	51
North Dakota	552	1,278	726	132
Oklahoma	730	1,538	808	111
Oregon	724	2,258	1,534	212
SouthDakota	597	900	303	51
Texas	830	2,017	1,187	143
Utah	520	1,596	1,076	206
Washington	909	2,000	1,091	121
Wisconsin	807	1,961	1,154	143
Wyoming	622	1,220	598	96

Source: Income data from U.S. Bureau of the Census, *U.S. Census of Population: 1950. Special Reports,* "Characteristics of the Non-White Population by Race." Table 21, pp. 72–75, Washington, D.C., 1953; *U.S. Census of Population. Subject Reports.* "Nonwhite Population by Race." Final Report PC(2)-1C table 56, 234–239.

The above data indicate that there has not been much change in the relative rankings of the states vis-a-vis Indian income; that is, the states which ranked highest or lowest in 1950 generally ranked the same in 1960. The rank correlation coefficient is .87. With the exception of New York, Indian incomes in 1960 were highest in the West Coast states of California, Oregon, and Washington. These western states experienced a rapid growth in manufacturing and services between 1950 and 1960 and Indians migrated to urban areas within those states to take advantage of job opportunities and increased incomes. Thus, between 1950 and 1960 median Indian incomes increased $1,698 in California, $1,534 in Oregon, and $1,091 in Washington.

Incomes grew very slowly in Mississippi and North Carolina (only slightly over $300) between 1950 and 1960. This was because many Indians have remained in relatively unremunerative agricultural occupations in those states. In Mississippi many of the Choctaw Indians (the principal Indian tribe in Mississippi) earn as little as $300 a year working as sharecroppers.[18]

---

[18] Income data furnished by Robert Murray, Director RCA Family Training Project, Philadelphia, Mississippi.

The low income of South Dakota Indians is due to the steady decline of agriculture in that state and on the reservations and the lack of industry to provide substitute employment. South Dakota ranks 50th in the nation industrially and its Indian reservations have some of the highest unemployment rates to be found on reservations anywhere in the nation.

PROSPECTS FOR THE FUTURE

It is difficult to predict whether future income gains for non-reservation Indians will be greater than future income gains for reservation Indians. For example, in the industrial centers of the West, where economic development and population growth are occurring more rapidly than in most sections of the country, an increasing number of high paying industrial and commercial jobs will be available for Indians who have left or are migrating from the reservation.

However, the rapid growth in recent years of industrial plants on the reservations, with prospects for sustained future growth, indicates the possibility that increasing numbers of reservations will become viable economic entities, particularly if agricultural land use can be enhanced.

It should be noted that even with expanding employment opportunities for Indians who prefer to remain on the reservations unemployment rates for adult Indians will likely remain above acceptable levels. What additional policies will the federal government undertake to ameliorate the economic conditions of these people?

Will a large scale road building and public works program be established on the reservations? Will a crash reservation home building program be developed to provide construction jobs as well as decent homes for thousands of Indians? [19] Or will the government perceive the poverty of the Indian as similar to that of non-Indian and attack this poverty with such measures as the negative income tax? The answer to these questions affect not only the Indian people but the nation as well.

---

[19] In 1966, according to a Task Force Report on Indian Housing, over 75 percent of all reservation homes were substandard, with over 50 percent needed to be replaced.

ROLE OF MANPOWER PROGRAMS IN ASSISTING THE AMERICAN INDIANS

U.S. Department of Labor*

FOREWORD

In 1966 and 1967, the Department of Labor conducted an extensive field survey and evaluation of the impact on American Indians of its manpower programs. The report resulting from this study, printed below, describes current programs and makes a number of recommendations for improvement. The recommendations include: an active effort to recruit Indians into higher level Manpower Administration positions; a manpower policy which will assist Indians in attaining work where they live but provide relocation assistance if desired; a greater availability of U.S. Employment Service programs on reservations and in rural areas; and a more vigorous program of followup after job placement.

SUMMARY OF FINDINGS

I. Introduction

A. THE STUDY

The general objective of this study was to determine the impact on American Indians of the manpower programs of the Department of Labor, the areas in which these programs have been most successful, the difficulties remaining, and possible solutions.

It was conducted through a series of visits by staff teams to 16 reservations, eight cities, and 11 nonreservation tribes, in the fall of 1966, and the spring and fall of 1967.

B. CULTURAL MATTERS AFFECTING MANPOWER PLANNING

An early conclusion was that in planning manpower programs any attempt to ignore the culturally determined behavior and life attitudes of Indians and shape the programs into the same mold as programs for other Americans represents a blueprint for failure.

Urge toward retention of culture

The Indians' desire to retain their heritage, their reluctance to be assimilated, their attachment to jobless reservations, their intense feeling of individual worth, their aversion to acquisitive aggressiveness and lack of orientation to time values, added to widespread illiteracy and lack of skill backgrounds, are factors which make manpower planning difficult for reservation Indians. Assumptions have been made that the objective of manpower programs should be the reloca-

---

*This evaluation study was conducted by Mr. Ralph Walker and Mr. Bernard Goudy of the Office of Evaluation. Miss Ruth Feder, Miss Janet Wegner, and Miss Jacqueline Buckman assisted at various times in the study.

The study was also conducted with the active collaboration of the national and field staffs of the Bureau of Employment Security, Bureau of Apprenticeship and Training, Bureau of Work Programs, and the State employment services involved.

The Bureau of Indian Affairs cooperated and assisted fully at the national level and in the field.

tion of the Indian off the reservation in areas of employment opportunity. But there are strong indications that the loss of identity resulting from this and the demoralizing effect of frenetic urban living are detrimental to Indians rather than beneficial.

There are significant variations between tribes in work habits, capacity for acculturation, traditions, and ability to adapt.

C. DISCRIMINATION STILL A PROBLEM

Discrimination against Indians in employment varies in degree and quality. But much prejudice, stereotyped thinking, and discrimination still exist, including some among officials administering programs.

II. RESERVATION INDIANS

A. CONDITIONS

Reservations are usually isolated from urban centers and without employment opportunities. Unemployment varies greatly, in some reservations running as high as 80 percent at times.

Where the jobs are

In the typical reservation, jobs are found with the Bureau of Indian Affairs, the tribal government, the CAP, and a small industry or two. Only in a few reservations are the crafts industries (pottery, silverwork, leatherwork, beadwork, basketry) of any consequence.

BIA schooling

The Bureau of Indian Affairs can offer extensive schooling to any tribal youth; much of this schooling, however, is off reservation and directed toward fitting the Indian youth to the white man's urban civilization.

B. MANPOWER PROGRAMS

On the reservations, manpower programs include the training administered by BIA, training under MDTA, the public employment program, the Neighborhood Youth Corps, Operation Mainstream, and various special projects under the community action agencies. Coordination of these programs between BIA, CAA's, and State ES offices is seldom close, although interpersonal relationships are generally good. Collaboration and integration of programs, although much to be desired, is the exception.

ES HRD personnel

As one result of intensified effort among Indians following the Indian Manpower Conference in Kansas City in February 1967, USES established 171 positions for State ES employees to serve Indians directly. More than half of these were filled at the time of the visits, but recruitment for many was lagging, apparently because of indifference on the part of some State ES staff.

Role of ES offices on reservations

Although some ES representatives on reservations were doing useful work, ES offices on the reservations were found to be fulfilling a passive and minimal role, recruiting for seasonal farm or firefighting work when available, taking little or no part in general manpower planning for the reservations, and not very well known to the Indians themselves. These offices, generally, were not serving as centers of information for the reservation Indians about the opportunities and demands of the world of work.

MDTA

MDTA training of reservation Indians, in the aggregate, is probably as great in proportionate volume as it is among the general population. However, the need is much greater, the employment opportunities are fewer, the results in permanent employment are much poorer, and little or no attempt has been made to adapt MDTA policy and structure to fit the needs of the reservations.

Policies and practices inhibiting training in crafts, training of "helpers" in the building trades, and training to build up training labor pools on reservation limit the usefulness of MDTA institutional training to reservation Indians. On-the-job training under MDTA is of negligible quantity.

Apprenticeship

Apprenticeship training for reservation youngsters is virtually unknown.

NYC

Neighborhood youth corps programs are very popular on reservations. They offer a return quite disproportionate to outlay in terms of increased pride and self-sufficiency, assistance to the tribal economies, prevention of school dropout and introduction to the demands of a work-oriented society.

Problems include the completely inadequate ratio of slots to need, lack of adequate orientation to work and life beyond the NYC stint, failure to use imagination in developing new and valuable kinds of work for the trainees, and the failure of leaders and Indian youth to realize the particular value of out-of-school programs for Indian dropouts.

In the existing out-of-school programs there are often formidable problems of alcoholism, absenteeism, dropout, which are actually illustrative of the need for this kind of program.

Main-stream

What NYC does for Indian youth, operation mainstream, where it exists, does for their indigent elders. The benefits to the individuals are great, occasional placements into regular employment are made, and where the programs are well-planned, appearance, comfort, and economy of the tribe are strengthened. The basic problem is that this program is not understood by many of the tribes.

III. URBAN INDIANS

Small numbers

The evaluators were surprised at the small numbers of Indians in actual residence in the large cities visited. Many, indeed most, Indians stay only a short while in the cities, then return to their reservations, so that the number of Indian residents at any one time is small. Reliable ethnic records, however, are nowhere available.

Manpower programs

Because of the small populations, the high turnover, the fact that many Indian urban residents are BIA relocates, the general ignorance of Indians concerning Federal programs, and their shyness about going through the complex forms of access to such programs in the cities.

there was little evidence of involvement of urban Indians in the manpower programs of the Department of Labor. In any case, applicable ethnic records are not kept.

Living conditions

In their contacts in Indian centers (organizations run by Indians in several cities) and areas of concentration of Indians the evaluators found few indications that a policy of relocation of Indians to large cities is advisable; conditions of slum living, frequent job discrimination, the prevalent alcoholism, the passivity and hopelessness of many Indians there argue against it.

IV. OKLAHOMA INDIANS

Uniqueness

Oklahoma, with 65 tribes of nonreservation but predominantly rural Indians, offers a different social and economic setting. There are radical differences in the education, social standing, and conditions of discrimination between the "Five Civilized Tribes" in eastern Oklahoma and the Plains Indians in the western part of the State.

Regional differences

Assimilation and acculturation are far advanced in Oklahoma, much to the distress of some Indian leaders, who feel that the loss of Indian identity can only be harmful. Manpower programs are easier here and present the same complex of problems they present in any rural or small-town setting.

ES and the Indians

The employment service in Oklahoma identifies well with Indians, but jobs in the rural areas are scarce, and the employment service has been of little help to people without marketable skills. Intensified moves to assist Indians by the national office seem to have had a beneficial effect there.

On the other hand, the resolute determination of the Oklahoma Employment Service to treat full-blood Indians, part Indians, and whites exactly alike, without keeping ethnic records, apparently has worked to the disadvantage of the poorly qualified, nonaggressive Indians, who need to be sought out and actively recruited. In other words, this disadvantaged minority group needs special attention, which cannot be given in an atmosphere of rigid equality of treatment.

Neighborhood Youth Corps

The Neighborhood Youth Corps is very popular among Oklahoma Indians, as it is on the reservations; the problems are essentially the same, except that in Oklahoma out-of-school programs are more plentiful and their potentialities better realized and more skillfully exploited. Some of the best run NYC programs encountered by the evaluators were sponsored by Oklahoma tribes.

There are recruitment problems, compounded by the lack of outreach of the ES in rural areas. There are a few effective examples of close collaboration between NYC sponsors and Employment offices in placement.

Dropout from the NYC out-of-school programs, as on reservations, is often heavy due to the same cultural and economic factors.

V. Testing of Indians

The tests being given Indians for employment screening and MDTA are generally acknowledged to be inadequate or improper for Indians, because of linguistic and cultural problems. However, the use of the tests persists, with the standard norms, because of the lack of anything else to use, and because of a belief that tests of some sort are necessary.

SUMMARY OF RECOMMENDATIONS

The evaluators endorse the 12 recommendations of the Ad Hoc Advisory Committee to USES on Indian Employment, with the reservation that the committee puts too much emphasis on moving Indians into urban environments and the mainstream.

The committee's recommendations concern (1) establishment of the duties of an Indian "desk," (2) establishment of halfway house program, (3) encouragement of in-service or out training, (4) analysis of human and natural resources of reservations, (5) full utilization HRD concept, (6) staffing of ES offices with Indians, (7) participation of organized labor, (8) preparation of information packets, (9) emphasis on employment, (10) encouraging employers to expand into reservations, (11) bringing groups of employer representatives to reservations, and (12) organization of Indian economic development corporations.

The recommendations of the authors of this report follow:

1. That mandatory sensitivity courses on Indian mores, psychology, traditions, and needs be developed and given officials who work with Indians;

2. That an active effort be made to recruit Indians for high-level Manpower Administration positions;

3. That the Department establish an Indian manpower policy which will assist Indians to attain work where they live, retaining their traditional values but will assist in relocation if desired by Indians;

4. That USES concentrate its efforts to aid Indians into the reservation and rural areas;

5. That USES prepare and issue guidelines for ES activity in serving Indians, covering policy, concept of service, and collaboration with tribal governments and other agencies;

6. That firm steps be taken to fill all of the jobs specially created by USES for serving Indians;

7. That continuing mechanisms be established for coordination of programs in Indian areas;

8. That USES vigorously promulgate the concept of followup after placement by Indian ES personnel, and that MDTA projects for Indians contain one "coach" or after-placement counselor for every 20 trainees.

9. That MDTA be made more responsive to the needs of reservation and rural Indians through the encouragement of (a) training in the traditional Indian crafts; (b) training of Indians as helpers in the building trades; (c) use of MDTA to establish labor pools; and (d) use of other valid means of selection than standard tests.

10. That a task force or study group be created to study and make recommendations on the advisability and feasibility of a separate NYC program for Indians.

I. INTRODUCTION

Background of study

This study was conducted in two stages:
1. Between August 1966 and February 1967 in the Southwest, and
2. From September to December 1967 in the Northern and Midwestern States in the South.

It was planned as part of the series of the role of manpower programs in relation to major minority groups in this country.

The first stage was conducted in conjunction with the study of the Spanish-speaking people of the Southwest and a preliminary report on manpower programs for Indians for highly restricted circulation was prepared in 1967. The present report incorporates the findings for the whole country.

How it was conducted

Field work included visits to 16 different Indian reservations, eight cities with substantial Indian populations, 10 tribes in Oklahoma, and Menominee County, Wisconsin.

In the areas visited, as many persons as possible were interviewed who might have been considered to have some knowledge of the economic situation of the Indians, their opportunities for training and employment, their attitudes toward manpower programs, and the results and effects of such programs. Discussions were held with State officials, regional officials and others responsible for manpower programs for the Indians. In addition, statistics and data were secured wherever available.

The overall objective was to determine the impact of the Department of Labor's manpower programs on the Indians, the successes these programs have had, and the difficulties they have encountered.

Upsurge of interest

One of the motivating factors behind the study was the upsurge of interest in the American Indian and his problems of poverty, unemployment and the cultural disorientation. Sociologists, anthropologists, labor economists, and others are attempting to come up with solutions to the American manpower dilemma concerning Indians. The Department of Labor itself in the last 2 years has undertaken materially to strengthen and to improve its service to Indians. Indians have been given special attention in antipoverty programs.

The conscience of Americans concerning the genocide of the last century and the continued aggressive swindling of the Indians by selfish interests, plus the impetus of the antipoverty movement of the past several years, resulted in heavy expenditures aimed at eliminating poverty and unemployment.

Problems created by Indian aversion to assimilation

The bewilderment of the American people, however, in confronting the general aversion of the Indians to assimilation into the so-called mainstream of American culture is clearly exemplified in the frustration of the managers of various manpower programs, who have attempted to speed up such assimilation, with indifferent results. We do not expect to advance a solution to the very basic policy question of whether the Indian should be assimilated into the dominant culture or whether he should be encouraged to retain his tribal and traditional identity. This question, which is several generations old already, may never be resolved, and will continue to create difficulties.

Coverage gaps

The particular strength of this evaluation study can be found in its broad coverage and the attempt it has made to obtain as many different points of view as possible. There are still gaps, however, because of lack of staff time to extend the coverage. For example, the Indians of New York State and other areas of the eastern part of the country were not visited. The Lumbee Indians of North Carolina and some Southwestern tribes such as the Apaches had to be omitted.

Attempts to learn Indian attitudes

We make no pretense that this quick study penetrates very deeply into Indian psychology. Indians generally are reserved and do not open up often on initial contact with strange officials. Often they say the things they believe they are expected to say. Only those who have been well acculturated and who know what is expected through such studies are likely to talk freely in interviews of the sort which we conducted. To alleviate this difficulty we solicited a great deal of second-hand information from Indian sponsors and managers of programs and others who had had an opportunity to sound out tribal sentiment.

Biases of the evaluators—admiration for Indians

Also, we must admit to certain biases which developed. We grew to admire the Indians tremendously as a group, to marvel at their courtesy and dignity even in the midst of abject poverty, and to appreciate their lack of aggressive acquisitiveness. Even their reserve appeared to be the symbol of an inner strength as well as an insulation against the deteriorating influences of white society.

Value of their heritage

The second bias is this: After visiting a few reservations, we began to sense the unique and priceless cultural heritage of the American Indian, battered and adulterated as it now is. We realized what a tremendous loss to mankind would be the obliteration of this culture, call the obliteration process what one will—assimilation, acculturation, or termination. We became strong partisans of the belief that the Indians should be encouraged and helped to preserve their culture and to retain their tribal cultures, if they wish. This position is, consistent with a great body of enlightened opinion in this country, and with prevailing opinion among the Indians themselves.

With the qualifications and limitations indicated above, some important insights were gained during the evaluation into the manpower problems of Indians as these problems are intensified by Indian aspirations, cultural characteristics, and the residue of a very unhappy recent history.

II. Reservation Indians

A. Variations Between Reservations

The truth—Wide variations

The general public tends to generalize too much about Indians, to assume erroneously that all Indians are alike. The truth is considerably different. Indians are not alike, and there are wide variations between reservations. There is as much difference between the enormous Navajo reservation (with an area the size of Belgium and the Netherlands combined) and some of the smallest reservations as there is between Russia and Switzerland. Ethnologically, linguistically, and culturally, the differences between the Apaches and the Eastern Cherokees are greater than between the Swedes and the Italians.

Economic variations

There are also great variations in the economic conditions of the places visited. The Mountain Utes of Colorado, for example, are wealthy enough to make an annual per capita payment of $1,200 to tribal members, while the per capita annual income of some of the tribes is so small as to be hardly measurable in American terms. Some reservations visited, notably the Salt River Reservation in Arizona, have the potential for considerable wealth because of the promixity of their land to burgeoning urban development, while others exist on isolated, infertile, and useless land with no usable mineral resources. Many reservations have potential for tourist development because of lakes, parks, and because of the attraction of the Indians themselves. But none of the others visited can remotely approach the volume of tourist business done on the Cherokee Reservation of North Carolina, where every summer on of the country's greatest tourist floods spills out of the Smoky Mountains National Park, and inundates the whole reservation.

Variations of prejudice

There are significant variations, too, in the relationships and attitudes of the reservation people with the white population around them. The prejudice against the reservation Indians in the northern part of the country is well known; here the stereotypes about the Indians are heard on every hand. Here there is possibly some justification in comparing the reservations to ghettos, although Indians can leave if they wish for larger cities and find housing without the blatant discrimination which afflicts the Negroes. The Choctaws of Mississippi are victims of the very strong prejudices of their neighbors against nonwhites, since the Choctaws have a mixture of Negro blood.

The fortunate ones

In the Southwest, on the other hand, it is often actually an advantage to be an Indian in looking for work outside the reservation, and there is little general prejudice against the Indians socially, in housing, or in educational institutions. The Cherokees of North Carolina, surrounded as they are by southern mountaineers, have to a considerable extent absorbed the mores and ways of thought of their neighbors, intermarry with their neighbors, and experience little or no discrimination when they move outside the reservation.

Variations in cultural retention

There are also variations between tribal groups in their attitude toward acculturation and their willingness and ability to adopt the methods of the white man in business, in religion, in language and in household economy. Thus the Zunis have maintained intact to this day one of the oldest genuine civilizations existing anywhere in the world, with their own culture and religion. Other tribes have virtually lost their traditions, language and any vestige of religious ceremonies or beliefs.

Similarities

Despite all these differences there are similarities and elements of uniformity. Generalizations can be made concerning the level of education; the attachment to the reservation way of life; the lack of tradition; knowledge and incentive toward making business profits; and the Indian tendency to adhere to his extended family or clan and to share his goods with members of the clan and the tribe. Also of late, under the leadership of groups of younger Indians, including the National Congress of American Indians, there has been developing a pan-Indian movement and "Indianness" stronger than ever before, so that today it is possible to look at the Indians as a group in considering some of their manpower problems.

Clinging to heritage

It is hard to escape the conclusion that the Indians have retrogressed under the stifling rule of the white man. In the sense that the Indian has lost his independence, much of his feelings of self-worth, and much of his identity as a person, this is true. But it is also true that the Indian has done a remarkable job of clinging to some of the best of his heritage, in spite of all the attempts of white society to make him over in the white man's image.

Manpower problems thus created

Whether one looks at the present divergence of Indian culture from white as being a preservation of the good or a clinging to obsolete values, it nevertheless poses real problems in the manpower picture. Many Indians lack what the white man calls "time sense." They often have a tendency to leave their jobs to return to the reservations because of some family illness, because of a religious ceremony, or because of plain homesickness. A few of them get drunk periodically. Most of them lack some kind of acquisitive ambition which the white man has. All of these pose problems to the white employer who feels that his employees should be on time, should work a steady 40 hours per week, and should attempt to progress on the job.

That many of the Indian workers, perhaps most of them, are good workers by any standards, assumes less importance in many areas than the reputation created by a few of the Indians who do not conform.

The cultural problems which appear to affect manpower programs most are those concerned with education, attachment to reservations and language.

Opportunities

1. *Education.* The educational possibilities for reservation Indians are usually considered rather good. Practically any Indian youngster who has the ability to be schooled can be sent to a school run by the

Bureau of Indian Affairs, either on the reservation or in a boarding school off the reservation. This system will take the youngster through high school and even through college. In addition, in many of the reservations we visited there are opportunities for reservation youngsters to attend public schools in the neighboring counties.

Breaking down tribal identity

Many Indians don't like the system of BIA schooling because to them it appears to be devoted to the principle of breaking down tribal identity and bringing the Indian youngster into the culture of the white man. In Indian boarding schools, youngsters from different tribes with different native languages and different backgrounds are brought together and are taught standard white school curriculums which do not emphasize to any great extent Indian culture and history. The theory has been that by giving the Indian youngster this kind of education the Indian youngster would be better equipped to make his way in the world.

The BIA system also provides some vocational education (to be distinguished from the vocational training given adult Indians by BIA to prepare them for relocation in urban settings). Some of the more affluent tribes have established their own schools on the reservation.

Literacy

Whatever the variations in the system and whatever its general efficacy, the result is increasing literacy, although dropout is very heavy in some tribes, and the results of the schooling are said to disappear after a few years of reservation life without the necessity to use the education.

Illiteracy

Illiteracy among the older generation in most tribes is still prevalent. There are tens of thousands of adult tribesmen who cannot read, write, or speak acceptable English.

Data on literacy

We attempted to find national statistics on Indian educational levels and literacy. Apparently, however, none are available from any source, except those which appear in the 1960 census. (See United States Census of Population, 1960, Nonwhite Population by Race, table 10.) Here it is indicated that 10 percent of all Indians over 14 have had no schooling and nearly 60 percent have had less than an eighth grade education. Half of all Indian children who enter do not finish high school, and despite ample scholarship funds from the BIA and other sources only 1 percent of those Indians over 14 had completed 4 or more years of college in 1960 (only one-third of those who entered). Indeed, according to the special census report of that year, the median number of school years completed by Indian males over 14 was 8.4, and by females, 8.5.

Causes for dropout

During our own visits we found indications generally of very heavy dropout from school. This was explained by our informants as being due to parental indifference, to drunkenness among Indian high school boys, to transportation problems, to the pull of the reservation on boarding school youngsters, to language problems, and, perhaps most of all, to a failure on the part of the youngster to see that his education would advantage him very much. Also, where Indian students are mixed with white in public school systems, there is often an attitude of superiority of the white children which is galling to the Indians. Their ever-present poverty keeps them from dressing so well as the whites. Their natural reserve is often associated with stupidity by inexperienced and insensitive teachers.

Why they don't like the city

2. *Attachment to reservations.* The Indian's attachment to his reservation is difficult for white people, particularly urban white people, to understand. It can only be understood by another Indian or by someone who has also grown up in a protective society with extended family ties and a distinctive way of life. The Indian likes reservation life better than city life—many of them have tried urban life and have returned—because despite its poverty, it is more satisfying to their sense of individual worth, more responsible to their tradition of communal interdependence and sharing, less hectic and antlike, and, even in the direst poverty, less ugly than life in city slums. There is something else which is perhaps more important than any of the comparative reactions noted above—outside the reservation, in the middle of white society, the Indian loses his identity as an Indian and as a member of his tribe. Identity based on what is left of the Indian tradition is important to them and for the most of them, according to Indian informants, have no desire to become imitation white people.

Manpower planning to relocate them

With his certain conviction that his own way of life is best, the average American finds it hard to understand this. Most Government policy and most Government planning, including manpower planning in the past, has been based on the proposition that it is in the Indian's best interest to move him out of the reservation into the "mainstream." The relocation and vocational education policies of the Bureau of Indian Affairs have been directed toward this end. The Indians have cooperated, then have returned to the reservation.

Those who stay outside

Some have stayed outside, of course, and a few have made good in the white man's sense of the term. In many municipalities there are small colonies of Indians who are trying desperately to retain something of their Indianness. What we saw in the study of the urban life of Indians does not lead us to the conclusion that it is best for the Indians to move to the cities. If the Indians are to be helped to the maximum by manpower programs, these programs will have to be meshed with other programs for improving conditions and opportunities for living on the reservations.

Survival of native tongues

3. *Language.* The persistence of the Indians in clinging to their ancestral languages is a cause of bafflement to persons who are convinced that the knowledge and use of English is essential to being an American. Even those who understand the survival of the native tongues believe that Indians will have to conquer their unemployment and poor living conditions in English. In the present social context

there is reason for this. The Government over the years has pursued policies of education designed to encourage the substitution of English for the tribal languages. There have been interludes in which, under tribal pressures or under particularly enlightened leadership, the Government has encouraged the writing of local languages, but efforts to teach the Indian languages in the schools have been sporadic and generally have died because of lack of impetus from those who make policy.

Interest in tribal tongues

Wherever we went in the course of this study, the gradual decline of the native languages, for the most part still unwritten, was deplored by tribal spokesmen. Some tribes are spending tribal funds to have grammars and vocabularies prepared.

Language of the elders

The general pattern on the reservations, as well as in the non-reservation areas of Oklahoma and Wisconsin, is that among the older people the knowledge of English is subordinate to that of their native languages. Many of them are unable to speak more than a few words of English.

Language of the younger

The young people, as might be expected, having gone to school in English use English more than the tribal language. Those in the middle age groups show varied patterns. In some tribes, such as the Navaho, the language problem is acute. In securing employment outside the reservation, they usually have to work in groups with a member who knows English acting as interpreter.

Illustrations of variations

The variation between reservations in the use of English can be illustrated on the one hand by some of the Pueblos of New Mexico where practically no English is spoken in everyday life, and on the other hand by the Fort Berthold Reservation where the coexistence of three different tribes with distinct languages has required the use of English as a *lingua franca*.

Possibly the Choctaw Reservation in Mississippi is fairly typical. A household survey there in 1963 showed that 4 percent of the families used excellent English, 57 percent used good, and 39 percent used poor English.

Language problems at work

The language problem is quite important in the manpower picture. For industry on the reservation, there are always interpreters and foremen who speak the native language. When uneducated or poorly educated Indians work outside the reservation, the problem of communication intensifies. The problem is compounded because of the natural reserve of the Indians. Rather than make any great attempt to explain themselves to their employers when a misunderstanding arises, they often will simply say nothing, or leave.

Materials and instruction in native languages

Because of the large diversity of distinct Indian languages, most of them are spoken by only a relatively small number of people. It is manifestly impractical to adapt manpower training or orientation materials to these languages, with the possible exception of those that are already written and spoken by the larger groups, particularly Navaho and Dakota. However, among Indians where the knowledge of English is not widespread or general, the use of native language instructors and counselors should be encouraged. Below (Section F) we discuss the role which speakers of native languages are playing and can play in connection with Employment Service activities, where it is important, even necessary, that there be a capability in an Indian language.

Other communication problems

Besides language there are other communication problems. Reservation Indians (except those who have been educated in white public schools and who know firsthand the white man's way and are prepared to imitate them) are usually slow to express their thoughts, ambitions and desires to strangers, to Employment Service officials, to well-meaning academicians making surveys on the reservations, or to instructors. Among these Indians throughout the country there seems to be an etiquette which requires slowness, deliberation and patience in communication. Few white people, particularly in the hurly-burly of the industrial milieu, possess it or understand it.

C. LIVELIHOOD AND UNEMPLOYMENT

It is difficult to generalize about the means of livelihood of Indians in diverse tribes in different locations of the country, in States with different economies. Some patterns are discernible, however.

Plants on reservations

Here and there factories and plants are located on the reservations. Some of them are tribally owned, some of them are owned by outsiders who have been induced by the tribes to come in. Some of them are wood manufacturing industries, some are electronic industries, some are needle trades industries and furniture plants. These employ limited numbers of Indians with mixed success. Many such industries have folded because of the lack of understanding of foremen and supervisors of the Indian's attitude toward work, some because of sales or transportation difficulties. Many, however, are still operating; practically all of these are small.

Just outside

Immediately outside the reservations, within commuting distance or at least close enough so that the workers can maintain their ties with the reservation, several thousand more are employed in places like Farmington, N. Mex., and Philadelphia, Miss.

BIA, CAA

Except for plants inside the reservations and immediately outside, the largest steady employers are the Bureau of Indian Affairs and the community action agencies. The latter have fused new vitality into the economies of many tribes, although the unemployment problem is much too great for a solution to be achieved this way.

Indian unemployment by any standard is catastrophic. When it is added to inadequate shelter, particularly in the rough climate of the Northern States, the poverty of the Indians has a quality which cannot be imagined until it is seen firsthand. The erroneous belief of so many Americans that, as wards of the Government, the Indians are supported by the Government, is prevalent even in communities bordering on the reservations and was actually encountered among some employment service officials close to reservations.

Unemployment

When all of the opportunities from steady year-round employment for reservation Indians are added together, the proportion is still very small. At various times of the year unemployment on the typical reservation is very heavy, sometimes running as high as 80 percent. When there is seasonal employment, the percentage goes down, of course. Seasonal employment includes the tourist industries (particularly on the Cherokee Reservation in North Carolina), firefighting (a lucrative and well-liked means of employment for many of the northern and southwestern Indians), and farmwork, much of which is done in the general area of the reservations, with a considerable amount done out of migrant camps in various locations. Self-employment by the reservation Indians is general, although many of them farm small plots. Business doesn't seem to be their forte, even where opportunities for small independently owned businesses are plentiful.

Craftsmanship died out—revived

At one time the tradition of craftsmanship among most of the Indians throughout the country was very strong, but it died out during the depressing years after the final conquest by the whites. The only area in the country where it has been generally and successfully revived is in the Southwest, where basketry has been revived among one or two tribes, pottery has continued strong among the Pueblos, and silversmithing, particularly among the Zuni, Hopis and Navajos, has procured a large worldwide market. In the shape seen by most tourists, silversmithing is really a modern industry which has been developed since the 1880's by enterprising Indian leaders and whites who foresaw the market.

Their own outlets

One difficulty is that, by the time the usual middlemen and retail outlets have made their profits, the amount which is left for the craftsmen is often not commensurate with the effort which went into the work. To offset middleman expenses, some of the tribes have developed their own arts and crafts organizations and their own outlets, with increasing skill in marketing distribution. Many tribes may eventually make craftsmanship a very important source of income. Even now some of the the smaller pueblos derive their principal income from their famous pottery.

D. DISCRIMINATION

The eagerness of so many white people interviewed, including some Employment Service officials, to deny that discrimination against Indians exists is indicative more of changing social values than of the actual situation.

Where discrimination is

There is widespread discrimination throughout the northern tier of States and in Mississippi against Indians socially and in employment. The discrimination is often as strong as that against Negroes and is justified on the basis of undependability in employment (see above) and the alleged dirtiness of the Indians themselves. We observed no more of the latter among Indians than we have observed among poor whites. It is really immaterial to the question of discrimination, which is rooted so deeply in the American tradition and history. Even if Indians overnight became paragons of cleanliness, sobriety, and conventional morality, they would still be discriminated against. This is illustrated by the fact that in the areas of greatest discrimination, those who live and act like whites are still considered second-class citizens by their neighbors.

Where discrimination is not (so much)

In the Southwest and among the Cherokees of North Carolina, the picture is somewhat different. Discrimination exists in employment, but is balanced somewhat by a kind of reverse discrimination which causes employers to want to employ Indians. Also, in these areas there is no racial antipathy, and North Carolina mountaineers or Southwestern Anglos who marry Indians lose no social status.

The pendulum swings full cycle in eastern Oklahoma, where to have even a small proportion of Indian blood is a matter of great pride among white people, and persons with one quarter or even one-eighth of Indian ancestry proclaim themselves to be Indians.

In many areas there is obvious police discrimination against Indians who are arrested on the slightest pretext when off the reservation. This frequency of arrest contributes to the stereotyped picture of the Indian as belonging to an undependable criminal element, and the arrest records, unfair as they may be, often mitigate against employment.

Employment service variations in attitude

Without intending to do so, many Employment Service officials in employment offices serving reservations betrayed their own prejudices against Indians by expressing irritation and disgust about matters concerning which, with a little understanding, they would have spoken differently. Again there seemed to be wide variations within States, ranging from the almost complete acceptance of Indians in the biggest Indian State, Arizona, to an attitude in one or two other States which approached rejection.

The concern and interest of the national leadership of the U.S. Employment Service (see below) must be translated somehow to all the States involved with Indians before the picture can be uniformly good.

Officials of Neighborhood Youth Corps programs and CAA programs, often Indians themselves, and BIA, appeared to have fewer problems of prejudice and identification.

Resentment

Resentment toward discrimination is building up among Indians, particularly the young Indians. So far it has not taken many overt forms, but this can be expected in the future.

E. CONNECTION BETWEEN BIA PROGRAMS AND LABOR DEPARTMENT PROGRAMS

Good points

Relations between the field staff of BIA, the State employment service and the NYC sponsors are generally friendly and cordial, and there are examples not only of coordination, but of collaboration between them. Thus, in a Phoenix licensed practical nurse course, the basic education of the 20 to 25 Indians in the course was provided under MDTA with BIA furnishing the vocational component. In Sandoval County, N. Mex., the coordinator of the concerted services program involves BIA from the Navaho Reservation and the United Pueblos very frequently in his projects for joint action. There are numerous instances where the employment service has done testing for students under the auspices of BIA. BIA officials frequently send Indians to the nearest employment service office. In Oklahoma some very successful NYC projects are run by the tribes with aid from BIA. On the reservations NYC projects are usually under the CAP, which in turn is under general tribe supervision, and in all of these cases, BIA has some input, sometimes actually assisting in drawing up proposals.

Bad points

The examples given above, however, should not convey the impression that collaboration between BIA and BIA programs and officials in Labor Department Government officials is the rule. The above are exceptions. There is a very great deal of inertia in this area—inertia due to the fact that for many years each has run an independent operation, without a great deal of interchange with other agencies. In the past there seems to have been a feeling that attempts to cooperate would signal to the other agency that someone was trying to move in on its territory. Partly for this reason, the attempts of the national office of the Employment Service to better the Employment Service's capability on reservations has been carried out with more diffidence than otherwise in the area of relationship between the Employment Service and the BIA.

Carryover of attitude toward BIA

The love-hate relationship of the Indians with BIA, well known to BIA officials and to others, is a complicating factor. Because of recent moves, the suspicion with which Indians generally have viewed BIA efforts toward assimilation may be lessening and many Indians may no longer believe that BIA's ultimate objective is the obliteration of tribal culture. But such feelings are still very strong. Indians generally, except the most knowledgeable leaders, make little distinction in their minds between BIA-sponsored programs and other manpower programs.

BIA and Employment Service placement

The BIA assistance program includes both manpower training and placement services. The placement services of BIA and of the Employment Service are often most effective when Indians are placed within commuting distance or at least within weekend visiting distance of the reservations.

Although the orientation of the BIA employment assistance program appears to be toward relocation, employment assistance officers and education officers often work hard to assist tribal members to get jobs near by so that they can stay on the reservation. Placement activities can be particularly effective when coordinated between a BIA employment assistance officer and the local Employment Service office.

More can be done

It would seem that much closer collaboration is possible. For example, BIA manpower training could be complemented by MDTA, or vice versa, and the use of BIA educational assistance in MDTA training sites would seem to be important. Very little of this is being done. We encountered occasional statements that officials on one side or the other felt that the other program was competitive. Where such a feeling exists in either agency, it hampers effective collaboration.

Relocation to small towns

Relocation to the larger cities, whether through BIA, through MDTA or through Employment Service placement action, found little support among the Indians with whom we discussed it. In fact it found little support among Employment Service people themselves. Some local office staff thought that Indians should be relocated into white society but in smaller towns and among rural societies instead of the cities, on the assumption that it would be easier and that they would not be contributing to the slum population of the cities. Also they felt the chances of their remaining would be increased.

The Muscatine relocation

An example of this, apparently successful, at least in its initial stages, was an arrangement between the Employment Service of South Dakota and BIA whereby three families moved to Muscatine, Iowa, from the Rosebud Reservation and worked for a tomato-processing plant. The BIA funded the relocation, but the State employment service found the jobs and arranged for the receiving community to establish an organization for counseling them and guiding them. This group will be built up if successful, and the project should be very carefully watched as showing a way to a possible better future for Indians who wish to be relocated.

F. THE U.S. EMPLOYMENT SERVICE AND THE INDIANS

How well the Indians know Employment Service

1. *Image.*—In our opinion there is no Indian "image" of the Employment Service, as there might be said to be among the Mexican-Americans or the ghetto Negroes. Until U.S. Employment Service began to station interviewers on all of the larger reservations, to most reservation Indians the Employment Service was a nebulous, uncertain organization concerned with unemployment compensation. In any case it was a white man's organization which didn't concern them much because they had their own employment assistance office in the BIA quarters.

Farm work through Employment Service

Many of the Indians know the employment offices in cities outside the reservations to be places where they go to get farm jobs. There are a few locations such as the Navajo Reservation in Arizona where representatives of the Employment Service have been stationed for years. These permanent stations were, and are, known as places where one can obtain seasonal farm work off the reservation, firefighting work at times, and the like. At no time, and not even now, have the Employment Service offices been considered places where the Indians can go to find permanent work in the cities or on the reservation. The BIA employment assistance office is still considered the place for that.

Varying degrees of dynamism

Some of the Employment Service representatives have acquired a reputation for being hardworking, cooperative people who are interested in the welfare of the Indians. Some, however (and this applies to the Indian representatives as well as the white representatives) of those who serve the reservations are not particularly active or dynamic in their efforts to think of ways to serve the Indians.

Expansion of services

2. *Extent of Employment Service services to Indians.*—Since the Kansas City conference in February 1967 U.S. Employment Service has tried to fill the gap which had been present in its services to Indians. An Indian desk was planned, although we understand that no one was placed in the job, and that now an Indian Office in the Manpower Administrator's Office has been created, 198 human resources development positions were established specifically to serve Indians and were distributed among the States. During our second round of visits in the north and the south, we encountered many of the persons who have been selected for these HRD positions. There were some patterns here which became apparent: The majority, although not all, were Indians (on September 15, 1967, 112 out of the 171 filled were Indians) and considerable difficulty was encountered in recruiting for Indians to fill these positons. This was because of (1) difficulty in finding Indians with sufficient education and desire to undertake this sort of job; (2) competition from community action agencies for this same type of Indian; (3) rigid State civil service requirements, which meant in many instances that the Indians did not meet the requirements for permanent positions, and if hired, had to be placed on temporary positions; and (4) indifferent recruitment efforts in a few locations.

Some foot-dragging

A majority of State employment services and local Employment Service offices having jurisdiction over Indian reservations have earnestly attempted to implement the directive. However, there were instances where people were obviously dragging their heels out of inertia or ignorance about what was needed. We believe that, despite the difficulties, all of the available positions should have been filled by the end of 1967 mostly with Indians.

Policy

Other efforts by the Employment Service included the encouragement of research, supplementing the smaller community program so that it can serve reservations, the establishment of seminars at the universities for Employment Service personnel, and the urging of manpower advisory committees to form subcommittees aimed at improving services to Indians.

An ad hoc Advisory Committee to U.S. Employment Service on Indian Employment Programs was established. It was chaired by Dr. Daniel Kruger, professor of industrial relations, Michigan State University, and consisting of four subcommittees (economic development, research, education and training, and job placement) with representatives from among tribal leaders, employers, educators, and individuals who represent employer organizations and appropriate Federal agencies. The committee was charged with the responsibility for advising on the development of employment and training opportunities for Indians on reservations and in communities with sizable Indian populations and the assistance of Indians with job-related problems.

A meeting of the advisory committee on June 19–20, 1967, in Washington, D.C., resulted in a number of important recommendations, which are listed in section VI of this report.

Positives in the new efforts

In view of this effort and all this interest on the part of the national office and some State offices, how effective actually is the service which is given to Indians on the reservations? The answer is: The result is not yet commensurate with the effort. Contact has been reestablished and coverage has been increased. The Indians who come to the area of tribal headquarters are now aware that there is an Employment Service, and everywhere the HRD personnel go over the reservations visiting people, awareness of the Employment Service and what is available is greater than it was before. These are all positives.

Recruiting for NYC and Job Corps and occasional MDTA training has been moderately successful although there were complaints. Also most of the employment testing done for the reservation Indians, whether for BIA, for employers, or for schools is done by the Employment Service. These are also positives.

Negatives

Negatives can be found in the persistent attitudes of some Employment Service personnel who cannot bring themselves to consider the problems of the Indians as seriously as they should, the lack of job opportunities which the Employment Service people have to offer the Indians, the lack of the close collaboration with employment assistance officers of the BIA, and the absence of a consistent idea of what the Employment Service is supposed to do for the Indians.

What is ES role

This last statement may startle some and it should be explained. The Employment Service role on the reservations is far from clear cut. Most of the employment offices serving Indians are concerned with finding jobs for Indians *off the reservation*, temporary jobs in agricultural work, lumbering, firefighting, and the like. Only a minimal part of the total Employment Service activity on the reservations is concerned with filling or developing jobs on the reservations in collaboration with BIA, the community action agencies, and others. There is general agreement that it is in the latter area that the employment future of the reservation Indian lies. Irritation was expressed by some Employment Service personnel stationed on reservations that Indians did not flock to the opportunities for temporary work which they advertised. Based on this, the conclusion was voiced more than once that the Indians do not really want to work.

What is needed most

What is lacking is a sense of direction, a guideline as to what they should do for the Indians. They are, in effect, trying to translate a regular employment office to the reservation, and the result is, inevitably, a feeling of futility. They should have guidelines related to Labor Department policy. (There are recommendations on both Labor Department policy and USES adaptation of it at the end of this report.)

Increase the Indian staff

How can the services the Employment Service renders to Indians be extended further? One answer is obvious. Fill the vacant positions at once; if necessary, working with State civil service systems to modify requirements. Whenever a moderately qualified Indian is found who knows the language of the tribe, this can be considered an asset so valuable that it should overbalance his lack of education. If State civil service requirements are not flexible enough to admit this, a strenuous effort should be made to get them changed. The Indians thus employed can be given special titles such as interviewer–interpreter (as they are given in Arizona) or ethnic specialist. In South Dakota at the time of the visit a job title of Employment Service aide was being developed to replace the interviewer 1 position for Indians. Many such devices are possible, and should be coupled with opportunities for training and education, so that Indians hired can have the opportunity for advancement.

Collaboration

The other principal way in which Employment Service services to reservation Indians can be extended will be discussed more in detail in a later section. Essentially it consists of closer collaboration of the Employment Service representatives with BIA and the community action agencies.

Outreach

3. *Other deficiencies and problems in Employment Service service to Indians.*—Several problems in Employment Service service to Indians on reservations have been mentioned in the previous section. One problem mentioned but not stressed above is difficulty in outreach. This has been partially solved by the addition of the HRD personnel, but remains a problem because of the isolation of many households on reservations and the difficulty in reaching them.

Counseling

One of the greatest deficiencies in Employment Service service to Indians is the lack of vocational counseling. The small size of the local offices serving reservations and the lack of professional qualifications of the personnel stationed on the reservations tend to make such service almost impossible. Also, the isolation of Employment Service personnel on reservations and their lack of contact with the fountainheads of employment make it difficult for them to communicate comprehensive information about the world of work to the Indian tribesmen.

Separate form CAP

Much could be done to remedy this deficiency by bringing someone periodically to the reservations, with the collaboration and the help of the community action agency, to counsel individuals or groups. In fact some CAP directors expressed their desire to have Employment Service people come in to do such counseling. It seems to us, in any case, that here is an opportunity for the Employment Service to work with the CAP directors. Employment officers could be set up in the vicinity of the CAP, sometimes in the same building, so that persons who visit one office can also visit the other. When the Employment Service representative is out, an Indian can receive the information he wants from a community action employee. As it is, Employment Services offices often are placed in separate little buildings on the reservations which are not in themselves centers of activity and which are not frequented by the Indians.

The service concept

Perhaps the most significant deficiency of Employment Service service to Indians is a subtle one, which we advance with the full knowledge that its concepts will be contested by many knowledgeable people. It is this: The Employment Service's offices which serve the reservation are still oriented to the idea that the heart of the Employment Service operation is to take job applicants who come into the office seeking jobs and find jobs for them.

What ES should concentrate on

That the ultimate object of practical ES activity is the finding of full-time work for individuals we do not deny. However, we submit that in view of the scarcity of actual concrete job opportunities at or near the reservations for Indians, the Employment Service could be much more useful and perform a much greater service if it concentrated its reservation efforts in the areas of job information and counseling about job opportunities, in developing information for the tribal leaders and for individuals about what is being done in other reservations concerning work opportunities, in holding training session on what white employers demand from their employees, in counseling young people about the kinds of training they might find most useful and where it could be obtained, and in other service activities not involving direct referral to jobs available for Indians.

This does not mean, of course, that they should not do the latter. It does mean that the personnel selected for serving the reservations should be chosen for their qualification for other aspects of service and their understanding of the people they are trying to serve. If these things were done in collaboration with BIA and with the community action orgaizations there would, we believe, be much improvement in employment services to reservation Indians.

G. MANPOWER TRAINING—MDTA ON THE RESERVATION

MDTA compared with Public Law 959

On the reservations it is generally considered easier to establish a manpower training project under BIA auspices than an MDTA project because only one agency, the Bureau of Indian Affairs, is involved.

Also the training conducted by BIA is better known and understood by the Indians, it can be explained to them by the BIA employment assistance representative at their tribal headquarters, whom they are accustomed to consult, and who frequently makes presentations at tribal council meetings.

Reasons for lack of MDTA activity

There is a conspicuous lack of MDTA activities on the reservations. The principal reasons on the reservation lie neither in fund shortages nor possible competition from BIA programs. Rather, they lie in (1) lack of employment opportunity within commuting distance, (2) the lack of interest, innovation, and vigorous attempts to overcome difficulties on the part of many (not all) ES personnel, particularly prior to the renewed emphasis on Indian matters in 1967.

Other difficulties

MDTA training for reservation Indians has also been plagued by a number of other difficulties. The most obvious opportunities have often been in the building trades because of fairly extensive building programs on the reservations. What is needed here are courses for training Indians to perform under the supervision of skilled journeymen. Yet the rigidity of the MDTA system, the requirements for union approval, etc., effectively preclude in many places such short, term training in the building trades. In one case the building trades union in the nearby city would give approval only if a guarantee was given that Indians would compete off the reservation. This obviously was impossible to give, since no one can control people in such a way. Besides it was discriminatory. The guarantee was not given and the training was not given.

MDTA for "helpers"

To help solve some of these difficulties, MDTA courses could be developed for "helper positions," particularly in the apprenticeable occupations.

There are other problems: There is apparently problems of competition for clients between OEO programs and MDTA. The OEO programs pay more. There is the problem of the Indian attitude toward any kind of training since long years of dependence have made many of them look upon any kind of training program as simply another opportunity for a livelihood rather than a bridge to productive wage earning employment.

Problems of training off the reservation

Dropouts from MDTA courses, particularly those courses given off the reservation, pose a particularly acute problem. From our visits, we recevied the impression that the record with respect to the taking of MDTA courses by Indians boarding off the reservation has been generally unsuccessful because of financial and social problems. The families of Indian primary wage earners want to be with them during training. (Indian families are usually very close.) There have been numerous mistakes made in sending heads of families to nearby cities without making provision for the drawing of subsistence by the trainees and their families at the training locations. In several instances the families have moved in without understanding the implications of what they did; thus the trainees lost their subsistence and dropped out. Part of this is due to lack of initiative on the part of ES personnel, part of it is due to lack of knowlege on their part, and part perhaps has been due at least at times in the past to a certain amount of indifference toward the problem.

Keeping them in MDTA courses

In MDTA courses, as in employment, Indians respond well to treatment as individuals of worth and react negatively to impersonal, condescending, or rude treatment. They have the same difficulties in attending MDTA courses regularly that they have in working regularly on the job, since they have not become accustomed to living their lives by the clock.

The record of ES personnel in Menominee County, Wis. (until recently a reservation), in counseling Indian MDTA trainees, coaching them, keeping them in training and on the job shows that, given enough interest and enough staff and enough sympathy for the problems of the Indians, excellent results can be achieved. Problems of attendance and dropout are less on reservations themselves where the tribal leaders themselves can be induced to help keep the Indians in training.

Why don't they respond?

We repeatedly encountered statements from Indian spokesmen and from employment service officials to the effect that Indians have not been responsive to MDTA. Apparently this statement is based on lack of response by Indians to courses advertised in cities near the reservation. Part of the lack of response is due to native reserve. Part of it probably is due to the confusion in the minds of tribesmen between MDTA and the manpower training programs of BIA and OEO. (In talking with Indians who are not directly involved in these programs, we found it almost impossible to get answers which distinguished between them.) There are indications that when Indians understand what the training is, what it is aimed at, and what it can do for them as individuals, they do respond.

The MDTA Indian question

Perhaps the most fundamental policy question concerning MDTA policy on courses for reservation Indians is whether these courses should be planned, directed, and focused on jobs in or near the reservation or for relocation outside the commuting distance in cities away from the reservation.

Relocation a debatable goal

We question the validity of the facile assumption we have encountered on the part of national office personnel and others that MDTA should imitate BIA's relocation program and attempt to train large numbers of Indians for relocation. The Indians are not likely to respond affirmatively to this in numbers. Those who do respond and are relocated are not likely to stay. There is also the deeper social question as to whether this sort of action actually benefits society. There is no real purpose in adding to the burdens of our inner cities by moving in poorly educated people with a completely different cultural tradition, whose adaptation will be next to impossible and whose children will inevitably deteriorate in the slums of the cities.

The direction we think MDTA should take

In our opinion, planning of MDTA training should be coordinated very closely with planning for industrial development in or near the reservations, and MDTA should make little or no effort toward training reservation Indians for relocation away from the reservations unless tribal leaders specifically request it. There are, of course, individual circumstances where this kind of thing may be feasible. However, the people planning our programs must divest themselves of the discredited idea that the only solution for the Indian problem is to train them to be like white people and to move them into the large cities.

Crafts training

Some OEO programs have encouraged craft work. Some of these have been successful, others have not; however, this is a field with which Labor Department programs have had little connection. Abortive attempts have been made at MDTA training in crafts work, but have generally been considered inconsistent with the principles and policies of the MDTA program. We believe another look should be taken at the MDTA policies concerning crafts training. It would help if the CAA's on the reservation could organize cooperatives for marketing and supervising production. BIA could also help. This would require initiative and collaboration to a greater extent than is now the general pattern. We are not attempting to minimize the difficulties of marketing. Often white people who work with Indians on craft programs have difficulty understanding the Indian psychology concerning work. An Indian manager of an arts and crafts shop may accept inferior work from a tribe and pay him just as much for his product as he pays the tribesmen who make superior goods, in order to avoid damage to the ego of the workman. Then, in sales to the tourists, the manager may have to adjust his prices as best he can.

Whatever the problems, there is potential here, as is illustrated on the Cherokee Reservation in North Carolina. There cheap foreign-made imitations of Indian arts and crafts compete in the shops alongside the not very plentiful objects made by the Indians on the reservation. Tourists will gladly pay much more for the genuine Indians goods.

A sad case of misdirected craft training

A particularly pathetic instance was encountered on one reservation where under MDTA about a dozen potters had been trained for a factory which some local people were attempting to establish under EDA funds. When we asked the people running this program whether or not there had been any attempt or there was going to be any attempt to have the Indians manufacture pottery with the traditional designs of this tribe, the answer was "no." They would be manufacturing only commercial pottery of standard design and competing with other conventional potters in this country. Yet this tribe had an old tradition of pottery with distinctive designs, and there is little doubt that it would have found a ready market at prices much higher than the machine-produced standard product they were intending to manufacture.

A labor pool from MDTA

The basic tenet of MDTA that training should be for available jobs can be challenged, insofar as the Indian reservations are concerned. We could make no study of the feasibility or advisability of building up a trained labor pool on the reservation which would serve to attract industry. If we consider only training in specific skills, the idea is probably impractical, since predictions of exactly what kind of skills will be likely to attract industry are difficult. However, building up the general work capability of adult Indians, their literacy, their ability to communicate in English, their knowledge of what is demanded in standard working situations in the white man's world—all of these could be done in advance of and in anticipation of employment opportunities on the reservation.

OJT

On-the-job training under MDTA is virtually nonexistent in some areas, particularly in the Southwest. At some places earnest efforts have been made to provide OJT for Indians. Success has not been of the same level as the OJT training for other elements of the population. Part of this was the problem of a proud people who cannot adjust to working conditions, who interpret, often rightly, the tone of voice of foremen and white fellow workmen as indicating contempt or condescension or disrespect for the Indian as a person.

Dropout

Part of it is due to the work habits of the Indian themselves, which include absenteeism and lack of dependability in the white man's sense. Dropout for these reasons is quite heavy. We encountered one plant manager who projected the most rabid prejudice against Indians, yet was managing a plant on a reservation which had and was going to have more OJT trainees.

Lack of communication

In a few instances, we found that on-the-job training which might have been made available to Indians in areas just outside the reservation was not provided because of the lack of knowledge of ES officials serving the reservation and of BIA employment assistance officers concerning the opportunities that were available. Obviously there was a lack of communication somewhere between the BAT representatives and the Employment Service and the Employment Service and BIA on the other. In one particularly flagrant instance where we had been assured by State BAT people that there were numerous opportunities available for Indians, we found an utter lack of knowledge on the part of the people who would have to refer the Indians to such training.

What OJT courses need

On-the-job training with respect to Indians needs much more basic education and orientation into the ways of work built into the courses than OJT ordinarily does even for disadvantaged people. The incidence of dropout, we believe, would be much less if this were done. We consider it essential that any on-the-job training programs in the future, whether done under MDAT under the concentrated employment program, the work incentive program, or any other manpower program, give due consideration to this factor.

H. APPRENTICESHIP

Ignorance about it

It has been our observation in the course of several evaluation studies that knowledge about the purposes of apprenticeship or the regulations governing it, is minimal or nonexistent in nearly all circles except those directly concerned with it. Misconceptions about apprenticeship are rife. Reservation Indians follow the pattern. As a rule they know nothing about apprenticeship. There are a few exceptions, a very few. For example, the construction staff of the Navaho tribe at one time had some apprentices.

At one reservation

At one place visited, the employment service official of a nearby local office serving the reservation did not know what apprenticeship was. In talking to him about it he kept responding in terms that had no relation whatever to an actual apprenticeship program. When apprenticeship was explained to him, he was rather surprised. At the same reservation, the employment assistance official of BIA did not understand the apprenticeship program.

Information about apprenticeship is part of a general body of information which Indian young people should get concerning training and job possibilities outside the reservation. The most apparent source of such information is through the Employment Service representatives on the reservation, if the reservation has one. The second most apparent source is through the employment assistance adviser of the BIA agency on the reservation. The third source is through the school counselors either of BIA schools or public schools. The giving of such information should not be part of a campaign to induce Indian youth to leave the reservation and become apprentices, which should continue to be a matter of individual choice. However, it should be part of the general effort to inform Indians about possibilities for work and training.

I. NEIGHBORHOOD YOUTH CORPS

The BIA school mix

Attempting to assess the overall impact and image of the Neighborhood Youth Corps among reservation Indians is complicated by the fact that many tribal youngsters of high school age attend off-reservation BIA boarding schools, some quite a distance away. The inschool projects conducted in these schools may or may not include the youngsters of a particular tribe.

Thus, in a high school at Ignacio in the Southern Ute Reservation, a number of Indian boarding school pupils live in dormitories on the reservation and attend the public high school there. Most of them are Navahos from the reservation. The inschool NYC project at Ignacio includes, in addition to Navahos, Utes, local Spanish Americans, and Anglos who live within the reservation.

Some reservations conduct inschool NYC projects for reservation youngsters who are attending high school off the reservation; in these cases the tribes furnish employment.

The importance of NYC

No matter how complicated the arrangement or the sponsorship may be, the inschool NYC program has been a godsend to the reservations. The income earned by these youngsters may not seem much to the more affluent, but it is tremendously important to tribal youngsters and constitutes a boost to the tribal economy.

Benefits

In addition to the usual benefits of increased self-confidence caused by having money and being able to buy better clothes, the work experience which these projects give to Indian youngsters is of immense value in bringing them out of their traditional reserve and giving them the ability to communicate better with employers and strangers. The prestige of NYC inschool programs on the reservations is enormous.

There are some objections to NYC wage levels, since adult Indians can't earn this much on the reservation or off, other than in federally sponsored programs.

Big deficiency

The principal deficiency of the inschool NYC projects on the reservations visited was that there simply were not enough slots even to begin to fulfill the need.

Some needs for help

Some school officials fear that if there were more slots, it might be difficult to find proper work-training assignments for the youngsters with an adequate distribution of supervisors. However, indications are that more teachers' aides are needed. Also (and to the best of our knowledge this has not been seriously considered by the Neighborhood Youth Corp leadership as being necessary or advisable), most of the reservations could use good Indian high school students as tutors for their youngsters who are falling behind and about to drop out, and for adults who wish to learn to read, write, and speak English. This could offer an excellent opportunity for some NYC youngsters not only to earn money but to be of particular use to their tribe.

Vacant slots and selection of relatives

On one fairly typical reservation CAP officials informed us that 500 youths on the reservation appeared to qualify for 30 NYC slots. Because of this they tried to select those from the poorest families. In many reservations all the Indian families meet the criteria for the Neighborhood Youth Corps. Yet, vacant slots exist sometimes because of misunderstandings and delays, and general lack of experience in dealing with the white man's mores and laws. Selection of relatives is a problem on most of the reservations, since what the white man calls "nepotism" with a derogatory connotation is an accepted ethical manner of behavior among Indians. They are often unable to understand why they should not select close relatives.

Politics

Tribal politics also enter into the NYC picture. At the time of our visit to the gigantic Navajo reservation they had no NYC project because of the conditions brought on by a hard-fought tribal election. In another reservation friction between the CAP leadership and the tribal council chairman was in effect ordering the NYC directors to report directly to him, bypassing the Community Action Agency.

Few out-of-school programs

Relatively few out-of-school programs have been set up. Those we encountered during our visits were on the Hopi, Cherokee, Rosebud, and Red Lake Reservations. One reason for the lag in out-of-school programs is that sometimes the out-of-school programs are in the hands of county and non-Indian local people who are only moderately aware of and sympathetic to the problems of Indians. In one instance the CAP Director stated flatly that he did not want an out-of-school program because he didn't want to reward school dropouts.

Where there are programs and slots, there sometimes appears to be difficulty in keeping them filled because of resistance to required educational activities and because the young Indians toward whom the program is aimed are oftentimes not conditioned to accepting steady work. NYC out-of-school assignments on the reservations are simply considered jobs. Yet the fact that these young Indians are reluctant to engage in this kind of "work" is in itself indicative of the need for these programs, in which they can be positively recruited and counseled to stay in the program, and to learn the obligations and privileges of work for wages, as these are seen by the dominant society.

Leading to later work

It is generally recognized that even with the best of supervision and the best of counseling, NYC can hardly lead to a real orientation to the kind of work which will be expected of these youngsters later on. In one small out-of-school reservation project, an innovative arrangement had been made with an employer under which the trainees would work 3 months, including 32 hours per week for NYC and 8 hours for the company, then they would enter full-time employment for the employer. Shortly before our arrival, however, legal questions had arisen because the trainees were in actual production during NYC hours, and the project had to be terminated. The employer did agree to hire all the trainees who were working for him, and thus the project achieved its purpose.

Opportunities for meaningful work

In traveling about over the reservations we saw numerous opportunities for NYC out-of-school work which would, we believe, fall within the legal requirements of these programs, offer a chance for some training even though rudimentary, and be of benefit to the tribe. For example, the roads on many of the larger reservations are very poorly marked or not marked at all. A stranger on the reservation often cannot determine which road to take even from the imperfect maps. A system of simple wooden road signs or streets signs painted and lettered by stencil would be of considerable benefit. The tribe or BIA could furnish the equipment and materials. The NYC trainees could do the work. Substandard housing could be repaired by NYC trainees, with BIA furnishing material and supervision. Recreation spots can be built.[1]

Any project is beneficial which provides an introduction to working for a supervisor under conditions requiring steady attendance. In-school or out-of-school trainees who work in tribal headquarters and for BIA on the reservation obtain valuable training. On the Navaho reservation where they were used as community aides and park recreation aides the additional benefits of these public contact jobs are apparent. Also on the Navaho reservation some of the youngsters in the previous NYC project worked at the Employment Service branch office where they could learn methods of applying for jobs and talking to people.

The matter of guidance

All of these assignments are valuable. They would be more valuable if they could be accompanied by effective counseling, guidance, and information about working conditions, working opportunities, limita-

[1] These possibilities for NYC out-of-school activities could as well be applied to Operation Mainstream.

tions on working opportunities and the like. Sometimes this is available through NYC officials who know the youngsters personally and talk to them individually when problems arise. Provided the NYC officials have sufficient knowledge, such informal guidance can be of immense value to the youth. The nominal role which the Employment Service plays in vocational counseling of NYC trainees should be increased. One of the principal needs of the Indian youngster is information about the outside world, what he might do there, what the pitfalls are, and what the opportunities are. Also, there is a need to dispel misconceptions.

The Boys' Club at Cherokee

One of the most imaginative and successful uses of the Neighborhood Youth Corps was encountered on the North Carolina Reservation where work for youngsters in the out-of-school program includes various jobs supervised by the Boys' Club: jobs in fish management, as safety aides, bus captains, lawnmower crews, and mechanics, and in construction work, carpentry work and the like. The Boys' Club, which began as the Boys' Farm Club, has been incorporated since 1964; it operates a cooperative fertilizer and feed business, building supplies cooperative, auto shop, school bus company, etc. The manager of the club is a former NYC director and vocational education teacher who often aids in the unofficial counseling of NYC youth. The majority of the supervisors in the club at one time were NYC trainees themselves. Several current bus drivers on the reservation were formerly bus captains or safety aides. The club sells farm and building supplies on a nonprofit basis. An NYC graduate is the manager of the farm and building supply section and NYC trainees deliver, and act as salesmen. The club repairs and maintains all vehicles of the tribe. Club buildings were built by the NYC trainees, who do wiring, plumbing, laying of foundations, carpentry work, and the like.

Features and advantages

The advantages of this type of operation are obvious, not only for the immediate tasks performed but also from the training. A feature of the trainees' experience here is that a number of the boys rotate jobs to obtain a wider range of experience. The club has classroom facilities which are useful in remedial and supplementary classes. This operation, which is so closely linked with the NYC program of the Cherokee Reservation, is of such significance that we urge that it be studied by BWTP officials and by other tribes.

NYC slots outside reservations for reservation Indians

The NYC projects on the reservations would be more valuable to the Indians if training slots could be established in nearby cities outside the reservations where the trainees could become better acquainted with the job expectations of white employers. This would not necessarily be aimed at encouraging the Indians to remove from the reservations. Most of these tribes are trying to bring industry and employment to the reservation, and this type of NYC training would create a better trained work force for prospective employers. Under the present NYC system this would be very difficult without the establishment of local coordinating groups. Also the transportation problem is very real for the reservations, and a busing system would probably have to be worked out.

Followup

Although in the reservation NYC projects visited there was very little post-training followup, the populations of most of the reservations were small enough for the officials to know rather well what happened to each youngster when he completed his NYC training. However, this informal followup should be firmed up and made a part of the NYC system.

Use of NYC earnings

An ingenious method of determining what is being done with the money earned by NYC in-school youngsters was tried in the Cherokee Reservation. There had been criticism that the NYC program simply provided money for buying alcohol and cars. In August 1966, the $8,000 payroll was made up entirely of rare $2 bills. It was possible to trace these bills and check on how the money was spent. It was discovered that most of it was turned over to grocery stores and some to clothing stores as far away as Asheville, North Carolina. Very little was discovered in taverns or liquor stores.

Alcoholism, however, is a problem in some reservations with out-of-school trainees. It causes absenteeism, and sometimes leads to dissipation of NYC earnings.

Criticisms

Criticism of the NYC program followed the usual lines: not enough counseling, sometimes inadequate supervision, and occasionally that the trainees didn't have to work hard enough. An intelligent criticism was given by a BIA official who said that many Indian youngsters are reluctant to meet the public and prefer the sheltered jobs which NYC now offers. He felt that a good counseling program might identify such youngsters and encourage them to get into jobs where they can meet the public.

Transportation

Transportation on the reservations is always a problem, particularly on the larger reservations, since NYC out-of-school trainees have to find a way to get to the work site.

Educational materials

Another problem is the difficulty in getting materials for remedial education. In one tribe where they attempted to start remedial education they had no guidance, tried local resources through GSA without result, went to nearby air bases and found that the materials were too advanced. This would seem to be an area where materials from the national office would be useful.

Personal difficulties

On the poorer reservations the conditions under which Indian youngsters have been reared and the cultural differences between them and the whites affect their response to training programs, whether labeled Neighborhood Youth Corps or something else. Their reserve and shrinking from contact which teachers and others often call backwardness, their sensitivity to charges that they are dirty and smell bad, and their feeling that they are rejected by white youngsters and by white supervisors, lead to extensive dropout from NYC and from school. Youth from many areas retain tribal religious feelings which are misunderstood and mocked, sometimes even by Mexican-American youths whose poverty may approach their own.

In passing, we should note that the summer N YC programs in all reservations were universally approved and generally considered successful. However, there was distress in several locations because more trainee slots were not made available in the summer.

Separate Indian NYC

The problems of N YC programs on the reservation as well as their potentialities are sufficiently different from those of N YC programs elsewhere in our society to warrant, we believe, serious consideration for the establishment of a separate N YC Indian program under much the same theory as the separate Indian CAP program in OEO.

Great potential

As we see the N YC program both in-school and out-of-school, it offers more at the present time to brighten the future of the reservation Indians than any other Department of Labor manpower program. The potential of the N YC program has hardly been tapped. There is opportunity here for some work in developing some really meaningful activity, staffed by youngsters, who can learn much that is valuable at the same time they are producing much that is beneficial to their tribes. The opportunity is far greater than the present limited allotment of slots can show.

J. OTHER MANPOWER PROGRAMS

Benefits of mainstream

1. *Operation Mainstream.* On reservations, work programs are needed for older Indians whose capabilities and prospects are much more limited than any of the younger Indians, who often have insurmountable language problems, and whose lack of skills has made them unemployable outside the reservations. There could hardly have been a better model developed for such people than Operation Mainstream as we have observed it on the reservations. Most of the projects have concerned the preparation of tourist facilities, cleaning up beside the roads, planting, and beautification. These are the kinds of things which older men without skills and without knowledge of English can do well under proper supervision. They are also the kinds of things in which they and the tribe can take pride. They add to the sum of self-respect on the reservation and in addition provide a source of funds and a boost to the tribal economy. Examples of Operation Mainstream participants obtaining work from other employers as a result of their mainstream experience are numerous enough to indicate that this kind of benefit should not be minimized. However, the most important benefit to the individual is to the older Indian of substandard health and capability who would have no chance whatever to earn any money for himself and his family without this.

Collaboration

Where cooperation with other Federal efforts on the reservation can be accomplished in skill training, language, and literacy training, legal advice, health assistance, and the like, the benefits of Operation Mainstream can be greatly enhanced.

Problems

There are not enough of these programs. Tribal leaders do not understand them; CAP officials, if they understand them, have sometimes been unable to muster the necessary enthusiasm or support for them; there are problems of organization, transportation, and supervision which are simply beyond the capabilities of many tribes. There is turnover, particularly in women who quit to take care of their families, and alcoholism often is present among these older Indians.

Need for information and models

Guidance is badly needed. The evaluators were asked repeatedly for information about Mainstream projects, how they could be gotten off the ground, and so forth. During the time of the visits and the recent transition of the program responsibility from OEO to BWP, the field representatives of BWP were not particularly well versed in Operation Mainstream and were unable to give often times the kind of details, advice, and guidance which was necessary. As this report is being written we hope this difficulty has been cleared up. If not, it is strongly suggested that BWTP officials should hold institutes or orientation courses for their field personnel on Operation Mainstream.

Problems of title V

2. *Title V of the Economic Opportunity Act.*—Although title V programs were being phased out in anticipation of the new work incentive program, its successor, some of the problems and lessons learned from the small number of title V programs in operation on the reservations are important. The rather generous payments to heads of families, and the certain knowledge of many that at the end of the title V program the wage earners would be unable, no matter what kind of jobs they got, to go into the job market and obtain as much money, were a hindrance to effective placement after the program. Transportation often has proved to be an almost insurmountable problem for Indian title V trainees. Differences in the administration of the welfare system between the local counties and BIA have effectively blocked programs in some places.

There was a real lack of imaginative thinking about what the title V program can do, and in none of the reservations visited did we see the highly successful rebuilding of homes of welfare clients which was being carried on in Sandoval County, N. Mex. There was also a real problem of coordinating aims between those administering the program and the Employment Service.

A problem concerning Indians

3. *Job Corps.*—Although the Job Corps is not a Labor Department manpower program, the Labor Department is involved, since Employment Service representatives often do recruiting for the Corps. We learned from our visits that there is a very real problem with respect to Indians and Job Corps which the Job Corps has apparently not solved. The problem is that the cultural differences between the Indians who go to the Job Corps camps and the larger number of Negroes there are so great that really beneficial results for the Indians are very difficult to achieve. Dropout is very heavy. Indian youngsters are naturally shy and reserved, and less addicted to the types of aggressive behavior which are learned in the ghettos. This contributes to the inevitable homesickness of the Indian youngster away from the reservation. Our very limited experience leads us to the suggestion that perhaps the Job Corps is unsuitable for reservation Indians and recruitment efforts there should be dropped. This is a suitable subject for further study by OEO.

Effect on tribes

4. *Other Community Action Programs on Reservation.*—Many of these with manpower components or overtones are well known and there is no need to describe them here. CAP projects on reservations have a general record of success. The CAA is usually one of the largest employers in the tribe, and much of the professional and administrative capability of educated members of the tribe is concentrated in the CAP leadership. With the exception of MDTA, the Labor Department manpower programs which have an effect of the reservation are practically always administered by CAP. Withdrawal of CAP funds and CAA leadership from reservations would be a very heavy blow to the Indians.

III. URBAN INDIANS

A. GENERAL SITUATION AND CONDITIONS

Small number

An attempt was made to study urban Indians, particularly the Indians in Denver, Albuquerque, Los Angeles, Phoenix, Oklahoma City, Tulsa, Minneapolis-St. Paul, and Seattle. Pieces of information were secured about Indians in smaller places in Duluth and Gallup. From the beginning we were surprised at the small numbers of Indians living in cities. Many figures concerning urban Indians which we have seen in books and have heard appear to be greatly exaggerated. That there are no reliable statistical sources for data on urban Indian population was discovered early in this study, and we had to depend upon the best local estimates we could find. In Denver, which we had been told was a principal center for urban Indians, the best estimate we could get was that the Indian population ranged from 2,500 to 3,000 and that the Indian population there had been close to this number for several years in spite of the very heavy influx and large turnover.

Examples

In the Los Angeles metropolitan area, there are possibly 15,000 to 20,000 altogether who have come from all parts of the Southwest. In Seattle, a major Indian center, there are 6,000, more or less; and in Minneapolis-St. Paul, 8,000 to 10,000. In Albuquerque, surrounded as it is by Indians, one would expect a large urban Indian population. However, there are only a few thousand. In Tulsa and Oklahoma City, valid statistics are impossible, because of the mixture in Indian blood in the general population; but it was stated that the number of persons on tribal rolls living in these cities is small. In Phoenix, the number is indeterminate; but there, as elsewhere, the best estimates indicate that the permanent Indian population is small.

Indian mobility

Indians come to the cities looking for work; they may find work; they may work for a while; then they go back to the reservation to be replaced by someone else. Those who are relocated by BIA to such centers as Los Angeles and Denver often return to the reservation after having worked a few months or years. During our visits, we did not encounter the floating summer Indian population created by the seasonal migration of Indians from Arizona and New Mexico into cities in Utah and elsewhere to work during the summer, but who return to their southwestern homes during the winter. This seasonal influx sometimes gives rise to exaggerated figures about urban Indian populations.

Reasons for urban turnover

Some reasons for the instability of the Indian population in the cities have been mentioned above—their attachment to the reservations, and (in Oklahoma and Wisconsin) to their rural tribal areas, their inability to adjust to the conditions of living in the city, their exploitation and cheating by unscrupulous white people in the cities their inability to get ahead because of the demands of visiting relatives, and their own lack of knowledge of how to manage their money. Another reason has only been hinted at—the overpowering pressure and ugliness of life in the slums where the Indians so often reside, and the contrast between this life and reservation life, which, although deprived economically, at least is relatively relaxed, with real values of friendship and a sense of belonging. The result is homesickness for the tribe, for the sheltered society of the reservation, for the comfort of the extended family, for the security which the tribal tradition and ceremonies can give.

Indians of various tribes in the cities

Since the Indians in the cities come from various tribes, they have an "Indianness" which is not so apparent on the reservations. That is, they look upon themselves as Indians to some degree, rather than as Papagos, Navajos, or Blackfeet, and will cooperate with numbers of other tribes. Most of the cities have Indian centers, some created by individual initiative, some by particular churches, or by other organizations. These centers attempt to offer places of gathering, places of consultation, and, in some instances, legal and even financial assistance. Their success depends a great deal upon the skill of the management. Many of the Indian managers have little experience in the kind of management which this kind of center requires: thus, some are successes; many are failures.

After BIA

The Indian who is brought to the city by a BIA relocation project finds it hard to shake off his BIA dependence. However, BIA has a time limit for assisting him, and after this has passed, he theoretically is dependent upon whatever apparatus is available to non-Indians in the city for employment and other assistance.

Discrimination

The matter of discrimination against Indians in the urban setting is very hard to define. Discrimination undoubtedly exists, and at places is quite heavy. Some of it is based on a few unfortunate experiences which employers have had with Indians, and the tendency of Americans to generalize on the basis of very limited experience. Thus, an employer who has had one Indian employee who was absent every Monday because he was in jail for drunkenness, may refuse to hire any other Indians in the fear that they're all that way. Employers in Oklahoma City might refuse to hire any Indians "who look like Indians" from any part of the State on the basis of a few unfavorable experiences with some of the less cultured Indians from the northwestern part of the State.

In the Southwest

In the Southwest, with the exception of western Oklahoma, we did not encounter as much discrimination based on racial antipathy, as is prevalent in some of the Northern States. The reverse discrimination mentioned above, in which employers are anxious to hire Indians, appears to be present only in the Southwest, particularly in Denver and Phoenix.

Variations in attitude toward Indians

In ethnically conglomerate cities like Gallup, racial discrimination is virtually nonexistent; Indians may even have an advantage in employment. Stores and other public institutions want Indians who can deal with their Indian customers; speak their language, and so forth. In Tulsa, the possession, of Indian blood, or being "full blood," is actually a mark of distinction, and may bring advancement. In California, the proportion of Indians is so small that attitudes pro or con do not seem to have crystallized. Here, however, Indians often share in prejudice against the Mexican-Americans. In Seattle, the visibility of the "skid row" Indians, mentioned by several informants and observed by us, leads to a stereotyped unfavorable Indian image which contributes to job discrimination, although it was reported that the Boeing Co., the principal employer, does not discriminate.

Their work

Occupations of urban Indians, like those of the white, range from unskilled to professional. The professionals are less visible, in the cities having merged into white society. The skilled workmen, often trained and relocated with BIA help, and their families furnish much of the clientele of the Indian centers and Indian organizations. The unskilled or poorly skilled, who drift in and out of the urban areas, can usually find only menial or day labor work in the cities, if they can find work at all.

B. EMPLOYMENT OFFICE CONTACTS

Little special effort

In the larger cities the small proportion of the Indian population minimizes their importance in regular employment office business. Ethnic records are not kept, there is little special effort made to serve Indians as such, and counselors and interviewers are not specially trained (with a very few exceptions) or oriented toward the problems of Indians. The misconceptions of the general population (that Indians are supported by the Government, that they are lazy and don't want to work, etc.) are often shared by ES personnel in the cities.

There is apparently no conscious discrimination by ES personnel, in the larger cities, and most of those we interviewed, seemed anxious to help Indians, but the insignificance of the group as an urban minority, plus the fact that the BIA employment assistance offices in the cities are concerned with relocatees for six months after relocation, has lessened the frequency of outreach and contact.

Need for orientation

ES personnel in cities with Indian population need orientation and training in the problems and characteristics of the Indians who move into their cities.

The Indians' point of view

On the other side of the coin, Indians who come from reservations have little knowledge of State Employment Services, and tend to ignore them in the cities, even when they are unemployed. They often try to obtain employment assistance from the BIA office, which may try to send them to the ES office. Rather than face the unknown, however, the unemployed Indian may simply drift back to the reservation.

C. URBAN INDIANS IN MDTA

Lack of visibility

In the larger cities Indians are hardly visible in MDTA courses, either institutional or OJT. There are never enough opportunities for all the disadvantaged, no special efforts are made in recruiting to reach the small concentrations of Indians in the cities, and records of Indian participation have usually not been maintained. In these cities, the person who is identifiable as an Indian because of his appearance, his self-proclaimed status, or his recent arrival from a reservation, seldom applies for MDTA training.

In smaller cities near reservations, natually, the proportion of Indian residents and of Indian MDTA enrollees is greater.

Not a priority in cities

We do not feel that the need to increase the participation of urban Indians in MDTA is urgent. The priorities for action in this area lie in the reservations and rural areas. But ES offices should continue to encourage Indians to take available courses, should collaborate more closely with the BIA employment assistance offices located in some of the cities to offer courses to relocatees or other Indians who are underemployed or unemployed. Indian centers should receive literature and visits from ES personnel.

D. APPRENTICESHIPS FOR URBAN INDIANS

Difficulty of spotting

Occasional traces were found of Indian apprentices. For example, out of 15 names picked at random in a spot check with the State Director of Apprenticeship in New Mexico, two individuals were identified as definitely Indian. These were carpenter apprentices. Four Indian ironworker apprentices were reported in Duluth. Generally, however, Indians are not very noticeable in apprentice jobs and in the city areas are hard to identify, particularly if they have common Spanish or British surnames.

Lack of knowledge

The statement was heard several times that Indians don't know about apprenticeships. However, considering the tiny Indian populations of these cities, it is doubtful that their ignorance is any greater than that of other population groups.

Opportunities for apprenticeships

Apparently, in the cities there is little or no prejudice against Indians in apprentice positions. In fact, many informants made the statement that they would be glad to get Indians provided they could do so. In Phoenix and Denver, we were told that those responsible for selecting apprentices would lean over backwards to secure Indian apprentices. In Denver, the opinion was advanced that the Indian youth who was educated well enough to be an apprentice would, like the Negro and the Spanish-American, prefer to get a white collar job because of the prestige attached.

E. URBAN INDIANS AND THE NEIGHBORHOOD YOUTH CORPS

The minuscule Indian urban population does not offer a fertile source for recruitment for NYC. There are a few here and there; usually, however, the urban Indian who loses his job and whose income drops below the family eligibility level for eligibility to NYC, usually returns to his reservation. There are NYC programs in the Indian schools located in the cities, of course, and these are very important for them. In the Oklahoma cities, where the dividing line between the Indian population and the non-Indian is difficult to discern, there are NYC trainees of all degrees of Indian blood, including a few full-bloods.

IV. OKLAHOMA INDIANS

A. GENERAL SITUATION AND CONDITIONS

Present status

The Oklahoma Indians do not live on reservations. This is a salient and important fact and a subject of much confusion. At the Kansas City Manpower Conference in February 1967, the representatives of the Oklahoma tribes were constantly frustrated because discussion all centered around the problems of reservations Indians. At the present time, there are about 65 tribes in Oklahoma, totaling about 65,000 people who own private property, live on farms, or live in the urban setting, and who have almost been assimilated into the dominant society. The tribes still have their special identities and their chairmen are recognized by the Bureau of Indian Affairs. As tribes, they often still own land or mineral rights; they continue to press suits against the U.S. Government; and they show worse conditions of unemployment and illiteracy than the dominant white culture of Oklahoma.

The progress of assimilation

The process toward assimilation is moving at a fast pace among the educated—slower among the less well educated. The children of one of the tribal leaders to whom we talked are in or are planning college, speak only a few words of their tribal language, know a few tribal dances, but have practically no knowledge of Indian culture. This man said, "In 30 years the Indian will be practically extinct. I hate to see the Indian culture go, but this is the price of successfully living in the white man's world." This attitude was frequently met among Indian people in Oklahoma who have achieved middle class educational and economic status.

Differences between East and West

Conditions in eastern Oklahoma, particularly among the "five civilized tribes" (Choctaws, Chickasaws, Cherokees, Seminoles, and Creeks) differ in many essential details from those in western Oklahoma, where most of the Indians are members of the Plains Tribes. The five civilized tribes, and the others associated with them, such as the Osage and the Delaware, are generally considered to have advanced further toward the white man's culture than the Plains Indians in the West. Their almost complete assimilation into the local society is not reflected in the West, particularly in the Northwest, where the Indians are still considered a race apart, and are subject to considerable discrimination. In the eastern part of the State the dividing line between the Indian part of the population and the white population is often impossible to discern. Many tribal members who are prominent in Indian affairs are only one-quarter Indian. The five civilized tribes have a long tradition of intermarriage with whites, some of the most famous chiefs in their history having had only a small fraction of Indian blood.

Wealth and poverty

For the Indians, Oklahoma is a land of contrasts. On one side, there are the wealthy millionaire Indians who have made money in oil; on the other hand, there are the poor, illiterate Indians who can barely speak English or who speak none at all, who must still converse in their own language, and who can read and write in no language, who still harbor considerable resentment against their treatment by the white man, and who resist assimilation.

Difficulty of generalization

In such a setting, statistics about "Indians" are hard to come by. Generalizations which are made by Oklahoma informants usually, upon further questioning, turn out to be made about those who are predominantly Indian; that is, those who are one-half Indian or more.

Rise and decline

For the past several decades, the Indians in Oklahoma have appeared to drop behind the white population in material and educational progress. There was a time in the history of the State when some of the tribes, particularly the five civilized tribes, were progressing faster than other Americans, and in the fullness of prosperity and cultural richness, their autonomous "nations" were rapidly reaching a pinnacle which would have created envy in most any group. However, the participation on the side of the Confederacy led to harsh action after the Civil War, and a gradual retrogression.

Many of the cultural characteristics of reservation Indians have been retained by the Oklahoma Indians. They still have the tendency to share their property with one another, the inclination to cling to their home communities and to return to them, the maintenance of the extended family, and the like.

Considering assimilation

Oklahoma is one of the centers of the "New Indians", representatives of a militant movement attempting to retain an Indian identity. There are also strong "conservative" Indian societies in Oklahoma ("Conservative" to an Indian, means one who is attempting to preserve Indian traditions, religion, and language). There is an unspoken but increasingly important alliance between the two groups.

Discrimination

Discrimination against the Indians in Oklahoma is present. In Oklahoma City it was reported by a Negro leader that there is widespread discrimination against Indians "who look like Indians", but little or no discrimination against Indians who look like white people.

We encountered at places the stereotyped conception that Indians are untrustworthy, drink a great deal, and generally make unreliable employees. Such opinions were more prevalent in the western portion, and for the most part has to do with Plains Indians who have not yet been so fully acculturated. One employment service official working in eastern Oklahoma, but who had come from western Oklahoma, said that he had been surprised at the difference in attitude.

Whether or not the reservation is a community with well-defined limits in which the Indian can maintain his own identity and to some extent rule his own destiny, or whether it is, as some contend, a continuing symbol of discrimination, the fact is that the lack of reservations in Oklahoma has created some special problems. The Indians for the most part are anxious to retain the racial and tribal identities, but find it more and more difficult. Where the tribes are intermixed in the same locality, as is the rule rather than the exception, the conflicts of tribal loyalties and the possibility of discrimination by officials with affiliations in one tribe against members of another tribe are always present.

Separate Indian identity

The Oklahoma Indians, at least their leaders, want to be considered as a separate group with separate problems. Yet, officially, most elements in Oklahoma have erased the outward symbols of segregation and differentiation so that many administrators take great pride in not knowing who is an Indian and who is not an Indian.

The problem this poses for Federal and State officials is mainly one of emphasis, direction, and identification.

B. EMPLOYMENT AND THE ES

Conditions of employment

Many of the Indians in Oklahoma do farm labor. This work is dwindling. Formerly, in the eastern portion, thousands of them worked in the timber industry, but the timber is now exhausted and this means of livelihood has disappeared. Most of the Indians who are employed in Oklahoma are employed in services outside the larger urban centers and in the factories scattered throughout the State. Much of their work is intermittent and seasonal, which partly explains their poverty. There is a consensus that the Indians in Oklahoma are unemployed and underemployed to a much greater extent than whites.

The close connections of the Employment Service of Oklahoma with Indian groups, the large number of ES employees who have varying portions of Indian blood, and the general lack of any kind of orientation toward discrimination insure that over most of the State Indians do not look upon the Employment Service as an agent of discrimination. Employment Service staff members encountered by us who expressed the stereotyped prejudices about Indians were few.

Employment Service and lower strata Indians

This identification with the Indians of Oklahoma by the Employment Service does not necessarily mean that the Indians look upon the Employment Service with a universally favorable image. The large number of Indians with poor education lack marketable skills. In the rural areas of Oklahoma there is little employment for them. In the urban areas such as Tulsa, practically any Indian who is willing to work can find a job. Often, however, his qualifications insure that the work to which the Employment Service can refer him must be of the casual laborer or lower paid service type. This creates some resentment, and there is some feeling on the part of Indians that they are being deliberately kept underemployed by the government structure.

Little help to unskilled Indians

A State welfare official said that the Employment Service offered no real help to people without marketable skills. An Urban League official said that the Employment Service is not effective with low-income groups. An Employment Service official stated that the disadvantaged are reticent about coming to the employment office to apply for work.

Favorable part of the image

A Cherokee tribal official, however, stated that even back in the hills, practically all of the Cherokees are familiar with the Employment Service, but they don't come in because the Employment Service can give them no jobs, and because they have no cars to travel to the employment office; they have no education, no mobility.

Favorable comments

A BIA official in Oklahoma stated that the State employment service is receptive toward doing everything possible toward helping the Indians. A chief of a prominent tribe said that he encourages Indians to register at the Employment Service because sometimes jobs outside the State result, that Indians hear about the Employment Service from word of mouth, that sometimes they use the Employment Service to get directions toward migrant work, then may go out on their own.

Negative part

Most of the Indians, irrespective of their feeling concerning the effectiveness of the Employment Service, indicated that the Employment Service had very few jobs for them. In western Oklahoma, where the Employment Service faces its greatest problems because of employer attitude toward Indians, this pessimism seemed to be greater.

New efforts

The moves of USES to strengthen its capability for serving Indians have benefited Oklahoma. Newly appointed Indian HRD representatives late in 1967 were making manpower surveys and analysis in areas of Indian population. The Oklahoma State Employment Service has prepared information packets for distribution to tribal groups and others.

Location of YOC's

The YOC's in Oklahoma City and Tulsa have made earnest efforts to improve their capacity for service to Indians, including Indians on the staff and outreach capability. However, both these YOC's are handicapped by extremely inconvenient locations on upper floors of downtown office buildings. The employment service role with respect to NYC youngsters in Oklahoma varies greatly from area to area. In most instances, the relationships are good, and the employment service will furnish whatever services are requested of them by the NYC sponsoring staff.

C. MDTA TRAINING

Lack of outreach

The employment service's lack of outreach capability affects enrollment in MDTA courses, since only those Indians who are alert enough, well-enough oriented to urban society, or who are brought to the employment office by knowledgeable friends or community organizations are in line for MDTA enrollments. The general lack of discrimination and race consciousness on the part of employment service personnel, prevalent in much of the State, strangely enough seems to work to the detriment of Indian participation in MDTA. The employment service officers are so conscientious about taking people who come to the office irrespective of race that the nonaggressive Indian who stays in the background and who would, were he approached, be quite anxious to enroll in an MDTA course, often doesn't get the opportunity.

MDTA boarding classes

In Oklahoma, much MDTA training is concentrated in training centers run by existing schools, such as Northeastern State College and the Okmulgee Technical Institute. The trainees are sent in from other parts of the State on a subsistence basis and are actually boarding students. This is a good device for a heavily rural State with limited vocational training facilities and is indicative of an earnest desire to make the benefits of MDTA available to all people in the State. It is also consistent with our recommendations in previous evaluation reports concerning the establishment of MDTA training centers.

Lack of ethnic data

However, attempts to determine the number of Indians who were benefiting from this arrangement fell rather flat. To begin with, the instructors didn't know who was an Indian and who was not; no ethnic record was kept. When knowledge was pooled and people's personal knowledge of who was an Indian and who was not was called upon, it was found that the number of actual Indians, that is, those one-quarter Indian or more, was proportionately quite small.

OJT in western Oklahoma

The OJT project at Sequoyah Mills Anadarko (400 slots plus proposal for 360 slots at Elk City funiture plant and negotiating 300 slots at another subsidiary) should be mentioned as an example of what can be done in training Indians for steady work on permanent jobs.

D. NYC

Where tribes sponsor NYC

The Neighborhood Youth Corps program in the Indian regions of Oklahoma has a bright and positive look, and is rather popular with the Indians. The Osages and Cherokees are sponsors of extensive NYC programs covering not only their own tribesmen, but members of other Indian tribes and white people, and Negroes as well, over several counties. Indians are proud of these programs, and very proud of the fact that the tribes are sponsoring them. Much of the initiative in sponsoring them is due to suggestions and assistance rendered by the Bureau of Indian Affairs in developing and preparing the proposals.

However, their administration has been in the hands of the Indians themselves, and has been carried on with imagination and initiative.

Followup at Pawhuska

The Osage project with headquarters at Pawhuska gave us a view of the most careful system of followup and the most positive connection with the employment service that we have yet found in NYC in-school or out-of-school projects. Very careful records are maintained the youngsters are followed after they leave both the in-school and out-of-school projects, and the directors of the project themselves do not hesitate to make special arrangements for a particular youngster to be given special attention at the employment office in Tulsa, or elsewhere in the area.

Early prejudice

In the early stages of the NYC program when the NYC sponsors attempted to find training slots for Indians and Negroes in Oklahoma City, it was stated that they encountered a great deal of prejudice against both Indians and Negroes, and that people were reluctant to work with either Indians or Negroes. Once the introduction was made, however, there was no more difficulty. Some officials indicated that they felt that NYC had done a lot around Oklahoma to break down some of the remaining prejudice.

Reductions

In Oklahoma, as in other Southwestern States we visited, there had been a substantial reduction in NYC slots during the second year of operation which caused a great deal of trauma.

Recruiting

Much of the recruiting was done by employment service in places where the employment service has the capability. However, the lack of outreach capability by the employment service, lack of travel funds, and so forth, has greatly inhibited employment service usefulness in recruitment. There is a problem in the recruitment of Indians in the rural areas. Unlike reservation Indians, they are reported to be suspicious of Federal programs and to pay very little attention to the average white who comes around attempting to persuade them to undertake some governmental program. Indian outreach personnel are needed.

Counseling

A substantial amount of counseling of out-of-school trainees is going on. Most of it, however, is not done by the employment service, but by counselors hired by the sponsors. The Indian youngsters badly need continuing advice and guidance.

Placement

Placement by the employment service is spotty. In some cases, particularly where there are close connections between the NYC sponsor and the employment service, it is fairly good. In other places, there is no real attempt to have the former NYC trainee placed by the employment service. In many instances, the NYC sponsors run their own job development centers to locate jobs. Followup, generally, except for the Indian-sponsored projects already mentioned, is nominal.

A report has been received from Oklahoma on 1966 high school graduates who were in the Cherokee NYC project. Out of a total of 623 graduates, 254 (41 percent) were in college, 178 (28 percent) were employed in industry, 69 (11 percent) were in the Armed Forces, 39 (6 percent) were unemployed, and the others were married, or could not be traced.

Indian boarding school

An interesting facet of the Osage project is that in their area they have a BIA Indian school which has 250 Eskimos in it. These Eskimo children did not arrive with clothing suitable for the climate. They, and many other children there, have no income source at all. NYC, for those who are fortunate enough to be chosen, furnishes an income for them. However, at the time of the visit there were 1,100 Indian children in school, most of them eligible for NYC, and only 10 NYC slots were available. This indicates the tremendous need. NYC sponsoring officials hoped that the summer NYC program would help this matter. They indicated that some of the Indian kids were so hungry for work, and needed any amount of money so badly, that they would ask for as little as 1 hour of work, although this was completely impractical. As a result of conditions at this boarding school, the dropout rate was very, very heavy.

Oklahoma City dropouts

Despite the popularity of NYC with Indians and despite the need which it fulfills, many of the Indian youngsters have real problems and the dropout from NYC's out-of-school program is relatively heavy. For example, in an NYC out-of-school project of 125 enrollees in Oklahoma City, of whom 12 were Indians, there were only four Indians left at the time of the visit. Eight other Indians had dropped out. Their reasons, as given by the sponsors:

(1) Male, on probation and ran away because he couldn't stay put;

(2) Female, irregular, ran off, picked up by the law, which took her back to the girl's training school;

(3) Female, irregular, became pregnant;

(4) Female, quit to enroll in an MDTA course;

(5) Male, was recommended for full-time employment but his police record was found out; after that he started straying off irregularly, and finally quit;

(6) Male, simply quit, no reason known;

(7) Female, disappeared and could not be located;

(8) Male, married, left for reasons not known.

The problems of many Indian families in an urban society are well illustrated by the above. The youngsters drift toward delinquency, the parents towards alcoholism, and it could be said that their urge to return to the reservation or their marginal farms is really an instinct for survival.

Rural dropout

But dropout problems are not confined to urban Indians. In two rural counties between Tulsa and Oklahoma City with almost exclusively Indian populations, 45 had been enrolled in the last 18 months, and practically all had dropped out. The field representative of the sponsor said that the principal cause underlying their dropping out was lack of home discipline, the permissiveness of the Indian family in which they had been raised was responsible, If they felt a little bad, they didn't come in. If they got drunk over the weekend, they wouldn't come in on Monday, and might not come back at all. They are also in constant trouble with the police. This description appeared to apply to one or two particular tribal groups in this area, and was not echoed in other counties within the same project. As indicated earlier in this report, there is a great deal of variation among tribes.

Inschool problems

The difficulties of adjustment are also noticeable in the inschool project. A county school official made almost the same statement as the out-of-school field representative concerning the lack of initiative, lack of concern, lack of discipline in the home.

NYC social problems

He said they were not dependable on the job. Many of them had very rough home situations. The marriage customs of the white people don't mean a whole lot in some of the tribes. One high school boy who was in the NYC program had been living in the home of a half-sister who was pregnant, father unknown. This boy himself had a 14-year-old girl living with him and she was pregnant. The school arranged the marriage, helped get them certificates, blood tests, and so forth, got some benefits from BIA, and the like. But at the last minute the girl's mother refused consent, and there was no marriage. These problems, of course, are not radically different from the problems which NYC sponsors face everywhere.

Remedial services

Shortly after our visit to Oklahoma, funds were made available by BWP for remedial services in some of the projects. However, there was no indication at the time that the sponsors would be able to extend this into future years. Remedial services and supportive services are very badly needed by the Indians.

Lack of vocational counseling

The lack of vocational counseling by experienced and knowledgeable vocational counselors, both for in-school trainees and out-of-school trainees, was freqently mentioned. In some cases they attempt to get this through BIA or the Employment Service. Wherever the sponsors have asked the Employment Service for group counseling sessions, it has always been available. Apparently, there have been few attempts to get individual vocational counseling from the Employment Service for other in-school trainees or out-of-school trainees. We were told that the Indian youngsters badly need the most elementary information concerning the world of work, the kind of jobs they can get, where they can get them, and the like.

Parent-child relationship

One of the difficulties is that the Indians want to be segregated. Their traditions includes more deference to their elders than is customary in white American society. This means that if an Indian youngster is counseled personally by a non-Indian, he may become confused and go home and report either incorrectly to his parents, or his parents will not understand this third-hand information about what the counselor has recommended. The youngsters are very hesistant to move without the consent of their elders. An Indian counselor will recognize this and take it into account, is more likely to put it into terms which the parents will understand, and may be in a position to talk with the parent themselves.

Trainability a criterion

One NYC sponsoring official presented what he considered a real problem. He said that with the increasing emphasis on education of NYC trainees instead of merely giving them work, a screening will be made for trainability, and thus the really hard-core kids, the retarded, the bottom-of-the-barrel will be eliminated. He said that there was a ruling that no out-of-school youngster can stay in the program more than 6 months unless he had at least 6 hours of supportive services, and that some of the enrollees really were not up to the level where they could take the supportive services which were needed. He could, he thought, get an exception for these, but the problem was illustrative of the growing emphasis on trainability.

If the basic purpose of NYC is simply to take the youngsters off the streets and give them an introduction to work and an income for a short time, this official's argument would make considerable sense. However, it does seem that the task of training NYC youngsters is an important one and so long as exceptions are possible from the rules, the emphasis on training should be continued.

Transfer out-of-school to inschool

It was in Oklahoma that the difficulty in transferring out-of-school NYC trainee enrollees to inschool slots became most dramatic. Instances were brought to our attention where out-of-school trainees wanted to return to school, should be encouraged to return to school, but could not return to school without some income. Attempts to work them into the local on-going inschool slots had run into difficulty because (1) the inschool slots were filled, and (2) there was a waiting list. Usually the inschool and out-of-school trainees had differing sponsors. In an instance where they had the same sponsor, the Osage project, it was stated that this could always be worked out. Elsewhere the necessity for some kind of flexibility to permit this was not apparent. Since one of the purposes of the NYC out-of-school program is to encourage youngsters to go back to school, it would seem that something should be done to make this kind of process easier.

V. TESTING OF INDIANS

Lower scores on GATB verbal

It is to be expected that Indians who are not completely fluent in English will score lower on the verbal portions of the general aptitude test battery, and such a result was reported by the Employment Service people who administered tests to Indians in the offices which we visited. The difficulty of the Indian in verbal tests is due to (1) usually English is not his native language, not the language in which he originally began to think, and often not the language spoken in his home; and (2) even if English is his natural language, his cultural background is often so different that he has difficulty getting into the proper psychological mood for the test, and in addition many of the questions, or situations, in the tests are foreign to him.

Are tests needed?

In most of the localities we visited, particularly in the Southwest, it was recognized that standard tests were inadequate, or even improper for Indians. Yet they were still given because anything else was lacking, and possibly because it was felt that they were required. There were indications that the more imaginative Employment Service people were using the test properly as only rough indications of certain abilities, and were not using them as screening devices for Indians. For example, the CAP director from one of the largest pueblos in New Mexico objected strongly to the use of testing on Indians in making selections for MDTA, but was told by the MDTA representative of the Employment Service that the tests were only rough guides, that they recognize the problems of Indians in taking tests, and that test results were ignored in some cases. This happened in other places too. It raises the question as to why the tests should be given at all. Would not other measuring devices, including interviewing, be sufficiently indicative?

Special uses of testing

A more defensible use of testing was apparently made in selecting people for positions in which manual dexterity was necessary. The electronics plant on the Navajo Reservation is an example. Indian women in particular are reputed to have extremely high manual finger dexterity, and apparently in the GATB, they test very highly in this faculty. In a few localities, there are agreements to test the BIA employment assistance clients. Most of these employment assistance clients who are not fluent in English do rather poorly on the verbal portions.

We found the State employment test technicians reluctant to make any comparisons of Indian verbal scores with those of other ethnic groups, since any opinions they have are not based on any kind of scientific evidence. However, it is obvious that the scores of Indians as a group on available tests are lower than those of whites. There are exceptions, especially among tribes where English is the normal language of the homes. Work sample testing was frequently mentioned as being part of the answer. Work was underway toward developing a special set of norms for the Navajos in connection with testing for electronic assembly work.

Some innovations—Why necessary?

There have been attempts to use the IPAT "Culture Fair" test with the Indians. Generally these efforts have not been considered successful. However, a particularly imaginative use of this with monolingual Cherokee speakers in Oklahoma is worthy of note. In recruiting NYC out-of-school trainees for the Wild Life Commission project, many of the youngsters didn't speak English well enough really to be tested. However, once they were persuaded to be tested, the employment service put those who could speak English between others, and reported the results as satisfactory. They then tried the same thing on migrants from Texas, 80 percent of whom had no English, and believed they had good luck there. Again, however, the question arises, if it is necessary in order to get any kind of results to go to such devices, why give the test at all? Why not simply make the selection on the basis of interviews?

VI. Recommendations

A. RECOMMENDATIONS OF AD HOC ADVISORY COMMITTEE

The recommendations of the ad hoc advisory committee to USES on Indian employment programs are repeated below:

1. The Indian desk should be situated at Department level and headed by a person of American Indian ancestry, who would have major responsibility for the coordination of activities between the Federal and State governments, industry, and the community-at-large to bring the Indian population into the mainstream of our economy,

(a) The desk should provide proper interstate coordination of funded programs (when more than one State would be involved), establish priorities and allocate funds as needed programwide rather than along narrow State considerations,

(b) The desk should work closely with unions to assure equal opportunity for Indians in all activities requiring union affiliation,

(c) The desk should help tribes in program development and should facilitate and assist in a fuller utilization of existing federal and State programs which can help to improve the socioeconomic status of Indians,

(d) Research and development should be important functions of the desk. These activities would serve to determine what services were needed in particular kinds of situations involving Indians on and off reservations, and allow for alterations and innovations in programs designed to help the target group. Indians who desire to stay on reservations should be given the opportunity to develop their talents in productive employment thereon. The same should apply to those who desire to seek opportunity elsewhere.

(e) As an extension of the Employment Service, the Indian desk should also be concerned with the administration and dissemination of job market information and should, therefore, be a source of direct assistance to Indians and employers alike,

(f) The desk should not only be concerned with establishing jobs or finding employment for the Indian people, but it should also look into vocational training, employability development, development, and the bringing of industry onto or near a reservation. The Indians should be given maximum exposure to job opportunities and training. Furthermore, considerable efforts must be made to facilitate the individual potential for growth and development, and

(g) The Indian desk should work in close cooperation with the Bureau of Indian Affairs, appropriate units of the Department of Health, Education, and Welfare, and other Federal agencies which have programs relating to the Indian. This will enable the Indian desk to become more involved in the total programs for American Indians.

2. A half-way house program should be established to ease the cultural shock of Indians moving from reservations to an urban environment.

3. Inservice training or OJT training should be encouraged and urged on employers of Indians to upgrade the skills of Indians and make them available to employers on or off reservations.

4. A thorough analysis of the problems and the human and natural resources should be made on the various Indian reservations and in communities with large Indian populations to get at the heart of the economic and social needs of the group.

5. The HRD concept should be utilized to the fullest extent possible to reach Indians, even in the most remote areas and ghettos on or off reservations.

6. The USES and its affiliated State agencies should make maximum use of Indians in staffing local offices and filling outreach positions.

7. Representatives of organized labor should be asked to participate on all committees and in economic development programs at every level—State, national, local.

8. The USES should prepare an information packet of all programs that touch on the problems of Indians. In addition, a packet of materials should be prepared which show success stories of tribal economic and industrial activities.

9. Since the problems of bringing Indians into the mainstream of our economy are so vast and will require the resources of many agencies, the Employment Service should be primarily involved with employability and job development.

10. With proper economic resource inducements, the Employment Service ought to look into the possibility of utilizing local employers as well as large national firms to expand their establishments onto reservations. The support of groups such as Plans for Progress, National Association of Manufacturers, and the Chamber of Commerce should be made available to these groups.

11. Groups of employer representatives should be brought to the reservations and exposed to first-hand information about the successful enterprises already established.

12. Economic Development Corporation should be encouraged and organized on reservations to help the Indians help themselves.

Our findings lead us to agree with all of these recommendations, although there seems to be too much emphasis on moving Indians into urban environments and into the "mainstream," concepts which, in our opinion are rapidly becoming outmoded, which in the past have led to a general record of failure in manpower development, and which will continue to do so in the future.

The committee's recommendations are, of course, general and need to be translated into a specific action program.

Our recommendations are as follows:

B. SENSITIVITY INDOCTRINATION

It is inevitable that the prevalent misconceptions of white people about Indians should be shared by many Federal and State officials. It is less excusable that Federal and State officials who have to work with Indians and to pass on Indian programs should be ignorant of Indian psychology, traditions, or conditions. and should therefore frequently make blunders of fact and relationships. Yet this is constantly happening.

The new Indian specialist heading the Indian desk in the Office of the Manpower Administration will be able to help at the national level. But very badly needed are indoctrination courses conducted by Indians and experts on Indians, somewhat like the seminars given for USES HRD Indian personnel, but more perhaps like the indoctrination given Indian trainees on how to live in the white man's world. The white man who works with Indians needs to know very much about them.

Recommendation No. 1

That the Manpower Administration's new "Indian desk" undertake as an urgent task the development of courses on Indian mores, psychology, traditions, and needs, organized roughly on a regional bases, and that attendance be mandatory for officials of national and regional offices who work with Indians, and strongly recommended for State ES officials.

C. RECRUITMENT OF INDIANS FOR THE MANPOWER ADMINISTRATION

To improve the Department's posture toward Indians, as well as increase the understanding of officials in the area of Indian problems, it is essential that more Indian spokesmen be available in higher level positions. Indians who are willing to work in the cities, and who have the requisite professional qualifications, are hard to find. Positive recruitment efforts are needed. The new Indian desk should take an active part in such recruitment, and the National Congress of American Indians should be called upon for assistance.

Recommendation No. 2

That an active effort be made to recruit knowledgeable and able Indians for high-level positions in the Manpower Administration, the national offices of USES and BWTP, and in the offices of Regional Manpower Administrators and Regional Directors who have Indian tribes in their regions, and that State ES offices be encouraged to do the same.

D. AN OVERALL DEPARTMENT POLICY FOR INDIANS

The conflict between the ideals of total acculturation and retention of tribal identity and traditions cannot be resolved by the Department of Labor, by the Bureau of Indian Affairs or any by other governmental agency. It should not be attempted. The Indians should do it themselves, and the Department of Labor, along with other Government agencies, should assist them, either as a group or as tribes, to attain their objectives.

The Manpower Administration, we believe, should establish a basic policy defining the purpose of manpower programs for Indians, to serve as a framework for planning, as follows:

Recommendation No. 3

That an overall Indian manpower policy of the Department of Labor be established in terms similar to the following: It is the policy of the Department of Labor to help American Indians attain the capability for steady work at standard wages in the locations where the Indians live or nearby, encouraging the Indians, if they wish, to retain their tribal traditions and values. At the same time, provided viable programs to do so can be mounted, and the tribal councils involved specifically request it, the Department of Labor will assist in manpower efforts leading to relocation of of trained Indian workers.

E. CONCENTRATION OF ES EFFORT

Whether or not the above is adopted as department policy, USES should channel its efforts for Indians in directions where they will do the most good.

We can only comment favorably on the earnestness of the national office of USES in its efforts to improve services to Indians. In these efforts, however, there is still considerable dissipation of efforts in the unproductive sphere of attempted assimilation. Badly needed is a sense of direction, a guideline for concentration of limited resources. Because of the above need, limited employment opportunities, and lack of interest by Indians in visiting the employment offices on reservations, some ES representatives lack opportunities for activity.

Recommendation No. 4

That USES concentrate its efforts for Indians into the reservation and rural Indian areas, with the aim of encouraging training and job development in these areas, assisting vigorously in efforts to develop or bring in industry, and counseling and guiding Indians in matters concerning work.

F. GUIDELINES FOR PERSONNEL SERVING INDIANS

The report discussed the feeling of futility resulting from the attempts of State ES personnel to translate regular employment offices to reservations without any real sense of direction or guideline as to what they are expected to do for Indians. The following recommendation results from this.

Recommendation No. 5

That USES prepare and issue guidelines for ES activity in serving Indians, covering items such as (1) department policy, (2) the concept of service by counseling and guiding Indians and helping bring in industry, and (3) the necessity for close collaboration with tribal councils, community action agencies, and BIA.

G. STAFFING ACTION

USES national office efforts to staff the new positions for Indian assistance with qualified Indians have, at a few places, apparently run afoul of State regulations and indifference, inertia, and ineptness on the part of those responsible for recruiting. USES needs to take vigorous action as follows:

Recommendation No. 6

That USES instruct its regional offices to have careful and thorough checks made into the staffing and operation of every position created for the purpose of serving Indians, and to take, or recommend, whatever steps are necessary to carry out the intent of the national office, including securing of changes in State civil service requirements.

H. COORDINATION

The problems of coordination of programs to serve Indians are, in a sense, like such problems everywhere, but there are unique features.

In the manpower field three agencies are primarily concerned; OEO, DOL, and BIA, and (very important) the tribe. Local education officials are concerned where MDTA is involved. Public Health and Department of Agriculture officials should also be involved. There should be a continuing mechanism for effecting coordination and collaboration, so that, among other things the ES and BIA employment staffs can work closely together, so that MDTA and community action programs can be meshed, the ES representatives can come out of their frequent semi-isolation and become a part of community action, and all Federal officials can plan jointly with the Indian tribes themselves.

Recommendation No. 7

That a system of local coordinating committees be developed and promulgated simultaneously by the Manpower Administration, the Office of Economic Opportunity, and the Bureau of Indian Affairs. The initiative should be taken by the Manpower Administrator, inviting the other agencies to participate in preliminary discussions.

I. USE OF COACHES

The problems of newly employed Indians in adapting to the demands of white employers result in heavy absenteeism and turnover. This can and has often been disastrous to OJT programs and continued placement efforts of ES and BIA.

In concentrated employment programs coaches are engaged who counsel newly employed persons, and work with the employers to keep the new employees productive, dependable, and on the job until they have adjusted to the working conditions. These coaches can explain working rules, classifications, union rules, the necessity for promptness and dependability, and so forth.

Something like this is needed generally for Indians. The new Indian personnel of the Employment Service stationed on reservations theoretically could perform this function, although their experience in industry may be limited.

We encountered one example of success in such endeavors by an Indian "community aide" under ES.

Recommendation No. 8

a. That USES actively and vigorously promulgate the concept of followup on the job by Indian ES personnel on reservations, furnishing these personnel needed training in methods of "coaching" and making sure that they have adequate transportation facilities to all parts of the reservations and to nearby cities.

b. That MDTA–OJT institutional projects for Indians include one such Indian "coach" or counselor for every 20 trainees. Such a person would work with the trainees during training, assist in their placement, and continue to work with them after placement.

J. CHANGES IN MDTA PROGRAMS

The handicaps and difficulties of MDTA programs in helping reservation Indians were discussed in the body of the report. Also discussed were the need for crafts training, and training for helper positions among Indians, and the inequities of testing prospective Indian MDTA trainees with standard tests.

Recommendation No. 9

That MDTA be made more responsive to the needs of reservation and rural Indians through the encouragement of:

 a. Training in the traditional Indian crafts;
 b. Training of Indians as helpers in the building trades;
 c. Use of MDTA to establish labor pools on reservations;
 d. Use of other valid means of selection than standard tests.

If there are impediments to any of the above in MDTA policy or in the attitudes of labor union locals, ways of overcoming these obstacles without harm to the overall objectives of MDTA should be vigorously sought.

K. SEPARATE INDIAN NYC PROGRAM

That the Neighborhood Youth Corps represents a shining hope to rural and reservation Indians is abundantly clear. The tragedy lies in the limited number of slots available. The words "drying up" applied to NYC programs for Indians seems to be adequately descriptive. Problems and benefits of NYC among Indians are sufficiently distinct from those of the rest of the population to warrant separate direction for it.

Recommendation No. 10

That the Manpower Administrator create a task force or study group, containing staff planning personnel, BWTP officials and experienced Indian NYC sponsors, to study and make recommendations on the advisability and feasibility of a separate NYC program for Indians.

AN ECONOMIC EVALUATION OF ON-THE-JOB TRAINING CONDUCTED UNDER THE AUSPICES OF THE BUREAU OF INDIAN AFFAIRS: CONCEPTS AND PRELIMINARY FINDINGS

By Loren C. Scott and David W. Stevens*

FOREWORD

In order to insure the effectiveness of Federal programs to assist the Indians, it is necessary to be able to systematically evaluate the the progress made under different programs. Lawrence Scott and David Stevens have developed a conceptual framework for evaluating the private and social benefits of the Bureau of Indian Affairs on-the-job training program. They have applied this model to a sample of 78 trainees, comparing number of months worked in the year and average monthly earnings before and after training. There was a significant increase in the number of months worked and in average earnings following training, but the evidence suggests that this was at least partly due to the recruitment and screening of the trainees, rather than to the training per se. The training periods appeared to be unnecessarily long. It may be that the same benefits could have been obtained with a smaller expenditure of Federal funds.

Introduction

This paper explores the evaluative methodology and preliminary findings from a study of the effectiveness of the Bureau of Indian Affairs on-the-job training program (BIA–OJT). Two other BIA employment assistance programs, direct employment assistance (DE) and adult vocational training (AVT), are not included in this analysis.

The evaluative framework is presented first, followed by a brief outline of the administrative procedures used in carrying out the statutory directives. The tentative findings from interviews with participating employers are presented in a third section, and preliminary analysis of responses to a mailed questionnaire by former trainees follows this. Tentative conclusions are presented in a final section.

I. An Evaluative Framework

Introduction.—The purpose of this section is to introduce the evaluative criteria set that will be used in subsequent pages to study the effectiveness of the BIA–OJT program in achieving its established

---

*David W. Stevens is Associate Professor of Economics, Oklahoma State University. Loren C. Scott is Assistant Professor of Economics, Louisiana State University. The authors wish to thank Jack Jayne and Darrell Williams, area employment assistance officers for the BIA in Oklahoma, for their cooperation during this study. Financial assistance was received from the Manpower Research and Training Center and the Research Foundation, Oklahoma State University, and the Oklahoma Economic Development Foundation.

objective(s). This presentation is a skeletal synthesis of relevant methodological contributions made by our predecessors in evaluating public sector programs.[1] No claim to originality is made although to our knowledge this paper represents the first *application* of economic analysis in evaluating the BIA–OJT program.[2]

PUBLIC SECTOR RESOURCE ALLOCATION AND THE BIA

Public Law 959 states in part, that—
> * * * in order to help adult Indians who reside on or near Indian reservations to obtain reasonable and satisfactory employment, the Secretary of the Interior is authorized to undertake a program of * * * on-the-job training * * * [3]

The Chief of the Branch of Employment Assistance, BIA, states that:
> All of the various activities of the employment assistance program are directed toward employment. * * * On-the-job training is the activity whereby employment is immediate and the individual learns while working.[4]

This statement of purpose, or single-factor objective, appears to be explicit enough at first glance. However, employment is not usually desired as an end itself, but rather serves as a surrogate for two other objective factors; namely, increased income (consumption) and a redistribution of income (consumption). [6, p. 23; and 4, pp. 177 ff.]

Recognition of a multifactor objective suggests the need for a quantitative weighing of the component elements. [3] Otherwise, there is no basis for evaluating the relative effectiveness of the program in achieving each of its multiple objectives. For purposes of this paper, it is assumed that only redistribution of income is considered in BIA–OJT program decisionmaking.[5]

Two levels of decisionmaking *are not* considered here, although it is recognized that social welfare maximization ultimately requires attention to these allocation decisions. [See 5.] It is assumed that the division of resources *between* the public and private sectors has already been accomplished. It is also assumed that the allocation of resources *within* the public sector has been determined among the competing broad objective factors such as national defense, law enforcement, and investment in human resources.

The decisions that *are* of interest in this paper are those that determine the division of public sector resources within the BIA between on-the-job training and other programs restricted to Indian participants, and those which allocate resources to substitute and complementary programs in public agencies other than the BIA which are available, but not restricted, to Indian participants.

---

[1] Selected references to the methodological literature on program evaluation are indicated by bracketed numbers in the text, which in turn refer to a bibliography at the end of the paper. Each source cited will be understood by noneconomists. Direction to the more technical literature on specific conceptual problems can be found in the citations in these sources. [See 10.]

[2] The authors are aware of, but have not seen, Alan Sorkin's manuscript for the Brookings Institution. Our understanding from a brief conversation with Sorkin is that his analysis is limted to the DE and AVT programs, and is based on records provided by the Employment Assistance Branch of the BIA. For reasons that will be made clear in the following pages, this would appear to be an inadequate source of evaluative data. For an economic evaluation of the AVT program in Oklahoma see Paul R. Blume, "An Evaluation of Institutional Training Received by American Indians Through the Muskogee, Okla., Area Office of the Bureau of Indian Affairs," unpublished Ph. D. dissertation, Oklahoma State University, 1968.

[3] 70 Stat. 986, U.S.C., sec. 309.

[4] Letter to Loren C. Scott, from Walter J. Knodel, dated Sept. 3, 1968.

[5] We will argue, however, that apparently even this factor has not been effectively introduced as a criterion for allocating program resources. See p. 32, below.

PROGRAM OBJECTIVES AND EVALUATIVE CRITERIA

It was shown above that Indian employment is the statutory objective of the Employment Assistance Branch of the BIA. The assumption was therefore introduced that Indian employment is sought without reference to the effect on non-Indian and total consumption. This is probably an accurate representation of the BIA objective, but it clearly does not reflect general social preferences. Therefore, third-party (external) effects of the BIA–OJT program must be considered. More will be said about these externalities below; temporarily it is assumed that increased Indian employment is the sole objective, and attention is directed in the following paragraphs to the evaluative criteria relevant to this narrowly conceived goal.

THE INDIAN EMPLOYMENT (CONSUMPTION) OBJECTIVE

One indicator of BIA–OJT program effectiveness would be the isolation of a level of earnings by Indian participants which exceeds what they would have earned in the absence of the program. However, such a measure is impossible to achieve directly because of an inability to determine what income *would have been*. Nevertheless, reasonable procedures have been developed to secure an acceptable proxy for this earnings concept.

Even with the estimation of a positive earnings differential that can be attributed to the training program, however, many important questions would remain unanswered. All that would be known is that the participating Indians' earnings stream had risen over the time period covered.

Did the participating Indians incur personal costs (or realize non-earnings benefits) in connection with the program that should be subtracted from (added to) the earnings increment in order to arrive at a more meaningful measure of *net private benefit?* [6]

Is the timespan that was used in the earnings comparison the appropriate one? It is almost certain that an earnings differential derived for a year soon after participation in the program would not continue at the same level through the remaining years of work. Therefore, assumptions must be made about both the direction and magnitude of change, and the time profile of the estimated differential. The latter assumption is necessitated by the fact that earnings (consumption) in the future are not valued as highly as income today. Therefore, future earnings must be discounted to obtain a present value transformation,[7] which in turn can be compared with costs.

Even assuming that these conceptual and data problems can be resolved, and that a satisfactory measure of the net private benefit of the BIA–OJT program has been determined, two major questions remain unanswered. Could the participating Indians have been helped to secure *larger* net benefits with the same expenditure of public sector

---

[6] It is not necessary, or even desirable in many instances, to limit the contributing cost and benefit factors to those which already have a dollar value. For instance, employment, and earnings derived from employment, allow environmental changes that affect future productivity of children in the household. The value of this effect should be considered in calculating the return to training. A monetary value can be placed on *any* factor, although there may be disagreement about the particular "shadow price" chosen. [4, pp. 33 ff.] It must also be recognized that the market price of those factors that do have existing price tags may also be a poor measure of the social valuation of the resources in question. See the section on "Opportunity Costs" below.

[7] This discounting procedure and the determination of an appropriate rate have received substantial attention in the technical literature. A good treatment of the issue, and further citations can be found in [6].

resources? [8] And, given the objective of increasing Indian employment (consumption), were the participating Indians the appropriate ones to achieve maximum gains from a given expenditure? The latter question introduces the importance of differentiating between private and social costs and benefits.

PRIVATE AND SOCIAL OPPORTUNITY COSTS

The opportunity cost concept refers to the pricing of a resource using the value that would be placed on it in the best alternative application. A given resource can only be applied to one use at a given time. Therefore, a good measure of the value placed on the resource in the chosen application should be the return that would have accrued if the best foregone alternative had been selected instead. In the context of the last question raised in the preceding section, it should be clear that a net *private* benefit to participating Indians is not synonymous with a net *social* benefit, even accepting the narrowly conceived objective of Indian employment. In addition, it will be shown below that when the objective is itself broadened the private and social measures of net benefit are likely to differ widely.

PROGRAM PRESENCE-ABSENCE AND THE MEASUREMENT OF EARNINGS DIFFERENCES

Practical techniques for isolating the effect of a given treatment (e.g., BIA sponsored OJT) on a specified objective (e.g., Indian employment) have received intensive consideration in the literature on public sector program evaluation. [See 10.] Two basic methods have been used to date. One technique, called the control-experimental method, involves the selection of a group of labor force participants whose experiences are considered to be comparable to what the treatment recipients would have experienced in the absence of the program. An alternative method, called the pre-post technique, compares the pretreatment and posttreatment experience of the participants themselves, usually with appropriate adjustments for factors that are thought to have influenced the objective measure but which cannot be attributed to the treatment itself. The experimental-control method will not receive further attention here because the alternative pre-post technique is adopted in subsequent sections. [9]

The pre-post earnings data are to be used to determine the with and without training difference in earnings. These are not the same concept, however. [11] Among the factors that contribute to a divergence of these two concepts are changes in the market environment in which the earnings accrue, assumptions about what the participants' market responses would have been in the absence of the program, and self-selection factors. Each of these factors is discussed below.

THE MARKET ENVIRONMENT

The earnings stream is a composite price-time measure. The price element is the money wage rate which is affected by a number of

---

[8] The technique discussed so far determines only the private return to the *existing* program, without pursuing the question of whether the program design is the *least-cost* method for attaining a given objective.
[9] The authors have recently secured information on 141 new entrants into the BIA–OJT program. These data will allow the introduction of the control-experimental technique in subsequent analysis, and a comparison of the results of the two techniques.

market factors such as the level of aggregate economic activity, net excess demand (positive or negative) for the skill complement in question, and a variety of institutional factors including minimum wage legislation, labor union activity, and labor mobility patterns. The time element is itself a composite of willingness to work (a supply response) and opportunity to work (the demand environment) and each of these elements is related to the price factor and its determinants.

The implication of this is that changes in these market environment factors should be quantified and the estimated difference in the earnings stream must be adjusted to reflect all changes which cannot be attributed to the training program. The net adjustment magnitude could either inflate or deflate this gross differential, depending upon the environmental changes that occurred.

RESPONSE TO SITUATION IN ABSENCE OF THE PROGRAM

Since the participating Indians did enter training it is necessary to make certain assumptions about what their market orientation would have been in the absence of the program.[10]

Given the market environment during the period from the inception of training until the time of data collection, what would the participants have done in the absence of training? Would they have continued their pretraining pattern of market activity? Or, would they have been geographically or occupationally mobile to take advantage of opportunities as they become available? Or, might they even have dropped out of the labor force altogether in response to an unsatisfactory return for work effort expended?

The choice of the appropriate assumption for the group in question requires intimate knowledge of the relationship of their labor force participation to the dynamics of local, regional, and national levels of economic activity. For instance, if the general level of economic activity has risen substantially during the training and posttraining periods, it might seem reasonable to deflate an estimated difference in preearnings and postearnings streams to account for the higher probability that a given number of months would have been worked even in the absence of the program, and probably at a higher wage rate since wages, prices, and aggregate demand are positively related. However, if a closer examination determines that the demand for labor services of the type the trainees embodied prior to their OJT participation was actually declining because of technological advances or shifts in productive activity, the prepost income stream differential should be *inflated* to indicate that the pretraining level could not have been maintained over the subsequent period, and that the contribution of the program to the participants' earnings stream is greater than the unadjusted comparison. Again, however, it is necessary to assume something about the individual's response to a decline in the demand for his services in the absence of the OJT program. Would he have become discouraged and withdrawn from the labor force, or would he have sought alternative opportunities in the growing economy. The assumption made influences the calculated return to participation in the training program.

---

[10] These assumptions are necessary regardless of the technique adopted. If the control-experimental technique is used the assumptions are necessary prior to selecting the appropriate control group. When the prepost method is used the assumptions determine what adjustments of the pretraining earnings stream are necessary.

SELF-SELECTION EFFECTS

Assuming all of the previously mentioned conceptual problems have been resolved, another barrier to the achievement of an accurate estimate of the private return to training remains. The very act of application for and completion of the program may indicate a higher motivational level that that exhibited by nonparticipants. If this is true, the generalizing the findings from past participants to other Indians may be inappropriate.[11]

It should be recognized that the pre-post technique effectively controls for this phenomenon in calculating the private return *to those who participated*, but the problem lies in generalizing these findings. In the use of the control-experimental method, the significance of this factor would lie in the necessity to recognize its presence as a criterion for selecting an appropriate control group.

PLACEMENT AND TRAINING COMPONENTS OF THE PROGRAM

It will be useful in the empirical sections of this paper to consider two separate functions of the BIA–OJT program. On the basis of the statutory enabling legislation, the primary function of the program is seen to be on-the-job *training*. The Chief of the Branch of Employment Assistance, BIA, interprets this as follows:

> On-the-job training may be defined as instruction in the performance of a job given to an employed worker by the employer during the usual working hours of the occupation and for which workers are paid. [12]

There is another less obvious, but perhaps more important function of the BIA–OJT program, however, and that is the *job placement* function. It is conceivable, and even likely, that some proportion of the estimated pre-post differential in earnings is attributable to the shift from low wage, perhaps intermittent, jobs to relatively higher wage jobs with greater associated employment stability.[13] The importance of this is that with no extraordinary increase in productivity; that is, no investment in training per se, there might still be an increase in earnings, if entry into the program shifts an Indian worker out of an isolated employment sector, defined as one that is not affected by the general pattern of economic activity, and into the mainstream of productive involvement.

TRAINING: GENERAL AND SPECIFIC ASPECTS

A distinction has been drawn in the literature between training that is specific to a firm and training that is transferable to other firms. [2] The criterion on which the distinction is based is whether the increase in worker productivity that accrues from the investment in

---

[11] This may not be relevant in the BIA–OJT program because initial application is frequently at the initiative of the Bureau.

[12] Letter to Loren C. Scott, from Walter J. Knodel, dated September 3, 1968.

[13] Our preliminary analysis suggests that the pretraining earnings of the Indian participants in the BIA–OJT program studied were unrelated to the trend of average earnings in selected Oklahoma employment sectors over the 1960–66 period. We interpret this to mean that the Indians' pretraining employment was isolated from the general regional trend of rising price levels associated with expanding aggregate demand. Therefore, if the posttraining Indian earnings stream is inflated by trend price and productivity increases, this component of the estimated prepost earnings differential *should not* be taken out in deriving the net return to the *program*. It *should* be taken out of the return attributed to training, though, because the "placement effect" alone would have produced this increase, without any extraordinary increase in productivity. The validity of this argument rests on the assumption that in the absence of the BIA–OJT program the Indians would have remained isolated from the regional trend of economic activity.

training can be restricted in whole or in part to the firm providing the training. To the extent that the productivity increase can be restricted to the firm, the wage rate can be held below the worker's net contribution to the value of production, because the best alternative employment opportunity would be at a lower level of productivity and a correspondingly lower wage.[14]

At one extreme, if the increase in productivity is completely specific to the firm offering training, the firm can pay a wage rate equal to what could be secured in the best alternative, and all returns to training would accrue to the firm. In this case, use of the observed wage rate as the price component of earnings would not capture any of the return to training.[15] Of course, if the *private* return to training is being calculated, this is desirable, because the private return is zero. However, the social return should include the increased output.

The other extreme would be a case where the increase in productivity is perfectly general (would accrue regardless of the employing firm), meaning that the firm offering training could not capture any of the return and would, therefore, force the trainee (or the BIA) to bear the full cost of training.

The relevant empirical procedure, therefore, becomes one of determining which parties bear what share of the training costs, and to whom the returns are accruing.

EARNINGS: EMPLOYMENT AND WAGE EFFECTS

It has been noted that "* * * the same increase in earnings can be obtained through expenditures which increase the probability of employment or increase worker productivity" [1, p. 82]. In one sense, this relates to the earlier distinction drawn between placement and training effects, but it also requires the analyst to separate the time and price components of the earnings measure. This is accomplished in this paper by presenting data on the average number of months worked annually for both the pretraining and posttraining periods. The posttraining data should be adjusted for the increased expectation (higher probability) that a given number of months would be worked because of the higher level of economic activity, *if* Indian expectations should be related to aggregate activity (see footnote 13). Again, the BIA–OJT program should not be credited with improvements in employment opportunity that are attributable to the dynamics of the general level of economic activity, nor should the return to the program be reduced if such a relationship does not exist.

THE BIA–OJT PROGRAM: THIRD-PARTY EFFECTS

Up to this point it has been assumed that the sole objective criterion was the private and social return to the BIA–OJT program as it has been conceived in the past. Conceptual issues involved in this evaluation have been discussed in detail, and appropriate references to the literature have been indicated. Little attention has been paid to specific

---

[14] This issue is complex, and may strike some readers as an unnecessary complication of the analysis. It should be noted, therefore, that the appropriateness of earnings as a measure of increased productivity depends on the assumptions made about firm behavior with regard to this issue. See [2].
[15] This assumes that the firm absorbed the costs of training in anticipation of receiving the returns from increased productivity. Since the trainee could always quit and leave the firm with incurred costs but no accruing returns, it is more likely that both the costs and returns will be shared by the firm and the employee. See [2].

cost issues because the data necessary for this aspect of the evaluation are not yet in a usable form. (See 2, 7.) It has been emphasized, however, that no matter how sophisticated the measurement of private or social benefits may be, these measures are meaningless for resource allocation decisions without knowing the resource costs involved in securing the benefits. It was also noted that even if we calculate a *net* return for the existing program, we still cannot say whether a higher net return could have been achieved for the same group under a modified program. Finally, it was stated that given the objective of Indian employment it might be desirable to alter the eligibility criteria as a means of increasing the return for a given expenditure.

The final issue that should be considered from a social welfare perspective is what effect the BIA–OJT program has on Indian non-participants and non-Indians. These effects are called externalities, or third-party effects. (See 9.) We are not urging that BIA decision makers adopt this perspective, but rather that the allocation of public sector resources at a higher level include the considerations explored below.

When an Indian enters training under the auspices of the BIA–OJT program what effect does this have on both his own situation and the employment opportunities of others? Would the Indian trainee have gotten the same job in the absence of the program? Would someone else have taken the job if the Indian had not? If so, does this person remain unemployed or introduce an iterative bumping effect by taking another job that would have been filled, et cetera? Does someone else take the trainee's previous job? If so, would he have remained unemployed otherwise, or does he leave a previous job open? Does entry into the training program remove a production bottleneck which thereby allows increased employment in other related occupations?

The small absolute size of the BIA-OJT program to date minimizes awareness of any bumping effect that may accompany Indian employment. However, the existence of a *scale effect* should not be overlooked. If Indian employment were to be rapidly expanded through the BIA-OJT program at the expense of non-Indian opportunity, acceptance of the program may be less easily secured, even though the resulting distribution may be considered socially desirable. The path of least resistance is obviously to place Indian trainees in new jobs that neither they nor anyone else would have secured otherwise. Questions were asked of both participating employers and former trainees to get at this question of what their respective market responses would have been in the absence of the program.

We do not want to leave the reader with the impression that all external effects are "disbenefits" (11), or undesirable. It has been suggested that the distribution effect itself may be desirable; but even if it is not, the supply of low productivity job seekers (and holders) is diminished by the BIA–OJT program, and this puts upward pressure on wage rates associated with these types of work. While the employment effect of this pressure, and resulting earnings, cannot be categorically predicted because of the possibility that the remaining low-skill level workers will be replaced by less costly capital equipment, it is likely that increased employment opportunities at higher wage rates will result. Similarly, transfer payments may be reduced by the investment in on-the-job training.

The purpose of this section has been to introduce the reader to selected techniques and problems associated with evaluating public sector resource allocation. The most readable items in the literature have been cited at appropriate places.

Perhaps the most important caution we can urge upon the reader before proceeding to the empirical sections is to recognize the tentative and partial nature of the data presented. Hasty conclusions based on inadequate data could lead to less effective programing, instead of improvement. We think the analysis presented does have important implications for the BIA–OJT program, and a forthcoming monograph (8) will include a more comprehensive methodological and empirical presentation.

With this conceptual introduction, attention is shifted in the next section to a brief outline of the administrative aspects of the BIA–OJT program.

II. ADMINISTRATION

PUBLIC LAW 959

In 1956, Congress passed Public Law 959 to provide vocational training for American Indians. After devoting 16 months to establishing the administrative framework, actual training began in January 1958. During the subsequent 8 years 19,519 Indians received training through funds appropriated under the auspices of Public Law 959.[16] Again, with respect to on-the-job training the law states:

> * * * in order to help adult Indians who reside on or near Indian reservations to obtain reasonable and satisfactory employment, the Secretary of the Interior is authorized to undertake a program of * * * apprenticeship, and on-the-job training, for periods that do not exceed 24 months. * * * For the purposes of this program the Secretary is authorized to enter into contracts or agreements with any * * * corporation or association which has an existing apprenticeship or on-the-job training program which is recognized by industry and labor as leading to skilled employment.[17]

The sole administrator of Public Law 959 is the Bureau of Indian Affairs. The BIA coordinates the activities of 10 *area offices*. The area offices formulate policy recommendations and supervise the activities of the *agency offices* which are the grass roots administrative branch of the BIA. There are numerous agency offices, including 11 in Oklahoma.

The Branch of Employment Assistance is the unit of the BIA which administers Public Law 959. Each agency office has an *agency employment assistance officer* who assists Indians in completing the application for on-the-job training (OJT). This officer either accepts or rejects the applicant. The opinion of the agency employment assistance officer is then reviewed by the *area employment assistance officer*. The area officer has veto power over the agency officer, but usually yields to the latter's judgment since the agency officer has more direct contact with the applicant.

---

[16] 14,640 participated in Adult Vocational Training (institutional) and 4,879 received on-the-job training.
[17] 70 Stat. 986, U.S.C. sec. 309.

THE OJT PROGRAM [18]

The sequence of events leading to an Indian entering the OJT program begins with the selection of a firm to undertake the training. Each area office employs an *area industrial development specialist* whose job is to make contacts with employers who might qualify to participate in the program. The manual which the BIA follows in administering the OJT program specifies that the participating firm must meet two basic standards: (1) it must not be owned by an individual and (2) it must have an existing OJT program which is recognized by industry and labor as leading to skilled employment. The industrial development specialist is not the contract negotiator. His job is exploratory in nature. He explains the availability of the program and if the employer is interested, he arranges a meeting with the contract negotiator.

The Commissioner, Area Director, or anyone to whom they have delegated their authority, is responsible for the negotiation of and compliance to the terms of the contract. The *area property and supply officer* is generally responsible for negotiating the terms of the contract. The *area employment assistance officer* then handles the OJT program phases and the administration of the contract.

The manual also specifies that the facilities of the prospective firm are to be inspected to determine if there is adequate heating, lighting, toilet facilities, and if safety practices are followed. Equipment and tools are to be inspected for safety and general condition. An attempt should be made to determine if adequate housing is available in the vicinity for the trainees. The firm's OJT program is to be investigated to determine the period of its existence, number of persons who have completed training, their present places of employment, the number now employed by the prospective firm, and the number of supervisors and instructors employed to furnish training.

Details are then to be worked out for the OJT program. Two variables in particular are negotiable: (1) the amount of the wage rate to be paid by the BIA and (2) the length of the training period for each skill. The manual stipulates that the portion of the wage rate subsidized is not to exceed one-half of the established minimum wage under the Fair Labor Standards Act of 1938, as amended, per week for each trainee, based on a 40-hour, 5-day workweek. For example, the present legal minimum wage is $1.60 per hour. If the trainee's starting wage rate was $2.50 per hour, the BIA would pay $0.80 of that hourly wage rate. If the trainee began at $1.50, the BIA would pay $0.75 of that hourly rate. If the trainee were to work 54 hours per week, the BIA could subsidize only 40 of those hours.

Once the details of the contract are worked out prospective trainees are referred to the participating firm. The screening, evaluation, and referral of trainees is the responsibility of the area employment assistance officer, although he is usually assisted by the agency employment assistance officer. The final selection of Indians to be trained is made by the participating employer. The employer is not required to hire every person referred to him by the BIA.

---

[18] *Indian Affairs Manual Release 43–159*, U.S. Department of the Interior, Bureau of Indian Affairs, Oct. 3, 1963.

III. The Demand for Indian Trainees: Participating Firms

BIA SELECTION OF ELIGIBLE FIRMS

The selection of the firm to conduct on-the-job training is one of the more crucial aspects of the BIA–OJT program. Many of the Bureau's trainees have experienced only seasonal employment, or have poor job stability records. They need the experience of having an 8-hour day, 5-day week job, with the accompanying regular paychecks. This cannot be accomplished in a firm which must shutdown and layoff workers from time to time due to lack of orders. Though BIA officials cannot predict future levels of economic activity, they should seek reasonable assurance that a chosen employer is financially secure and expects sufficient work-force stability so that the probability of trainee termination due to inadequate product demand is low.

Six of the nine firms included in this study are still in operation. Five of these were visited and the person in charge of the OJT project was interviewed. The other operating firm, which trained only one Indian, was not visited. The requirement that all firms be equal opportunity employers was roughly confirmed by observation while touring their respective facilities. With respect to other legal requirements, none of the firms were owned by an individual. Only two of the firms visited indicated they had an established training program of any sort. This is a period of time, beginning with initial placement, during which the trainee acquires and perfects a skill. The other three firms visited did not speak directly of an apprenticeship training program, but their method of training new employees was essentially the same as for those who said they had an established program. A man is hired and works closely with a supervisor until his task is mastered.

None of the firms contacted became aware of the BIA–OJT program through the Area Industrial Specialist. Two were solicited by an Area Employment Assistance Officer, one became aware of the program through other financial dealings with the BIA, another inherited the program with a firm it bought out, and the fifth was managed by a man who is a former BIA Area Industrial Specialist.

CONTRACT NEGOTIATIONS

Once a firm is selected, two variables are to be negotiated—the portion of the wage rate to be borne by the BIA and the length of the training period. In the past, only the latter has been negotiated. The participating firms have been granted the maximum hourly subsidy and then the length of the training period for which the subsidy is to be paid is negotiated. A comparison of the length of these negotiated training periods with the time subjectively estimated to be necessary to master the skill suggests that the negotiated time period is frequently longer than the time required to learn a task. Two of the more striking comparisons are illustrated in the following job descriptions taken from actual contracts:

Taper (cardboard box maker): *32 week training period.* Folds ready-cut box blanks along scored lines and fastens edges together by one of the following methods: (1) coats flaps with glue and presses them together. (2) interlocks corners by means of tabs. (3) seals edges with strip of gummed tape.

Furniture Assembler: 12 month training course. Assembles and fastens together prefabricated parts into frames, section or complete articles of furniture. Trims and sands component parts to make them fit together forming sections or subassemblies, and clamps parts tightly together with hand or machine clamps. May drive nails, screws or dowels through joints or reinforce them.

Further evidence is presented in table 1. In the post-training mailed questionnaire, former trainees were asked to respond to the following question:

When you were in the on-the-job training program, how many weeks did it take you to learn to do your job without help?

It should be noted that trainees are generally not aware of the length of their negotiated training period. The replies of 72 respondents are listed opposite the length of training period negotiated for their particular OJT skill.

TABLE 1.—*A comparison of negotiated training periods with amount of time trainees think was required to learn task*

Number of weeks trainees indicated was required to learn task

Length of negotiated training peroid (weeks):

6	4, [1] 24
8	3
11	1
12	1, 1, 2
13	1, 2, 2, 4
14	2, 2, 3, 4, 6
26	1, 2, 2
32	1, 2, 2, 3, [2] 32
39	1, 1, 1, 1, 1, 2, 6
46	1, 1, 3, 4, 5, 6, 8, 12
52	1, 1, 1, 1, 1, 2, 2, 2, 2, 2, 2, 3, 3, 3, 3, 3, 3, 3, 3, 4, 4, 4, 4, 6, 12, 16, [2] 52
78	1, 6, 7

[1] The only respondent whose estimate exceeded the contract time.
[2] Respondent's estimate identical with negotiated period, suggesting knowledge of the contrac s ulat no

One respondent indicated it took him longer to learn a task than the time period negotiated. An additional two respondents indicated it took them the full length of the negotiated training period to learn their task.

While touring the facilities of the five plants which were visited, employees and plant managers were asked to estimate the length of time required to learn given tasks. Their answers were similar to those illustrated in table 1. In only one case did a plant manager estimate a training period longer than the negotiated training period for a particular task.

The length of the negotiated time is based on information given in the *Dictionary of Occupational Titles* (DOT) [19] and the knowledge and experience of the representatives of the firm and the area employment assistance officer.

[19] *Dictionary of Occupational Titles: Occupational Classification and Industry Index*, 3d ed., vol. II, 1965, U.S. Department of Labor. The training time periods shown in the DOT are themselves questionable in some cases. For example, the DOT suggests a training period of "over 30 days" to become an usher, p. 509.

SELECTION OF TRAINEES

Once the terms of employment have been determined, Indians desiring OJT are screened by the Bureau and referred to the participating firm for employment and training. One plant manager felt this was the most valuable aspect of the program. He wanted to train a core staff and the Bureau sent him the best people they had available. A less enthusiastic response was expressed by another plant manager, who recalled that the first round of referrals included "every drunk in town." This BIA prescreening aspect of the program appears to have varied widely among the firms. For instance, sometimes this BIA screening-referral function is not involved at all in placing the trainees. Two firms (whose contracts involved 121 trainees) indicated that if an Indian comes to the firm looking for a job and if he appears employable, the firm hires him, then contacts the local BIA office to determine if he is eligible for subsidy.[20] This firm-to-Bureau method might be partially explained by an inadequate number of referrals being made from the Bureau to the firm. In fact, one of these firms indicated the reason they no longer had an OJT contract with the BIA was because the Bureau could not provide them with enough trainees.

All five firms stated they were actively hiring other personnel at the time they began participation in the BIA–OJT program. Each also stated that hiring was carried out only to fill normal vacancies and that the subsidy had not encouraged the creation of new jobs.

SUMMARY

Table 2 shows the rankings in five categories of the BIA trainees by the representatives of the firms visited, relative to other new employees. BIA trainees were estimated to have compiled higher absentee rates and poorer punctuality records than other new employees. These were generally thought to be inherent characteristics of Indian employees which tend to improve the longer the employees stay with the firm. Those trainess who completed their training were given above-average ratings on productivity and work attitudes by all five firms. No consensus was discernible with respect to turnover rates. On the whole, all five firms believed the program was a success in their plants.

TABLE 2.—A COMPARISON OF BIA TRAINEES RELATIVE TO OTHER NEW EMPLOYEES

	Firm				
	1	3	4	5	9
Turnover	Higher	Lower	Same	Higher	Same.
Absenteeism	do	do	do	do	Higher.
Punctuality	Poorer	Better	Better	Poorer	Poorer.
Work attitudes	Higher	Higher	Higher	Higher	Much higher.
Productivity	Same	do	Same	do	Higher.

[20] One trainee wrote that he was working for a participating firm and one day he was called into the office and informed that he was now a BIA trainee and his wage would be paid in part by the Bureau.

IV. Pre-Post Comparisons: A Preliminary Analysis

TRAINING CHARACTERISTICS

By 1968, the Oklahoma area offices of the BIA had initiated and completed nine OJT contracts with firms located in Mississippi and Oklahoma. A firm-by-firm breakdown of the number of entering trainees, completions, dropouts, percentage completing training, and BIA subsidy payments is shown in table 3. Of the 226 Indians who participated in the program, 118, or 52 percent, completed their training. The total cost to the Bureau of servicing these nine contracts totaled $228,159, of which $82,000 represented administrative costs.

TABLE 3.—TRAINEE ENTRANTS, COMPLETIONS, DROPOUTS, PERCENTAGE OF COMPLETIONS, AND SUBSIDY PAYMENTS BY FIRMS

	Number entering training	Number of completions	Number of dropouts	Percent completing training	BIA subsidy payments
Firm:					
1	76	43	33	57	$64,068
2	19	3	16	16	5,348
3	21	11	10	52	4,103
4	18	7	11	39	4,093
5	8	6	2	75	2,210
6	26	9	17	35	17,130
7	12	10	2	83	8,161
8	1	1	0	100	2,600
9	45	28	17	62	38,446
Total	226	118	108	52	146,159
BIA administrative cost					82,000
Total, BIA outlay for OJT program					228,159

Firm No. 2, which went out of business before several of the trainees had completed their training, was the first firm granted an OJT contract by the Oklahoma BIA offices. Two other firms are also no longer in operation. An accurate count of the number of trainees still employed by their training firm is not available.

Data on the personal characteristics of the 226 trainees are available from their employment assistance applications. These applications also provided pretraining employment and monthly earnings records on 151 of the trainees. The remainder of the pretraining data and all the posttraining data were secured through the use of a mailed questionnaire. Seventy-eight usable replies were received. This is a 35 percent response rate which is reasonable for this method of data collection.

Selected characteristics of these 78 respondents when they entered training are illustrated in table 4. Public Law 959 states that this program is "* * * primarily for Indians who are not less than 18 and not more than 35 years of age." None of the respondents were under 18 years old and only 17 were over 35 years of age.[21] Forty-six had not completed their high school education. Seventy-three percent of the respondents were married, and 78 percent were males, indicating an emphasis on providing training for those who have persons depending on them for economic support.

[21] Of the total population of 226 trainees, 1 was 17 and 34 were over 35 years of age.

TABLE 4.—SELECTED CHARACTERISTICS OF THE 78 RESPONDENTS AT THE TIME OF ENTERING TRAINING

Description	Number	Percent
Total	78	100
Sex:		
Male	61	78
Female	17	22
Age:		
18 to 20	8	10
20 to 25	23	29
26 to 30	20	26
31 to 35	10	13
36 to 40	9	12
Over 40	8	10
Education (highest grade completed):		
0 to 8	24	31
9 to 11	22	28
12 or more	32	41
Marital status:		
Married	57	73
Single	17	22
Widowed, divorced, separated	4	5

PRE-POST COMPARISONS, TOTAL RESPONDING GROUP [22]

The comparisons presented in this subsection group together responding male and female trainees ranging along the age continuum, who have widely differing educational attainment, and who may or may not have completed the full on-the-job training period. Subsequent sections present sex, age, education, and did–did not complete comparisons, of these same measures separately. A time constraint has precluded the presentation of the results of multiple regression analysis, but this evaluative technique represents the core of the forthcoming monograph (8).

The responding Indians had been employed an average [23] of 7.4 months annually prior to entering the BIA–OJT program.[24]

During the posttraining period covered the responding trainees (N=78) were employed an average (mean) of 10.8 months annually.

[22] The findings reported here refer only to the records of former trainees who responded to the mailed questionnaire. Since data are available on the pretraining experience of nonrespondents also, statistical tests will be conducted of the randomness of the respondent sample taken from the total trainee population. If significant differences are found the findings reported here cannot be generalized beyond the group studied. These statistical tests, dispersion measures of averages presented here, and tests of statistical significance of differences between measures shown in this paper, will be included in (8). In the absence of these procedures, the reader is urged to interpret all figures shown here with great caution.

[23] All averages presented in this section are arithmetic means, $\dfrac{\sum\limits_{i=1}^{N} n_i}{N}$

[24] The number of months employed, both pre- and post-, were regressed separately on the national nonwhite unemployment rate to test for a relationship between Indian employment opportunity and the aggregate level of economic activity. The nonwhite unemployment rate was adopted as the best available proxy for minority group employment opportunity. In neither case was a statistically significant relationship estimated. (See 8.) Therefore, the data on number of months employed have not been adjusted to reflect changes in the aggregate level of economic activity. See footnote 13 for a discussion of the rationale for using a similar procedure to test the relationship of earnings to the level of activity. In this case, the posttraining level of earnings of Indian trainees was found to be significantly related to the aggregate index used (a time-series composite of the average weekly earnings in selected Oklahoma employment sectors), and appropriate adjustments will be made in (8) to separate the placement effect from the training effect. Both posttraining earnings and employment have been adjusted for age on the basis of a relationship estimated by regressing the pretraining values of each on age. These adjustments may be biased because tests for collinearity of age with other factors affecting earnings and employment have not been conducted yet, but such tests will be included in (8).

The average (mean) monthly earned income prior to training was $185, while the average post-training level (adjusted for age) is $323.[25] Thus the respective mean differences between pre- and post-training periods are 3.4 months annually and $138 a month.[26]

PRE-POST COMPARISONS, BY SEX

When the comparisons made in the preceding paragraph are separated into male and female groups, interesting differences appear,[27] as shown in table 5. Because of the small number of observations and absence of statistical tests of differences, we are reluctant to state conclusions from the data in table 5, but it is difficult to resist introducing one speculative hypothesis to explain the size of the observed increase in female earnings. It is likely that the extremely low pretraining earnings level is based on part-time as well as intermittant work, and that entry into the BIA–OJT program precluded continuation of this time preference.[28] Note that the large increase for females is due to a lower pretraining base, not to higher posttraining earnings.

TABLE 5.—PRE-POST COMPARISONS OF EARNINGS AND EMPLOYMENT, BY SEX

	Male (N=61)	Female (N=17)
Average (mean) number of months employed annually prior to training	7.8	6.5
Average (mean) number of months employed annually after training	10.7	10.6
Mean difference (months)	2.9	4.1
Average (mean) monthly earned income prior to training	$205	$125
Average (mean) monthly earned income after training	$333	$308
Mean difference	$128	$183

PRE-POST COMPARISONS, BY DID OR DID NOT COMPLETE TRAINING

Continuing the cross-tabulation presentation, table 6 presents the prepost comparative data by whether or not the training program was completed.

TABLE 6.—PRE-POST COMPARISONS OF EARNINGS AND EMPLOYMENT, BY COMPLETION OF TRAINING

	Completed (52 persons)	Did not complete (26 persons)
Average (mean) number of months employed annually prior to training	7.2 mos.	8 mos.
Average (mean) number of months employed annually after training	10.8 mos.	10.5 mos.
Mean difference	3.6 mos.	2.5 mos.
Average (mean) monthly earned income prior to training	$188	$186.
Average (mean) monthly earned income after training	$327	$330.
Mean difference	$139	$144.

When combined with our findings from the employer interviews and the subjective estimates by the responding trainees about the length of time it took to actually learn to perform their job assignment without unusual supervision, this comparison strongly suggests that

[25] The length of the posttraining period differs among the 78 respondents, thus there is an upward bias in the earnings data reported here. As was indicated in section I above, assumptions have to be made explicit about the predicted direction and magnitude of the prepost differential beyond the coverage of the follow-up contact. Several alternative assumptions will be introduced in (8) to show the effect of the premises on calculated returns.

[26] Again, no statistical tests have been conducted on these estimated differences, and they are gross measures of the private return to training with no netting out of private or social costs incurred in achieving these gains or addition of nonearnings benefits accrued, and there has been incomplete adjustment for influencing factors other than training.

[27] See footnote 25 for interpretive precautions.

[28] This possibility will be explored in (8).

the Indian trainee who fails to complete the prescribed training timetable has nevertheless achieved a plateau of achievement comparable to what the Indian who completes the schedule attains. This could mean that the entire productivity increase accrues very soon after initial employment, as suggested by both the trainees and present employees in the firms.[29]

PRE-POST COMPARISONS, BY EDUCATIONAL ATTAINMENT

Still another way of looking at the pre-post differences is to distinguish between high school graduates and nongraduates.[30] Do the trainees need a high school diploma to benefit from the BIA–OJT program? Or, if both groups realize an increase in earnings, do the graduates realize a relatively greater advantage? Our preliminary findings are shown in table 7.

TABLE 7.—PRE-POST COMPARISONS OF EARNINGS AND EMPLOYMENT, BY EDUCATIONAL ATTAINMENT

	High-school graduates (N=32)	Nongraduate (N=46)
Average (mean) number of months employed annually prior to training	8.4 mos	6.9 mos.
Average (mean) number of months employed annually after training	10.6 mos	10.8 mos.
Mean difference	2.2 mos	3.9 mos.
Average (mean) monthly earned income prior to training	$189	$186.
Average (mean) monthly earned income after training	$340	$319.
Mean difference	$151	$133.

These preliminary data suggest virtually no difference in the post-training experience of the respective groups.

PRE-POST COMPARISONS, BY AGE

The final breakout presented in this paper is by age, since the program is explicitly directed toward the 18 to 35 age range. These data are presented in table 8, below.

TABLE 8.—PRE-POST COMPARISONS OF EARNINGS AND EMPLOYMENT, BY AGE

	18 to 20 (N=8)	21 to 25 (N=23)	26 to 30 (N=20)	31 to 35 (N=10)	36 to 40 (N=9)	Over 40 (N=8)
Average (mean) number of months employed annually prior to training.	7.3 mos	7.0 mos	7.5 mos	6.7 mos	8.9 mos	8.6 mos.
Average (mean) number of months employed annually after training.	11.0 mos	10.7 mos	11.1 mos	10.2 mos	10.8 mos	10.3 mos.
Mean difference	3.7 mos	3.7 mos	3.6 mos	3.5 mos	1.9 mos	1.7 mos.
Average (mean) monthly earned income prior to training.	$122	$187	$171	$223	$241	$189.
Average (mean) monthly earned income after training.	$335	$338	$344	$337	$306	$265.
Mean difference	$212	$152	$173	$113	$65	$76.

[29] Measurement of productivity increases is extremely difficult. While the presence or absence of wage rate increases cannot be accepted as the sole criterion of productivity changes, they do provide an indicator of such changes. For instance, if the appropriate comparative earnings index remains constant while wages rise in a given occupation, this suggests that productivity may be rising in this sector. The analyst should then go beyond the numbers to see whether institutional changes such as union organization, or altered market conditions have occurred. If not, then more confidence can be placed in the actual training effect on wage rates. Again, this issue is explored at greater length in (8).

[30] Once again, we caution the reader that the relationships shown are not net effects. Multiple-regression analysis is necessary to effectively control for the effect of other relevant factors. For example, all of the nongraduates may be females, who have been shown to have had fewer months of pretraining employment annually than males. There is, then, an interaction here that would have to be controlled before net influences of one or the other factor could be determined.

The number in each age classification is so small that we do not think it is appropriate to state even tentative conclusions. In particular the reader is urged to look at both the pre- and post-training *levels* of earnings, as well as the difference.

V. CONCLUSIONS

Our objectives in writing this paper have been to present a conceptual framework, or set of criteria, for evaluating the BIA–OJT program; to briefly describe BIA administrative directives for entering into contractual agreements with participating employers; and to explore information secured from participating employers and former trainees in response to questions about their unemployment and training related experiences.

The time constraint imposed by the publication deadline has precluded the completion of many analytical procedures the authors think are essential to an understanding of the relationships among the factors investigated. For this reason, we have repeatedly referred the interested reader to Mr. Scott's forthcoming monograph [8]. Nevertheless, we cannot assume that all readers will have access to this more comprehensive treatment of the issues explored here. Thus we are obligated to state tentative conclusions here that may prove to be false under further scrutiny. With this final caution, our assessment of the BIA–OJT program at this time follows.

With regard to the two partial measures of economic achievement, the prepost *change* in average number of months employed annually and the prepost *change* in average monthly earnings, the program appears to have had a positive effect. On the average, the Indian trainees were employed 3.4 more months each year and earned an additional $138 each month, compared with their experience before receiving training. Of the 78 respondents, 49 were fully employed during the posttraining period, compared with 11 in the pretraining period. These appear to be substantial gross private benefit figures. However, conclusions concerning net private and social returns require an awareness of the resource costs incurred in achieving these benefits. These cost data are not available at this time, so no cost-benefit derivations can be presented here. However, see [8].

We got a distinct impression from participating employers that the training slots filled by BIA subsidized Indian trainees would have been filled anyway, by qualified Indians or non-Indians. This brings the subsidy issue into question. It may be that the training slots would have been filled by others, but that it is socially desirable to move further down the productivity queue and make up the difference between the value to the employer of the designated less productive Indian and the employer's best alternative applicant. No evidence was uncovered that indicates the existence of such a productivity differential. In fact, in some instances a trainee was recruited and hired by the firm and then placed on the roster of subsidized Indian employees.

Additional evidence strongly suggests that the most attractive aspect of the program was the recruiting and screening function, since the time span covered has been one of increasingly tight labor markets (an increasing relative scarcity of qualified applicants for job openings at current market wage rates). We do not have evidence to suggest that *no* subsidization is needed, but we are concerned by the observed pattern of contractual subsidy at the statutory limit in all cases. There is a hierarchy of embodied productivity represented among Indian applicants for OJT, which suggests that a continuum of subsidy rates, as a proportion of the market wage (up to twice the subsidy amount), should be observed. This is not the case.

We are also concerned that the negotiated length of the prescribed training periods may be unnecessarily long. Evidence to this effect was presented in Section III, above. Again, in light of the responses received from both participating employers and former trainees, the job duties were usually performed competently (i.e., without extraordinary supervision) within a few weeks from the date of initial employment. If this is so, and if the job slot was not a new one designed specifically for the Indian trainee, the employer could reasonably be expected to bear the full wage cost after the extraordinary supervision is withdrawn.

With regard to the recruitment of employers and potential trainees we are concerned because not one of the employers was recruited by the BIA person assigned to this task. On the supply side, it is apparent that the Adult Vocational Training program is more popular among the eligible Indian population. There is a long waiting list for that program, compared with an inability to recruit enough qualified applicants for the OJT program in some cases. This is why doubt was expressed in footnote 5, above, about the effectiveness of achieving even the narrowly conceived objective.

On what basis is AVT so much more popular than OJT? BIA officials cite mobility characteristics of the respective applicant groups as one determining factor. It is quite possible that self-selection should be constrained in some ways to direct Indian applicants into the program that will best meet the combined objectives of private and community preferences.

Again, then, we are back to the expression of a need for a quantitative specification of the multiple factors contributing to social welfare maximization. Once the multi-faceted objective is explicitly stated we must seek information about how a given amount of resources can make a maximum contribution to achieving this objective, or from another perspective, how the objective can be attained with the least amount of resources. We think this paper constitutes a step in that direction.

BIBLIOGRAPHY

1. Bateman, Worth, "An Application of Cost-Benefit Analysis to the Work-Experience Program," *American Economic Review*, Vol. 57 (May 1967), pp. 80–90.
2. Becker, Gary S., "Investment in Human Capital: A Theoretical Analysis," *The Journal of Political Economy*, Vol. 70 (October 1962, Supplement), pp. 9–49.
3. Brandl, John E., "On Budget Allocation in Government Agencies," unpublished paper presented at the Catholic Economic Association meetings, San Francisco, California, December 1966, 15 pp.
4. Chase, Samuel B., Jr., (Ed.), *Problems in Public Expenditure Analysis*, Studies of Government Finance, The Brookings Institution, Washington, D.C., 1968, 269 pp.
5. Maass, Arthur, "Benefit-Cost Analysis: Its Relevance to Public Investment Decisions," *Quarterly Journal of Economics*, Vol. 80 (May 1966), pp. 208–226.

6. Marglin, Stephen A., *Public Investment Criteria: Benefit-Cost Analysis for Planned Economic Growth*, The M.I.T. Press, Cambridge, Massachusetts, 1968, 101 pp.

7. Mincer, Jacob, "On-the-Job Training: Costs, Returns, and Some Implications," *The Journal of Political Economy*, Vol. 70 (October 1962, Supplement), pp. 50–79.

8. Scott, Loren C., An Economic Evaluation of On-the-Job Training Conducted Under the Auspices of the Bureau of Indian Affairs in Oklahoma, Ph.D. dissertation, Oklahoma State University, (forthcoming).

9. Sewell, David O., "A Critique of Cost-Benefit Analyses of Training," *Monthly Labor Review*, Vol. 90 (September 1967), pp. 45–51.

10. Somers, Gerald G., (Ed.), *Retraining the Unemployed*, University of Wisconsin Press, Madison, Wisconsin, 1968, 351 pp.

11. Weisbrod, Burton A., "Conceptual Issues in Evaluating Training Programs," *Monthly Labor Review*, Vol. 89 (October 1966), pp. 1091–1097.

LAWYERS ON THE RESERVATION: SOME IMPLICATIONS FOR THE LEGAL PROFESSION*

By Monroe E. Price**

FOREWORD

Among the many projects of the Office of Economic Opportunity has been the provision of legal services for Indian reservations. The position of the lawyer on a reservation is much different from that of the lawyer for the urban poor, both because of the Indian culture and because of the vast potential and actual natural resources held by Indians. Professor Price, who is closely connected with California Indian Legal Services, examines the program and some of its unique cultural problems and obstacles. He then discusses the proper role of the legal services lawyer on the reservation and concludes that he must act as architect in helping to define, effect, and manage economic development of the reservation's resources.

Introduction

This is an essay on a tiny corner of the legal profession, a small but growing band of lawyers financed by the Office of Economic Opportunity to provide legal services for American Indians. But, as is sometimes the case, a part can illuminate the whole, and here, in the hothouse of the reservation context, important questions about the law and lawyers can be treated in a comparative way within a domestic setting. The experience of the OEO lawyers provides some insight into the relationship between law and economic development and also into the role of a lawyer where there is substantial social and institutional change.

The lawyers, about 40 in number, are distributed throughout the country: there are OEO programs at the Choctaw Reservation in Philadelphia, Mississippi; at Cheyenne River, Crow Creek, and Rosebud in South Dakota; at Zuni Pueblo in New Mexico, Papago and Navajo in Arizona, Wind River in Wyoming; and in a statewide program in California. In addition, the Alaska, Montana, and Wisconsin statewide OEO programs have a heavy Indian emphasis. These OEO lawyers have been at large in a setting where the major question is the creation of climate where the tribal governments, long blighted, weakened by heavyhanded intervention and by an intolerably ambiguous role, are beginning to show signs of health and strength. The lawyers are in an environment where the tools of a legal system designed to assist in the representation of individuals against one another or against the State may not contribute, and may in fact conflict, with OEO's primary strategy of hastening the process of tribal development and independence. The activities of these lawyers, the cases they bring, and the difficulties they face provide opportunities for analysis of longstanding problems from a

*Printed with the permission of *The Journal of Law and the Social Order* Arizona State University (Copyrighted).

** Professor of Law, University of California at Los Angeles.

new perspective. In some ways, the lawyers in the legal service programs have represented a significant infusion of new influences into a closed society composed of Government officials and Indians.

It would be repetitious in this article to include the usual litany of statistics about the conditions of poverty among American Indians. There is general agreement on the matter. [1]* Yet a few introductory words about the legal systems involved will be helpful. We expect that the relationship between Government and citizenry is normally controlled by systematized law, at least in theory, and this has been true—also in theory—of the relationships between the Federal Government and the tribe and between the Federal Government and the individual Indian. [2] Indeed, the spillover or hangover of this lengthy relationship is a mountain of dusty regulations, obsolete doctrine, unique theories of supervision, and subtle and pervasive over regulation and dependence. Because the very existence of Indian organizations is now dependent on the pleasure of Congress, law has taken on a role in the life of Indians that it has thankfully not assumed over the life of almost any other group except for those involved in subversive activities. The Government's power is of life and death dimensions. When Congress, in a fit of rancor, decides there shall be no more Menominee Tribe, then it can, as it did in 1954, alter Menominee existence; [3] if it thinks that the small pieces of land set aside in California have served their purposes and should now be distributed in a way that will make the land (if not its owners) come into the mainstream of American society, it can unilaterally do so. [4] And the draconian power of law stretches far beyond the land. If the Congress decides that the internal law administered by the tribal authorities is not good enough for American citizens, it can decree that those laws will be of no effect unless they comport with Federal standards or are approved by the Secretary of Interior. [5] The Secretary of Interior, through his minions, intervenes in the activities of reservation governments and individual decisions in intimate and debilitating ways.

What all this power means is that the legal system, as a whole, has done exactly what law is usually intended to prevent: it has contributed uncertainty and provided an abrasive influence. It has been invoked as a weapon of denial—the agent of the Bureau of Indian Affairs decreeing what a group of people cannot do, what action it cannot take.[6] In that sense, it has impeded the development of political organization. Federal law has also damaged the normal growth of relationships between persons because of its definitions of crimes, its scheme of remedies, and its establishment of status, for it has been the legal system of an alien culture, imposing rules about behavior that may have been at odds with customary practice.[7] If the genius of the common law at large has been its ability through slow growth to conform ideals to societal mores, then that genius has not had a chance to flourish in the reservation setting; the goal, virtually from the beginning, was to use law to mold behavior—to make Indians more like white men—rather than to make a law that codified or respected behavior.[8]

This history accounts, in large part, for what might be called the rustiness of the legal process. A principal feature of the legal system has been the fact that the usual adversary, the Bureau of Indian Affairs, is unused to combat and, as a consequence, does not always respond

---

*See notes, beginning p. 213.

in the expected fashion. For example, when a lawyer for a small tribe called a local official of the Bureau in California to protest a decision, the official suggested that he did not have to talk to the lawyer; it was the official, not the attorney, who had the best interests of the Indians at heart. Because the Bureau officials have matured in a system that is colonial and not adversary, they have difficulty in summoning forth the appropriate response. When an Internal Revenue Service agent calls, a lawyer can attempt to explain what lies at the base of the misunderstanding. There may be an argument between the two, but areas of disagreement will emerge and the scope of the contest will be virtually certain. Furthermore, there is a general awareness of when the process of informal tug and pull and appeal has ended and formal steps must be taken. And the lawyer has some idea of the formal steps within the Government hierarchy before a court action will ensue.

In the Indian context, this structuring aspect of potential litigation is absent. There is rarely a concept of time, a concept of the limits of regulation, or a concept of meaningful response. The "Secretary's discretion" becomes the rallying point for any kind of action, no matter how unwarranted. And at the lower levels of the service, each agent tries to protect his decision or lack of decision by delay. Reservations, by and large, are scarred with unsolved legal matters. Title to land is littered with unanswered questions. The lawyer faces the maddening prospect of educating his adversary to the meaning of dealing with citizens who have attorneys. Bureau officials have trained their Indian wards to accept, almost without question, their statements. The "law" has been a distant force that sanctified their decisions rather than one that could place limits upon them. [9] Examples are legion. In land management, in education, in every field the problem is the same. The local agent has had unlimited power without meaningful challenge to his exercise of discretion. As a consequence, he has forgotten that there are boundaries placed by law on his conduct and his decisions. The relationship is colonial in that sense.

I. The Lawyer and the Tribe

The principal characteristic of the environment faced by the lawyer on the Indian reservation is the tenuously constructed, unsure tribal organization. For the smaller reservations, there may be virtually no organization at all; factionalism may be rampant, leading to an inability to build a constitutional structure.[10] On the larger reservations, the problems are more predictable. The governments are inadequately funded, and the leaders, with outstanding exceptions, suffer from lack of experience and education. They are, moreover, under great pressure. The revolution of rising expectations is just about to come to the reservation, and tribal governments have started to feel the momentum for change. The long tradition, partly cultural, partly encouraged by the Bureau, that it was not right for Indians to picket and demonstrate, to be uncivil like "other" minoirty groups, is beginning to be shattered.[11] Furthermore, the lands where the reservations are located—no matter how poor at the time of investiture—are now starting to fall in the suburbs of cities, along freeways, near airport sites, and are becoming potentially valuable in numérous other ways. Consequently, there are great questions about the direction to be taken in land use, and because land use and culture are so closely related, the new debate has intensified friction between traditionalists and less traditional groups on the reservation.

The tribal governments, then, find themselves besieged by problems at a time when many still have feelings of inferiority and dependence, and the prospect they face is far more severe problems in the future. The potential for internal conflict is especially evident in three areas: (a) the division of resources; (b) the political process of the tribe; and (c) the administration of justice. In resource allocation, the Oglala Sioux of Pine Ridge, S. Dak., passed an ordinance several years ago that would have changed the system of allocating grazing permits to give a significant preference to members of the tribe with at least one-quarter blood quantum. [12] Other members who held substantial cattle interests complained bitterly and alleged that the council action was discriminatory. Their position, which implied constitutional limits to tribal action, was favorably viewed by the Secretary of the Interior, who disapproved the tribal ordinance. [13] More generally, where there is now a substantial off-reservation population (such as at the Yakima Reservation in Washington), there are frequent charges that the tribal leadership favors the on-reservation group in the disbursement of income or reserves for capital improvement. [14] An example of the potential for political conflict is the method for selecting tribal council members. Reservations are often fragmented into chapters or other political subdivisions from which representatives are selected. It may be that the system of apportionment, as in the Cheyenne River Reservation, is so unfair that by almost any standard the scheme raises serious constitutional questions. [15] In the administration of justice, conflict between individual and group arises where the tribe and the tribal judiciary seek to keep professional attorneys out of the litigative process. [16]

These conflicts between individual and tribe, often affecting the future course of political leadership and economic development, have presented the young OEO lawyers on the reservations with frequent dilemmas. They have been hired, ostensibly, to protect the interests of individual Indians who qualify for service; under a predominant view of their responsibility, they have little right to discriminate among appropriate applicants for their services. Yet in the reservation context, where the lawyer is a particularly important figure, where there may be few other non-Indians who are not connected with the Bureau of Indian Affairs or the Public Health Service, they can scarcely help having some important influence on the existing tribal structure. They must make subtle decisions concerning how much to attack and how much to support the present structure. They must decide how much to identify with the present leadership and strenghen it and how much time to devote to those who seek change. They must determine how much effort to devote to building the social organization and how much effort to devote to the servicing of the needs of individuals.

To suggest the difficulty of these problems in greater detail, I will discuss two fairly current matters. The first issue involves the recently passed Civil Rights Act of 1968, the "right to counsel" requirement, and its relationship to the tribe. The second is the crisis-filled history of the largest Indian legal service program in the country, the Navajos' DNA. [17]

A. THE CIVIL RIGHTS ACT AND THE RIGHT TO COUNSEL

Title II of the Civil Rights Act of 1968 [18] sets forth a series of standards to govern the powers of the tribal councils and tribal courts. Heralded as a "Bill of Rights for Indians," it was the culmination of a long effort by Senator Sam Ervin of North Carolina. Senator Ervin's subcommittee on constitutional rights had determined that "one of tne most serious inadequacies of tribal government arises from its failure to conform to traditional safeguards which apply to State and Federal Action." [19]

In addition to other important standards, the Act requires by section 202(6) that "No Indian tribe * * * deny to any person in a criminal proceeding the right * * * at his own expense to have the assistance of counsel for his defense." On the surface, this seems a simple and logical requirement and one that should be implemented immediately. [20] The meaning seems fairly clear, and an OEO-funded lawyer on a reservatior, representing a client convicted of a crime in tribal court, would seem to have no choice, but to challenge any reservation rule that did not permit a lawyer to appear in a criminal prosecution. But let us assume the following circumstances: The reservation has a rule, passed by the tribal council, prohibiting professional attorneys from appearing in tribal courts. The tribal judges are not lawyers, and they do not have an extensive formal education, but they are wise and good judges who have developed techniques for seeking a just solution that may be sharply different from the techniques of the normal adversary process. [21] Moreover, there may be a cadre of tribal members—almost professional—who appear in the courts as advocates, who have some training and experience, but who are not lawyers. (Indeed, several of the OEO-funded programs are expanding and professionalizing such lay counsel for more effective representation in the tribal courts.) Furthermore, there probably is no prosecutor in the courts to purify through contest the contentions of defense counsel, nor is there money in the tribal coffers to expand the system by hiring a prosecuting attorney.

Those are the first level contextual problems that a tribe faces with section 202(6). But there are more subtle issues, too. The provision guarantees counsel (at defendant's expense) only in criminal prosecutions. It is only clear that there are criminal prosecutions by the Indian Courts because of terms and practices that have been imposed from the outside. We may start with the easy assumption that there has to be some system of dispute settling, and some of the settlements must involve the imposition of certain sanctions. Yet the customary approach in many Indian settings was far richer in the range of sanctions, in the choice of alternatives, than was the non-Indian equivalent. Indeed, even at present, as Mary Shepardson has documented, there are nonformal methods of dispute settling in the interior of the Navajo reservation in cases that we would call criminal. [22] The dispute or the violation of mores was presented to some figure respected in the community—perhaps a medicine man—who announced some disposition. It may have involved certain degrees of shame, or banishment, or compensation to the injured party. Federal officials who viewed the reservation as a place to impart ideas of civilization found this barbarian practice of informal settlement of disputes intolerable. Indeed, the whole system of tribal courts developed as an educational device to teach the heathen about law and order, so that they would know about written rules, judges, and due process of law. Then, on that great day when all Indians would be civilized, when the reservation would vanish, an Indian would not be surprised when he had to obey the laws of Wisconsin, nor would he be shocked when he entered the marble halls of a municipal court judge. Criminal trials were imposed on reservations in this century, for the most part, and have only provided a partial method for the adjudication of disputes. It would not be unfair to say that if the reservations could regress in their method of adjudicating disputes, they would be replicating some of the experiments in alternate tracks and noncriminal dispositions that are now the vogue among commentators on American criminal law. [23] What I mean to suggest is that on the reservations there may be a loose and sometimes nonexistent line between criminal and noncriminal trials, particularly because those terms are so clearly non-Indian in both origin and significance. The want of a sharp line is beneficial, perhaps something that should be encouraged. Yet the Civil Rights Act, by requiring counsel in a "criminal proceeding," may force a hardening of the categories prematurely. It may be the role of the OEO-funded attorney, or any attorney with some institutional connection with the tribe, to urge ways in which the tribal council and tribal courts can minimize the scope of section 202(6) rather than to argue the circumstances in which counsel must appear. [24]

There is a third set of problems posed by section 202(6), which springs from the extraordinary nature of Indian tribes. Assuming that we can answer the question of what constitutes a criminal proceeding, still the tribe, the defendant, and the lawyer for the defendant must decide what constitutes "counsel." Indeed, that is now a problem of great significance, for a number of tribes, including the Navajos, are presently making rules concerning who may practice in tribal courts. And here there is an important principle of sovereignty at stake. One of the nice powers of being a State, or being a State court, is deciding who can practice law within the State and who can appear in the State's courts. It is a power that should not be underestimated, because the decision determines the scope of the monopoly practitioners hold, the extent of their financial and political possibilities, the shape and course of the judicial system. [25] As part of the process of imposing counsel on the tribal courts, there is some indication that the Federal Government is also trying to say what the qualifications for counsel should be. To be sure, counsel in a criminal proceeding might mean nothing less than a regular lawyer, certified, for example, by the Arizona or New Mexico bar. It seemed a simple matter. But since the passage of the act, and partly to blunt its impact, serious thought has been given to the power of the reservation to determine who shall practice law in its courts. A number of restrictions have been suggested, all of them with some degree of reason. First, it might be useful for a tribe to require that counsel practicing in its courts pass an examination that demonstrates some familiarity with tribal law.

Second, there might be some language requirement since many clients will speak only or predominantly the Indian dialect. Third, there might be some sort of residence requirement. These are not unusual requirements; they mirror the restrictions normally placed on the practice of law by the several States. [26] Yet there is some reluctance to allow the Indian tribes to impose them. The Office of the Solicitor for the Department has informally notified tribes that counsel means what one would normally consider it to mean, lawyers admitted to practice in the State in which the reservation is located. Language requirements are completely discouraged, and residence requirements are not even contemplated. Yet the issue is rife with important considerations of soverignty. It is not only the theoretical power than is important, but the exercise of that power. If there is a substantial interest in developing strong and meaningful Indian courts that have an independent validity, that are more than pale carbons of inferior State tribunals, then the tribal development of standards governing who should practice before the courts is exceedingly important.

Because these rules are important to the reservation, they should be important to the OEO-funded lawyer who may be considering a complaint in a habeas corpus action that his client was not represented. [27] In this respect, the OEO lawyer is slightly different from the lawyer who is retained on a one-time basis by a particular tribal member. The OEO lawyer, because of his continuing relationship with the tribe, with his dual interest—both in his client and with all potential clients—sometimes must think twice about the position he should espouse. If he, in his role as lawyer, as architect, has fixed views concerning the pace and form with which lawyers should be introduced into tribal courts, then he may not make all the arguments that he would otherwise make if his sole objective were to reverse a conviction or to obtain a new trail. As a lawyer, he has the opportunity to bring a variety of traditional reservation practices before the stern gaze of an often ununderstanding non-Indian judge in a non-Indian court. [28] Which issues he brings, and when, will have an enormous impact on the tribe. The lawyer can take a laissez-faire view and do what coldly seems necessary, but there seems to be a consensus among the OCO lawyers on the reservations that such a position is irresponsible. In each reservation, there are cases that should be brought sooner and cases that should never be brought, for one of the functions of the OEO lawyer on the reservation is to contribute to the growth and health of the tribe. He is part of a community action program that is very specifically designed to build an organization.

Thus, the OEO-funded lawyer confronted with section 202(6) of the Civil Rights Act has responded differently, depending on the reservation he serves. At Rosebud, S. Dak., the legal services attorney has pressed for the full representation of criminal defendants before the tribal court, offering to serve as counsel in those cases where the defendant cannot secure a retained attorney. The grounds for his position are largely the existing legalization of the tribal court at Rosebud. Indeed, that reservation is one of the few in the Nation that has an attorney sitting as judge—a non-Indian from a nearby town who sits in an appeal capacity under appointment of the tribe. Furthermore, the criminal trials are *really* criminal trials, with incarceration in a most unpleasant jail the result of conviction. Finally, on the Rosebud Reservation, there are no advocates experienced in the tribal courts who are able to defend people accused of crimes for a small fee. The OEO lawyer is also seeking to aid the tribe in securing funds for a prosecutor so that there will be a full-blown adversary system to assist the judge, a far better system than defense counsel pitted directly against the bench. [29].

On the Navajo Reservation, the situation is quite different, and the position of the legal services program, DNA, is also quite different. In addition to the rules for professional attorneys adopted by the court [30] with assistance from the University of New Mexico School of Law and others, there is now a complement of lay counselors who have experience and skill in the tribal courts. [31] Furthermore, the tribal judges on the Navajo Reservation often view their role in a "criminal" prosecution as one of mediating between the defendant and the complainant and seeking a solution under which both parties walk out of the court happy. In this climate, DNA, not surprisingly, has taken the attitude that the sharp intervention of counsel, forcing a solution through the dictate of a Federal district judge, is not wise at the moment.

B. THE NAVAJO LEGAL SERVICES PROGRAM

The second example of the effect of OEO attorneys on the tribe involves not a single issue, but an entire program. It involves the potential for conflict between reservation establishment, tribal members, and OEO lawyers, which arises almost by the very existence of a powerful legal services program.

In 1964, Theodore Mitchell, a graduate of the Harvard Law School and a tough westerner, undertook the monumental task of building a $1 million a year program to provide adequate legal services to the 100,000 indigent Navajos stretched across a reservation as big as West Virginia. There were incredible obstacles—recruiting a first-class staff to what was widely considered a desolate area, securing adequate housing on a reservation where there was hardly enough housing for tribal personnel, coping with the difficult problem of dealing with a client population many of whom spoke a different tongue, and setting up a parallel Navajo-manned legal service system for the tribal courts. With courage, bluster, and bravado, Mitchell moved toward what most people would have considered impossible. The rigor and romance of the program turned its remoteness from a liability into an asset; idealistic young lawyers began to flock to the program until Mitchell had a staff—including VISTA lawyers—of more than 20 professional attorneys. An excellent cadre of Navajo administrators was assembled, which developed substantial grassroots support for the program through the community education effort. It has become one of the biggest and most striking of the legal services programs in the country.

At the apex of the development, Mitchell, in August 1968, was banished from the reservation. [32] It was clear from the outset that at the heart of the controversy was a dispute over power. The OEO-funded program had become strong in such an important sense that it challenged the importance of the tribe. Whether the challenge took an overt form or not, it was implicit in the gleaming strength of the energetic attorneys, in their wide support throughout the reservation, in their thousands of dollars worth of equipment and books, in the acknowledged fact that the OEO lawyers could accomplish things that other people could not—that, in fact, often a person should come to DNA rather than to the tribe or the Bureau for help and assistance. In a society that is exceedingly sensitive to symbols, the emblems of strength displayed by the legal services program were too striking.

Again, the historic context is important. The reservation governments have had a shaky existence, suffering the whims of Congress and the overarching impostions of impolite bureaucrats from the Bureau of Indian Affairs. The tribal chairman, in all this, has often been something of a cog, a powerless representative with the seeming responsibility of leadership. While strong leadership has in fact developed in some reservation contexts, the tendency has been for an uneasy wearing of the crown. While the Indian Reorganization Act of 1934 [33] made some improvements in the relationship between Federal Government and tribal government, the goal of strong tribal governments has not been realized. Indeed, the Economic Opportunity Act, with its hope of providing more adequate financial assistance directly to the tribe and curtailing dependence on the Department of the Interior, was the most important effort since 1934 toward strengthening the tribal structure.

The actions involving DNA should be viewed in this historical context. At least as far as the Indian desk at OEO was concerned, [34] the large amounts of money that were being funneled by OEO to the tribes were designed to improve the sense of sovereignty, to indicate, in a sense, that tribal governments as well as other governments were free to err, to make mistakes in spending public funds. The community action programs became, on many reservations, the funding vehicle for vast efforts that the tribe had wanted to undertake, but could never finance, such as housing programs and training programs; cultural programs were begun that could never have been approved through the staid and sterile chain of command at the Department of the Interior. In large part, this was true at the Navajo Reservation. The community action program (CAP) soon became the second largest employer on the reservation. A vast homebuilding and home repairing program was undertaken. An enormous pioneering educational effort was begun, first through Operation Headstart, then through the funding of a pioneer Rough Rock School, which introduced experimental techniques quite exciting in nature, and finally through the beginning of the first Indian junior college. Other large and striking programs were also undertaken. All these were under Navajo control; at the critical points in the development of the dispute the community action program was, in fact, closely alined with the tribe.

In this setting, the legal services program presented a striking contrast. If all other programs were under close tribal control, then the legal services program can be said to have striven for independence. As was the normal reaction of all the lawyers placed in reservation settings, and in urban settings as well, the idea that an attorney who was to represent indigents would be controlled by the community action program was anathema. Throughout the whole legal services system there was an effort to insure that the CAP's priorities would not control the priorities of the legal services program, nor that CAP's strategy become its strategy. The effect of the independence, however, was that instead of supplementing the power of the tribe, the legal services program, in a crucial sense, detracted from it. It did so formally by disagreeing to certain decisions and suggesting that certain lawsuits be brought; [35] it did so politically by developing grassroots strength at the chapter level, [36] which could be interpreted as providing the base for political challenge to the incumbent chairman of the tribe; and it provided a challenge informally by becoming, through the accumulation of excellence, a sounder, more certain dispenser of results than the tribe. Finally, the legal services program had a payroll that rivaled that of the tribe.

The conflict between the Navajo Tribe and DNA seems, at one level to be exactly the sort of confrontation where caution by the lawyers was counseled in the previous discussion of the Civil Rights Act. Yet the confrontation between DNA and the tribe should be seen as involving not a withering of the strength of the tribe, but a strengthening of the normal political process within the reservation. The paradox of the OEO-funded lawyer on the reservation is such that despite these seeming symbolic attacks on the sovereignty of the tribe, the DNA program was in far more important ways a buttress to sovereignty, a reinforcer of the tribal structure. This was particularly true as DNA, under severe attack, demonstrated the enormous amount of community support that it had developed in its short span. Indeed, the supportive aspect of DNA's politicization helps to explain how legal services programs, acting at their best, are effective parts of community action programs.

One of the peculiar questions, conceptually, from the beginning of the Community Action Program was the relationship between the goals of the CAP Board of Directors and legal services, or stated differently, how legal services could fit into an overall strategy to use CAP funds to organize and channel the political energies of the community. It was always hard to understand how legal services programs could serve as integral portions of the CAP efforts; normally they perceived their role as totally unrelated. [37] The standard legal aid effort was the worst offender. Hiding behind the slogan that its mission was to provide for poor people the same kind of legal services that people who had money could afford—that it should provide the best legal service possible for the people who walked through the door—the legal aid agencies asserted independence from the CAP as a way of keeping social reformers out of their hair. The legal aid lawyer religiously avoided working with the CAP personnel; indeed, there was usually conversation between them only at refunding time. [38]

DNA took another course, a course that made it effective, but also brought it into conflict with the tribe. In essence, the Director of DNA, its staff, and its Board viewed the legal services program as itself a community action program. It was to be concerned in a broad way with education, economic development, cultural growth, and political strengthening. The lawyers were not to rely solely on the flow of cases into the offices. They were to ask the architectural question that was at the base of OEO: how can we, guided by the board of directors, and given close to $1 million in Federal funds, deploy our forces and our money in a way that will contribute to the elimination of poverty on the reservation? The asking of that question meant that the legal services program, rather than merely serving as lawyer to indigents, would become a political force, with a viewpoint that would likely differ from that of the tribe itself. DNA became an effective program, not because it provided good legal services to people who came to the door, but because it provided the political functions that the CAP was designed to produce, the creation of a political effort toward change, toward redistribution of resources, toward less reliance on the Federal Government, toward the training of new political leaders. The presence of conflict forced the program to become intensely political. An enormous proportion of time was spent in self-preservation to gain the support of the people. And through the process of gaining that support, DNA created attitudes and forces that will have a long-range impact on the future of the Navajo reservation. [39]

II. The OEO Lawyer and Economic Development

As difficult as are the attitudinal issues confronting an OEO lawyer who participates in legal conflicts within the reservation, the ambivalences surrounding the lawyer's role in economic development are even greater. These problems are particularly striking because an important characteristic of providing legal services on Indian reservations (distinguishing it from OEO's urban role) is the quite different potential for economic development. Unlike the urban poor, the reservation poor normally possess a considerable common asset, usually land. [40] It would be natural if the presence of this resource encouraged a different strategy for the legal services attorney.

The problem in economic development of the proper role of the OEO lawyer is so complex that OEO lawyers on the reservations have been more or less stymied. Impediment after impediment has prevented or discouraged applying legal skills in a way that will have an appreciable impact on income levels. For example, the restriction against taking fee-bearing cases is sometimes, although falsely, perceived as a barrier to significant involvement in the economic development task by OEO lawyers. A substantial impediment has also resulted from the historic tendency of the Federal Government to leave development goals undefined, or perversely to shift from one definition to another without the substantial and considered participation of the Indian group involved. [41] Indeed, it is possible to say that the concept of economic development itself has fluctuated from period to period, reflecting central prejudices concerning the style of life on Indian reservations. Although "economic development" as a matter of fashion now summons forth rather unanimous concord, the term masks important differences about such questions as the relationship between work and income, the conflict between cultural growth and economic growth, and political prerequisites for reservation development. Because those questions have rarely been sharply faced, the function of the lawyer is treacherous.

In this section, an attempt is made to define certain aspects of the economic development role that reservation lawyers must confront. First, as has been indicated, there is the basic problem, rooted in deeply held attitudes, of assisting in the definition of the economic development goals; second, there is the function, close to the lawyer's heart, of expanding the resources available for development and the closely related function of unraveling the legal complexities that make the use of the resources almost impossible. Third, there is the necessity of encouraging the growth of adequate managerial expertise. The lawyer must understand all these aspects of his role if he is to be able to advise his clients on establishing the legal forms appropriate to their desires and needs.

A. DEFINITIONAL PROBLEMS

The current approach of most officials of the Bureau of Indian Affairs, as well as of those in other Government agencies, is to emphasize development of a sort that maximizes the opportunity for work rather than the opportunity for income. [42] As a consequence, development plans often have little or no relation to the cultural and political goals of the reservation. [43] This approach is a matter of substantial consequence to the legal services attorney since Federal goals are a significant limit on the strategies he must pursue. In the absence of the prejudice in favor of work-related development, the existence of natural resources could mean that his function would be to help make a poor man rich, rather than just a little less poor. But such a view raises cultural hackles. On the procedural level, there is the nagging problem of representing poor people where there is a chance of a payoff in the future out of which a nice fee could have been drawn. [44] Naturally, there was continuous concern in the beginning of the legal services programs generally that these programs were driving marginal lawyers out of business. Their concern was extended to the reservations, and at one time there was a general rule proscribing legal services programs form representing tribes rather than individuals. Culturally, income-directed development was upsetting because of a deep-seated feeling, in Americans in general and in lawyers as products of America, that the road up for poor people is (and should be) long and hard, and that work, not income, is the direction that must be taken. Because the mental set is for OEO lawyers to alleviate conditions of poverty by eliminating discrimination that may prevent a client from getting an entry level job that pays slightly above subsistence salary, or providing a little greater security so that the client will not be arbitrarily ejected from his dwelling, or providing modest opportunities for self-employment and management, or assisting by offering welfare benefits, there is little thought given to using legal techniques to change the allocation of resources radically and provide a comfortable source of funds for the formerly poor. In the urban context, it is almost impossible for the legal services lawyer to find any means whereby the latter strategy of rapid income change would succeed. In the reservation context, that did not have to be the case, yet the influence of strongly held attitudes often produced roughly similar approaches.

It is important for a legal services attorney to understand the development goals of the reservation he serves; otherwise he will be unable to advise his clients on matters that are resource oriented, such as how assignments and allocations of land should be made, what challenges or suggestions to offer concerning an internal tax system or even concerning the nature of the educational system. In California, particularly in the southern reservations, California Indian Legal Services has begun encouraging the sharper definition of development goals. When CILS began, the OEO-funded lawyers expected the package of legal problems that normally accompany poverty. California Indians were reported to be at the bottom of the economic barrel with annual income, life expectancy, educational level—all the normal indicators of mainstream participation—suggesting abysmal poverty and despair. But there were immediately sharp distinguishing characteristics. At least the leadership of the California Indians shared in the dream that a way out would still be found; that under more or less free enterprise, they would be able to develop their resources in a way that would make them independent of Government interference. They began to conceive of a lawyer in an entirely different way.

For the urban poor, the function of the lawyer is to force the establishment to invent quasi-entitlements to resources that the middle class now controls. The pool of jobs has to be shared; the universities built for the middle class must be made accessible to the poor; and there are those who argue bravely that, beyond all else there must be a sharing of income, regardless of the distribution of work. It is exceedingly difficult to construct the necessary legal, as opposed to political argument to compel such sharing. The lawyer for the Indian poor may often find these themes of "sharing" inapposite. The California Indians living on reservations, for example, have resources and are often entitled to additional resources under traditional legal doctrines. For them, the problem is somewhat different. To be sure, the Indians of California are plagued with problems concerning education, welfare payments, landlord-tenant, and so forth. But in an interesting process of interaction between lawyer and client, the attention of the lawyers has been directed to far more developmental issues. For example, the leaders of the Morongo Reservation, between Palm Springs and Riverside, became concerned over the fact that the slippage of land out of trust status and into non-Indian ownership gives the reservation a pock-marked quality that impeded optimal use and the most satisfactory planning of resources; more important, the land slippage was eroding the base of young members of the band who, deprived of land, moved to nearby cities. The preparation of a more sensible tenure pattern might permit the preservation of zones free of the indirect fallout from development. Tribal leaders sought advice on the possibility of devising some sophisticated scheme that would help in preserving the integrity of the remaining Indian land. [45]

It is hard for lawyers for the poor to take on such assignment for several reasons. First, as has already been indicated, the fierceness of the Protestant ethic influences greatly the strategies that are usually considered. Tne Bureau of Indian Affairs, the Congress, the Economic Development Administration, the prevailing mood, all seek progress in terms of jobs. The Bureau will not show California reservation lands to prospective industrial users as part of its promotional task largely because there is not an ample Indian labor supply for development. Even though the lands are often in excellent industrial-potential zones, and even though the chief industrial development office of the Bureau is in Los Angeles, the Bureau encourages Fairchild, General Dynamics, and others to locate in the Southwest, the Dakotas, and other areas, such as the Navajo Reservation, where Indian unemployment is found in large numbers. Since the Los Angeles office is largely ineffective, the point is not exceedingly important, but the underlying philosophy is indicative. There is no public interest in making the California reservations financially comfortable without work. It is viewed as peculiar and bizarre that the Palm Springs Indians should now be "rich" without having worked their way up some well-accepted ladder.

Debate concerning economic development, then, is plagued by ambivalence—ambivalence about the relationship between work and income that pervades discussion in other contexts of welfare payments and the preferability of a job. This ambivalence toward substantial wealth for poor reservation Indians is reflected in the process of adjudicating Indian claims against the Federal Government. Because this problem is basic to development, it is worth dwelling a moment on the claims process. California Indians, for example, have claimed considerable land within the State for the last century; to the factory worker in Downey, the claim—that the Indians are entitled to large chunks of metropolitan and rural California—appears extravagant. In the 20th century, afflicted with some sense of guilt, the Nation provided for limited opportunities for the assertion of these Indian claims. [47] If there had been full compensation, the Indians would have gathered enormous wealth, either in land or money. Economic development—in the sense of providing immediate financial security of the highest sort—would have been assured. The solution, embodying a compromise in the form of limited compensation, reflects the reluctance to see development in such grand nonlabor terms. On the one hand, the response allowed continuation of the idea that we are a fair and square country that believes in law and certainly in property rights—for that reason alone, some recognition had to be given to the Indian claims. On the other hand, it was preposterous to recognize fully such extraordinary claims of a handful of poor people, even to the extent that these were based on legitimate entitlement. [48]

Pervading the entire process is the particular kind of phoniness and condescension that pervades many economic development efforts. There was the knowledge from the beginning that the claims, even if they went through trial, could not produce what they would have been worth if they had been the claims of non-Indian property owners claiming, in the 20th century, a taking without compensation in violation of the 14th amendment. Even the pooling of claimants and the per capita distribution process have a certain cynical and simplifying aspect. It would have been too tedious and burdensome to process each claim separately—there must have been over 100 separate California claimants; yet pooling and per capita distributions ignore handsome differences among the groups and individuals in terms of what happened and what their rights are. And for some litigants, lower claims were made simply because of the incredible size of the claims if normal rules were applied.

Just as the claims process was manipulated to provide some compromise between the obligation of conscience and the extraordinary change in living conditions that might occur if full compensation were made, economic development efforts represent a compromise as well. There must be enough industry, enough effort directed to encouraging industry to move to reservations, that our consciences will be collectively healed, but only that sort of industry should be encouraged that permits the proper kind of healing. And that has meant, traditionally, the sort of development that provides the slow entrance into the "mainstream" of American society through work and saving.

Indeed, the impetus towards mainstream is so great that encouragement of industry has an added complexity. Development must be sufficient to make life on the reservation adequate, but not so adequate that persons will be discouraged from leaving the reservation and assimilating into American society. As conceived and as pushed by the Federal Government, and as has been impressed upon the tribes, economic development means traditionally this kind of shifty compromise. The legal services attorney should not be satisfied with such a compromise, at least to the extent that it is Bureau-imposed. It presents the greatest likelihood of disintegrating and emasculating the reservation even further, for the trade of work for income diminishes rather than expands the opportunity for the cultural growth of the reservation. [49]

B. EXPANDING RESOURCES

It is quite natural for a lawyer to expand the resources available for development once the primary goal is clarified. This function includes more than conquest as a means of adding to the tribal domain; it means, also, extricating existing resources from legal and political snarls that render them virtually useless. The claims of the Alaskan natives provide one example. In the act giving statehood to Alaska, [50] the Congress authorized the State to select about 100 million acres of federally owned land. It was generally agreed that the State selection process was crucial to Alaska's economic development. When the government in Juneau began the long process of picking and choosing from the massive Federal reserves, it almost immediately was faced with objections from natives to every selection. It was the natives' contention that when the United States bought Alaska from Russia in 1867, the United States assured continuing rights of use and occupancy to the natives. [51] The purchase agreement has never been fully and adequately interpreted. But the claims that the natives are now making are far from unreasonable; moreover, they have been packaged in a manner that makes them extremely appealing. [52] As a consequence, the Secretary of Interior has frozen all State selections until there is a settlement of the claims. [53] The function of the Alaskan claims is to provide a permanent base of financial security and a guarantee that the Eskimos and Indians will have a continuing stake in the economic future use of the State. The security provides the opportunity to fashion the cultural future of the group in a way that makes it less dependent on migration to urban areas and marginal employment for subsistence.

There are probably similar, well-based claims in numerous States. In South Dakota, the Oglala Sioux of Pine Ridge Reservation are pressing for the return of valuable Black Hills land "temporarily" borrowed by the United States for an artillery range during World War II. In Maine, a venturesome lawyer, on behalf of the few remnants of the Passamaquoddy, has sued the State for $150 million for improper trusteeship of timberland held for the benefit of the tribe. Several years ago in Utah, a group of Navajos successfully attacked the decisions of a State Indian commission that was using trust funds to benefit individuals other than the true beneficiaries. [54] As a categorical matter, residual rights under treaties that still have force have never been adequately explored. Certain areas, including Montana, Oklahoma, and the checkerboard area of the Navajo reservation, are pregnant with uncertainties that flow from the overlapping settlements, and where there is uncertainty, the chances are good that non-Indians have acted affirmatively, leaving it to the Indians to raise later objections. Throughout the West, the rights of Indians to precious water should almost certainly be the subject of more extensive litigation.

Closely tied to these areas for legal ingenuity are the problems linked to the fallowness of present resources held in Indian hands. In southern California, a drive from Indio to El Centro along the Salton Sea is dramatic demonstration of the special problems of Indian land. Alternate sections are Indian-held; those sections owned by non-Indians flourish with date palms, other agricultural uses, and some industrial and residential improvements, while the Indian-held land languishes in the grip of restrictive leasing policy, the ensnarlment of distrust, the heavy hand of cautious bureaucracy, and the crippling uncertainty of informal and formally conflicting claims. A small piece of land is subject not only to statutory restrictions on long-term leasing [55], but its ownership may be fragmented among numerous heirs who cannot be brought together for the purpose of reaching a common business decision. In other places, there may be historic assignments of land, so that on an informal or customary basis, the tribe may not be able to control land that is nominally "tribal." The prospect of working with large chunks of land—a first impression—is quickly corrected by experience. Here there is an important and difficult task for lawyers. Some way must be found to improve the power to make decisions that can rationalize land assignments and land use on the reservation. Some technique must be devised to allow at least the possibility of reassignment of existing rights within the reservation so that the people feel a sense of participation in the planning, a knowledge that their interests are protected, and some sense that through cooperation and rearrangement of entitlement there is some likelihood that not only the group but the individuals within the group will prosper. On most reservations, such a task will require a complete examination of tenure patterns and a wholesale reassessment of the way land is held.

C. LAWYERS AND MANAGERIAL GUIDANCE

In addition to clarification of development goals and improvement of resources, there is a third important function OEO lawyers should fulfill: the providing of managerial guidance. One failure of Federal policy, only partly remedied in the onrush of programs in the 1960's, has been the failure to provide adequate technical assistance so that resources, once exploited and realized, would have a good chance at sensible management. The counsel for Indians must help to close the gap. Two examples will provide background: the Palm Springs Indians and the claims award process.

In Palm Springs, it had been clear since the late 1940's that at some time in the future there would be a partition of tribal assets (mainly land) that had soared in value, and that members of the Agua Caliente Band would face new and intense responsibilities. [56] Indeed, by the time the partition actually took place, the per capita share was in excess of $300,000. The United States, in the exercise of its trust capacity, was quite careful in making sure—under direction from Congress—that the distribution of land was meticulous and fair; men were employed fulltime for several years to supervise the real estate affairs of the Agua Caliente Band. Yet no attention was given to providing the Indians with any skill, education, or training concerning the management of the resource once the trust status was severed. At the time of the distribution, no member of the Band was a college graduate; juvenile delinquency was beginning to be a serious matter. The void in management skills was quickly filled by a group of lawyers under the supervision of a State judge. [57] The group, or at least most of its members, was later charged by the Federal Government with bilking the Indians by extracting from them exorbitant fees for management and legal services. [58] The dependency relationship had been transferred from one group (the Federal Bureau) to another (the local lawyers and bankers). The major consequence of the Federal investigation in 1967 and 1968 into the practice of the Palm Springs bar was castigation and a resumption of the Federal trust relationship. There has yet to be an important effort to prepare the Agua Caliente Band for its new responsibilities. There has been no effort to provide experience or exposure to various investment opportunities or development strategies.

The same thing is true under the practice of the Indian Claims Commission. By and large, its processes consist of long discussions among Washington lawyers for the Indians, Washington lawyers for the Justice Department, anthropologists, and Commission members. At the end of the discussion—which may take over 20 years— checks are sent out to the Indians. On the occasion of the distribution, it is the practice of journalists for some clever press service bureau to go out to the Indian community to see how quickly the paltry sum is spent; it always makes an amusing story. What no one has reported is the shameful fact that the Indian Claims Commission has now distributed $251 million [59], and neither it nor the Congress has given any consideration to the consequences of distribution.

Although Congress does review the plan for distribution before appropriating money, it has generally treated the claims process as if it were an ordinary judgment; and ordinarily neither the judge nor the defendant cares what the plaintiff does with the money he has secured. Yet, in a sense, the Indian Claims Commission Act can be looked upon a precursor of the Economic Opportunity Act. Problems of obligation aside, there was a perceived need to use a greater amount of Federal funds to correct the vast discrepancy between the living standards of Indians and the living standards of other Americans. [60] Perhaps it is wise to look at the Indian Claims Commission Act as a technique for justifying needed expenditures based on entitlements rather than on charity; the claims justification, in this sense, aided only in obtaining passage for the act. If the Commission was a prototype OEO, then it and Congress have failed miserably. The most important goal of such a mission would be to see that the money expended contributed to independence, self-sufficiency, and development. Yet that aspect of the job was totally and completely neglected until the development of the poverty program. The Congress assumed that the awards would mean that there was little need for continued Federal help through the Bureau of Indian Affairs; indeed, the Indian

Claims Commission was often a threshold for termination of the Federal trust status.[61] But the assumption was wholly erroneous. The award of a large sum of money, by itself, almost nowhere provided the ability to survive independently of Federal trusteeship. As a consequence, the money awarded by the Claims Commission was virtually thrown to the winds. It was a salve to our collective conscience, but little else. It did not do what it could have done—provide the basis, the start for meaningful development.

What should be done about this lack of training in development? It is virtually impossible for the Bureau of Indian Affairs, as presently constituted, to correct this problem. Its local agents, by and large, are capable of distributing only misinformation, particularly on issues of economic development. They have no experience and certainly no outstanding expertise in matters like banking, land finance, and land planning. At times the Bureau attempts to progress through changes in nomenclature. At one agency on the Navajo Reservation, for example, the supervisor received word that there must be a town planning officer, but no budget was provided; to satisfy the order, the local realty agent whose job was to file and keep track of allotments and assignments was appointed director of urban and town planning. In many instances, the Indians view the Bureau as attempting to secure a solution that will mean the end to any land-related integrity of the Indian organization, and the businessmen considering enterprises together with Indian communities look at the Bureau as the symbol of redtape and oversupervision. Furthermore, the Bureau is trapped within its own conflicts. It is impossible to service one reservation well as a development advocate when there is a mandate to provide assistance to "all Indians." The Bureau may have different goals in mind from those of the reservation itself—for example, it may be concerned with terminating the Federal trust relationship, curtailing Federal expenditures, creating jobs rather than income, providing incentives for Indians to leave the reservation. It is responsible not to the reservation, but to the Congress and more particularly to the Committees on Interior and Insular Affairs and to the Appropriations Committees. Its policies are designed to produce results and statistics that the committees will find satisfying—but that may conflict with the needs of the reservation. Infrastructure investments, for transportation and water for example, require large Federal expenditures with sometimes remote likelihood of return. Within the Department of Interior, the Bureau must compete for attention, prestige, and funds with agencies that have more muscle and economic power behind them. Within the Department, Indians must fight livestock owners, conservationists, water planners, advocates of every interest other than that of the particular reservation.

D. APPLYING THE LAWYER'S SKILLS

By default, development advocacy falls in part to the lawyer not only in assisting the tribe in obtaining and securing resources, but also in assisting in the management of the resources. If the presence of natural resources constitutes an important distinguishing characteristic between reservations and other poverty contexts, it is fair to ask whether the reservation counsel, OEO-financed or not, is capable of fulfilling this role. What skills, in other words, are necessary for the task?

First, the architectural skills of the lawyer are much in demand. He should constantly consider the sorts of innovative legal constructs that will provide for exploitation of resources in a way that is compatible with the cultural needs of his clients. Here, as in other respects, the lawyer for the Indian poor must be as resourceful as the lawyer for the wealthy. Lawyers for the rich have devised schemes to allow a culture to continue: the spendthrift trust; the personal holding company; the foundation; the Philadelphia nun; the generation-skipping trust—all designed to allow a group of people to live in the style to which it has grown accustomed, hindered as little as possible by the incursions of change in the society at large. Moreover, the rich have often taken the perspective that their way of life should be available not only for them, but for generations to come as well. They ask not only that their assets be preserved, but that they grow, and they ask as well that those assets produce a sufficiently ample income to give the owners freedom to pursue activities of their own choice.

The Indians ask no less of their lawyers. They seek economic development that is consistent with their style of life, but only seldom is it provided. The Palm Springs Agua Caliente Band may serve, again, as an example. The land of the Band and of its members is rapidly being "developed." Lavish new houses, new hotels, new golf courses have appeared where not long ago barren vacant lands existed. But none of the houses are inhabited by Indians and the comfortable country clubs have no Indian members. There is money, but it is obtained at the expense of the continuing existence of the Band as a political and cultural entity. Similar difficulties are encountered in the pellmell effort to induce industry—any industry—to locate on reservations. The fact that the jobs created may be rendered obsolete in 5 or 10 years is often overlooked, even though technological change may leave in its wake the same kind of brutalization and haphazard urbanization that has occurred in many instances in small towns and cities throughout the country. And some reservations, without wise counsel, expose themselves to the sort of raping of their natural resources that has saddened the lives and future of Appalachia. [62]

There are more hopeful examples. In Alaska, the legal services program was asked to provide a legal entity that would develop Nelson Island, located in the western part of the State. The Indians of the village sought a vehicle for development that would not defeat traditional concepts of property and life. The legal services program devised a new kind of entity tailored to the traditional forms of organization and political decisionmaking in the area. Most important, all property except personal property will eventually be held in trust on behalf of all the members of the Nelson Island Corp. [63] The corporate form provides the atmosphere for development while honoring customary ways in which the members of the village consider the property of the commune. Together with Z. Simpson Cox, a Phoenix attorney, the Gila River Reservation has formed a complex 5-year plan for development, including careful decisions concerning what reservation land should be used for homesites, where industrial development would be most desirable, and how transportation, water, and income changes relate to education, tribal organization, and housing. Largely as a consequence of the basic planning, Gila River was selected for inclusion in the Federal model cities program.

In California, there are special circumstances for economic development that limit the capacity of the Indians of the State to employ the substantial funds that have been gained through the claims process. The prime limitation has been the understandable desire of the Indians with an interest in the fund to obtain a per capita distribution. Deprived for 100 years of both land and money, they now have little tolerance for an intangible right to a fund. On the other hand, it is clear that the potential for development is almost wholly dissipated when the $29 million is spread at the rate of about $800 per claimant. Still, some leaders, particularly in the southern part of the State, are interested in seeking ways to achieve both goals. The OEO-funded program in California, California Indian Legal Services, is presently exploring the possibility of creating a special savings bank, in the nature of a California Indian Development Fund, that would allow withdrawals by individual Indians, but would also permit accumulations for investment purposes.

III. CONCLUSION

The process of shifting from a service orientation to a development orientation is not easy for the lawyer. First of all, there are service needs that, because they result from immediate pains, often must be met. Furthermore, the lawyers themselves may not be trained to take a developmental view of their skills. A corporate lawyer, in the company of titans, may plot with his client the conquest of certain worlds, but the lawyer for the poor normally views his role more humbly. To argue, on behalf of a group of poor people that they, rather than a major city, are entitled to the flow from a major river is a luxury that is local to those representing Indians. Yet in some California valleys where substantial diversions have taken place, such an argument undoubtedly has great merit.

It would be excellent if the charge to lawyers could rest with the mandate to maximize resource use consistent with the cultural needs of the reservation client. Unfortunately, there are complications. Quite clearly, many reservations, smitten by the same ambivalencies that have diseased the non-Indian administrators, may not be able to present the profile of a lifestyle that they wish to nourish and preserve. In some cases, such as the Colville Reservation in Washington, the membership is riven. A large sector has already accomplished the acculturation process and is loathe to stand by while a significant proportion of tribal assets is dedicated to the development of the reservation, but there are others, usually those still on the reservation, who see the need to use common resources in ways that assist the tribal members who are living , as treaties used to say, "in the Indian manner." Again, the use of land becomes central. If the land is not to be sold, the wholly assimilated members of the band may wish to have it exploited in a way that maximizes income, whether the land use is consistent with traditional needs or not. Before long-term action can be taken, before the lawyer-as-architect has any idea of the direction he should take, there must be some approximate resolution among the vying forces concerning the uses of reservation resources.

The resolution is not necessarily in terms of a blueprint and full plan for development; that will rarely occur. It may occur through the political process with the leadership selected largely because of its capacity to mediate between the two sides. But there is almost certainly a prior role for the lawyer to play in some settings—assisting in the articulation process. For example, the dissention in some reservation contexts may be attributable to the fact that no one is aware of all the alternatives; presented with a meager set of choices, the opportunity for polarization is increased. Furthermore, the continuing uncertainty about Federal policy contributes to a false sense of urgency when it appears that policy may change quite drastically. If the lawyer seeks to be guided by the reservation concerning the use of his architectural skills, he must increase the richness of the choices available to the tribe. He has to encourage the tribe to look at issues from a development perspective, he must enhance the ability to criticize the proposals of the Government, of consultants, of lawyers, and of private developers.

Partly, this is a problem of Indian perception of the Bureau of Indian Affairs. In the past, the Bureau was the exclusive provender of Federal Government largess. The superintendent of the agency was the man from whom all money had to be coaxed, and who approved all decisions. The political consequences of this colonial relationship were disastrous. In the recent past, there has been an effort to fragment the notion of dependence by encouraging Indian tribes to go elsewhere with proposals for a change. The Economic Development Administration, the Department of Labor, the Department of Health, Education, and Welfare, as well as the Office of Economic Opportunity, have become principal sources for tribal funding. As a consequence, the economic importance of the Bureau personnel on the reservation has diminished. But the legacy of subservience and overobedience still remains. It will be impossible for economic development to occur, and it will be impossible for the lawyer to obtain a useful picture of tribal goals, so long as the singleness of the relationship exists. [64] As part of his function of demonstrating the richness of alternatives, the lawyer must indicate the richness of institutional choices that the reservation can make—that it is not necessary to be so dependent on the Bureau of Indian Affairs. [65]

The task, breaking the psychological stranglehold of the Bureau, the legacy of dependence even after the fact of dependence has disappeared, will be most difficult. To a large extent, it will be the function of the lawyer to demonstrate that the Bureau is vulnerable not invincible, and that its decisions concerning development are often faulty and overly conservative. Such a strategy can be implemented in several ways. First, the lawyer can encourage the establishment of model projects that proceed wholly independent of Bureau involvement, hoping to demonstrate the effect of the Bureau's dead hand. Second, there is the exposition of the truth, making known to the tribal leadership aspects of the Bureau-tribal relationship that have probably never come to light. [66] There are few developmental aspects of the Bureau's stewardship that would not bear serious scrutiny. [67]

The task, however, is not only changing the reservations' view of the Bureau, but also the Bureau's attitude toward the reservations. An Indian reservation, Judge Deady said in *United States* v. *Clapox* [68], is in the nature of a school, and the Indians are gathered there, under the charge of an agent, for the purpose of acquiring the habits, ideas, and aspirations that distinguish the civilized from the uncivilized man. That has been the view of the Bureau, virtually since its inception. It has looked at the reservation as a campus—to be terminated when the graduates all attain sufficient degree of civilization. In terms of economic development, however, there are special perils because of the Bureau's definition of civilization. It must be a definition that flows from the collective ideas and attitudes of the personnel. It is a view of civilization and development that is humble and modest, an attitude toward the pupils that one might expect from a third-grade teacher toward her class. It is an attitude based on Horatio Alger and hard work, professional ambitions for the few, but virtually no ambition for the many. Development of the land, like development of the political institutions, is desirable only to the extent that it increases the freedom of the reservation clients—freedom from hunger and privation, but also freedom to pursue a culture or style of life considered worth while. It is no feat to fill the reservation with another suburb, or to line the reservations with industrial buildings assembling electronic components, just as it is no feat to superimpose American-style courts and educational institutions upon the political structure of the tribe. What is needed, rather, is a subtle understanding on behalf of the reservation, its lawyers, and the Government agencies, of the capacity to manipulate progress so as to provide a greater degree of meaningful self-determination.

NOTES

1. *See generally* Commission on the Rights, Liberties, & Responsibilities of the American Indian, Report: The Indian: America's Unfinished Business, 67–72, 138–41, 159–70 (W. Brophy & S. Aberle eds. 1966).

2. The best justification of United States policy towards Indians as consistent with a rule of law is contained in Felix Cohen's collection of essays, The Legal Conscience (1953). While Cohen's views will always remain a landmark contribution to the understanding of American Indian legal history, it is time for an attempt at revisionism. As a crusader for increased justice, Felix Cohen sought to build on what he perceived to be a consistent strain of fair dealings (with unfortunate aberrations) beginning with the Northwest Ordinance of 1787, Ch. 8, 1 Stat. 50. It is possible, however, that the unfortunate aberrations were the rule and the fair dealings the exception.

3. Menominee Termination Act of 1954, 68 Stat. 250, *as amended*, 25 U.S.C. §§ 891–902 (1964).

4. *See, e.g.*, the Rancheria Act of 1958, Pub. L. No. 85–671, 72 Stat. 619, which governed the mechanism for dissolving certain Indian land collectives in California. The most expansive legislation governing internal tribal organization is the Indian Reorganization Act of 1934, 25 U.S.C. §§ 461–79 (1964).

5. *See, e.g.*, 25 C.F.R. pt. 52.

6. Reported authority on the spirit of negativism is sparse, but examples abound. Local agents tell the Indian governments what laws they cannot pass, what rights they do not have, what trust moneys they cannot reach. The most tangible evidence of negativism is the recurring theme in presidential and secretarial statements declaring a "new way," allowing Indians to control their own destinies. Candidate Nixon, in a speech given October 9, 1968, for example, said "I will see to it that local programs and Federal budgets are operated with minimum bureaucratic restraint and in full consultation with the Indian people who should achieve increasing authority and responsibility over programs affecting them."

7. *See, e.g.*, R. BRANDT, HOPI ETHICS: A THEORETICAL ANALYSIS 200–01 (1954); Van Valkenburgh, *Navajo Common Law*, III MUSEUM NOTES (Museum of N. Ariz.) 39 (1938).

8. *See United States* v. *Clapox*, 35 F. 575 (D. Ore. 1888).

9. A California reservation that sought a license to sell beer on fiesta days asked secretarial approval of an ordinance that would limit the sale to specified parts of the reservation. The Bureau official claimed that only a wholesale lifting of prohibition would be approved, and as a consequence, he refused to pass the ordinance to the next highest office. In defense of his position, he invoked his superior knowledge of departmental regulations. A challenge by an attorney produced no better results; only by an appeal directly to the Secretary of Interior could the application be dislodged from the local official's desk.

The maddening slowness of the process is even present in criminal prosecutions. In a recent case on the Choctaw reservation, the body of a Choctaw woman was found near the house at an RCA Training Center. Soon thereafter, her husband, also a Choctaw, was arrested by Sheriff's deputies of Neshoba County, Mississippi, where the reservation is located. It is fairly clear that the State did not have jurisdiction to prosecute if the murder took place on the reservation, and it was clear to all that the murder did in fact take place near the reservation. Yet the Federal Government—in this case the United States Attorney—sought a survey of the land before he would accept jurisdiction, and the State took the position that they would not drop prosecution until the Federal Government moved in. For two months, the Federal Government moved the case back and forth between the Department of Interior and the Department of Justice while the defendant sat in the Neshoba County Jail. Finally, the OEO-funded lawyer filed an action under the Civil Rights Act of 1871, 42 U.S.C. § 1983 (1964), to obtain his client's release.

10. There are a number of sources for the difficulty in constitution-making, and not the least of them has been the conflicting directions for Indian development proffered by the United States. Division of the land into small individual holdings has created attitudes that conflict with attitudes of those who would rather see the preservation of the land as an entity. The policy of lumping various distinct Indian groups on a single reservation—as on the Colorado River Reservation in Arizona and California and on the Rocky Boy Reservation in Montana—also contributes to the difficulty. Disputes about enrollment of members, as on the San Pasquale Reservation in Southern California, produce sharp and intense conflict that lasts over many decades. And the demand for a constitutional structure, which means the binding quality of a majority vote, often yields an embittered minority.

11. The National Congress of American Indians disassociated itself from the Poor People's March on Washington partly because of a commitment to change through the normal processes of appeal; on the other hand, groups such as the National Indian Youth Council and the fish-in protesters in the State of Washington have been more sympathetic toward demonstration methods.

12. Oglala Sioux Tribe of Pine Ridge Resolution 67-3. Grazing land is a major resource of the reservation, an expanse of land about 5,000 square miles in southwest South Dakota. The decision concerning the terms and conditions of leases of the land have been a consistent issue in elections for the tribal council that has the principal authority. *See* Note, *The Indian: The Forgotten American*, 81 HARV. L. REV. 1818, 1827 (1968).

13. The Assistant Secretary of the Interior wrote the tribal attorney that "the relation a blood factor bears to the qualifications of members of the tribe is not apparent; and no showing has been made that blood degree classification relates to qualifications for a grazing allocation. . . ." The Department sloughed off the argument that the Federal Government establishes blood quantum tests for determining entitlement to Federal benefits such as attendance at Bureau of Indian Affairs schools. The Assistant Secretary relied on Colliflower v. Garland, 342 F. 2d 369 (9th Cir. 1965), to support his argument. *See* M. PRICE, AMERICAN INDIAN LEGAL PROBLEMS: CASES AND MATERIALS ch. I, at 79–82 (tent. mimeo. ed. 1968).

14. It was pressure from off-reservation groups that persuaded the Secretary of Interior to include in the ill-fated Omnibus Bill of 1967 a section that would authorize tribes to vote to distribute shares of commonly-held assets to individuals who wished to withdraw their interest in the reservation. The section would have been divisive and destructive because of its incentive for increased fragmentation, but the bill did not prosper in Congress.

15. The tribal council may be selected with one representative from each particular culture group or historical band on the reservation, regardless of numerical representation. It would be interesting to see if the reservations are a haven from the ferocity of the one-man one-vote rule. The question, of course, has not yet arisen; but the passage of the Rights of Indians title to the Civil Rights Act of 1968, 25 U.S.C.A. §§ 1301–03 (1968), suggests that the equal protection standard of Reynolds v. Sims, 377 U.S. 533 (1964), could be made applicable.

16. The Navajo tribe is currently engaged in a serious dispute on this issue, primarily involving the impact of the Civil Rights Act of 1968 on a tribal rule that prohibited lawyers from practicing in tribal courts. *See* p. xxx, *infra.*

17. The Navajo Tribe has approved a plan for hiring a professional attorney as a tribal prosecutor. DNA stands for Dinebeiina Nahiilna be Agaditahe, which means "Program for the Economic Revitalization of the People." The name was suggested by a Navajo member of the Board of Directors.

18. 25 U.S.C.A. §§ 1301–03 (1968).

19. Subcomm. on Constitutional Rights of Senate Comm. on the Judiciary, 88th Cong., 2d Sess., Report 1 (1964).

20. Of course, there are serious questions as to the scope of the right to counsel generally, particularly in the area where a misdemeanor might involve a serious punishment. At the present time, the tribal courts do not take criminal jurisdiction over serious offenses, which are prosecuted by the Federal Government under the Major Crimes Act, 18 U.S.C. § 1153 (1964). But some feel that the criminal jurisdiction over serious crimes may be concurrent. *See* Davis, *Criminal Jurisdiction Over Indian Country in Arizona*, 1 Ariz. L. Rev. 62, 89 (1959), an excellent article. If the jurisdiction is concurrent, and if the Indian tribes were

to exercise their power, then there would certainly be problems in that aspect of the Civil Rights Act of 1968 that promises an attorney only at the Indian defendant's "own expense." Assuming that the Federal Government has sole jurisdiction over serious offenses, the statute can be read as giving Indian defendants merely the opportunity to hire counsel in any criminal case including misdemeanors. Needless to say, the fundamental question, both before and after the passage of the Rights of Indians sections of the Civil Rights Act of 1968, is whether the *real* Bill of Rights applies to the acts of tribal governments either as instrumentalities of the Federal Government or through the fourteenth amendment. *See, e.g., Colliflower* v. *Garland*, 342 F. 2d 369 (9th Cir. 1965); Fretz, *The Bill of Rights and American Indian Tribal Governments*, 6 Nat. Res. J. 581 (1966); Note, *The Indian Bill of Rights and the Constitutional Status of Tribal Governments*, 82 Harv. L. Rev. 1343 (1969).

21. The best expositions of the judicial systems of the reservations are to be found in various cases that deal with the powers of the courts. *See, e.g.,* Colliflower v. Garland, *supra* note 22; Iron Crow v. Ogallala Sioux Tribe, 129 F. Supp. 15 (D.S.D. 1955); Application of Jimerson, 4 Misc. 2d 1028, 255 N.Y.S. 2d 627 (Sup. Ct. 1963), *aff'd*, 22 App. Div. 2d 417, 255 N.Y.S. 2d 959 (1965). *See also* Lednicer, *The Peacemaker Court in New York State*, 14 N.Y.U. Intra. L. Rev. 189 (1959).

22. Shepardson, *Problems of the Navajo Tribal Courts in Transition*, Human Organization 250 (1950).

23. *See, e.g.*, President's Comm'n on Law Enforcement & the Administration of Justice, Task Force Report on the Courts 97 (1967).

24. The Taos Pueblo may serve as an example. The Pueblo has resisted the imposition of the tribal court structure, and the Governor of the Pueblo settles cases as they are brought before him. It is doubtful that the Governor divides the cases into criminal or non-criminal, for that distinction has only limited utility in a small, closely-knit society where all infractions have antisocial consequences—where, in fact, law and religion are closely intertwined. Similarly, the non-Indian judicial system is beginning to understand the disutility of classifying the problems of chronic alcoholics and the vagrant poor as "criminal" ones.

25. In Sanders v. Russell, 401 F. 2d 241 (5th Cir. 1968), the court struck down extraordinarily restrictive rules announced by the Federal judge in Mississippi that would have made it difficult for regular representation of civil rights litigants; the rules were designed principally, of course, to prevent disruption of patterns of culture, much the same purpose as reservation rules excluding professional attorneys. *Cf.* Spanos v. Skouras Theatres Corp., 364 F. 2d 161 (2d Cir. 1966).

26. Because they may be of assistance in the preparation of rules for other reservations, significant portions of the new Rules of Admission to the Practice of Law on the Navajo Reservation are reprinted in Appendix A. These rules are not now in effect.

27. The power to file an application for a writ of habeas corpus has been strengthened by section 203 of the Civil Rights Act of 1968, 25 U.S.C.A. §1303 (1968): "The privilege of the writ of habeas corpus shall be available to any person, in a court of the United States, to test the legality of his detention by order of an Indian tribe." For an indication of the scope of the writ prior to the Civil Rights Act, see Colliflower v. Garland, 342 F. 2d 369 (9th Cir. 1965).

28. A famous example of a refusal to understand Indian justice is *Ex parte* Crow Dog, 109 U.S. 556 (1883), where a great rivalry between two leaders of the Brule Sioux resulted in the killing of Spotted Tail by Crow Dog. There was a customary form of retribution, including the surrender of horses and other property by the family of Crow Dog, but this was not sufficient punishment for the Federal Government. A Federal murder indictment was brought.

29. Some reservations are planning to make application for funds for prosecutorial services under the Safe Streets and Crime Control Act of 1968, Pub. L. No. 90–351, 82 Stat. 197. The Navajo Tribe has approved a plan for hiring a professional attorney as a tribal prosecutor.

30. See note 26, *supra*, and Appendix A.

31. Indeed, the OEO legal services program, from the outset, has considered itself a combination of professional Anglo attorneys and talented lay advocates recruited from the reservation. As part of the DNA program, these lay counsel are given additional training by the professional attorneys.

32. The Advisory Committee of the tribe, invoking the tribe's inherent power to exclude any non-Indian from the reservation, passed a rule forbidding Mitchell from coming on Navajo land. The very circumstances of the expulsion underscore the otherworldly quality of practice on the reservation. At a meeting in the Navajo Council Chamber shortly before his expulsion, Mrs. Annie Wauneka, an elderly and important member of the tribe's central Advisory Committee, was questioning certain Washington officials about the power of the tribe to exclude non-Indians. In the process of the conversation, Mitchell, who was sitting at the back of the room, laughed. He laughed, he said later, out of embarrassment; Mrs. Wauneka said it was "the silliest, dirtiest laugh I have ever heard." At any rate, after brooding about the matter, Mrs. Wauneka walked up to Mitchell at another session and began pounding him about the head. The next day, August 7, 1968, the Committee passed a resolution that Mitchell's

> ridicule of the Advisory Committe and other selected officers of the Navajo Tribe has increased tensions among the Navajo people to the point where there has even been a breach of the peace and violent disturbances during a meeting of the Advisory Committee.

> such defiance, ridicule, tensions and violence seem destined to continue and grow worse, thus threatening the peace and well-being of the Navajo people and manifestly leading to grave danger to the life and health of members of the Navajo Tribe.

The resolution was a prelude to an order for "forcible removal" pursuant to section 1786 of the Tribal Code, which permits the Chairman, with the concurrence of the Bureau, "in extreme cases involving grave danger to the life, health, morals or property of the Tribe," to order exclusion from the reservation. The formal charge, then, leading to banishment was ridicule, a not infrequently used tool of lawyers. Mitchell moved his office to a trailer outside the reservation, and OEO has hired a lawyer to defend him. In Dodge v. Nakai, 298 F. Supp. 17 (D. Ariz. 1969), the Federal court held that the tribe's action had violated the Civil Rights Act, and directed that Mitchell be readmitted to the reservation. The decision is now on appeal.

33. 25 U.S.C. §§ 461-79 (1964).

34. The Indian Desk was an early creation of Sargent Shriver, then Director of the Office of Economic Opportunity, designed to ensure that there was some coordinated philosophy behind OEO grants for the benefit of Indian reservations. The Desk had its greatest influence on the design and funding of applications establishing community action agencies, such as the Office of Navajo Economic Opportunity. Head Start programs were also approved through the Indian Desk. Legal Services programs were treated slightly differently. The predominant planning and funding function rested with the Legal Services Branch of OEO in Washington; the Indian Desk had the right to renew and complain, but not the power to veto. The director of the Indian Desk during the formative years was Dr. Jim Wilson, an Oglala Sioux.

35. Various areas of friction developed; among them was the pace of recognition of the Native American Church and its use of peyote; DNA seemed to encourage greater haste toward legalization than did the tribe's general counsel.

36. The Navajo tribe is divided into 98 chapters with roughly 1,000 members each. DNA sought to reach the people with an effective community legal education program through the chapters. Furthermore the chapters elected Navajo members to the Board of Directors of DNA. Because of the service, the close contact, and the appointment of effective young Navajos to leadership positions in DNA, the bonds to the people were strong.

37. Thus, the Legal Services Bureau in Washington made it a fairly strict rule that the OEO-funded lawyers were not to provide legal advice to CAP officials. Furthermore, the CAP normally had, at the most, only token representation on the legal services board. Ethical problems, such as the interposition of a non-lawyer decision-maker between the lawyer and his client, were thereby blunted. But the Washington office made it clear that there was supposed to be some relationship with the CAP. In metaphorical terms, the legal services program was one weapon in the war on poverty; if the CAP director was the General, then surely he must have some influence on what his divisions do.

38. It is true, however, that the CAP executives rarely knew how to use a legal services program in an integrated way with other programs even if the lawyers would have been willing.

39. The theme of this section has been to develop examples that indicate the differences between OEO experience on Indian reservations and in other legal services contexts. A final contrast relating to conflict may be useful. A major question for OEO has been the acceptability of a condition in grants to legal services programs prohibiting suits against State officials. This issue was epitomized in the struggle between Governor Ronald Reagan and California Rural Legal Assistance. At the heart of the fight, at least in its last incarnation, was the demand by the Governor that the CRLA lawyers promise that they would not sue government agencies. At one level, the Governor was protesting the use of government funds to finance attacks on government programs, but the basis of the attack was some sentiment about the right of the State to develop, for example, the Medicaid program free of substantial interference from another official agency. It was easy at the time for those fighting poverty to point out the folly of the Governor's position since transactions between the government and the poor were often the root of a felt injustice or oppression, to exclude that area of litigation from the activities of lawyers for the poor would be to gut the effort and to substitute a patina of assistance for the real thing. Advocates of CRLA summoned forth numerous examples of State subvention of legal attacks, primarily in the area of criminal defense. Since the 1920's there has not been much fashion in the position that the government is entitled to some special protection or some preferred position in the defense of law suits. The CRLA struggle, was not an occasion where reasonable men could differ; if anything, the CRLA experience, the challenges to the State and to the Federal Department of Labor, emphasized the need for an adequately financed group of lawyers whose prime function was to attack the government.

Yet there is a haunting difference between CRLA's experience with Governor Reagan and suits against the tribal government on Indian reservations. For example, the Office of Economic Opportunity, through promotional and training programs established at Arizona State University, approached eight pueblos in northern New Mexico to determine whether they would be interested in a legal services program as a delegate agency of the community action effort. The pueblos, including the Taos Pueblo, contain strong traditional leadership that has measured carefully the introduction of each modern development. The pueblos listened carefully to the OEO proposals and then indicated acceptance with a limitation that sounded strangely Reaganesque: the OEO-funded lawyers in the pueblos must agree not to bring any action against the tribal organizations. The pueblos argued that they could not trust lawyers from an alien culture, taking internal issues into foreign courts, upsetting delicate balances, providing the image that the tribal government is not only fallible, but can easily be brought to task before non-Indian decisionmakers. What at first seems like a similar condition— that the federally-funded lawyer forbear from challenging a governmental decision—may thus turn out to have different roots and to be defensible here.

40. The land is held, as will be indicated below, under serious disability. All in all, there are about 50 million acres of Indian land (outside Alaska) that fall under trust status with the Bureau of Indian Affairs. Commission on the Rights, Liberties, & Responsibilities of the American Indian, Report: The Indian: America's Unfinished Business 72 (W. Brophy & S. Aberle eds. 1966). Some of the land is owned in common by the reservation; some is allotted into units and owned, subject to the Federal trust relationship, by individual Indians; some land is assigned to Indian families, formally or informally, but with the impact that assigned land is not open to reassignment at the tribe's whim. See Gilbert & Taylor, Indian Land Questions, 8 Ariz. L. Rev. 101 (1966).

41. "Development" is a magic word that rarely receives interpretation. It is incanted to persuade electronic assembly plants to remove to reservations where nimble fingers can be placed at the disposal of transistor radios. "Development" as a concept is swallowed uncritically, not rubbed and examined to determine what kind of development is good for what kinds of reasons. Indeed, there is the possibility that economic development—as widely understood—is itself chimerical, as remote, romantic, and false a goal as "civilization" was in the nineteenth century. It wraps up inapplicable values in a dignified cloak, obscuring the basic crudity of our understanding. In the nineteenth century, private property was the *summmum bonum*, the doorway to civilization and progress, the prerequisite to education, thrift, and enterprise. Since private property in land was so elevated, it was forced upon the Indians, primarily through the Dawes Act, 24 Stat. 388 (1887), with disastrous consequences. Today, it is thought, sophistication is rampant, and our planners would not repeat the simplistic mistakes of the past.

Yet the Bureau planners now have the solution wrapped up in development with the formation of "corporations" being the successful technique. The attitude toward development fluctuated with the predominant feeling about the good life in the United States. In its 1904 regulations, for example, the Department of Interior claimed that the act passed in 1887 was designed to "give the Indian a tract of land that he could call his own; in which he would feel a personal interest and from the cultivation of which, by the labor of his own hands, he might gain a subsistence and at the same time acquire the arts of civilization." U.S. Dep't of the Interior, Regulations of the Indian Office § 599 (1904). The regulations continued: "To permit the indiscriminate leasing of these allotments would defeat the purpose for which they were made." This virtual prohibition on leasing is far different from the 99-year leases now being indulged on various reservations designed to encourage economic development, 1960's style.

42. The current style in economic development is for the location of industries that will provide jobs on the reservation. In important ways, this is not a departure from the nineteenth century approach outlined in the prior footnote. Instead that will provide jobs on the reservation. In important ways, this is not a departure from the nineteenth century approach outlined in the prior footnote. Instead of a farmer, the Indian becomes a worker; either way, he finds his way to civilization.

43. The location of various industries in the area near Shiprock on the Navajo reservation has meant important changes in population distribution and, often, an increase in the number of single women who are employed in a quasi-urban area. While there is certainly nothing "wrong" with the trend towards urbanization on the Navajo reservation, and towards the creation of a new supply of jobs, for women, the tribe does not ask a great deal about the social implications before it encourages General Dynamics or Fairchild to establish a plant.

44. It is possible that all that is implied is that the development chore is for private rather than OEO-financed attorneys. But it has been clear on almost all reservations (except for those that have ever-present private attorneys) that the OEO lawyer can do a great deal to establish the basis for development, draft some of the early papers, and introduce some important choices for organization among other things, leaving to the private lawyer the remaining functions when the enterprise begins to be profitable.

45. At Soboba to the southeast, the problem was just as encompassing. Reservation population had decreased and income per capita had fallen precipitously since the early twentieth century when a water-carrying tunnel destined for Los Angeles, driven through the mountains above Soboba, dried up the springs that fed the land immediately below it. From a plush orchard, the land became dry and rocky. Now, 50 years later, negotiations are still in process to restore an adequate water supply and to obtain compensation.

46. In fact, the California claims have an unusual and fairly clear historical validity. Shortly after the Treaty of Guadalupe Hidalgo, in an effort to quiet title, the Federal Government dispatched a group of treaty commissioners to California to persuade the Indians to surrender their claims to immense areas for the guarantee of peace and tranquility in more modest zones. By and large, the Indians agreed, questions of the adequacy of consideration aside, in 18 treaties. But in the spirit of the Gold Rush, there was opposition to assuring Indian hegemony even over the limited parcels guaranteed in the treaties; as a consequence the treaties were never ratified by the Senate. Because the treaties were rejected, the former rights of the Indians were theoretically preserved.

47. 60 Stat. 1049 (1946), as amended, 25 U.S.C. § 70–70v (1964).

48. The California claims cases are typical of the compromise inherent in the response. In the first suit, under a special jurisdictional act, a portion of the California Indians obtained a judgment of $17 million against the United States, based on a valuation of land at the time of taking of $1.25 per acre; the figure of $1.25 was justified by peculiarly legalistic notions such as the price that could have been commanded if all the land had been sold at one time and the sorts of buyers that were available in 1851. There was never any question of receiving land back, of course, nor was there interest on the judgment. And to add legalistic insult to injury, the Congress "set off" against the judgment $12 million for items such as education, blankets, and support for BIA bureaucrats. The result was a "victory" for the litigating California Indians of $5 million. Through such contortions was the American legal conscience satisfied, while preventing a particular group of poor people from asserting fully and adequately an entitlement against the Government.

A "compromise" is now coming to fruition in the remaining California claims cases. Under a law establishing an Indian Claims Commission in 1946, ch. 959, 60 Stat. 1049, all claims not included in the 1944 judgment could be filed for recovery. The claims were pooled, and lengthy research proceedings began. By 1963, the lawyers for the California Indians (there were over 70 lawyers involved in one capacity or another) agreed with the Department of Justice that a settlement offer of $0.47 per acre should be presented to the Indians. While some estimates of the entitlement ran to half a billion dollars, the settlement offer was finally accepted although a plebiscite among the plaintiffs revealed a significant dissent. In the fall of 1968, Congress passed the necessary legislation ordering that a roll of California Indians be brought up to date and that the $29 million be distributed on a per capita basis. It is expected that there will be about $800 distributed per person by 1970 and that that will be the end of the land settlement.

49. At the Choctaw Reservation near Philadelphia, Mississippi, development takes the form of taking six new families each month into a year-long skill development program with an eye to eventual jobs in New Orleans and Cleveland. There are only 300 Choctaw families left. Six families each month is a steady sort of cultural attrition.

50. The Alaska Statehood Act, 72 Stat. 339 (1958).

51. The Alaska Organization Act of 1884, 23 Stat. 24, 26, declared that "the Indians . . . shall not be disturbed in the possession of lands actually in their use or occupation or now claimed by them but the terms under which such persons may acquire title to such lands is reserved for future legislation by Congress. . . ." The Statehood Act, in addition to providing that the State could select about 100 million acres from the public domain, provided that the State must disclaim right and title to lands or other property if the right or title is held by Natives or by the United States in trust for them. Since it was unclear which land was public and which was Native-owned, there was a stalemate.

52. The Alaska Federation of Natives, together with then Governor Walter J. Hickel, now the Secretary of the Interior, established a Land Claims Task Force to develop a legislative proposal in cooperation with the States. The report of the Task Force was far-reaching and imaginative. It would provide land security by withdrawing lands in extensive measure surrounding Eskimo and Indian villages. In addition, there would be the receipt of a percentage of revenues from the exploitation of offshore oil wells with the money administered through a development corporation run by the native people. Finally, there would be some per capita cash distribution.

53. *See generally* Henninger, *Alaska: Share the Oil,* THE NEW REPUBLIC, June 28, 1969, at 15.

54. Sakezzie v. Utah State Indian Affairs Comm'n, 215 F. Supp. 12 (D. Utah 1963).

55. *See* 25 U.S.C. § 415 (1964).

56. *See* Arenas v. United States, 322 U.S. 419 (1944).

57. The process of turning the Indian estates from Federal trust status to local guardianships and conservatorships under the control of the Palm Springs bench and bar was outlined in a series of Pulitzer Prize winning stories by George Ringwald of the Riverside Enterprise. *See also* N.Y. Times, May 20, 1967, at 16, col. 4.

58. *See* Report to the Solicitor of the United States Department of the Interior, from the Special Palm Springs Task Force, September 26, 1967. The Task Force reviewed the following complaints about the conservatorship and guardianship program: (1) high fees assessed against the estates; (2) lack of knowledge by the wards about their estate affairs; (3) confusion and misunderstanding of Indian rights under the program; (4) failure of the program to train and educate Indians to handle their own affairs; (5) frustration at not being able to foresee an end to the program.

59. 1968 INDIAN CLAIMS COMM'N ANN. REP.

60. There was also an effort to improve the world public view of the United States. Karl Mundt, then a Congressman and now a Senator, urged that "if any Indian tribe can prove it has been unfairly and dishonorably dealt with by the United States, it is entitled to recover. This ought to be an example for all the world to follow in its treatment of minorities." 92 CONG. REC. A492 (1946).

61. *See* Pawnee Tribe v. United States, 124 F. Supp. 860 (Ct. Cl. 1953).

62. On the Muckleshoot reservation in Washington, beautiful land with historical significance is being cleared for trailer parks. Another example is the Big River project of the Colorado River Reservation, straddling the Arizona and California border. The most valuable sector of the reservation, along a scenic bend in the river, has been turned over to developers for the building of yet another suburban-type leisure city, with some opportunity, some time in the future, for the Indians to be paid. In the meantime, the developers have given the tribe a new gymnasium, the 1969 equivalent of glass beads. There was not even the attempt, indulged frequently by underdeveloped countries elsewhere in the world, to require that the developer employ and train the indigenous population at all levels of his enterprise.

63. Summary of achievements, Alaska Legal Services Program (undated memorandum). Similar problems arose in American Samoa. The Samoan Constitution, approved by the United States Secretary of Interior, proclaims that no law shall be passed that is inconsistent with Samoan customs and land ownership. Specifically, Samoan land cannot be owned by anyone with less than 50% Samoan blood. The constitutionality of this provision under the United States Constitution has not been tested.

64. Indeed, the idea that in 1968 a Government functionary can bear the title "superintendent" of a reservation (as if it were a huge prison farm) approximates the absurd.

65. For example, a reservation in the Northwest has a substantial timber business with a potential income of $10 million per year. The management of the resources is now conducted by the Bureau of Indian Affairs; for the past 25 years, the tribe has eschewed obtaining expert private management assistance because it thought it was obtaining aid from the Bureau free of charge. Recently the tribe learned that the Bureau is deducting 10% of income to cover administrative expenses. Furthermore, the Bureau, in providing management assistance, often has unusual ideas about the limits on development strategies; it has, for example, discouraged vertical integration of the tribe's lumber business because of the possibility of distressing the white community near the reservation. It is possible and likely that the Bureau will change its views, but the monopoly aspect of the situation stifles the atmosphere in which the highest, most creative thought concerning development can take place.

66. Often this will center about the administration of trust land or trust money by the Bureau. California Indian Legal Services, for example, has filed suit against the government for paying only 4% interest on Indian funds on deposit in the United States Treasury while no other creditor is paid at so low a rate.

67. The lawyer might encourage more critical appraisals of Bureau proposals. In California, the Bureau of Indian Affairs found $15,000 remaining at the end of a fiscal year that would have to be returned to the Treasury if it were not used or obligated. Rather than turn back the funds, the Bureau spent the money to hire a retired land planner to do an economic development profile of five reservations in the Pauma Valley. It was a hopeless task from the outset—the contract was signed before the Indians were consulted; there was not enough money to do a decent study; the contract plan was pregnant with the possibility that the planner would devise land uses incompatible with Indian wishes. With little at risk, it would have been possible to recommend to the over-studied California bands that they reject the contract, that they state why it was inadequate and inefficient, and that they ask for an accounting from the General Accounting Office of the procedures under which the contract was let.

68. 35 F. 575 (D. Ore. 1888).

APPENDIX I

Rules of **Admission** to the **Practice** of **Law** on the **Navajo Reservation**

I. *Definitions*

A. "Attorney" shall mean any person who has been licensed to practice law by any State.

B. "Advocate" shall mean any person who is not a licensed attorney in at least one of the states of the United States, who appears for another and practices law upon lands subject to the jurisdiction of the Navajo Tribe by arguing causes, presenting motions or otherwise appearing before the Navajo Tribal Courts, whether such arguments, motions or other appearances is made orally or by written documents.

C. "Practice of Law" shall mean giving legal advise or counsel; or appearing in a representative capacity in proceedings before any court; board, body or commission; or acting professionally in legal formalities, negotiations or proceedings for a client; or preparing or drafting legal instruments or contracts by which legal rights are secured; or taking any action for another in matters connected with the law.

II. *Self Representation*

Any person may appear before the courts of the Navajo Tribe without the assistance of a regularly licensed attorney or advocate and present or defend any action wherein he is plaintiff or defendent. One who acts only for himself in legal matters is not practicing law contrary to these rules. An owner representing a business entity other than a sole proprietorship, or a person prosecuting a claim procured by assignment or a claim not originally his own is engaged in the practice of law, and must be licensed according to these provisions.

III. *License To Practice*

A. Only persons licensed to practice by the Board of Legal Examiners shall practice law upon lands subject to the jurisdiction of the Navajo Tribe. The practice of law is a privilege bestowed upon qualified persons for the benefit of the Navajo Tribe in accordance with its duty to assure that a high standard of justice and order is maintained.

B. An attorney shall be licensed to practice upon lands subject to the jurisdiction of the Navajo Tribe who furnishes satisfactory proof to the Board of Legal Examiners that:

1. He has a professional knowledge of the laws, court rules and procedures of the Navajo Tribe, and is a licensed member in good standing of at least one state bar, or, he is a licensed member in good standing of at least one state bar and has engaged in the practice of law for 5 years continuously prior to his applications;

2. He is of good moral character, and

3. (a) He has maintained his continuous domicile upon the Navajo Reservation for a period of four months immediately prior to his application, or (b) He has been permanently and continuously employed on the Navajo Reservation on a full time basis under the supervision of an attorney who is duly licensed to practice pursuant to these rules for a period of four months immediately prior to his application.

C. An advocate shall be licensed to practice upon lands subject to the jurisdiction of the Navajo Tribe who furnishes satisfactory proof that:

1. He has a professional knowledge of the laws, customs, and court rules and procedures of the Navajo Tribe, and

2. He has a fluent command of the Navajo and English languages, and

3. He has maintained his continuous domicile upon the Navajo Reservation for a period of six months immediately prior to his application, and

4. He is of good moral character.

D. Advocates and attorneys currently practicing law upon the lands subject to the jurisdiction of the Navajo Tribe may be licensed notwithstanding any other licensing requirements set forth in these rules upon:

1. Payment of the application filing too, and

2. Furnishing satisfactory proof that: (a) If the application is for license as an advocate, the applicant has been regularly practicing before the courts of the Navajo Tribe since (insert date 6 months prior to effective date of these rules), or (b) If the application is for license as an attorney, the applicant has been regularly practicing law on the Navajo reservation, other than by appearing in tribal courts, on a full-time basis since (insert date 3 months prior to effective date of these rules).

E. Upon motion to the court hearing the case a duly licensed member of a state bar who is sponsored by an attorney or an advocate who is licensed to practice on lands subject to the jurisdiction of the Navajo Tribe may be permitted to appear as an associate to a duly licensed advocate.

The motion to appear must be accompanied by a statement showing that the applying attorney is sponsored by an attorney or advocate duly licensed pursuant to these rules to practice upon lands subject to the jurisdiction of the Navajo Tribe. The statement of sponsorship shall state that the sponsoring attorney vouches for the good character and professional good standing of the applicant, and that the sponsoring attorney will be personally responsible for the professional conduct of the applicant.

The motion must specify the advocate with whom the applicant is associating, and the applicant may not associate with a different advocate except upon motion to the court. The association shall be only for the purposes of the trial or hearing of the cause then before the court, and the attorney who has been granted permission to associate shall at all times be under the direct personal supervision of the advocate with whom he is associated, pursuant to the provisions of Section IV of these rules. Time spent on the lands subject to the jurisdiction of the Navajo Tribe while associated shall not be included in computing time requirements for domicil or practice periods under Section III B of these rules. Nor shall permission to associate confirm any rights to practice law on the lands subject to the jurisdiction of the Navajo Tribe other than those given to participate as an associate in the cause in which permission to associate has been given. Any person upon lands subject to the jurisdiction of the Navajo Tribe pursuant to a permission to associate shall be subject to the provisions of Section X of these rules.

IV. Motions and Arguments

All motions and arguments before courts of the Navajo Tribe, whether oral or written, shall be presented only by the following persons:

A. In criminal or juvenile cases by an advocate, or by an attorney under the direct personal supervision of the advocate.

B. In civil cases by an advocate, or pursuant to a motion if the court specifically grants permission for the purposes of the case before it, by an attorney under the direct personal supervision of an advocate.

C. This section shall not be construed as limiting the scope of Section I.

A PLAN FOR NAVAJO ECONOMIC DEVELOPMENT

By DAVID F. ABERLE*

FOREWORD

For many years, Navajo economic development has been hampered by rapid population growth and an eroding agricultural resource base. Although in recent years the tribe has derived substantially increased revenues from oil leases, the economy remains essentially that of an underdeveloped region. David Aberle argues that the Navajos are in what is essentially a colonial situation, with the chief benefits of natural resource exploitation going to outsiders. Aberle outlines a development approach which would involve the Navajos in planning for their own economic development and would allow the tribe to exploit their own mineral resources and control their own industrial development. Other development needs he identifies include rapid expansion of transportation facilities and public utilities and improvements in health services and the educational system. Aberle stresses that no major development effort can succeed without a commitment by Congress—not only a sustained commitment of funds, but a commitment to let the Navajos manage their own affairs.

CONTENTS

*Department of Anthropology and Sociology, University of British Columbia, Vancouver, B.C.

PREFACE

This report was prepared at the request of the Joint Economic Committee of the U.S. Congress. I was asked to prepare a plan for economic development for the Navajo Tribe to aid the committee in its deliberations. As I understood the request, it was that an anthropologist undertake to say what kinds of things needed to be done for a satisfactory development of the reservation: that is, one that would contribute to a more satisfying life for Navajos. I did not think that I was to prepare budget estimates, and I have not done so. The report was prepared without staff or funds. Work began in October 1968, a first draft was circulated to a large number of people in December of 1968, and the final draft was completed in March of 1969.

My qualifications for preparing it are nearly 30 years of intermittent contact with hundreds of Navajos, including past and present members of the Tribal Council and past and present Chapter officers, with officials of the Bureau of Indian Affairs, and especially of the Navajo Area Office, and with traders, missionaries, and border-town Anglos. The report is based on recollections of the Navajo scene in 1940 and 1941, and on eight summers' field work at the community level (1949–53, 1965, 1966, and 1968), the last three explicitly concerned with the effects of the contemporary economy on Navajo family and kinship organization. It is also based on several years' research on the history of the Navajo economy (Aberle, 1966, esp. pp. 23–106), and on a good deal of reflection on the condition of underdeveloped economies in the world today.

The first draft has been extensively revised in the light of comments from BIA officials, officials of the Navajo Tribe, and social scientists, and in the light of documents submitted by the Navajo Area Office of the Bureau of Indian Affairs, asterisked in the bibliography at the end of this report.

The report has been prepared under time pressure and without access to a great many important facts—indeed without a knowledge whether some of those facts are available without further firsthand research. It has, however, benefited by the new information received since December.

I should like specifically to acknowledge the assistance of the following individuals, none of whom would agree with everything in this report, and some of whom would disagree with most of it. None can be held accountable for the opinions I have expressed, nor for errors of fact or interpretation that may follow. They are: Graham Holmes, Russell E. Kilgore, and Val McBroom, of the Navajo Area Office, BIA; Paul W. Hand, Chinle Agency, BIA; Wayne Holm, Rock Point School, BIA; Walter O. Olson, Robert W. Young, and F. D. Shannon; Albuquerque Area Office, BIA; Ed Darby, Navajo Tribal Office, Edward B. Danson, Museum of Northern Arizona; Jerrold Levy, Museum of Northern Arizona and Portland State University; Mary Shepardson, San Francisco State University; Elizabeth Colson,

University of California at Berkeley; Louise Lamphere, Brown University; William Willmott, Cyril S. Belshaw, Braxton Alfred, and Terry Reynolds, University of British Columbia; my wife, Kathleen Gough, Simon Fraser University; Stephen Kunitz, Yale University, Robert Bergman, U.S. Public Health Service; and Tom T. Sasaki; the Johns Hopkins University. Allan McMillan assisted greatly in collating the comments received from all of these sources.

It is a matter of concern to me that this report inevitably criticizes some of the very people who have helped me: Bureau officials, traders, and members of the Tribal Council in particular—not by name but by category. In spite of the criticism, however, I see the Bureau, the traders, and the Tribal Council as locked into a situation that they can change less than it needs to be changed. The tragedy of the Bureau is that so much intelligence and humane concern should have been channeled into an organization that has largely lacked the power to take necessary steps and has often failed to take steps that might have made a modest, favorable difference, because of political pressures engendered by local interests. The traders' tragedy is that although many have a decent attitude toward the Navajos, they themselves are the next to bottom rung in a chain of exploitation that they cannot break. The tragedy of the Council is that, with resources now to control, they have become so preoccupied with the mechanics of this operation that they have lost sight of their own constituencies—or so the constituents tell me. In addition, they have been exposed to only one approach to development—that through external, private business exploitation of Navajo resources—and they have accepted this outlook with too little question.

Having dealt with the deficiencies of planning and action of all of these parties to present Navajo problems throughout this report, I should like to say at this point that the primary responsibility finally falls on that arm of the Government that provides funds; that is, the Congress of the United States. It is possible to add up appropriations for the benefit of American Indians over the years and to claim that a great deal has been done—but not if one is forced to contemplate the results. In terms of political muscle, the BIA is one of the weakest arms of the executive branch. Only Congress could strengthen it, but it has been sensitive to the demands of national and local business and to local politicians, far more than to the needs of Indians.

This report suggests some ways of breaking out of the present frame of reference. As I write it, however, I am aware that the preparation of plans too often has been a substitute for action, rather than a basis for action, in the case of American Indians. A plan was recently developed by Abt Associates (see Radov 1968 in the bibliography of this report); the tribe has recently hired consultants to assist in its planning; now Congress has this report. Similar multiple efforts could be found for the 1930's, 1940's, and 1950's. The question is, When will resources be made available so that some plan can go forward?

It is barely possible that some Navajo readers will regard this document as lacking respect for their way of life: as an outsider's view that they must be "uplifted." This is not the case. I like Navajo life styles. I find living with Navajo families a blessed relief from some of the pressures of an academic existence. But Navajos complain to me about their diet, as to its quantity, quality, and variety, about their deficient housing, medical care, and education, about their lack of control over their own affairs, and about their difficulties in earning a living. This report is dedicated to showing the roots of these miseries and suggesting some remedies.

It is, however, a report by an American anthropologist, not by a Navajo. If my definition of Navajos' needs disagrees with their own, my views must yield. Finally, although this report was prepared at the request of the Joint Economic Committee, it is prepared *for* the Navajos—for the Tribal Council and for any Navajo who wants to read it and use it.

This last point must be underscored for the benefit of Navajo readers. I view this report as one man's view of what is needed for Navajo development, not as a plan to be imposed on Navajos. The Joint Economic Committee is, of course, not a committee with a responsibility for detailed planning of Navajo development. The aim of the report is to stimulate the committee's thinking, and, far more, to provide suggestions to Navajos interested in planning their own future. The remainder of this report will, I trust, make it fully clear that I think that the right and the responsibility for planning (but not for fundraising) rests with Navajos.

I. INTRODUCTION

The Navajo Reservation has rich resources; the Navajo Tribal Council receives sizable revenues from a portion of these; there are more to be utilized in the future; but the per capita income of reservation Navajos is perhaps a third of that of Anglos in the Southwest (see U.S. Census for 1960). To understand this apparent paradox we must first examine their natural environment, their history, and their current pattern of relations with the larger society. It will then be possible to discuss their needs, to speak of the kind of technological development that would meet those needs, and to explore some ways of arriving at the desired end state.

Economically speaking, the Navajo constitute an underdeveloped group. They are an underdeveloped, internal U.S. colony. They show the marks of it. Their poverty and their undereducation are not causes of their underdevelopment but results of it. The underdevelopment results from their relations with the larger society, which limit the economic options open to them, drain off their resources, and fail to provide them with the education, the technological base, and the organizational forms necessary for satisfactory development.

Because I view the Navajo Reservation as an underdeveloped economy, I have put stress on programs related to mineral exploitation, industry, and commerce, above all. Farming and livestock improvements are important and urgent, but less so than these matters. Educational changes are vital, but are seen here primarily as an instrument for local economic development, rather than treated primarily as a means to remove Navajos from the reservation as a part of the labor force. The option of migration under satisfactory conditions should, of course, be open to Navajos. Tourism is not stressed, although it is in much tribal planning, because Navajos have much more significant assets than the excess cash brought by tourists, and more important and humanly significant tasks open to them than acting as living examples of their culture for the benefit of Anglo visitors. Health and welfare programs are seen as sustaining economic development, rather than viewing the Navajo future as one of major dependency on individual doles. In sum, the program recommended, which is summarized near the end of this report, is one that would put Navajos in control of their own economic destinies and create a developed economy in the area. Before detailed recommendations can be supplied, however, a good deal of background information must be supplied. That is the purpose of sections II–V.

II. ENVIRONMENT

The Navajo probably number in excess of 120,000 people, most of whom reside for at least part of the year on a reservation in northern Arizona and New Mexico and southern Utah, and in off-reservation checkerboarded allotted areas to the east and south of the reservation.

A handful live off reservation in southwestern Colorado. Many work off reservation for a part of the year, and some have relocated, permanently or temporarily, in border towns and in such major American urban centers as Los Angeles, San Francisco, Denver, Dallas, and Chicago.

The entire Navajo-Hopi Reservation area includes about 23,600 square miles, of which about 19,400 square miles is clearly Navajo-owned and about 1,500 square miles is clearly Hopi-owned. The remainder has been allocated by court decision (Jones vs. Healing) to the two tribes to work out their way of allocating surface and subsurface rights. They have not succeeded in doing so. Hence a definitive area for the Navajo Reservation cannot be supplied. The Hopi Reservation, however defined, exists entirely surrounded by Navajo lands. An additional 3,000 square miles of allotted land occupied by Navajos is in New Mexico, adjoining the reservation. There are additional Navajo groups at Ramah (230 square miles), Canoncito (120 square miles), and Puertocito or Alamo (100 square miles), the last two remote geographically from the main body of the Navajo.

Altitude ranges from 4,500 feet above sea level to 10,000 feet on the mountain peaks, with the bulk of the area between 5,000 and 7,000 feet. Rainfall varies from averages of 7 inches per annum (lows down to 1.5) up to averages of 27 inches, a figure reached only at the highest elevations. A tabular presentation will clarify conditions.

TABLE 1.—CLIMATE, SOIL, AND VEGETATION

Type	Percent of area	Temperature			Vegetation	Uses
		Annual average	Average summer maximum	Average winter minimum		
Semidesert_____	55	50–60	95–105	11–30	Chamise, greasewood, weeds, barren.	Herding.
Steppe_____	37	45–50	80–88	10–25	Grassland, weed, sagebrush, chamise, greasewood.	Farming and herding.
Humid_____	8	43–50	70–80	4–15	Timber, meadow, woodland, aspen.	Farming, herding, forest products.

Note: The presence of irrigated or irrigable land makes farming possible in any zone except at altitudes too high for a reliable growing season. About 2,600 square miles of the Navajo and Hopi Reservations are barren or inaccessible or both.

Source: The Navajo Yearbook, 1961: 358–366.

The land can be divided into the following kinds of use areas from the point of view of food production: over half is suitable for livestock (principally sheep) but minimally satisfactory for subsistence agriculture; over one-third is suitable for livestock with better agricultural potential than the first; some is suitable for relatively productive agriculture on irrigated farmland, with livestock subsidiary. In addition, two other types of production should be mentioned: a few good forests of timber, principally Yellow Pine (*pinus ponderosa*) stand on the reservation, notably in the Chuskas and Lukachukais, and mineral resources are found in various areas: the reservation presently produces oil, natural gas, helium, uranium, and coal. Other minerals are known.

The scanty and fluctuating rainfall that characterizes most of the reservation makes for uncertain production and occasional catastrophe in both farming and livestock management.

III. History of the Navajo Economic Scene

The original homeland of the Navajo is far to the north, where most of the Athapaskan languages are found today, in Canada and Alaska. (Navajo is one of the languages of Apachean; Apachean is a subgroup of the Athapaskan language family.) Ancestral to present-day Navajo culture is a hunting and gathering technology. The Navajos acquired agriculture either en route to the Southwest or when they arrived here, adding cultivation to their hunting and gathering pattern. Probably about 1600 A.D. the Navajos acquired Spanish techniques of riding and herding horses, using them for hunting and warfare, and shortly afterward, Spanish techniques of managing sheep, cattle, burros, and so forth.

When the Navajos arrived in the Southwest, they found that the best watered sites (those capable of supporting farming villages like those of the modern Pueblo Indians) were already mainly occupied by the Pueblos. The Navajo therefore settled in an inter-Pueblo niche. They had to live on relatively small, scattered spots where they could use floodwater runoff for farming, while they continued to hunt and raid. The scattered residence pattern created by this pressure from their natural and cultural environment was reinforced when they began to build up their herds (sizeable by 1750), since a concentration of several hundred people around a compact village would require each herdsman to take his animals out far from the village and remain in an isolated and dangerous situation for the sake of pasture. Otherwise the forage area around the village would be .denuded. Consequently, from the beginning of their recorded history until today, they have lived scattered about over the countryside in large family units, some as small as two members, but many with 20 or more men, women, and children. Seasonal moves to new pasture were also required—two, three, or more per year.

This pattern of exploitation of the natural environment remains the basic one for the majority of the onreservation population. It means that, although the reservation grows constantly more crowded, the population remains spread out, in separate clusters of kin, dispersed by its own livelihood pursuits, rather than concentrated in villages. The partial exceptions occur where a different kind of resource is involved: the closer clustering of individual homesteads on the irrigated land of Shiprock, Fruitland, and Many Farms; and the town pattern of various agency headquarters, where Navajos depend on steady wagework, predominantly for the Bureau of Indian Affairs, the U.S. Public Health Service, and the Navajo Tribe.

Competition between Mexicans and Navajos must have begun fairly early. It was certainly a chronic feature of the scene by the time of the American occupation of the area in 1846 and following. Although Mexicans and Navajos raided each other for stock and slaves, the U.S. Government patently considered the Navajo raids the primary issue, not the Mexican. Kit Carson, who was the planner of the American conquest of the Navajos in 1863, viewed this as unjust; yet under his leadership in 1863, American troops burned off Navajo crops, drove off Navajo stock, and invited Navajos to come to Fort Sumner if they did not wish to starve in the winter. Some eight thousand made the trek to eastern New Mexico. A number—variously estimated from a handful to five thousand—stayed out in the hills. Called a resettlement project at the time, Fort Sumner could in no wise accommodate the Navajos and other Indians incarcerated in what can better be called a nonlethal concentration camp, nor could it protect them from the raids of still other Indians, such as the Comanches. In 1868 a U.S. Army commission, headed by General Sherman, finally decided that they should be released. A peace treaty was signed, and the Navajos were returned to a portion of their former homeland, with an agency headquarters at Fort Defiance. Livestock were issued to them, and they commenced to rebuild their lives. They lost large amounts of their best eastern territory, but over the years they spilled out over the reservation borders, to be repeatedly confirmed in the possession of new territories, until expanding white settlers and Navajos reached an approximate territorial equilibrium in the early 20th century. The last major addition occurred in 1907, the eastern off-reservation area was restored to the public domain in 1908–11, and thereafter there were only minor additions up to 1934, when Government additions ended.

Warfare disappeared from the Navajo techniques of livelihood after 1868; there were no further serious breaches of the peace. Involvement with the American market began in the 1870's with Navajos selling increasing amounts of wool blankets and later silver, to procure various trade goods on which they came increasingly to depend. Still later pinon nuts became a significant item of sale as well. The agents connecting Navajos with the American economy were the traders, who sold a wide range of goods to Navajos and bought their goods from them. The traders sold coffee, fat, flour, potatoes, cooking utensils, water barrels, wagons, farm implements, horse gear, clothing, cloth, etc. The prime medium of exchange was credit and trader script: that is, the trader extended credit until time for wool sales or until rugs were brought in, or he purchased these items from the Navajo with "tin" or "paper money" good only at his trading post—a practice finally halted only in the late 1930's. In addition, Navajos pawned their turquoise and hand-crafted jewelery to the trader. Navajos in the late 19th Century, then, combined subsistence farming and herding with commercial herding and crafts and entered the American economy.

As far back as the 1850's and presumably far earlier, some Navajos had many sheep and others had few. It was presumably those with least who were willing, from the turn of the century on, to enter the job market, seeking part-time employment initially on the railroad as it was extended west through the Navajo country. The absolute number and the percentage of Navajos involved in the off-reservation job market has increased steadily, with a big jump during World War II; indeed among able-bodied Navajo men 60 and younger at present, it would be hard to find one, English-speaking or not, who has not worked at least part time, off reservation for several years— on the railroad, in the beet, bean, or carrot fields, or elsewhere. I have known Navajos with no command of English who have worked for the railroad as far afield as Chicago and The Dalles, in Oregon. The traders act as labor recruiters.

In this way, Navajos have developed a dependency not only on their reservation subsistence resources and on the sale of native products, but also on the larger job market. In the process, one mode of livelihood has not replaced another, but outside sources have supplemented the exploitation of on-reservation resources. This theme will be discussed further below.

Beginning in the 1930's, the Navajos suffered a major economic dislocation, in their own view second only to Fort Sumner as a hardship. This was the livestock reduction program of the Bureau of Indian Affairs. To understand this program we must go back some decades. From the modest beginnings of Navajo herds in the issue of livestock by the Government to the Indians immediately following the return from Fort Sumner in 1868, the herd had grown rapidly. By the 1880's agents had begun to comment about the overgrazing of the range. Although the reservation grew, the herds grew faster. By the late 1920's, when there was a total of perhaps 1,300,000 head of sheep and goats, including immature animals, plus 60,000 to 75,000 cattle and horses, the Bureau regarded the situation as critical. The depression following 1929 resulted in a lower level of sales and herd buildup, and drought or bad winters caused major livestock losses on the overcrowded reservation land—and, for that matter, in the equally crowded off-reservation allotted areas.

By the 1930's, then, the range showed marked effects of overgrazing. The quality of the forage had deteriotated. Areas that once produced hay now produced Russian thistle. What had once been runoff flood plains in wet weather had turned to deep arroyos. Loss of plant cover was causing wind erosion of topsoil, as well as dissection of the country by water. This was also the period of the dustbowl in American farming. A conservation-minded administration turned to livestock reduction and control for the Navajos, 50 years after the problem had first been noted.

The Bureau asked for, and got Navajo Tribal Council consent for reduction—but what consent meant in this case is problematic: the Councilmen received an explanation of the value and importance of a reduction program, were told that if they were genuinely interested in the welfare of their people they would accept reduction, but were also told that even if they did not accept it, the herds would be reduced. They also understood that the people would be able to secure Government jobs to compensate for their livestock losses. Work for the Civilian Conservation Corps and Emergency Conservation Works did provide them with new income, but did not supply the amount or duration of employment that the Navajos had expected. The Council accepted. Between the mid 1930's and the mid 1940's, Navajo herds were reduced from nearly 940,000 mature sheep units to below 450,000 mature sheep units. (A sheep or a goat is one sheep unit. Cattle are rated at four units, horses at five.) The quality of the sheep was improved by Bureau efforts, so that the total amount of meat and wool on the hoof on the reservation actually increased—even if there were fewer hooves—but since Navajo population was growing rapidly, the net effect was a per capita decrease of some magnitude, and one that has, by and large, continued ever since: herds have varied somewhat, rising slightly in the past few years, but population has risen constantly. (In 1967 there were 585,000 mature sheep units on reservation and 131,000 on Navajo lands in districts bordering the reservation. The reservation was 18 percent over estimated carrying capacity.)

Along with reduction went New Deal on-reservation government-supported employment: Emergency Conservation Work, expanded

Bureau payroll, and so on. But, as some Navajos said, it was not necessarily those who lost the stock who got the jobs. As the United States began to prepare for World War II, Government job supplements to the reservation economy decreased. There might have been a crisis, but the war itself averted it. Many Navajos were drafted or volunteered, and in the labor shortage situation of the wartime economy, many more Navajos left the reservation to work in industrial plants. This is a phenomenon to be stressed: when the economic situation was advantageous, when jobs with good pay were abundant, Navajos who were, on average, of lower educational attainment than is the present Navajo population, could be induced to do wagework off reservation and could perform successfully. No relocation program since has operated under these economically advantageous conditions.

The effects of peace in 1945 and after, created a near disaster. Veterans and wartime industrial workers returned to a still more overpopulated reservation, with no local reservoir of jobs, with sharp limitations on the livestock economy in the form of livestock regulation, and with a level of local technological development well behind the non-Indian parts of Arizona, New Mexico, and Utah, and even farther behind the more developed sectors of the United States: to a roadless country with little water development and no electricity other than that suppled by local generator systems, for traders and the Bureau.

The Navajo-Hopi 10-year rehabilitation program was instituted in 1950 to attempt to cope with the crisis. Over a period of 11 fiscal years it supplied a total of just short of $90,000,000 (of the $108,570,000 authorized in 1951 and 1958, not all allocated by Congress). It is doubtful that this level of expenditure would have had much effect, had it not been that tribal income increased rapidly during the same period. There was a small jump with the discovery of uranium ores on the reservation (visible in 1952 and after), and a much larger jump, especially in 1953 and after, when rich oil fields were discovered—not the first in Navajoland, but incomparably more productive than earlier finds. The tribe deployed some of these funds for various forms of relief and part-time employment and expanded its organizations. In addition, through Federal payment to the Southwestern States of unusually large proportions of welfare funds, beginning in 1950, Navajos and other Indians became eligible for State relief funds (old age, aid to dependent children, aid to the needy blind) even if resident on reservation. They were also eligible for social security, old age and survivor's benefits, etc., if they could qualify on the basis of employment or as selfemployed. In 1961, however, an estimated 30 percent of qualified Navajos did not receive social security or old age and survivors' benefits because they did not know about their eligibility. Since then the tribe has employed some Navajos to explain the system and to deal with complex cases. Whereas between 1951 and 1960 the number of payments to the aged and the blind remained more or less level, there was a striking increase in aid to dependent children. No more recent figures are available to me, but the trend doubtless continues.

More recently a major school building program in the 1960's has afforded new jobs for construction workers and instructional aids, and the OEO program (Office of *Navajo* Opportunity, or ONEO, in the Navajo country) has created a large number of part-time jobs.

Tribal public works programs are a significant source of short-term employment.

Mineral resources have been exploited almost entirely by private, nontribal capital. Income from minerals comes to the tribe in the form of rents, royalties, and bonuses. Betewen 1935 and 1956, some $19 million accrued. Between 1957 and 1968, the total was $217 million. The upturn is obvious. The first period shows an average of less than $100,000 per annum, the second, an average of about $18 million per annum, with a range from less than $9 million to nearly $35 million.

It would be a mistake to believe that these royalties could substantially benefit individual Navajos if they were divided on a *per capita* basis. The principal reason for this lies in the present economic condition and economic opportunities of Navajos (described below). Per capita divisions would be dissipated at once to meet such consumer needs as trucks, furniture, and clothing, leaving each family with precisely its present inadequate economic base. The principal beneficiaries would be border town merchants. The average benefit would vary around $200 per person, or $1,000 per family, per annum. As will be shown later the tribe has not divided these funds but instead has used them for a variety of useful purposes.

There is some tribal industry. And there is now some private industrial development on the reservation.

The result of income from uranium, oil, gas, and coal is recent years has been to transform the role of the Tribal Council and to make some progress toward breaking down the barriers to development engendered by the lack of the necessary technological base (infrastructure) on the reservation.

The tribe has used its funds in imaginative ways: For emergency relief, for housing grants to those unable to afford materials (limited to $600), for relief of impoverished families whose homes are destroyed by fire, for prostheses, which the Public Health Service will not supply, for baby layettes and clothing for schoolchildren whose parents cannot afford them—for a range of social services. It has set aside a large principal sum the income of which provides scholarships and loans for college students. It has enacted enabling legislation to permit it to cooperate in industrial development on reservation and in border towns where this development would result in Navajo employment. It has set up a revolving credit fund. It pays the Navajo law and order (police) staff and the tribal judges. It supports the construction and improvement of chapter houses (for community organization headquarters and community functions). It has put money into Tribal enterprises, of which a Forest Products Industry, a Tribal Utility Authority, an Arts and Crafts Board, some motels, and a housing project are successful examples, and a cement products, clay products, leather products, wood products, and wool textile industry are unsuccessful examples, together with four trading posts once owned by the Tribe. It is engaged in water development. The Tribal public works program supports activities that improve a variety of local conditions, including work on dirt roads whose maintenance is vital for community travel. And more projects could be named.

Furthermore, it has negotiated successfully for access to gas pipelines running from reservation gas sources to the west coast. Electrical power is generated on the reservation by coal, by Utah Construction

Co., and the Arizona Public Service Co., and a portion of this is reserved for tribal use in the future. Electricity has been run in from Farmington as well, and the Navajo Tribal Utility Authority deals with electrification, natural gas systems, and water and sewage facilities.

Indeed development projects undertaken by the Tribe since the 1950's would require a volume for description and evaluation.

There is ONEO money, as has been said, furnishing part-time employment to many Navajos.

The result of this period of expansion is the existence of a number of new foci of power on the reservation. Prior to 1920 the foci were the BIA, the traders, the missions, the border town financial interests, and influential Navajo leaders. In the 1920's the tribal council and the local chapters began to be slight forces, and in the 1930's larger ones. At the same time, with the first oil leases, large corporate business began to be a force on the reservation, with interests in council decisions. Today, in addition to traders, missions, and border town financial interests, there is still the BIA, there is a well-organized Tribal Council, there are local chapters, there are a variety of major corporate financial interests, there is ONEO (Office of Navajo Economic Opportunity), which is not under BIA control and becomes a new power element, there is DNA, a legal aid organization funded by ONEO but with its own board of directors. Needless to say the powers clash, and the results of the clash are visible in conflicts within the Tribal Council, since each non-Navajo force seeks support within the Council.

To read the preface to the Navajo Tribal Code (published in 1962) written by the former attorney to the Navajo Tribe, is to feel that tremendous progress has been made. Yet the per capita income figures are discouraging, both as to relative amounts and as to source.

Perhaps the most important point to be made is that Navajo income is probably in the neighborhood of one-third to one-quarter of various white comparison groups. The second important point is that nearly three-quarters of that income comes from wagework and another sixth comes from welfare, social security, railroad retirement, etc. This is, then, a low-income group, one of the very lowest in the country, and one that spends a great deal of its time in maintaining herds and farms but gets most of its income from elsewhere.

Young, for example, estimated Navajo per capita income in 1960 at $521 net and at $645 if the value of "free" Government services and surplus commodities was included. This includes the value of livestock and farm products consumed by the producers. The State of New Mexico (including Navajos) had a per capita of $1,812; McKinley Country (including Navajos) had a per capita of $1,709, and the United States as a whole had a per capita of $2,116 (TNY 1961: 229). U.S. Census figures for 1960 are not computed separately for Navajos, but are for rural Indians in Arizona and elsewhere. They show higher per capita figures, but these are based on all individuals 14 or over and are not directly comparable with Young's. Indian figures run at one-third to one-quarter of white figures in Arizona. Adams' figures for Shonto in 1955 (Adams 1963: 137–148) run lower than Young's but are for an isolated area with relatively little wagework income. Belaboring the point will not change it; Navajo figures are probably low among American Indian groups, but not at the absolute bottom; their incomes are below Negro and Spanish-American incomes and far below Anglo incomes. No figures for more recent years are available.

Young has estimates for percentages of income from various sources for Navajos in 1958 (TNY 1961: 100–109), regrouped in Aberle (1966: 81). Only 10 percent of income came from livestock and agriculture; only 1 percent from arts and crafts; 68 percent from wages; 5 percent from mineral leases; but 16 percent from railroad retirement, social security, welfare, etc. Over 60 percent of wages were derived from off-reservation work, and two-thirds of off-reservation wages were then from railroad work. Furthermore nearly two-thirds of on-reservation wages were derived from Federal and tribal employment: 40 percent from Federal and 23 percent from tribal sources. (In 1967–68, the BIA employed 3,300 Indians, most of them Navajos, out of an estimated labor force of 32,000, over 10 percent of employables. Apparently 50 percent of that force was seeking employment. Navajo Area Office 1968a: 12, 14.)

The figures for 1958 on farming and livestock include estimates for the value of products consumed and do not reflect sales only. Thus in 1958 the two dominant sources of income were wages and welfare, which made up 84 percent of all income in goods and cash. This is no subsistence economy. I have no comparable figures for the present period. They would show a rise in terms of on-reservation wagework, because of ONEO funds (about $11,500,000 in 1968), Tribal public works programs, Federal building programs, and increase in the number of school employees. Welfare would also rise. The percentage derived from farming and herding would fall. Yet under present circumstances, for reasons to be set forth, many Navajos will not give up and dare not give up their farming and herding, although on a dollar accounting basis it is relatively trivial. Instead, the characteristic pattern for Navajo families is the necessity to depend on a multiplicity of income sources, no one of which yields a stable and predictable income.

IV. The Reservation as an Underdeveloped Area

What are the equities of the Navajo situation? There are several ways of looking at this. In earlier decades, a plea for improvement of Indian conditions was often based on the fact that since Western European settlers took the continent from the Indians, we owed a special debt to them. A later plea was based on the argument that we have a moral obligation to "lift the Indian to our level." To each of these the counter argument has been made that the Indians could have done for themselves what various immigrant groups did for themselves. This ignores the fact that Indians were not immigrants, but on the contrary fighting a losing battle against immigrants backed initially by various colonial forces and later by the Federal Government.

The argument set forth here is that the Navajo country is an underdeveloped area, and that the cause of its underdevelopment is its historical and current relations with the larger polity, economy, and society. If this is so, the issue becomes relatively clear: either these relationships must be changed, or we must openly decide that the dispossession and deprivation of the Navojo sector (and many other submerged sectors of our society) is something the consequences of which the rest of the society is prepared to accept.

The basic reason for this hundred-year period of underdevelopment is that the Navajos did not have the capital or the know-how to achieve development, Congress would not provide the Bureau with the funds necessary for development, nor would the States, and until the 1950's private industry had little interest in exploiting reservation resources. Various features of the reservation will be examined in turn.

A. THE TECHNOLOGICAL BASE

The Government did not, and for many decades the Navajos could not create the technological base that would make it possible for the area to be developed by Navajos, rather than by outside forces.

1. *Livestock.*—Virtually no effort was made to avert the eventual catastrophe that overtook the Navajo livestock industry in the 1930's. Many steps could have been taken. First, although there were sporadic efforts to bring larger and more productive sheep on the reservation in earlier days, these failed because the sheep could not cope with Navajo environmental conditions. In a crisis it was possible to develop a sheep that provided a much increased meat and wool yield and could cope with the reservation environment, and when it was developed, the Navajos accepted it: the barriers to improved livestock, then, were not just Navajo conservatism, but American. Earlier development of this breed could have made it possible to reduce the livestock painlessly if certain other steps had been taken as well. Incentive payments for culling, incentive payments for raising improved breeds, parity payments for livestock—all these, combined with livestock regulation, could have created improved livestock practices and economic yields. Government subsidies to farmers in other areas have proved to benefit large, rather than small owners. It is, therefore, no particular surprise that a tribe of small holders was not the beneficiary of such a program as has been outlined.

2. *Roads.*—The road system has always been inadequate. There were no paved roads on the reservation except for Highway 666, which was needed to connect nonreservation communities, until the 1950's. Today the reservation has about 30 percent as many miles of surfaced road per 1,000 square miles as the surrounding rural areas. The States receive Federal supplements to their highway programs, nominally to build reservation roads; the Indians pay State gasoline tax, which goes toward road building; but the State does little to build reservation roads, which are primarily built by the Federal Government. The inadequacy of the system of paved roads handicaps every phase of Navajo life: job seeking, transportation of children to schools, trips to medical facilities, livestock marketing, and so on. As one indication, when a single black-top road was built in one community, half the boarders in the local school became day pupils.

3. *Water.*—The water system remains totally inadequate, whether in terms of domestic water or stock water. As respects domestic water, in 1960, a survey of over 1,400 homes indicates that less than 12 percent had a water source $\frac{1}{4}$ mile or less from the home; another 36 percent had a source between $\frac{1}{4}$ mile and 2 miles, so that less than half of the houses had a water source closer than 2 miles. The remaining

52 percent were drawing on water sources more than 2 miles distant, and indeed over 17 percent traveled more than 4 miles (TNY 1961: 306). We are speaking here of water for drinking, cooking, dishwashing, laundry, and for washing hands, face, hair, feet, et cetera. (Most bathing is done in sweat baths or by using a chapter or schoolhouse bath facility—or the trailer of a friend working in the school.) At one time this perhaps made not too much difference. Today, hauling water requires the use of male labor and at times ties men down who might otherwise take off-reservation jobs (see below under *Fuel, light, and heat*).

It is unlikely that much can be done about running water in homes while Navajos live scattered as they do. Where sizable concentrations of population are found—as at agency headquarters—there is running water in the homes. Expansion of water systems beyond agency headquarters proper is a function of the Navajo Tribal Utility Authority, founded in 1966. It had about 1,000 customers in 1967, or perhaps a maximum of four families out of 100. Only increase in the number and percentage of people living in concentrated clusters of residences will make it possible to reduce the number of people who must carry their water. There has been a considerable improvement in recent years in the number of Government wells from which people can draw domestic water, but they are not inspected frequently enough. As a corollary of the lack of running water, there is a serious sewage problem. Population densities have tripled since 1930, but Navajos outside agency headquarters use outhouses for the most part (they once followed a more salubrious practice of burying wastes), which promises serious health problems in the future. NTUA is developing sewage systems, but these are, of course, for concentrated populations.

The failure to develop adquate stock water resources contributes to the erosion of the reservation and makes rational use of pasture quite impossible. Undeveloped water is a resource that Navajos do not regard as the exclusive property of anyone. If they did, one man's flocks could die when his source was dry, and his neighbor's on a similar occasion. Hence people have traditional rights to move across another man's customary pasture to get to water in that pasture, treading out and consuming fodder in the process. I have known men who had to move their own stock to a winter pasture area in the summer because, during a dry spell, their neighbor's sheep were going to and fro so often. Government-developed wells are protected for common use by current grazing regulations. The results are conflict, treading out of pasture, and inability to plan the use of pasture. The topics of water for industry and irrigation are discussed elsewhere.

4. *Fuel, light, and heat.*—The Federal failure to develop local electrification in a largely electrified Nation is conspicuous. There is an increasing amount of electrification on the reservation today—as a result of Tribal Council, not Federal action. The NTUA had 7,000 electric customers in 1967, or about 30 out of 100 families.

In the absence of highways, the gathering of wood is unduly difficult, which again ties men at home who might find positions in the extra-reservation labor force. Today some Navajos begin to use propane, for heat, light, and cooking in their homes, but the delivery of large gas supplies remains a problem—this for a tribe that is at one end of a gas pipeline that reaches to the west coast and was constructed at a cost of $140 million (TNY 1965: 266). Some of the natural gas leases make provision for Navajo tapping of the pipeline, but relatively little has yet been done to pipe gas to homes. NTUA had about 1,300 customers in 1967, or about five families out of 100. This situation is again partly a problem of scattered population.

The cost of this pipeline is sometimes used as a figure to justify the fact that Navajos receive royalties on their minerals rather than exploiting them themselves. If one considers, on the contrary, that private capital can pay for the lease, the exploitation, the processing, the royalties, and the pipeline and still realize a profit, the picture alters somewhat. And when the $140 million used by private capital for this one pipeline is put alongside the $90 million allocated to rehabilitate the Navajo and Hopi combined from 1951 to 1961, serious questions arise as to how to spend rehabilitation funds, and as to how much money is required.

5. *Miscellaneous.*—The list of underdevelopment could go on and on; it is worth mentioning housing and communications, in order to say that both are sadly underdeveloped. Some progress in housing has been made recently.

Under these circumstances, commercial, industrial, and agricultural and livestock development on the reservation necessarily lags: it has nothing to "hook up to" and, because of the educational deficit (see below), until recently it could rely on almost no supply of adequately trained local labor.

B. THE COURSE OF MINERAL EXPLOITATION

It is only by luck that the Navajos have mineral wealth. In the 1870's Agent Arny tried to release a strip across the northern end of the reservation of those days, because he thought there were minerals there. Alerted by traders married into the tribe, the Navajos succeeded in having him removed. From 1889 to 1891 there were efforts to find minerals in the northern reservation, illegally and legally, and the agent foresaw a fate for the Navajos like the dispossession of the Sioux when gold was found in the Black Hills. A cession of part of the reservation in 1892 occurred because it was thought that there were minerals there.

The Navajos were fortunate, however. No significant mineral finds on the reservation were made until the 1920's, when the Federal Government created a Tribal Council for the specific purpose of having a legal body to sign mineral leases. (The Council was not always willing to do so, however; see Kelly, 1968.) They were also fortunate that a protracted series of battles in Congress raised the allowable percentage of oil royalties going to Indians living on reservation land created by Executive order (see Kelly, 1968). Until recently, royalty rates ran at a normal rate of 12.5 percent by Federal law, except in individually negotiated instances. In 1961 the rate was raised to 16⅔ percent, with the possibility of higher rates in some instances (TNY 1961: 265). In addition, the tribe receives bonuses. On unproven land these sometimes run up to $5,500 per acre. On proven lands they run at a fixed rate of $500, but royalties are negotiable, and under certain conditions some of them reportedly brought high royalty bids, averaging as much as 50 percent (Navajo Tribal Code, I (1962): xiii).

The dollar costs of these leases have been low. For example, in 1960 about $114,000 was spent for the salaries of Federal and Tribal employees who expedited leasing. This, of course, does not include such concealed costs as the per diem figures for Councilmen meeting to consider the acceptance of bids nor the salary of the Tribe's legal staff insofar as that staff spent time in providing general advice to the tribe in these matters. Even so, additional concealed costs would still represent a relatively small figure compared with the $12 million of income from leases, bonuses, and royalties received in 1960. The costs of exploitation of the oil fields, on the contrary, is high: $100,000 to $300,000 per completed well in the Aneth area, and $140 million for a gas pipeline to the west coast. It has become an accepted dictum, to be challenged here, that leasing is the appropriate, sound, and economical way to exploit Navajo mineral resources (see, for example, Hough, 1967).

The point to be made, however, is that the entire operation has been run with primary concern for non-Navajo needs. Had minerals been discovered earlier on Navajo land, the land would not have remained Navajo. The rate of exploitation is determined by the needs of private industry and Government, without consideration of any controlled rate of exploitation for the sake of Navajo budgetary planning. And the producer receives a tax benefit, a depletion allowance, although it is Navajo resources that are being depleted. In sum, through tax loopholes the American public underwrites a not inconsiderable part of the expenses, the Navajos get the royalties, and the oil companies get the profits.

The answer to all this might well be that since the Navajos have little, they cannot afford the experts, equipment, roads, gaslines, and so forth, necessary to exploit the fields. This would be a reasonable argument, were it not that the U.S. Government subsidizes many well-endowed enterprises. It runs an agricultural subsidy program that has been repeatedly shown to benefit large producers more than small. It pays the research and development expenses of large corporations manufacturing novel military equipment and then pays a profit to these same corporations when they sell to the Government (see Nieburg, 1966) and so on. Under these circumstances, it would seem reasonable to redress the equities somewhat, to consider a subsidy sufficient to permit Navajos to develop their own mineral industry.

Instead, although a joint development program with a private firm was considered and rejected by the Bureau and the Tribe a few years ago, so far as I know Navajo management has never been proposed to the Tribe by the Government, and there is reason to believe that Federal officials emphasize the advantages of leasing and the difficulties of native development, so that by now everyone is convinced of the efficiency, economy, and equity of the present arrangements.

C. EDUCATION

1. Early in this report it was said that undereducation was a result, not a cause of underdevelopment. That is true in the sense that the Federal Government has not supplied Navajos with an adequate school system, and that this failure is a part of a general undernourishment of the reservation's economy and society. It is also true that an undereducated population is one of the factors that slows development.

In sum, the Navajos were provided with insufficient schools for their children from 1868 until the 1950's, when, for the first time, there were enough seats in schools for almost all the children. About 90 percent of Navajo children of school age are now in school, the remainder being largely the physically or mentally handicapped and the children of parents who avoid sending them to school.

There was early Navajo resistance to schooling, partly because the labor of children was an asset for the livestock economy, but also because the early schools were often brutally run, fed the children miserably, and created conditions that resulted in many deaths from infectious deseases. From 1946 on, as children became an economic liability and as wartime exposure of a part of the population to the outside world showed them the disadvantages of undereducation, Navajos began to plead for schools. Now they demand an adequate educational system. The long-term lack of education has meant a lack of opportunity to compete successfully in the larger society.

2. Only in the last few years has there been the beginnings of a broadscale effort to introduce special methods for the teaching of English (English as a second language), although the vast majority of entering pupils speak only Navajo. Early, promising efforts by Willard Beatty in the 1930's and early 1940's did not take hold. As a result, there is often little relationship between the language competence of a pupil and his nominal grade level. I know seventh-graders who can barely understand simple English in a face-to-face situation with a familiar person. Clearly they cannot cope with seventh-grade instruction in mathematics, history, and science.

3. In the 1930's and early 1940's, under Willard Beatty's aegis, there was an effort to introduce curricular material that would encourage a feeling of pride in being a Navajo and an Indian. Again, this effort did not take hold. There is now some revival of such efforts, which find slightly more acceptance among teachers today as America's general ethnic problems multiply. Meantime, however, most Navajos passed through school under conditions that led them to believe that they and their culture were regarded as inferior. Some people pass through such an experience hardened and tempered in their opposition to the larger society, but a commoner result is a feeling of defeat early instilled.

4. The pattern of schooling makes unusual demands on both parents and children. The early approach in the Navajo country was on-reservation boarding schools, later supplemented by off-reservation boarding schools. These early schools (from the 1870's to the early 1930's) had unfavorable characteristics mentioned above. In addition, they demanded the separation of parents and children. Yet few families in the larger society would accept a similar separation from their young children by Government edict.

Later, a day school program in the 1930's foundered for lack of a technological base: the roads were so poor that pupils could not be bussed to school, nor, given weather conditions on the reservation, could they walk in winter, nor did their parents have adequate ways to bring them. Today in some areas a child is in boarding school near his home until eighth grade and may then be in boarding school some distance from his home. In other areas, he must leave his home region after third grade. A notable exception is found in major administrative centers where many agency and tribal personnel live. There,

242

public high schools are to be found, so that this group of parents does not have to part with its children. Some 50 to 60 percent of Navajo children attend boarding schools.

It is true that boarding schools permit parents, all of whose children are in school, to seek winter off-reservation employment, but this marginal employment pattern, further discussed below, is not a desirable one.

5. The first community college was opened in 1969, although as yet it has no building of its own: it now occupies part of a large high school that has not yet been filled. It is good to note that it is directed by a Navajo board of regents.

6. There has never been an adequate Bureau-operated college for Indians off reservation.

7. There has never been a proper college preparatory program on reservation.

8. Only in recent years has there been a Federal scholarship program for Indian students. In recent years BIA scholarship support has increased. On some agencies it is able to support all students admitted to college or university. In the case of the Navajo, the tribe's mineral wealth has been used in part for a scholarship fund, which supports about 500 students. The BIA, in the Navajo case, uses its scholarship funds to support those students to whom the tribe is unable to make grants, which is a reasonable approach, and one that has provided funds for a number of successful students. It is the lateness of Federal entry into this field, however, that I wish to stress.

D. EMPLOYMENT

Navajos are subject to the racial discrimination so common in American society when they seek jobs in the off-reservation world. They are thereby reduced in their capacity to secure income through employment. They are discriminated against in hiring, in wage levels, and in working conditions. Furthermore, this discrimination is most marked in the border towns, precisely in the areas that would be most convenient for Navajos seeking work—and also in the very communities most dependent on Indian customers for income. The *Navajo Times*, the tribe's own newspaper, characteristically carries ads for consumer goods from border towns and help wanted ads from remote communities. Although the Bureau is the largest single employer of Navajo workers, charges of discrimination have been made even there.

E. THE REGION

Section VI of this report deals with proposals for the development of the reservation. A proper perspective on development, however, requires attention to the towns bordering the reservation, since the reservation is not an isolated enclave. These towns are themselves relatively underdeveloped, with a heavy reliance on tourism and on an impoverished Indian clientele and an emphasis on retail and wholesale facilities. (Farmington relies as well on the newly developed oil and gas industry.) They have contributed to reservation underdevelopment, since they have been jealous of competing on-reservation facilities. In the long run, a prosperous Indian population will, however, benefit them. As things now stand, the reservation is an underdeveloped vacuum standing inside a larger partial vacuum: the border towns.

F. SUMMARY

The Federal Government is responsible for the situation on the reservation. It has been in charge of the land and the people for a hundred years. At the end of this time we find an undereducated, unhealthy, overcrowded population with a primitive livestock and farming pattern, with no technological substratum for development, and with almost no development save for the exploitation of mineral resources by outside private capital. Furthermore, Navajos have not been protected from the relatively monopolistic situation created by trading posts, for pressures to enter the job market on unequal terms, or from an unplanned draining off of their resources. They are, then, a population that is exploited and underdeveloped.

It should be noted that I have referred here, and in many, but not all other places in this report, to the Federal Government, rather than to the BIA. The BIA is what local and national popular pressures and Congress have made it: an understaffed, underbudgeted operation with no control over many of the salient factors that would make a difference in Indian economic development. It is not encouraged to set up tribal businesses of any scale, it is not in a position to exert much pressure on border town populations, and so on. In the Navajo case, what water, roads, police, schools, agricultural extension work, livestock extension work, and planning were to be found in the area until the 1950's, when tribal income increased, were the product of the Bureau and its resources. I have tried to show that what it was able to do was totally inadequate, in spite of the labors of many men of good conscience and intelligence.

The inability of the BIA to proceed with development with its own resources is amply evident from the most recent budget available to me, that for fiscal year 1968. The total is $54,715,490. Nearly 70 percent of that budget is for "education and welfare services," almost all of the 70 percent for education. Another 12 percent is for resources management and repair and maintenance. Only a little over 18 percent is allocated to construction (buildings and utilities—a little over 1 percent) and road construction (the remainder). It is notable that development funds came from the Economic Development Administration ($8.5 million, with plans to apply for another $21 million). The point is not necessarily that the Bureau's budget should include development funds (although I will later argue that in the past it certainly should have), but that unless generous funds on a preferential basis can be made available to the Navajos and other Indian tribes, development must lag hopelessly.

We turn from the overall picture to a closer examination of the local economy.

V. THE LOCAL ECONOMY

A. THE STYLE OF LIFE

The effects of all these factors promoting underdevelopment in the Navajo country are, at the local level, a particular style of economic and social life—one often criticized by Anglos as evidence of backwardness, or praised by some as "the Navajo way." It has some roots in custom, but it has its present causes in current economic conditions and represents an adjustment to them.

It is a curiosity that so much energy has been expended by agents of American society—Bureau officials (particularly in the past), missionaries, sometimes traders, and others—to push Navajos to give up "Navajo ways" like long hair, ceremonials, and even mother-in-law avoidance, and so little has been expended in giving them an opportunity to take on those parts of American life that they so evidently want: Roads, plumbing, electric lights, sewing machines, and so on. The aim has been too often to rob them of cultural identity while depriving them of material benefits, where it should so clearly be a matter of providing them with the opportunities for materially improved conditions while allowing them cultural identity and pride in being Navajo.

The key items that promote the Navajo style are—

    (1) shortages of material equipment, stemming from a shortage of cash;

    (2) simple logistic problems in running the household and the subsistence economy, resulting from a need for some wage labor and from the difficulties involved in herding, getting water, and hauling fuel; and

    (3) fluctuating income.

By shortages of equipment I refer to a number of things. Navajo families have difficulty managing without access to a pickup truck, which is often needed for such mutually contradictory purposes as hauling wood and water, getting to and from a job, and procuring supplies from the trading post or the town. Yet by no means every unit of husband, wife, and immature children can afford a pickup. Hence a cluster of such families (an extended family) is advantageous, since it can share the pickup and often can pool sporadic contributions to maintain the payments on a pickup. (In effect, Navajos today are involved in the lifetime rental of a pickup truck, at about $200 per month. It takes about 3 years to pay for a pickup, and by the end of that time, road conditions being what they are, it is uneconomical to keep it. It is traded, and payments on a new one begin.) But not only pickups are involved. I have seen gas irons, gas lamps, tarpaulins, water barrels, sewing machines, automobile tools, etc., borrowed from family to family to meet temporary exigencies.

The absence of running water, of adequate stock water, and of fuel except in the form of firewood, all require the labor of some men in the family for at least a day or two a week. Again the extended family is useful as labor pool. There are, however, families where, for one reason or another, there are no resident adult males: Where there are a set of related women all of whom are divorced or widowed, whose younger male relatives have married out or taken jobs far away. In one such case, as an example, a woman's married son is the major source of labor for firewood and water hauling, for her and several female descendants with small children. He lives an hour's drive away and has a major commitment to his own children and his wife's family as well. Meantime he certainly cannot seek employment.

Along the same lines, many Navajos do not believe that they dare to give up their livestock. But someone must herd it. Within limits this work can be done by women, although it is seldom done exclusively by women. Particularly in winter, and when sheep are lost, herding is arduous in the extreme. To have only *one* possibly herder in a family is to tie the herder permanently to the home, without opportunity even to go to the trading post, and to invite disaster if that one should fall ill. Again the labor pool afforded by the extended family is valuable.

As for fluctuating income there is, for most Navajos, no stable and predictable single source of income. Weather, disease, and fluctuating prices for wool, mohair, and sheep and cattle cause wide variations in both the food supply and the income from livestock. In an arid environment, crops often fail as well. The wagework market is variable. Even Government jobs (BIA and Office of Navajo Economic Opportunity) fluctuate in accordance with budgetary variation. Furthermore a man receiving disability pay may experience no change in his physical condition yet be cut off the welfare lists, through the occasional "re-evaluations" of conditions like bad backs that occur.

Not only is there continual gift giving and borrowing within the extended family to cope with these variations, but there is a wide circle of kin who depend on each other, who ask for help when they need it and give help when they can. This style of economic life we may call reciprocity—the Navajos call it "helping out" when they speak of it in English—and the ethic that accompanies it is generosity. No more than among other peoples does every Navajo do what is expected of him, but this ethic dominates the Navajo values at present. The behavior that accompanies it is often seen by whites as foolishly improvident. It is not: it is the best way for people thus circumstanced to survive.

Thus in a typical extended family—parents, some of their children (usually daughters) and their mates, and their children's children— multiple economic dependencies are the rule: Livestock, farming, weaving, part-time off-reservation work, and welfare are frequently found as income and subsistence sources in the same unit. No one of these can be relinquished—that is, efficient specialization is impossible—because none is certain and none is sufficient.

Three hundred years of history leave the Navajo in one sense exactly where they started: In the 1660's they depended on multiple, fluctuating resources—the farm, the herd, the hunt, the raid, and in the 1960's the sources have only partly changed—the farm, the herd, the hunt to a small extent, the job, the wood, rug, silver, and pinon nut market, and the welfare check.

B. THE ROLE OF THE TRADER

Any institution may be a force for progress in one era and a conservative force in another, without changing its basic form. That is what has happened to the traders. Once they were the primary channel for introducing Navajos to the elements of Western technology, food, clothing, utensils, and so forth, that they could use; assisted Navajos in their land struggles—some still do; and explained the ways of white men and Government to them. Today, as the center of each community's credit system, they are forced into being conservative forces by their quest for market security. Each attitude was tied to opportunities for profit—the first to gain, the second to retain a market. And their situation is becoming increasingly difficult.

Traders aim at keeping a certain volume of Navajo business, which they manage by judicious use of credit. There is no long-term debt peonage in the Navajo country: Navajos are allowed credit only in amounts that they can repay in the relatively near future. The trader supplies his customers with credit sufficient to absorb their short-run (6 months to a year) future income, extending credit for expectable income that is likely to pass through the trader's own hands. This income includes wool sales, rug sales, sheep sales, and to some degree cattle sales (when these go through the trader), welfare and railroad retirement checks, and Federal and tribal paychecks in areas where he is the only easily available agent for cashing checks. Although tribal law requires a trader to give the Navajo payee the full amount of a check he cashes for him, this law is certainly widely violated. (Traders could have been more tightly regulated by the BIA. Regulations permit this, but U.S. attorneys have not pushed enforcement.) The trader allows credit on future wools, rugs, sheep, and cattle, and on future checks, and balances off the credit when the Navajo sells to him or when the checks come in. He serves as a pawnbroker for Navajo jewelry.

The trader is in a position to put pressure on Navajos to take off-reservation jobs so that they can pay off debts to him, and he can apply pressure on men working off reservation to remit money by informing the man's family that credit will be cut off if no money comes in. This is riskier than the livestock and wool sales and local checks (often mailed care of the trading post), but traders learn eventually who are good and who are poor credit risks in these situations.

As every trader is well aware, he is the community's bank, and apparently the Tribe, the Government, and the local financial interests in the towns are willing for this arrangement to continue, since they have developed no feasible alternatives, such as a fully adequate Tribal or Federal loan program. The Tribal revolving credit program had outstanding loans of $1,123,000 at the end of fiscal year 1967–68, according to the Navajo area office. It is not clear whether this included loans to Tribal businesses or not. Even if we assume that these are all loans to individuals, it should be noted that in 1961 Young (TNY 1961: 245) estimated a need of $2,500,000 to $3 million to support an adequate loan program. The Area Office also mentions that in 1967 "outside sources" provided financing in excess of $47 million, but without further particulars one does not know what to make of this figure, which includes loans to the tribe.

The trader maintains his position, insofar as he can, by credit saturation, as Adams (1963) calls it. (Most of my information on trading comes from this source; some comes from observation of a number of posts from 1949 on.) Credit saturation is the practice of soaking up a man's future earnings by judicious extension of credit, since this tends to result in a monopoly over that man's purchasing power. His interest in credit saturation is demonstrated by the willingness to give a man a higher dollar value for his livestock in credit than in cash.

He compensates for his role as banker—for the costs of his credit to him—in a variety of ways. One way is *high markup*. Prices on reservation are high in comparison with the border towns. At one post, where prices averaged 10–15 percent above town prices, markups ranged from 35 percent for groceries to 75 percent for dry goods, 100 percent for hardware, and 100–200 percent for remedies (Adams, 1963). Traders justify their high markup on two bases, transportation costs and credit risks. Both are certainly elements in traders' costs. So, of course, are the traders' own interest rates. What a reasonable markup would be, of course, has not been established. Some traders add to their markup a credit charge, sometimes a flat 10 percent of the purchase. Some give to regular Anglo customers, cash or credit, discounts as high as 20 percent. Some also give discounts to Navajos who regularly pay cash or who pay cash often, but these are smaller—about 10 percent. There is no evident reason why Anglos should get a higher discount than Navajos, except as a way for the trader to separate "us" from "them".

What it does in addition, of course, is to make costs lower for Anglos, who have higher incomes, than for Navajos, who have lower ones. Perhaps it preserves more business for the trader, inducing Anglos to postpone fewer purchases until their next trip to town. But if there is still a profit after a 20 percent discount, one is curious about the entire operation. Both Navajos and Anglos who have been given discounts are discouraged by the trader from discussing the practice with others. Since they do not wish to lose the discount, they are likely to talk about it only to a limited extent.

At present the reservation situation is highly variable from one place to another. In many areas, Navajos are served by local retailing facilities with the characteristics of a general store in a rural community in the 1930's. Still others are served by facilities like small super-markets. At Window Rock a new Fed-Mart store, opened in fall of 1968, provides a combined discount house and supermarket facility for Navajos from that area on a day-to-day basis and from a much larger area for occasional shopping trips. (Tribal funds were used to attract this business, which has undertaken to hire Navajo staff for middle managerial, as well as lower positions.)

In the hinterlands, there is an increasing number of cafes attached to trading posts; closer to town are restaurants or drive-ins not so attached. In larger centers there are tourist courts. Some trading posts run garages.

In the hinterlands, only trading posts serve to cash checks. In Ship-rock and Window Rock there are banks, in the founding of which the Tribe has played an economic role.

Nevertheless, much of the population must travel distances of 20 to 150 miles for boot and shoe repairs, radio repairs, complex automotive repairs, haircuts (except for the amateur jobs, often quite good, that Navajos supply to each other), beauty parlors, even duplicate keys. For all these trivial items, as well as for major items like furniture, men's suits, women's dresses (except for the simpler ones), they must travel, for the most part, to border towns or, with the new Fed-Mart, to Window Rock. This means gross inefficiency for Navajos in their daily living (since they must run hither and yon for quite minor items), a high cost of living (since they must pay transportation costs), and finally the siphoning off of cash to the border towns, so that Navajo income has no "multiplier" effect for Navajos: the range of customer services that could be provided by Navajos on reservation are sup-plied by non-Navajos, primarily in border towns. There are many reasons for this lack of facilities. One is the trader's fear of over-expansion; another the poverty of the population; a third the potential

Navajo entrepreneur's lack of capital; a fourth is the relative scarcity of trained Navajos to run local businesses. For a visitor to Shiprock or Window Rock, or even a smaller center like Chinle, the situation has changed enormously in the last 20 years. At points farther from the reservation borders the change is far too slow.

To summarize thus far, the trader is the center of the credit system of many communities. He serves the purpose of extending credit to compensate for the fact that Navajo income comes in irregular amounts. He therefore controls a good deal in the community: pressures for off-reservation employment, for example, may emanate from him, and his attitude toward extending credit controls a family's ability to undertake a large ceremony. He has changed from a "fashion leader" to a reluctant fashion follower, whose customers seek more kinds of goods than he wishes to stock. The reservation lacks many important consumer facilities, which are located in border towns.

The trader's situation, however, is complicated today by three factors: (1) There is more ready cash available to Navajos. Although they must often cash Federal and Tribal paychecks with the trader, they do not always do so. (2) Transportation is easier with better roads, and more pickups and larger trucks, making it possible for Navajos to do quantity buying in town or at more distant posts, and even to sell cattle and sheep in small quantities in town. (3) His own credit costs are rising, so that his credit business is probably more costly to him today (no figures available).

Nowadays some relatively well-to-do Navajos use the trading posts as they would the corner grocery—for the occasional loaf of bread or bottle of milk—doing their major shopping in supermarkets, sometimes a hundred miles or more away. They do so because it saves money. Others, ordinarily not at all well off, use the credit arrangement to insure larger amounts of disposable cash at particular times. Thus a woman may get credit on a rug at one post but sell it at another, or in town. Eventually she must pay off the debt with another rug, but temporarily she has the credit and the cash as well. If this can be done at a time when she has to clothe her children for school or meet some other emergency, the delay may be worth while. The restriction of inventory also leads to shopping in town, and such shopping clearly is not likely to be for the odd item but for a large order. (Among the goods one might not find in some out-of-the-way posts are dental floss, ashtrays, and mailing labels, all of which are nevertheless used by some Navajos and some non-Navajos in the community.)

In the early 1950's the Tribal Council talked as if it might fail to renew a number of trading post leases or renew them only on a short-term basis. In the end, however, it set up provisions for 25-year leases, with no option for renewal except where a case was made that capital could not be recovered in 25 years. It also set up some anti-monopoly provisions. Leases can be canceled for cause (see Navajo Tribal Code). These leases will expire, for the most part, in 1978–79.

The trader is at the bottom of a business hierarchy in the Southwest. Above him are wholesalers and banks. In the power hierarchy of the Southwestern States, few actual traders are to be found, although many significant figures come from what were once trading families.

Traders are kings only on the reservation, and their position is certainly undermined today. Adams argues that many traders could survive in no other setting because they are not sufficiently up to date as businessmen. This may be true for some; it does not seem to be true for most of those I have known. Furthermore, Tribal regulations would appear to make it difficult for a reservationwide or regional monopoly to be set up, but many traders are united by kinship and marriage. Shared interests and personal ties do now, and will increasingly in the future, create a tendency towary,anp ooillgo d toward a "monopoly" by a few people united among themselves and able to compete successfully with new outsiders and with potential Navajo traders, but perhaps not with an expansion in the number of stores like Fed-Mart.

It must be noted that traders do many things not in the repertory of the corner grocer or supermarket manager. They advise Navajos who receive bafflling documents from the Government, notify people about meetings, drive them to the hospital in emergencies, turn out to rescue them from snow and flooded arroyos, provide their own telephone at cost per call to members of the community, deliver individual messages, give wedding presents, sometimes bury the dead, and bear with some patience the trials of daily life.

Nevertheless, Navajos are served by a relatively expensive, inventory-constricted set of retailers. These retailers control the credit network and operate with high interest charges that are neither regulated not clearly visible to the customer. (A 10-percent credit charge on any credit purchase—not a universal practice by any means—is not a clear charge, since it might in different cases amount to 10 percent per day, per month, or per year.) Consumer facilities situation on the reservation are underdeveloped. The trader's position is being weakened, but traders form a relatively well-consolidated interest bloc on the reservation. Traders of Navaio origin, it should be made clear, are few and far between.

C. SUMMARY

Let us suppose that we could cut a cross section through the reservation territory extending about 8,000 feet below ground, and that we could make a rapid-motion picture of the flow of population, money, and resources from about 1900 on. What would we see? First, we would see a population doubled thrice between 1870 and 1958: hogans and houses would multiply before our eyes. Plant cover would disappear; huge washes would appear and increase in size; topsoil would disappear. An ebb and flow of the population off the reservation to employment sites could be observed. But money would flow predominantly to the trader and from the trader to the larger economy, balanced only by a flow necessary to sustain life and (in recent years) somewhat to enhance the standard of living. Sheep would increase rapidly—and then decrease suddenly in the 1930's, to remain more or less steady in quantity. Horses would increase until the 1930's and dwindle rapidly thereafter, while pickup trucks would partly replace them. Wagons would increase to the 1930's and almost disappear by the 1960's. Timber for firewood and house construction would dwindle fairly rapidly, commercial timber less so. Meantime, below ground, we would see oil, helium, coal, uranium, and vanadium draining off into the surrounding economy; we would see rents and royalties flowing into the tribal treasury, but, of course, major profits accruing to the corporations exploiting the reservation. We would see the slow development of roads, water for stock and drinking, government facilities, and so forth, and a flow of welfare funds coming in, to go out again via the trader. The net flow of many physical resources would be outward; the flow of profits would be outward; and the only major increase to be seen would be population, with a minor increment in physical facilities and consumer goods.

This is the picture of a colony. It can be duplicated time after time, place after place, in Africa, Asia, Latin America, and the Caribbean (for not all colonies are formally the political property of the country that dominates them), and, of course for other American Indian groups. Where do we go from here?

VI. Possibilities for Development

A. WHO SHOULD PLAN DEVELOPMENT?

Planning with Navajos has been a major aim for the Navajo Area Office for several decades. *Navajo Progress* (see bibliography) and other Area Office documents make it evident that efforts at joint planning with Navajos are to be found at every level from reservation-wide planning to the local community, and in every area, from industrial development to schools and roads. How much actual devolution of power there has been, however, is another question.

It is not satisfactory, however, to grant Navajos a share in the planning process. The solution is for Navajos to plan for themselves, drawing on such advice as they wish, whether from the Bureau and other Federal agencies, Congressmen, universities, management consultants, private industry, and whatever experts they need. The reason for this is that whereas Navajos may make mistakes, only Navajos are primarily concerned for Navajos. Congressmen are primarily concerned with their constituents, only a minority of whom are Indians. Bureau officials are constrained in many ways: they wish to be primarily concerned for Navajos, but they must be concerned lest they violate their role as trustees for Indian property, and lest they upset local interests, who in turn will put pressure on Congress, which will put pressure on them. Furthermore, neither Congress nor Federal officials have to live with mistakes in dealing with Navajo resources as closely as Navajos do.

To say that Navajos must plan does not mean that all planning should reside in the Tribal Council. There are now two levels at which planning occurs and a third seems to be emerging and should be encouraged. There is the Council and there are the Chapters, or, approximately speaking, a tribewide and a communitywide level. Regional groups are beginning to appear: Agency councils, presently made up of chapter officers and local tribal delegates. (There are five agencies in the Navajo Area Office: Fort Defiance, Crownpoint, Shiprock, Chinle, and Tuba City, and five agency councils.) Under present circumstances these councils are not elective, nor are they strong. A variety of possibilities exist for altering this situation, but it would be premature to discuss them here.

A responsive, responsible, and flexible system for Navajo planning would involve all three levels, since some issues are purely local, far more are regional, and some are tribal. The advantages of the regional (agency) council would be that it would permit new leadership to emerge, that it would be attuned to local issues, and that it would be a counterforce for grassroots level Navajos to the Tribal Council, whose concern with development in recent years has put it somewhat out of touch with local Navajos—or so they tell me. The Council is also unduly sensitive to the opinions of the Bureau and of private industry, and new regional councils might break that mold. Such a step, however, should be undertaken by Navajos, and not be external pressure.

The Bureau's reaction to this sort of recommendation is that it is "bringing Navajos along" as fast as it can. Nevertheless, it is true that I have found a great deal of frustration among Navajos who have definite ideas about what needs to be done and no way of influencing events: there are signs, then, of a great deal of frustrated energy on the reservation, where the Bureau seems to find apathy and hesitancy. It is also said that the Council tend to distrust Anglo employees of the Tribe and that they therefore show a high rate of turnover. But surely it is better for the Tribe to draw on experts whose sole responsibility is to the Tribe than to depend on those whom it did not hire and cannot fire.

The plan submitted below, then, is one man's version of what needs to be done. But it is assumed that the final plan, if there is to be a sound one, will be made by Navajos.

A necessary adjunct to Tribal planning is a Tribally operated unit capable of undertaking sample surveys to determine relevant characteristics of the Navajo population and Navajo reactions to possible plans. The recently completed Navajo manpower survey is an excellent start. It was begun in spring of 1967 and should soon be available. The tribe, the Bureau, ONEO, USPHS, and the Arizona State Employment Service joined forces to carry out this work.

It is evident from the work that Navajos have done as interpreters, census takers for the U.S. Government and for the chapters and the BIA schools, ONEO and social security investigators, and so on, that literate Navajos, some with only a sixth-grade education, are capable after brief training of working as interviewers. A sample of 1,000 to 2,000 Navajos should be adequate for quite complex surveys. What is needed are funds and a few experts—initially from outside, perhaps, but later Navajos—who can plan the sampling technique to be used and cope with the problem of wording interview schedules and of translating them into Navajo. The Tribe should not have to depend on the interests of outside investigators for data of this sort.

The Tribe also badly needs resource surveys. It seems that the USGS will not conduct surveys of Navajo mineral assets. Neither will the BIA. The Tribe should have its own experts, responsible to it, rather than depending on surveys by private businesses for their own purposes.

It should be noted that the Tribe is already carrying out its own planning activities and hiring its own experts. This should continue at an accelerated rate.

B. THE POPULATION CONTEXT OF DEVELOPMENT

Navajo population doubled between 1870 and 1898 (28 years); between 1898 and 1932 (34 years—slowed down by the terrible influenza epidemic after World War I); and between 1932 and 1958 (26 years). Its present rate of growth is probably on the order of $2\frac{3}{4}$ to $3\frac{1}{4}$

percent per annum (doubling in 22–26 years). No forces are evident that would slow the rate of growth; on the contrary with 55 percent of the population below 19 and 79 percent below 34, growth should accelerate in the future. Since the present population, on and off reservation, is in the neighborhood of 120,000, about 90 percent of whom spend some part of each year on reservation, any plans developed should be on the assumption that by 1990 (only a little more than 20 years away) there will be about 240,000, and that unless the external economy and the educational system alike have been enormously improved, 80 to 90 percent of these will wish to have a place on the reservation. Over 3,000 should enter the potential labor force this year, and about 4,500 in 1979. Any planning must be done on the basis of a maximum estimate of population and population growth and a minimum assumption respecting emigration from the reservation. These assumptions are necessary for humane, rational planning. Too many plans for the enhancement of standards of living in underdeveloped areas have foundered through a failure to allow for population growth. To develop a plan for extensive migration is easy but inhumane. It is also to a considerable extent unnecessary. With no planning at all, emigration will be forced. Navajos, however, are living in their homeland. They have significant resources. A rational and humane plan will be one that makes migration a matter of choice and provides maximum opportunity for them to gain an adequate livelihood from their own resources.

This report has not discussed organized planning for emigration because it deals with reservation development. It is, nevertheless, true that Navajos will wish to migrate, and that the educational system should be one that gives sufficient opportunity to prepare for this option. There should also be efforts to assist Navajos desiring to migrate to find jobs, housing, and so forth, job training opportunities such as now go on (see below), and perhaps planned efforts to locate Navajo migrants in groups in cities, instead of scattered about, as is typical now. Such enclaves seem to have made for a good urban adjustment for some Pueblo Indians, for example the Laguna colony in Barstow.

C. MINERAL EXPLOITATION

Since only a fraction of the projected population can achieve a decent standard of living based on farming or herding, we will begin with mineral exploitation, industry, and commerce.

In my opinion, the present pattern of leasing mineral rights drains both resources and wealth from the reservation, in spite of the residue that remains in the Tribal treasury. The mineral wealth of the Navajo country is not unlimited, and the yield will decline. All the more reason why it should be managed by Navajos and its profits devoted to them. At present the tempo of exploitation is set by oil and coal companies, and the product used largely for fuel. Yet the oil and coal have potential use for the manufacture of synthetic products. By the time the reservation is ready to take advantage of the potential for more complex use of these minerals, they may well be largely gone or entirely under the control of enterprises whose interests lie many miles from Navajo country.

Although the initial outlay would be considerable, and would require Government support, and although trained personnel would initially have to come from outside, the rational procedure for a planned program of economic development would be for the Navajo Tribe, as a corporate body, to own and operate its own petroleum, gas, coal, vanadium, and so forth, industries, to set its own pace for extraction, to process the products in as large part as possible, to sell them, and to utilize the profits for the benefit of members of the tribe.

At present, Navajo assets are used to enrich non-Navajo enterprises. Tax funds enter the reservation in relatively "soft" forms like ONEO part-time employment funds. The use of Federal funds, whether as subsidy or as low-interest rate loans, for Tribal enterprises of this sort could reverse the present impoverishment of the Navajos and their dependence on welfare and "soft" Government money, like ONEO.

The Tribe operates the Navajo Forest Products Industries and the Navajo Tribal Utilities Authority. Thus it is not Tribal enterprise as such that constitutes a block to Tribal exploitation of minearl resources. The obstacles lie elsewhere. First, the Federal Government's trustee obligations to the tribe are such that legislation would be needed for approval of enterprises involving higher risk than the present ones. Second, shortage of capital would have to be remedied by Federal action. Third, managerial staff would be needed.

There are, however, still other obstacles. Most Federal employees and most Council members are at present persuaded that the low risk and infinitesimal investment involved in present leasing arrangements are preferable to the higher risk and large investment otherwise needed. Both of these attitudes are supported by the reactions of private industry, which undoubtedly would like to use the mineral wealth of the reservation for their highly profitable operations. This last point, I believe, is very important. By and large, private industry and local interests alike resist the development of competitive economic activities by Indian tribes. Thus a sawmill is acceptable because it is a small operation with relatively small profits and hence has little opposition from the lumber industry. The present mineral operation is a very large one with very large profits, and it can be anticipated that there would be great pressure against development of Tribal mineral enterprises. Hence it would be necessary to insure a sales outlet for Navajo oil, gas, and coal. Since the U.S. Government is one of the larger users of all three commodities, it would be in a position to guarantee the purchase of Navajo supplies at fair market prices.

To anticipate somewhat, on the Navajo Reservation at present are various industrial plants in defense-related industries. So far as I know, a considerable part of the product of the companies involved is produced on a cost-plus basis for the Federal Government. This is a tax-subsidized business operation. If this can be done for defense purposes, it would seem that tax money could be used to develop Navajo resources, particularly since in the end the reservation would be far less dependent on Federal funds than it is at present. The fact that Tribal enterprises are not presently subject to Federal tax would also provide a badly needed advantage in establishing tribal industries.

As things now stand, even the manner of exploitation of Navajo resources lies outside the control of the people. There is strip mining of coal near Window Rock, and there will be strip mining by Peabody Coal at the north end of Black Mesa. When I was there the local population did not know anything about strip mining plans, but only about mining, in some general way, nor did they have information (nor do I) as to arrangements, if any, for disposition of toxic wastes, backfilling, contouring, or reforestation. Yet Navajos have been using this area for their own purposes. The entire subject needs wider discussion among Navajos. (I am informed that future strip mining contracts will contain restoration clauses, but how enforceable these will be I do not know.)

Conceivably Navajos would be more prudent in their rates of consumption of these rare and limited resources and more careful in considering the effects of the manner of exploitation than is private industry. Possibly they would prove less prudent and careful. In either case, however, decisions would be based on local considerations and not on the needs of particular corporations. This seems vital for the Navajo future.

I have earlier mentioned processing. What we are seeking here is the well-known multiplier effect: that the extraction itself should employ as many Navajos as possible, that the refined rather than the crude product should, insofar as possible, be produced on the reservation, so that more jobs for Navajos are created on all levels, labor and managerial, that centers of production of this kind become population centers demanding various service industries (stores, garages, and so forth), which in turn would be Navajo-run, and so on.

For this processing to come off, of course, further capital is needed, and the technological substratum of roads, power, et cetera, previously mentioned in virtually every section of this report, is required.

No proposal in this report has encountered more objections from BIA officials than that for Tribal exploitation of minerals. Alternative suggestions made to me are that the Tribe might operate processing plants but not the basic extractive industries, or that management of the entire operation might be Tribal but the capital be external. The objections to these plans, each of which has advantages compared with the present situation, are twofold: neither curbs the outflow of profits from Navajo resources to non-Navajo recipients, and neither places control of the pattern of exploitation in Navajo hands.

There are a number of oil leases on the reservation. Peabody Coal, Pittsburgh and Midway Coal, Utah Mining and Construction Co., and El Paso Natural Gas Co., are all involved in coal exploitation. Other mining interests are represented by Kerr-McGee, Climax Uranium, and Vanadium Corp. of America.

El Paso Natural Gas Co. owns pipeline booster stations, and Shell Oil operates a refinery at Aneth, Utah.

D. INDUSTRY

As much processing of minerals as possible should occur on the reservation, for the sake of multiplier effects. In addition, there should be development of the manufacture of various kinds of finished goods and components.

The past few years have seen a rapid but somewhat special growth of industry in the Navajo country.

The Tribe itself operates Navajo Forest Products Industries, at Navajo, N. Mex. It runs the Navajo Tribal Utilities Authority (NTUA), providing electricity, gas, water, and sewage to an increasing number of customers. It runs the Arts and Crafts Guild, one of the best outlets for high quality Navajo silver, rugs, and other crafts products in the Southwest. And it runs motels and restaurants at Window Rock and Shiprock.

The size of the NTUA operation has been described. In line with what has been said before about Navajo control of Navajo resources, NTUA has one interesting feature. It buys power from the Arizona Public Service Co., which runs a powerplant near Fruitland, N. Mex., with a present capacity of about 570,000 kilowatts, soon to be increased to 2,080,000 kilowatts. Arizona Public Service is headquartered in Phoenix. Ownership of the expanded facility will include APS and Southern California Edison Co., Salt River project, Tucson Gas & Electric Co., Public Service Co. of New Mexico, and El Paso Electric Co. Coal for the plant is supplied by Utah Construction & Mining Co. from Navajo mineral leases. Current will be transmitted to southern California. By about 1970, it is said, the payroll will include 800 persons involved in plant construction, and thereafter the present payroll for the plant proper will double. "The combination of the new power units and the mine will mean an additional $1,041,600 annually in rents and royalties to the Navajo Tribe. The coal reserves will last through the economic life of the powerplant" (Anonymous, 1966a; Destination: the Twentieth Century, p. 3).

This means that Navajos lease mines to Utah Construction & Mining Co., that they receive the royalties on these leases, whereas Utah Construction & Mining Co. receives the profits, and that they then buy back the coal in the form of electric current, which they sell at a profit locally. NTUA is indeed an important achievement for the Tribe. But is there not some less roundabout way for the Tribe to use its own coal and to hold a larger margin of the profits from it? Furthermore, should Navajos relinquish so much of their coal for the sake of power users in California, so that at a later date they can pay for the import of power to the reservation when their own needs expand?

Navajo Forest Products Industries employs about 500 people, over 90 percent of them Navajo; I do not have figures on NTUA employees, save that 93 percent are Navajo. It will probably expand to make particle board, door and window frames, and other products. It should.

There are a number of private industries in the Navajo country. One is a utility, already discussed; Arizona Public Service Co.'s Four Corners Powerplant at Fruitland, presently employing about 120 people, less than 20 percent of whom are Navajos. One is Navajo Furniture Industries, Inc., which manufactures juvenile furniture in Gallup, with about 25 employees, almost all of them Navajo.

There is, as has been said, an oil refinery at Aneth, Utah.

Finally, there are three manufacturing plants, all of them in defense-oriented industries. Fairchild Semiconductor Division, Fairchild Instrument and Camera Corp. manufactures semiconductors in a plant at Shiprock, employing 850 people, 800 of them Navajos. It expects to expand to 1,200 employees. General Dynamics Corp., Pomona Division, has an electronic assembly plant at Fort Defiance, Ariz., employing 150 people, 125 of them Navajos. And Vostron Electronic Packaging Industries carries on electronics assembly at Page, Ariz. It employs 36 people, all but the manager being Navajo. (Data on industries from Navajo Area Office, BIA.)

In the past the Tribe began industrial operations that were later canceled, all of them involving substantially less complex processes than the private plants just mentioned: Cement, clay, leather, and wood products, and wool textiles. I have been told that these enterprises were terminated because they were losing money—through lack of local markets for products, because of high transportation costs for finished products, etc. I have also been told that in the 1950's, when they were stopped, the Bureau was less than wholehearted in its support for Tribal enterprises.

At present, then, Tribal enterprises employ well over 500 Navajos (no figures for NTUA), and private industry on reservation in the neighborhood of 1,000. This is an enormous change from a few years ago, but it represents only a tiny fraction of the potential labor force, or even of the total of Navajos now employed part and full time.

However pleased one may be about this rise in employment opportunities and about the Tribal and Bureau enterprise that helped to bring about these results, there are some significant features of industrial developments to date that deserve considerable thought. First, the electronics plants, the major industrial employers, hire almost entirely women. Thus, opportunities for steady employment for men on reservation are not improved by these industries. There is nothing about the employment of women that is undesirable, either from the point of view of development or from a Navajo point of view. But unless parallel opportunities arise for men, demoralization of the male labor force will continue.

Second, once again private industry rather than Tribal industry has been let in on the ground floor, so that payroll comes on the reservation but profits go off. Furthermore, to the degree that water is a limiting factor for industrial development in the Navajo country, these firms inhibit any later possibilities for Tribal industries to arise.

Third, concentration of Tribal industrial employment in defense-oriented industries would seem unwise unless the United States is to maintain present levels of military spending indefinitely—in itself an unhappy prospect.

Fourth, since there is reason to believe that tax money has been used to finance the development of defense-oriented private enterprise on the reservation, the question arises why it could not be used to finance Tribal enterprise. In brief, Federal funds paid for on the job training; the firms in question carry on a considerable portion of their activities on a cost-plus basis; their location on the reservation seems to have been a product of Kennedy administration policy to spread the locations of defense-oriented industry to hardship areas. The net result appears to be that the Navajos have secured a payroll for about 1,000 employees (at fairly low wages), that in order to do so they have deployed reservation land and water, that the Federal Government has footed the bill for the employment training and, in one way or another, underwritten the profits of the firms in question—profits that do not accrue to the Tribe. (See H. L. Nieburg, "In the Name of Science" (1966), for substantiation of the general position taken here.)

It would appear, then, that a more frontal approach to industrial development on the reservation might be attempted through the creation of Tribal industries—one that would (as at present) use Federal funds to assist in employee training, perhaps one that would provide cost-plus contracts initially, but certainly far better one that would provide low-interest loans initially. Furthermore, the development program should be less one-sided than the present defense orientation. Tribal industry would be highly advantageous in retaining profits in the area. Finally there should be employment for men, as well as for women.

There are many possible ways, instead of, or in addition to the above, for the Tribe to acquire more control over its own industrial development. It could begin as a minority or majority shareholder, instead of an owner. In that case there could be built-in opportunities for the Tribe to purchase increasing quantities of stock on an option basis at a fixed price until it became majority shareholder or owner, as might be deemed desirable. Since options are granted to corporation officials for their services, they could equally well be granted to the Tribe in exchange for its site, roads, and relatively cheap, non-unionized labor (unions are forbidden by Tribal law). There is Tribal enabling legislation for partnerships with private concerns now on the books.

It might be said that trained Navajo manpower would constitute a relatively stable labor supply, since Navajos are strongly desirous in so many cases of finding work on the reservation.

It is evident that in the early phases of Navajo-owned complex manufacturing, non-Navajo know-how would be needed. It can be hired, as it has been for the Forest Products operation. The greatest obstacle, of course, would be the difficulties of marketing products in the face of a distaste for competition on the part of large corporations, and the simplicity that arises for private and governmental purchasing agents in going to large corporations to satisfy their needs. But if this problem cannot be met, the Navajo country cannot be developed except in the present highly exploitative fashion.

It should be noted that each of the private plants is located on the periphery of the reservation, and the same is true of the Tribal ones. A Tribally planned development could be based on a system of plant locations that took account of the Navajos' own needs. The present pattern benefits only selected portions of the reservation, except for those Navajos who relocate to take advantage of employment. Light industry has a wider potential range of placement than it has yet achieved in the Navajo country.

If there is to be well-developed cash-crop farming in the land made available by the Navajo Indian irrigation project (see below), and if the livestock industry is to be improved (see below), food processing plants and meat-packing plants would be highly desirable.

The Navajo Forest Products Industries, the Tribe's most successful enterprise to date, now has Navajo employees capable of assuming major responsibilities. One, at least, has been offered an excellent job in an outside wood products company but has refused and is staying on the reservation for lower wages than he could make elsewhere. He was trained on the job. There is, however, no particular reason to assume that local loyalty will operate to keep well-trained Navajos in the Navajo country: It is likely that some are as vulnerable to "brain drain" salary offers as are Englishmen and Canadians, now that the United States pays top dollar. Hence salaries must be competitively high. But more important, on-the-job training opportunities must exist in all industries, so that, as rapidly as possible, Navajos may assume responsible jobs. Responsibility is not learned except in responsible positions. Preparation for jobs should also occur in schools. (See education, below.)

D. THE TECHNOLOGICAL BASE

Further mineral exploitation and industrial development, as well as topics discussed below, such as commerce, education, and health programs, demand rapid movement to create an adequate technological base, in terms of roads, electrical service, gas service, and a variety of other features. Mineral exploitation, industrial development, and improvement of the livestock industry and of farming all demand water development.

The 20-year road plan jointly developed by the Tribe and the Bureau will cost $300 million and provide an expansion from the present 430 miles of paved road to about 4,000 miles. This would seem urgent, and 20 years too long a time. A bus service is needed. The basis for expanded electrical and gas service now exists. The water situation is more complicated.

Since 1961, water development has been largely in the hands of the Tribe, with cooperation from the U.S. Public Health Service, which provides technical guidance in developing and protecting shallow water sources. A report by Heinrich J. Thiele & Associates (Thiele, 1966) supplies a detailed picture of the situation in 1966 and of future prospects. It recommends the establishing of a Navajo Tribal Water Authority, and the removal of water development and service from the Navajo Tribal Utilities Authority and all other programs now dealing with water. I can only concur. The Thiele report indicates clearly that planning for water use is a prerequisite for the development of urban centers, industry, commerce, irrigated farming and pasture, and tourism on the reservation. The picture as respects quality and abundance of water is far too complex to present here. Suffice it to say that relatively abundant, potable water can be found on only about 39 percent of the reservation's area, that portion in which about 66 percent of the population was living in 1966. Thirty-two percent of the area brings in brackish water, and 29 percent has almost no water potential. Under these circumstances, planned locations for denser aggregates of the population, for schools, and for industry are an urgent need. Furthermore, there is potential competition for water as respects the demands for livestock, farming, mineral exploitation, industry, and domestic use.

The Thiele report makes mention of future industrial needs but contains few projections on this score. It indicates that since wells were first dug on the reservation, neither selection of sites, construction methods, materials, nor maintenance has been adequate. It is expected that use of water in rural area on the reservation will increase from 6,000 acre-feet in 1966 to 30,000 or more in the year 2000. No figure for industrial and urban use is supplied by the report.

The Navajo Indian irrigation project is supposed to supply about 508,000 acre-feet of water for 110,000 acres of land when it is completed (according to BIA projections, in 1981; according to some newspaper accounts, in the 1990's a date discouraging to Navajos). Originally 23,000 acre-feet in addition was set aside for municipal and industrial use, a figure that did not allow for the domestic water needs of people making use of the irrigated land. This was later increased to 100,000 acre-feet. Of this amount, 51,500 acre-feet has already been allocated to Public Service Co. of New Mexico, Southern Union Gas Co., and Utah Construction & Mining Co., for thermal electric uses, leaving not very much for future domestic and industrial use. (See Public Law 90–272, 90th Cong., S.J. Res. 123 of Mar 22, 1968).

Meantime, Peabody Coal's operation, to slurry coal to Nevada, draws on deep wells in the Black Mesa territory. Full details are not available to me, but there are apparently at least four wells, to depths of 2,500 feet, providing 2,000 gallons per minute each, and costing $250,000 each. Thus scarce water resources are being used to shunt Navajo resources to Nevada, without, so far as can be determined, any overall water plan having been adopted by the Tribe.

To sum up: There is far more water in the Navajo country than might be supposed; much of it is at a considerable depth; it is not evenly distributed; and a water plan and a water authority are urgent needs underlying every phase of development.

F. COMMERCE

At present on the Navajo Reservation there are a large number of trading posts, some with cafes and garages, some private motels (at Tuba City, Monument Valley, and Chinle at least), two Tribal motel-restaurant combinations at Window Rock and Shiprock, two banks, at Window Rock and Crownpoint, brought there through the efforts of the Tribal Council, assorted small businesses like laundromats, and the new Fed-Mart store in Window Rock. There is also the Navajo Arts and Crafts Guild, run by the Tribe.

The perspective for development is a 25-year period, at the end of which time there will be an estimated 240,000 Navajos, most of whom will spend at least a portion of the year on the reservation.

About 10 years from now, a major decision point will arise. The traders' 25-year leases were mainly negotiated in 1953–54 and will expire in 1978–79.

If development occurs on other fronts, principally industrial and livestock, there will be an increasingly prosperous and an increasingly large population to be served by retail facilities of one sort and another. Furthermore, if there is industrial development, there will be (as there already are) population shifts on reservation creating a number of more densely populated centers. Finally, if livestock management were carried out on a suprafamilial level, even in relatively out-of-the-way communities there could be a less scattered pattern of residence, all of which would make retail activities more inviting.

There are dilemmas in the various plans that come to mind for future commercial development. The Fed-Mart store is a new factor that will condition the next few years to a marked extent. If, as appears likely, it is a success, it seems probable that Fed-Mart will build additional outlets in such population centers as Shiprock and Tuba City. And if these succeed, other agency headquarters afford additional possibilities. Each such move will create a small increment of jobs (60 in the Window Rock facility at present) and will draw Navajo business that might otherwise have gone to traders or to the border towns. This is likely to make the traders' position less attractive.

One can envisage the possibility, then, that as the traders' situation, already undermined to some degree, becomes less viable, and as leases expire, the new occupants will be either Anglos content with quite small-scale operations or Navajos willing to operate on a low margin of profit. The advantage of the Fed-Mart development is that it provides consumer goods to Navajos at far lower prices than they have paid to traders and border-town merchants in the past. The disadvantage is that again an outside interest will achieve a position of dominance on the reservation. While this may well make more commercial establishments available to Navajos, it will preempt large-scale commerce, since Navajos will not be able to compete with Fed-Mart in terms of range of goods. The likelihood is, however, that Fed-Mart will have secured its advantage well before any alternative possibility could be realized.

This being the case, there seem to be three areas of planning available. The first is the possibility of Tribal or individual Navajo control of trading posts as their leases expire. The second is an effort to reserve for Navajos the wide range of small business opportunities that ought to open up at an accelerating rate: Such facilities as laundromats, barber shops, beauty parlors, clothing stores, appliance repair shops, etcetera—some needed already, some not feasible for some years. This requires tribal control of licensing (which it has), an education program that will provide appropriate training in skills and particularly in business management, and a loan program on a considerable scale. The third is to modify the trader's role in the credit system, either by regularizing his interest charges or by displacing him as the community "bank" by providing a far more extensive tribal loan system, which would require underwriting by the Government. Navajos ought to have other resources to turn to for futures in meat and wool, for example. This would make it possible for Navajos to have more control over their own economic lives and would free the trader from a credit squeeze that begins to create problems for him. If, however, the credit now supplied by traders were to disappear without a substitute (and it has been argued here that *more* credit is needed than is now available, not the same amount by different means), Navajo families would suffer terrible hardships. At present trader and Navajo are "locked into" the system.

G. LIVESTOCK INDUSTRY

Most Navajos today are not in the livestock business in the sense in which a commercial farmer is in the wheat business. Their production is for a combination of use and sale. The sale is not, in any simple sense, for the sake of making a profit, but to buy the necessities of life at the trading post and the store. Neither mentally nor by means of bookkeeping is there a separation of the herd as a cash-and-credit enterprise, the herd as a source of food, and the herd as a form of insurance—to be used for an emergency, or to fall back on when a man loses his job. This can be seen in the arrangements in some extended families with respect to the yield from livestock. The sheep are earmarked for various members of the family, and each such member would claim that the sheep so marked were his. They may be used in any of the following ways: They may be eaten by family members, contributed for the ceremonies of relatives outside the family, or used for ceremonies within the family. The wool may be sheared and sold. The sheep may be sold. As for cattle, they are produced mainly for sale. Sometimes they are used for ceremonies. They are seldom killed for ordinary family consumption, because they are too large to be used before spoiling occurs. A given family member ordinarily allows decisions about killing sheep for meat or giving them for ceremonies to be vested in the senior member of the extended family. He also makes claims of his own for food and gifts. He may or may not shear his own sheep separately and sell the wool separately. If his parents' needs are great and he has a steady job, he may well allow the wool profits to remain with the parents. He may even allow the money from the sale of lambs to accrue to the parents. He will ordinarily claim the right to sell his own cattle and utilize the proceeds: cattle are seen in more of a business context. In sum, considerations of equity, far more than of profit, dominate the procedures of the family livestock industry.

Nevertheless, more and more people wish to be in the livestock business properly speaking. This often means conversion from sheep to cattle. There are several factors pushing people in this direction. First, so many Navajos are engaged in at least part-time wagework that a shortage of herders is on the way. Cattle require less daily management; they can be run with only occasional mass mobilization of manpower, to count, brand, castrate, dehorn, et cetera. Furthermore, it is often asserted that if the family unit cannot manage livestock operation of high quality, it can make more money from a herd of cattle than from a herd of sheep. (It is also asserted that under optimal conditions for the sheep, they would be more profitable than cattle.) In addition—why I do not know—cattle are viewed differently from sheep: it seems to be considered normal for a person to realize his own money from sales of his own cattle, rather than turning over the proceeds to a parent.

Cattle, however, have one major disadvantage compared to sheep: they cannot be casually killed for a few days' meat. The older people are keenly aware of this; the thought of having only cattle, or very few sheep alarms them. They survive on the sheep. (It is also true that most Navajos like mutton better than beef. Many non-Navajos who have eaten range mutton and range beef would agree with them.)

For adequate economic development of the livestock base, there must be more water development in order for any rational use of pasturage to take place. Fencing is impossible without water development. This need not always mean deep wells, or even shallow ones. Plastic catchment basins draining into stock tanks can in fact provide adequate stock water in many areas. Under these circumstances it would be possible to fence and to plan the use of the range, regulating by season and responding to weather conditions, without the present problems created by few watering spots.

This, however, is not sufficient. At present the Navajo range can support an amount of livestock that was less than adequate for 40,000 people. There are now about 120,000 Navajos, with doubling in prospect in 22 to 26 years.

There are, however, possibilities of increasing the forage yield two-fold to fortyfold. At present in some 25 locations on the Navajo Reservation this is being done. It involves chaining off pinon and juniper trees or uprooting sage and reseeding with hardy grasses. But for the grasses to survive, controlled grazing must be achieved, by making water available in each pasture and by fencing. Further work along these lines is certainly desirable.

One difficulty already evident in some areas where fencing, chaining, and seeding have gone on involves the disposition of the dead pinons resulting from chaining. Ideally these should be left initially as obstacles to prevent excessive runoff, and ultimately to decay and enrich the soil. Unfortunately, the shortage of firewood results in the speedy clearance of these trees for fuel.

There are, however, special social and economic consequences that follow from these practices that have not, in my opinion, been thought through. At present, each reseeded area is an extended or nuclear family pasture, that is, a customary use-right area of such a family, fenced only by permission of the neighbors. The reservation is not allotted in severalty at present. Nevertheless, the effects of fencing are to confirm a specific use right for a specific family with a clarity that is not found in other areas. Such families take the position that trespass is involved if other herds move on to the area. Without any doubt they will come to think that these use rights are subject to hereditary transmission. And in time the typical problems of fractionation of heirship will arise. Furthermore, it is probable that if the fencing continues, some individuals will find themselves without grazing areas in the not too distant future. It is by no means clear (a) that systematic family allotment on a *de facto* basis is a sound practice, or (b) that the alternatives to such allotment have been discussed, or (c) that the consequences of family allotments have been made clear to the Navajos. Instead, the BIA seems to prefer to let the system grow on the assumption, no doubt, that it will make Navajo property patterns conform more closely to those of the dominant society.

Rational use of the range, with water development and seeding, could be based on the *community* as a unit, or on the *set of contiguous related families* and their pasture as the unit, or (as at present) the *single extended or nuclear family* as a unit. The present program of range improvement should continue, but not without a thorough airing of the consequences. The technical possibilities of this program *and* the issue of the proper management unit should be raised in discussions between the BIA, Tribal officials, and local Navajos, so that the consequences of the alternative management patterns are fully explored. Decisions about range management should be reached only after this step. The issue is always a sensitive one for Navajos, but that is one reason it needs to be discussed. At present, the Bureau is sliding into a policy the ramifications of which are not clear to Navajos, whether or not they are to the Bureau.

One significant and favorable feature of present policy should be mentioned. The tribe has permitted the issuing of "conservation use permits" to people who chain, fence, and seed—permits based on a survey of the range in the fenced area. These permits are renewable at 3-year intervals: At each review they may be increased, reduced, or eliminated, depending on range conditions and the conservation efforts of the users. It appears that these permits make it possible for more livestock to be raised in a given area and serve as an important incentive for conservation practices. Not every part of the reservation is ecologically suited to chaining and seeding. The practice is not a cure-all, but it seems to have value.

There is no reason why range management, adult education in range management, education in livestock care, and so forth, could not be turned over to the tribe more rapidly than is being done. The Federal Government has recently turned over many of these activities to the States. It would be better in the long run to supply the funds it provides to the States, or additional funds, to employ experts selected and paid by the Tribe. The experts should be answerable to the Tribe. Well-trained interpreters should be developed by the educational program (a step never undertaken), to serve as an effective communications link between experts, governmental or other, and the people. The educational system should be oriented to producing young Navajos trained as range management and livestock specialists to take over the positions now occupied by others.

The Tribe will also have to become sensitive to the future potentialities of the livestock market in planning along these lines. It would be possible to undertake an unwise expansion of the livestock industry: One that does not take into account its inelasticities or the significance of foreign and local competition. The balance of sheep, mohair goats, and cattle must be considered in this context.

The Navajo Indian Irrigation Project, scheduled for completion in 1981, will provide irrigation water for about 110,630 acres of land. It is apparently planned to use some of this land for irrigated pasture, which would make it possible for Navajos to raise grain-fed beef locally.

At present the tribe sponsors cattle auctions through the Cattlemen's Association. Considerably more could be done in the way of organized marketing activities by the tribe (for example, as respects wool and mohair), or in terms of cattle and sheep marketing cooperatives or management cooperatives at the local level. It is important that there be vigorous local organizations; as the tribal council takes on more functions, it is likely to become excessively dominant, unless the mission of chapters is expanded or other local, suprakin organizations emerge, or regional organizations appear—or all of these.

In the past, local cooperatives have not been successful. There are, however, special reasons for local opposition and apathy in most cases. Several cooperatives began by removing part of the pastureland of a given area from the control of families that had used it for many years and putting it under cooperative control. This step guaranteed undying opposition on the part of a segment of the community. The issue, however, should be reopened without this obstacle, so that Navajos may consider whether they wish a local economic unit larger than the family (whether for marketing or management or both), to give them leverage in dealing with traders, border-town businessmen, and tribal and BIA officials.

Finally, as respects both herding and farming (see below for farming), planning cannot be based on the assumption that Navajos need only a subsistence economy. Whereas they may derive food from farming and herding, these activities must be planned to yield a living, and not merely foodstuffs. Evidently there will come a time when family herds will not be the most economical or efficient way to use the range: When, by one means or another, aggregations of herds and of pastures will become desirable. All the more reason that this should be considered now, and from now on.

H. FARMING

There are two distinct issues connected with farming. The first is the likely fate of subsistence farming; the second is the question of the use of scarce and valuable irrigated farmland.

As to subsistence farming, there is some decrease in the number of farms per capita in many areas, and indeed probably an absolute decrease in the number of farms. One factor that probably contributes to this phenomenon wherever it is found is labor shortage. Many younger people are working on and off reservation at wage labor jobs or are in school during such critical periods as those for the preparation of fields, for cultivating, and for harvesting. This leaves a shortage of labor for herding. Older people prefer to concentrate on the livestock industry in many parts of the reservation and hence decide not to try to prepare fields. There are additional local factors, such as the short growing season on the slopes of Black Mesa, which makes farming marginal there, irregular and unpredictable water supply, and lowering of the water table, which has destroyed the utility of some fields good a generation ago.

In other areas, farming is probably holding its own. In a few, where irrigated farming is to be found, principally at Shiprock, Fruitland, and Many Farms, it is supplemented by cash crop farming, and new kinds of crops are being introduced. These areas are, however, inefficiently planned. The farms are small enough to require the family to produce partly for use and partly for sale and in addition to supplement their farming with wagework labor (cf. Sasaki, 1960). The result is an inefficient farmer, an inefficient wageworker, and an inefficient irrigation system.

If the livestock industry were to improve, would subsistence farming in nonirrigated areas increase or decline? Possibly, with more income from livestock, families would rely more on purchasing food and less on subsistence farming. On the other hand, if families had more income, there might be less part-time summer employment and more labor available to farm. These two possibilities should be considered.

Irrigated farming, however, is another matter—not so much for Fruitland, Shiprock, and Many Farms, unless there is to be a great deal of reorganization there—in the case of the Navajo Indian irrigation project.

There are today about 35,000 acres of irrigable land on the reservation, of which perhaps a third is utilized. Low utilization results from such factors as farm units too small for effective commercial farming (as at Fruitland) and uneven and unpredictable water supply (as in the Chinle Wash area). The Navajo Indian irrigation project (based on the San Juan-Chama diversion) is planned to increase irrigable land greatly. It is to supply 110,630 acres of land with 580,000 acre-feet of water by 1981. The work on this project has lagged by comparison with other portions of the San Juan-Chama development. An additional 13,000 irrigated acres could be supplied in other ways. Thus, there is a potential 158,000 acres of irrigable land, by comparison with today's 35,000.

The Navajo Indian Irrigation Project raises a number of planning issues. First, as BIA officials readily recognize, the area must be used for commercial, not subsistence farming. This, however, raises the question whether it should be cut up into small holder plots of reason-

able size with, say, farm machinery and marketing cooperatives, or
worked in very large plots as corporate enterprises, or what. There is
also the question, mentioned before, of using a part of it for irrigated
pasture. If, in fact, it is to be used efficiently, it will have to have a far
better technological base than Navajo farming heretofore.

Even before the land has become available, there is some talk of
using a portion of the 508,000 acre-feet for do'mestic or industrial
purposes, which disturbs Navajos who wish to farm there considerably.
But the balance between potential use of that water for farming, herding, industry, and domestic purposes must soon be settled.

In irrigated farmland areas, adult education for farmers is desirable.
Responsibility for agricultural extension work was transferred from the
BIA to the State extension services July 1, 1968, with Federal funding
continuing. It would seem desirable that it should soon pass into
Navajo hands, and that the education system should produce Navajo
stock experts and agricultural extension workers—still with Federal
funding.

I. SOME LAND PROBLEMS

1. *Off-reservation groups.*—The existence of off-reservation groups
(other than urban migrants) creates special problems for any development plan. These groups include (*a*) Navajos in Grazing Districts 16,
19, and 20, east and south of the reservation on allotted land, and
(*b*) Navajos in the separate enclaves at Ramah, Puertocito, and
Canoncito.

For purposes of development, it would be valuable to be able to
work in terms of a contiguous area. The enclaves make this impossible,
but the borders of the reservation could be extended to create a
continuous reservation that would include the groups enumerated in
(*a*) above. This, however, would not lead to any simple solution, because these lands are allotted. The kind of mineral, industrial, and
commercial development described in this report requires the ability
to deal with fairly large tracts of land, and allotment would hence
constitute a problem. (Allotment of the entire reservation is no solution at all, although the fencing now being carried out in some areas
seems to be moving Navajos toward a *de facto* allotment system without prior discussion of its probable effects. Allotment in the areas
mentioned above was necessary to preserve Indian claims to this land,
but in the *general* history of American Indians under the U.S. Government, allotment has not led to the solution of Indian problems, but to a
transfer of Federal headaches to Indian heads, and to loss of Indian
lands to non-Indians.) The Tribe seems inclined to extend such benefits
as Tribal police and public works programs to at least some of these
enclaves, but there would be problems of extending the general benefits of a reservation development program to them. All that can be
done here is to point to the existence of a problem.

2. *The Executive order territory (Executive order of December 16,
1882).*—This area is a large rectangle surrounding the territory presently
occupied by the Hopi Indians (District 6). It was established by the
Executive order of December 16, 1882, at which time it bordered the
Navajo Reservation as enlarged in 1878 and 1880. It was established
for the Hopi Indians and other Indians dwelling in the area (not a
quotation). As a result of a suit, *Jones* v. *Healing*, the area now presents
a difficult problem for the planning of development. The court threw

on the Hopi and the Navajo Tribes the burden of arriving at a joint decision respecting the exploitation of surface and subsurface resources. To date they have been unable to do so. It is unlikely that they will be able to reach a solution without long congressional legislation clarifying the situation. Thus at present rational overall planning by either Tribe seems difficult. The building of roads, gaslines, powerlines, and so on, should be planned to benefit this entire area, either, and, indeed, for this reason the Executive order area is the most inaccessible and underdeveloped sector of the entire reservation with respect to roads, electricity, schools, medical facilities, commercial establishments, etc. The issue must be resolved. Some Navajos and Hopis say they could solve it were it not for white lawyers. The ideal solution would be joint planning by the two Tribes.

J. POPULATION MOVEMENT AND LABOR MIGRATION

Everything proposed previously should result in a more concentrated pattern for the population. It is evident that on-reservation mineral, industrial, and commercial development will result in internal migration and denser aggregations of the population. A combination of adequate roads and patterns of management of livestock and farming in larger units would make it possible for families to live in more of a town or village pattern, with farming and herding territories around the towns. This in turn would make a day school program feasible as well as great expansion of the electric, gas, water, and sewage systems to family dwellings, now so scattered that even under more favorable circumstances few could be served. This concentration is another advantage of the proposal for cooperative livestock ventures and corporate or cooperative farming on irrigated lands. The educational program should train people for the many new kinds of expertise that this living pattern would require.

Whereas the thrust of this report is to make the reservation more liveable for more Navajos, many will wish to migrate not within the reservation but outside its boundaries. The educational system (see below) should provide not only the adult vocational training programs that now exist, but the guidance in career planning and the training that would enable Navajos who desire to do so to relocate. They should, however, be given as much psychological armament as possible against the prejudice they will encounter in the larger society.

K. EDUCATION

Most of the foregoing material relates directly to economic development. Education, health, and welfare are necessary for development but do not constitute development in any direct sense. Education in particular, is too often viewed as a substitute for development: it is too often reasoned that if Navajos are given sufficient education so that (in theory) they can leave the reservation, there need be no development of the reservation. In the present report, education is treated primarily as a means to development, not as an alternative for it.

There is evident need for an expanded, updated, and experimental program of education in the Navajo country. It should be said that the BIA is making some efforts to achieve many of the goals listed below. Nevertheless, while the BIA is understandably optimistic in comparing its present efforts with its past performance, people not directly involved in education but with an opportunity to observe the system and its fruits are quite discouraged. The recommendations below reflect the latter state of mind, but should not be understood to ignore what is being done.

1. There seems no reason why the entire school system should not come under the managerial control of the Tribe and of local Navajo school boards. The Bureau has said for decades that it is trying to put Indians in a position where they can manage their own affairs and it can go out of business. Nevertheless, a program of actual withdrawal is not feasible, because it removes essential protection from Indians. There is, however, no reason why there should not be a vastly increased role for the Tribe and for the local community, and a vastly decreased direct role for the Government in the immediate future.

There are nominal school boards attached to most reservation schools, but there has been relatively little devolution of authority to date. Local school boards will not be workable unless they have fiscal control and sizable funds.

In education, modest results have been achieved by creating corporations that administer Federal funds and use them to operate Navajo school facilities on an experimental basis. The first Navajo-run school has already been created at Rough Rock, with a school board some of whose members do not speak English but who seem quite competent to deal with the issues. Experimental programs can be found at other schools—for example, English as a second language is particularly strongly developed at Rock Point. Turning over the school system to the Tribe seems a reasonable prospect for the immediate future. Training of Navajo teachers and administrators in greatly increased numbers is therefore a must. Upgrading of Navajo employees is also needed. The Bureau recognizes this, but much more needs to be done.

2. Closely associated with the first, the education program should be one that attunes Navajo Indians to pride in their own language and culture and gives them a realistic understanding of their situation. An announced goal of the BIA, this is scarcely realizable when so many teachers are in fact firmly ethnocentric; when social life of Navajo and non-Navajo employees remains de facto largely separate, and when few teachers have any experience of the actual daily life of Navajos. Nor is it realizable when there are penalties for children who speak Navajo in school, to name but one of the many points where policy and practice are at variance.

3. Experimentation in the teaching of English is a must. Different schools could well utilize different approaches, which could then be evaluated. One school might experiment with a full development of teaching English as a second language, another with teaching young children in Navajo and making them literate in Navajo, with a subsequent transition to English (as has been done for Spanish-Americans) and so on. While it is true that some experimentation now goes on at Rough Rock and Rock Point, there is room for more. There is a need for better teaching materials and better teachers for the English as a second language program, which remains more of a slogan than an actuality.

4. The salary levels for teachers should be raised so as to attract a higher caliber of teachers and other conditions changed to make it possible to hold them. The school system is fortunate in the number of dedicated people it does draw, but there are a number of inhibitory factors: salary levels, a smothering bureaucratic atmosphere that discourages initiative and experimental variation, and a censorious concern with the personal lives of employees that drives some new teachers away in short order.

5. Several junior colleges on reservation seem desirable in the immediate future. (There is one, now, at Many Farms with a Navajo Board of Regents.) They could and should recruit *part* of their staff on short contracts from the better universities around the country, as visitors. These universities should be encouraged to pay the salaries of such visitors.

6. There should be a concentrated effort at better preparation of students for a variety of vocational and career opportunities and a much enlarged program of vocational guidance. A variety of trained Navajos will be needed in the near future: stockmen and extension workers, teachers and counselors, managers and forestry workers, computer specialists, statisticians, draftsmen, interpreters, and so on. Furthermore, some Navajos will wish to find their place in the larger society. As things now stand the school system is not geared to potential Navajo careers, vocational guidance personnel are few and undertrained, and Navajos are often discouraged from such careers as law and medicine. This is not wise.

7. The amount and quality of personal counseling available in the schools should be raised.

8. Occupational training for those who have left school should continue and be expanded. The Federal Government at present runs a program that prepares Navajos for over 150 occupations, under the aegis of the Branch of Employment Assistance.

9. Adult education classes now in existence should be continued and enlarged.

10. The combination of Tribal and Federal funds (which now provides college scholarships for about 650 students per annum 500 of them supported by tribal funds) should be continued and expanded. But the tribe should be encouraged to set its sights higher. It tends to select the poorer quality local universities as optimal places for its scholarship students. In some cases this may be wise, but able students should be encouraged to go to first-class institutions in any part of the country. It should also encourage some high school students to go to off-reservation private schools that welcome them, as is true at certain Quaker schools (George School and Westtown) and Verde Valley. The tribe should also encourage academic, as well as vocational programs as choices for college students, and should provide support for graduate work, even if this means a more selective approach to college scholarships. Tribal scholarships and vocational guidance work should be integrated.

11. Various universities in the Southwest should be encouraged to do far more than has been done to meet the special problems of Indian students. The document, Indian Education Research Projects and Action Programs, compiled by the Southwestern Cooperative Education Laboratory, includes information from only five colleges and

universities, and may not be representative. There is evidence of efforts to provide special training for some people and in a few instances of language programs for Indian college students. It is evident, however, from what is happening in several American universities, that the curriculum and atmosphere they provide is not acceptable to ethnic minorities. It would be pleasant to hear of Southwestern universities' taking steps to remedy the situation before student strikes or sit-ins force their hands. Indians are already involved in various "third world" curriculum demands on the west coast. The time for action is now.

12. It should be assumed that Navajo children are variable in ability, outlook, and personality: that different programs, different modes of teaching, and different approaches to educating an American minority group will appeal to different children. A pluralistic, not a monolithic approach seems indicated, with an effort to match the child and the program, or the child and the teacher. Since American education as a whole does not seem to be able to manage this, perhaps it is too much to expect of the reservation program, but such an approach should be the target.

A school program for Navajos should be designed on the assumption that will be far more expensive per capita, not less expensive, than the program in the "best" (i.e., wealthiest) sections of urban centers. This will necessarily be the case in any bilingual situation.

L. HEALTH

The reservation program has the following major needs.

(1) Many more doctors.

(2) Many more nurses, nurses' aides, and health education personnel.

(3) An increase from almost none to many medical interpreters. The work of Prof. Oswald Werner of Northwestern University, Prof. Jerrold Levy of Portland State University, and Dr. Stephen Kunitz of Yale University is relevant here. They have shown that, given a competent, trained interpreter and a doctor who listens, an adequate medical history and explication of symptoms can be obtained from Navajos. With present interpreting facilities, however, this is not often possible. Prof. John Adair of San Francisco State University and Dr. Kurt Deuschle of Mount Sinai Medical School, New York City, have shown that with sufficient staff to inform Navajos and undertake casefinding, Navajos can be induced to use public health facilities wisely and frequently enough to merit great expansion of present resources.

(4) If possible, some reduction in the likelihood that a Navajo who is ill will see Doctor X on one visit and Doctor Y on the next, something that Navajos, like others, find disheartening. And a change in attitude on the part of some doctors and nurses. Many are superb, but some make Navajos feel that they are the subjects of veterinary medicine practiced on not too worthwhile animals.

(5) A vast expansion of preventive medicine and health education. More public health nurses concerned with preventive medicine and health education are needed, more Navajo personnel capable of instructing in Navajo are badly needed, better

inspection, of drinking water is needed, and a whole series of fields of instruction need development. These include prenatal and maternal care, sex, contraceptive, and venereal disease education for adults and adolescents, accident prevention, etc. Adequate visual aids, including film strips and movies with Navajo oral text, are vital for health education programs.

(6) An improvement of dental care. Whereas children are seen routinely in school, most adults are not adequately informed about dental care and go to the dentist only when their teeth are so bad as to require extraction.

(7) A program of free prostheses: eyeglasses, dentures, hearing aids, and false limbs. At present medical care and drugs are free, but these are not, yet they are reasonable features of any public health program and any approach to habilitation and rehabilitation. Eyeglasses are sometimes provided to school-children, but often too late in the year to be much help. At present this gap in the PHS program is filled to some degree by Tribal funds, but not adequately.

(8) A considerable rise in the availability of ambulance and air ambulance service.

(9) More psychiatrists—there are two at present, the first ever to be attached to the PHS on the Navajo Reservation.

(50) A systematic program of recruitment, integrated with the vocational guidance program, and the scholarship program, to secure more Navajo doctors, nurses, nurses' aides, health education personnel, and medical interpreters.

It should be emphasized that there has been a tremendous improvement in medical care beginning in 1947, when physicians subject to the draft began to be assigned to work with Indians. The improvement continued after 1954, when the PHS took over from the Indian Bureau PHS. What was once an unqualified disaster has become merely inadequate in all respects mentioned. The quality of the physicians themselves, however, has improved strikingly. This will not continue to be the case if physicians are not subject to the draft unless PHS stipends are raised—since PHS service is presently an alternative to military service for physicians.

M. WELFARE

It is assumed that in terms of eligibility and amounts the welfare program for Navajos will be that of the State and Federal programs, and that some emergency welfare will be available from tribal sources. Far less emphasis has been put on welfare in this presentation than would be made if the stress were not on the development of the reservation economy. Were the steps described to be taken, the welfare load would be considerably lightened over a 25-year period. If they are not, it will increase. If numerous Navajos are to remain permanent welfare clientele, as seems likely under present conditions, then a vastly expanded welfare program would be necessary. Present amounts are totally inadequate, Navajos are removed unpredictably from the rolls, and many do not know their rights.

N. MISCELLANEOUS

1. *Housing.*—The traditional Navajo house was the hogan, a circular, single-room, dirt-floored dwelling made of wood or stone and used both for living and for ceremonial practices. Today most Navajos and most of their ceremonial practitioners insist on the use of a hogan for ceremonial purposes, so that many Navajo clusters of kin maintain at least one hogan. Shortage of the timbers necessary for a good hogan, desire for larger structures, and need for floors as more and more families have furniture and stoves, have led to the building of increasing numbers of dewllings built of machine-processed frame materials. In this building program people have been aided by tribal funds for those with minimum income and by ONEO funds and labor force. Furthermore, the ONEO program has provided training in house-building skills for many Navajo men (Home Improvement Training Program).

The present houses, however, have serious deficiencies. These include cordless, badly fitted windows, that are difficult to open or keep open, concrete floors, which are cold, and uninsulated houses both hotter in summer and colder in winter than the mud-chinked timbered houses of the past. An experimental program in housing is needed for the reservation (and for the United States at large, which lags in this respect). The BIA and ONEO are now developing model homes, which is a beginning.

The industrial and commercial development suggested in this document will require housing projects in the centers where this development occurs; so will an expanding population elsewhere. An improved housing program would be beneficial in terms of employment and for those housed, and would be essential for families working in newly developed centers. Such a program should develop under Tribal aegis. A fair amount of housing has been built in various centers by the Bureau and the Tribe.

2. *Experts and the training of experts.*—Mention has been made of hiring experts for various purposes. In some cases these would be consultants; in others they would occupy managerial roles. In either case, the Tribe would be well-advised to consider experts whose experiences are particularly relevant to their situation: Livestock and farming experts with experience in arid lands, whether in the United States or in the Near East, for example. By the same token, the Tribe might wish to send some of its scholarship students to areas where parallel geographical conditions must be met (for example, Israel), or where industrialization with slender means has made progress. The tendency to use consultants and managers whose prior experience is that of operating with maximal resources and under optimal conditions should be avoided.

O. SUMMARY OF THE PURPOSE, NATURE, AND ADVANTAGES OF THE PLAN OUTLINED

The purposes of this plan are (1) to allow Navajos to utilize their own resources to improve their own livelihood; (2) to give Navajos control over the utilization of their own resources; (3) to increase the level of income by increasing the number of jobs on the reservation and by improving the range; (4) to permit individuals to specialize occupationally in the interests of greater efficiency.

1. First, and foremost, it is proposed that any planning, along lines proposed here or other lines, should involve the Tribal Council, regional organizations, and chapters or other community-level organizations as primary planners. This is not a call for joint planning with the Bureau but for primary rights and responsibilities to be vested in Navajos.

2. It is proposed that the Navajo Tribe undertake future exploitation of its own minerals, process them, market them, and enjoy the profits from them.

3. It is proposed that future industrial development be Tribal in character, whether at once or on a phased basis.

4. It is proposed that there be a rapid development of roads, bus ines, and utilities as a basis for all other developments, and that the ssue of water allocation be carefully considered.

5. It is proposed that commercial development of a more specialized type than is found today is necessary and feasible for the reservation population, and that such development might place major emphasis on individual Navajos, Navajo partnerships and corporations, or the Tribe itself; for development and control.

6. Range improvement is proposed. This must be combined with stock water development, transition from sheep to cattle for many people, enhancement of the quality of the stock, and fencing. It is urgent to discuss and decide whether the management units should be nuclear families, extended families, larger kin groups, cooperatives, or community corporations. In all events except the last, heirship problems will arise with respect to improved, fenced range.

7. The irrigated farmland already in prospect raises questions respecting the efficient unit of management. Again the question of family units, larger kinship units, cooperatives, or large corporate farms arises.

8. It is proposed that an expanded and experimental educational program be carried out, that health facilities be expanded and improved, and that welfare operate at the level characteristic for non-Indians.

The advantages of the plan proposed are, first and foremost, to make Navajos responsible for their own economic affairs by giving them control thereof. Let us be clear: Responsibility is not doing what some one else wants one to do; it is being able to think about the consequences of one's acts, calculating the effects of those acts on others and on oneself, and being willing to live with the consequences. There is no such thing as preparing a *people* for responsibility. The capacity to deal with the group's affairs grows only by performance, not by rehearsal. The other advantages are a heightened standard of living, a more variegated series of occupational niches on reservation, and a decrease of dependency on welfare and disguised welfare programs.

P. SUMMARY OF DISADVANTAGES

There are two major disadvantages to the proposal. The first is that given some economic freedom, there will be individual Navajos who will prove as foolish, as corrupt, and as greedy as some people in the larger society. Some plans will go awry, and some Navajos will be guilty of breach of trust. This is a necessary risk. The second is that if planning is to be vested in Navajo hands, at present the principal agent of planning would be the Tribal Council. The Council is, however, out of touch with many sentiments at the grass roots level, or so I am told by many noncouncil Navajos. In addition, in a number of cases, members of the Council have come to believe that the interests of the Tribe and those of corporations interested in the Tribe's assets are identical. Remedies lie in the use of regional and local planning units where possible.

Q. REQUIREMENTS FOR IMPLEMENTING THIS PLAN

Since this is by no means the first plan for Navajo economic development, we must ask what must be dealt with so that this (or any other likely plan of any scale) can be implemented.

1. Congressional behavior will have to change. It will have to expend funds for Indians on a scale much greater than in the past, particularly to back the Tribe in the development of its own mineral exploitation and industry. Furthermore, funds will have to be predictable from year to year, which is not a congressional habit.

2. Considerable opposition will have to be met—from U.S. Senators and Representatives, national business interests, local business and livestock interests, State political figures, some members of the Navajo Tribal Council, and some other Navajos. The kinds of attitudes that must be overcome include at least the following.

(a) It is too expensive. (It is expensive for some years to come, but not in the long run.)

(b) It allows Navajos certain advantages or protections at the taxpayer's expense in competing with national and local business and local livestock interests. (It should. A close examination of a hundred years of history—the so-called long walk to progress celebrated by the Navajo Tribe in 1968, the anniversary of their release from Fort Sumner, indicates clearly that the U.S. Government has failed to give Navajos the material and educational tools to cope with the larger society and has responded to pressures from powerful national and local interests to make that competition more difficult. After 100 years, the Navajos are undereducated, unhealthy, living in a downgraded environment, living in part on unconsolidated checkerboard fee patent lands in unequal competition with surrounding ranchers, and passive participants in the exploitation of their own lands for mineral resources, a passivity encouraged by the Federal Government. This plan attempts to redress the balance. At least 25 years will be required to do so.)

(c) It will undermine native life. (This objection is not too likely from Navajos. Poverty, overgrazing, and overpopulation with the attendant need for more and more of the population to move off the reservation part time will, in time, not so much erode as corrode native life. Navajo life is bound to change in significant respects during the next 25 years. The question is not whether it should change, but in what respects it will change under different conditions.)

(d) It interferes with the natural processes of a market economy. (That is why we are where we are today: these very forces have, with relatively little Government interference, created the urban mess, pollution, a stagnant rural economy in many places, and a widening wealth differentiation that, while it accompanies a general rise in the

standard of living, leaves the underprivileged increasingly badly off
by comparison with the rest of the society.)

(e) It is not aimed at integration but at segregation; it is racist.
(This objection is particularly likely from liberals. The plan is in fact
consonant with a decided tendency toward ethnic solidarity on the
part of the Navajo. It is also consonant with the fact that it is easier to
gain acceptance in the larger society and to feel secure there if one has
an adequate base to operate from. It is consonant with the obvious general increase in ethnic movements in the United States. And it makes
sense when one realizes that at present Navajos are not being integrated as a tribe into the larger society, but being squeezed dry by it,
and that they are being neither integrated nor assimilated into the
larger society as individuals, but pushed into its lower echelons on
most unfavorable terms.

(f) Perhaps the most insidious argument, one that has already been
raised by some BIA officials, is that everything suggested is already
being done. Clearly anything that is being done along these lines is to
the good; it is unfortunate to criticize the Bureau for not doing what
it is doing—but without a tremendous boost, it is too little and too
late. Communications from the area office make it evident that
priorities established there include the same broad elements as are
brought out here: education, roads, industries and commerce, community facilities, and agriculture (in that order for the area office,
but not in my mind). It is not so much lack of understanding that
impedes the Bureau, but lack of instrumentalities.

3. A well-coordinated development program will require that funding be more centralized—vested in fewer Federal agencies than is
presently the case. To read the roster of agencies to which the BIA
and the tribe must appeal to get support for each piecemeal program
in housing, education, or health is to be amazed by the endurance of
officials who, in the end, get even a part of what they need.

R. THE ALTERNATIVE

Under present circumstances and without a major development
thrust, the Navajo economic situation will continue to develop much
as at present, but with continually increasing pressure on its surface
resources. That is, there will be some development of irrigation, which
will absorb a few people into cash crop farming. There will be a
gradually increasing amount of land fenced, chained, seeded, and
developed for water in some areas but in no planned fashion, so that
there will have been no thought given as to optimal units of management, consequences in terms of transition from use ownership to
effective ownership, and consequences in terms of heirship. Inefficiency will characterize many such operations because of the need of
many men to seek part-time employment off-reservation. Mineral
exploitation will continue along present lines, but at a pace that is not
Navajo-determined, and in a manner that produces a minimum of
multiplier effect. Outside forces will gain a stranglehold on somewhat
expanded Navajo retail economy. And support of Navajos by part-
time works projects based on "soft" money, uncertain from year to
year, and by welfare, will involve an increased amount of money,
without development of the reservation. It is not to be expected that
for some time to come Navajos will be absorbed into the external

economic scene on favorable terms. Unemployment rates tend to be relatively high in the economy except through war booms, and Navajos, because of educational handicaps and prejudice, are unfavorably placed for job competition. The attendant political consequences, which will to some degree occur in any case, will involve an increasing conjunction of Navajos in a Navajo power movement, of Indians in a red power movement, and of Indians, Mexicans, and Blacks in a generalized movement of oppressed ethnic groups.

S. THE PRICE TAG

It was understood that this report was to deal with the manner of economic development rather than with the budget for development. Some idea of the order of magnitude can be gained from the fact that the combined Navajo Area Office-Tribal 20-year plan for road improvement would cost over $300 million in 1968 dollars. Evidently a 25-year plan to encompass roads, schools, industry, commerce, credit, utilities, range improvement, and so forth, would cost a great deal more. There would be short run range compensations in reduction of soft money programs, like ONEO. If ONEO remained at its present level, it would expend over $250 million in 1968 dollars over 25 years, in ways that would sustain families and improve morale but that would contribute only modestly to development. In the long run, of course, the development plan would be less expensive than the present modes of sustaining the Navajo population at a minimum level

REFERENCES

The meager list below consists of references cited in the text and of current materials, not all cited, supplied by the Navajo Area Office. It does not attempt to include a list of every publication relevant for the the subject, nor even of the various publications consulted in the course of writing this document. For a full bibliography on the Navajos see Brugge, Correll, and Watson (1967). Starred items were kindly supplied by the Navajo Area Office.

ABERLE, DAVID F. 1966. The Peyote Religion among the Navaho. Chicago Aldine Publishing Co.

ADAMS, WILLIAM Y. 1963. Shonto: Study of the Role of the Trader in a Modern Navaho Community. Bureau of American Ethnology Bulletin 188. Washington, G.P.O.

*ANONYMOUS. n.d. Navajoland, Business Frontier. (A publication on industrial and commercial opportunities in the Navajo Country, with a foreword signed by Raymond Nakai, Chairman, Navajo Tribal Council, and Graham Holmes, Navajo Area Director. Probable date, 1968.)

Anonymous. 1962. Navajo Tribal Code. 2 vols. Orford, New Hampshire, Equity Publishing Co. (Together with 1967 Cumulative Pocket Supplements, Vols. 1 and 2.)

*Anonymous. 1966a. Destination: The Twentieth Century. Phoenix Cement News, 4, no. 1: 1–3.

*Anonymous. 1966b. Four Corners Goes West. Phoenix Cement News, 4, no. 3: 1–3.

BROPHY, WILLIAM A. and SOPHIE D. ABERLE, comp. 1966: The Indian, America's Unfinished Business. Norman, Oklahoma, University of Oklahoma Press.

BRUGGE, DAVID M., J. LEE CORRELL, and EDITHA L. WATSON. 1967. Navajo Bibliography. Window Rock, Arizona, Navajo Tribal Museum (mimeo).

HOUGH, HENRY W. 1967. Development of Indian Resources. Denver, World Press, Inc.

276

KELLY, LAWRENCE C. 1968. The Navajo Indians and Federal Indian Policy, 1900–1935. Tucson, The University of Arizona Press.

*KUTNEWSKY, FREMONT. 1966. Industry in Indian Land. New Mexico Magazine, September, pp. 16–19, 38–39.

*Navajo Area Office. n.d. Roads on the Navajo Reservation. Mimeo, 5 pp.

*Navajo Area Office. 1967. History of the Navajo Indian Irrigation Project (March, 1967). Prepared by J. Y. CHRISTIANSEN. Mimeo, 22 pp.

*Navajo Area Office. 1968a. Navajo Progress (deals with Fiscal Year 1967–68).

*Navajo Area Office. 1968b. Irrigation Agriculture in the Arizona part of the Upper Colorado River Compact Area (December, 1968). Prepared as a one-page information sheet for the Navajo Tribal Council.

*Navajo Forest Products Industries. 1967. Navajo Pine: Navajo Forest Products Industries Annual Report (Eighth Annual Report).

*Navajo Tribal Utility Authority. 1967. Annual Report to the Navajo People.

The Navajo Yearbook (See Young 1961).

NIEBURG, H. L. 1966. In the Name of Science. Chicago, Quadrangle Books.

OHANNESSIAN, SIRARPI, prep. and ed. 1967. The Study of the Problems of Teaching English to American Indians, Report and Recommendations, July 1976. Washington, Center for Applied Linguistics.

*RADOV, KARL. 1968. Economic Development Possibilities of the Navajo Reservation. ms., 6 pp. From a report prepared by ABT Associates, Inc., 55 Wheeler St., Cambridge, Mass.

SASAKI, TOM T. 1960. Fruitland, New Mexico: A Navaho Community in Transition. Ithaca, New York, Cornell University Press.

*THIELE, HEINRICH J. and Associates. 1966. Navajo Water Resources, Supplies and Management and the Proposed Navajo Tribal Water Authority (NTWA), A Reservation-Wide Water Study. (Heinrich J. Thiele and Associates, Consulting Engineers, Economists and Hydrologists, Scottsdale, Arizona, July 1, 1966. Published by the Navaju Tribe, Raymond Nakai, Chairman, Navajo Tribal Council, Window Rock, Arizona.) Although published by the Navajo Tribe, this report has not been accepted officially by the Navajo Tribal Council.

TNY (See Young 1961).

U.S. Bureau of the Census. 1963. U.S. Census of Population: 1960. Vol. 1, Characteristics of the Population. Part 4, Arizona. Washington, G.P.O.

U.S. Bureau of the Census. 1963. U.S. Census of Population: 1960. Subject Reports. Nonwhite Population by Race. Final Report PC(2)–1C. Washington, G.P.O.

*U.S. Congress, 1968. Public Law 90–272, 90th Congress, S. J. Res. 123, March 22, 1968. Joint Resolution to approve long-term contracts for delivery of water from Navajo Reservoir in the State of New Mexico, and for other purposes.

*U.S. Department of the Interior, Bureau of Reclamation, Navajo Indian Irrigation Project, P.O. Box 28, Farmington, New Mexico, 87401. 1967. Information Summary on Navajo Indian Irrigation Project (revised March, 1967). Mimeo, 7 pp.

WERNER, OSWALD. 1967. Some Cultural Prerequisites to Teaching English as a Second Language in BIA Schools. Mimeo, 26 pp.

YOUNG, ROBERT W., comp. 1961. The Navajo Yearbook, Report No. viii, 1951–1961, A Decade of Progress. Window Rock, Arizona, The Navajo Agency. (Cited as TNY.)

THE LUMBEE INDIANS: PATTERNS OF ADJUSTMENT

By MOHAMMOD AMANULLAH[*]

FOREWORD

The Lumbee Indians of Baltimore represent an Indian group which has attempted to assimilate into an urban environment. Although these Lumbees came to Baltimore from rural North Carolina in search of better jobs and a higher standard of living, they find themselves at the bottom of urban society. Mohammod Amanullah's study, based on extensive interviews with Lumbee families, reveals that they live in extreme poverty and have few contacts with persons outside their own ethnic group. In many cases, they are unaware of available employment opportunities and social services. Their greatest needs would appear to be the development of leadership within the group and concentrated assistance in obtaining available social, educational, and employment assistance.

CONTENTS

PROBLEM

The Lumbee Indians of Baltimore came from North Carolina some 18 years ago, congregating in the slum sections around Baltimore Street off Broadway. The Lumbees are but one of the many minority groups in this neighborhood, which is composed of families of Negro, Polish, Greek, and German descent, and their population is estimated at 1,500. The Lumbees, coming from an essentially rural agricultural background, have had to make an adjustment to urban society. The fact that they are Indians means that they are not accepted by the dominant urban group—the whites in general and the various neighborhood ethnic groups in particular—and the fact that they are anti-Negro means that the Negroes do not look upon them with favor.

[*]Assistant Professor, Department of Sociology, Morgan State College, Baltimore, Md.

The Lumbees, by and large, are unskilled, therefore, their earnings do not enable them to meet the urban standard of living. Still, their standard of living is perhaps a much higher standard as compared with the Southern rural standard of North Carolina. Economically, they are poor and a portion of the group continually live on welfare. Their educational aspirations are far too limited. Lack of education, a lack of skills and concomitant poor wages combined with poor housing conditions and early marriages create situations which produce constant anxiety and hardships.

Purpose

It is the purpose of this study to examine the kinds of opportunities that prevail for intergroup relations between the Lumbees and the minority and majority groups of Baltimore and primarily to determine the actual intergroup relations between the Lumbees and their urban neighbors as a process of social adjustment.*

Objectives

As the first exploratory study of this group, the study will set guidelines for future research. It is hoped the investigation will discover those situations which aggravate ingroup-outgroup tension and those relations which bridge the gap between the groups. It is believed that certain patterns of behavior will emerge which will provide clues for the improvement of intergroup relations.

Sample

The sample consists of Lumbees who live within the confines of Broadway on the east, Madeira Street and Patterson Park on the west, Madison Street on the north, and Eastern Avenue on the south. The sample is composed of 60 cases (37 males and 23 females). Subjects were chosen on a random sampling basis after a sampling frame was made. Alternates were selected when an attempt to interview first-choice subjects failed. There are common factors in the sample in that 90 percent of the subjects belong to the lower-lower class of Baltimore society; 12 percent belong to the upper-lower class because the heads of the household are skilled. The age range in this sample was 18–56 for men and 18–62 for women,** with an average of 32.6 years for men; 57 of the respondents are married and three are unmarried.

Methods and Data Collection

Methods used in the study are participant observation and the use of a schedule. Each interview lasted from 1 hour and 15 minutes to 2

---

*The city is seen as a system of interaction and a web of social relationships. Adjustment is seen in the process of social interaction. The individual acts in consideration of others, that is, he modifies his behavior to the extent that is presentable and acceptable to the rest.

**At the time of the initial interviews, two respondents were 15 years old, married, and the parents of one child. They were seen often during the period of the study because they lived in an extended family and at the time this is being written they are approximately 18 years old. A set of 15-year-old twins were also interviewed, but for sample purposes, only the parents are considered.

hours (an average of 1 hour and 40 minutes) and each interview was conducted in the home of the subject. For relevant information, social agencies such as the church, the school, the police department, and the social welfare administration were approached. In order to determine patterns of adjustment among the Lumbees of Baltimore, it was felt that a visit to North Carolina, the Lumbees' original home, would throw some light on the subject. The author visited North Carolina and interviewed several prominent Lumbees in the area. He also secured information in the Pembroke State College Library and in the North Carolina University Library at Raleigh. This information helped him to understand native Lumbee culture as it exists in Robeson County.

WHY CHOOSE LUMBEES?

The Lumbees are an Indian group who have very few Indian traditions. They have, in large measure, adopted white ways. They are moving beyond acculturation in the direction of assimilation with the dominant society. They now live in several large cities such as Baltimore, Detroit, and New York. Therefore, the findings on Lumbee intergroup behavior in one city may provide clues to their behavior in other cities. Further, the author's own interest in the Indians of the United States and the accessibility of the Lumbees as one of Baltimore's minority groups made them a particularly favorable choice for study.

DATA HANDLING AND OBJECTIVITY

The data consist of responses which came from those who were interviewed. In the interviews the interviewer maintained a friendly but uncommitted attitude. Respondents were asked questions from a schedule. The interviewer also recorded his observations of the subject's home such as household effects, tidiness (or otherwise), children, telephone calls, or any visitors at the time of the interview. Interpretation of the survey is based on actual data through the use of cross tabulation. However, the analysis is also influenced by the author's observation and participation.

Part of the data refer to the same respondent at two or more points in time. Data of this nature help ascertain changes in attitude or interaction of the person. By and large, the discussion focuses on the information gathered at a single point in time.

SOME LIMITATIONS IN THE STUDY

Some of the responses do not always reveal the truth nor do they throw light on the subject in which the investigator is directly interested. It is also true that sometimes answers are given to questions which are socially approved and desirable. For instance, one parent who outwardly displays a high regard for education yet did not help any of his six children to finish high school actually discouraged each of them from continuing his education. Second, the respondents are quite frequently vague when answering any question which requires some conjecture on their part. Additional difficulty resulted from the Lumbees' suspicion of "outsiders"; as in any other group, there is an outgroup hostility among Lumbees.

Lack of cooperation from social agencies such as the police department, school authorities, and social welfare agencies placed limitations in the study in some areas.

Background of the Lumbees

Of all the groups that mingle in Baltimore's melting pot, perhaps none have such an intriguing history as the Lumbees who claim descent from Sir Walter Raleigh's Lost Colony. "The universal tradition among the Indians," writes Hamilton McMillan, "found in Robeson County and counties adjoining, is that they are the descendants of English people and the Cherokees." [1]

"The language of these people is old English and similar to that used in the time of Chaucer." [2]

The result of this intermingling is evidenced by the presence of a number of blue-eyed, blonde people among the Lumbees.

The people now known as Lumbees have only recently been recognized as a separate group of Indians by an act of the North Carolina Legislature in 1954. Previously, they had been referred to as Cherokee, Croatan, and "Indians of the Robeson County". [3] The Cherokees, however, do not recognize them as Cherokees—perhaps because of the latter's racial mixture. They were designated as "colored" under North Carolina law and thus were supposed to go to Negro schools. The Lumbees refused to associate with Negroes in any way and so they were an isolated group, claimed by none. The name "Lumbee" derives either from the Lumber River or from the town of Lumberton, N.C. The Lumbees were officially named and recognized by the State in 1954. [4]

It is believed that the Lumbees began to migrate to larger cities, such as Baltimore, apparently to find a better livelihood. The life of the Lumbees in the Pembroke area is even now far below the American standard of living. The bulk of the Lumbee population is engaged in farm work. Socially, there are three classes: (1) the very poor, even poverty stricken, class which is the majority; (2) the lower middle class; and (3) the extremely small elite class. The elites are those Lumbees who have become teachers, authors, doctors, or ministers and the power structure in Pembroke, N.C., is in their hands.

The Lumbees in Baltimore

It is estimated that there are 1,500 Lumbees in Baltimore, concentrated in a radius of 5 miles around Broadway and Baltimore Street. Generally, they are a hospitable people. They welcome guests and readily offer a drink and something to eat. The investigator soon discovered that it was wise to avoid interviewing around mealtimes for one family would insist that he join them for "early" supper and the next would equally insist that he join them for a "late" supper. Unaccustomed to drinking, he felt safer on the drive home if he confined himself to only two or three interviews a day. The best in the house is laid before the guest—the husband is jovial, expansive, and

---

[1] *Sir Walter Raleigh's Lost Colony*, Edwards and Broughton Printing Company, Raleigh (1894), p. 42.
[2] *Ibid.*, p. 44.
[3] McLean, A. W., "Historical Sketch of the Indians of Robeson County," in: McPherson, O. M., *Indians of North Carolina*, Washington (1915).
[4] *Ibid.*

full of talk while the wife, in a little flurry of excitement, hurries in and out of the room, anxious that her cooking should please. Children are sent to borrow supplies from the neighbors. Borrowing was carried on in the belief that if someone had what was needed he would share, secure that if he was ever in need, the favor would be returned in kind. At one home, there was no food and the husband borrowed $5 from the investigator for the evening meal. One family with a baby called the investigator to borrow money for medicine for the child. Once, a young man offered the investigator some tea but there was no sugar in the house and no one nearby had any. They do not apologize if their offering seems meager. One teabag will be carried between three or more cups and used again for seconds and no embarrassment will be displayed. Usually, the host does most of the talking and he is a good conversationalist. The only time that the wife talked was during the "ladies' section" of the questionnaire or when she was interviewed during her husband's absence. Otherwise, the man dominated the conversation and relished it.

Most of the respondents live in rented apartments. The appearance of the homes could be characterized as "lacking." Every family had a television set and some had color television. The majority of the families interviewed did not have telephones. During the winter, interviews were conducted in the kitchens because of the inadequate heating and the gas stove would be burning to supplement the heat. Whether the walls were wallpapered or painted, they were cracked and peeling. One family mentioned that the landlord would not furnish paint even when requested. Most of the homes were clean and neat, even though the furnishings were worn. In one home, the back door was hanging off its hinges with the cold air coming in and the gas jets burning. The sink, stove, floor, and counters were greasy. Few dishes and less food was displayed in the open cabinets. There was no door at all between the kitchen and bathroom. The stool had no seat, the window did not close completely, there were holes in the wall. This family had no tub or shower. There were two rooms upstairs, used as bedrooms, and three rooms downstairs: the kitchen, living room, and a dining room converted into a bedroom. The living room was sparsely furnished and contained a well-worn couch and one chair. One or two pictures and a calendar hung lopsidedly on the walls. The floors were bare, unvarnished wood and faded linoleum was on the kitchen floor. Twelve people live in this apartment, including the parents and their children, two married children and their spouses, and a girl who lived with the family. During the time of the investigation, a married son with his wife and child moved in as well. There were no facilities for washing clothes. The family used a nearby laundromat. Utilities were paid for separately from the rent which was $25 a week. During the period of the investigation, two families are known to have been evicted for being a week late with the rent.

There were over a hundred cases on welfare among Lumbees at the time of the investigation. This is estimated to be one-third of the total families. Many of the employed men are seasonal workers and they go on welfare or collect unemployment during part of the year. Thus, the caseload varies from season to season.

Approximately one-third of the sample had automobiles. Their jobs are located nearby or as faraway as 15 miles from where they live. They shop locally at small neighborhood stores and frequent local bars, movies, restaurants, and churches. The Lumbees have two churches of their own, one Baptist and one Church of God. Children in the sample families attend public neighborhood schools No. 23 and No. 27 At the time of the study, 65 children were in school (28 were in grades 1 through 3) and there were seven dropouts in the case families.

THE LUMBEE FAMILY

Sociologists classify the family as either nuclear or joint. The pattern of the American middle-class family falls in the category called nuclear family where the parents and their unmarried children live together.

Lumbees do not fit these nuclear or extended family types. Twenty percent of the sample families are extended families. In one such extended family, the mother and two of her married daughters lived together in a three-story apartment. The two daughters together had 14 children. Only one of the three women was working at the time of the interview—she was a waitress. The daughter with 11 children had not lived with her husband for a considerable length of time, yet she had quite small children. A white man was seen in the apartment, but he was not the husband of any of the women. A number of the children were blond and blue-eyed. It was not clear how they managed economically with only one person employed in the family. There are some Lumbees who belong to nuclear families as well. The difficulty of placing them in one or another cateogry lies in the fact that if and when the Lumbees are not members of extended families, they live in close proximity to other family members. Parents and their married children live (1) in an apartment in the same building, (2) on the same street, or (3) within a distance of a few blocks. Of the 1,500 Lumbees, approximately 900 of them live within six blocks of Baltimore Street alone and the rest within an area of 10 to 15 blocks around Baltimore Street.

It is quite common for family members to visit each other every day and they frequently eat at one another's homes. A daughter may visit her mother in the morning and spend the rest of the day with her until her husband comes. Together they may eat supper and then they return to their own home, which is perhaps in the same block. It does not appear that the mother influences the daughter in any vital decisionmaking; rather, a mother is available whenever any assistance in the form of advice is needed. The mother-in-law and son-in-law relationship is, therefore, not usually one of unresolved conflict, nor is there a sore feeling between them. The son-in-law realizes that the mother-in-law acts in good faith and that she is a well-meaning person. She is not Young and Willmott's "Mum" of the East London family. Father-in-law and son-in-law relation is, on the surface, a friendly relation. They may be seen together in a restaurant or going to the doctor's or lawyer's together. However, this surface appearance is deceiving, especially if they are living in a joint family. The father is the head of his household and that includes his daughters' husbands. He advises them on the jobs they should take, collects "rent" from their paychecks, and either delights in or complains about pregnancy of the daughter. The son-in-law commonly gives so much of his paycheck to the father that he is unable to move out on his own. In those few instances where relations were strained between the husband and his wife's family, the husband attributed it to the "old man's interference." He blamed this "interference" as the reason they were living separately from the wife's family. One son-in-law repeatedly stated that he hated his father-in-law, but in economic stress, he matter-of-factly moved in with his wife's family. He complained that the father-in-law did not work and just collected from the daughters' husbands. He also felt that his father-in-law unfairly made his wife do most of the housework and was angry enough to air his dispute with the entire family.

Husband-Wife Relationship.—The relationship between a husband and wife is based on a clear division of labor—clearer than that which exists in the middle-class American family. A middle-class husband at home generally helps his wife in a variety of ways such as cleaning the house, drying dishes, ironing, changing diapers, etc. This, however, is not the case with the Lumbees. Most household jobs are strictly the wife's. In the study, a very small percentage (15 percent) of the husbands mentioned helping their wives in drying the dishes or doing the laundry. The general pattern then seems to be a segregation of the sphere of duties and responsibilities. A Lumbee father is a relatively free man. He is the head of the house in every sense, the one who makes decisions, and his wife obeys. Of the 60 families (cases) studied, only one wife displayed antagonism and disobedience to her husband. She seemed sulky and seldom spoke except to criticize or correct her husband. Most wives, in front of the interviewer, deferred to their husbands in conversation, never openly disagreed with their statements, and seemed generally to be quiet and unassuming. During the "ladies' only" portion of the interview a wife might mention some incident in disciplining the children or about community relations but if the husband later told a different version, she always agreed with his viewpoint. This one wife took her family's side against her husband and when he defended her right not to be overworked by her father, she took her father's side.

Few of the men in the sample had full-time, year-round jobs. They were occupationally unskilled and educationally deficient. Approximately one-third of the total Lumbee population is estimated to be on welfare. At the time of the study, eight families were on welfare and two of these were long-term cases. In one family the father had not worked in 10 years. In another family the husband was a young man in his twenties who had not held a job in 2 years. Both men are "medically unfit" for work and have the medical evidence to support their claims. (However, the investigator learned that for a price anyone can receive such medical evidence. There are stories told about other Lumbees who "work" 1 or 2 days, become "injured," and then collect compensation. Only one respondent would admit that he was guilty of such a charge, in fact he was proud of it and thought that he ought not to work. A lawyer is available to assist Lumbees in claiming damages or compensation and one such case was underway at the time of the study.) Both these men do not want their wives to work. The welfare check is not sufficient to cover all the expenses connected with a home and children. Yet, the young husband, unable to pay the week's rent or to buy groceries, insists that his wife go to work. She works anywhere from 1 day to 2 weeks, depending on how much the family needs to see them through the latest crisis. If she complains that the work is too hard or the job too far away, he insists that she stop working, but she cannot stop if she has not earned enough for the week's rent. When the wife was sick, this man called upon the investigator for help. Advised about agencies which offer short-term relief, he sent his wife to three charitable organizations for money and food. She was gone nearly the entire day while he complained about her slowness and stupidity. He was positive that she was unable to tell a story convincing enough to secure food and when she did return with staples and money he berated her for not bringing enough. The wife calmly accepted his accusations and never once suggested that he get a job so that such incidents would not occur.

Parent-Child Relationship.—Lumbee parents are generally permissive and yet they use harsh punishment on children. Physical punishment such as spanking and whipping with a belt is not uncommon. Parents are heard to threaten the children by saying, "You want me to get the belt?" Even very young children of a year and a half or 2 are so threatened. Some parents use punishment such as no television, no candy or other treats, or sending the child to his room. They allow the children to stay out late, to play or chat on street corners as they please, to come and go without direct supervision. Yet, a child cannot overtly disobey the parents, particularly in front of visitors, without experiencing immediate retribution. Crimes include sassing, crying when told to stop, or refusing to do chores. Chores are given to all the children in the family, even the youngest. They are expected to clean their rooms, sweep the floors, run errands, mind the younger siblings, and do the dishes. There is a definite difference between boys' chores and girls' chores: boys run errands for cigarettes or Coke, girls make coffee or clean and dress the baby. In only one or two cases were the children given an allowance, none received "pay" for work done around the house. Punishment is swift for bad behavior, but little reward or incentive for good behavior is offered.

It was difficult to gauge the effect of child-rearing practices on the children. Most children were shy, spoke seldom, preferred to leave the room rather than stay and visit. Boys of thirteen sat on the fringes of the men's group, absorbing the talk, but not contributing even if directly questioned.

Parents outwardly place a high value on education. However, their lack of interest or supervision regarding homework or school attendance more adequately reveals their true feelings. They tell the children to do their school work but make no effort to check it for neatness, etc. In the entire sample, hardly ten percent of the parents of school-attending children knew what their children were doing at school. Parents say they want an education for their children higher than what they themselves had. But they do not have a clear set of educational goals and when they do have such goals they do not know how to go about obtaining their realizations. Eighty-five percent of the parents wanted their children to get a high school education and fifteen percent wanted them to have a college education. Those parents who want a college education for their children are the ones who themselves had some college.

The Lumbees and Education

Educationally, the Lumbees of Baltimore are one of the backward groups in the nation. In the sample, only 8.33 percent attended college for a year or two. No one in the sample has finished college, nor does anyone in the entire area under our definition have a college degree.[5] Interestingly enough, the same percentage (8.33 percent) in the sample had had no formal education, that is, they were illiterate. Women attending college at one time or another numbered 5 percent and the total for men was 3.33 percent. The reverse was true for the illiterates, there were more male than female illiterates. The highest percentage of the population (36.66 percent) comprised those who had completed a sixth-grade education.

Several reasons were given for not continuing with education. Most of the men said they were needed to work on the farm. Their parents had insisted on their working in the fields and for some education was a financial burden their families could not afford. A small number of men, however, said they did not like school and nothing at school attracted them. The women also said that they were required to help out at home by cooking, cleaning, or helping with the younger children. Seven of the women (30.43 percent) were married before they could finish school. Two of them admitted being pregnant when they got married at 15. In Baltimore, the young people were still faced with economic pressures and they often quit school to go to work. Girls usually marry rather than go out to work.

The Lumbees realize that education is necessary if they are to obtain good jobs and they know that their children will find life even more difficult if they do not have good educations. They tell the investigator that they want their children to have a better education than they themselves had, yet they do nothing to encourage or assist their children in reaching this goal. Only 21 percent show some seriousness about helping the children get an education—they talk about the value of school, they see education as a worthwhile goal. Yet, only one mother in the survey said that her children had to finish their homework before playing. A very small 10 percent was aware of what their children were doing in school in terms of grades, subjects, teacher's name, etc. The goal was entirely abstract for these concerned parents had no idea of what they could do to reach fulfillment of their goal. All parents with some college education wanted their children to go to college; parents whose hopes for college were never realized still wanted such an education for their children.

Lumbee parents did not participate in school activities such as the PTA and they did not send cakes or cookies for the school bazaar, etc.

Enrollment of Lumbee children (grades 1 through 10)

Grade:	Number of children
1	10
2	8
3	10
4	6
5	8
6	7
7	5
8	8
9	3
10	0
Total	65

[5] There is a Lumbee social worker with an M.S.W. who works for Baltimore City. He, however, does not live in the area which we defined elsewhere in this study. Many Lumbees know his name and they mentioned his name when asked to name three well-known Lumbees.

There are 228 children in 57 families in the sample, with an average of four children per family. The youngest family represented consists of one 18-year-old couple and their two children. Both the parents quit school at 13. They live with the wife's family and are supported by welfare. At the time of the study, there were 65 children attending public schools No. 23 and No. 27. The chart above shows the number of children enrolled in each grade. The majority of the Lumbee children attend school No. 27, which has been called the "worst" school in the Baltimore public school system. Conditions are so deplorable that No. 27 lacks even the bare essentials for education. Teachers are unqualified. There are no library or cafeteria facilities. Further, the building itself is structurally unsafe. Some parents expressed their concern about school No. 27 in particular and about the poor quality of teaching generally. They have no idea what they can do or whom to approach for improvement of the school conditions. They do not have the money to send the children to another school for bus fares and other incidentals. The Lumbees, as well as all the children in the vicinity, are the victims of the poor school system. It was not determined how much of an effect the poor facilities might have had on the children's eagerness to leave school. The lack of a library is especially evident for no adult in the sample has ever gone to the library. Only two of the children have been to a library, but they have not spent their lives in the Baltimore-Broadway area.

School dropouts.—School officials were asked for information regarding the Lumbee children, their number, the number of dropouts, etc., with little success. The school was very uncooperative and said that such information (based on race or color) was no longer being kept.

Thus, information on dropouts was gathered indirectly. At one time during the investigation, there were two boys (ages 13 and 14) who were put in reform school. One of the two has since been released. Neither boy went to school. Another boy (age undetermined) was identified as a dropout. There were four female dropouts. Two 15-year-old twins said that they had dropped out of school because there were Negroes in their class and they refused to go to a school in which there were Negroes. The other two girls said that their families had wanted them to help out at home. It was said, but not confirmed by the girl in question, that one of the 15-year-old girls was pregnant at the time she quit school.

Lack of motivation was the common factor in these seven cases of dropouts. The lack of motivation was reinforced by the inferior school situation and the parents' unconcern. Economic conditions are certainly a factor in these children's dropping out of school where parents are forced to encourage their children to take odd jobs to supplement family income. It is not unusual to see the Lumbee family in economic distress, trying to obtain money from churches, emergency centers, and other charitable organizations.

The following chart briefly summarizes the investigator's findings on the educational background of the Lumbees in the sample.

EDUCATIONAL ACHIEVEMENT AMONG LUMBEES

[Number of persons, 60]

Sex, type of education, and number of persons	Percentage in the sample	Percentage in the total population	Percentage for every 100 males and females combined
Male:			
College (1 year or more) (2)	5.4	3.33	
High school (6)	16.2	10.00	
Junior high (15)	40.5	25.00	
Some schooling (11)	29.8	18.33	
No schooling (3)	8.1	5.00	
Total (37)	100	61.66	
Female:			
College (1 year or more) (3)	13.04	5.00	8.33
High school (2)	8.70	3.33	13.33
Junior high (7)	30.43	11.66	36.66
Some schooling (9)	39.13	15.00	33.33
No schooling (2)	8.70	3.33	8.33
Total (23)	100.00	38.32	100.00

ECONOMIC STATUS OF THE LUMBEES

The Lumbees, as a group, are economically poor. Income ranges between $2,000 and $4,000 a year. Only five cases in the sample had an income over $4,000 a year. Two of these five were white men married to Lumbee women. In view of the America standard of living, the bulk of the Lumbee population lives on an income which Congress has termed "poverty level".

Approximately one-third of the Lumbees in Baltimore are on welfare. In the sample eight familes were on welfare. This number, however, varies from season to season since the men work at unskilled seasonal jobs. Among men only 7.3 percent are engaged in skilled jobs and only 4.86 percent of the women work at skilled jobs. More than 80 percent of the Lumbees are unskilled. Sixty percent of the Lumbees in the sample work in three areas: boxmaking, painting, and roofing. Both painting and roofing are seasonal jobs; thus, appioximately 57 percent of these men are jobless during the year. During their offseason, the men receive unemployment compensation and welfare. (In the total sample, approximately 35 percent of the men are jobless during the year who work at painting and roofing.)

Social class determinants include occupation, income, dwelling area, house type, education, and style of life. Any or all of these determinants clearly indicate that the Lumbees are a low-income group and that they inhabit the lowest strata of Baltimore's class structure.

Occupationally, only 12.16 percent of the sample hold skilled jobs: IBM keypunch operator, machine operator, clerk, and auto mechanic. Eighty-seven percent can be classified as unskilled. Special efforts were made to determine how many held steady, full-time jobs. Questions were asked such as, "Since painting is a seasonal job, what do you do off-season?" Few of the men make any effort to find another job preferring to collect unemployment compensation or go on welfare. Two of the men in the sample claim medical disability and have not worked anywhere from 2 to 10 years. It is known that medical certificates are available under a "mutual benefit" agreement to help them in securing fraudulent compensation. All of the respondents gave rosy answers and inflated income figures when questioned about annual income. By observation and indirect questioning, the investigator was able to determine the true extent of their earnings.

None of the Lumbees interviewed owned his own home. All lived in old, rundown apartment buildings. No home presented evidence of affluence, color television notwithstanding, for the furniture was uniformily worn and in need of immediate repair or replacement. Not everyone had a telephone and no one owned a washing machine. Car ownership, no longer a reliable determinant of social class in today's "buy today, pay tomorrow" market, still appears to be adequate as far as the subjects of this study are concerned. Only 36.7 percent of the Lumbees owned automobiles, while 63.3 were without a car.

Their style of life is very meager. Children were shabbily dressed. One 2-year-old only child wore her mother's blouses and stockings. Her hair was long, dirty, and unkempt. She was sickly and her parents would take her to the free clinic but be unable to buy the medicine prescribed. Her diapers consisted of torn up blankets, sheets, and men's shirts. She is a pretty and affectionate child. In only one family were the two children neatly and stylishly dressed with clothing that fit. They had an advantage in that their mother had had an education and she was especially concerned that the children have a nice appearance. She also required them to study daily and had dreams of their going to college someday. As the children grew older and were able to find jobs their appearance improved. Even so, the prettiest dress was often torn and dirty. The investigator did not observe sewing machines in any of the homes and was unable to determine if there were any.

OCCUPATIONS OF THE BALTIMORE LUMBEES

Jobs	Number of men employed	Percent	Number of women employed	Percent	Total number and percentage
Machine operator	2	6. 45	0	0	2–4. 87
Painting	7	22. 61	0	0	7–17. 03
Boxmaking and other factory work	8	25. 80	3	30	11–26. 76
Maid	0	0	2	20	2–4. 87
Clerk	0	0	1	10	1–2. 43
Janitorial	3	9. 67	0	0	3–7. 30
IBM keypunch operator	0	0	1	10	1–2. 43
Exotic dancer	0	0	1	10	1–2. 43
Waitress	0	0	1	10	1–2. 43
Bartender	1	3. 22	0	0	1–2. 43
Orderly	2	6. 45	0	0	2–4. 87
Auto mechanic	1	3. 22	0	0	1–2. 43
Roofers	4	12. 90	0	0	4–9. 74
Gas station attendant	1	3. 22	0	0	1–2. 43
Homemaker	0	0	1	10	1–2. 43
Minister	2	6. 45	0	0	2–4. 87
Total	31	100. 00	10	100	41–100. 0

MARRIAGE

Lumbees marry at an early age; according to the sample, the average age of marriage for women was fifteen and for men seventeen. Girls go steady as soon as they attain puberty. Most frequently, dating takes place with those who live in the neighborhood or with those who are in some way related with the family. Very little time elapses between engagement and marriage. A very large number of girls are already pregnant at the time of marriage. It was not possible to determine the exact number of premarital pregnancies because all of the information came to the investigator secondhand, except for two girls who said that they had deliberately gotten pregnant at fifteen in order to escape parental pressure at home, but it appears that perhaps one-half of the marriages take place because the girl is pregnant. The ceremony of marriage is not elaborate. A wedding gown is not worn and large numbers of guests are not invited. It is very much a family affair and a wedding cake and the minister's blessing are sufficient. The wedding is performed in the minister's home (part of which is used as a church) and the bride and groom go directly home. Their economic conditions seldom allow for such extras as an elaborate wedding or a honeymoon trip.

"I think it is better to marry in one's own race," sums up the feelings expressed by Lumbees with regard to intermarriage. While opposed to mixed-marriage generally, they are specifically and vehemently opposed to any Lumbee-Negro marriage. The investigator has knowledge of two cases of Lumbee-Negro intermarriage* but they are not included in this sample. There are 16 cases of intermarriage in the sample, all between Lumbee and white. The expressed adherence to endogamy is more idealistic than actual since more than one-fourth of all the marriages in the sample are mixed marriages. Lumbee-white marriage is quite common among the upper class Lumbees in North Carolina. The mayor of Pembroke—a Lumbee—informed the investigator that all of his children married whites. Such intermarriages have been taking place since the time of Sir Walter Raleigh and it is difficult to visually distinguish a Lumbee from a white among the upper class Lumbees of Pembroke.

A Lumbee is not disgraced by marrying a white. In fact, he acquires a sense of superiority toward other Lumbees. Intermarried couples do not visit each other. The white spouse is willing to have the nearest relatives and the closest friends of the Lumbee over to the house. On the other hand, the white person's relatives do not invite the couple and they do not visit the couple, although they do invite the white partner alone. One white woman married to a Lumbee said, "My friends deliberately ignore me if they happen to see me in the store or on the street." Only one of the whites mentioned taking his wife to his family's home and he said that she was well received. None of the white spouses had visited the Lumbee partner's home in Pembroke. For the Lumbee, intermarriage with a white raises him in the eyes of other Lumbees, insofar as social status is concerned, but he gains no recognition at all from the dominant white group and finds that his white partner's social status can be considerably diminished.

Divorce and separation.—The Lumbee rate of divorce and separation is not different from the national trend. There were 14 cases of divorce (23.3 percent) and four cases of separation (6.7 percent) in the sample.

---

*There are four Negro families whose last name is Locklear. The Lumbees stated to the author that Negroes took the name in order to establish themselves as Indian. One of the Negro Locklears is herself the child of a mixed marriage. She is married to a Negro college graduate, has had 2 years of college, and did not in any way try to impress the author that she was Indian. She related that about 50 years ago her parents and aunt came from Rocky Island, N.C., and that she herself was born and raised in Baltimore. She visited Pembroke only once, when she was four, and considers herself Negro. She lives in a middle class Negro neighborhood. Another Locklear is a male who has completed 4 years of college and is now doing part-time graduate study. His Negro wife is a nurse. He is proud of his Indian ancestry and says that he is Negro-Indian. (His wife, however, emphasizes the point that her husband is a Lumbee.) He lives in a middle class integrated neighborhood and sends his children to private school.

The rate of divorce is higher among mixed marriages. There are 16 Lumbee-white marriages in the sample and the divorce rate is 37.5 percent. For Lumbee-Lumbee marriages, the divorce rate is 18.2 percent.

DIVORCE AND SEPARATION (N-60)

	Divorces	Percent	Separations	Percent
Lumbee-Lumbee	8	13.3	4	6.7
Mixed couples	6	10.0	0	0
Total	14	23.3	4	6.7

DIVORCE RATE BY COUPLE COMPOSITION—N-44 (LUMBEE-LUMBEE); N-16 (MIXED COUPLES)

	Divorces	Percent	Separations	Percent
Lumbee-Lumbee	8	18.2	4	9.1
Mixed couples	6	37.5	0	0

The Lumbees felt that there were several reasons for their rate of divorce. These are listed below in descending order:
1. "Not marrying their own kind."
2. Infidelity.
3. Husband drinks too much.
4. Husband stays away from his job, is not a good provider.
5. Couple does not get along.
6. Husband beats up on wife.

The Lumbees do not approve of divorce but they agree that when "things do not go right" it is perhaps better to get a divorce. Part of the reason for their rate of divorce may be that the role of the woman in the Lumbee family has considerably altered since the Lumbees came to Baltimore. In the rural agricultural environment of North Carolina, mothers do not work; grandmothers, sisters, aunts, nieces, and other female relatives help each other with their work and take care of the children. In an urban setting, however, wives are more dependent on their own resources. All too often the husband is unable to adequately support his family due to his lack of skills and education and the wife is forced to seek work. A woman with no skills can work as a janitoress, maid, waitress, nurses' aide, or factory worker. These are all low-paying jobs but if a woman is fortunate enough to have her mother or another female relative nearby she can avoid paying for child care. In one family, both parents work in a factory and they freely admit that the wife's mother was asked to come from Pembroke in order to care for the children. The wife felt that the children received the best care and the husband agreed. The wife's role as a working partner makes her somewhat financially independent from her husband. If she is the sole money-earner, her voice becomes increasingly more important in terms of how the money is spent and this diminishes the man's importance as the provider and decision-maker.

It may be assumed that there is a loss of role as the result of urban impact. Men find that they cannot go home to rest in the middle of the working day and women cannot bring their husbands' lunches to the job as they did when the men worked in the fields. They find themselves confused in the anonymity of urban life. One woman spoke about the magnitude of "things" in the urban setting, the great profusion of bars, stores, and restaurants, the mass of traffic and people constantly passing by. She made a distinction between the relationship of people in North Carolina and in Baltimore. In North Carolina, she felt, people are friendly because they want to be your friend. In the city people were "out to get you" and no one could be really trusted as a friend. Unsure of how they "fit" into the urban scheme of things, they become overly sensitive to the impersonal and formal urban ways.

INTERGROUP RELATIONS

Acculturation is the imposition of the culture of the dominant group on a subordinate group. In Baltimore the Lumbees definitely find themselves in a subordinate role. Because they live in a city, they are subjected to an inescapable "voluntary" acceptance of urban ways. Therefore, in any intergroup contact, the Lumbees feel a sense of insecurity, anxiety, hostility, and suspicion. In this atmosphere of hostility and insecurity, much of the intergroup relationship is not fruitful. The investigator faced rather strange and unforeseen problems during the period of study. After walking along Baltimore Street for several hours, talking to people who denied that they had ever heard of the Lumbees, the investigator was told by a policeman that the Moonlight Restaurant was a Lumbee gathering place. In the restaurant, he was able to meet and talk to two Lumbees who were rather reticent about themselves but who did give their names and phone numbers. Later, the investigator tried to contact them without success.

After several more fruitless visits to the area, the investigator finally found a church selling secondhand clothes on a Saturday morning and approached the minister. He was introduced to an old gray-haired lady who then invited him to her house. After talking to her for several hours, he learned that there were three churches serving the Lumbees and he decided to attend Sunday church services to make more contacts. Soon it was discovered that all three groups, except for a few individuals, were highly suspicious of him. Repeated attendance at church led to some confidence among a few members of the group, but on the whole there was very little trust by the Lumbees that the investigator was indeed seeking only information.

After about 6 weeks of observation, a schedule was constructed dealing with various aspects of their lives. Some names and addresses were obtained and attempts were made to interview respondents. Many still shied away, giving various excuses, and there were two people who were violently opposed to anyone studying the Lumbees. Unfortunately, these people were group leaders and many contacts were blighted by this resistance. Their opposition stemmed in part from the publication in Ebony of two articles showing Lumbee-Negro interaction, and from a series of Sunpapers' articles which they felt were uncomplimentary. Added to these expressed reasons was the deeply ingrained suspicion and distrust the Lumbees felt toward any "outsider". Wild rumors spread that the investigator was a welfare worker checking on fraudulent claims, that he was a plainsclothesman, a fire inspector, and even an insurance inspector checking on phony broken arms and legs.

It was with patience and perseverance that two informants were hired with the understanding that they would be paid for each interview they arranged. It was only through the intervention of the informants that doors were opened. Together, we would go to the subject's home for coffee and small talk. During the conversation we would try to set up an interview time during the next day or two. The investigator would then return alone to conduct the interview. Once this rapport had been established the interviewing could proceed. Otherwise, the investigator was given the cold shoulder if he attempted to speak to families on his own. Use of the informants was not altogether successful. One in particular was not universally popular and the investigator was told that he would receive no help if he were ———'s friend.

Intergroup relations may be approached in terms of social participation. In the church, in school, in recreational activities, and other community functions some participation is expected. Perhaps the most intensive interaction is between intermarried couples and their friends and relatives. This does not represent the bulk of the population and we will attempt to discuss interaction outside intermarital relations.[6]

Religion is an integral part of Lumbee life. Their religious and social life centers around the church. The initial interviews for this study were arranged through contacts made in church. Presently they have two churches—one Baptist and one Church of God.[7] Both are storefront churches. One is attended exclusively by Lumbees while the other has some white and Negro members as well. Attendance ranges from 30 to 50, including the children. It is reasonable to assume that the church having white, Negro, and Lumbee members does provide opportunities for interaction. Some white parishioners do visit the Lumbee minister, but the investigator was otherwise unable to determine the quality or extent of interaction.

The Lumbee children participate in some form of interaction during their time at school. The school should also provide a forum for interaction on the parents' part. In the entire sample only one mother replied that she went to the school to check on the children's progress and to talk with the teacher. None of the parents attend PTA meetings. There does not appear to be any adult-level interaction between the Lumbees and the school community. The children, of course, play with children at school and in the neighborhood but this interaction is with white children only. None of the children visit the home of his white friends and only two reported that they had a white friend over to visit their home.

Recreation is considered to be another major form of interaction. The interviewees were asked if they participated in activities of the Y, the Little League, scouting, or structured recreation such as bowling or group sports. A response of 100 percent was elicited to the effect that no one participates in such activities. They mentioned spending spare time in the Moonlight Restaurant or the Volcano Bar. They

[6] In any process of acculturation, a dominant and subordinate role relationship is involved between the two groups of people. In assimilation, however, the differences between the groups are forgotten for all practical purposes. In Pembroke, N.C., the elite class is assimilated to the extent that intermarriage is a regular and uneventful part of life. Such intermingling has been going on for decades. The elite class has participated in such a high degree of intermarriage that it is hard to distinguish a Lumbee from a white. The elites hold the power in Pembroke and, in comparison, the Baltimore Lumbees appear to have regressed in patterns of interaction.

[7] At the beginning of the study there were three churches serving Lumbees. One of these storefront churches was condemned by the city as being unsafe.

occasionally go to the White Coffee Pot or Gino's, but none said they went to larger restaurants. They mentioned watching baseball on television but when asked if they attend games at the stadium, the response was negative. The women do not belong to any ladies' groups.

Social distance between the Lumbees and other groups is believed to be the result of a lack of interaction. Interaction between Lumbees and whites is considerably different from interaction between Lumbees and Negroes.

The Lumbees are aware of discrimination in society. They are also aware that the Negroes are the most discriminated against. Therefore, the Lumbees do not want to associate with the Negroes lest they be labeled as Negroes.[8] The Lumbees make special efforts in Baltimore to be away from areas where Negroes have apartments. No Lumbee family lives in the public housing project in Baltimore because public housing has a heavy Negro concentration. In *The Newcomers*, Oscar Handlin states, "The colored Puerto Rican wished above all to avoid the stigma of identification with the Negro and he could do so only by establishing himself as a Spanish-speaking Puerto Rican." [9]

There is a belief among Lumbees that by disassociating themselves completely from the Negroes that their own identity becomes closer to the whites. They believe that they become more acceptable to the whites the more closely they live near them. It is quite common for a Lumbee to brag, "I am the only Indian in the building, the rest of the people are all white."

There are, however, differences among individual Lumbees in terms of the kind of interaction they have with others. For instance, it was found that Lumbees with steady jobs more frequently interact than those who have no steady jobs. Seventy-five percent of those with a steady job considered a white as a friend. Twenty-five percent expressed friendship with a Negro. It is significant that 25 percent of those with steady jobs considered a Negro a friend, since only 10 percent of the entire sample had the same feeling.

Also, it was observed that educational attainments and social interaction are interrelated; thus, people with a high school education and those with a college education have more interaction with other groups than those whose educations are limited. Everyone in the sample having a college education expressed a high level of interaction with the whites.

---

[8] Many whites in the Baltimore Street-Broadway area regard Lumbees, except for those who can pass as white, as "colored". The white minister of a Methodist church in the area was unable to distinguish a Lumbee from a Negro, while in fact the facial features and hair of the two groups are markedly dissimilar. The Lumbees resent the epithet "colored" and do not want to be in any way identified with the Negroes. They say that some Negroes want to capitalize on their heritage by claiming to be Lumbees. They disavow any discriminatory actions against themselves, but two men did say that they had faced discrimination in housing and jobs because they are dark skinned.

[9] *The Newcomers: Negroes and Puerto Ricans in a Changing Metropolis*, Doubleday & Co., Inc., Garden City, N.Y., 1962, p. 60.

LUMBEE INTERACTION WITH WHITES AND NEGROES

[Number of persons, 60]

	Number	Percent
No interaction with negroes	45	75
Some contact with negroes	15	25
Casual relationship	5	33.3
Repeated contact	10	66.7
Not considered friend	4	40
Considered friend	6	[1] 60
No interaction with whites	0	0
Some contact with whites	60	100
Casual relationship	12	20
Repeated contact	48	80
Not considered friend	38	79.2
Considered friend	10	[2] 20.8

[1] Considered friend in the total sample is 10 percent.
[2] Considered friend in the total sample is 16.7 percent.

Note: Friendship does not include any members among relatives, such as resulting from marriage.

RECOMMENDATIONS

The Lumbees are not happy with the existing order of things. They are not happy with the job market or with the income they earn. They have very basic needs: food, clothing, housing, and education of their children. But these needs are not being adequately met. In every area, the Lumbee is at the furthest extremity of the social and economic ladder. They feel that they have grievances which need immediate redress.

Because of the lack of proper leadership, the Lumbees are unable to articulate their grievances. They are so engrossed with making a bare living that they are unable to examine their difficulties or to find solutions. It is not that they are indifferent and do not care. Rather, their poor education and lack of ease with regard to the dominant society stifles their abilities to express themselves. Even the educated Lumbees do not know how to apply for a job, do not know who to see for a better paying job, do not know which jobs pay more. They tend to work together—one man works for a contractor and his friend applies at the same company. They do not regard their failure in the job market as "discrimination," only two respondents said that they were discriminated against in housing and jobs, but they do feel that "there's nothing a man can do about it" and so they accept the inevitable.

Clearly, they are in need. Perhaps an agency could be set up strictly for the purpose of helping the Lumbees find a more rewarding and socially productive place in urban life, providing them with opportunities to develop their own solutions, by giving them answers to questions such as "Where do I go to get a job as a housekeeper?" This agency could approach various public and private social organizations for their help.

It is a fact that groups in the lower strata of urban society need help in satisfying their barest needs. The Baltimore Urban Renewal Agency has initiated a specific program in a specific area with a specific purpose in mind—to encourage residents of the urban renewal area (Harlem Park) to see a doctor. Each year the agency sponsors two social gatherings of the community to discuss any disease which members had not discussed with a doctor. These people lack the habit of consulting a doctor for medical advice and diseases such as cancer and TB are cured only by early diagnosis and treatment. The agency feels that the program is successful, particularly in the detection of TB, as it orients community members to seeking medical help when they feel ill. In the same way, the Lumbees could be encouraged to more fully utilize the opportunities available in an urban setting. They do take their children to the clinic of a nearby hospital but, due to the setup of the free clinics (long lines, long waits), they avoid taking the children for routine checkups or in the early stages of illness. Some hospitals are now in the process of revitalizing their clinic programs and it is hoped that the families dependent on the clinics for their health care will find that the "too poor to pay" indignities of clinic care will have been alleviated. In one instance, the investigator found a 63-year-old woman who had a large boil on her leg. She went to a doctor once a month to have it cleaned and bandaged. Unable to pay the $10 fee, she did not come back weekly as the doctor suggested, and so the boil did not heal. The investigator called several agencies to secure help for this woman who did not know anything about medicare. The very next day someone came with the forms and helped her to fill them out. She then received medical attention through medicare. There might be many in similar situations who, with a little help in defining their needs, could secure benefits to ease the problems they face.

The Lumbees need assistance in realizing the importance of education. Lumbee children should be given additional counseling in school and encouraged to finish their high school programs. Efforts should be made to place them in better schools. There is no distinction in attending the worst school in the city. Since parents cannot afford bus fares, busing might be provided. School must be made meaningful and attractive to both children and parents.

Recreation is essential in the inner city. Few of the Lumbees have cars and their limited resources do not permit them to take advantage of the recreational activities available. Through coordination of programs with the Y, the Girl and Boy Scouts, and so forth, activities such as camping, swimming, picnicking, and sports could be made available to the children.

Perhaps an agency such as VISTA would extend its help to Lumbee families. VISTA volunteers could be assigned to these neighborhoods to aid the people and define their needs. After these needs were identified then programs could be designed to meet them.

Both the Community Action Agency and Model Cities receive large sums of money from the Federal Government. Thus far their attention has not been drawn to the Lumbees. The investigator spoke to leaders of these programs and discovered that they had no plans even in the distant future for the Lumbees. Social welfare's help does not go beyond the monthly check as determined in this study. It might be strongly suggested that these agencies, either separately or together, set up an office on a temporary basis to work extensively with the Lumbees. Such an office could institute a door-to-door survey of the Lumbees regarding their needs in jobs, education, housing, and all the related areas of social living.

The Lumbees, as a minority, are nowhere represented. This group is alienated in the sense that they cannot effectively participate in their society due to a (1) lack of education, (2) lack of effective organization,

(3) lack of effective leadership, (4) halfhearted acceptance in society and because (5) they are a group for whom special provisions should be made since they are Indians—original inhabitants of North America. They also suffer from a latent sense of inferiority and a consequent lack of interaction.

Once they are recognized as a group unrepresented, as a group that badly needs public assistance to better their lives, special efforts can and should be made to find remedies. They are not aware of programs such as the Job Corps and the Manpower Training Act but they could be given information and encouragement to join these programs.

Not all help necessarily should be governmental. Private agencies could easily fill these needs. The New York Archdiocese formulated "a policy to provide all possible assistance to the Puerto Ricans to help them become integrated into established parishes. The archdiocese is not following a policy of setting up separate parishes for the Puerto Ricans, but is making an extraordinary effort to train priests, sisters, and lay workers to work with the Puerto Ricans as they seek to become active members together with older parishioners in existing parishes." [10] Such an experiment in integration has never been tried by Baltimore's religious institutions, yet because of the Lumbees intense interest in religion, this could be a starting point.

SUMMARY

PROBLEM

The Lumbees of Baltimore migrated from North Carolina some 18 years ago and settled in the slum section around Baltimore Street and Broadway. The Lumbees are but one of the many minority groups in this neighborhood which is composed of families of Negro, Polish, Greek, and German descent. The Lumbee population is estimated at 1,500. Coming from a rural background, with very little skill for urban employment, they have had to make a large measure of adjustment to urban society.

PURPOSE

It is the purpose of this study to examine kinds of opportunities that exist for intergroup relations between Lumbees and the other groups as a process of social adjustment.

OBJECTIVES

As the first exploratory study of this group, the study will set guidelines for future research. It is hoped the investigation will discover those situations which aggravate ingroup-outgroup tension and those relations which bridge the gap between the groups. It is believed that certain patterns of behavior will emerge which will provide clues for the improvement of intergroup relations.

SAMPLE

The sample consists of Lumbees who live within the confines of Broadway on the east, Madeira Street and Patterson Park on the west,

[10] Milton L. Barron, *Minorities in a Changing World*, Alfred A. Knopf, Inc., New York, 1967, p. 284.

Madison Street on the north, and Eastern Avenue on the south. The sample is composed of 60 cases (37 male, 23 female). After a sampling frame was made, subjects were chosen on a random sampling basis. Alternates were selected when an attempt to interview failed. There are common factors in the sample in that 90 percent of the subjects belong to the lower-lower strata of Baltimore society. The remaining 10 percent are white men married to Lumbee women and Lumbee women who belong to the upper-lower class. Three men out of the 37 are skilled and two women out of 23 are skilled. The age range was 18–56 (male) and 18–62 (female). Fifty-seven of the respondents are married and three are unmarried.

METHODOLOGY AND DATA COLLECTION

Methods used in the study are participant observation, use of a schedule, and printed materials. Each interview averaged 1 hour and 40 minutes and was conducted in the subject's home. The author visited Pembroke, N.C., for comparison of native Lumbee culture as it exists in Robeson County and the patterns of adjustment found among Lumbees in Baltimore.

FINDINGS

Economically, Lumbees are poor, averaging $2,000 income a year. They live in crowded slum housing, paying average rents of $102 monthly. Redfield and Wirth generalized that, as people migrate from a rural to an urban location, the primary group relation generally changes into secondary group behavior; urban characteristics effect a decline in the importance of a primary group. However, Lumbees, even though from many parts of North Carolina, are very informal with each other and 20 percent still live in extended families, a primary group characteristic. About 88 percent of them are engaged in jobs which call for manual labor. The remaining 12 percent is composed of 2 percent clerical, 2 percent homemaking, 2 percent auto mechanics, 4 percent machine operators, and 2 percent keypunch operators. Education among Lumbees is still at a very low level. Only 5 percent female and 3.33 percent male have a year or two of college; 10 percent male and 3.3 percent female are high school graduates; 36.7 percent have a sixth-grade education, and 8.33 percent are illiterate.

The Lumbee father is the head of the patriarchal family in every sense. Women find themselves in a subordinate role—even those who have a job and economically are the family's sole support. About 24 percent of the marriages end in divorce and a further 7 percent were separated. However, in terms of the total marriages, the rate of divorce for mixed marriages is much higher. There is a general permissiveness in the Lumbee families and the children, according to age, are expected to do a number of chores.

If social interactions reduce group tension, this is clearly evidenced with Lumbees and their relations to other groups. Those Lumbees who have a steady job are the ones who are secure and make a better adjustment. The people with steady jobs and a high school (or beyond) education have a much higher degree of contact with other groups. People with higher intergroup contacts show less outgroup hostility and aggressive behavior. Places of interaction are the church, job, restaurants, bars, and grocery stores. The frequency of Lumbee-white contacts: Casual, 20 percent; repeated, 80 percent; and considered friend, 16.7 percent. However, the trend of interaction with Negroes varies from that of the whites. Thus, Lumbee-Negro contacts are: No interaction, 75 percent; some interaction, 25 percent, and considered friend, 10 percent.

BIBLIOGRAPHY

BARRON, MILTON L. *Minorities in a Changing World.* Alfred A. Knopf. New York. 1967.

GLAZER, NATHAN and MOYNIHAN, D. P. *Beyond the Melting Pot.* The M. I. T. Press. Cambridge, Massachusetts. 1965.

HANDLIN, OSCAR. *The Newcomers: Negroes and Puerto Ricans in a Changing Metropolis.* Doubleday & Company, Inc. New York. 1962.

KOMAROVSKY, MIRRA. *Blue Collar Marriage.* Random House. New York. 1967.

MCKAY, ARNOLD A. "Nobody Knows Anything about the Croatans," in *The State.* Raleigh, North Carolina. February 24, 1934.

MCMILLAN, HAMILTON. "The Croatans," in the North Carolina Booklet Vol. X, No. 3. January, 1911.

MCMILLAN, HAMILTON. *Sir Walter Raleigh's Lost Colony.* Edwards & Broughton Printing Company. Raleigh, North Carolina. 1911.

MCPHERSON, O. M. *Indians of North Carolina.* Washington. 1915.

MEAD, MARGARET. *Growing Up in New Guinea.* The New American Library. New York. 1953.

MEAD, MARGARET. *New Lives for Old.* Dell Publishing House. New York. 1956.

MEYER, G. and MARDEN, C. F. *Minorities in American Society.* American Book Company. New York. 1962.

OXENDINE, CLIFFTON. "Pembroke State College for Indians," in *North Carolina Historical Review.* January, 1945.

PARK, ROBERT EZRA. *Race and Culture.* The Free Press. Glencoe, Illinois. 1964.

The Robesonian, a newspaper published in Lumberton, North Carolina.

ROBIN, WILLIAM, JR. *Strangers Next Door.* Prentice Hall. Englewood Cliffs, New Jersey. 1965.

SIMPSON, G. and YINGER, J. M. *Racial and Cultural Minorities.* Harper and Row. New York. 1965.

WEEKS, STEPHEN B. The Knicker Bocker Press. New York. 1897.

YINGER, J. MILTON. *A Minority Group in American Society.* McGraw Hill, Inc. New York. 1965.

YOUNG, MICHAEL and WILLMOTT, PETER. *Family and Kinship in East London.* Penguin Books, Inc. Baltimore, Maryland. 1967.

TAX INCENTIVES FOR INDUSTRIAL DEVELOPMENT

By HON. E. Y. BERRY*

FOREWORD

Despite large Federal expenditure on Indian programs, poverty and unemployment remain severe on the Indian reservations. In his statement prepared for this compendium, Representative Berry argues that the solution lies in attracting industry to the reservations. Tax incentives, similar to those which have been so successful in encouraging Puerto Rican industrialization, offer a promising means of helping industry overcome the added costs of locating in remote reservation areas. Together with Representative Morris Udall of Arizona, Representative Berry has introduced legislation authorizing a pilot program of 10-year tax exemptions for industries locating on Indian reservations in South Dakota and Arizona.

Introduction

The purpose of this statement is to set before this subcommittee the absolute need for an "Operation Bootstrap—Indian Style" industrial program on the Indian reservations of America. I propose a tax incentive law which will be an inducement for industry to search out reservation areas. It is an inducement for industry to provide employment, salaries and income for the Indian people, permitting them to lift themselves by their own bootstraps from the quagmire of despair and the hopeless welfare existence in which they find themselves today, and from which there is no possibility of improvement through the programs in effect today.

THE INDIAN PROBLEM?

One of the oldest cliches in the American lexicon is "the Indian problem." There is no Indian problem—what is glibly referred to as an "Indian problem" is purely and simply a white man's problem. It has been created by the white man through the bureaucracy of the white man's government.

The difficulty is that when Congress sees a bad situation—whether it be domestic or international—the tendency is to throw money at it and hope the problem will disappear. Millions of dollars have been thrown at the "Indian problem," only to find that the problem has grown worse and worse. This is true primarily because the activities of the Bureau of Indian Affairs have been geared basically toward the use of land rather than toward the improvement of the lives of the Indian people. We found the Indian on the land—we thought that all Indians should be farmers.

Because of this policy by the Bureau, the plight of the individual Indian has worsened year after year because there is nothing for the individual Indian to look forward to. There is probably enough land on

---

*A Representative in the Congress of the United States from the Second Congressional District, South Dakota.

each reservation to provide a livelihood for 5 percent of the enrolled Indians on that reservation, and the Bureau has geared their entire program to that 5 percent. The other 95 percent have been kicked from pillar to post. They are much worse off today than they were 40 years ago when I made my home on an Indian reservation and first became interested in trying to help solve their problems.

Through recent years such programs as relocation have captured the imagination of the Bureau. The Indian people have been taken to the cities where jobs have been found for them. But because these people have no friends there, and because they soon become homesick for someone with whom to associate, they soon return to the reservation where they can live in the only surroundings they know, and where they can associate with people they know. The reservation is the only homeland they have ever had.

In every instance where industry has gone to these reservations, and provided jobs, salaries and opportunity, we have seen a complete transformation of the Indian people and of the Indian community. Absenteeism is lower in these plants than in any like plant anywhere in America. They have used their money to improve their homes, feed and clothe their children, and instead of spending their meager relief check on liquor, they spend their salaries on improving their own lot and the lot of their families.

The difficulty with human beings—regardless of the color of their skin—is that if they have no future to look forward to they try to drown their failure in liquor, or some method of mental relief.

Now the question is, how do we, as a government, promote the industrial development of these reservation areas? It must be remembered that almost every reservation is located in some remote area where the cost of transportation of the raw material, and the cost of the transportation of the finished product, is very high. Because of this situation, industry is unable to compete with like production in the more accessible areas of the Nation, with the result that industry shies away from reservations in spite of the fact there is a great pool of possible employment.

The only way this cost differential can be compensated for is either through a *direct subsidy* to *industry* coming to the reservation, or else in the use of a *tax benefit* similar to those tax benefits offered to industry by the emerging nations, and by such other areas as Puerto Rico, and so forth.

The Bureau for several years has been working on a program of locating industries on Indian reservations, with some minor success, but the program will never be a success, and will have only scattered results until there is some offset for the added cost of production on these reservation areas.

The only inducement the Bureau has today is an Indian Trades Training and on-the-job training program wherein a portion of the salary of the employee can be paid by the Department during the time such employee is learning the trade. This, of course, is some little inducement for industry, but the inducement is so very small because of the fact that when the employee has learned the job sufficiently well to fill the proper niche, this subsidy is removed, so that actually, while this is very beneficial to the Indian employee, it is of very little permanent benefit to the industry itself.

For several years I have had legislation pending which would provide a tax incentive in the form of a complete Federal tax exemption for a 10-year period. However, the Treasury has always opposed it on the grounds that it has no way of knowing what the cost would be to the Federal Government. As a pilot program to determine what might be expected in the way of cost, Representative Morris Udall of Arizona and I have, for the past 4 years, had legislation pending which would provide a pilot program, giving a 10-year tax exemption to any industry that would come onto Indian reservations in South Dakota and Arizona, employing Indian help for at least 50 percent of their staff. By this pilot method Treasury and the Bureau of Indian Affairs would have a good idea as to what the cost of a national program would be.

The advantages of such a program are primarily that it would provide training, industrial education, jobs, and salaries, and do it in the home area of these people where they can stand erect once again, as they did before the white man forced them into concentration camps, later referred to as reservations. It would give them an opportunity to again have pride in themselves and their family, providing education and equal opportunity for their children and give them an opportunity to lift themselves by their own "moccasin straps" from the shame of dole to the pride of production.

Congress and the Bureau have tried everything else and everything else has failed. While Congress has passed dozens of integration laws that apply to the colored man, we have passed twice that many laws *forcing segregation* of the Indian people. We have forced the Indian to attend segregated schools where non-Indians are not permitted. We have forced them to live on segregated reservations where non-Indians are almost entirely excluded, and we have forced them to live on the dole if they want to be among their own people rather than going out into an unknown world without training, without a job, and without friends.

Bringing industry to these reservation areas would also bring non-Indians to these reservations to manage the business ventures. This would mean non-Indian children living and playing with the Indian boys and girls. It would give the Indian youth an opportunity to learn that the non-Indian can be a friend, and it would integrate these reservations. Another thing, as the Indian becomes trained and skilled in the job provided by industry, he would be transferred to other areas off the reservation in managerial capacities. In other words you would eventually have complete integration, complete opportunity, and a race of people with a future, instead of a government forced, segregated, welfare existence.

THE ROLE OF THE FEDERAL GOVERNMENT IN PRESENT-DAY INDIAN INDUSTRIAL AND COMMERCIAL DEVELOPMENT: A DISCUSSION

By MAURICE SONNENBERG*

FOREWORD

The apparent inefficiency of many of the Federal Indian programs is disturbing. Among the problems identified by Maurice Sonnenberg are lack of statistics needed for intelligent planning, duplication of effort, excessive time lags in processing project applications, and inadequate accounting of funds expended. Sonnenberg suggests that all Federal programs relating to Indian economic development be brought together under a newly created Indian Economic Development Administration. An Indian development company and an Indian development bank should be part of this agency, and the agency should seek private as well as governmental advice and assistance. Among the programs Sonnenberg would like to see this new agency emphasize are tribal equity in industrial and commercial enterprises on Indian reservations, financing and guarantees, a tax exemption board, and a "data bank." He also suggests that Indian reservations be given the same authority to issue bonds that other local governments enjoy. The new IEDA should work closely with the Indian tribes, giving the Indians full opportunity to manage their own affairs.

It is well known that a large segment of the American Indian population suffers severe economic deprivation.

Approximately 40 to 50 percent of the national Indian labor force, 16 years or older, is unemployed. This compares with a national unemployment average of less than 4 percent. In addition to the serious problem of unemployment, there is extensive underemployment. Indian health conditions are depressing: Life expectancy for the American Indian averages 50–52 years, an excessive infant mortality rate, a high rate of pulmonary disease and an apparently high incidence, on certain reservations, of illnesses that fall into the category of psychological ills (alcoholism, depression, etc.).

Alternatively, the facts show there has been a great deal of improvement in these conditions in recent years. For as bad as conditions in the area of health and education have been they are improving. It is the rate of time which is of concern. This has been the result of a greater awareness and effort on the part of tribal leaders, the increasing role of the Federal Government through its various agencies, in assisting the tribes to achieve greater self-sufficiency, and the efforts of private organizations, such as the National Congress of American Indians and the Association on American Indian Affairs, Inc.

---

*An investment consultant primarily engaged in the business of encouraging capital flow of investment into underdeveloped areas of the United States, Latin America and the Caribbean. His consultative work has permitted him to become involved in the field of economic development as it affects American Indian reservations and lands.

Let us reflect on some of the methods used to alleviate this obvious inequity in our present day society. At the outset, however, it should be pointed out, I am not an expert in the field of American Indian problems (as a matter of fact, I am moved to point out the recent appearance of a plethora of quasi-American Indian experts, most of whom are of a non-Indian background!).

Since the Federal Government plays such an enormous role in the lives of the American Indian, I would ask how can the Federal resources be better utilized to eradicate the obvious social injustice and deprivation so long endured by this group of people?

The answer lies in a thorough examination of some of the benefits and defects I have observed in the application of Federal resources to Indian reservations and communities, and then, a perusal of some recommendations for alternative programs.

The most startling observation and point of concern is the fact that the Federal Government is spending well over one-half billion dollars, on an annual basis, through its various agencies, Bureau of Indian Affairs (BIA), Economic Development Administration (EDA). Office of Economic Opportunity (OEO), and others, in Indian lands and reservations. There are approximately 600,000 Indians in America today, of which an estimated 400,000 to 450,000 live on these lands and theoretically receive the benefits of this munificent expenditure. I am moved to ask whether this expenditure, while not necessarily unjustified, is commensurate to the return? The question is even more pertinent when it has been established that there is approximately one Federal employee working on Indian programs for every six Indians, granting the fact that the Federal Government employs many Indians.

To digress a moment, I would like to note that my observations will be confined primarily to the area of industrial and commercial development in the direct sense of the word. Therefore, I would be remiss if I did not also mention the appalling inadequacies that exist in the area of formal and technical education, be it academic, psychological, or cultural. Likewise, that this has a direct bearing on the fact that there are few trained Indian individuals and leaders. This condition, if not dramatically improved, may irreparably slow down the development of tribally developed leadership from which to draw managerial and supervisory skills, let alone advance skills on the production line level. In addition there is abundant evidence of the need in the near future for basic and adequate housing. Especially, if the expenditures to be made in the area of industrial and commercial development are to be fruitful. In short, the community factors of development cannot be isolated from the subject at hand.

As said before, hundreds of millions of dollars have been spent by BIA, OEO, and EDA on Indian communities, a small part of which goes into direct economic development. Before these expenditures are made there is a necessity for adequate planning based on substantive analysis. This is predicated on the availability of adequate statistical information. Mr. Henry W. Hough recently wrote, "If all Indians living on reservations had a total income of $9,248,255 from agriculture in 1939, and the comparable figure for 1944 increased to $22,038,111, the figure for 1966 should be highly interesting and significant; unfortunately, it is impossible to obtain recent figures." [1]

---

[1] Hough, Henry W., *Development of Indian Resources*, World Press, Inc., Denver, 1967, p. 72.

Mr. Hough quotes a Bureau official who says that "these statistical series came to a halt after 1944 and our recently instituted surveys have yet to provide current counterparts." [2] Mr. Hough goes on to say, and I concur, "that in much the same way it is impossible to obtain information for the total income of Indian tribes, in various categories of income such as from rentals and royalties, from forest lands, from trust funds and other investments, and from operation of tribally owned enterprises."

Only this past year an attorney for one tribe informed me of the tribe's having entered into a research contract with an institute involved in community and economic planning, and of an official of the company receiving "population figures that were almost 100 percent higher in the tribe's files than in Washington files at the Bureau." The tribe has an adult population of less than 5,500.

Statistics in all phases of social and economic concern are deplorable, at best, inadequate. Certainly, with the present amount and method of funding, there should exist some sort of "data bank." A national registry of this type is indispensable to any sensible planning.

Another area in which I find a need for serious revamping is the inefficient handling of Federal moneys due to duplication of efforts. By way of example, one large tribe has three "industrial development specialists." The benefactors of the "experts" are OEO, EDA and BIA. A visit by a former Indian Council member and myself to these gentlemen provided us with contradictory basic information on the subject of existing factors necessary for someone contemplating an economic venture—for example, one actually told us a small factory was in operation "with about 45 employees," while the other expert claimed no one had been working there for at least 6 weeks. Furthermore, there existed a rivalry that rather than assisting in development here proved counterproductive.

My Indian friend and I found that an estimated $70,000 payroll was being squandered in this manner in view of the serious needs of the community for decent housing and improved education. An absurd situation when one is aware of the fact that less than 1,500 adults are available for employment at this reservation.

While it appears to me that it is the function of the Small Business Administration (SBA) to develop programs to encourage the development of small entrepreneur enterprises, I was puzzled when I discovered EDA and OEO have found this an area of their concern.

I would point out that I am not against another agency fulfilling this need should the assumed agency for this kind of activity be remiss in its duties to the community.

Duplication again manifests itself in the unfortunate tendency to claim successful projects as belonging to that agency preparing its list of accomplishments. The 1968 Progress Report of one agency, for example, discusses the agency's role in American Indian work by naming one plant it claims is the "result" of two coastal "EDA and OEO sponsored industrial conferences." The fact is that the plant, (the only one mentioned in this brief account) was in operation before these conferences were held, largely due to the efforts of a third agency. Furthermore, the tribe put up the money for buildings, machinery and equipment.

[2] *Ibid.*, p. 72.

While on the subject of those conferences, the appearance of almost as many Federal employees as Indians, and a grossly exaggerated figure of the number of industrialists that appeared, only seems to emphasize the need for centralizing and professionalizing the role of these agencies.[3]

Then there is the example of simultaneous studies for the same project, by two agencies having an interest on the same reservation. The studies were completed before either agency knew what the other was doing! Downgrading by one agency's efforts of the other, is the natural consequence of this circumstance.

This leads to another area that needs a thorough examination, that of the "feasibility studies" or a variation thereof.

There exists a mimeographed compilation (no identifiable source), entitled, "Tabulation of Studies and Surveys Conducted on Indian Reservations and in Indian Areas (Including Alaska Native Areas) 1961 to March 1, 1967." Funding agencies are listed, for the more than 200 studies, as the BIA, Area Redevelopment Administration (ARA) and two or three tribal contributions costing hundreds of thousands of dollars. Requests by me for some of these studies revealed that more than half of the 20 I requested were not to be found. I understand that this is not an uncommon experience for others who inquire about such studies. But far more serious is the fact that the Indians will probably not really benefit by most of these studies because of the lack of quality inherent in these productions. It might be of value to examine the firms that received these awards and whether they are actively and seriously engaged in the "consulting business," and what followup occurred, if any.

I would caution the reader to not construe my comments as a call for curtailment of necessary feasibility research in the area of economic development. Quite the contrary, the expenditure in this area should be increased. However, this expenditure should be aimed at a more fruitful return and benefit for the Indian rather than for the contractor.

I am reminded of one Indian who in a rare fit of anger said, "we are tired of being studied to death." These are cries, whether accurate or not, of frustration at the apparent lack of efficacy in some of this monumental planning.

It would be unfair of me to leave this subject without pointing out the fact that there have been numerous projects that have been developed from some of these studies and in all likelihood they would not have come to fruition had it not been for such preparatory activity.

One agency has attempted to activate economic development through grants and loans for public works projects, as well as loans for working capital. Its "Directory of Approved Projects" reveals some interesting aspects in regard to its activities in Indian reservations. It has "selected 15 reservations that have the greatest potential for economic and social development." [4] I am not sure that this is the proper and fair course to follow although, from the agency point of view, the chances of success are more likely!

This directory is interesting in that it allows for examination of another facet of possible abuse, that of the subject of accurate re-

[3] *1968 Progress Report of the Economic Development Administration*, U.S. Department of Commerce, U.S. Government Printing Office, Washington, D.C., 1968, p. 28.
[4] "1968 Progress Report of the Economic Development Administration" U.S. Department of Commerce, U.S. Government Printing Office, Washington, D.C., 1968, p. 28.

porting there is no room for misleading accounts of activities that are being engaged in by these agencies. EDA "Directory of Approved Projects," as of September 1969, lists awards made throughout the country under "Public Works," "Grants" and "Loan" and another heading referred to as "Business Development." This report is somewhat misleading in the sense that when one glances at this directory, one would assume, for example, that these approved loans were on their way to the recipient of the project described.

The fact remains that a number of approved projects on Indian reservations have yet to receive their funds. An explanation given is that "these are conditional and they're holding up the loan by failing to comply." I believe this information should be so stated in the directory. In some cases, the time has extended over more than 1 year. Furthermore, this inordinate amount of time for processing has resulted in time-consuming activities that have discouraged applications and terminated interest in projects. The protracted time for processing of these applications seems to exist in virtually every Indian land in the country.

Since the assumed purpose of this expenditure is job production, there should be a reporting of how many jobs were created, in addition to an accurate accounting of the disposition of this money.

In one area in the Southwest, public works' grants "approved" totaled more than $2.2 million, and loans of well over $400,000. In addition, business development loans of over $2 million were likewise approved during the years of 1967–68. Perhaps this approval becomes more significant when one is informed of the fact that a 1963 population census compiled by the BIA lists this area as a reservation of having a population of less than 7,000: Wouldn't it be worthwhile to see how many *Indian* jobs were created as a result of these approved EDA expenditures in the past 3 years?

I took the time to call the BIA about one large loan (over $800,000) approved in 1967, and was told that the operation so funded has not yet produced a job. I do not propose, nor have the time to run through this complete listing, but I would presume that this Senate subcommittee could recommend a thorough examination of how efficiently these funds are being used.

As said before, the Government should, I believe, share the responsibility of assisting in these enterprises, although in a more discriminating manner. The EDA led project in Bethel, Alaska, to give natives decent housing, is undoubtedly worthwhile and the 1968 approved public works loans and grants of over $500,000 would seem to be warranted in this situation. By way of contrast, to the prior example, the population here is less than 9,000.

A better and more accurate reporting system of what plants or industrial firms are actually on reservations or nearby lands is mandatory. Just to have agencies breast-beating their promotions on a published list of named accomplishments is meaningless unless one knows not just the firm name, but relationship to parent firm, if any, how many are employed (10 or more?), constantly revised so as to indicate how many are actually operating, who funded the project (Indians?), and by exact percentage. (One list I have seen indicates a firm with 200 or more employed that has since gone broke, and needless to say, with it, the various approved agency fundings.)

In short, agencies should stop trying to set phony track records!

Finally, there is the agency that has been repeatedly asked for a breakdown of figures in regard to its expenditures on Indian lands and consistently sends a "Summary of Indian Participation in OEO Programs," with no figures: The other day I was informed of two senatorial requests that have been made in the past 6 months for these figures, with no success.

A BIA official said simply, "they make block grants and that ends that." Where some of these programs are indeed of value, for example, Headstart, CAP, job training, et cetera, how efficient are they if the administrators cannot be called upon to give an account of their activities in terms of the expenditure? Or worse, as was pointed out to me by a reservation Indian official, "what real voice have we got in these Indian programs?" I countered by saying that many Indians were employed in these programs on the reservation, and he said yes, but "must do and say what they're told by that Indian Division."

Other agency practices that bear some investigation are as follows:

The Bureau of Indian Affairs administers the forests of the Flathead Reservation and takes ten percent of gross receipts as its "contribution" from the Indians toward the total cost. . . .

The imposing total of these "deductions" is seen clearly when an Indian group receives its final settlement after receiving a judgment for a claim won by the Indians. The "costs" levied against the Indians by the Bureau of Indian Affairs frequently use up nearly all of the judgment funds, leaving a relatively small amount of money that actually reaches the Indian beneficiaries.[5]

Then there is the refusal of one agency to give prior credit, financial and feasibility information to an attorney who requested it more than 9 months ago in relation to his clients purchase of this particular agency's sponsored industrial project, previously gone broke.

This is further complicated by the charge of misrepresentation against the agency as regards the value and resources being conveyed.

Meanwhile, the Indians are not working.

Or the case of a tribe where one agency pledged Indian trust funds to another agency, so that the second agency might finance a project that the tribe's attorney claimed, was just a method of financing a continued nonreservation white man's operation. A threat of suit against the first agency brought a restoration of the funds removed without the tribe's authority.

Or the case of the agency recommending use of limited tribe funds in a business run to the ground by its non-Indian "operator." The marginal nature of the business and its operators doomed it from the beginning.

In fairness to the agencies, these are cases I have come across and do not suggest to me a general practice. However, even if isolated, they must be corrected by tightening of agency activities.

The budget of the United States, under the heading of Department of the Interior presents some interesting figures with regard to "commercial and industrial development." The following table appears:

	1968 actual	1969 estimated
New industrial enterprises established	36	29
New Indian jobs created	2,138	1,560

---

[5] "Development of Indian Resources," p. 155.

With the need for more than 65,000 jobs in the next 5 years to normalize the unemployment situation among Indians, one can ask how much progress has really been achieved?

So much for the criticism. What can be offered that is constructive?

Without question, the training programs are needed expenses. The BIA, I was informed, spent approximately $24 million on training activities this past year. I have no knowledge as to the amount of funds expended under the Manpower Development Training Act (MDTA) or OEO in this area. In any event, this seems to me to be a form of expenditure where the returns are inherent in the investment.

There is a necessity to enlarge these expenditures outside of the area of the traditional on-the-job and apprentice training.

For example, there should be training in areas of job opportunity that are not directly related to immediate income-producing activity. The severe shortage of housing will have to be met and therefore, skills in this area might perhaps be improved to allow the Indians participation in greater numbers in this potential employment activity.

Furthermore, as a basic economy develops, due to the increased return from agriculture, use of mineral and timber resources, and/or industry, there will hopefully arise a commercial middle class. This means more Indian shopkeepers and other entrepreneurs. Training in the skills necessary for these activities should be established now (by one agency). One reservation I visited had 90 percent non-Indian ownership of commercial enterprises on its reservation. Some skills and funding could expedite the needed change in this area.

The subject of future Indian management and supervisory personnel should also be given priorities. There should be more training programs available in the area of advanced management skills. Funds should be also made available to send a number of promising Indians through courses in advanced business and public administration. Likewise, a number of promising Indians should be exposed to actual management situations through association with off-reservation corporate management activities.

The development of trained management offers the future possibility of greater participation, with those tribes so able and inclined, for joint-venture, and the creation of indigenous enterprises and commercial intrepreneurship.

I would like now to consider an area which I feel can increase, immeasurably, the number of job-producing enterprises and at the least cost to the Government. This is the area of more capital availability. I refer specifically to the area of tax incentives and bond financing power.

The experience of "Operation Bootstrap" in Puerto Rico has proved that corporate tax exemption for a limited period of time has been instrumental in turning this largely agrarian populace of 20 years ago into a viable industrial society.

Its problems were not too disimilar to those of the Indian Reservation. A possession territory (vis-a-vis a trust territory), which had a need to find adequate employment opportunities for its out of proportion unemployed population * * * a need for substantial investment in capital resources and educational activity to compensate for the lack of natural resources and usable land, sensitivity to transportation costs due to its comparitive isolation as well as the prior mentioned lack of natural resources and a comparatively small economic size for its local market.

In 1959, the per capita income of this island was only $469 per year, and now it is well over $1,100. The percentage of unemployment had been cut in half.

The success lies primarily in the industrial development program of Puerto Rico. A canvass I personally conducted a few years ago of about 30 manufacturers in the Island, revealed that 25 would not have located their facilities in Puerto Rico were it not for the tax exemption.

This does not mean that I advocate a tax exemption on the same basis as exists in Puerto Rico. However, there appears to be a need for the use of tax incentives (or credits) to stimulate the employment that will become necessary if this deprivation is to come to an end.

Incentives can take the form of tax credits on machinery, equipment or number employed, if the exemption for an across-the-board corporate taxes meets with too much opposition. (Although I personally favor this as the most dramatic and fruitful approach.) In any event, any of these exemptions or credits would have a period of duration for the industrial facility of perhaps 10 years.

There would be a need and ability to attract serious industry, rather than marginal firms that have already caused the Indians added grief. This could be controlled by a criteria of eligibility for tax exemption (or credit). For example, the firm is to be a legitimate subsidiary of an established corporation, not a runaway plant, with an anticipated minimum employment at commencement of operation.

Opponents of this method of subsidized financing, who oppose it on the grounds that good business does not seek "avoidance" of tax, should be informed of the fact that any tax exemption or credit given in this area is, in reality, more of a tax transfer than a giveaway, especially when one considers the expenditures presently coming from the national treasury.[6] The Indians would really be receiving a direct tax benefit.

Next the tribes should have the right of raising their own financing; this would result in increased independence from unwieldly bureacratic purse strings. If municipalities and counties have the right to issue tax exempt bonds, why shouldn't the reservations? These bonds have been a sine qua non to the island of Puerto Rico in its successful departure from the poverty line.

The present Revolving Loan Fund of the BIA does not seem to be adequate to the needs of the Indians. As one official in the BIA pointed out to me, very little money has gone into the industrial and commercial development area from this fund. The $450 million fund (as authorized by section 1 of act of 1963, as amended), is set up to provide a source of financing for Indians [7] who cannot borrow from other credit agencies or commercial lenders. Loans are made to tribes for relending purposes in such areas as economic development, education, preparation and trial of claims pending before the Indian Claims Commission, etc.

While this is indeed a commendable approach, it is not enough.

A bill introduced in the 90th Congress (H.R. 539), would provide for guarantee and insurance of loans to Indians and Indian organiza-

---

[6] Contrary to some expressed views, there has been little exodus of successful plant operations due to expiration of tax exemption in Puerto Rico.
[7] "Authorized" does not mean appropriated.

tions. This approach, has been very successful in financing industrial enterprises in the States of Connecticut and Rhode Island.

It is apparent that a combination of these methods or one alone could make significant inroads into present existing conditions on these reservations.

I now return to one of the subjects of my initial complaint. The plethora of organizations involved in the development of Indian reservations on the Federal and State level.

I feel almost all of these functions should be placed in one all encompassing Indian Economic Development Administration (IEDA). This administration should be charged with the function of overseeing the use of Federal funds in this area. I believe that an Indian development company and an Indian development bank should be part of this administration. Financing and guarantees, equity ownership, industrial construction, assistance to local development projects in progress should be made through this organization. There should be a tax exemption or credit board that will pass on the merits of the projects requesting such relief, as being in the best interest of the Indians. This board should have as its members some Government officials, some Indians and representatives of industry. Likewise, another board should be created to assess the merits of assisting finanancially any projects which can further advance the economic growth of Indian lands.

A "data bank" should be immediately established within this Indian Economic Development Administration so that sensible feasibility studies can be made and research done in an industry-like manner, that is, research and development unit.

Furthermore, a small crack unit, of industrial location experts should be established. These are to be well-knowledgeable and connected individuals who can approach the very top echelons of industry. They should be hired on a consultive basis, except for a skeleton staff. If necessary, contracts should be attached to their performance; i.e., results.

Any tribe requesting assistance should be able to apply to what I call an "intelligence" unit to get free consulting on project inquiries. These inquiries are to be in the province of the tribe and the IEDA agency, only.

The development of tourism should be placed under the IEDA as a legitimate function of its activities.

Finally, the board (or other IEDA designate) should work closely with tribes during and *after* projects are activated. Since it is presumed the board would not engage in rivalry with another agency, it would be better able to ride through the occasional difficulty of tribal politics.

I note that while the tribe is sometimes to blame for the difficulties arising in development plans, it has not been beyond the scope of an agency to engage in mischievous activity through deliberate or negligent conduct on the part of its agents.

If the IEDA were not empowered to give out training labor funds through its industrial development company, then it must have direct liaison with one agency—for example Departmentof Labor—so that these funds can be made accessible in quick time. In short IEDA is to be a one-stop agency!

All education, health, and welfare matters would presumably remain in other agencies so charged with that responsibility. However, it would not be out of the province of IEDA to exert influence upon other agencies having responsibilities in the area of community development, and this is where the greatest effort must be placed. Closer liaison with housing and education agencies—not rivalry—is essential.

There should exist the possibility of tribes being able to draw on professional management, from the private sector, if they so desire. As previously pointed out, a number of industrial projects have failed and with it the loss sometimes, of limited Indian tribal capital because the so-called Government Indian experts were not up to the job of giving the Indians sound economic advice. Furthermore, projects that should have been considered more seriously were summarily turned aside or procrastinated upon so that the interested investor lost interest. An outside management adviser might also have the effect of lessening detrimental tribal political situations.

In closing, I offer some observations. It has been my experience that one cannot generalize about a monolithic American Indian. The tribes have different cultures and mores. They are trying and should be allowed to develop on their own terms, and in their own way. Their unique attachment to their land is nonexistent with any other ethnic group in this country. It is their security, their religion, their hope. The policy of the Government has for too many years been heavyhanded and when beneficial, at times, clouded by a kind of oppressive paternalism.

Yes, I realize the attitudes of many of the Federal employees is changing and the ward concept of Indian care is diminishing. However, I recall only last month of the refusal of two tribal officials to challenge what was an obviously detrimental policy of Federal officials in the area of economic development of that tribe for fear of retaliation by the local Federal authorities.

The policy in general should, I believe, be to phase the Federal Government off the reservation, except where health and related services are necessary.

The time has come for the Federal Government to be there to assist the Indian rather than lead or push him. It is sometimes a cycle where the massive presence of the Government over the Indian, inhibits the initiative to develop his own economic destinies. I emphasize that this generalization does not apply to all reservations or indicate present government policy.

I want to just touch briefly upon the reorganization plans that have been discussed in this area.

Whether the BIA should remain as an entity, needs close examination. And, likewise, whether these other agencies in the Indian business should continue their present functions, should certainly be the subject of concern.

I realize there are proposals to place the education and welfare functions of BIA in HEW, and these may have merit. My proposal for an IEDA would certainly necessitate a separate agency if it were adopted in full detail.

This would encompass a transfer and dissolution of present functions, in other agencies now charged with these areas of economic development activities.

However, my economic incentive measures could be acted upon under present organizational structure.

It is simple to conclude that what appears to be needed is a more dramatic and efficient use of the funds presently available for Indian development projects. This calls for a thorough examination of the past expenditures by these agencies. The General Accounting Office could aid considerably in evaluating the raison d'etre for their continued involvement in these programs.

Furthermore, there must be a greater effort to bring—with assistance from the Federal government—the currents of American business and industry into more of a partnership with the Indians. The goal in mind is an uprooting of those officials whose practices border on delinquent management of Indian affairs.

Finally, I reiterate, there must be a greater awareness of the individuality of the Indian and his tribe, and a respect for the right of the Indian to choose his own destinies. At best, the assistance he receives should increase his options in arriving at that choice. For surely, as the choice expands so will the pride that is so richly buried within the soul of this group of Americans.

This concomitant independence will inevitably result in the greater well-being and prosperity of this forgotten American, the first American.

ECONOMIC DEVELOPMENT AND ALASKAN NATIVES*

By Arlon R. Tussing and Douglas N. Jones

FOREWORD

New discoveries of mineral wealth in Alaska create exciting prospects for that State and for its Native groups. In this excerpt from the Report of the Federal Field Committee for Development Planning in Alaska, Arlon Tussing and Douglas Jones describe the Alaskan economy and the economic position of the Natives in the various regions of Alaska. They then discuss the possible economic damage which may be being incurred due to the current freeze on the leasing of mineral rights, and the development possibilities which an eventual settlement will present for the Alaskan Natives.

The meaning of the native protests for economic development in Alaska is necessarily a central issue in their resolution. There is hardly any aspect of the general problem of the protests which is the subject of deeper and more persistent controversy. One source of conflict is the fact that the notion of economic development holds *different meanings* for different groups. To some it means factories, to others the commercial use of land resources, and to still others a self-sufficient homestead. The question in other terms is *whose* economic development is to be fostered.

Another difficulty is that even if the meaning of economic development can be agreed upon there are differing views as to its *proper measurement*. Typically, the measures are changes in employment and income. But the *distribution* of these gains—the labor force and population base against which they are measured—is equally important. Alaska natives cannot be expected to feel a stake in a pattern of economic growth in which the new jobs are almost exclusively filled by white in-migrants. Other less direct, but no less important, quasi-economic tests might be used if other values—say, the political and psychological dimensions—are given emphasis. In this case, a wider distribution of landownership and a greater feeling of participation in one's economic affairs might be the desired change.

A final problem is that of the *time frame* which is chosen for evaluating the economic consequences of development, however defined and however measured. Is it a short term, intermediate term, or long run time horizon that is the backdrop within which we progress? Economic development is, after all, a process; and this implies that longer term gains later on may come at the expense of short term gains now. Conflicts arising from different time horizons are not resolved simply by choosing a single "rate of discount" by which the present and the future can be compared. Such a procedure may be meaningful for the State or for a large corporation which can borrow or lend on the basis of future expectations, but it is meaningless to people without commercial assets or commercial attitudes.

The burden of analysis of the economic implications of the native protest and the attendant claims legislation involves at least four tasks,

---

*From *Alaska Natives & the Land*, report of the Federal Field Committee for Development Planning in Alaska, Anchorage, 1968.

314

and these are. the ones around which the subsequent writing centers. These are:

- To summarize the most important features of Alaska's economy and recent economic development;
- To discover whether or not corporate or governmental behavior has been different as a *result* of native protest and whether such different behavior has had an effect on economic development in Alaska; and to indicate whether or not sustained, unresolved. controversy on the issue would affect economic development in Alaska;
- To evaluate the implications for Alaska natives of the most likely patterns of regional economic development; and
- To appraise the likely effects on economic development of various possible legislative provisions.

ALASKA'S ECONOMIC DEVELOPMENT

One of the most important points to understand about the Alaska economy is its *enclave* or insular character. Population and productive activity are mostly concentrated in a very few locations at tidewater and in a narrow belt about 100 miles long, stretching from Palmer to Kenai, and centering in the city of Anchorage.

Economic activity is even more concentrated than population, both spatially and sectorally. The proportion of all employment in the State contributed by all commodity-producing industries is extremely low. A table showing Alaska's gross domestic product for 1965 (Figure VI–1) shows the particularly undeveloped and unbalanced nature of the economy in more striking detail. Less than 1 percent of the product came from agriculture, forestry, and fisheries combined; and mining accounted for less than 4 percent of the total, despite the fact that it is for the latter two industries that Alaska is most noted.

FIGURE VI-1.—ALASKA GROSS PRODUCT, 1960-65

[Millions of current dollars]

	1960	1961	1962	1963	1964	1965
Agriculture, forestry, and fishery	4.3	5.7	6.3	5.2	5.8	8.3
	.6	*.8*	*.8*	*.6*	*.6*	*.8*
Mining	28.3	34.4	38.8	37.2	36.2	38.3
	3.8	*4.6*	*4.8*	*4.5*	*3.9*	*3.7*
Contract construction	98.9	64.1	64.8	69.2	105.3	117.5
	13.2	*8.7*	*8.4*	*8.4*	*11.2*	*11.4*
Manufacturing	65.4	58.0	61.0	65.1	68.7	82.3
	8.8	*7.8*	*7.9*	*7.9*	*7.3*	*8.0*
Transportation	45.0	42.7	45.0	47.6	52.6	56.4
	6.0	*5.8*	*5.8*	*5.8*	*5.6*	*5.5*
Communications	34.2	59.8	55.1	55.5	53.0	55.0
	4.6	*8.1*	*7.2*	*6.7*	*5.6*	*5.3*
Electric, gas, and sanitary services	9.4	11.0	13.8	15.7	18.2	21.0
	1.3	*1.5*	*1.8*	*1.9*	*1.9*	*2.0*
Wholesale and retail trade	85.2	96.1	95.3	100.2	109.3	126.1
	11.4	*13.0*	*12.4*	*12.1*	*11.6*	*12.3*
Finance, insurance, and real estate	42.6	44.8	51.1	58.4	66.6	77.4
	5.7	*6.0*	*6.6*	*7.1*	*7.1*	*7.5*
Services	42.6	44.8	50.4	51.4	66.9	74.5
	5.7	*6.0*	*6.5*	*6.2*	*7.1*	*7.2*
Government and government enterprise	290.8	279.8	291.0	321.0	369.9	372.2
	39.9	*37.7*	*37.8*	*38.8*	*38.2*	*36.2*
Total	746.8	741.2	770.7	826.5	942.1	1029.5
	100.0	*100.0*	*100.0*	*100.0*	*100.0*	*100.0*

Source: Bradford H. Tuck, *An Aggregate Income Model of a Semi-Autonomous Alaskan Economy*, prepared for the Federal Field Committee for Development Planning in Alaska, Anchorage, 1967, p. 68.

Note: Italics denote percent.

Manufacturing, including the processing of primary products (fish packing, lumber, and pulp manufacture, etc.), and the so-called support industries (like baking, soft-drink bottling, and printing and publishing), contributed 8 percent of value added. Commodity production in its totality, then, made up only about one-eighth of the total volume of activity in Alaska's economy.

On the other hand, Government employment alone was directly responsible for well over one-third of Alaska gross income and product; and Government activity alone accounts for about two-fifths of all employment and for about half of all wage and salary payments in Alaska. In addition, the activity of the service sectors of the private economy and of construction ultimately depends largely upon the income injected into the State from Government expenditures. Government must ultimately account for substantially more than half of all economic activity in Alaska.

The large role played in Alaska's economy by the Federal Government, and particularly by defense activities and defense construction, together with the relatively small role of the State's resource industries, is *not*, however, representative of the forces for growth in the State. As shown in figure VI–2, the gross value of product in Alaska's extractive industries about doubled between 1960 and 1966.

FIGURE VI-2.—GROWTH IN COMMODITY INDUSTRIES BY VALUE OF PRODUCT

[Millions of dollars]

Industry	1960	1961	1962	1963	1964	1965	1966
Fisheries	$96.5	$128.7	$126.5	$104.7	$125.0	$166.5	$185.0
Forest products	47.3	44.7	49.7	50.1	58.0	57.5	67.8
Minerals	20.6	17.8	18.8	35.2	35.5	[1] 47.6	34.7
Oil and gas	1.3	17.0	28.4	32.7	35.5	35.6	50.2
Agriculture	5.4	5.5	5.8	5.5	5.6	5.2	5.5
Furs	4.8	4.2	4.3	4.4	4.4	5.8	[2] 7.0
Total	175.9	217.9	233.7	232.6	264.0	318.2	350.2

[1] Reflects postearthquake construction.
[2] Largely an increase in unit prices.
Source: Alaska Development Corporation, *Annual Report*.

Figures on *investment* rather than production would show an even more spectacular contrast and lead to the conclusion that it was oil and gas and their derivatives above all—exploration, development, and processing, as well as production—which are now the main engine of economic growth in Alaska. The discovery in 1968 of what appears to be the biggest oil field in North America certainly does not modify this judgment.

There has also been an expansion of Alaska-based fisheries operations, formerly concentrated almost wholly on salmon, into other species such as king crab, shrimp, and scallops.

Logging, pulp manufacture, and the cutting of roughly squared lumber for export to Japan have also expanded substantially so that by the fall of 1968 almost two-thirds of the State's allowable timber cut had been committed to production.

It cannot be too heavily emphasized that the above three resource groups—oil and gas, fish and timber—and their processing are now, together with tourism, the State's *only* basic growth industries and that the benefits from their growth are distributed exceedingly unevenly within the State. The growth of these resource-based activities has, of course, greatly stimulated the growth of supporting manufactures and services and of State and local government; but it is only mildly exaggerating to say that this growth of the "infrastructure and superstructure" has occurred entirely in the Anchorage-Kenai area.

On the whole, this concentration—indeed urbanization—has been beneficial to Alaska's overall development. It has reduced costs through economies of scale and through greater competition and has provided the Anchorage area with virtually all of the amenities of modern urban life. The developments of the last decade have, in addition, reduced the relative amplitude of seasonal fluctuations in income and employment.

This growth has, however, meant little to most Alaska natives. There has been some influx of natives into the urban centers, but most natives still live in small villages apart from the continental land transportation network and almost totally outside the mainstream of the economy.

Even more significant, however, is the *composition* of new employment. A comprehensive manpower and manpower-demand study of Alaska has yet to be done, but there is little doubt that the education and skill requirements for entry into the jobs being created by economic growth in Alaska are, on the average, exceptionally high, and are rising year by year. This circumstance was reflected already in the 1960 census by Alaska's median educational attainment for whites of 12.4 years compared with 10.9 for the United States as a whole.

The leading growth industry—oil and gas—is one of the most capital intensive and technology intensive of all commodity-producing industries and employs almost no unskilled or semiskilled labor.

Alaska's economic growth is expected to continue at a rapid pace along its present lines, and some of the most serious problems of economic backwardness and isolation (for instance, high prices and costs, and violent seasonal fluctuations) may be effectively mitigated in the urban core over the next few years. But it would not be surprising if this development took place without adding at all to the number of jobs which can be filled by persons without at least the equivalent of a high school education.[1]

SUBREGIONAL ASPECTS

The important economic aspects of each of Alaska's five subregions, defined in figure VI-3 (of the report), as they touch the native protests, are considered below.[2]

[1] This is not to say that there will not be *any* new jobs created at minimum entry levels. The point is that any new positions of this type may well be more than offset by the disappearance of unskilled and semiskilled jobs in declining industries or trades, and resulting from automation, modernization, and upgrading of work in general. Under these circumstances, programs to place additional natives in minimum-entry jobs may succeed only to the extent they *redistribute* unemployment rather than alleviate it.

[2] The regional subdivision of Alaska used here is that prepared for the Federal field committee's "A Subregional Economic Analysis of Alaska," Anchorage, September 1968, which study provides a detailed description, analysis, and projection of the economies of the respective subregions.

Region I—*Southeastern Alaska*

The economy of southeastern Alaska is heavily dependent on government and distributive activities; virtually the State's entire timber industry and a large proportion of fishing activity are also based in the region. Commercial fishing is the most important occupation of the native people, and the subsistence economy is less important here than it is elsewhere in the State.

Because the bulk of the productive land in the region is national forest land, and because at least a partial resolution of the claims of the Haida and Tlingit Indians has already been achieved judicially, the "land freeze" has little effect here.

Region II—*Southcentral Alaska*

Southcentral Alaska comprises the economic heartland of the State. With the State's largest city, about half its population, virtually the entire oil and gas industry, and the bulk of its fishing industry, any action related to Native claims which affects the magnitude and pace of economic activity in this region cannot help but have a significant effect on the total economic and fiscal strength of the State. The effect of the land freeze on the oil and gas industry is treated a few pages hence; we take up here its impact in other fields.

The whole of the Chugach National Forest lies within the bounds of region II. The estimated allowable cut for the Chugach is 67 million board feet. Only a fraction of this has been cut. In the opinion of the U.S. Forest Service, the national forest will be unaffected by native land claims. In large part this view stems from the fact that the present Native claims legislation does not contemplate disturbing the national forests. The Congress could, of course, make a different settlement. The Statehood Act provides that communities may, for purposes of expansion, select "* * * from lands within national forests in Alaska which are vacant and unappropriated at the time of their selection not to exceed four hundred thousand acres of land * * *." So far the State has made requests amounting to fewer than 40,000 acres under this provision.

The State of Alaska has received tentative approval for its selected timberlands on the Kenai Peninsula, Shuyak Island, the Susitna Valley, and the Yakataga area. Major State sales include 96 million board feet on the Kenai and 100 million in the Susitna Valley. A sale in conjunction with a U.S. Forest Service sale was planned to include 100 million board feet of State timber on Shuyak Island, but was not consummated. Within a year the State expected to offer the Yakataga timber for sale. Estimated allowable cut there is about 29 million board feet yer year.

Unless present policy is changed, the State will not receive approval on any further timberland selections that it might make until the land claims have been settled.

The areas mentioned above should provide adequate inventory from the present to at least 2 years hence. When the time period 3 to 6 years is reached, the land claims may well have an effect. By that time, cutting on sales which have already been made may be in full swing.

Some additional demand could be met by further sales on land the State now controls. Should the resource be seriously depleted, however, it is quite possible that potential buyers would look to national forest timber for supply where they might normally have sought out State timber.

The major land selection which would be delayed by the land claims is the Copper River Valley area. The Bureau of Land Management is presently surveying and classifying this land area. It is understood that the State would like to select this land in about 5 years.

As to the Alaska Peninsula and the Aleutian Chain areas, it is concluded that there is no appreciable effect of the pending native land claims legislation. It did not deter investment in plant and equipment during the past 2 years, nor did it have an effect on the recent sale of the Dutch Harbor property by the General Services Administration; although these properties are outside the delineated land claims.

People in the fishing industry do not seem concerned. They are far more concerned about the fisheries resource than they are about lands on which to establish plants. It is anticipated that lands would be made available to the fishing industry, taking into consideration impending land claims, as long as they offered employment.

Other problems such as townsite planning, the use of wildlife refuges, and the relationship and use of military lands appear to play a greater role than do native land claims in this area.

Region III—*Kuskokwim Area*

The population of region III is about 13,000, about nine-tenths of whom are Alaska natives. Bluntly put, the region has no apparent base for economic growth. It has a rapidly growing population without local employment prospects and generally without the cultural, educational, and skill prerequisites for successful out-migration. In the foreseeable future, outside of the conversion of the present subsistence fishery in the Kuskokwim and Yukon Rivers to a more efficient commercial operation, any growth of opportunity either for employment or for enterprise in the region, will result directly from Government action. The only prospect for expansion of the public sector, in turn, can be anticipated as a result of efforts to overcome the cultural and economic handicaps of the region's population.

No instance is known in which the "land freeze" has hindered, delayed, or prevented any economic development project in the region. There can be no assurance, however, that a prolongation of the freeze for several years would not deter programs which depend on acquisition of mineral title or on timber sales. It should be pointed out, however, that there is no immediate prospect for action in either area under any circumstance.

Region IV—*Interior Alaska*

The economy of interior Alaska is concentrated in the Fairbanks area and is dominated by Government and distributive activities. The only conspicuous source of economic growth in recent years has been the University of Alaska and a Government-technical-scientific complex growing up around the University campus. Mining and agriculture have minor and declining roles in the area.

Interior Alaska's native population is approximately 6,500, or 13 percent of the total population. Outside of Fairbanks proper, most natives are still attached to the subsistence economy; and their most conspicuous sources of cash income are occasional construction work and Government employment together with welfare payments.

No instance is known in which the "land freeze" has prevented any commercial development. Its continuation would, of course, be an obstacle to mineral development in this highly mineralized area, assuming, of course, that significant discoveries would otherwise be made and produced.

Region V—*Northwest Alaska*

This area, with a population of about 12,300, of which about nine-tenths are Eskimos, is almost totally undeveloped; but it is the site of the recent spectacular oil discoveries. The potential for economic development rests largely in minerals and tourism. At present no mineral production is being carried out, but the north slope as a whole may turn out to be one of the world's richest petroleum provinces and the general geology of the Brooks Ranges suggests the possibility of major developments in metallic ores. Actual production of either is unlikely within 4 or 5 years, and the future of the mineral industries in the area is still highly speculative. In the present primitive state of mapping, surveys, and exploration, statements about the regions' "vast mineral wealth" are prophesies of the faithful more than asser-tion of fact. Nevertheless, indications of oil and gas and of other commerce mineral prospects are sufficient to encourage substantial pri-vate investment in exploration. Discounting for the uncertainties of discovery and eventual production, the present value in the private market of all petroleum and natural gas rights on north slope land yet to be leased, including Naval Petroleum Reserve No. 4, is prob-ably in the order of hundreds of millions of dollars.

Even in advance of possible production, the exploration investment in region V and the public revenues generated from leases will be enormous in resident *per capita* terms, as will the gross value of prod-uct and public royalties and revenues when any production begins. But these flows will not generate a direct demand for the labor of local Eskimos *at their present levels of acculturation, education, and skills,* and in conformity with their present customs of employment and livelihood, so that the constructive impact on the indigenous economy may not be great.

No instance in which the "land freeze" has hindered, delayed, or prevented any economic development project has been found. All present or anticipated programs are being carried out or are planned offshore, on private land, or on existing leases or withdrawals. There can, however, be no assurance that prolongation of the freeze for sev-eral years will deter programs which depend on acquisition of new mineral title or lease.

GOVERNMENT AND OIL INDUSTRY PERCEPTIONS

Perhaps as important as whether or how the fact of native protest or the provisions of the attending legislation "should" have implica-tions for the economic development of Alaska is how decisional parties—governmental and corporate—*perceive* implications to the protest and claims. Two quotations are representative of the State's view. The Alaska Division of Lands recent annual report contains the remarks:

> The State's land selection program continues to be restricted by a Federal policy of refusal to take final action on lands which are under recorded native land claims. There are now 40 such claims. They cover most of Alaska's 365 million acres, and because of overlapping, total more than the State's entire acreage.
>
> The Interior Department's policy of "no final action" means that tentative approval is not granted on State selections, and without tentative approval the State has not been able to assume management of the selected land. This, of course, means the State is not able to proceed as rapidly as desired in moving land into the hands of private ownership.[3]

In this last connection it should be pointed out that Interior's policy derives from the Administrative Procedures Act which requires a *finding* on protested government actions and is, therefore, not to be viewed as arbitrary and capricious.

In the same publication, the section on oil and gas leasing activity contains the observation:

> The decision of the Federal Government to suspend issue of leases in cases where the land is under native claim has had a definite. adverse effect on rental revenues to the State. Alaska is entitled to 90 percent of oil and gas lease revenues, but the total revenue continues to decline because expiring leases are not renewed and new leases are not issued. The rental income to Alaska from Federal oil and gas leases, topped $4 million in 1966, but dropped to $3,526,398.20 in 1967.[4]

Less conclusive is the University of Alaska's recent analysis of the impact of the freeze. The university publication states:

> Actual effect of the freeze on future oil and gas development is open to conjecture. Presently the freeze is stimulating drilling on some Federal leases, especially the Alaska Peninsula. This increased activity has resulted because the Federal leases in this area will be the first to expire and oil companies want to eliminate these areas from their list of prospects before the expiration dates do so automatically. If production is developed on a Federal leasehold, the lease is automatically renewable and, therefore, not subject to the restrictions of the freeze. Present indications are that the only districts in which oil company activity is actually slowing down are the Copper River Basin and along the Gulf of Alaska shoreline—and activity in these areas may have slowed without the freeze. However, if the freeze continues over a period of years, gaps will occur in potential drilling blocks in these and other areas that could depress future explorations in Alaska.[5]

It is notoriously difficult to get the industry view of any issue on the Alaska petroleum scene. This is not usually a matter of secretiveness on the part of the industry but more frequently a recognition of

---

[3] *Alaska Division of Lands 1967 Annual Report,* State of Alaska, Department of Natural Resources, Anchorage, Alaska, pp. 9–10.

[4] *Ibid,* p. 4.

[5] Judy Brady, "Native Land Claims," *Alaska Monthly Review of Business and Economic Conditions,* vol. IV, No. 6 (November 1967), University of Alaska, Institute of Social, Economic and Government Research, pp. 8–9.

the fact that individual members—and, indeed, individuals within a single company—have quite divergent views on most questions at issue. In an effort to get some insight into what some members of the oil and gas industry see as the effect of native protest on their activities, a group (35) of landmen responsible for advising their corporations on land availability, leasing and acquiring rights, negotiating land contracts, and the like was contacted. The questions posed each member and the distribution of responses follow:

Question.—What effect, if any, has the native land protest—and the land freeze—had on your company's behavior in Alaska?

Sixty-two percent of the respondents advised that the land freeze had an adverse effect on their company's exploratory activities in Alaska. Thirty-one percent advised that the land freeze had no noticeable effect to date. Seven percent advised the question was not applicable to the company's operations.

Question.—What effect could it have on your company's behavior in Alaska in the future?

Ninety-three percent of the respondents felt that the continuance of the land freeze would seriously limit and possibly halt their company's efforts in Alaska. Seven percent advised the question was not applicable to the company's operations.

Question.—Do you believe the recent California lease activity on the part of the industry in any way involves committing corporate monies there that might have been directed to Alaska in the absence of native protest and land freeze?

Fifty-three percent of the respondents advised that the land freeze did not affect their company's participation in recent California lease activity. Twenty-three percent advised that they felt their company spent more money at the recent California sale than they would have had they been otherwise committed in Alaska. Three respondents advised that they feel the land freeze has released exploration monies not only for use in California but in other areas in the United States as well. Seven percent of the respondents advised that there was little comparison between the recent Santa Barbara sale and oil activities in Alaska. They felt that their companies were purchasing known producing structures as opposed to attempting to delineate such oil fields in Alaska.

Within these generalized conclusions, several particular responses brought out the move to substitute exploration of Outer Continental Shelf lands in Alaska for onshore lands, the difficulty and cost of altering the 5-year budget plans which typify the exploration process—on the point of forecasting corporate activity in foreign or other domestic areas—and the all-pervasive mood of uncertainty and instability they see as surrounding land matters.

Almost all comments from any source on the economic effects of native protest cite the so-called land freeze as the central source of immediate difficulty. It seems fair to say that the freeze is looked upon by business as a much greater obstacle to development than cloudiness of land titles. This, of course, is understandable- in that the freeze is explicit and certain and the ultimate resolution of ownership is quite unclear.

The freeze affects all land disposal cases situated in claim areas, including State selection; final action on homesteads, homesites, trade and manufacturing, power and airport sites; road rights-of-way; mining claims; and the like. The freeze does not directly affect Federal lands already under lease nor does it affect State-owned lands, including tidal and submerged lands. Further leasing of federally administered lands and tentative-approval lands was stopped, however.[6]

The prevailing view of the actual and potential results of this paralysis is captured in the testimony of one former senior State official in the land field. He writes:

* * * The welfare of all Alaskans and the economic stability of the State itself is dependent upon accelerated rather than delayed development of the resources * * *. [The] recent freeze on issuing oil and gas leases on land covered by native claims, has proven costly financially to the Federal and State governments. It promises to be far more costly in delayed resource development.[7]

Further, he concludes:

Although the Federal Government can tolerate delays resulting from decisions, cumbersome legal proceedings or from lack of appropriations, Alaska cannot permit such delays which often mean lost opportunity for securing commitments of development capital.[8]

On the face of it, one might imagine that the question of ownership of land—or, indeed, even the matter of land in disputed ownership—might not "make any difference" to the interested business party (for example, oil companies) as long as it was leaseable. But even here there are economic implications that turn on the nature and provisions of ownership. Lease payments would be 50 cents per acre per year with State ownership. Similarly, royalty payments would be at a rate of 16½ percent. The terms of leases under possible native association ownership are today simply conjectural. Further, there is the question of the patterns of offerings, their frequency, size, and location, and how these might differ under varying ownership. Finally, the issue of the administrative and managerial skill levels and experiences under different ownership arrangements is probably viewed by most State and industry officials along the lines of the following quotation:

Once the "freeze is lifted," mineral exploration and development can proceed promptly if established and tested laws and regulations are in effect * * *. If the mineral rights are transferred to Native groups, development will unquestionably be delayed and discouraged simply because of the uncertainties attendant upon drafting and adoption of rules, regulations, and operating procedures. The significance of Alaskan mineral re-

---

[6] Writing to this point, the University of Alaska analysis of Native claims includes the comment: "The history of leasing in Alaska has shown that 20 to 25 per cent of the federal leases are dropped or expire each year. These leases have been replaced by enough new leases to keep the level fairly stable. Under the freeze, with virtually no new federal leases being issued to replace those dropped, the acreage under federal lease has dropped from approximately 10 million in May of 1966 to about 7.8 million at the end of May 1967." *Ibid.*, p. 8.

[7] Testimony of Roscoe E. Bell, consultant to the Alaska Land Law Study team of the Public Land Law Review Commission and lecturer in natural resources, University of Wisconsin, on S-2906 in letter to Senator Henry Jackson, chairman of the committee holding hearings on the legislation.

[8] *Ibid.*

source development justifies retention of the mineral rights by the Federal or State government or at least mineral management by the Government agencies.[9]

It should be explicitly acknowledged, of course, that judgments about the character and quality of native management of land resources that might be granted by legislative settlement are highly speculative. So long as land and mineral title is not so fragmented as to make rational management impossible, there is no reason to expect the quality of business talent engaged by native groups to be inferior to that of the State. On the contrary, the management of native investment corporations might be expected to be more single-mindedly devoted to maximizing the commercial value of their assets than would management agencies of the Federal or State government, which face many more conflicting policy objectives and constraints.

There is another important dimension to the whole "supply side" of the equation that is generally discussed above. This is the behavior of Government—State and local agencies and other Federal agencies—in the face of native protest, the Department of the Interior's "land freeze," and pending claims legislation. Here, too, the effects are several, with varying degrees of impact on the orderly growth and development of the State. One is the conflict between claims legislation and land selection rights granted by the Statehood Act, that is, given the fact that land suitable for selection is not unlimited in quantity, a large acreage grant to native claims could reduce the amount of desirable land available for State selection.

A second and related item is the fact that the extensive existing Federal land withdrawals around the State will be seen as increasingly desirable in the competition for land of value. Earlier withdrawals will very likely come under growing pressure for review and reclassification. This, of course, is quite consonant with the charge of the Public Land Law Review Commission.

A third effect is that agencies may well pursue their normal program in the land-management or related fields with less vigor than they otherwise would or may redirect their efforts away from some areas in favor of others on the basis of native protests. Examples here might be found in airport facilities work, grazing permits, land classification, and wilderness and parks and recreation activities. Any relative retrenchment on the part of agency programs in a State where government is such a dominant phenomenon in the economy cannot have neutral effects.

A "demand analysis" of the issue points up several considerations. There is a danger of viewing corporate (and, perhaps, Government) behavior in too narrow a context. It could well be the case that industry conditions of prices, markets, costs, and internal company concerns of budgets, cash flow, utilization of facilities, and substitute opportunities elsewhere may be more determinative of business behavior than the fact of native protest and legislation—or at least the latter may be only governing at the margin. Then, too, there is the possibility that the native protest may be used as a handy scapegoat—a ready explanation for business to taper off the level of their activities contemplated for other reasons.

---

[9] *Ibid.*

USE AND MANAGEMENT OF RESOURCES

Alaska's wildlife resources which are of national significance are afforded habitat preservation and management by the Federal Government. While Alaska native populations depend in whole or in part upon biotic resources in order to sustain life and while many of Alaska's wildlife resources are of national significance, there is little conflict between the national wildlife objectives and native subsistence requirements, with the possible exception of some migratory bird nesting populations. Increasing conflict between the sport or commercial harvest of wildlife resources and the subsistence harvest of these same resources by the native people is, however, developing.

Legislative jurisdiction for all wildlife resources, except for migratory birds, is vested in the State of Alaska. On the other hand, proprietary jurisdiction of most of Alaska, the habitat of wildlife, is vested, at this point in time, primarily in the Federal Government which has the right to prescribe who, where, and in what manner persons may enter, travel across, and conduct activities upon land within its jurisdiction.

As in the case of wildlife resources, the native "property right" in the fishery resource was "taken" when legislative jurisdiction over fish and wildlife resources passed to the State by virtue of the Statehood Act. Alaska's native people rely heavily upon the fisheries, but they share in these resources only as members of the general public.

The fishery resource is a natural resource which offers immediate direct promise for major economic participation; one in which natives can compete as wage earners with moderate outlays of capital. It is a renewable resource with which natives are familiar.

The general development and allocation of Alaska water resources is essential to economic growth and community welfare in Alaska. Furthermore, Alaska is a region of water surplus and is considered as a future potential continental water source for water-deficient areas in the western United States and Canada. While the largest possible use for Alaska water resources is hydroelectric power development, this, with the exception of a few sites, does not exhibit favorable cost-benefit ratios. The Federal withdrawal of many hydroelectric power sites which have no foreseeable reservoir areas, however, prevents a conflict with potential land ownership to many native groups and villages.

Many Alaska aboriginal groups recognized a "user right" to individuals or families for a net, weir, or other fish catching place on a river or lake; no such exclusive "right" now exists on navigable waters because the Statehood Act extinguished any personal proprietorship and vested general ownership of lands beneath navigable waters in the State.

There is need to provide watershed protection to water source supplies for Alaska's cities, towns, and villages. Depending upon location and physiography, community watersheds may have to be of considerable size in order to provide for safe and adequate supplies in the future. There is need also to provide land for public flood plain zoning in many regions of Alaska as economic and community growth increases.

Alaska possesses 16 percent of all U.S. forest resources. Nearly all forest resources of Alaska are subject to Federal jurisdiction. The important commercial forests of the coastal zone are administered by the U.S. Forest Service within the Chugach and Tongass National Forests. Interior forests on the public domain, comprising 32 percent of the total land area of Alaska, 21 percent of which is commercial timber, are administered by the Bureau of Land Management. These interior forests are subject to State selection and also offer a possible resource to native claimants.

Almost all available cropland in Alaska has been selected by the State or patented to private interests. The undeveloped agricultural resource significant to native claimants and nonnatives alike, however, is grazing land—particularly on the Alaska Peninsula, Kodiak Island, and the Aleutian Islands. With improved transportation and changing economic feasibility, livestock production (cattle and sheep) is a potential expandable use for the grasslands of western Alaska. However, conflict with wildlife use of the same lands is probable; and at the present time, wildlife is the more economically valuable resource. A particularly important grazing land use occurs on lands of the Seward Peninsula, St. Lawrence Island, and Nunivak Island and a few other small areas of western Alaska where native reindeer husbandry is practiced.

Although present areas of intensive recreational use cover less than one-sixth of Alaska—chiefly in areas adjoining the major communities—the recreational resources of the State are one of the most potentially valuable economic assets of the Nation, State, and natives in the years ahead. Estimates are that by 1980 nearly three-quarters of a million tourists will have visited Alaska, adding thereby $225 million to the Alaskan economy in the 15 years following 1964.

The potential wealth of Alaska mineral and oil and gas resources is not known, although it is estimated to be many billions of dollars. So little of the State's geology is understood—many regions of the State being virtually unexplored—that it is impossible to pattern a rational distribution of land based upon mineral wealth. Nevertheless, sufficient knowledge exists to say that geologic distribution of known deposits is extremely unequal and variable.

ECONOMIC CONSEQUENCES OF SETTLEMENT

Any forecast of the pace and pattern of economic development in Alaska is limited by the accuracy of its assumptions and must be accepted with great caution. The same caution is required with respect to forecasts of the economic consequences of any legislative package designed to settle the native claims. The following remarks are intended to set out in what general *direction* will be the probable effect on the economic status of the natives and on Alaska's general economic development of the individual elements of various settlement proposals, including those before the Congress.

PROTECTION OF SUBSISTENCE RESOURCES

None of the legislation introduced so far deals in a definitive way with protection of fish and wildlife stocks used in the indigenous economy, or with protection of native access to these stocks. With the partial exception of migratory wildfowl, fish and game are a matter of

State title and State responsibility. Article VIII, section 3, of the State constitution appears to preclude establishing proprietary rights in fish or wildlife harvests.[12] Under these circumstances, the only provisions of any of the existing bills which might affect *exclusive* native access to fish or wildlife resources would be large grants of land in fee simple, or unrestricted grants of the surface estate. Such measures, while not conveying a property right in fish or wildlife, would enable native proprietors to post the land against entry by others for hunting, fishing, or trapping.

Congress might, however, protect public access, native and non-native, to fish and wildlife by providing that State-selected land and other land withdrawn from the public domain in Alaska for other purposes remain open in perpetuity to (all) the public for hunting, fishing, and trapping. Under either of these provisions, the harvest in fact available to natives would still depend upon State management and regulations.

The general economic impact of legislation in this area would depend upon the amount and location of lands and waters involved. There might conceivably be local effects on recreation and tourist-oriented enterprise, but these effects in the aggregate are not likely to be large.

GRANTS OF HOMESITES, TOWNSITES, AND SPECIAL-PURPOSE LOCATIONS

The absence of title to land occupied by natives in Alaska villages is clearly an obstacle to financing homes, businesses, and community facilities. The grant of title to these lands would just as clearly have a beneficial effect on the village economy. The same is true of grants of land for expansion in the vicinity of each village. One necessary reservation here is that, unless some provision is made for future exchanges of land or otherwise for the occupation of new sites, families and communities may be tied to places which turn out to be poorly located from an economic or some other standpoint.

Grants of land title for homesites, businesses, community facilities, and special-purpose locations such as fish camps and burial grounds should not be expected to have any negative effects on general economic development. Some question might be raised about sites in existing withdrawals such as national forests. The total area of land involved is so small, however, that we can find no instance in which such transfers would subvert the purposes of the original withdrawal.

INDIVIDUAL LAND GRANTS

The aggregate impact of granting individuals fee simple ownership, or title to either the surface estate or the mineral estate, on large tracts of land is extremely difficult to predict. It is obvious, however, that the benefits would be very unevenly distributed, both because of the wide differences in value of land resource, and because of wide differences in individuals' ability to manage and exploit these resources. Some individuals would undoubtedly become very wealthy, while a great number would probably not benefit at all.

---

[13] *"Common use.* Wherever occurring in a natural state, fish, wildlife, and waters are reserved to the people for common use." In addition, sec. 15 of the same article reads, *"No exclusive right of fishery.* No exclusive right or special privilege of fisheries shall be created or authorized in the natural waters of the State." *Alaska State Constitution.*

It is not clear whether such a provision would on balance speed up or retard commercial development of Alaska resources. What probably can be said is that the time horizons of individual proprietors would be shorter, and their focus narrower, than would be the case with Government management.

LAND GRANTS TO NATIVE CORPORATIONS OR NATIVE ASSOCIATIONS

There is no reason to expect the quality of management employed by native associations to be on the average inferior to that available to the State. Generalizations about management policy, however, are extremely speculative. On balance, ownership by native corporations, like private ownership in general, would probably result in a more rapid rate of development and a greater concern for maximizing the economic returns from the land resources than would management by Government agencies. For instance, native corporations would probably not require primary processing of extractive products or "sustained-yield" timber management except where they were clearly justified in dollar terms. Native corporations in attempting to maximize their net incomes from the land would pursue a multiple-use policy, and in doing so would probably be able to resolve conflicts among competing *commercial* land uses more economically and more satisfactorily than would Government. On the other hand, to the extent their policies reflected a single-minded concern with the commercial revenues of the land, they might be less concerned than would Government with such nonmonetary and collective values as those of wilderness and scenery.

The previous treatment assumes that native corporations would manage their land grants for their income rather than distributing them to individuals or selling out in order to distribute the proceeds. The impact of either of these policies on native welfare would approximate that of individual land grants and individual cash settlements, respectively. Grants of commercially valuable land managed for its income by native corporations could be expected to provide an income flow to individual families and to provide a source of capital which native enterprise could invest in other lines of business and capital for community improvements. It would also provide openings for the development of native managerial talent.

INDIVIDUAL LUMP-SUM SETTLEMENTS

It is again difficult to generalize about the impact of lump-sum individual payments on native welfare except to say that the effects would vary immensely among individuals. Some natives undoubtedly would invest their money very effectively; but because of poverty, lack of education and of commercial attitudes, a great number of recipients would undoubtedly soon be no better off than they were before receiving the grant.

For the same reason (i.e., the natives' high propensity to consume), the lump-sum settlement to individuals would probably be a sharp stimulus to the general Alaska economy, but this stimulus would be of a "once-and-for-all" nature and would leave little lasting impact on Alaska income or employment.

INDIVIDUAL CASH ANNUITIES

Substantial cash grants to individuals, distributed regularly over a long period of time, might be expected to make a contribution to native living standards proportionate to the size of the grant, and to be a corresponding stimulus to the regional economy. It is not clear, however, that such payments would be any different in principle or in effect from increased, universal, public-assistance distributions.[13]

CASH SETTLEMENTS TO NATIVE ASSOCIATIONS OR CORPORATIONS

A large cash settlement distributed to a native corporation or corporations, if treated as investment capital rather than distributed to individuals, could be expected to provide a continuing stream of income to individuals as well as a source of funds for enterprise and for community development. It would also provide openings for the development of native management talent. Beyond this it is difficult to generalize, because the impact both on welfare of individual natives and on overall economic development would depend on the investment policies pursued, and on the managerial skills provided by, or hired by, the native groups.

SHARE OF REVENUES FROM PUBLIC LANDS (AND/OR OUTER CONTINENTAL SHELF)

Distribution to natives of a specified share of revenues from all or from certain kinds of public lands in Alaska would have effects on native welfare similar to that of cash disbursements and would vary similarly depending on whether the payments were to individuals or to a native corporations. In the latter case, they would vary depending on the managerial skills available to, and the policies of, those corporations. Unlike grants of commercially valuable lands to individuals or to native corporations, land and resource management would remain a government responsibility and would probably be pursued with a broader range of policy objectives than would be the case under private ownership. The flow of funds to native individuals or groups would begin sooner than they would in the case of grants of land title, unless the latter included lands presently under mineral lease.

Any increased investment or expenditure in the State resulting from these payments would clearly be an impetus to overall economic development, except to the extent they preempted a share of royalties, lease payments, or timber sales revenues which would otherwise accrue to State or local government. The net effect on economic development in the latter case is not clear.

[13] This study is not the proper place for a full discussion of the philosophy and economics of welfare. Existing public-assistance programs are under critical examination throughout the United States, and several alternatives are being widely considered. It is appropriate to point out here, however, that some kind of family income maintenance program will be required in rural Alaska for many years. We would hesitate to generalize about the relationship of public-assistance payments to the feelings of self-respect and to the economic motivations of Alaska natives, but it is clear there is a close connnection among them in the thinking on the cultural majority in America. Unearned income is regarded as degrading and disgraceful if the recipient gets it because he is poor and unemployed. But such income is highly respectable if it comes from the ownership of land or of securities. This consideration suggests that, dollar for dollar, public funds distributed to Alaska natives may be more effective in raising ther social and economc status if done wisely as part of a land-claims settlement than if done as public assistance.

TAX EXEMPTION

Tax exemptions *could* have significant fiscal implications for the State and local government. The real estate exemption of S.B. 3586, for instance, keeps all the lands granted off the property tax rolls whether they are "in fee or in trust." This provision applies as well to any minerals associated with the land grant which could otherwise be made subject to *ad valorem* levies where tax bodies existed. Conceivably, these sums might amount to considerable amounts of public receipts foregone. Some caution is appropriate here, however, in that too early and too much land taxation can result in confiscation of the land, which result would clearly be counterproductive to the policy resolution intended.

The problem here seems to be to distinguish among the different purposes for which land might be granted. In the case of homesites, fishing camps, and the like, or of lands granted to protect subsistence activities, maximum insurance is required against confiscation because of the owner's inability to pay taxes. In the case of grants of commercially valuable land for income purposes, however, the point is to get them into a productive, income-earning position, and, indeed, to get them *on* the tax rolls. To the extent that these lands are in fact capable of producing income, there is no obvious justification for keeping them off the tax rolls simply because they happen to be owned by natives or native groups.

Any provision, however, that initial cash payments under the Act are not taxable means simply that any monetary settlement is effectively larger in disposable income than its nominal dollar amount.

The provision in S.B. 3586 relating to section 501 of the Internal Revenue Code indicates that another nonprofit enterprise would be created, a corporate status which is currently under serious review by government and public-finance scholars alike. In a State the vast bulk of whose land and a great proportion of whose capital assets are already exempt from taxation, there seems to be no economic justification for this further departure from tax uniformity.

CORPORATE ORGANIZATION, TRUSTEESHIP, AND PROPERTY ALIENATION

To the extent that lump sums, tracts of commercially valuable land, or a share of the revenue from public lands in Alaska are transferred to native corporations, a major purpose is to assist the natives as a group to get a firm footing within the money economy and the capitalistic organization of the United States. Other aspects of the claims settlement may be designed to protect those natives and native communities which wish to maintain intact their nonmarket economy and their distinctive ways of life. But legislation providing a special role for native development corporations is directed toward economic equality for natives with other Americans, and toward their economic integration into the life of the Nation. For this reason, provisions establishing any trusteeship over the capital assets of the natives, including land, or establishing a special status for native development corporations, should be carefully examined and the time span of these provisions carefully considered.

The desire to protect a vulnerable people from exploitation or expropriation must be balanced against the desirability of giving them early control over their own livelihood and their own assets, and against the community's interest in avoiding franchise to private monopolies and special privilege. While restrictions on land transfer or stock sales to nonnative provide some protection to the improvident and the gullible, these restrictions will sharply reduce the *value* of the assets involved. Land which cannot be alienated cannot be mortgaged. If the land is the owner's only capital assets, he is tied to it economically as securely as if he were a serf. Stock in a native corporation which can be sold only to eligible natives is *ceteris paribus* worth less than stock which can be sold to anyone; stock which cannot be sold at all is, of course, worth even less. To the extent that the property of individual natives or of native corporations is encumbered either by law or by covenant, the value of that property will be reduced, the economic freedom of the natives impaired, and the most productive use of land and capital discouraged.

The bills so far presented to Congress for settlement of the land claims include two distinct approaches to protecting both native assets and the public interest during a prolonged transition to full equality. One approach would hold much of the natives' assets in trust and would rely heavily on the discretion of the Secretary of the Interior. The second approach, together with or separate from the first, provides a multitude of special provisions for native development corporations, including tax exemptions and restrictions on the disposal of their assets and on stock ownership. Congress may wish to consider whether either apparatus is really necessary, if the native development corporations commence with sufficient economic scale in terms of cash, land title, revenue shares, or some combination thereof, to reduce uncertainty about future income to acceptable levels, to distribute its benefits widely among the native communities of Alaska, and to engage first-rate professional management. In this case, the public interest, native and nonnative alike, might best be served by the early transformation of the native development corporation into one with all the rights and responsibilities of other businesses in our economy.

O

Part II: DEVELOPMENT PROGRAMS AND PLANS

Toward Economic Development for Native American Communities

Part II: DEVELOPMENT PROGRAMS AND PLANS

ECONOMIC DEVELOPMENT OF INDIAN COMMUNITIES

By BUREAU OF INDIAN AFFAIRS: U.S. DEPARTMENT OF THE INTERIOR

FOREWORD

The Bureau of Indian Affairs is the Federal agency having the primary responsibility for Indian programs. In this statement, the BIA describes the economic and social conditions found on Indian reservations, pointing out the ways in which the Indians are in a unique situation, requiring unique policies of development assistance. The statement describes the present programs of the BIA and of other Government agencies and suggests some future policy needs.

I. NATIONAL POLICY FOR DISTINCTIVE COMMUNITIES

The economic development of American Indian communities on the lands held in trust by the Secretary of the Interior, is encouraged and advanced by programs of the communities themselves and of the Bureau of Indian Affairs. Bureau programs, increasingly supportive, rather than directive in nature, are designed to enable the Indians to realize their full potential as citizens of the United States. Realization of this potential—economic, political, social, and cultural—is recognized by the Bureau and the Department of the Interior as a goal of national policy. This goal received support from President Johnson in his Message on Indian Opportunity, of March 6, 1968, and from President Nixon, as a candidate, in his statement of September 27, 1968, concerning American Indians.

The programs of the Bureau of Indian Affairs are authorized and funded by Congress for the benefit of all Indians, living on or near trust land. In the administration of these programs, however, the Bureau must take into account both the differences to be found between typical Indian communities and non-Indian America and the significant differences that exist among Indian communities themselves. Otherwise, program resources would not be applied as effectively as possible to the achievement of these policy goals.

POVERTY: CONDITIONS AND CONSEQUENCES

Most Indian families live in varying degrees of poverty that stem from varied sources—cultural differences from the non-Indian society, lack of educational opportunities, and lack of development of reservation-based resources. These handicaps are aggravated by geographical isolation from the rest of society and a set of values, that has been characterized as "an intense attachment to native soil, a reverent disposition toward habitat and ancestral ways, and a restraint

(331)

on individual self-seekings in favor of family and community." The Federal Government holds title, in trust for Indians, to approximately 40-million acres of tribally owned land and 11-million acres of individually owned land. Possession of land gives Indians a sense of security, not necessarily related to its present or prospective economic contribution. This phychological fact, which has its counterpart in some non-Indian depressed areas, helps explain why Indians often choose to remain on land which currently offers limited economic support.

Education.—Indian people, in general, have not been well educated. The educational level among adults is only two-thirds that of other Americans. Indians must overcome severe handicaps to secure the education demanded by today's sophisticated and specialized society.

Indian children start to school with handicaps springing from a different culture, poverty, and physical isolation. The evidence is disorganized families, low levels of education among parents and in the community, few books or newspapers in the home, meager modern facilities, and a general isolation from the larger world brought about by poor roads and communication.

Beyond these handicaps, which are common to rural poverty areas, the Indian child has unique problems of cultural isolation. He must learn to bridge two cultures—the ancient, satifying, Indian heritage, and the customs of the majority of our society. Indian values differ markedly from those typical of the white majority. Individual excellence in classroom achievement, for example, may run counter to the Indian ideal of group solidarity and cooperation. Indians revere the traditions of the past, are reluctant to accept new customs, and resist change. An additional problem of adjustment for many Indians is learning English as a second language. Symptoms of strain under cultural conflict are apathy, feelings of powerlessness, avoidance of non-Indian contact, substandard educational achievement, expectation of failure, and a high dropout rate from school.

Lack of Resource Development.—Indian people suffer from unemployment and inadequate income, as a result of lack of resources, both natural and human, or their underdevelopment. A shortage in the quantity and quality of skills exists on many reservations. As a result, widespread unemployment (10 times and more the national average) is typical. Underemployment is extensive, with many workers in low-paying and seasonal jobs.

Deficiency of Resources.—Many Indian people living on reservations occupy poor, barren land, lacking exploitable resources. Other reservations, while rich in resources, are overpopulated. Resident Indian population growth exceeds the Nation's average. When combined with inadequate natural resources and an inadequately skilled labor force, the growing population compounds a severe economic problem for the Indian people.

Inadequate Credit.—This problem is further compounded by a lack of credit, which limits investment both in economic ventures and in social overhead capital. Indian people, unaccustomed to ordinary business practices and lacking in management or technical training, have great difficulty in obtaining credit. Protective devices placed around Indians, such as their inability to sue or be sued, and the lack of authority for tribes to use land, their main asset, as security, sometimes makes it impractical for lenders to provide financing.

Fractionated Ownership of Land.—Heirship procedures on allotted Indian lands have created highly fractionated ownership, which hampers their efficient use for various business ventures or agriculture. Multiple ownership makes the consolidation of Indian-owned lands for productive use difficult and in many cases impossible.

Physical Isolation.—The physical isolation of many Indians living on reservations also handicaps economic growth. Typically isolated from central labor and consumer markets, Indians have fewer job opportunities and must pay high prices for consumer goods. Poor transportation facilities, air, rail, and highway, have discouraged many concerns otherwise interested in establishing industries. Indian communities generally have fewer roads per square mile of territory than surrounding States and many roads on reservations cannot be used in bad weather. School days are missed and social contacts held back to an extent not typical of the rest of society.

A cumulative result of extended unemployment is the lack of work experience. This disadvantage is manifest in a large number of dropouts from employment training programs and from apprentice-type jobs. When coupled with the cultural isolation, the lack of work habits and experience becomes a primary limiting factor in achieving continuous employment for individuals.

Housing.—A recent survey indicated that only one out of four Indian families was adequately housed. Approximately 19,000 families live in homes that can be brought up to acceptable standards by renovation, and 49,000 families must have new housing. Low income, high unemployment, and physical isolation have limited the Indians' participation in normal channels that provide long-term mortgage capital.

Health Problems.—The health level of the Indian is the lowest of any major population group in the United States. It is evidenced by a high infant mortality rate, 34.5 per 1,000 births, 12 points worse than the national average. A high incidence of pneumonia, viral infections, and malnutrition is common among Indian children. Tuberculosis among Indians and Alaska natives is more than five times as common as the national average. Alcoholism is a major problem and becoming more prevalent. More than half of the Indians obtain water from contaminated or potentially dangerous sources, and waste disposal facilities are grossly inadequate.

The foregoing are quantifiable differences that are characteristic of the residents of Indian communities. They have their roots in the basic cultural differences that have led to such serious divergence between these communities and their non-Indian neighbors. Cultural differences are deep and lasting; they yield only slowly to the influence of the surrounding culture. Indian economic development can proceed only as the process of acculturation allows. Following are three illustrations of older culture concepts found among most Indian tribes and Alaska natives which still influence economic development.

Material wealth does not embody the same values or have the same attraction for the native cultures as in present-day American culture. Prestige is acquired primarily by other means; therefore, the promise of payrolls and other forms of material reward often does not provide the motivation needed to encourage economic growth.

Social pressures discourage acquisitions of material goods. Thus, demands of the family will not infrequently discourage individual initiative, particularly where family obligations range over a wide network of persons.

A preference for leisure (that is, for contemplative time) is evident among most native cultures. Time is measured in hours and seasons, not in sweeps of the second hand. The desire for time to contemplate need not be hostile to the desire for economic progress, but can strongly influence the direction and pace of economic change and the view as to what directions constitute wholesome economic change.

The differences, both visible and underlying, between Indians and non-Indians are marked and significant. These differences are manifest in the social and cultural patterns of the Indian community. It is a collective, cooperative system, as contrasted with the competitive, individualistic system of non-Indian communities. Yet, despite these common characteristics distinguishing them from non-Indian society, there are also many difference among Indian communities, differences that are significant for their attitudes toward and capability of economic development.

VARIED TYPES OF INDIAN COMMUNITIES

Essential for an overview of the problems faced in economic development of Indian communities is recognition of the vast range of reservation community types—their varying sizes of population and land area, their differening degrees of cultural or geographic isolation from the larger national community, and the enormous differences in the quality, quantity, and strategic location of resources.

There are 270 Indian "reservations" in the "lower 48" States. Another 24 trust reserves, along with 100 federally owned land areas, have been set aside for Indians, Eskimos, and Aleuts in Alaska. These range in size from the 14-million acre Navajo Reservation, upon which 100,000 Indian people live, to single-acre California "rancherias" with no resident populations. Some, as is true of most of the Alaskan areas, are distant from larger communities and further cut off from them by the most tenuous systems of transportation and communications. Others, as in the instance of certain of the Nevada colonies, some of the reservations in Washington, Arizona, New Mexico, Michigan, Wisconsin, New York, and the Indian area of western Oklahoma, are contiguous to or surrounded areas already urban or becoming urbanized.

In still other locations, notably where reservations were allotted to individuals (before this practice was curtailed by law in the early 1930's), much Indian land has been alienated to non-Indians, who outnumber Indians many times over within the external boundaries of the old reservations. For example, on the Flathead Reservation in Montana, where considerable economic development activities on behalf of Indians have taken place, whites outnumber Indians roughly 10 to 1. The same holds true on the Sisseton Reservation in North and South Dakota, where only 10 percent of the old reserve remains in ownership by the Indians. On the South Dakota Pine Ridge and Rosebud Sioux Reservations, with aggregate Indian populations in excess of 10,000, less than 50 percent of the land remains in Indian hands. Much of the economic control in the areas is by whites or by so-called "mixed bloods" who in some instances maintain only the most nominal sort of tribal identities.

Of 129 reservation areas with populations of at least 200 Indian people and with at least 1,000 acres of land base, 25 have greater non-Indian than Indian population within their original boundaries, 45 are adjacent to or in close proximity to urban areas, and 38 have lost 50 percent or more of their original reservation area to non-Indians. These figures do not include the situation in Oklahoma, where land alienation and residence in close proximity to larger non-Indian populations is the rule.

Also of importance in seeking a direction for reservation economic development is an awareness of the rather significant mobility of many reservation Indian populations. At present, roughly one-third of all Indians, most of them recently from the reservations, no longer live in their home communities. Many now live in the larger urban areas of the west coast, the upper Midwest, or in the Southwest—particularly in Oklahoma and Texas. By far the largest off-reservation population is in Los Angeles County, where between 30,000 and 40,000 Indians, especially Sioux, Navajo, and native Oklahomans presently live. Less than half have moved there with the Bureau's assistance, although its assistance program has undoubtedly been influential in attracting nonparticipants to the urban areas. The influence of these urban Indian colonies in attracting others from the rural areas is only beginning to be appreciated; some observers expect that 1970, the decennial census year, will see for the first time in history more American Indians living and earning their living in small towns and urban areas than on their home reservations.

The relevance of these differences among Indian communities to the subject under discussion lies in the fact that much of what we have learned about economic development is derived from experience in typical American communities. If Indian communities represent a generally different type, then any assumptions based on general American experience must be open to reexamination. And the significant differences among Indian communities constitute clear warning that each case must be considered on its own terms, with minimum assumptions concerning what factors are controlling. In short, none of the usual assumptions for economic development may be taken as automatically valid when we come to deal with the requirements of Indian economic development.

Skepticism here is reinforced by experience with similar development situations overseas. An eminent American economist, with long experience in the field, asserts, "not as an hypothesis, but as an empirical fact" that:

> To adapt almost any technique (even the spade, to replace the digging hoe) so that it will work well in a society with a quite different social and cultural complex and quite different personalities requires a very high degree of creativity.[1]

If spade instead of digging hoe, what of time-clock instead of the four seasons?

POLICY CHANGES AFFECTING INDIAN RESOURCES

Current programs of economic development made available to Indian communities by the Bureau and other public agencies do not yet reflect full practical recognition of the differences that have been

---

[1] E. E. Hagen, "What we do not know about the economics of development in low income societies," in *The Teaching of Development Economics*, Aldine, Chicago, 1967, p. 56.

identified in the preceding paragraphs. Some beginning has been made, however, from a starting point years ago that was essentially nondevelopmental in attitude and policy. Three significant changes are worth discussion.

For many decades the Secretary's trust responsibility for Indian lands was carried out essentially in terms of custodianship rather than of stewardship—of protection against loss rather as of responsible use for maximum Indian welfare and advancement. In recent decades, the Bureau has increasingly recognized an obligation to work with the Indians, not only in preventing deterioration of the physical resources of their lands, but also in bringing them up to optimum use and return. A successful claims action brought by a Wisconsin tribe whose forest had been poorly managed may have been the precipitating factor in this change of policy.

A second change relates to recognition of the resources of each Indian community as constituting an organic whole, not as a collection of range land, farm land, and forest land, each to be managed as though it stood alone. Recognition of a community's resources as a single complex has been promoted by the third significant change in approach, which is that of shifting emphasis from the Bureau to the Indians themselves.

This third change in policy has entailed the involvement of Federal agencies other than the Bureau of Indian Affairs and the Public Health Service in Indian programs and has had far broader impact than on resource use. Under this emphasis Indian communities have been enabled and encouraged to take full advantage of all Federal programs, not only those historically the responsibility of the Bureau of Indian Affairs and of the Indian Health Service in the Department of Health, Education, and Welfare, but those also of such agencies as the Economic Development Administration, Office of Economic Opportunity, Housing Assistance Administration, and Manpower Administration.

Reflecting these changes in attitude and policy toward Indian resources and the role of Indian communities in resource development have been at least two other alterations of Federal policy that are important for economic development. These affect education of Indians, both as children and as young adults, and the Indian community as a social organism requiring attention and development.

EDUCATION AND ECONOMIC DEVELOPMENT

Federal schools for Indian children have existed for nearly 100 years and in recent decades education has accounted for more than half of the Bureau's annual budget. The purpose of Indian education varied during the early years. One Secretary of the Interior explained its objective as being to "civilize" the Indians by training them for farming, homemaking, and the trades. Evidence of this narrow attitude is still found today among the influences brought to bear on our school programs and funding. Once there had been a persistent effort to de-Indianize the Indian child who attended a Federal school, particularly a boarding school. He was forbidden to use his native tongue and the classroom instruction, including such vocational emphasis as was found appropriate, followed lines and used textbooks originally designed for non-Indian children. Indeed, "Dick and Jane" primers continued in use down to only a few years ago.

There was a brief period, about 30 years ago, when the emphasis was markedly changed. The native tongue was encouraged and in some cases was used in the classroom. Primers told stories about Indians and were illustrated to show them in their native environment. Indian crafts were drawn upon for teaching materials and Indian lore was taught in the context of science and history studies. Vocational education was oriented to the needs of the community, as, for example, the unprecedented seafaring and commercial fishing training once offered at Wrangell Institute in Alaska.

This period was soon brought to an end by the criticism, from Indians as well as non-Indians, that the Bureau was attempting to keep the Indians as blanket Indians. It is only during the past few years that this ground has again been broken, Indian materials have again been introduced in the Bureau schools, and it has been recognized that English must be taught children as a second language. During the past year, for the first time, the Bureau has been able to open kindergartens, so that Indian children may avoid the lag in educational achievement that in the past has typically opened up during early years of schooling between them and non-Indian pupils. Support is also being given public school systems, which account for two-thirds of total Indian enrollment, for the introduction of kindergartens.

These are improvements, undertaken as essential for the education of the Indian child as a member of a community and of a culture, that also increase his capability as an adult to adapt himself to the economic requirements and opportunities of the Indian community and thus also of whatever other community he may later join. It is only in recent years that this basic contribution of education to the processes of community development, including its economic aspects, has been made.

ADULT VOCATIONAL TRAINING

Alongside the schooling of Indian children, including opportunities for vocational training, there has been introduced, beginning in 1956, adult vocational training, for Indians of ages 18–35. Such training was originally designed to make up for the deficiencies of the Bureau's program to assist Indians in finding employment in distant urban centers, relocating families who were willing to try their luck away from the Indian community. Adult vocational training continues to be focused primarily on such workers and their families. For some years, however, it has included on-the-job training for Indians employed at plants located on or near the community under the Bureau's industrial development program, which is discussed below. Moreover, the early emphasis upon relocating the Indian family at as great a distance as possible from its home community, has been ended. Vocational training now enables Indians to prepare for work wherever it may be found. The result is that a growing number find employment near enough their home community as never to lose their sense of identification with it or their availability to participate in its affairs and responsibilities. The AVT program, while continuing to open the way for the ambitious Indian wishing to join the outside world also helps strengthen the Indian community by enabling others to improve their incomes without abandoning their relatives and homeland.

The relationship of these policy and program elements to economic development may be judged in light of experience. This indicates that

Indian youth who keep up with school requirements and thereby complete high school satisfactorily, and who thereafter complete an AVT course, are exceptionally successful in finding and holding good jobs at good wages. To the extent they do so near the home community, the community is strengthened. To the extent they do so at a distance, the community benefits psychologically from the increasing demonstration that Indians who genuinely undertake to do so are fully capable of successfully competing in the non-Indian society.

COMMUNITY DEVELOPMENT

Community development, as recognized by the Bureau, is less a program in itself than a philosophy affecting all Bureau programs. Other Federal agencies—notably the Office of Economic Opportunity and the Economic Development Administration—are similarly groping toward the encouragement and support of constructive community effort among the Indian people. Results thus far are very encouraging. The nature and extent of participation by community members in the shaping and execution of development programs varies widely. In many communities such participation is still disappointingly low. The examples that follow are drawn from the many others, where the Indian people are learning to accept responsibility rather than to look to the Bureau for answers. In community after community, it is the Indian people themselves who decide what the programs shall be.

Navajo Experience.—We may begin with the Navajo, largest tribe of all, numbering about 100,000 members on the reservation. Here the shift of Bureau programs from custodianship to development has been accompanied by a change in the Bureau's role to that of technical adviser, real direction being provided by the Navajo themselves. The Navajo have become more than participants—they are innovators and leaders. Mistakes are made, recognized, and dealt with. Successes are frequent and rewarding, leading the way to further development.

Today, nearly all Federal schools on the Navajo Reservation are advised by local school boards. They make suggestions for goals and programs and assist in solution of problems. A listing of the accomplishments of these groups would be almost endless—setting up parental visitation schedules, arranging for discussions on scheduling, talking through the need for and importance of report cards, appearing in school assembly programs, trying to find solutions to the problem of absenteeism. Representatives from the boards have joined together at agency level to discuss common problems. These ventures are strengthened both by encouragement and guidance of the Bureau staff and by the Tribal Education Committee, an arm of the Navajo Tribal Council. The committee meets jointly on a regular basis with Bureau Education Staff, sharing ideas and programs. It conducts an annual enrollment drive to be certain that all Navajo children are in school. A recent major decision, accepted by the Bureau, was that new boarding school construction should be halted in favor of a master road system. Such a move would provide means for more children to attend on a day basis rather than living in boarding schools.

For many years the Navajo Tribe has recognized the industrial potential of the reservation. In order to conserve their vast timber resources they developed a commercial sawmill which was the forerunner of the present Navajo Forest Products Industries. This wholly owned tribal enterprise is directed by a Management Board of nine members, including five Navajo. Assets of the industry exceed $12 million. The Board is responsible for all aspects of the operation— mill management, capital expansion, and townsite development. More than nine out of 10 of the 500 employees are Navajo. A second venture of the tribe, along the same organizational pattern, is the Navajo Tribal Utility Authority. Assets of this facility now exceed $20 million and the present staff numbers nearly 200, only a few being non-Navajo.

Meeting employment needs of the Navajo people in the expanding economy has largely been an activity of the tribal relocation and placement committee, the personnel department, the apprenticeship coordinator, and an interagency committee on migrant labor. Although industrialization and urbanization have brought new jobs to the reservation, and local on-the-job training has increased tremendously, many Navajo people continue to move elsewhere for the types of employment they seek. At the same time, an adult education program is supplementing cooperative Bureau and tribal efforts to provide basic education needs for a growing labor force. It almost goes without saying that the adult education courses are designed to meet local demands, such as basic skills, driver education, and community living. Such efforts prepare people to adjust to the many new living situations being created both on and off the reservation.

The Navajo people are expressing themselves through all channels of government, both tribal and Federal, but a most important ingredient has been added with the implementation of the community development program. While it began as a Bureau program, the Navajo people accepted it, from the first seminar, as their own, naming a tribal community development committee and local committee at each agency. By July 1969, community development seminars, planned largely by Navajo people, will have been held at each of the five agencies. Suggestions from the completed seminars are already being incorporated in existing programs. Full impact of these new voices of the people will be felt in the new Navajo way of life.

Billings area.—In another jurisdiction, that of our Billings area office, tribal housing authorities have been established on all reservations. The membership of these authorities is predominantly tribal, but also includes local non-Indians. All housing authorities in this area have assumed primary responsibility for the conduct of the housing programs financed by the Housing Assistance Administration, Department of Housing and Urban Development. On several reservations the Bureau's housing improvement program, HIP, has been contracted to the housing authorities. We are moving in the direction of contracting with housing authorities also for the employment of housing construction representatives, which heretofore have been Federal employees. Thus, on a number of reservations in this area the tribes have taken over almost complete management of the construction and rehabilitation of Indian housing.

On Crow, Northern Cheyenne, Blackfeet, and Fort Peck Reservations, the tribes have been very active in the planning and implementing of industrial development. Perhaps the best illustration is the Crow Industrial Development Commission, which was created at the time the tribe received $10 million of judgment funds. This commission was given full responsibility for the use of $1 million of tribal funds dedicated for industrial development. This commission has not been a rubberstamp organization, but has actually assumed full manage responsibility for the program, with Bureau employees serving only as technical advisors.

The commission's first accomplishment, establishment of a manufacturing plant, proved abortive when the company failed, but the tribe and commission have persisted, with encouraging results. The Big Horn Carpet Co., after initial difficulties leading to a change of management, is operating satisfactorily, with prospect that employment may eventually reach 400 rather than the earlier target of 100. In recent months, the Crow Industries Feed Mill has been established with tribal participation; it also appears solidly grounded, though offering less employment potential.

Warm Springs.—In the Pacific Northwest, the Confederated Tribes of Warm Springs, Oreg., provide a case study, perhaps a model, for Indian comprehensive planning through their experiences in active participation in such planning during the past 3 years. Nowhere among the tribes of the Northwest is there an equivalent example of direct Indian control and participation in developmental planning.

For many years, the Warm Springs Tribes have made steady progress in the general area of economic development, but it was not until mid-1967 that they embarked upon a truly integrated comprehensive planning program. Prior to mid-1967, a variety of planning reports, feasibility studies, basic data compilations, and the like had been developed by the tribes through various means. These included both tribally funded and Bureau-funded studies, both tribally conceived and Bureau-conceived studies.

The Warm Springs Tribes were, in effect, trailbreakers in the Northwest in comprehensive planning for Indian tribes, and the path was not always easy. From the time of the resolution (1963) to the date of the actual application to the Department of Housing and Urban Development (DHUD), some 4 years elapsed during which laborious steps were taken and severe obstacles overcome. Probably the most difficult and time-consuming effort was devoted to the establishment of a tribal planning committee and that committee's subsequent development of statements of tribal objectives and goals. These statements served to clarify and make more concrete in the minds of the planning committee and the tribal council both what problems were to be faced and, essentially, what kind of reservation and communities the Warm Springs people wanted for themselves and their children in the coming years.

Among other obstacles that were overcome during this period were the need for modification of existing Federal legislation to make Indian tribes eligible for planning assistance under section 701 of the Housing Act of 1954 and the lack in Oregon of enabling legislation that would allow the State planning agency to contract with DHUD on behalf of Indian tribes in Oregon. During this period, however, the tribes and the Bureau worked with the State planning agency to develop a planning program that met State and DHUD requirements and, at the same time, came as near as possible to meeting tribal goals and objectives.

Perhaps the most significant aspect of the Warm Springs planning saga was the control and participation exercised by the tribes along each step of the way. The tribes set the operation in motion, objectives and goals were established by the tribes, enabling legislation was introduced at the specific request of the tribes, and a consulting firm to assist in planning was selected by the tribes. As of March 1969, the first phase of the comprehensive plan was nearing completion and the entire effort continued to revolve around tribal control and participation.

II. COMMUNITY PROGRESS AND BROADENED FEDERAL PROGRAMS

As a result of many factors, specifically including the community efforts of the Indian people themselves, their lag in achievement behind national norms has been reduced in recent years. The current lag continues, however, to present difficulties for economic development. These require special program efforts, and a high degree of interagency cooperation to maximize Indian opportunities, capability, and participation.

A most encouraging aspect is the continuing improvement in education. In 1960 such improvement was manifest in the fact that 73 percent of young adult Indians, ages 20 to 24, had completed eighth grade, as compared with only 51 percent for Indians aged 25 and over. Similarly, 30 percent of the young adults had completed high school, compared to only 9 percent for the older population. The 1970 census of population will unquestionably disclose continued progress; we already know that secondary school enrollment of Indians increased, as a percentage of the secondary-school-age population, from 47 percent in 1960 to 69 percent in 1967.

The improvement in education is reflected in the increasing social and political responsibilities exemplified in the community situations described in preceding pages. In a crucial aspect, however, Indian progress remains disappointingly slow, that of income. Although Indian incomes have risen in recent years, there has been no lessening of the gap between them and those typical of the United States. Thus, it is estimated that in 1967 per capita income of Indians in the Bureau's service population was somewhat less than $850, to be compared with the United States average of $3,159 and of $1,896 for the State having the lowest average (Mississippi). Put in the more familiar terms of family income, the Bureau estimates that 75 percent of the families in Indian communities have incomes below $3,000, which is one of the poverty benchmarks. The official U.S. poverty percentage, 24 in 1959, had declined to 16 by 1967.

The great and continuing lack that accounts for substantially lower incomes in the Indian communities is that of wage employment; no prospective improvement in the management of resources or employment of Indians in resource use can yield the equivalent of the absorption of the idle reservation labor force (running to 40 percent and more) through such employment at standard wage rates.

CHARACTERISTICS OF THE RESERVATION LABOR FORCE

Wage employment on the reservations, or sufficiently nearby to permit commuting, requires both job opportunities and employable skills. Both are in short supply. This is especially true of employable skills when account is taken of typical Indian disinclination to conform to the daily regimen required by modern factory production; possession of a skill is not enough to make it truly employable. It is important also to recognize that industrial employment is in continuing competition with other payroll opportunities.

The most significant source of income to Indians on virtually all of the larger reservations is employment with the Bureau of Indian Affairs and the Indian Health Service. Not only are most permanent nonskilled or semiskilled agency jobs filled by local Indian people (bus drivers, school support staff, hospital support staffs, maintenance workers, road crews, and a variety of professional aids, etc.) but each year many part-time employees are hired for special construction projects, forest fire suppression, et ceteria. Usually more than half of all Federal employees, although by no means the best paid employees, of the major Federal agencies are recruited from local community members.

Since 1963, first with Area Redevelopment Administration projects, and more recently through local employment opportunities funded by OEO, EDA, and other agencies, the number of intermittent jobs for reservation Indians has expanded dramatically. On the Navajo Reservation, for example, almost 4,000 Indian people, mostly Navajo, work for the Bureau of Indian Affairs; another 650 are employed by the Indian Health Service; and more than 2,900 jobs have been funded for Navajos under the CAP programs sponsored by the Office of Navajo Economic Opportunity. A total of 2,250 are employed by the Navajo Tribe itself—an aggregate of more than 9,000 tribal or Federally funded jobs. (Not included in these figures are those Navajo employed for shorter periods in the Neighborhood Youth Corps activities, in work training programs under title V, or in other sorts of training activities for which subsistence is paid.)

The varied activities alluded to above are far more under the control of the Indian employees than may appear on the surface. Indian concepts about time, production standards, attitudes toward absenteeism—all tend to prevail. This logically derives from the fact that none of these activities produces a product against which production standards can be measured realistically and that supervisory performance in large measure is evaluated against employee satisfaction.

"*Income Maintenance.*"—A second factor which must be evaluated in considering industrial development activities derives from the *de facto* program of income maintenance that is inherent in the reservation system. The mass of indian unemployed or underemployed have minimal but nonetheless very real income subsidies, which have developed gradually and which have been pretty much integrated into the cultural life of the group. Most Indians pay no rent on their inadequate homes, nor are taxes paid on the trust land they own. Comprehensive medical services are available, as is virtually free education for Indian children. In the instance of children from the poorest of Indian families, and for those from broken or disrupted homes, Federal boarding schools further stretch limited cash income.

Thus, welfare payments, to which no significant social stigma is attached, permanent or intermittent work or training activities funded by various Federal agencies, and seasonal or casual labor in agriculture, forestry, or whatever unskilled jobs are available in the community area, are the economic "knowns" against which industrial employment must compete.

Indian Sharing.—Another factor that has an unknown effect on the sorts of economic reorientation that industrial employment implies, derives from our almost total ignorance about how incomes from multiple sources are allocated and distributed to the members of an Indian nuclear or an extended family. That Indians share what they have with relatives is widely accepted; we need to know more about how. A hypothetical Indian extended family, not necessarily living under one roof, might be composed of parents, sons and daughters with children of their own, as well as minor children. Between them they have a BIA bus driver's salary, some income allotted from farm lands leased to non-Indians, seasonal income from agricultural labor, two aid-to-dependent children allotments, some limited income from the sale of cattle, as well as intermittent wages from a local CAP program funded by the Office of Economic Opportunity. We have no idea how far this income from all such varied sources goes toward meeting the felt economic needs of this family; we have no objective basis for assuming that the "unemployed" members of this not atypical reservation family will be drawn to industrial jobs, should they become available.

Social disorganization, with accompanying manifestations such as drinking, broken homes, fatherless children, etc., are the rule rather than the exception in many Indian communities. In this social environment, women not uncommonly are the active family heads, and as such, provide a better potential for developing a work force, than do Indian men. Indian men with a long history of unemployment, or of intermittent or casual labor, seem to treat the prospects of steady employment with considerable trepidation. Typically, they fear that they cannot handle the job, often hiding their fear behind a good deal of bluster and rationalization that the job is "woman's work"; that it lacks status, etc.

Indian men, of the sort referred to above, must be supported by a good deal more "training," to make them competitive, industrial employees than simply teaching them the vocational skills associated with the job itself. Assisting socially and psychologically handicapped persons permanently to join an industrial work force, whether they be from an urban ghetto or a rural reservation, is both complex and expensive. To reject the hard-to-employ leaves unsolved major social problems; too often this happens in attracting industry to a reservation or to an area near a reservation.

There is wide agreement that many reservation Indians view open-air jobs, in which they can work with other Indians in large groups, under easy-going supervision, without too much attention paid to absenteeism or tardiness, as offering ideal working conditions. The Indian Division of the Civilian Conservation Corps, provided jobs of this sort in the 1930's and early 1940's; this period is looked back upon by many Indians as the high point in their work experience. The widespread employment of many Indians in the wartime economy in no small way, resulted from the job-conditioning gained in CCC work. That this sort of activity remains popular with Indians was clearly established in the early 1960's when CCC-type activities were briefly reintroduced in the Accelerated Public Works Program under ARA. Administrators on many reservations where these activities were initiated, reported that Indian men lined up, many bringing their own axes or other tools, well ahead of the announced hour. In addition, many others who had left the community, including some who had been employed steadily for some time, returned to the reservation to join APW labor gangs.

It is safe to generalize, that Indian workers tend to prefer comfortable and satisfying employment at a lesser wage to a high income derived from less satisfactory working conditions. Thus, in more than a few instances, employment in newly established reservation factories, has been seen as interim employment until such time as BIA, OEO, or tribal jobs become available.

OVERCOMING GEOGRAPHIC ISOLATION

Despite the relative isolation of most Indian communities, there are many lines of production that today can realistically consider establishment of plants on or near reservations. However, difficulties of two types must be faced. On the one hand, small plants, reasonably geared to the size of the reservation labor force, are likely to be characterized by marginal management and shaky financing. On the other, companies that are well managed, are likely to be of such size that even a single plant may dominate the Indian community, involving serious disadvantages, at least until adjustments can be made, that tend to offset the advantages of employment and income. With the steady expansion of the Bureau's industrial development program (see part III, below), it has proved possible to protect Indian tribes and communities against the riskier opportunities offered to them. And to date, only one example of the second type of problem has arisen to require community adjustment to the wholly new problem of major expansion of job opportunities.

It is the high value and low bulk of a wide range of products, characteristics that permit reliance on air transportation, that explains the increased feasibility of establishing plants on the reservations. Equally important, the Bureau has had substantial success in on-the-job training of reservation residents for employment in nearby plants. Under most circumstances, indeed, it is such training that provides the final inducement to the manufacturer to locate in or near an Indian community.

PROGRAMS OF OTHER FEDERAL AGENCIES

Economic development of Indian communities has been supported since 1962 by other Federal agencies, beginning that year with the Area Redevelopment Administration, predecessor of the Economic Development Administration, in the Department of Commerce. For the first time, a non-Indian program was made available to Indian communities. In the following year, legal difficulties that for 25 years had barred construction of public housing on Indian trust lands, were overcome and this non-Indian program also was opened up to Indian communities. Such programs have not only been important in themselves—substandard housing in particular being a major adverse social, educational, and economic factor—but have benefited the Indians by altering the setting in which they now participate in programs of the Federal Government and other public agencies and deal generally with the "outside world."

The public resources devoted to the development of Indian communities have been substantially expanded by the contributions of the major agencies already identified and by lesser programs of the Department of Agriculture, the Department of Health, Education, and Welfare, and the Small Business Administration.

American Indians, though this is less true of tribal members than of leaders, have come to recognize, that their communities now have access to many programs other than those of the Bureau and the Indian Health Service. The introduction of new and supplementary programs has helped both the Indians and the Bureau move away from the patronage-dependency relationship that for decades held progress to an intolerably slow pace.

Although the Indians' reliance on Federal support is as great as ever, they no longer equate the Bureau with the entire Government and they are learning to approach the Bureau as well as other agencies on terms similar to those characteristic of other groups in their dealings with government. In the process, they are discovering more and more that they can do for themselves. The Bureau, for its part, is benefiting from demonstration that adequate and flexible funding can transform programs, that Indians can be given responsibilities comparable to those of other American groups, and that Indian efforts that cannot be reinforced through traditional programs may receive necessary assistance through new ones.

INTERAGENCY COORDINATION

The rapid expansion of programs available for Indian community and economic development poses matters of coordination of such programs and of the efforts of all parties to assure their effective operation. Coordination has several aspects, of which three have thus far been recognized and acted upon.

The core of program coordination must be handled on the reservation and by the Indian tribal council or other responsible body that speaks for the community. This is not only the logical focus, but without it programs would continue to be for the Indians rather than by the community and could hardly be expected to succeed over time. Such a core responsibility, moreover, conforms completely with the preference of all agencies for dealing directly with the tribe; it does not preclude the tribe from seeking advice and counsel from familiar quarters. The Bureau has stressed both the tribe's role in deciding how programs shall be combined to serve Indian goals and the tribe's direct responsibility toward each participating agency for fulfillment of commitments that may be undertaken.

Administration of agency programs to supply the mix that is decided upon by tribal authorities calls for coordination among the agencies. The pragmatic approach here is provided by the Indian desk of each major agency contributing to Indian development and, for the Bureau, an Assistant to the Commissioner who has interagency relations as his major assignment. Typically, this is an assignment to assist the agency head and his principal staff in keeping lines of communication open, to monitor daily interagency developments, and to assure that practical problems requiring conference table discussions get such attention. Responsibility for promoting decent harmony among Indian program operations—one definition of practical coordination—is shared by all line officials of the participating agencies; it cannot feasibly be limited to a single office or staff.

The creation of the national council for Indian opportunity in March 1968, provided a capstone to the structure of program coordination. This body, composed of seven cabinet members and six Indian leaders, enables a continual review to be made of Indian needs and programs and permits decisions to be reached concerning administrative policy and program implementation that should be binding on all agencies represented on the council.

III. Joint Development—Progress and Prospect

Supporting and reinforcing the developmental efforts of Indian tribes and communities, the Bureau of Indian Affairs directly encourages and promotes Indian economic development. It does so through programs of resource development and management, of training in marketable skills, and for the creation of opportunities for wage employment in establishments induced to locate in "Indian country," as well as in tribal enterprises. Particularly with respect to the industrial aspects of these programs and to the public works needed to provide essential "social overhead," the Bureau's programs have in recent years been greatly exceeded by those of other Federal agencies that now also serve Indian communities, especially the Economic Development Administration and the Department of Housing and Urban Development.

NATURAL RESOURCE USE

Early in the Bureau's history, major emphasis was placed on making farmers of the Indians, but only in the Southwest have they generally taken to agriculture in earnest. Elsewhere the greatest success has been with livestock production. On only a few reservations have Indian farmers done well with dryfarming. Where grazing is a more common activity of Indians, irrigated agriculture, involving the integration of dryland grazing with irrigated pasture and hay production, has been very successful. Recently, however, Indian farmers in the Great Plains States have also become receptive to irrigated agriculture. Some are now assuming the initiative in developing irrigated agriculture, making use of pump irrigation, which demands precise and efficient management. Demands are now being heard, too, that small farm units be consolidated into larger operating units for improved and efficient production; action which the Bureau has urged upon the Indians for years. But small farm units and fractionated ownership continue as major problems requiring attention. Possibly the most obvious need in all aspects of Indian agriculture throughout the West is the upgrading of productivity. To meet the need of extended instruction and information for Indian farmers and ranchers, existing inventories of land resources must be completed through expanded technical assistance. On the basis of such complete data, progress can be speeded in the improvement of cultivation, cropping practices, rotation, farm enterprise combinations, and of management practices in general.

Water is rapidly becoming the most important and valuable resource in much of Indian country. Progress has been made in the past decade in stabilizing and improving Indian economies through expanded use of water for irrigated agriculture. Streams and lakes have been made valuable recreational assets to attract increasing numbers of paying hunters, fishermen, and vacationers to utilize associated facilities. Increasing use is also being made of water supplies for Indian domestic, commercial, and industrial uses. While Indians are looking forward to making greater use of their waters, others have put them to prior uses, thus jeopardizing Indian water rights. This is currently delaying Indian economic development activities. An excellent illustration is the situation at the Pyramid Lake Reservation, Nev. Here, despite efforts to stabilize the lake's water level to permit the establishment of comprehensive recreational development, the flow of water into the lake is being reduced by increasing upstream diversions for irrigation development of non-Indian lands. Throughout the areas where water rights are essential to the full development of Indian lands, accelerated development is needed to protect Indian water rights, by prior Indian use, from continuation of such encroachment.

Among other Indian natural resources are forests and minerals. Both are under use—at several reservations, under intensive use—creating sizable income and employment opportunities. An excellent example is the Navajo Forest Products Industry on the Navajo Reservation, which in fiscal year 1968 employed 452 Navajo Indians and paid $1,526,000 in wages to Indians. The tribe received $330,000 for stumpage payments, and $533,000 in net proceeds above costs. The capital value of the plant in that fiscal year was estimated to be $12 million. A continuing vital need in the forestry program is funding for timber inventories and growth projections. This is a similar need with reference to minerals. Minerals investigations to date are inadequate and much more survey work is needed.

Under the influence of Bureau resource programs, substantial gains have been made in the conservation and improvement of Indian natural resources and in the income derived from them.

• Total gross value of annual agricultural production on Indian reservations increased from $133 to $171 million during the period 1962–68. Production by Indian operators increased from $46 to $59 million.

• Lands used by Indians for agricultural purposes increased from 30.5 to 46 million acres.

• Annual value of livestock production from Indian lands increased from $47 to $61 million. Of this total, livestock production by Indian operators increased from $22.8 to $32.5 million.

• Production by Indians using irrigated lands increased from $8 to $11.3 million annually.

• Indian income from outdoor recreation and wildlife use-fees increased from $1.2 to $2.1 million yearly.

• More visitors using outdoor recreation resources came to the reservations, the number rising by 1966 to 7.1 million visitor days, from 3.7 million days in 1962.

Dramatic increases occurred during 1962–68 in Indian timber harvests and related benefits, which included stumpage income, employment, and wages.

- Between fiscal years 1961 and 1968, the annual Indian timber harvest increased from 490 to 952 million board feet.
- Annual stumpage income nearly doubled—from $8.5 to $21.1 million.
- Permanent year-long jobs increased from 3,430 to 6,440.
- Related wages rose from $17 to $32 million a year.

INDUSTRIAL DEVELOPMENT

In addition to this noteworthy improvement in the economic utilization of Indian natural resources, progress at what may prove to be an accelerating rate has been recorded in the field of industrial development. Because of the wage employment at stake, such development, as already noted, is especially important. This progress has been achieved against the unusual cultural background that has been described in preceding pages, which clearly is weighted rather seriously against the introduction of modern industry, with its time clocks, assembly lines, and production norms. With the advantage of a period of unprecedented sustained national prosperity, however, and with increasing support from other Federal agencies, the Bureau has succeeded in helping the Indian tribes add 132 plants to the 18 that at the end of 1961 were operating on or near the reservations. Indian employment in such plants increased from 1,050 to 4,630 by the end of 1968. Compared with the total reservation labor force of about 130,000, employment of 4,600 is a small figure; compared with 1,050 jobs in 1961, however, it represents a more than fourfold increase in 7 years. Continuation at this rate would bring industrial employment to close to 20,000 by 1975.

The record of this period provides clear evidence that, with training, Indian manpower can become a highly productive labor resource even for rather complex operations. For example, during 1965, the Fairchild Camera & Instrument Corp. located a branch plant of its semiconductor Division at Shiprock, N. Mex. on the Navaho Indian Reservation; by early 1969, this company had increased its Indian work force from 477 a year earlier to more than 1,000. Within the next 6 months the Bureau planned to help the company recruit and train an additional 500 Indian workers to be employed in a new $750,000 plant financed by the tribe.

The Bureau programs contributing to this impressive result are shared among the agency's several constituent offices. There is close operating rapport between the Economic Development and the Community Services Offices, respectively responsible for the industrial development and the employment assistance programs, the latter including on-the-job training. Similarly the Education Office of the Bureau is not only aware of the contribution that general educational advance makes to economic as to other community development, but is also actively cooperating with the Economic Development Office in such innovations as courses in distributive education. These are only the latest of vocationally oriented courses that help Indian youth learn about the American economy and prepare to find their place in its Indian variant.[2]

The Bureau's industrial development program is the joint responsibility of the Economic Development and Community Services Offices, as just noted. Their joint goal is to establish wage employment opportunities on or near the reservations and to enable members of the Indian labor force to acquire the skills necessary for such employment.

The role of the Office of Economic Development with respect to industrial and commercial development (apart from tribal enterprises, to be discussed below) is basically that of assisting the Indian communities to improve their physical facilites for industrial purposes and to bring their advantages of labor supply, facilities, and location, particularly the first of these, to the attention of industrial concerns. This entails competition with literally huundreds of communities throughtout the country which similarly seek to attract new and larger payrolls and thereby to strengthen and perhaps also to diversify and stabilize their economies. In light of the keeness of this competition, the expansion of industrial employment in the Indian communities at an average compound rate of 20 percent during the past 7 years is particularly remarkable. This office also works closely with the tribal authorities to provide financing from the Bureau's revolving loan fund and assistance in negotiating financing from other Federal or from commercial sources. as well as to provide expert counsel and technical advice in their negotiations with industrial prospects, other Federal agencies, and State and local authorities.

The lack of dependable and adequate financing has been a serious deterrent to Indian economic development. The Bureau's credit program is presently limited to (a) administration of a revolving fund for loans involving a total of $25.1 million appropriated over a period of 34 years; (b) use of tribal funds for the same purposes as loans made from the revolving fund; and (c) assistance in obtaining financing from customary lenders, both governmental and private. The significance of the foregoing amounts appropriated for the revolving fund is apparent when compared with the total financing of $324.5 million used in 1968. The revolving loan fund was the source of only 7.8 percent of the total, while Indian funds represented 28.4 percent, and funds from customary lenders amounted to 63.8 percent of the total. The 1968 total represents an increase of $33.6 million from 1967, of which amount less than $500,000 was available, under the heavy demands of other needs, for industrial development.

---

[2] It may be worth noting that the interdependence of the several Bureau programs is recognized not only in the daily working relationships among the several divisions of the 3 program offices, and within the more tightly knit staffs of the area offices and agencies, but in the Washington office, through the device of the Commissioner's small staff. This is composed of the Deputy Commissioner, the Assistant Commissioners in charge of programs of community services, economic development, and education, and those responsible for the staff functions of administration, engineering, and program coordination, one or more assistants to the Commissioner, and the information and congressional relations officers.

Meetings of the small staff are held at call of the Commissioner, rather than being scheduled periodically for routine reporting on current activities. Once the major policy or program item occasioning the call has been disposed of, the opportunity is regularly used to canvass all participants for matters that are of general concern and that may at a later stage themselves call for a meeting of the small staff. To supplement working relationships and such conferences, there is distributed daily to each member of the small staff the Commissioner's reading file, made up of copies of all correspondence of the preceding day that is regarded by the Commissioner or any member of the small staff, as meriting such attention. This selectivity avoids the circulation of a bulky complete daily file and makes it possible for each member of the small staff readily to follow the flow of key correspondence arising from Bureau operations.

It is estimated that Indian financing requirements will expand over the next 5 years by more than $660 million, to a total of nearly $990 million. Of this increase, $98 million is expected to be needed by the end of 1969. A bill submitted by the Department of the Interior is now before the Congress providing for a $100 million increase in Indian financing. Of that total, $85 million would be utilized in increasing the revolving loan fund, and $15 million would be used in the guarantee and insurance of loans from private lending sources. It is estimated that the $15 million guarantee and insurance fund will generate an additional $105 million in loans to the Indian people.

The labor force of the typical Indian community (see pages 26–28, above), has been found to possess aptitudes that are particularly attractive to makers of a wide variety of products. The general aptitude tests (GAT) of the U.S. Department of Labor are comprised of 12 tests that have been found to yield a useful measure of nine aptitudes shown to be important for successful performance in a wide variety of occupations. Tests of Indian workers tend rather uniformly to disclose above-normal aptitude for spatial perception, form perception, manual dexterity, and eye-hand coordination. Such aptitudes are particularly relevant to such occupations as machinist, sheet metal worker, carpenter, office machine serviceman, equipment assembler, and machine operator, among others. In recent years numerous electrical equipment, radio manufacturing, electronics equipment manufacturing, and plastics products manufacturing industries have been induced to locate on reservations to take advantage of the attractive manpower opportunities.

It is the role of the Office of Community Services to work with the tribal authorities in identifying the skills already available in the Indian labor force and the aptitudes and vocational interests in on-the-job training, so that an approach to industrial prospects may be well documented. Thereafter, when such a prospect has been persuaded of the advantages offered, the two offices share responsibility in negotiating contracts for such training on the premises of the plant that is to go into operation. Here, too, the Bureau finds itself providing counsel and technical assistance in the related negotiations between the tribe, perhaps also the employer, and the Department of Labor, State authorities, et cetera.

The physical development of the community, with respect to housing, roads, and community facilities, is commonly very important to specific industrial development negotiations. Programs for these purposes, substantially supplemented by programs of other Federal agencies, are the responsibility of other parts of the Bureau, with which the industrial development and on-the-job training staffs work closely.

COMMERCIAL DEVELOPMENT AND TRIBAL ENTERPRISE

The 150 enterprises operating in "Indian country" at the end of 1968 included 17 commercial establishments, employing 150 Indian workers. The total also included four tribal enterprises, none of them commercial, employing 253 Indians.

These categories include only those ventures that have been undertaken with the Bureau's assistance and that reflect the use of Bureau resources for development purposes. An additional number of both

351

types of enterprise represent Indian initiative, in which the Bureau has played an advisory role apart from any specifically developmental program. An important example of tribal enterprise is the Navajo Forest Products Industries, already described. It is appropriate to omit such enterprises from the records of program accomplishments. Bureau field reports are being revised currently to provide both broader and more detailed coverage of all aspects of the reservations and their development. Such important aspects as the establishment of enterprises outside the Bureau's own programs will be included in this broadened scope.

PROGRAMS OF OTHER AGENCIES

Since 1962, as observed earlier, the role of other Federal agencies in providing assistance and support to Indian communities has expanded greatly. Much of this assistance, particularly from the Office of Economic Opportunity, has promoted the largely noneconomic aspects of community development. Other contributions have had a more direct impact on economic development, through the provision of roads and housing. Still other programs have related directly to economic and indeed industrial and commercial development, the latter including recreation and tourist-oriented facilities. Programs of this last category are almost exclusively those of the Economic Development Administration in the Department of Commerce.

The results of these programs, which in view of their size can only awkwardly be termed supplementary to the Bureau's efforts, are of substantial benefit to the Indian people. Some perspective on the relative role played by the Bureau and the Economic Development Administration may be gained by comparison between the funds currently being made available by the two agencies.

The Bureau's industrial development program currently has less than $800,000 for the entire range of its promotional, advisory, and negotiating services. This is supplemented from two other Bureau sources, the credit and the on-the-job training programs. Due to the extreme stringency of funds of the Bureau's revolving fund for loans, the extension of credit for purposes of industrial development amounted during 1968 to less than $500,000 while funds for on-the-job training were less than $2,250,000. The total of all Bureau funds comparable to those available through EDA was thus about $3.5 million. In fiscal 1968, EDA funded Indian industrial development, through grants and loans, in a total amount of nearly $19 million; for 1969 the allotted amount is $30 million, compared to $26 million allotted in 1968.

It is significant that the Bureau's industrial development program currently accounts for only $800,000 of a total of about $3.5 million (between one-fifth and one-fourth) of the Bureau's total funding of such efforts. The Bureau's funding, in turn, is only about one-sixth as great as that supplied last year by EDA. On the reasonable assumption that the Bureau's promotional, advisory, and negotiating services are essential, it may well be that EDA would have come closer last year to its allotment of $26 million and this year would fully achieve its target of $30 million for Indians, if Bureau funds had been larger.

It has often been argued that Bureau programs are inadequately financed. Experience since 1962, when such financing has been provided in this massive "supplementary" fashion, with such impressive initial results, yet falling short of reasonable targets, tends to support this view.

Ignoring at this stage the complex matter of assuring community situations, that in themselves are reasonably conducive to development along economic as well as more general lines, it may be useful to outline the steps that have been found effective as a systematic approach to economic development:

(1) Evaluation of economic potentials and alternatives;

(2) Coordination with State and local development agencies and groups;

(3) Establishment of priorities for development—taking into account not only resources to be developed, but schools, homes, medical services, recreational services, etc.

(4) A sophisticated promotional program integrated with the overall program.

As fully as possible, this is the approach now being used by the Bureau. Under it, the following activities are receiving attention as essential to continued success and improvement on the past record:

Community inventories.—For each Indian area we need more reliable current information on population, labor force, unemployment, prevailing wage rates, existing commerce and industry, transportation facilities in relation to regional and national markets, utilities and water services, State and local tax rates, composition of local governments, availability of raw materials, schools and medical services and quality of each, and culture and recreational facilities and services.

Much of the data required is now being gathered by the Bureau through a reporting system instituted in 1967. A uniform format is used in the preparation of Reservation Development Studies (RDS) for the principal reservations. These are designed to assemble and set forth such data as described above and any other information that may be found necessary for comprehensive planning and economic development. Thus, it is planned for the RDS to be updated annually and expanded to include additional diverse elements, such as data on housing, investment and consumer credit requirements, migration estimates, and educational and skill levels.

Other data require systematic gathering and statistical reporting by other agencies. The Bureau has consulted closely with the Bureau of the Census in its planning of the 1970 census of population and housing, to assure that the reports will be as valuable as possible for purposes of the Indians and of the Bureau. It is planned, moreover, to build on the 1970 census through interim compilation, in cooperation with the Census Bureau, of data yielding even more complete information on Indian communities.

The Reservation Development Studies are the responsibility of the Agency staffs, which are benefiting from increasing Indian participation. A particularly important example of Indian involvement in the comprehensive development approach is that of Zuni Pueblo in New Mexico, which is participating in the process of formulating a planning model for reservation development planning. Zuni Pueblo was selected as representative in terms of significant area and population, geographic isolation, and need. In addition, the Zuni have a leadership that has demonstrated a desire to participate actively in the development of comprehensive planning techniques. Also, the Zuni have formulated shortrun development goals and have a self-imposed tax system designed to augment local financing. Further, the Zuni Pueblo has been designated by the Economic Development Administration as an EDA action area. An area policy paper required by EDA was completed in 1967, providing additional planning impetus.

In addition to Indian involvement, one of the ingredients essential to the success of a comprehensive reservation development operation is the participation of appropriate Federal, State, and local government agencies. At the Zuni Pueblo contact at the field level has already been made with several agencies, including New Mexico State officials, Indian Health Service, EDA and HUD. The Office of Economic Opportunity has a staff member assigned to Zuni who is a primary participant on the tribal planning staff. Other exploratory discussions have been held with field staff representatives of Federal Water Pollution Control Administration (Interior) and the Soil Conservation and Forest Services (Agriculture).

Other community inventory items.—A program of modern large-scale topographic mapping has been developed jointly with the U.S. Geographic Survey. With adequate funding and accelerated execution, it can be completed throughout Indian country by 1973. A series of reports has been planned to identify specific business opportunities in various areas of Indian country. Such reports will pinpoint industries able to use the unique combination of natural resources, labor supply, and market potential existing in specific Indian areas.

Urban and regional planning.—In addition to new programs already underway, up-to-date plans must be developed, including master plans and adequate zoning regulations for all Indian lands capable of urban development. Area-wide planning and the employment of professional urban planners is necessary.

Community organization.—In each region an industrial development team is needed, comprised not only of tribal and Federal representatives but also of economic development specialists of State governments, railroads, utilities, local governments, businessmen, and organizations such as Chambers of Commerce. One of the important benefits of such an organization is an increase in the gainful employment of local Indians by local private industry and business.

Equalizing Indian job opportunities.—The Bureau has become aware both of relatively high employment of Indians by a few of the many enterprises located in the vicinity of Indian communities and of the generally low Indian employment in such establishments. Preliminary work is underway for a survey to provide reliable information defining the situation and opening the way for concerted efforts to correct it.

Equalizing Indian job opportunities is something the Bureau can help accomplish. It will involve closer cooperation with local officials and businessmen and an intensified counseling and training program for Indians in their home communities.

Training Indians.—Large pools of trainable labor can be decisive in our efforts to attract new industrial payrolls to Indian communities. However, a labor pool that not only is unskilled but is totally unconditioned to the concept of regularly scheduled work, continues to be a serious obstacle to maximum commercial-industrial development of some otherwise promising Indian communities. In the long run, it is the social climate of the community and the social health of the community's residents that suffer from on-again off-again employment situations.

Current Indian training programs are not adequately designed to meet all the specific needs of particular employers—and this is sometimes the crux of the absentee and drop-out problem. There is discontent on the part both of the employee and of the employer, which eventually results in strained employee-employer relations in the industry as a whole. Some of these problems unquestionably could be overcome by a more flexible and varied training service that will:

- Send Indians for specific training to an existing plant operation off the reservation, if this is required.
- Provide preinduction training in basic education and skills, in cooperation with the employer if he so desires.
- Provide onsite and on-the-job training with the employer's supervisors as instructors. (The Bureau's current training program generally operates this way.)
- Provide vocational training centers in Indian country to offer continual opportunities for skill training and a manpower pool for industrial selection.
- Provide followup services in counseling and employee relations with the local employers.

Developing Indian-owned commercial enterprises.—Training for managerial and submanagerial skills is equally important to creation of viable economies and balanced social structures in Indian communities. Except for the limited number of higher education scholarships the Bureau now offers Indian youth, which are aimed at fostering professional skills, little if any attention has been given to the need for preparing Indians to manage their own business and personal affairs.

The Bureau is therefore giving close attention to the areas of business management training and distributive education (sales, marketing, and merchandising). For example, during 1968, as a modest step, a 10-week program was completed, in cooperation with the University of Wisconsin and the American Cooperative League, to train at least one Indian from each Bureau area how to set up and manage marketing cooperatives for the benefit of large numbers of Indian people.

Developing tourist opportunities.—The development of a modern tourist industry under Indian ownership will be sponsored to take advantage of the tremendous tourist potential growing annually in the United States. This development calls for building facilities, roads, and other capital investments, combined with planning and control of land use to prevent improper development of commercial facilities detrimental to the most productive use of Indian properties.

Underway is an effort to extend franchise operations into Indian country. Indians, trained in management by the chain operator, would in time become the managers of motels and restaurants located on or near reservations which offer tourist potentials.

General promotion.—Indian lands and the Indian labor force suffer from neglect of the responsibility to carry on a sophisticated promotional effort. Such haphazard publicity as they do receive is either romanticized or in the form of unfounded attacks like those made in a recent television series.

A promotional effort aimed at the business community and sophisticated enough to compete successfully for such attention, is urgently needed. It should focus national attention on the Indian problem and identify solution through :

- Advertising in newspapers, magazines, radio, and television.
- An organized speakers' bureau to reach business and industrial organizations regionally and nationally and provide continuing liaison.
- High-quality publications—brochures, flyers, and reports to meet specific needs.
- Documentary films and slides, as well as feature stories, to illustrate opportunities and developments in Indian country.
- Well organized forums and other meetings between representatives of business, industry, and Government with Indian leaders. A first step in the latter phase of a national promotion effort was the meeting for industrial leaders held in New York in March 1968. Another national meeting is planned with State economic development officials to be held in 1969 to promote a more aggressive interest and use of State staff and other facilities for developing Indian land and manpower.

IV. Conclusion

The preceding parts of this paper have indicated, first, the general nature of the pursuit of a national policy of development with and for the benefit of communities of Indians, which in many ways are different from typical American communities as they are generally known and which also differ significantly among themselves, second, have identified the constraints—particularly cultural factors affecting economic behavior—that must be dealt with in carrying out such a policy, and, third, have recorded certain achievements and needs for further progress.

It may be useful to underscore the entire subject by pointing out, as former Commissioner Bennett has done in another paper in this compendium, that "a clear distinction should be made between those poor in America who are outside the productive life of the economy and those who are poor despite their ability to participate in the labor force." These are, indeed, "different aspects of the problem and require different treatment." It is in the determination, jointly with the Indians, of appropriately different treatment, in the adaptation of existing general programs to the requirements of distinctive community situations, and in the identification of opportunities for public support of Indian initiative, that the future of economic development lies for them.

Indications to date are favorable. The Indians and all who are concerned for their welfare and progress must hope that, after many decades of turns and shifts of policy, the Federal Government, with the participation of other public agencies and private organizations, is now embarked on a settled course of encouragement and support that in the foreseeable future will enable the American Indians to realize their full potential, economic as well as social and political, as citizens of the United States.

INDIAN DEVELOPMENT PROGRAM

By Economic Development Administration, Department of Commerce

FOREWORD

The Economic Development Administration's program to encourage industries to locate on Indian reservations was substantially expanded in 1967. Emphasis was placed on the importance of an overall development plan for each reservation and on the involvement of the tribal leadership in this planning process. In order to achieve an effective concentration of limited budget resources, the EDA program has been directed primarily at a selected list of reservations, which now includes about 66 percent of the total reservation Indian population. An effort has been made to closely coordinate the economic and social programs managed by various Federal agencies on these reservations. In particular, the Economic Development Administration and the Office of Economic Opportunity have closely coordinated their efforts. The types of assistance provided by the EDA include public works development, business loans, and planning grants. Provision of a public works infrastructure is especially crucial at the current early stage of industrial development. Efforts to provide this infrastructure have included the establishment of facilities for industrial parks on 12 of the selected reservations.

The Problem

The social and economic problems facing the American Indian are varied and pervasive. Because of the remoteness of so many reservations the Indian has often been isolated from the economic and social systems within which he lives. There has been little incentive for the reservation population to move toward self-sustained economic growth. Stagnation, hopelessness, and poverty characterize the lives of America's Indians—even those who have left the reservations.

Perhaps the greatest single element impeding the development of solutions to the problems facing the American Indian has been the evolution of a reservation subculture which transcends individual tribal lines. This subculture has produced individuals who are apathetic, have low self-images, tend to be failure-oriented, and feel that they have little or no control over the future. Bare subsistence is accepted as the normal condition of reservation life; poverty is a self-fulfilling prophecy. Consider, briefly, the nature of the social and economic problems which the Indian must face.*

PHYSICAL AND SOCIAL CAPITAL

Indian Lands and Resources.—Indian lands and resources have been severely depleted. Some experts attribute this fact to the Allotment Act of 1887, which was one of the first official attempts to provide for

---

* Much of the data contained in this section is taken from the unpublished Report of the Interagency Task Force on the American Indian, October 1967.

assimilation of the Indian into American life and formed the basis
for what many feel was the final expropriation of Indian lands.

Under the act, each Indian family head who applied was to receive
80 acres of farming or 160 of grazing land, cut out and allotted from
tribal lands. For all tribes, allotment reduced 140 million acres of
Indian land holdings in 1886 to fewer than 56 million acres in 1965.
Further division of Indian land has taken place through leasing, sale,
and inheritance. Although Indians as a group are not land poor,
little of it is of good quality. This has made it difficult to assemble
areas suitable for ranching, let alone for comprehensive agricultural
or industrial planning.*

Infrastructure.—Lack of public investments in infrastructure re-
inforces low-land value. Intrareservation transportation systems are
grossly inadequate. As a result, the distances from potential industry
sites on the reservations to most major markets bring high-transporta-
tion costs. Utilities and other public facilities are also relatively undeveloped. Basic capital facilities essential for growth can be provided,
but they will be expensive.

Capital and Credit Availability.—Capital and credit shortages further limit reservations development potential; Indians, having little
to begin with, are poor risks.

Urban Development.—Relocation of Indians from their reservations
to urban areas has not proved successful, even with vocational training and various kinds of financial assistance. Even so, reservations
populations tend to be widely scattered. Few Indian communities
have as many as 3,000 people. The average reservation population
density is quite low—only one person per 4.2 square miles.

Housing.—More than 50 percent of Indian and Alaskan natives live
in one- or two-room houses, tar paper or mud shacks, old car bodies,
or similar substandard housing. Approximately three-fourths of the
76,000 units of housing on reservations and trust lands fall below
minimum standards.

Water for more than 50 percent of Indian families comes from
open wells or ditches, or from potentially contaminated sources; cock-
roaches and rats are continuous problems; and, at least 80 percent
of Indian and Alaskan native housing is constructed of inferior
material.

Overcrowding is chronic: On the average five or six people spend
their nights in the same room, often in the same beds. More than 70
percent of Indian houses appear to be too dilapidated to repair.

The result is that deterioration of homes and Indian population
growth consistently outstrip new house construction on reservations.
The Indians themselves are unable to meet housing needs. Perhaps only
1,000 Indian family heads could afford low-interest, long-term Federal Government loans for rehabilitation or expansion of their homes.
Further, most Indians would have difficulty obtaining financing from
other sources and repaying at the higher interest rates. This is a small
percentage of the estimated need of 16,000 units needing repair.

High FHA construction standards designed for an urban environment often make Indian housing costs prohibitively high and exclude
the building of traditional adobe or log structures where desired. On

* For example, 37 percent of the Sioux's grazing land, and all but 13 percent
of his cultivable acreage (which is only one-ninth of the Sioux's combined
acreage to begin with) is now in enterprises run by non-Indians.

a $15,000 house, the costs of meeting these standards on a reservation are $3,000 to $6,000 per unit higher than they would be in a city.

HUMAN CAPITAL

Employment.—Indian social history gives grim testimony to the devastating effects of sustained, hard-core unemployment on the individual, the family, and the group.

The Indian labor force is estimated at 120,000, approximately 30 percent of the total Indian population. Of these, almost 50 percent are chronically unemployed, compared with unemployment among all nonwhites of around 7.5 percent and United States of 3.5 percent. Because of limited skills, much Indian employment is seasonal or temporary; as such, 50 percent of the Indians who *do* work are "underemployed." Underemployment causes low incomes: only 10 percent of Indian families have annual incomes of $5,000; half have wage incomes below $2,000 a year, and 74 percent are below $3,000.

Skill Levels.—Management skills and business know-how is a scarce commodity in the Indian reservations. Most of the Indian labor force is unskilled and much of it unaccustomed to the requirements of steady employment.

Relocation.—Most Indians are unwilling—and as yet, probably unprepared—to leave their lands. Moreover Indian migration to cities in large numbers, and without adequate training, merely increases the number of urban unskilled unemployed.

Some relocation has begun. Those Indians who have left the reservation most often settled in Indian enclaves, often living in conditions equaling the worst reservation—bad housing, unemployment, unstable family lives—but without Federal reservation support. These Indians often find themselves neglected by State ad local governments and, like many other minority groups, are often discriminated against by local citizens.

Since 1952, a relocation program sponsored by the BIA has provided employment services in approximately 10 large cities across the United States. More than 10,000 Indian families have moved to cities under this program. By the end of fiscal year 1966, 62,000 Indians had been relocated and provided with vocational training. An additional 18,000 single Indians and family heads received special institutional vocational training. Approximately 11,000 of the 18,000 who started institutional vocational training completed the training; some 81 percent of these were placed in permanent jobs.

But relocation has not been an altogether effective solution to the Indians' social and economic problems. The program siphons off the more aggressive and able men from the reservations. Moreover, when compared with Indian population growth—averaging 3 percent each year since 1950—existing relocation programs do not offer a substantial solution to the problem of increasing numbers on the limited reservation resource base. Off-reservation migration for all causes amounts to about 2 percent of the population in any year. Indians have the highest birth rate (41.9 per 1,000) of any group in the Nation.

Nor does relocation, even when it is backed with vocational training, necessarily solve unemployment. In some areas, off-reservation Indian unemployment equals the high-jobless rate on reservations. Also, in locales with large Indian populations, many relocatees appear to experience race prejudice. For a variety of reasons, therefore, one out of every three relocatees eventually returns to the reservation, embittered and often more determined than previously to withdraw into welfare dependency.

Health and Medical Care.—In 1965, Indian infant mortality was placed at 35.9 deaths per 1,000 live births—11 points higher than the national average, and 20 higher than the rate in middle class neighborhoods where high home sanitation standards prevail.

Childhood disease prevention is also a serious need. Recent research suggests that children who recover from childhood diseases nevertheless may have been permanently damaged. For example, viral infections, complications of diarrhea-pneumonia, and inadequate protein supply have all been shown capable of leading to mental retardation.

Indian Education.—One-third of the 150,000 Indian children in States where BIA operates schools attend 245 Bureau schools. More than 23,000 go to BIA boarding institutions, thus removing them from their native culture and language. About 8,000 attend private (mainly church-sponsored) schools. The remainder are in the public system. In addition, upwards of 4,000 Indian children live in 18 bordertown dormitories and attend public schools.

The quality of this education is low. For example, average pupil-teacher ratios in BIA elementary schools are comparatively high—about 27 : 1. Moreover, in many instances Indian alienation is evident. Studies show very high correlation between measures of alienation and low academic achievement for a large sample of Indian students. This alienation is caused in part by the low number of Indian teachers. Only 1 percent of Indian children in public elementary schools have Indian teachers; only 1 percent an Indian principal.

Disinterest by non-Indian teachers may be another cause of the low quality of Indian education. By their own report, 25 percent of elementary and 24 percent of secondary school teachers preferred not to be teaching Indians.

Parents of children contend that they have little influence on the educational programs provided to their children. Whatever the cause, the result too often is that a chasm exists between the child's home culture—Indian, tribal, usually non-English speaking—and the white culture represented by the teacher. Frequently Indians neither understand what is expected of their children as students, nor of themselves as parents. Most have, at best, ambivalent attitudes toward the schools their children attend.

Curriculums, books and teaching materials, and underlying educational objectives for the most part reflects life in non-Indian, middle-class American society. Emotional pressures generated by this cultural conflict help account for the high Indian drop-out rates and low achievement levels. Especially significant is the tendency among Indians to drop out just before or during high school. The rate is double the national average. The adolescent often simply decides to withdraw back into the tribe and the reservation. That he chooses the tribal community in preference to "assimilation," even in the demoralized condition in which the tribe survives today, testifies to the difficulties of adapting to an alien non-Indian culture.

It is evident that the Federal Government has not designed policies and programs which have dealt adequately with the problems and conditions outlined above. This is not due to a lack of funds but rather to the difficulty of the problem and a lack of direction on the part of interested Federal agencies.

On a per capita basis, current expenditures for programs and services to Indians are the highest in the Nation—over $1,000 per Indian annually. There are approximately 20,000 total Federal employees from a number of different agencies and some half billion dollars per year in resources expended to help deal with the problems of approximately 400,000 Indians on reservations.

In spite of the extremely heavy rate of assistance to the Indian, approaching $5,000 per family unit per year, the amount of income per family averages around $3,000 per year. Thus, Federal investment in programs for the American Indian does not even result in a one-to-one ratio between dollars spent and family income.

Renewed efforts to attack the Indian problems can succeed only if Indians can be assisted in becoming productive members of the American society.

Since substantial relocation of Indians to producing economic areas is not viable at present, the only way to enhance Indian productivity is to bring the means to produce to Indian areas. Governmental experience and recent economic indications show that industrial and tourist development efforts can succeed on many reservations if reinforced by other community and social programs.

First, programs such as the Area Redevelopment Administration, Economic Development Administration have shown that Government efforts can assist industry and tourism enterprises to locate in previously unproductive areas. For example, EDA has assisted many firms to locate on Indian reservations by means of 23 business loans totaling $11 million and 7 working capital guarantees in the amount of $2 million.

Second, well documented industrial trends show that due to the decreasing importance of transportation and other location costs, many industries are increasingly locating in remote areas not unlike Indian reservations.

Third, there are numerous cases of successful location of industries on Indian reservations. Firms such as IBM, Fairchild Semi-Conductor, General Dynamics, Alaska-Pacific Timber Co., and Spartus Corporation have moved to Indian lands and are providing a significant number of jobs for Indians.

In sum, although vast economic problems exist in Indian areas, carefully directed policies and programs can make a significant impact on the problems of poverty and unemployment on many of the reservations.

Development of Present EDA Strategy

In 1967, EDA realized that if it was to effectively assist the Indian reservations to achieve economic growth—more jobs, higher salaries, and a higher standard of living—it would have to develop a more effective strategy. Prior ARA and EDA experience had shown that the Indian reservations could not come up with enough good project applications to which the agency could react. This resulted in few project approvals and the fairly low level of EDA expenditure on reservations up to fiscal year 1967 (see chart, p. 367, infra.)

For a variety of reasons and because few Indians were actually involved in the development and implementation of programs directed toward their wellbeing, most reservations lacked the internal capacity to plan for their own development, that is, to establish the goals, priorities and projects, which together constitute the tribes' long-range programs or outlines of action to be undertaken over a period of several years.

EDA decided to take a more active role in the development of projects on Indian reservations. The Agency felt that it was only by working with the reservations in the development of a capacity to plan for their future and by providing them with an incentive to move toward self-sustained economic growth, that they would be able to receive EDA assistance at a level equivalent to other redevelopment areas.

STRATEGY

EDA's strategy was based on the following assumptions: First, economic development should be predicated on the participation of the Indian people, the Indian family, and the Indian community in solving the problems. Experience has shown that for any program to be successful, the Indians themselves must assume the leadership in developing and implementing it.

Second, a comprehensive, coordinated effort should be mobilized from the many groups, agencies and departments within the Federal Government in support of Indian programs. Emphasis must be directed toward the need for integrated planning aimed at altering the conditions in the home, the school, the community, and the geographic areas as a whole.

EDA's long range goal is a single planning requirement for each reservation upon which all Federal investments would be based. In the past the various Federal Indian programs were not coordinated; each department or agency decided what was best for each Indian reservation and proceeded to devise and implement its own particular programs without the benefit of the desires of the Indian themselves or of the experience of other interested parties. This resulted in duplication of effort in many areas and a complete lack of attention in others.

Also, in order to make sure that Indian reservations received EDA program funds on a basis equal to that of other EDA redevelopment areas, it was decided to allocate specific funds for use on Indian reservations. Considering the reservation population and the investments required to have an impact on their economic development, in fiscal year 1968, EDA allocated $19 million to a selected number of reservations which had the greatest potential for economic growth. This allocation of funds demonstrated to these reservations that EDA was ready to assist them in their development efforts. Furthermore, the agency as a whole was informed that a priority had been set for economic development on Indian reservation projects.

In October 1967, an Indian desk was established within the Office of Policy Coordination. The Indian desk was charged with responsibility for coordinating EDA's Indian program with other Federal agencies, State Indian commissions, private industry, consultants, et cetera. This desk was headed by an Indian program manager, who has overall responsibility for the development of the special program.

The Selected Indian Reservation Program

To implement this new strategy, EDA set up the Selected Indian Reservation Program. Because of the larger number of Indian reservations and its limited funds, it was obvious to EDA that a distribution of its resources among all eligible reservations would not provide any one with a sufficiently massive input to overcome the conditions which were currently inhibiting growth. Further, in order to maximize the return from the Federal funds invested on Indian reservations, the combined resources of several Federal agencies working jointly under a single comprehensive development plan was needed.

ACTION LIST RESERVATIONS

In the late spring of 1967, an agreement was reached between OEO and EDA to combine their resources in helping a select number of Indian reservations referred to as the "action list." Fifteen reservations which demonstrated the greatest potential for sustained economic growth and viability were chosen to participate. These reservations are located in various parts of the Western United States and have a population of 185,000 or 53 percent of all Indians living on reservations:

Reservation	State	Population	Percent unemployed
Navajo	Arizona	125,000	39.0
San Carlos	do	4,473	74.0
Salt River	do	2,212	43.0
Gila River	do	7,113	55.0
Annette Island	Alaska	1,000	19.3
Zuni Pueblo	New Mexico	5,000	77.0
Mescalero	do	1,559	61.0
Blackfeet	Montana	6,381	39.0
Crow	do	4,097	44.0
Red Lake	Minnesota	2,538	38.0
Fort Berthold	North Dakota	2,657	79.0
Standing Rock	South Dakota	4,720	47.0
Pine Ridge	do	10,496	32.0
Rosebud	do	5,432	61.5
Lower Brule and Crow Creek	do	1,731	70.5

The criteria used in delineating these reservations included:
1. Community factors:
  (*a*) Tribal leadership interest in economic development.
  (*b*) Manpower pool.
  (*c*) Education facilities.
  (*d*) Training programs.
  (*e*) Availability of management skills, within the community and adjacent to it.
2. Material resource factors:
  (*a*) Status of reservations facilities.
  (*b*) Availability of significant qualitative amounts of appropriate raw materials.

(c) Current industrial activities.

(d) Probability of adequate financing—availability of tribal, other agency, private funds.

3. Physical location factors:

(a) Proximity to regional growth centers (market factors).

(b) Transportation between the reservation and these centers.

The main advantages of the Selected Indian Reservation Program are:

The *concentration* of Federal agency resources in a number of selected reservations is intended to accelerate the planning for future development and the approval of needed programs.

The *cooperation* of Federal agencies in this effort is aimed at overcoming the disjointed nature of multiple Federal program inputs on the reservations.

The *acceleration* of Federal investments is intended to generate greater impact in a shorter period of time.

The *selectivity* of the program is designed to provide an incentive to those reservations with the greatest potential, so that economic and social viability can be achieved as quickly as possible.

The following principles guide the development efforts of the program:

1. Investments on Indian reservations should be based on a comprehensive development strategy containing an outline of action to be undertaken over several years and specifying the tribes' priorities regarding its goals and the specific projects to be implemented. These plans are continually updated as economic conditions of the reservations change and improve.

2. The goal should be a single planning requirement upon which all Federal investments are based.

3. The means to achieve a catalytic effect should be based on a responsiveness to the desires, needs and plans of the Indians as expressed through their tribal councils.

EDA recognizes that the tribal attitude toward change will, in the long run, make a more positive contribution to the progress, or lack thereof, than will any other single resource. Thus, tribal involvement is an essential element of the selected Indian reservation program. Both long range planning and project selection must be based on a response to the Indians' desires, as expressed through their leadership. No coercive cultural or economic assimilation is intended—in fact, the program is designed to avoid such coercion.

Work was begun to prepare the action plans for each of the selected reservations. These plans are for EDA's internal use and specify projects which it would consider funding over the next 3 to 5 years. The tribal leadership on each of the 15 reservations was deeply involved in the development of the plans. Meetings were held on each reservation with tribal leaders and officials of EDA, OEO, BIA, SBA, HUD and PHS. Several months later, tribal leaders were called to locations in the Southwest and North Central parts of the country to discuss as a group, the developments to date and their priorities for economic development. Draft action plans were then prepared by the tribes in conjunction with EDA economic development specialists and the area offices. The first action plans for the 15 action list reservations were completed by 1968. These reservations have submitted applications to the appropriate Federal agencies for the loans and grants outlined in their plans and funding has been accomplished on numerous projects to assist the Indian reservation's economic development programs.

PLANNING LIST RESERVATIONS

In July 1968, 14 additional reservations and groups of small reservations were selected to take part in the Selected Indian Reservation program:

Reservation	State	Population	Percent unemployed
Cheyenne River	do	4,008	25
Turtle Mountain	North Dakota	7,187	52
Leech Lake	Minnesota	2,796	26
Papago	Arizona	5,358	23
Fort Apache	do	5,407	43
Hopi	do	5,556	48
Colorado River	do	1,628	47
Eight Northern Pueblos	New Mexico	3,301	(¹)
Jicarilla	do	1,474	43
Nevada reservations (22)	Nevada	4,418	(¹)
Fort Yuma (Quechan)	Arizona	1,634	35
Rocky Boys	Montana	1,149	50
Fort Peck	do	4,196	51
Flathead	do	2,761	34
Fort Belknap	do	1,585	30
Northern Cheyenne	do	2,448	22

¹ Not applicable.

This second group, called the "Planning List", is working to develop the internal capacity necessary to formulate overall economic development plans. These tribes will concentrate on establishing goals, priorities and projects, which constitute their long range development programs. In order to assist in these efforts, Federal officials have been meeting with the leaders of these reservations to outline the program and to assist them in developing a planning capacity.

The Selected Indian Reservation program, both action and planning lists, includes 52 reservations having a population of 240,000, comprising 66% of all reservation Indians. An additional 50 reservations, having a population of 20,000 are also designated as redevelopment areas by EDA. While these latter reservations are eligible for EDA economic assistance, because of their relative lack of economic potential, EDA has decided that they should not receive the specialized consideration given to the selected Indian program reservations. Thus, EDA is presently giving assistance to tribes representing approximately 75% of all reservation Indians. The remaining Indian reservations not presently designated are too small in population to justify EDA assistance. However, where they are located in a fairly compact geographic area, EDA will designate them as a single unit and will assist them in planning for their common economic development.

Reservations will move into and out of the Selected Indian Reservation program. For example, when a reservation on the "action list" has developed a sound economy or sustained growth, it will no longer need the special attention of this program and will be removed from the "action list". The vacancy created may be filled by a reservation from the "planning list"; another reservation will then be chosen to fill the vacancy in the planning list. Conversely, if a reservation does not participate effectively in the Selected Indian Reservation program, it will be replaced by another reservation.

PROGRAM ACTIVITIES

One of the major concerns and aims of the Selected Indian Reservation program is to help tribes develop industrial development potential. To provide tribal leaders and tribally-employed development professionals with a sound understanding of industrial development procedures, EDA and OEO jointly sponsored the basic and advanced industrial development courses conducted by the American Industrial Development Council. These courses were conducted in February and December 1968, respectively, for the "action list" reservations. The basic course was repeated for the "planning list" reservations in January 1969; they were given the advanced course in April 1969.

EDA and OEO have also initiated a series of industrial development conferences which permit the selected reservation leaders to promote their industrial opportunities with major industrial firms. Conferences were held in Los Angeles and New York in the spring of 1968 for the "action list" under the auspices of the National Congress of American Indians and five conferences are scheduled in 1969 for both "lists". Tribes set up booths displaying examples of products they manufacture and tribal leaders outlined the advantages of locating branch plants on their reservations to some 300 industrialists during the show and at a cocktail party and luncheon.

EDA made certain that government officials were not present at any of the meetings between industrialists and tribal leaders. This forced the Indians to act on their own and lead them to realize many of the problems they must confront in implementing any industrialization. program. To improve the capacity of the selected reservations to help themselves, EDA has funded planning grants in 1968, which provides 62 planners serving 45 reservations. These individuals are employed by the tribes and provide the Indian leadership with needed staff assistance in planning and implementing sound economic development programs. Planning staffs are provided specialized training in economic development on reservations at EDA conducted planning seminars, the first of which was held at Bartlesville, Okla., in October 1968. The emphasis in this seminar and the courses is upon sound planning by the tribal leadership and effective and coordinated development.

Reservation program reviews were held in February and December, 1968, for the "action list" and for the "planning list" in January, 1969, to further assist in sound planning and the efficient use of Federal resources. The program reviews provide an opportunity for the tribal leaders to present their overall development program to key personnel from FHA, Labor, SBA, HUD, HEW, BIA, PHS, OEO, and EDA and then to discuss the soundness of their programs and the possible roles of the various agencies. These have proved most valuable in strengthening the reservation programs and in stimulating inter-agency coordination.

TYPE OF EDA ASSISTANCE

Over the past 2 years all EDA designated Indian reservations have received the following types and percentages of economic assistance: Public works, 72 percent; Business loans, 25 percent; and planning grants and technical assistance, 3 percent.

Estimated allocations for fiscal year 69 are approximately the same.

These allocations are based on EDA's evaluation of the needs of the reservations as outlined in their action plans. Due to the lack of any appreciable economic infrastructure and the extreme poverty exhibited on most reservations, most of the assistance has necessarily been given to provide a basis for future investment. For example, industrial parks have been constructed on 12 of the 15 "action list" reservations.

The following are examples of projects on Indian reservations which EDA has already funded:

Public Works:

Aid in construction of:

Industrial parks
Recreational/tourist complexes
Water and sewage systems
Airports
Fire protection systems
Access roads
Training and community centers

Business Loans:

Assistance in establishing:

Copper mining operations
Furniture plants
Tribal stores
Printing plants
Plants producing electronic controls and valves
Cattle feed lots
Sawmills
Electronic firm
Plants manufacturing prepared feed
Citrus groves
Planning assistance and technical assistance:
Feasibility studies for various types of manufacturing operations
Studies to help establish job planning offices
Grants to staff and implement industrial development programs and to plan for economic growth
Grants to help expand the skill-training programs
Water impoundment studies
Prefabricated plant studies

EDA also provides grants to various tribes to pay up to 75 percent of the cost of hiring planners in the areas of industrial development, tourist and planning. Planning grants are also given for hiring planners for the four newly developed districts, such as the Indian Development District of Arizona (IDDA) and the United Tribes of North Dakota. If EDA is not able to provide such planning grants, OEO has done so.

For fiscal year 1969, EDA allocated $30 million for all Indian reservations, whereas the prior fiscal year funds had only been allocated to the selected Indian reservations.

INDIAN PROGRAM EXPENDITURES

In keeping with the philosophy that economic development assistance should be directed to those reservations having the greatest potential, $18 million has been allocated to those reservations on the selected Indian reservation program's "action list." There is no specific allocation for those reservations on the "planning list," since the main thrust of EDA's involvement is to assist them in developing a planning capacity. For other qualified reservations, economic assistance is given on a project by project basis. The following chart indicates EDA investments on Indian reservations since 1966:

```
Fiscal year 1966:¹ EDA total appropriated funds_____ $332,425,000
Fiscal year 1966: EDA expenditures on Indian reservations_____    3,295,000
Fiscal year 1967: EDA total appropriated funds_____  296,100,000
Fiscal year 1967: EDA expenditures on Indian reservations_____   18,040,000
Fiscal year 1968: EDA total appropriated funds_____  275,000,000
Fiscal year 1968: EDA expenditures on Indian reservations____   18,873,000
Fiscal year 1969: EDA total appropriated funds_____  274,740,000
Fiscal year 1969: Allocation for Indian reservations_____   30,000,000
        (Selected Indian reservation "action list"
        allocation) _____    (18,000,000)
```

¹ Expenditures for the period fiscal years 1961–65 are not available as Indian reservation projects were not separated from overall commitment of funds.

Apart from the selected Indian reservations, a total of 50 reservations are presently qualified by EDA. This compares with 41 reservations at the end of fiscal year 1968 and 29 at the end of fiscal year 1967. While the present thrust of EDA's involvement is directed toward the selected Indian reservations, to date it has invested a total of $16 million in these other designated reservations.

EDA development assistance to these selected Indian reservations during fiscal year 1968 was approximately 70 percent of grants and loans to all Indian reservations. Since July 1, 1967, EDA has provided assistance to the following groups of reservations:

	Number of reservations	Expenditures since July 1967 (as of Nov. 30, 1968)	Applications pending (as of Nov. 30, 1968)
Action list	15	$10,660,000	$8,907,000
Planning list	44	9,061,000	1,270,500
Other reservations	50	5,675,780	3,918,000
Total		25,397,000	14,095,000

While it is too early to adequately evaluate the results of the Indian program, EDA has assisted the "action list" reservations in developing the institutional capabilities for planning their own economic and community development. The tribes on these reservations now understand their own problems, have planned for their future development, and are able to effectively work with the private sector and all levels of government—Federal, State, and local—in obtaining needed assistance. Equally as important, EDA has instilled all reservations with a sense of change—an attitude that they can effectively plan for their future and that the Federal Government will assist them in carrying out their efforts.

OFFICE OF ECONOMIC OPPORTUNITY

As EDA's partner in the Selected Indian Reservation program during fiscal year 1968, OEO committed $22,136,063 in funds providing 6,871 nonprofessionals and 1,114 professionals full time jobs on the 31 selected Indian reservations. Most of the projects will be in operation in fiscal year 1969 and will develop jobs in a variety of areas:

Mutual help housing.
Community beautification.
Headstart programs (full-year and summer).
Health education.
Community development.
Ranger corps.
Home management.
Parent child centers.
Home improvement program.
C & A.
Alcoholism.
Migrant program.
Emergency food programs.
Business management assistance.
Legal services.
Multi-purpose neighborhood centers.
Trailer park and land development.
Adult education.
Juvenile counseling.

This total does not include OEO's funding or Neighborhood Youth Corps, Operation Mainstream, work incentive programs, Upward Bound, VISTA or Job Corps. If funds allocated to these projects were included, OEO funding of the selected Indian reservation program would double. As mentioned previously, OEO also provides funds for the hiring of planners on the reservations.

THE INDIAN DESK

In addition to having the general responsibility of coordinating EDA's Indian program with other Federal agencies, State Indian commissions, private industry, consultants, etc., as the central point for all EDA Indian activities, the Indian program manager has jurisdiction of the $30 million allocated to all Indian reservations and works with all seven regional offices in establishing target allocations. The Indian desk also continually provides advice on all problems and projects and follows up on project applications until they are finally approved. To aid in this latter activity, the Indian program manager has set up an Indian working committee, comprised of representatives form the various Washington offices of EDA which work with Indian reservations. This committee meets periodically on all aspects of the Indian program and provides an effective vehicle for the Indian program manager to coordinate EDA Indian activities.

The Indian program manager has also strengthened relations with other Federal agencies, particularly with OEO, Labor, HUD, and HEW, which have appointed individuals to work specifically with their Indian programs. Discussions are currently being held with a view of extending relations with other agencies which have ongoing activities on Indian reservations.

The Indian program manager also meets periodically with the National Council of Indian Opportunity. This organization was set up by President Johnson in 1966, with the Vice President as Chairman. It is composed of six Indian leaders and six Cabinet officers and provides an effective vehicle for strengthening contact between the Federal Government and Indian leadership and for coordinating the efforts of all interested Federal agencies.

Although, at the present time EDA has done little with State Indian reservations, it is expanding its efforts in this area with the recent addition to the Indian desk of personnel who will work exclusively in this area.

While projects are important, they are only of lasting value if they accurately reflect a comprehensive development strategy as outlined in the various action plans. The Indian desk is constantly reevaluating these plans to insure that they reflect the most effective means of achieving the goal of economic self-sufficiency and community development. Further, even with its concentrated effort toward Indian reservations, EDA's resources are not in themselves sufficient to insure the success of such action plans, no matter how perceptive they may be. The Indian desk is, therefore, in contact with other Federal agencies with the object of bringing them into active participation in the implementation of these plans. However, even though EDA efforts have been partially successful over the past 2 years, any complete coordination of Federal investments on Indian reservations must be directed from above. EDA would like to see all Federal investments based on reservation development priorities and the projects set forth in the action plans which have been completed for the 15 action list reservations. Once action plans have been completed for the planning list reservations, Federal investment could be based on them as well.

It cannot be stressed too strongly that the essential aspect of the success or failure of EDA's program is that the Indians themselves must be brought into the initial planning process. The tribal attitude toward change will, in the long run, determine their progress and allow them to move toward self-sustained economic growth.

THE ROLE OF INDIAN TRIBES IN ECONOMIC DEVELOPMENT AND THE EFFORTS OF THE INDIAN DIVISION OF THE COMMUNITY ACTION PROGRAM OF THE OFFICE OF ECONOMIC OPPORTUNITY TO ASSIST IN INDIAN RESERVATION ECONOMIC DEVELOPMENT

By James J. Wilson *

FOREWORD

In keeping with the Office of Economic Opportunity's mandate to be an innovative agency, the OEO's Community Action Programs on Indian reservations have encompassed a variety of economic and social activities. In cooperation with the Economic Development Administration, the OEO has concentrated its activities on a selected group of reservations judged to have the greatest development potential. The OEO has stressed the importance of a reservation development plan created by the tribe itself, and among its basic objectives, the OEO has included assisting the tribal leadership to develop both the administrative sophistication necessary to deal successfully with Federal agencies and the sense of social concern required to carry out their responsibilities to the reservation residents. Among the specific economic development needs identified in this OEO statement are additional Federal investment in basic public utility systems on the reservations, special waiver authority for reservations to participate in Federal grant programs without providing the normal local matching funds, and special tax incentives to encourage industry to locate on reservations.

Introduction

The Office of Economic Opportunity does not have an economic development policy of the type generally associated with professional economic developers. The OEO had been given the legislation to be the command post for a continuing Federal attack on all of the causes of poverty. OEO was to engage in comprehensive, cooperative planning and to bring purpose and effectiveness to the many ongoing, but separate, efforts throughout the Government. The economic development policy of OEO should have been a composite or concensus of the interagency efforts. The community action program was to allow "maximum feasible participation of the residents to be served." The OEO was to make financial assistance available to local communities for purposes of "Community Action" to solve local community problems.

---

*Director, Indian Division, Office of Special Field Programs, Community Action Program, Office of Economic Opportunity.

The OEO established "guidelines" for programs to be developed locally. Some "national emphasis" programs were initiated by OEO. Community action programs took many forms. Interagency cooperation was not always possible because of either specific legislation or interpretation of intent of the legislation. The OEO general policy became one of total human resource development. Frequently, economic development was associated with industrial development and the fear of exploitation. Emphasis within human resource development moved toward social and educational development and away from economic development. The need for jobs with earned income has within the last 2 years caused major shifts in an opposite policy direction.

The remainder of this document will deal with recent and current topics. The subject to be dealt with will be delimited to Federal Indian reservations participating in OEO community action programs. The following material is organized in this manner: (1) A brief review of the recent and current economic development situation of Federal Indian reservations; (2) a brief discussion of the OEO/CAP Indian division philosophy and funding policies relating to Indian reservation economic development; and (3) specific recommendations.

I. RECENT AND CURRENT ECONOMIC DEVELOPMENT EFFORTS ON FEDERAL INDIAN RESERVATIONS

Every Indian tribe on a federally supervised reservation has had either a limited development plan or an overall economic development plan (OEDP). Nearly every Indian reservation has made attempts to create jobs on the reservation for tribal members. Because of lack of basic facilities, transportation, community services, and frequently extreme isolation, relatively few successes could be reported of industry moving onto reservations. Where interest was shown by private industry, there often existed situations of limited financial assistance and the relative lack of knowledge on the part of both tribal officials and Government officials of the specific needs and expectations of private industry when every community in America was also competing to attract new industry. Tribal resources, human, financial, and natural, frequently went undeveloped while learned men studied "the Indian problem" from the sociological and anthropological angles. Windfalls from the Indian Claims Commission awards frequently are distributed on a per capita basis or doled out for family plans resulting in almost no appreciable long-range gain to either the individual or the reservation community. Until very recently, tribal funds held in reserve were deposited with the U.S. Treasury at minimal interest rates. Present efforts are being made to invest in short-term bonds with rates considerably higher than U.S. Treasury rates.

Current efforts find many tribes using tribal funds to put up matching shares for basic facilities such as water, roads, buildings, powerlines, etc. Many tribes are or have gone deeply into debt on loans for such basic facilities, frequently failing (or unable) to arrange margins of safety in the repayment schedules. Many tribes have used OEO funds to employ economic development staffs; others have secured grants from agencies such as the Economic Development Administration (EDA) for economic planning staffs.

Presently, under an agreement between OEO and EDA, there are 31 tribes participating in the Selected Indian Reservation program (SIR) of economic development with 15 tribes in the action group (these tribes emphasizing implementation of existing OEDP's) and 16 tribes in the planning group (these tribes emphasizing the development of updated OEDP's). The tribes in the SIR program have participated in training programs conducted by the American Industrial Development Council sponsored by OEO and the National Congress of American Indians (NCAI). The tribes in the action group of the SIR program have participated in four Indian industrial development conferences sponsored by NCAI under a grant from OEO. Early reports on the Indian industrial development conferences indicate favorable results.

II. The OEO/CAP Philosophy and Funding Policy Relating to Indian Reservation Economic Development

The present Indian division philosophy and funding policies are not new but are simply reflective of a point in time of an evolutionary process. It is expected that this process will evolve further as new experiences develop and that at no time will there be either a fixed policy or detailed, written policies in regard to either tribal programs or economic development.

Relevancy of programing is dependent on a continuous process of reevaluation. To enable an administrator to meet special needs in programing, there needs to be a relatively simple and basic philosophy to which a funding policy is then adapted.

The basic philosophy of the Indian division has been defined thus: (a) To direct-fund Indian tribes to allow tribal governments to develop the program sophistication necessary for all levels of government to develop in their relationship to the Federal Government and (b) to develop, through a process of conditioning, the social responsibility of the tribal-governing body to the reservation residents (both Indian and non-Indian) expected of local governments in non-reservation communities.

Conditioning of behavior requires incentives so the funding policy adapted to the philosophy calls for distribution of grant funds on a formula basis. After some experimentation, the following funding policy has been developed for the present time: 80 percent of the funds are distributed on a per capita basis amongst all participating reservations; 20 percent of the funds are held back for incentive grants to stimulate desired behavior and to provide certain special group services, such as the AIDC and NCAI services.

In the application of this basic philosophy and funding policy to economic development on Indian reservations, there are many considerations which result in the vital necessity of considering each reservation program individually. However, thereare a number of considerations and questions which have applicability in each reservation situation. Some of the many considerations and questions which the Indian division has considered and/or dealt with follows:

How should a situation be assessed to assure a relevant reference point?—This is particularly important in dealing with tribes which have maintain a strong tribal cultural identity. Wherever possible, we seek to have as much of the assessment as possible made by people from within the community. Where local residents lack skills, we should train them.

Determining relationships identifies relative roles.—There are many relationships which must be clarified before effective economic development can be undertaken. The relationship of the reservation to surrounding communities, the tribal leaders to surrounding community leaders, etc. With role identification, a more accurate evaluation of the potential of development can be made. Some reservations probably should not think about economic development (Santa Ana and Sandia in New Mexico, Salt River in Arizona).

What can a single Federal agency do to adjust its rate of development to the timing of other agencies?—This seems to be the crucial question facing the Federal Government since every agency of Government has a role to play. The Director of the OEO/CAP Indian Division recommended over 2 years ago that an Office of Indian Program Coordination be established in the Executive Office of the President. In March of 1968, the National Council on Indian Opportunity was set up with the Vice President as chairman. This Council has not met as of this date under the new administration.

Should the level of program sophistication of the tribes be a major determinant in programing? The idea of conditioning and incentives emphasizes differences in program sophistication and makes it absolutely necessary to program according to this factor.

Economic development on a communitywide basis is a competitive undertaking for which both the leadership and the community must be prepared.

Human development probably leads to economic development but economic development doesn't necessarily lead to human development.

Tribal plans must have philosophic goals in relation to Indianess, culture, and reservations.

A plan alone is never enough.

Should job development be concentrated on male jobs?

Should efforts to attract industry be specialized by industry?; by size?; new industry or branch plants?

What are roles for individuals and private agencies in assisting tribal economic development?

Do you wait for leaders to appear or do you attempt to develop leadership?

These and hundreds of other questions and considerations come up when Indian reservations consider economic development in the full context of total community development and the economic betterment of the members of the community. Where successful economic development is taking place, there is to be found a combination of factors which economic development specialists can presently quite accurately define.

III. Specific Recommendations

With the present capability of economic development specialists to determine what factors must exist within a community to enhance such development, it can be fairly well determined what kinds of actions the Federal Government might profitably undertake to assist Indian reservations in their efforts of economic development. Some needs may not exist in every situation, but every situation has some needs. The following recommendations are suggestive and are not intended to be totally inclusive:

Special tax credits.—New legislation is needed to give business and industry incentives beyond offerings presently being made to offset factors of isolation, transportation, and services. The areas of application could be (1) employment tax credits, (2) transportation tax credits, and (3) accelerated plant and equipment depreciation allowances. The tax credits should be for a specific number of years and should be scaled to factors of area economic depression and the company earnings situation.

Federal investment in basic facilities.—To ease the rate of movement of population from rural to urban centers it is going to be necessary that the Federal Government make substantial investments in rural growth centers for essential basic facilities such as roads, water systems, sewage systems, heavy power systems, and in some cases railroad spurs and warehousing facilities.

Special waiver authority for matching funds grant programs.—The Secretary of each Department making matching funds grants should have legislative authority to waive part or all of the required local non-Federal share. We frequently find that without the existing waiver authority of OEO, Indian tribes would be too poor to participate in the poverty program.

The National Council on Indian Opportunity be given specific legislative direction and funds to establish a two-part American Institute (of Tribal Affairs and of Indian Studies).—Legislative direction should be given the NCIO to truly establish it as the command post of coordination of Federal Indian programs. The NCIO should have funds to operate a two-part American Indian Institute to deal in two specific areas: The American Institute of Tribal Affairs should deal with upgrading tribal government, tribal courts, and tribal business management. The American Indian Institute of Indian Studies (located at the same place in the same plant which should be a converted existing Bureau of Indian Affairs boarding school) would engage in studies of a nature to allow a coordinated approach to research and to make available for early application the more important research findings and feasibility study results.

Specific legislation allowing private industry and business tax deductions for providing technical assistance to tribal groups.—The Department of Commerce should be given legislative authority to initiate and monitor a program of matching the management know-how and technical assistance of America's 300 biggest corporations, with the management and technical assistance needs of America's 300 or so Indian reservations. Tax deductions should be allowed on a schedule to be worked out considering factors of minimal and maximal rates per man-day of assistance and minimal and maximal numbers of man-days of assistance.

Even with all needed permissive legislation and needed funds available, the final problem of economic development on Federal Indian reservations will be a human problem with the related problems of communication, hopes, plans, and community aspirations slowing, halting, or preventing development.

PEOPLE AND PROGRAMS: THE INDIAN EFFORT IN THE DEPARTMENT OF HEALTH, EDUCATION, AND WELFARE

FOREWORD

The Department of Health, Education, and Welfare administers the extensive Public Health Service program for the provision of health services and the construction of health care facilities on Indian reservations. In addition, HEW has recently established on Office of Indian Affairs, the purpose of which is to assure that Indians are aware of, and full participants in, all of HEW's programs. In support of this objective, HEW is undertaking a program to train the Indians to assume leadership roles in programs serving them and a program to gather and disseminate badly needed statistical data on Indian economic and social conditions.

Introduction

Optimum economic development in American Indian communities is a process dependent on a healthy, well educated, and socially sound population. Consequently, the Department of Health, Education, and Welfare as the Federal Government's primary focusing agency for programs of human development, has a key role to play in supporting this process.

There are over 600,000 citizens who identify themselves as Indians, Eskimos and Aleuts (hereafter referred to collectively as "Indian"). Some are found in each State. About 400,000 reside on or adjacent to Federal Indian reservations, and in communities in Oklahoma and Alaska. These 400,000 people, for complex legal and historical reasons, bear a unique relationship to the Federal Government and can participate in its special Federal Indian programs. Another 200,000 Indians live on State reservations, mainly along the Eastern seaboard, and in towns and cities throughout the Nation. These 200,000 people do not have a unique relationship to the Federal Government, and do not participate in special Federal Indian programs. Place of residence and unique Federal-Indian relationships notwithstanding, all 600,000 of these people, as citizens, are entitled to participate in the full range of HEW's more than 200 regular programs on the same basis as all other Americans.

BACKGROUND

The Department's involvement with the problems of Indians is long standing. The Public Health Service in the 1920's began to assign physicians to work in the health service of the Bureau of Indian Affairs, Department of Interior. During the 1930's the predecessors of HEW's Social Security Administration and Social and Rehabilitation Services began to extend services to Indians who qualified for them.

HEW involvement with Indians and their problems was intensified during the 1950's. Responsibility for health services for Indians was transferred by congressional action from the Bureau of Indian Affairs to the U.S. Public Health Service on July 1, 1955, resulting in the establishment of the Division of Indian Health, now designated, The Indian Health Service. This development represented the Department's first program specially organized and operated for Indians. Later in the decade, additional legislation authorized construction of community hospitals to serve both Indians and non-Indians. Further legislation authorized construction of safe water supplies and sanitary waste disposal facilities for Indian communities and individual homes. Another milestone of the era was the extension of Federal Impact Aid for Education to include Indian children enrolled in public school districts.

The trend of HEW's broadening concern for the problems of Indians has been extended into the 1960's. Recent legislation which has increased the Department's services and benefits to the general public has had the effect of increasing services and benefits to Indians. For example, amendments to the Elementary and Secondary Education Act have made special service and aids available to Federal and other schools with Indian students. The Education Professions Development Act, the Vocational Education Act and the Higher Education Act, similarly, make it possible to put forth intensified efforts in Indian education. In the field of health, medicare and medicaid have been extended to thousands of Indians living both on and off Federal Indian reservations.

Thus, in recent decades, the potential for Indian growth and development through the programs of HEW and its predecessors has substantially increased. However, in the recent past, evidence has emerged which indicates that this potential was not being fully realized. A major constraint to this realization has been the traditional social, cultural, and geographic isolation of Indian people. Another major constraint has been the widespread, but inaccurate belief that Indian people could turn to the special Federal Indian programs for all services needed by the individual, the family, and the community.

Former Secretary of HEW, John W. Gardner, addressed himself to this unfullfilled potential at a meeting of tribal leaders, Kansas City, Mo., February 17, 1967. While there to discuss a White House Task Force recommendation that the Bureau of Indian Affairs be transferred from the Department of Interior to the Department of Health, Education, and Welfare, he stated:

Wherever the major responsibility for Indian Affairs ultimately rests, you may be sure that my Department intends to throw its energies and resources toward solving the problems that Indians tell us are the real problems.

Although the task force recommendation did not come to fruition, the Department took definitive action to meet its commitment to the needs of Indians.

A thorough review of the Department's programs in relation to Indian needs was promptly undertaken. During the course of the review, HEW responsibility for Indian Affairs was officially assigned to the Office of the Assistant Secretary for Education in August 1967. Subsequently, this responsibility was transferred to the Office of the Assistant Secretary for Planning and Evaluation.

A charter setting forth responsibilities was developed and, late in 1967, the Office for Indian Progress, now designated the Office of Indian Affairs, was established. The purpose of establishing a departmental focal point for Indian Affairs was to assure that Indians are aware of, and full participants in all of HEW's programs, and when necessary, that the programs are combined and adapted to meet the Indians' special needs.

The office was charged with several broad areas of responsibility:

    1. Developing Department goals in the provision of services to Indians, and securing coordination in the achievement of such goals by operating agencies.

    2. Coordinating HEW research, demonstration, and action programs in the field of Indian affairs.

    3. Reflecting the special needs of the Indian community, on and off Federal Indian reservations, in operational decisions within the Department.

The Department's strategy for meeting Indian needs more effectively and efficiently was developed around the above purpose and responsibilities.

Elements of Strategy

The strategy was predicated, in part, on the Department's conviction that, in order for its programs and actions to be optimally effective and efficient relative to Indians, they must, in fact, take into account the ways in which these people perceive their needs and their ideas and beliefs about ways in which programs can be made appropriate to their unique social, cultural and geographic settings.

In essence, the elements of the strategy are:

    That existing operating agencies and their established procedures provide the means for carrying out program and administrative actions to meet Indian needs.

    That complementary and supplementary authorities, arts, sciences and funds of one or more individual operating agencies will be packaged in order that their cumulative effects, properly coordinated, can best meet Indian needs.

    That operating agencies' resources will be concentrated in areas of intense need so as to maximize their effect.

The Deparment's actions in the field of Indian affairs have been guided by this strategy.

Implementation of Strategy

DELINEATION OF INDIANS VIEWS

The first step taken in evolving a plan of action to implement the departmental strategy was a delineation of Indian views relative to their needs and HEW programs. This action necessitated a critical decision about selecting a method for delineating Indian views. The options open to the Department fell into three broad types:

    1. Conducting massive surveys.

    2. Holding workshops, forums, and similar hearings, and

    3 Using available information and public records.

The value of surveys and of hearings and similar meetings was clearly recognized. The necessity for conducting such activities was questioned, however, because this had already been done repeatedly and recently for the broad spectrum of social and similar needs in the Indian field. Also, the advisability and feasability was questioned because Indian people were under the impression that they had already provided information about their views in the above mentioned surveys and meetings. Thus additional surveys and hearings would appear to be superfluous and would indicate that this would become another fruitless exercise.

The results of numerous surveys over the years are available. These, combined with tribal and intertribal government resolutions, correspondence, proceedings from a variety of Indian meetings and other Indian expressions, have yielded a clear picture of Indian views about their needs and the way they relate to Federal programs both on a trend and a current basis. Therefore, the decision was made to utilize this information in the important step of delineating Indian views.

An analysis of this information identified five broad areas of concern to which the Indians appeared to want Government agencies to direct special attention. These five areas of concern indicate that:

1. Quantities and types of services are variably insufficient or unavailable at levels required to meet needs.

2. Needed services are often reached only with great hardship due to distance and time required to reach places where services are available.

3. Opportunities to constructively participate in planning, operating, and evaluating programs aimed at meeting needs are inadequately developed. The Indians want to be of substantial support to the agencies working to meet their needs.

4. Understanding of Indians' cultures and related problems and circumstances on the part of service personnel is insufficient to promote optimum growth and development of client confidence in the professional worker and the services and service systems which he represents. The Indians feel that this high level of confidence is indispensable and deserved.

5. Kinds of available, accessible services sometimes are not optimally appropriate to needs of Indian individuals and communities.

These areas of concern provide a reasonable basis for the manifold and divergent programs of the Department to view their relationships to the needs of Indians.

AREAS FOR EMPHASIS

As a means of facilitating the consideration of Indians' views in the Department, the five broad concerns were recast as areas for emphasis. The areas for Department-wide emphasis are, broadly, to develop, extend, improve and implement mechanisms to—

1. Assure that HEW services and benefits are available to Indians in need.

2. Increase the Indians' accessibility to HEW services and benefits.

3. Expand the ranges and methods of Indian involvement in programs which serve them.

4. Increase the effectiveness of program personnel, and the effectiveness of Indians involved in program planning, operation, and evaluation.

5. Increase the appropriateness of programs, and program delivery and management systems, to the needs of Indians.

Thus, the stage was set for designing and implementing a plan of action for pursuing the responsibilities inherent in the areas for emphasis.

PLAN OF ACTION

The HEW plan for Indian affairs consists of one basic and two supportive components. The basic component is program development aimed at generating actions which will assure that the Department's services and benefits are delivered to Indian people in consonance with the areas for emphasis.

The first of the two supporting components represents a critically needed effort. It would provide necessary orientation and learning experiences for Indians who are ill equipped to assume leadership roles in programs serving them; and for those who serve, or are to serve Indian people.

The second supporting component would provide for gathering, storing, retrieving, and disseminating statistical data on Indian populations, their needs and services to meet needs. This information is critically needed for the planning, operation, and evaluation of programs.

PROGRAM DEVELOPMENT

A special mechanism was devised to serve as the foundation for the Department-wide Indian program development component. The central feature of this mechanism is the five areas for emphasis. It is closely attuned to the departmental planning and budgeting systems and cycles.

In March 1968, a booklet, "Improving the Quality of Life Among Indians," was developed which provides guidance to operating agencies for preparing their plans to make substantive progress in each of the areas for emphasis—see exhibit (I).

In the booklet, agencies were requested to set objectives, identify specific program actions which they proposed to take to reach the objectives, and to estimate funds required to carry out the planned activities. Also, they were requested to identify policy and administrative constraints to achieving objectives.

This initial effort provided the Department for the first time with program and management information about the applicability and adaptability of its programs to the needs of Indians. Also, for the first time on a Department-wide basis, many operating agencies, with widely divergent missions, authorities, regulations, and methods of operations, developed specific planned efforts to meet needs of Indians within a common context; that is, the areas for emphasis.

An ongoing effort was organized and implemented in order to identify policy constraints to program development within the context of the areas for emphasis. Many such constraints have been identified through this process. Among those which have been resolved, two stand out as crucial to furthering basic Indian program development insofar as they established or affirmed the entitlement of qualified

Indians for health and welfare services available to other Americans in need—see exhibits II and III.

TRAINING AND ORIENTATION

A concept was developed to give substance to the training component of the plan. Its basic feature is the establishment of a National Indian Training and Research Center.

In collaboration with a number of Federal departments, private groups and foundations, the Department of HEW laid the conceptual groundwork in the form of a working draft for this effort. Both Indian and non-Indian groups were called upon to contribute ideas about the needs and possibilities that should determine the character of the Center.

An all-Indian steering committee was formed. The 20 committee members represented a cross section of Indian America. They were invited to critically evaluate the working draft and to give guidance on the most feasible method of implementing the concept which it represented. This was accomplished during two separate working sessions.

A decision emerged from the committee's deliberations calling for the establishment of a nonprofit corporation, the National Indian Training and Research Center. Incorporators and a Board of Directors were elected from the Steering Committee and authorized to proceed with the implementation of the proposal.

STATISTICS AND RELATED DATA

The rudiments of a mechanism were designed in connection with the statistical and related data component. This component is still in the process of development.

CONCLUSION

The Department of Health, Education, and Welfare has designed a strategy aimed at assuring that Indians are aware of, and full participants in all of HEW's programs, and when necessary, that the programs are combined and adapted to meet the Indians' special needs. A plan of action has been devised to translate the strategy into meaningful program action. In developing the plan of action, special mechanisms and techniques have been constructed and employed. These mechanisms and techniques are subject to continuing evaluation and refinement in order to achieve full realization of the departmental strategy in the field of Indian Affairs.

The efficacy of the Department's strategy and its implementation will determine, in part, the extent to which the Indian populations become characterized as healthy, well educated and socially sound. Such populations are best prepared to contribute to the success of economic development in American Indian communities.

[Exhibits follow.]

EXHIBIT I

IMPROVING THE QUALITY OF LIFE AMONG INDIANS

GUIDANCE FOR PLANS IN AREAS FOR EMPHASIS AFFECTING INDIANS

By U.S. DEPARTMENT OF HEALTH, EDUCATION, AND WELFARE

Introduction

American Indians * were present at the beginning of our country's development. Because of the shape of history, however, they have not shared fully in the benefits of the Nation's progress. Their levels of health, education, and related well being, as measured by a wide variety of indices, are among the lowest in America.

For many years the Buerau of Indian Affairs, Department of the Interior, was the sole Federal agency working with problems of poverty, poor health, and ignorance among Indians. Several decades ago, however, other agencies gradually became involved in Indian affairs. The predecessor of the Department of Health, Education, and Welfare was among the earliest of these. Today the Public Health Service—especially its Division of Indian Health, the Office of Education, the Social and Rehabilitation Service, and the Social Security Administration, are all closely involved. Many agencies of the Federal Government—the Department of the Interior, Housing and Urban Development, Labor, Commerce, Agriculture, and the Office of Economic Opportunity—provide a wide variety of services and benefits in response to Indians' needs.

Considerable progress has been made in helping Indians overcome their basic health, education, and social problems. However, in spite of progress, much remains to be done. For example:

    1. Indian infant death rates have declined 41 percent since 1955. However, the Indian rate of 40 per 1,000 live births is still 12 points above the national average.

    2. Indian life expectancy has risen from 62.5 years to 63.9 years since 1960. However, it is still over 6 years under the life expectancy as a whole.

    3. Indians are attending school in ever-increasing numbers. However, nearly 60 percent have less than an eighth grade education, and the drop-out rate is 50 percent.

---

* The term "Indian" includes Indians, Eskimos, and Aleuts.

4. Almost 100 industries have been encouraged to expand into Indian communities. However, the unemployment rate is almost 40 percent—10 times the national rate.

PROBLEMS

The Indians are well aware of the benefits resulting from the high quality of Department of Health, Education, and Welfare programs which reach them. They have expressed, however, through a variety of media such as tribal and intertribal government resolutions, conferences, special studies, and meetings with Federal and other Officials, problems to which, in their views, special Department of Health, Education, and Welfare service program attention should be directed. Some of the more frequently expressed problems have been grouped into several broad areas.

1. Quantities and types of services are variably insufficient or unavailable at levels required to meet needs.

2. Needed services are often reached only with great hardship due to distance and time required to reach places where services are available.

3. Opportunities to constructively participate in planning, operating, and evaluating programs aimed at meeting needs are inadequately developed. The Indians want to be of substantial support to the agencies working to meet their needs.

4. Understanding of Indians' cultures and related problems and circumstances on the part of service personnel is insufficient to promote optimum growth and development of client confidence in the professional worker and the services and service systems which he represents. The Indians feel that this high level of confidence is indispensable and deserved.

5. Kinds of available, accessible services sometimes are not optimally appropriate to needs of Indian individuals and communities.

These problems, recast as areas for emphasis, are shown in attachment I, along with program thrusts which departmental efforts concerning Indians will take.

POLICY

It is the policy of the Department to place special, continuing emphasis on reducing the problem areas cited above, through direct and supporting program and management actions.

It is the policy of the Department that its agencies will work closely among themselves and with other Federal agencies, State and local agencies, tribal governments and other appropriate organizations to the end of assuring coordinated intra- and inter-agency plans and collaborative actions aimed at reducing problem areas cited above.

It is the policy of the Department to direct its activities to Indians both on and off Federal Indian reservations.

IMPLEMENTATION

The Office of Education, Public Health Service, Social and Rehabilitation Service, and Social Security Administration should reexamine activity which took place in fiscal year 1967; was completed, is underway or planned for fiscal year 1968; and which is planned for fiscal year 1969, in order to:

1. Identify more precisely program content which has had, is having or will have a direct impact on Indian people as a target group, or as significant segments of larger target groups,

2. Identify resources (within the fiscal year 1968 appropriation and the President's budget for fiscal year 1969) and activities which can be directed or focused to address one or more areas for emphasis among Indians.

3. Set the stage for addressing intensified, expanded, and innovative efforts in each area for emphasis and reflecting these efforts in forthcoming plans for fiscal year 1970–1974.

These things can be done best within the framework of the departmental planning-programing-budgeting system. Instructions, forms, and related materials have been developed to that end.

Significant impact on Indian people can and does result from established efforts of individual DHEW agencies. This impact is strengthened in many instances, however, through the cumulative effort of intra- and interagency collaboration, as well as that of an interdepartmental nature. Thus, each DHEW agency should examine not only its own capacities to carry out programs within each area for emphasis, but, in addition, the potential for increased effectiveness of its efforts when coordinated with efforts of other parties working in related programs affecting Indians.

INSTRUCTIONS

PLANS IN AREAS FOR EMPHASIS AFFECTING INDIANS

This form is used for recording descriptions and data specific to a three or four digit program element, i.e., to one operating program of one organization, and one of the program categories to which it applies.

Program structure, codes, and definitions used in preparing the form are the same as those of the departmental planning-programing-budgeting system instructions, as revised, February 1968, except where otherwise noted.

Forms should be prepared for the lowest relevant organizational level—usually the bureau or division.

Box or column	*Instruction*
DHEW agency_____	Enter OE, PHS, SRS, or SSA.
Prepared by_____	Enter the name and organizational title of the person who coordinates preparation of the document.
Approved by_____	Enter the name and organizational title of the person who approves the document on behalf of the agency.
Date submitted_____	Enter the date on which the document is forwarded to OS.
(1) PPBS category code_____	Enter PPBS codes applicable to the agency at the following levels: OE, PHS—Third digit level. SRS, SSA—Fourth digit level. This is similar to the PPBS summary program and financial plan developed last fall.
(2) Areas for emphasis code_____	For each PPBS category code entered in column (1), enter codes of areas for emphasis within which the agency has taken, is taking, or plans to take action relative to Indians in fiscal year 1967, fiscal year 1968, or fiscal year 1969. Enter the number and NA (e.g., 3NA) for areas for emphasis within which the agency plans no action. (See attachment I for codes.)
(3) Objectives_____	Each agency should study each applicable area for emphasis (those not coded NA) entered in column (2) and the program thrust associated with it (see attachment I) to determine what it can do by the end of fiscal year 1969, alone or as a part of collaborative effort, and reflect its findings as one or more objectives. Each objective should specify, also, as exactly as possible, the amount of progress which is expected by the end of fiscal year 1968, as well as the situation as it was at the end of fiscal year 1967. Where feasible, objectives should include units of output as defined in instructions pertaining to PPBS form HEW 494 (Rev. 2/68), "Program and Financial Plan Output Data."

Constraints

In any cases where lack of, or inappropriate legislative authority is a constraint to addressing an area for emphasis, indicate the problem and its relationship to needed legislation. Do the same relative to administrative policy or any other constraint.

(4) PPBS activity code_____	For each objective shown in Column (3) enter PPBS activity code (two digits) for each type of activity involved in specific actions to be employed in achieving the objective.

Box or column	Instruction
(5) Brief description	For each Activity code shown in Column (4), describe in one or two lines the specific nature of each major action to be taken by the agency preparing the form. Collaborative efforts with other agencies or Departments should be cited, too. Work done under earned reimbursements should be so identified. Do not just name the PPBS Activity, e.g., Programmed Research. Rather, briefly describe what is to be done about Programmed Research during the plan period. Indicate plan period years during which each activity will take place.
(6) Responsible organizational unit	For each action shown in Column (5), indicate the organizational unit having closest immediate responsibility for undertaking or coordinating the action. This usually will be at the Division level. Identify the organizational unit by three digit PPBS organization codes.
(7) Program budget code	For each action shown in Column (5), enter six digit codes for funds to be tapped to support the action.
(8), (9), (10) Dollars	For each program budget code entry in Column (7) show total estimated funds to be used, by year of appropriation, in carrying out action during the specified fiscal years. Earned reimbursement funds should be indicated with a capital "R" preceding dollars shown, and the corresponding space in Column (7) left blank. FY 1967 data should go in Column (8), FY 1968 in Column (9), and FY 1969 in Column (10). Columns (11) and (12) are left blank.

Submission.—Requested materials, in duplicate, are due in the Office for Indian Progress, OS, Room 5721, DHEW North Building, by c.o.b., March 29, 1968.

AREAS FOR EMPHASIS AND PROGRAM THRUST IN ACTIVITIES RELATING TO INDIANS, DEPARTMENT OF HEALTH EDUCATION, AND WELFARE

Code	Areas for emphasis—Description	Program thrust
1	Availability to Indians of HEW service programs.	Develop, extend, improve, and implement mechanisms to assure that services and benefits provided through HEW supported programs are actually available to all Indians who qualify for them. Develop, extend, improve, and implement communications systems to assure that current information about services and benefits and eligibility requirement is meaningfully publicized among Indians.
2	Accessibility to Indians of HEW service programs.	Develop, extend, improve, and implement mechanisms for reducing time-distance gaps between residence of service population and points at which services are available.
3	Involvement of Indians in program planning, operation, and evaluation.	Develop, extend, improve, and implement mechanisms for expanding ranges and methods of Indian involvement at all levels of organization in planning, operation, and evaluation of programs affecting them.
4	Effectiveness of participation by personnel and Indians in service systems.	Develop, extend, improve, and implement mechanisms to increase effectiveness of service systems through improvement of the interrelationship between personnel dealing with Indians and Indians themselves, focusing on increasing non-Indian personnel understanding of Indians and their problems, and on increasing Indians' knowledge and skills prerequisite to their effective involvement in policy development and program guidance.
5	Appropriateness of programs to needs of Indians.	Develop, extend, improve, and implement mechanisms to stimulate and conduct research, development, testing, demonstration, and related scientific, statistical, and analytical activities aimed at yielding better ways of identifying potential Indian beneficiaries and their needs in health, education, and other areas related to HEW programs; and at yielding better procedures for planning, organizing, directing, and evaluating high quality service programs for achieving identified program objectives related to reducing needs and improving services to Indians.

ATTACHMENT II

DHEW Agency _____

Approved by _____

Page _____ of _____ Pages

Prepared by _____

Date Submitted _____

Areas for Emphasis

PPDS Activities to Achieve Objectives

PPDS Category Code (1)	Area for emphasis Code (2)	Objectives (3)	PPDS Activity Code (4)	Brief Description of Activities (5)	Resp. Org. Code (6)	Program Budget Code (7)	Budget Dollars (1,000's FY)				
							19 (8)	19 (9)	19 (10)	19 (11)	19 (12)

PLANS IN AREAS FOR EMPHASIS AFFECTING INDIANS

(2 of)

EXHIBIT II

DEPARTMENT OF HEALTH, EDUCATION, AND WELFARE,
SOCIAL AND REHABILITATION SERVICE,
Washington, D.C., April 18, 1968.

State Letter No. 1031

To: State agencies administering approved public assistance plans.

Subject: Eligibility of Indians, Including Those Living on Reservations, for Medical Care and Services Under Provisions of Social Security Act.

Questions have been raised which indicate States may not be clear as to the eligibility of Indians for medical care and services provided under the Social Security Act.

The following interpretations are aimed at resolving any uncertainty in this regard:

1. Indians shall have the same rights to receipt of medical services under a State plan approved under any of the public assistance titles of the Social Security Act, including title XIX, as do all other individuals in the State who meet the State's eligibility requirements.

2. In the case of a person who qualifies as an Indian beneficiary, the Division of Indian Health, Public Health Service, Department of Health, Education, and Welfare, may assume *residual* responsibility for medical care and services not included in the appropriate State plan, and for items that are encompassed by the plan, if such Indian chooses to utilize the Indian health facilities, without affecting the eligibility of the Indian under the State's medical assistance or other public assistance program.

3. Under the provisions of its approved medical assistance plan or other public assistance plans, the State agency responsible for such plans has *primary* responsibility for meeting the cost of the services provided therein for all individuals, regardless of race, who apply and are found eligible.

Sincerely,

STEPHEN P. SIMONDS, *Commissioner.*

EXHIBIT III

DEPARTMENT OF HEALTH, EDUCATION, AND WELFARE,
SOCIAL AND REHABILITATION SERVICE,
Washington, D.C., March 3, 1969.

State Letter No. 1062

To: State agencies administering approved public assistance plans.

Subject: Eligibility of Indians, Including Those Living on Reservations, for Assistance and Services Under Provisions of the Social Security Act.

Questions have been raised which indicate States may not be clear as to the eligibility of Indians for financial assistance and services provided under the Social Security Act.

The following interpretations are aimed at resolving any uncertainty in this regard:

1. State plan provision putting into effect titles I, IV, X, XIV, XVI, and XIX must be available State-wide to all eligible individuals. This includes State plan provisions added as a result of the 1967 legislation with reference to AFDC-Emergency assistance, unemployed fathers, and foster care.

2. Financial assistance through the Bureau of Indian Affairs, U.S. Department of the Interior (as well as medical assistance through Indian Health Service, Public Health Service, U.S. Department of Health, Education, and Welfare (see State Letter No. 1031)), is not available to individuals eligible for assistance from any other source.

Assistance, therefore from the Bureau of Indian Affairs, Department of the Interior, cannot be considered a basic resource in determining an individual's eligibility for a federally assisted program under the Social Security Act, since that resource is not actually available to persons eligible for the public assistance programs.

3. The Social Security Act provides that Federal sharing is available, under certain conditions when a child has been removed from his own home as the result of a judicial determination. The court or other judicial authority must have jurisdiction in such matters. Indian tribal courts and courts of Indian

offenses are courts of competent jurisdiction in this respect, and are so recognized by the laws and regulations of the United States.

Therefore, on Indian reservations, the authority of the tribal court to make such judicial determinations must be recognized by the State welfare agency as a proper authority for this provision of the Act.

4. This issuance does not replace or in any way modify State Letter No. 1031 which relates to medical assistance.

Sincerely,

STEPHEN P. SIMONDS, *Commissioner.*

MANPOWER PROGRAMS FOR INDIANS ADMINISTERED BY THE DEPARTMENT OF LABOR

FOREWORD

Indians participate in all the regular manpower training and employment programs administered by the Department of Labor. The Neighborhood Youth Corps and Operation Mainstream programs have been particularly popular on Indian reservations, and the results have been encouraging. Institutional and on-the-job training programs have produced mixed results, with subsequent job placement for enrollees sometimes presenting a difficult problem. Currently, various manpower programs are being coordinated into the Comprehensive Area Manpower Planning System, and efforts are being made to assure that Indians participate fully in this system and that they are represented on the various area, State, and regional CAMPS committees.

Introduction

While greatly increased efforts have been made by the Department of Labor to assist Indians to improve their employment situation, particularly in rural areas, a continued massive effort is still needed. Full employment of all American Indians may never become a reality in our lifetime. The present program being pursued in the Department of Labor, although a positive step in the direction of finding solutions to the "Indian problem," is inadequately funded to serve identified needs.

Indian population, according to the 1960 census, has been recorded at 552,000 persons. Three hundred thousand of these reside on Federal Indian reservations. The remaining 252,000 Indians reside in urban areas or on Indian reservations established through treaties with the States (thereafter under State jurisdiction). These State Indians are located along the east coast of the United States.

The Indian labor force—defined as all Indians of employable age neither in school nor prevented from working by retirement, ill health, or child care obligations—is estimated at 130,000 individuals. About 82,500 of these were at work in 1967. Estimates of Indian unemployment range from a low of 12 percent to a high of 74 percent, with an average unemployment rate of 38 percent. This is about 10 times the current national average unemployment rate.

In 1967, of a 10 percent sample of the total Navajo population, 88 percent of the men and 78 percent of the women age 14 and over, representing the Navajos actually in the labor force, 32.2 percent of the men and 51 percent of the women professed no knowledge of English, either written or oral. The average educational level (years of schooling) for American Indians was 5 years in 1966. Urban Indians tend to have higher academic achievement level and a slightly lower unemployment rate than the Indians from rural areas.

In an effort to prevent discrimination in the provision of placement services to minorities in the past, no records have been kept by State employment security officers on the employment status of Indians who reside in urban areas, or on State or Federal Indian reservations. This practice has been modified only recently to permit the collection of statistics on services to Indians and other minorities.

The tri-partite nature of Indian groups, i.e., (1) Federal reservation Indians, (2) off-reservation urban Indians, and (3) State reservation Indians, suggest diverse factors which have a bearing on Indian manpower programs. An example of the problem is provided by unenrolled members of the Cocopah Tribe in southwestern Arizona, numbering approximately 360, who live outside the urban communities but are not eligible for the services extended reservation Indians.

The Department of Labor has undertaken a number of manpower and employability programs to serve the disparate needs of the Indian groups in recent years. Program goals have been reoriented and delivery systems restructured to recognize the right of self-determination of the Indian people and to encourage their participation in planning their own destiny. Coordination of job training with economic development programs which create jobs on Indian reservations is being improved. Better ways of training of the Indian people for meaningful employment both on and off the reservation are being sought. A major thrust of the Department, over the past few years, has been directed toward assistance to Indians.

DEPARTMENT OF LABOR PROGRAM ACTIVITIES

Programs for Indians or other ethnic groups are not shown as separate and identifiable categories in the Department's budget; Indians participate in all the regular manpower training and employment programs administered by the Department. Following is a summary of the programs for Indians which can be identified for specific Indian reservations for fiscal years 1967 and 1968, and for fiscal year 1969 (through December 1968):

	Slots	Funds
Manpower Development and Training Act	4,380	$6,693,935
Neighborhood Youth Corps (in school and out of school)	19,488	12,777,097
Operation Mainstream	1,222	4,273,923

The impact of NYC and Operation Mainstream has been more immediate and apparent on Federal Indian reservations and consequently these programs have been extremely popular. The results of institutional and on-the-job training have been mixed; most problems have developed with placement of enrollees who have marginal qualifications.

Other Labor Department activities include:

(1) Two concentrated employment programs (CEP's) directly affecting Indian reservations, with $2 million obligated for each, one on the Navajo Reservation, Ariz.; the other in rural northern New Mexico.

(2) Two rural CEP's which are expected to serve a large number of Indians, although the projects are not specifically located on reservations. These are for a 10-county area in northern Wisconsin and a 10-county area of northern Minnesota. The latter covers several reservations.

(3) One hundred and ninety-eight positions have been established and funded to State employment security agencies to provide direct services to Indians.

(4) Indians are participating in the JOBS program in approximately 25 cities. New careers programs have been started on the Cherokee Reservation in North Carolina and the Navajo Reservation in Arizona. One project has been funded for $176,000 to establish a work incentive program for Indians eligible under AFDC in Nevada.

(5) The National Council on Indian Opportunity under the Executive Office of the Vice President has asked the DOL to look into the development of an apprenticeship program on Indian reservations where the construction being conducted on Indian reservations would provide the work opportunity necessary for apprenticeship training to take place. Presently the Arizona State office of the Bureau of Apprenticeship and Training is doing an analysis on the Arizona reservations and recommendations on how to develop an apprenticeship effort in the State for Indian reservations will be made shortly.

(6) The Department has cooperated with the Bureau of Indian Affairs through joint funding of training projects located at Missoula, Mont.; Roswell, N. Mex.; and Bismarck, N. Dak.

DELIVERY OF SERVICES

Adequate outreach services, testing, job orientation, guidance and counseling were unavailable to rural Indians for a number of years. Because of this neglect, funding of special programs for Indians is expensive—seemingly far out of proportion to their population base. Much is now being done, however, to improve utilization of available resources by providing the machinery which will make these services more readily available to Indians. Among steps taken within the past year to improve services to Indians are:

(1) A special assistant for Indian affairs has been appointed to serve on the manpower administrator's staff and to act on his behalf in all manpower matters relating to Indians. This position was filled by an American Indian.

(2) The Department of Labor is represented on the National Council on Indian Opportunity under the Executive Office of the Vice President by the special assistant for Indian affairs.

(3) Discussions have been initiated with the Bureau of Indian Affairs to identify the location and service areas for field staff outreach deployed by BIA and to compare this with positions allocated for Indian services by State employment security offices. The purpose is to find out whether any significant Indian communities are being grossly neglected and to recommend changes or reassignment of staff where necessary to provide service.

(4) Regional Manpower Administration representatives for Indian affairs have been designated in various regions of the DOL where concentrated Indian populations live and work.

(5) Steps are being taken to have Labor Department Indian representatives designated at State and local levels.

(6) In a separate but coordinated effort, the Department has recommended to the National Congress of American Indians that tribal manpower representatives be designated by the tribal councils as prime contact persons for the tribe with State and local employment security agency officials.

(7) The Labor Department has combined its efforts to give further attention to the Indian problem through the creation of an intra-departmental committee on Indian affairs to deal with Indian problems. It is chaired by the special assistant for Indian affairs.

The development of this structure which threads from the national office through regional offices to the State and local employment security offices, and the identification of specific persons within each tribal complex to deal with manpower programs round out the substructure which is necessary to go forward toward program objectives.

Through this organization will flow the information necessary to maximize the options for action available to Indian tribes and groups. The Federal assistance available will be put into sharper focus by the Indian tribes as they develop and implement their plans for overall economic development of their reservations.

JOINT PLANNING EFFORTS

Because of the changing character of national funding, varying statutory and administrative requirements, and conflicting agency jurisdictions, for Federal programs on Indian reservations, planning efforts have been thwarted and this causes problems in meeting objectives developed by Indians. Experience has dictated that short-range goals are necessary. Comprehensive long-range plans are critical to real growth on the reservations and must be given due attention.

Indian tribal plans must include a coordinated input from the several Federal agencies which now provide funds and services to Indians. Thus, the second step, after the development of the organizational structure to maximize services to Indians outlined above, is to develop a system which recognizes and uses options for planning and funding for Indian programs, through interagency coordination, with full participation of tribal groups. To this end, several agencies, including DOL, are cooperating in a joint effort with the Economic Development Administration which has developed a pilot program for 31 selected Indian reservation programs, specifically geared to meeting the select needs of a group of Indian tribes:

(1) EDA, OEO, and BIA have assisted the 31 tribes to formulate area action papers. Projects which are job producing projects have been identified by each of the tribes in each area action paper. The projects which have been identified have been assigned a priority listing by the tribes.

(2) Newly designated Regional Manpower Administrators' representatives for Indian affairs and members of the Intra-departmental Committee on Indian Affairs met with 16 reserva-

tions and groups in Phoenix in January 1969. The event was a Federal panel review of Indian Economic Development programs for the 16 Indian reservations and groups. This served as an orientation and workshop for DOL officials involved in Indian programs as an in-service training exercise for DOL staff.

(3) The Intradepartmental Committee on Indian Affairs plans follow-up on the Phoenix meeting.

DOL is now developing an annual program for Indian manpower services for the select Indian reservation program (see attachment 1).

INDIAN PARTICIPATION IN THE COMPREHENSIVE AREA MANPOWER PLANNING SYSTEM (CAMPS)

Care is being taken to assure a tie-in between the planning efforts described above with those of other manpower programs and that these plans are in turn coordinated through CAMPS. Attention is also being focused on adequate representation for Indians on the various area, State, and regional CAMPS committees.

After careful study of the problems reported by Indians in securing adequate representation in the CAMPS process, four recommendations to the Interagency CAMPS Committee are being considered, to afford more complete involvement of Indians in the system which affects their reservation development programs. They are:

(1) Designation of Indian tribal representatives from each tribe participating in EDA activities to the appropriate State CAMPS committee, and adequate representation of these groups on a technical subcommittee of the State committe involved. This would insure that reservation manpower plans of training and services have been coordinated with other planning. Representation for Indian tribes on the State level as well as the region is vital because the reservations are considered political subdivisions of the State under EOA title I–B.

(2) Some secretariat positions assigned to the State CAMPS committee to provide technical assistance in the development and preparation of the Indian component of the CAMPS plans for State and region. Indian reservations are under Federal jurisdiction, and therefore are eligible for special Federal program grants and aids for Indians. The Indian tribes are required to develop their own plans under these programs.

(3) Indian representation on the *Regional* CAMPS committees primarily because their reservations, and consequently their problems, transcend State lines.

The National Congress of American Indians during their executive council session, January 21–23, 1969, resolved that "whereas recent panel discussions have pointed out the difference between Indian and non-Indian values as to the importance of material possessions and the need of educators to understand these Indian matters in DOL training programs; that the DOL use such criteria for its education training programs other than the more material rewards so that these programs will be of greater interest to Indian participants." Behind this resolution is the conviction that Indians are culturally different more than culturally disadvantaged. In a society which is monoculturally oriented there are evidences that traditional methods need to be viewed in the face of bicultural characteristics and needs. Condemnation of the system alien to the Indians offers no solution in itself but may pave the way for some sound analysis.

The Indians intense desire to remain unchanged, to ignore the clock, to keep their customs intact, their heritage in high repute, and, their deep-seated attachment to their land, have augmented their fear that trusteeship by the Federal Government will be terminated, and have caused Indians to be wary of Federal Government program efforts. Prejudice experienced by Indians near reservation areas has contributed to defensive, negative attitudes toward instant outside help. Comprehensive planning by Indians, quality implementation by Indians, and effective followup by Indians, which have only recently become part of our policy in the conduct of Federal manpower programs on Indian reservations, must become the established pattern if we are to reverse the long years of distrust and bring about a climate for change which will make it possible for Indians to share more fully in a variety of employment opportunities.

Concentrated effort is being made to assist Indian youth in bridging the cultural gap without loss of identity. Attempts are being made to allow Indian people to make use of the best of both cultures while remaining firmly rooted in the Indian environment—if this is their choice—in order to lay the foundation for a healthier adjustment to the world of work than has heretofore been made.

However, any gains in this area will be lost unless the local Employment Service offices, which have Indian employment service staffs, recognize the role the Indian employment service staff must assume in relation to the tribal manpower plans and to be delegated the authority to act on behalf of the Employment Service organization so that tribal members will feel confident in turning to the employment service for assistance.

USDA PROGRAMS DIRECTED TO THE INDIAN COMMUNITY WITH ATTENTION TO THE RELATIONSHIPS AMONG USDA PROGRAMS AND THE HUMAN AND ECONOMIC DEVELOPMENT EFFORTS OF OTHER FEDERAL AGENCIES

FOREWORD

The Department of Agriculture operates no exclusively Indian programs, but the Department is giving increasing attention to problems of the rural poor and of rural economic development. Thus, emphasis on programs which are of benefit to Indians both on and off reservations is increasing. These programs include food assistance, rural housing assistance, forest service programs, soil and water conservation, and rural electric and telephone programs.

USDA PROGRAMS AVAILABLE TO THE INDIAN COMMUNITY

Although the Department of Agriculture operates no programs designed specifically for American Indian participation, most of our programs benefit the American Indian people. To the extent they constitute part of the target groups of programs, they benefit directly. As we continue to increase our attention to rural development and to the rural poor, programs of increasing benefit to Indians both on and off reservations have become available. A few examples of our more significant programs follow:

1. *Food assistance programs.*—Indians both on and off reservations have access to family food assistance programs. We expect that these programs will be available in the near future to low-income families in all parts of the Nation. Indians in needy families are included in this target group.

2. *Housing assistance.*—Loans to build or buy housing; to rehabilitate substandard homes; and to assist nonprofit groups in the development of rental housing in rural areas are available at sharply reduced interest rates to rural residents who are unable to find or afford adequate private credit. This program is being expanded sharply as part of the national housing program based on the Housing and Urban Development Act of 1968. It is available to Indians, as well as other low-income rural families.

3. *Forest Service programs.*—The Forest Service provides regular employment to around 400 American Indians. Last summer over 550 Indian youth were hired under the youth opportunity campaign. The Forest Service has also provided part-time firefighting employment for around 3,500 Indians in the Southwest and the Northern Plains area. Members of several reservations have participated in range management, land use, and technical assistance programs. Forest Service

research has recently designed plans for low-cost housing that will be of direct benefit to the Indian people. Over 100 Indian youth are enrolled in Job Corps Centers administered by the Forest Service.

4. *Rural electric and telephone.*—It is estimated that in September 1966, over 26,000 Indians were served by local electric cooperatives financed through the Department's Rural Electrification Administration. The REA, in coperation with OEO, HEW, and the Department of Labor, is presently developing a system that will provide electric service by the end of 1970 to some 67 small remote Alaskan communities.

5. *Soil and water conservation.*—Indians are major recipients of several of our resource conservation and development projects in Oklahoma, South Dakota, New Mexico, Idaho and Washington. It is estimated that our assistance under these programs in the coming fiscal year will be increased by about 10 percent over that of last year. Many Indians, particularly in the Southwest, are participating in the agricultural conservation program. To illustrate, about $1 million in cost-sharing funds has been made available in the past 5 years to assist the Navajo improve the productivity of their rangeland. This program will also be increased in fiscal year 1969. The Department is also cooperating with the Four Corners Regional Commission in developing the agricultural economy of that area.

6. *Water and sewer loans and grants.*—The Farmers Home Administration makes loans to associations and rural small towns for water and sewer facilities. For communities that are unable to repay the full cost of the loan, some grant funds are available to reduce the indebtedness to a level the community can afford. In designated areas, Farmers Home Administration loans are made in conjunction with grants from HUD, Interior, or the Department of Commerce. Legislation presently before Congress would change the present collateral requirement to facilitate loans for these and other purposes involving tribal corporations and tribal lands.

7. *Commodity programs.*—Many Indians participate in the Department's commodity programs, including the wool, wheat, feed grain, cotton and price support programs. In the event of natural disaster, the Department provides eligible farmers, including many Indians, with emergency livestock feed at reduced prices.

8. *Agricultural cooperatives.*—The Department is presently providing managerial and organizational assistance to several cooperatives having Indian membership.

9. *Other credit programs.*—The Farmers Home Administration makes loans to farmers and to rural residents who are unable to obtain credit elsewhere at reasonable rates. The loans are made for purposes of farm ownership, farm operating expenses, and small nonfarm enterprises.

10. *Extension programs.*—The Extension Service provides special programs designed to serve the particular needs of the Indian people in the specific situations where they live. These programs are concerned with improved family nutrition, improved housing and agricultural and community development. In fiscal year 1968, 84 extension workers provided training under contract to the BIA on specific reservations in 17 States having an Indian population of 313,592.

How USDA Programs Are Related to the Efforts of Other Federal Agencies

In the Department of Agriculture a substantial "outreach" effort is carried out to help rural residents, including Indians, gain convenient access to all programs of local, State, and Federal departments and agencies.

At the direction of the President, the Secretary of Agriculture is utilizing all the facilities of USDA field offices in the task of assisting other Federal agencies in making their programs fully effective in rural areas.

The principal mechanism is the technical action panel—a working group of representatives of all USDA agencies and interested local, State, and other Federal agencies located in a county or district. Over 3,000 of these groups are functioning at the county level in the 50 States and Puerto Rico.

These panels take the initiative in identifying problems of nonmetropolitan communities and rural parts of metropolitan communities which require the coordinated efforts of various departments and agencies for their effective solution.

At the Washington level, outreach is performed by the rural communities development staff which is responsible for identifying programs of other agencies and departments which will benefit rural citizens and for maintaining close liaison with the Washington level departments and the technical action panels in the field. An intradepartmental board with the Assistant Secretary for Rural Development and Conservation as chairman, is responsible for supplying local technical action panels the up-to-date information they need to perform their outreach function.

Two recent examples of successful TAP field operation are the work with the medicare program and cooperation with the Department of Labor in recruiting for manpower development programs. In both cases, the TAP's across the Nation effectively made available to many rural residents, who very likely would otherwise not have had it, information on important programs. Furthermore, rural residents who needed specific assistance in making application or following through on applications were helped.

This activity has been increasingly effective in helping rural residents gain access to non-USDA programs. The Department is continuing an extensive training effort to familiarize USDA employees with programs of other Departments and the particular needs of rural people these programs can best fill. USDA surveys indicate that TAP personnel are increasingly focusing their efforts and attentions on outreach and community development problems.

USDA Desk Officer for Minority Groups

In addition to the office of the Assistant to the Secretary for Civil Rights, the Secretary has designated the Deputy Assistant Secretary for Rural Development and Conservation as chairman of a departmentwide task force on problems of minority groups. One function of this officer is to represent the Secretary on the National Council on Indian Opportunity. In addition, this Deputy Assistant Secretary devotes special attention to the continuing problems of the Indian community and is charged with maintaining a constant review of agricultural programs to be sure that Indian benefit to the maximum extent possible.

ECONOMIC DEVELOPMENT IN THE AMERICAN INDIAN COMMUNITY; ROLE OF THE SMALL BUSINESS ADMINISTRATION

FOREWORD

Recent efforts by the Small Business Administration to encourage minority business enterprise have resulted in a substantially higher volume of lending to Indian-owned businesses. The SBA coordinates its lending program with the planning efforts of the Bureau of Indian Affairs and the Economic Development Administration. In addition to financial assistance, the SBA provides management assistance and technical training.

The Small Business Administration was created by Congress to insure free competition as the essence of the American economic system of private enterprise, and to strengthen the overall economy of the Nation. Through its 73 field offices, SBA offers financial assistance, management assistance, aid in obtaining Government contracts, counseling services and more than 500 publications covering successful practices in every small business field. These services are available, generally, to all small businesses throughout the country.

For many years, SBA has been particularly concerned with providing its assistance to disadvantaged persons. Our efforts have culminated in a bold new thrust to foster and encourage the development and expansion of small businesses among the socially and economically deprived segments of our population with special attention to small business concerns located in areas with high proportions of unemployed or low-income individuals, or owned by low-income individuals. The SBA effort to foster minority business enterprise involves all existing SBA authority and combines the efforts of private industry, banks, local communities, and the Federal Government, and is known as Operation Business Mainstream.

This new effort officially began on August 13, 1968, and has, thus far, been successful. In fiscal year 1968, prior to this new effort, 45 loans, totaling $1,296,880 were made to businesses owned by Indians. In only 7 months of this new effort (August 1968 through February 1969), these amounts were almost equaled with 42 loans for a total of $1,256,800 having been made. During this latter period the average loan size to Indian borrowers was $29,924 while the average loan size to all minorities was $21,813. There is every indication that the rate already achieved in the first 8 months of 1969 will continue and probably be exceeded.

Fostering minority business enterprise requires no new lending authority. It utilizes all lending, management and other assistance programs now operated by SBA. The program represents the current emphasis of the Agency with the additional factor of actively seeking assistance from the private sector of the economy. The SBA recognizes that the Federal Government, despite its vast resources, cannot, and indeed should not attempt to do the job alone.

Economic development among the underprivileged must be carefully planned if it is to accomplish its primary purpose, viz., bringing the economically deprived into the mainstream of our free enterprise economy. We realize that economic conditions vary around the country, between areas and cities, from city to city, between Indian reservations and surrounding areas. In any given area, the most immediate need may be for retail and service establishments to provide the residents of a deprived area with needed sources of goods and services. By assisting in the establishment of such small businesses by residents of the area, located in the area, the services are supplied and the profits to be made thereby are kept in the area and recirculated rather than being drawn off into more affluent surrounding areas. In other locations, however, more sophisticated labor-intensive businesses are needed to provide funds with which to purchase locally available goods and services. In addition, such light manufacturing and wholesale industries, owned and operated by area residents will provide a flow of new funds into the deprived area. The major thrust of economic development in deprived areas must be to encourage the inflow of funds from other more prosperous areas and to insure the availability of needed goods and services in that area, thereby keeping all or a good part of these new funds circulating within the area.

SBA's experience indicates that economic development in the American Indian community, as with all economically and socially disadvantaged communities, requires a special effort to—

(1) Seek out potential entrepreneurs and existing ones that wish to, and can successfully expand;

(2) Assist potential entrepreneurs in finding appropriate business opportunities; and

(3) Help provide the needed capital and management and technical training.

OUTREACH EFFORTS

To accomplish the first two items above, the agency must be knowledgeable about the communities involved and their inhabitants must be aware of the programs offered through SBA.

SBA is basically a resource agency, not a planning one. Once the decision has been made to start a new business or expand an existing one, SBA can provide financial and other assistance. However, we do actively assist those groups, both public and private, that exercise an economic planning function. For the most part, our assistance programs are wholly decentralized with operating authority vested in our 62 regional offices. Recognizing the diversity of local problems and local priorities, our regional office personnel have been encouraged to, and in fact do maintain close liaison with relevant planning groups. Our personnel meet on a regular basis with cognizant BIA personnel, EDA personnel and tribal officials. We also maintain a close working relationship with State development agencies and intertribal groups.

The primary purpose of these close contacts is to inform the knowledgeable planners and the representatives of the economically deprived areas of the assistance available through SBA and the requirements that must be satisfied before such assistance can be forthcoming. An additional benefit of such liaison is the fact that any request for assistance resulting from these planning sessions will be processed by an office that is aware of the background of and the need for the enterprise as well as the aspirations of the community and the individuals involved. In this manner, we can assist and encourage proper economic planning and be sure that the obstacles as well as the benefits are understood and have been considered in proper perspective.

Although our offices are located in urban areas, we have participated in meetings, conferences, briefings, and similar gatherings in any location where our assistance has been requested and where it appears appropriate. When the demand warrants it, we have established regular time periods on Indian reservations and elsewhere when a loan officer is present to answer all inquiries, and assist prospective borrowers in their dealings with SBA.

Specific SBA Programs

As a general rule, members of economically deprived groups lack both the needed capital to become small businessmen and the management and technical expertise necessary to be successful as entrepreneurs. Indian reservations are not generally located in proximity to sizable urban areas and are not routinely serviced by major banks or other financial institutions. The proper business climate that is part of the environment found in many urban and rural areas is woefully lacking on reservations. Although the will to succeed in business may be present, the drive will be wasted without proper financing and management and technical assistance.

Financial Assistance

SBA has three financial assistance programs that are particularly applicable to economic development in Indian areas; the Regular Business Loan program (RBL), the Economic Opportunity Loan program (EOL), and the Local Development Company program (LDC). These are all loan programs whereby SBA can loan money to, or guarantee loans by banks and other lending institutions to small businesses. With the exception of LDC's, the business must be organized on a profitmaking basis and financing must be unavailable on reasonable terms from other sources. The loans cannot be used for certain purposes, viz., to finance speculation, certain amusement or recreational facilities, newspapers, radio or television, gambling, relending or investing, agriculture, etc. And most importantly, there must be reasonable assurance of repayment of the loan.

Recently, relaxed criteria have been established for the RBL program to bring such loans more in line with the EOL program. The maximum loan to any one business under EOL is $25,000, under RBL, $350,000. These loans are for long terms, generally providing for amortization over a period of 10 years. For new businesses, a private equity injection of 15 percent of the amount of the loan requested is generally required. However, loans can be and have been made with smaller private equity injections where the circumstances warrant. The private equity injection can be in the form of cash, assets, or loans, provided the loans are subordinated to the SBA debt.

The LDC program is particularly applicable to assist Indian economic development. It affords the community an opportunity to establish industrial parks, shopping centers, and similar multibusiness developments as well as to provide aid to small businesses. Twenty-five or more citizens may form an LDC either as a profit or nonprofit corporation, whose basic purpose is to benefit the community involved by placing a new business (or keeping an existing one) in the community. SBA may lend up to $350,000 for each small business to be aided, for up to 25 years. On Indian reservations, the LDC must provide only 10 percent of the cost of the project for each identifiable small business. Funds may be used for plant construction, expansion, modernization, or conversion, including the purchase of land, building, equipment, and machinery. Simultaneously, SBA may make a working capital RBL or EOL loan to the independent small business. The advantages of the 502 program in economic development in Indian areas is self-evident. It is a program specifically designed to support community initiative, foster economic development, and create employment through new industries.

Other SBA financing programs, such as displaced business loans, lease guarantees, and small business investment companies may also make a substantial contribution to economic development of Indian areas in particular situations.

It should be noted that SBA's emphasis has been on guaranteeing loans by banks rather than on making direct loans. SBA can guarantee up to 90 percent of a bank loan under the RBL and LDC programs and up to 100 percent under the EOL program. By using this method, a small business becomes accustomed to dealing with banks and can reap the benefits connected with an appropriate bank relationship. Additionally, the bank can acquire a new customer and provide it with the full range of bank services, helping it to assume a competitive position in our economy and lessening the business' reliance on the Government. These positive factors together with considerations of governmental priorities and the enormous capital needs of the economically underprivileged have caused SBA to rely on its guarantee program rather than on its direct lending program.

Unfortunately, there are few banks doing business on Indian reservations and there has been a marked reluctance on behalf of many nearby banks to make loans on Indian reservations or to individual Indians. While recent Government and private efforts under Operation Business Mainstream have resulted in greater bank willingness to make loans in the area of Indian economic development, the flow of these funds is still not sufficient to meet the demand. Reasons given by banks for their reluctance to participate with SBA include the expense of servicing high-risk small loans to Indians and also, the fact that the Indian's best asset, his land, is unavailable for use as collateral in seeking bank loans. This matter requires serious and immediate attention. Perhaps consideration should be given to establishing a national Indian bank where tribal funds, trusteed funds, and even private funds could be channeled into SBA and similar lending programs.

MANAGEMENT ASSISTANCE

The lack of management and technical training of Indians presents an equally serious obstacle to economic development. Without such training, businesses are generally doomed to failure, even if provided with adequate capital. SBA's management assistance programs, including individual advice and group instruction, are aimed specifically at strengthening small business and improving the management capability of small businessmen.

Assistance on an individual basis is provided both by SBA employees and by SCORE (Service Corps of Retired Executives). SBA specialists make periodic visits to many remote communities to provide assistance to businesses on problems of marketing, accounting, product analysis, production methods, and research and development. SCORE provides expert advice of retired, successful businessmen to all businessmen who might otherwise not be able to hire experts to help them with their business difficulties. This service is voluntary by SCORE personnel, and is free to SBA, except for direct expenses.

On a group basis, SBA has sponsored and cosponsored conferences, workshops, and clinics for existing and potential small businessmen. Many of these programs are aimed at prospective small businessmen and deal with matters of importance to them, such as capital requirements and sources of financing, forms of business, organization, location, and so forth. In addition, SBA distributes many publications of general interest to prospective small businessmen, and publications which deal with specific management problems.

While these programs all contribute to supplying needed management expertise, they have not been able to compensate for the lack of business background prevalent in so many Indian communities. SBA's resources are insufficient to overcome this major obstacle. The voluntary SCORE program has not filled the gap due mainly to the distances involved and the absence of SCORE chapters in proximity to Indian communities. Other government agencies, notably the Economic Development Administration, have addressed themselves to this problem, but even the combined effort has not alleviated it.

Although the existing statutory authority appears adequate, the available resources do not permit measures sufficient to adequately cope with this problem. In this instance, private sector participation could close the gap. A VISTA-type volunteer program of experienced business or professional men, or voluntary donations of professional, management, and technical personnel time by private business organizations or groups should be fostered. Private industry, by its business success, has demonstrated its technical and managerial expertise and should be encouraged to share its knowledge, on a direct one-to-one basis, with less fortunate elements of our society.

PROCUREMENT ASSISTANCE

Each year the Federal Government does billions of dollars worth of business with private companies. The SBA helps small businessmen obtain a share of this Government business. Specialists in our field offices counsel small businessmen on prime contracting and subcontracting. They advise on which Government agencies buy the products or services supplied by a small business, guide the business in having its name placed on appropriate bidders' lists, help the small business to obtain drawings and specifications for proposed purchases, and assist in other ways.

The Government-wide "set-aside" program has helped this effort considerably. Under this program, the major Government purchasing agencies voluntarily set aside contracts or portions of contracts for small business. To augment this unilateral action, SBA has its own representatives stationed in major military and civilian procurement installations. They recommend additional set-asides, provide small business sources to contract officers, assist small concerns with contracting problems, recommend relaxation of unduly restrictive specifications, and so forth. SBA periodically checks the effectiveness of small business programs administered by procurement activities.

The fact that a small concern may be the low bidder on a Federal contract does not insure that it will in fact receive the contract. The contracting officer may question the low bidder's ability to perform the contract. In such cases, the concern may ask SBA for a "Certificate of Competency" (COC). Before a COC is issued, SBA specialists make an on-site survey of its facilities, management, performance record, and financial status. If SBA concludes that the company has, or can obtain, the necessary credit and productive capacity to perform the contract successfully, it issues the COC. The small business is then awarded the contract.

Subcontracting on Government procurements also offers an excellent opportunity for small business. SBA develops subcontract opportunities for small businesses by maintaining close contact with prime contractors and referring qualified small firms to them. We work closely with the largest contract-awarding agencies: The Department of Defense, General Services Administration, NASA, Atomic Energy Commission, and others. Under regulation established by these agencies, Government prime contractors must give small concerns an adequate opportunity to compete for subcontracts.

Under the Small Business Act, SBA also has authority to act as prime contractor on Government procurement contracts and may then subcontract with small firms which may be owned by economically deprived individuals or which will provide jobs for the hard-core unemployed. If necessary, labor training funds can also be utilized in this effort. The object of this program is to train unemployed people in depressed areas in skills which are salable in the normal labor markets. In the case of business owned by Indians or other deprived individuals, SBA seeks contracts for goods and services with continuing requirements and contracts that will enable the small business to raise its management and technical expertise to the level where it will be able to successfully compete in its chosen industry independent of direct SBA assistance.

This program, known as the 8(a) program, is being implemented in cooperation with the private sector. American industry is being asked to put all its expertise and all possible resources and energy behind this effort, and already there has been a gratifying response from numerous major corporations.

In addition to Federal Government procurement, there is enormous potential for small business in procurements by State and local government. Although SBA has no statutory authority in this area, many of our regional offices have made their local governments aware of the potential benetfis to underprivileged individuals and underdeveloped areas of awarding procurement contracts to small business owned and operated by, or employing such individuals or located in such areas. This potential market for goods and services produced by or in Indian communities should be exploited to the fullest extent possible.

FUTURE EFFORTS

Minority business ownership will continue to be a major emphasis of SBA. The agency will increase its efforts to encourage new small business enterprises and upgrade existing ones owned and operated by socially and economically deprived individuals. In those regions with substantial Indian populations or where reservations are located, major emphasis will continue to be placed on whatever assistance we can provide to Indian entrepreneurs, potential and existing, in cooperation with all other cognizant groups, public or private. The successes of the program during its relatively short existence and the cooperation which has been generated from other Government agencies, the financial community, and private industry have encouraged our efforts. Of course, improvements need to be made, new ideas and programs must be encouraged. The 8-month existence of the program to put minorities in business has been marked by constant innovation and change to meet particular problems of economic development among Indians and other underprivileged groups.

In recent months, we have witnessed a marked increase in efforts being made to coordinate economic development programs for Indians. We applaud these efforts and will continue to support them to the best of our ability. Because our basic function is as a resource agency rather than planning agency, until recently we have not been in the mainstream of this coordinating effort. We feel, however, that it is essential and should be bolstered.

It should also be recognized that coordination is necessary both on the national and local level. Major programs and goals should be interphased at the national level, particularly including detailed information as to the specific goals and programs of each agency involved in this effort. Hopefully, this exchange of information will permit the planners to identify necessary areas that are being ignored and areas of overlap and duplication between agencies. Once identified, remedial steps can be taken.

It would not be appropriate, however, to impose strict program operation and inflexible instructions, even in the area of coordination, from the national level. Policy and guidelines must be flexible. Conditions and circumstances differ from State to State, from city to city, and from reservation to reservation. Coordination at the local level by field personnel should be encouraged.

The key feature of a coordinated economic development approach in Indian affairs must be adaptability. The approach must be dynamic, not static. In this manner, the Indian community can be assisted in its attempts to reverse the trend of decay, and the American ethic of equality will have a practical and visible meaning to the Indian community and to individual Indians. Given an opportunity and help from the Government and from the private sector, the Indian can join the economic mainstream of our society.

[Appendixes follow:]

APPENDIX I

Correspondence between the Commissioner of the Bureau of Indian Affairs and the Small Business Administration:

U.S. DEPARTMENT OF THE INTERIOR,
BUREAU OF INDIAN AFFAIRS,
Washington, D.C., September 6, 1968.

Hon. HOWARD J. SAMUELS,
Administrator, Small Business Administration,
Washington, D.C.

DEAR MR. SAMUELS: Your new program, "Project Own," has just come to my attention. Although it is described in terms of serving the needs of the urban inner core, I am confident that you intend also to include Indians in its goal of increasing the number of business enterprises to be owned and operated by members of minority groups.

Indian areas need business enterprises owned and operated by tribal residents as desperately as any urban slum. Although our program of industrial development has been in operation for over 10 years and has to its credit today a total of more than 100 enterprises, employing over 4,000 Indians, much remains to be done. In recent months we have been giving special emphasis to the development of entrepreneurial franchise operations on the reservations. We welcome the opportunity offered by your agency in the form of loans to finance franchise operations and other small businesses.

So that our two agencies may explore the most effective means of assuring the inclusion of Indians among the economically disadvantaged groups benefiting from "Project Own," please let me know whom on your staff we may contact.

Sincerely yours,

ROBERT L. BENNETT, *Commissioner.*

DEPARTMENT OF THE INTERIOR,
BUREAU OF INDIAN AFFAIRS,
Washington, D.C., September 12, 1968.

Hon. ROBERT L. BENNETT,
Commissioner, Bureau of Indian Affairs, U.S. Department of the Interior,
Washington, D.C.

DEAR MR. BENNETT: Administrator Samuels has asked me to reply to your letter of September 6, 1968.

Your point that Indians should be included in the goal of increasing the number of businesses to be owned and operated by members of minority groups is well taken. The Administrator wholeheartedly agrees.

In announcing the program, Mr. Samuels pointed out that SBA would not use a set formula for every area of the country, but would vary its approach from community to community, not only in urban areas but also in rural areas having high proportions of unemployed, low-income, or disadvantaged individuals.

The opportunities under "Project Own" will be available across the country through our 77 field offices. In a limited number of locations, it is our plan to establish Minority Entrepreneurship Teams, with personnel to be stationed in the heart of the disadvantaged area (urban or rural). However, the absence of such a Team in a given location will in no way deny the benefits of the program to that location.

We welcome your suggestion that our two agencies explore together the most effective means of assuring the inclusion of Indians among the beneficiaries of this program. Please advise your staff to communicate with the undersigned to arrange a meeting. My telephone number is (code) 128-7267.

Sincerely,

MURRAY W. KRAMER,
Acting Director, Office of Operations Development.

APPENDIX II

The following are excerpts from recent reports by SBA field offices concerning their involvement in economic development in the American Indian community:

General

The experience on these loans has been quite satisfactory. A few have been slow in making payments, but this is primarily due to weather conditions which adversely affect certain operations in this area. Very few have ended in liquidation. At present there are several small proposals that are being developed. (*Wisconsin*)

There appears to be a good future for SBA aid in the American Indian community, but it also is evident that qualified capable businessmen may be lacking to carry out the daily operations. Some consideration should be given to an SBA program to provide aid to tribe-owned and operated businesses. This may be a future SBA lending program. (*California*)

We have found that programs progress much more successfully when cleared through the proper "Tribal Council officials" and believe valuable data in regard to applicants—both pro and con—can be developed through these sources. Without the cooperation of tribal officials, our loan programs in these communities could be disastrous. (*South Dakota*)

There was a recent flood in Marietta, Washington, which is an Indian village. We immediately called upon the Leaders, made a survey of the damage, had it declared a disaster area, and made 14 disaster loans to repair some of the damage to their homes, furniture and fishing gear. SBA was the only Agency, except the Red Cross, active in assisting the tribe in this flood disaster. In addition, it turns out that the tribe had some problems which would require the services of a lawyer beyond any authorities of SBA. Arrangements were made through the Seattle Bar Association for an attorney to be delegated to assist them in clearing title to some land they were unable to use due to the title being clouded by a faulty transfer of the land more than a 100 years ago to the Tribal Chief as an individual rather than to the Tribe. They were very grateful for this assistance. In addition to the assistance under the disaster loan program, we have made three regular business loans to Indian-owned and operated businesses. (*Washington*)

We have found by experience that the "most good" can be done by establishment of industry. This provides employment for a relatively large group of Indians. (*South Dakota*)

One recent development of importance was the approval of a loan to Inupiat Arts and Crafts, Inc. of Teller, Alaska, a business corporation which resembles a cooperative. Its incorporators, stockholders, directors and officers are (except for one Caucasian) Alaska Eskimos. The members (or owners) are ivory carvers and producers of artifacts. The corporation will purchase raw materials and market finished products, and also provide for its members' use some larger equipment which could not economically be owned by any one of them. (*Alaska*)

The immediate prospects for loan activity (on the) reservations are not good. There has been little or no initiative on the part of the tribal governments. It is foreseeable that the example of the Mohawks . . . may impel the other tribes to some action with respect to economic development. We will continue to encourage and assist fully such effort. (*New York*)

Other Agencies

The Bureau of Indian Affairs' officials work closely with the SBA regional office and attend pertinent staff conferences at the SBA office. SBA personnel attend meetings at BIA and both agencies frequently travel together on joint projects for Indian economic development. The Regional Director serves on the Commission for the development of certain property owned by IDDA (Indian Development District of Arizona). (*Arizona*)

We maintain close relationship with the Tribal Councils and the BIA. Banks are often reticent to make loans on reservations. We are working to overcome this hesitation through our guarantee plan in 502, EOL, ME and 7(a) loans. We are making good headway in most states, except Montana where the old distrust is harder to dissipate than anywhere else. We believe that time and our continued efforts will bear fruit here also. (*Rocky Mountain Area*)

Personnel of our office have coordinated and worked with the Bureau of Indian Affairs; Office of Economic Opportunity; Economic Development Administration; Forest Service (USDA); Farm Home Administration; Manpower Development Training . . . We have worked with the following State Agencies: State Coordinator of Indian Affairs; the Governor's Office; University System; State Technical Services; Unemployment Compensation Commission, and Consortium located at the University of Montana. (*Montana*)

This office has worked closely with the Bureau of Indian Affairs in developing areas where we can be of assistance. We have attended and provided speakers at various Economic Development workshops sponsored by the Indian Community Action Project. We have attended and discussed SBA programs with special emphasis on EOL and Project OWN programs with Technical Action Panels. These panels are made up of various Federal, State, and local organizations who are in a position to disseminate information about the SBA and its programs. We have met with Reservation Development Coordinators and Tribal Councils in order to advance the availability of our program. (*Wisconsin*)

A good deal of confusion could be avoided if possibly a memorandum of understanding between SBA and BIA could be enacted. This memorandum clearly would explain BIA restrictions on financial dealings concerning Indian lands of various types and Tribal and individual Indian funds. (*California*)

We also work closely with the Bureau of Indian Affairs. There is an agency office on each Indian reservation and they have generally designated one person to work closely with SBA. They not only provide leads for us but also provide assistance in putting a loan package together. (*North Dakota*)

Outreach

In order to inform the American Indian community of the assistance available through the Small Business Administration, this Regional Office has arranged to meet with interested Indians at the various reservations. Originally, a specific day each month was allocated to each reservation. Because of the lack of attendance, this policy was discontinued except for three reservations. However, arrangements have been made that when we are aware of any Indian or group of Indians who are interested in what SBA has to offer, we arrange for the most appropriate SBA personnel to meet with these interested parties at a place most convenient to them. This is usually at the reservation. This has resulted in several meetings which, hopefully, will develop into a concerte financial or other type SBA assistance. In addition to these specific meetings with interested Indians, the regular circuit-rider interviews are held in areas, some of which are close to the various reservations. SBA personnel have participated in workshops sponsored by groups interested in the Indian community. As a result of these outreach programs, this Regional Office has provided financial assistance to 21 businesses operated by the American Indian. (*Minnesota*)

This office is operating with the Rural Alaska Community Action Program in presenting the SBA story to remote villages and with VISTA attorneys attached to Alaska Legal Services for assistance in preparing applications and presentations. (*Alaska*)

Management Training

The remaining and most serious problem with which we are faced at present is our endeavor to provide sufficient follow-up once the loan has been made. As mentioned above, the applicant-borrower is competent in his trade, skill, or, as the case may be, he knows his product. The problem he faces is lack of business management know-how. (*North Dakota*)

Time would not permit a detailed study of Manpower Training Act directives, however, as a general statement, we believe the criteria for providing training to Indians should be extremely liberal since one of our problems is in finding prospective entrepreneurs with training and experience qualified to manage a small business. (*Montana*)

The greatest problem now facing our Indian economic assistance program is to make management assistance available. Due to distance and rural aspects of reservations SCORE assistance is difficult to provide. Staff personnel in MA because of the varied demands on their time can allot only a limited amount to Indian entrepreneurs and reservations. For an office servicing the number of Indian loans and Indian people that this office does, it is suggested that a Management Assistant Specialist for Indians only be provided. (*Arizona*)

It is difficult to measure counseling results; however, we have made seven loans. One of our loan officers is currently counseling a Winnebago group in regard to a homecraft effort and another of our loan officers has interviewed a prospective retail food dealer. Several of our loans in Menominee County have been for the transportation of forest products. The Menominee owned sawmill at Neopit is the sole industry in that county. Emphasis has been given Menominee County since its members number approximately 2500 persons whereas the other tribal groups are quite small (Oneida 361, Stockbridge-Munsee 214). Other current efforts in process involve small service businesses, including barber shop, filling station and a retail full service store. (*Wisconsin*)

One disadvantage for implementation of the course in management has been the difficulty of communicating with these people in using only the English language for instruction. By using bi-lingual abilities of the chosen coordinators, we are of the firm opinion that we have found the solution to management improvement in the out-lying areas where this training is so sorely needed. (*Alaska*)

Banks

Since it is still difficult to get private lending institutions involved, a loosening of funds for direct loans on Indian reservations is vital in all of our lending programs. (*Rocky Mountain Area*)

All banks near or on Indian Reservations have been contacted, both personally and through writing by personnel of our office. In most cases, contacts with the banks have not been encouraging. The banks have not participated in any way with the loans that have been made to individual Indians and do not plan to participate under the active inquiries mentioned above. A suggestion has been forwarded by a Loan Officer of this office, that SBA guarantee small business loans made by Indian tribes. (*Montana*)

Some success in securing bank participation has been experienced. However, banks are 20 to 30 miles from the reservations, and since they are small, with limited personnel, these banks find it difficult to service this type of participation loan. (*Wisconsin*)

Currently a plan has been developed whereby the leading bank in Arizona has designated a bank officer to work with SBA on minority loans with SBA guarantees. These will include loans to Indians on and off the reservations. (*Arizona*)

In addition we have had some inquiries during our Outreach to the Northern Counties of Siskiyou, Humboldt, and Trinity. The major problem here is that the banks are reluctant to participate and, according to the Loan Officer, the loans are not of the EOL nature. (*California*)

502 Program

In 1968, ten 502 Local Development Company loans were made to individual members (SBCs) of the Makah Indian Tribe. These are fishing vessel enterprises designed to adequately equip Indians to fish competitively on a commercial basis. An important factor in these projects was an opportunity which allowed the Indian to operate in a natural environment in or near his community rather than displacing him to urban areas of unfamiliar competition. This project reached capability through the knowledge that certain tribal assets are available to individual members only through projects that are beneficial to the tribe as a whole, such as community projects. A whole new dimension of assistance is open to a tribe functioning through the Local Development 502 Program. (*Washington*)

The Development Company Assistance Program has been a prime vehicle in the Rocky Mountain Area in the economic development of the American Indian communities. We have approved eight loans to local development companies on Indian reservations to assist manufacturing firms to locate there. These firms have provided 607 jobs for American Indians. Typical of these is the loan made in F/Y 1968 to the Omaha Tribal Opportunities Corporation, Walthill, Nebraska. A plant was constructed for Omahaline Hydraulic Corporation, a subsidiary of Prince Manufacturing Corporation of Sioux City, Iowa. It will provide 80 new jobs for members of the Omaha Tribe. Similar projects are now pending in South Dakota and Montana, as will no doubt be discussed in the answers you will receive from the Regional Directors in those states. (*Rocky Mountain Area*).

Some of our projects have contributed greatly to the Indian economy. We have just recently approved a 502 loan to the Cannon Ball Development Corporation (a wholly-owned Indian development company). Cannon Ball is a small community located on the Standing Rock Indian Reservation. The small business concern to be assisted, Chief Manufacturing, anticipates employment of 20 to 25 Indians. The $25,000 loan will assist the small business concern in the manufacture of novelty and souvenir items. The product will be imprinted with the Sioux Indian Tribe emblem. (*North Dakota*).

ECONOMIC DEVELOPMENT OF THE AMERICAN INDIAN AND HIS LANDS

Position Paper of the National Congress of American Indians

FOREWORD

The National Congress of American Indians is composed of 105 Indian tribes, containing more than 350,000 American Indians, and providing services to an even larger proportion of the Indian population. In its position paper, the NCAI states that efforts to assist the American Indians to become economically self-sufficient—efforts which now date back more than 100 years—have been in large measure a failure. The severe poverty and deprivation in which many Indian people live today "almost defy comprehension." Particularly urgent are the problems of the smaller and poorer tribes which have been completely unable to institute programs of economic development. Recently introduced programs of Federal assistance have enabled some tribes to achieve a greater degree of self-government and economic independence, but, in general, this progress has been limited to those tribes which have had the funds necessary to employ adequate legal counsel and to support economic program planning. The NCAI sponsors programs designed to assist the Indian tribes with economic planning, to provide technical assistance in applying for Federal and private development funds, and to encourage intertribal efforts to find joint solutions to problems of a regional nature. With the help of a grant from the Economic Development Administration, the NCAI is currently undertaking to establish a National Indian Development Organization which would make credit available for economic development programs.

The National Congress of American Indians (NCAI) is the only private, national Indian-directed organization limiting its voting power membership to Indian tribes and individuals. Serving as the speaking voice of the American Indian people, we include within our membership 105 Indian tribes, representing over 350,000 American Indians, and we provide services which reach even more of the Indian population.

NCAI has pledged itself to an economic development policy which contains the following principles: (1) Self-determination by the Indian people in their quest for social and economic equality; (2) protection of Indian tribal and individual ownership of Indian lands and resources, and maintenance of tax-exempt status for income derived from such lands, and for the lands themselves; (3) maximum development of the human and natural resources of Indians with the assistance of the BIA and all other Federal agencies offering programs and services designed to relieve conditions of poverty among all Americans.

We have spoken out often on this matter of Indian self-determination with respect to the matters affecting the lives and destiny of Indians, and there has been much lipservice, but little real substance, given to this concept by the officials of the Government.

Far too often, we have found the Congress voting on Indian matters with little knowledge of our views, and with no sensitivity to, or understanding of, them. We cannot contend more strongly that Congress cannot legislate or otherwise establish a successful program of Indian economic development without significant Indian input, or without recognition that success in the final analysis will depend, not on what the Congress thinks is good for the Indians, but what the Indian thinks is good for himself.

For over 100 years, it has been the policy of the U.S. Government to assist the American Indian to become economically self-sufficient. In large measure, as the statistics which follow will reveal, this policy has been a failure. At the root of this failure is the fact that the Indian's goals and cultural attitudes have largely been ignored in the perpetuation of this policy. It has never occurred to the majority of those pronouncing this policy that many Indians may not want to swim in a mainstream they largely regard as polluted and that they should be free to refuse; or that there might exist an Indian culture, which not only rejects the materialistic value system of the White Man, but has positive values in terms of brotherhood, and preservation of one's environment, from which the White Man could learn, if he were willing to listen.

Let us dispel another frequently made, yet erroneous assumption; that there is a close analogy to be drawn between the economic problems of Indians and those of other minority groups, and that, therefore, the same solutions will apply. To be sure, Indians bear the same mantle of alienation borne by other minorities: this is a product of rejection and discrimination against them by the dominant culture on the one hand, and denigration by the country's educational system of minority group status and values on the other; so that, for perhaps one-third of the country's Indians, the urban Indians who have attempted to make it in the main economy, and frequently are found, as President Nixon has said, "confined to hopeless city reservations of despair," the problems are similar, if not identical, to those of other minority groups in urban ghettos. But, for the remainder, the two-thirds of the American Indians living on reservations, attempting to retain their cultural identity, the problems of economic development are substantially different. These differences arise not only out of the cultural heritage that we have mentioned; and the unique attachment to the land that it has created, but out of the trust relationship of the Indian to the Federal Government, and the tax-exempt, restricted status of Indian land, which many people would hastily forget was bought and paid for by the cession of close to 2 billion acres of Indian-owned land to the Federal Government.

All too often, Second Class Status in the dominant culture has been the sole alternative offered to starvation on the reservation. NCAI believes that a successful economic development program must, on the one hand, provide for the Indian who desires to leave the reservation and enter into the general economy, a fair-fighting chance and equal opportunity for success, while, on the other hand providing the opportunity for the reservation economy to develop, in ways compatible with its own cultural values, to a point where it is capable of self-support at a level which will provide an equitable share of the bounty of our homeland—the world's richest Nation.

Let us look for a moment at what the late Senator Robert F. Kennedy called "the cold statistics which illuminate a national tragedy and a national disgrace":

The average Indian income is $1,500 annually, which is 74% below the national average; his unemployment rate hovers around 50%, which is ten times the national average, and on some reservations reaches 70–80%. The average American Indians life expectancy is 10 years less than the National average.

Even more startling were the observations of author Stan Steiner, in his recently published book, *The New Indians*, in which he related statistics from a 1962–63 Government study of employment among tribal Indians. The statistics have not changed much. Let us look at them:

"* * * on the plains of the Dakotas, the Pine Ridge Sioux had 2,175 of 3,400 tribal adults unemployed (yearly family income was $105), the Rosebud Sioux has 1,720 of 2,996 unemployed (yearly family income, $1,000—though the tribe, 4 years later, estimated $600 was more accurate); the Standing Rock Sioux had 500 of 880 heads of households unemployed (yearly family income, $190) * * *

"To the north, on the Blackfeet Reservation of Montana, the 'Permanent unemployment' rate was 72.5 percent. The yearly tribal income was 'less than $500 per family.'

"Down in Mississippi, on the Choctaw Reservation, of 1,225 adults there were 1,055 jobless. Unemployment rate: 86.1 percent.

"Where the tranquil and ancient Pueblos of New Mexico stood, seemingly impervious to the economic winds, there were 10,699 jobless out of 13,711. Unemployment among these, perhaps the oldest of the country's inhabitants, was 77 percent. The Hopis, too, those idyllic 'peaceful people,' had a less than idyllic unemployment rate of 71.7 percent.

"In the Pueblo de Acoma, the 'City in the Sky,' unemployment stood at 89.6 percent.

"In the mythology of the oil-rich Indians so credulously huzzahed by television comedians and popular legends, none are supposedly wealthier than the Oklahoma tribes. And yet, the Five Civilized Tribes reported an annual unemployment rate of 55 percent, and an annual income per family, including the fabled oil-lease payments, that came to little more than $1,200 * * *.

"Of 19,000 adult Indians in eastern Oklahoma, between the ages of 18 and 55, an estimated 10,000, or 52.6 percent, were unemployed; of the 10,000 jobless adult Indians, well over half received no unemployment insurance, or any other welfare assistance—whatsoever.

"So it went from tribe to tribe. Unemployment rates from 40 to 80 percent; incomes from $105 to $1,200.

"These are statistics neither new nor surprising. However, the mixture of the old poverty and the new Indians who have seen the material riches of the outside world, and who are angered and impatient, has created an explosive situation. 'If something isn't done, the young men may go to violence * * *.' "

At its 1968 25th Annual Convention NCAI made it clear that:

"The social and economic conditions of many Indian people when compared to that of the general population, almost defy comprehension. Adult Indians living on reservations are, as a group, only half as well educated as other citizens, their life expectancy is one-third less and their average annual income two-thirds less. Nine out of 10 of their homes are comparatively unfit for human habitation and their unemployment rate is several times above the national average."

It is time that these critical problems were faced and programs funded which will overcome them, without exacting a price so high that the status quo is preferable.

Although many significant proposals have been placed in the Congressional hopper which would, perhaps, improve the economic situation of the Indian, few of these have the support of the Indians. Members of Congress have often been frustrated by what appears to them to be the ultraconservatism of the Indians. And, to some extent, the Indian *is* afraid of change—chiefly because proposals for change emanating from Congress have, regardless of the language in which they were couched, usually been schemes to liberate the Indian from his land, and because the Indian desires to design his own program for change.

Linked to the preservation of Indian land rights is the whole question of termination. Nothing has been more threatening to long-range tribal planning than the hovering specter of termination. On the one hand, the Federal Government has talked of itself as a partner available to work with the Indians in economic expansion and future development; on the other hand, the Congressional policy of termination has lingered like a death sentence under constant appeal by the Indian for commutation.

To be sure, the Omnibus Bill of the last session, reintroduced as separate bills H.R. 6717, 6718, 6719, and 6720 in this session, was rejected by Indians in part because of objections to the way it was presented. But the real objections were and remain substantive:

For example, the proposed "Indian Financing Act" offers the Indian an important new source of credit, not unlike a Small Business Administration for Indians, but on an unacceptable condition that the tribes be authorized to mortgage trust land, or any other land to which the tribe has title, subject to foreclosure.

This is no solution to the difficult problem of finding a way to broaden the sources of available credit for Indians *without* requiring tribal assets to be subject to foreclosure. Under such legislation, the Indian would be worse off than he is now. For he is compelled to risk everything, with a high chance of failure, for a limited possibility of success.

The same bill contains authorization much sought after for tribes to issue tax-exempt bonds: but limits such issuance to industrial or commercial purposes while only non-tax-exempt bonds may be issued to provide entertainment, recreation or civic facilities, transportation facilities, or to supply electric energy, gas, water, or sewage disposal or other utility services to the tribe. NCAI sees no valid reason for this distinction. The authority to issue tax-exempt bonds would be a valuable stimulant to capitalization of these desperate needs of the Indian community, for it offers an easy way to bring in outside capital, at relatively low cost to the tribe. But this proposal has individual merits, and should be considered apart from the loan fund.

In large measure, the past 8 years have shown a great stride forward by American Indians in attaining a greater degree of self-government and economic independence. But, the extent of progress and programs has reached only a small number of Indian tribes. Generally, those tribes that have had the funds to employ adequate legal counsel, and that have had a significant income for use in program planning, have been able to move forward with programs funded by a variety of Government agencies.

As of December 31, 1968, there were 150 industrial and commercial enterprises established on or near reservations as a result of Indian industrial development programs; of these 140, or 93 percent, had been established since the beginning of 1962.

At the present time these enterprises have created approximately 10,000 new jobs, of which only 4,700 are held by Indians. If industrial development seems like a panacea to the problem of the reservation Indians, we remind you that in 1962 there were 10,699 unemployed Pueblos alone; and in 1968, there were approximately 45,000 Indians in the 14-to-21 age bracket.

For the industrial enterprises now in existence, it is projected that eventually these will provide a total of 15,000 jobs of which, it is hoped, 65 percent will be held by Indians. Twice, or even three times, this number of jobs will not solve the problem. And, at the same time that jobs are created, Indians must be trained for employability.

There are approximately 600,000 Indians living in the United States, and in recent years the Indian population has been increasing faster than among any other minority group. The Indian labor force numbers approximately 100,000 with the unemployment rate hovering around 50 percent, more than 10 times the national average. "Industrial development of reservations" has often meant economic exploitation of cheap Indian labor for the benefit of white capitalists, leaving in its wake sociological disaster. We should point out further that some reservations have frequently been unable to share in the expanded opportunities for community and economic development which have been provided in recent years. Not only do they lack the wherewithal to make their needs known, but they are frequently unable to meet matching fund requirements, or other strings, which limit development.

Among our other activities, NCAI has undertaken a program to assist the tribes which have not been able to begin programs on their reservations, with the hope that, in short order, they will be able to generate sufficient income as tribal bodies to plan and carry out their own programs and attain greater measures of self-sufficiency and self-government. Note, however, that our purpose is to strengthen tribes, not weaken them, as Congress so frequently has tried to do.

In general, the Indians who have been overlooked are in small Federal tribes or eastern non-Federal surviving groups. We do not believe that because Congress denies these Indians Federal recognition, they cease to be Indians. From our contact with these groups over the past several years, we believe that, with some technical and financial assistance, these groups can be placed on the road to total self-sufficiency. Indeed, they could be made totally independent in some cases with the financial assistance and expanded reservation or group programs to fit their immediate needs.

On the other hand, there are a number of instances of tribes so disconsolate, and dejected, and with such a feeling of general helplessness, that they must first be convinced that effort is worth making. It is a mistake to assume, as Congress frequently has, that progress will be easy of attainment, and that results must show up immediately if a project is to be continued. The very uncertainty of congressional appropriations, and vacillation in Federal programing has bred distrust among the Indians, and led to the failure of some potentially viable programs.

In years when there is a change of administration, these feelings necessarily multiply.

It has too often been the fate of Indian groups that Government agencies have tried to create "showcases" of gigantic programs of employment on reservations, when the need has been much simpler and more basic. We believe that the "shotgun" approach to community development has not paid off in the past, and we have no reason to anticipate sudden success in the future for this type of operation.

We have initiated a program of national scope funded by a Ford Foundation grant to zero in on the problems of small tribes and non-Federal surviving groups to work on the basic problems of the Indian community, as viewed by that community. Our orientation is directed to total community involvement and development, with primary emphasis on one simple goal—increase of tribal income and subsequent development of tribal assets with that increased income.

We are continually finding that there are specific legal, economic administrative and social problems that are hampering smaller tribes and particular Indian groups, which never come to the fore until we actually have contact with the Indian community concerned. If these groups are to make any significant progress in the years to come, someone must bring them into the picture of national economic and social development in the very near future. We believe this can be done, without sacrificing tribal values. Indeed, in most instances, it can be done only tribally.

NCAI, among its other goals, hopes to serve as a central clearinghouse operation, in economic planning and development among American Indians, supporting the efforts of member tribes to develop viable economic programs with technical advice and funding, by being a central agency with capabilities in these dimensions. As our staffing on separate projects increases, our capacity to play this role increases.

Our overall economic program evolves from three factors: First, the staff capabilities and funding of the organization, and its relationship with Indian leadership; second, the limited number of people in the Indian community familiar with the private enterprise money concept and economy, and the many intricate mechanisms it requires in economic planning; third, the shortage of socioeconomic data on the American Indians, which is generally regarded as a prerequisite base from which to establish sound and sensible economic design. Although the Bureau of Indian Affairs has been in the business, nominally at least, for many years, of economic development on Indian reservations, the Bureau itself has developed no meaningful and reliable statistics to serve this need. We are hopeful that the newly funded Office of Minority Business Enterprises in the Department of Commerce, through its Rural Division, will begin to amass and supply this data.

Because it is in the interest of efficiency and economic progress to maximize both the coordination of Federal interagency resources and Indian organization resources for economic development, we are in the process of expanding the scope and capacity of the NCAI Fund to make it the focal point and repository of nongovernmental funds allocated to assist the American Indian in the development and implementation of economic plans. We have thus been in a position to monitor grants to other smaller Indian organizations serving special needs. But the Indian community cannot meet its economic needs by itself; at best, we can hope to provide seed money or matching funds. The bulk of this effort must of necessity come from the Federal Government.

In both 1968 and 1969, NCAI has cosponsored two National Economic Development Conferences for 31 selected Indian Reservations, which were attended by representatives of major firms in the private sector. This program is funded by a separate grant from the Office of Economic Opportunity. The major aim of these conferences was to help tribes attract industry into locations within communities, in accord with the economic plans of such communities. The conferences also serve to give a major boost to the economic plans which have been endorsed or funded by NCAI.

In addition to the economic programs we have described, NCAI is involved in community planning activities among its constituent groups. We believe that no economic plan can succeed which takes into account merely the economic and industrial implications of a proposed activity, without considering the sociological implications as well—that is, the impact which the development of such a plan will have on the tribe itself. Too often in the past, such consequences have been heedlessly disregarded.

Where such implications are not considered, what may be a successful economic venture for a visiting industrialist, can turn into a sociological disaster for the tribe.

NCAI also provides technical assistance, in such diverse forms as interpreting the regulations of the BIA for tribes who do not understand them; helping tribes receive certificates of eligibility for EDA or OEO programs; providing legal research assistance with respect to Federal Indian Laws applicable to particular situations; providing practical assistance on the familiar problems of land consolidations; Law and Order Codes, program development—land leasing—credit unions, and other tribal enterprises: supporting and assisting the creation and maintenance of intertribal ventures to attack regional problems: and providing a referral service between tribes and appropriate private, State and Federal agencies, which can provide assistance with particular problems.

Our approach is to define specific areas of concern in community development, designating Indian groups eligible to receive assistance from the program. Tribal groups are asked to define and clarify immediate problems and long-range goals. Technical and financial assistance is available only until the group has reached the point where it has sufficient resources to begin programing and funding by itself. Then, program support ceases, thereby canceling out dependency upon the program for continued survival.

Financial assistance for accelerated community development consists of grants for capital improvements to enable tribes to overhaul community facilities and to provide matching grants "in kind" for programs; to assist unorganized communities to plan basic community organization; to enable Indian groups to employ professional service people in particular cases of need. as, for incorporation of enterprises, formation of credit unions, establishment of leasing programs or writing of tribal constitutions, and, for travel by tribal representatives to enable them to follow up on program applications, where necessary.

One priority area is the number of small tribes whose members are, for the most part employed, but the tribe as a governing body is too poor to begin a program of housing on a community basis; so, nothing is done. With some assistance in developing a housing program, and formulation of a plan to establish either a credit union or a tribal tax on the members, such a tribe could create housing for its people, with the program generating enough momentum to set up a basic community development program for the future. Once the program is undertaken, counselling and financial assistance can be provided to assist the tribe in building a basic tribal income to cover such future services as the members require. Such a tribe would then be, for all predictable purposes, self-sufficient.

Having waited in vain for Congress to approve a Federal Government endorsed, chartered and underwritten all-Indian Development Corporation, in accord with the recommendations of the Striner Report, NCAI has just obtained a substantial grant from EDA to study the feasibility of, and assuming a feasible method is found, to establish a National Indian Development Organization. Although the terms of the proposal require an organization to be established within existing law (if feasible), we will undoubtedly be seeking Congressional assistance to strengthen the significance of this organization. We see this as potentially the single most significant development in the field of Indian economic development. The need for a financial institution which can accommodate the unique requirements of the Indian for credit and other needs is quite apparent. To the extent that such an organization can be developed in the private sector under Indian direction, we think it will be the most useful. Some sort of Federal subsidization may well be needed, at least in the early stages, to make the organization feasible, and to that extent, we will turn to Congress for support.

In closing, we would like to remind you of the words President John F. Kennedy used in his inaugural address: "If a free society cannot help the many who are poor, it cannot save the few who are rich."

OKLAHOMANS FOR INDIAN OPPORTUNITY, INCORPORATED AND ECONOMIC DEVELOPMENT FOR NONRESERVATION INDIAN PEOPLE

By WILLIAM G. HAYDEN*

FOREWORD

Oklahomans for Indian Opportunity was organized in 1965 to represent and assist Oklahoma Indians. Oklahoma has no Indian reservations, but it has by far the largest nonreservation Indian population of any State. William Hayden here describes how white settlement and statehood for Oklahoma were accompanied by white encroachment on Indian lands, causing the Indians to become an exploited and poverty-stricken minority. He criticizes current Federal programs for continuing to promote white-owned industries, which employ Indians at low wages. A primary objective of the Oklahomans for Indian Opportunity is to promote Indian ownership and control of local commerce and industry. The OIO has already assisted in the establishment of a number of Indian-owned small businesses. Other OIO activities include an Indian youth council, which helps young people to develop the skills and self-confidence needed for scholastic success, and a community action program which helps Indian people to take better advantage of the social services provided by State and Federal agencies. In addition to describing the numerous activities of the OIO, Mr. Hayden's article includes extensive historical and statistical material on the economic, social, and educational status of the Oklahoma Indians.

Introduction

Oklahomans for Indian Opportunity, Inc., is a private nonprofit corporation organized under the laws of the State of Oklahoma. In Oklahoma there are 67 tribes of Indians and over 25 official tribal organizations. There are no reservations in the State of Oklahoma. Estimates of the Indian population of the State range anywhere from the official 64,000 of the 1960 Census to over 200,000. At any rate Oklahoma has the second largest Indian population of any State, and certainly the largest nonreservation Indian population of any State by far.

Prior to the organization of Oklahomans for Indian Opportunity there had been no single organization that really crossed traditional tribal barriers to the point that Indians from many different tribal groups could be galvanized into successful group action. Traditionally, Indian people have been divided by tribal and clan factionalism. It is the philosophy of Oklahomans for Indian Opportunity that Indian people need to have the opportunity to go beyond these things—to work together to promote their own social, economic, and

*Deputy Director, Oklahomans for Indian Opportunity—Rural Development Programs.

political well-being—regardless of whether they be tribal Indians, urban or rural; Pow-Wow Indians or church oriented; progressive Indians or what have you.

There is a popular myth in Oklahoma that since there are no Indian reservations in the State then there is no "Indian problem." According to the myth, Indians are rapidly being assimilated into the dominant society. Since technically, Indians are eligible for the same services as non-Indians and are on an equal footing legally in society as non-Indians, there is a widespread belief among Oklahomans that there is no such thing as discrimination against Indians. But such is not the truth. The occasional Indian who does "make it" in the dominant society is used to prove that all the others could also if they would just "try." In many areas cruel stereotypes are still operative: "Indians are lazy," "The drunk Indian"; any kind of erratic behavior on the part of an Indian individual can be explained simply by saying, "Well, he's an Indian." And tragically many Indians hold these same attitudes about themselves. For many years a sign was prominently placed on the outside of a tavern near Ponca City; it said "No Beer Sold to Indians." It was only removed a few months ago, but for years Indian people passed that sign everyday. It still happens that indigent Indian persons with serious or emergency health needs are turned away from hospitals with the explanation that they should go to the Indian hospital. The Indian hospital might be 30 miles away or it might be 100 miles away and how are the indigent to pay for transportation?

For an Indian to live in Oklahoma means that practically every phase of his life is controlled by white people: the school, State and local government, the police, the courts, the hospitals, the public welfare social worker, his boss where he works—always white. The fact that there are no reservations in Oklahoma simply means that Indian people control that much less, that they have little that they can call their own, and that there are fewer places to retreat from white insensitivity to whatever way of life they choose to live.

One could go on and on and on listing problems and incidents that Indian people have endured but suffice it to say it was because of these things that Indian people brought Oklahomans for Indian Opportunity into being. In the summer of 1965 over 500 Indian people from around the State of Oklahoma gathered at the University of Oklahoma in Norman, Okla. and voted to organize Oklahomans for Indian Opportunity for the purpose of promoting the advancement of Oklahoma Indians on a statewide level. OIO is an Indian-dominated organization—of the 41-member board of directors, 36 are Indian people from around the State of Oklahoma. OIO currently employs 47 people; and of these, 35 are Indian or approximately 75 percent. In the past 3 years, with the help of funds from the Federal Government, OIO has inaugurated a number of programs designed by Indian people for the benefit of Indian people. Some of these are:

The Oklahomans for Indian Opportunity *Community Organization Program* has selected several target areas with a high percentage of Indian population. In each area an Indian person who has not had the benefit of professional training and who shares in the viewpoint of his fellow Indians has been employed to serve as an advocate for the Indian poor. These persons help Indian people take better advantage of State and Federal programs, take up their cause with agencies like the welfare department or the Bureau of Indian Affairs and they are frequently called upon to gather facts in cases of discrimination.

The Oklahomans for Indian Opportunity *Youth Program* has organized over 70 youth councils in schools with a large Indian enrollment. The public school system of Oklahoma is, by and large, unresponsive to the needs of Oklahoma Indian young people. The fact that some school systems have a 70- to 90-percent dropout rate for Indian students is ample proof of this. In most of these schools with large Indian enrollment very few Indian students participate in extracurricular activities. OIO seeks to organize youth councils for the Indian students in these schools. The youth council then becomes a vehicle whereby Indian students can develop self-confidence, skills of leadership, and self-expression. The youth councils themselves are organized on a statewide level and the Indian young people elect statewide officers. The popularity of this program can be seen in the fact that nearly 1,700 Indian high school students recently attended the OIO Statewide Youth Conference at the University of Oklahoma.

The Oklahomans for Indian Opportunity *Work Orientation Program* seeks to train and find employment for young Indian men and women in areas where it is difficult for Indians to find jobs. The OIO staff people attempt to convince local employers that Indian people are good employees. Frequently employers are reluctant to hire Indians because they have been led to believe that Indians are not dependable or are lacking in initiative in a job situation. The OIO Program seeks to break down these stereotypes while at the same time attempting to develop a realistic understanding and commitment on the part of the young Indians to the "world of work." In some cases persons have been successfully placed on the job that had previously failed in some other type of job training program. One of the best results of the program has been that many of the trainees have come to the realization that they really need more education and training and have gone back to school either to gain a high school, college education, or more specialized vocational training.

The Oklahomans for Indian Opportunity *Referral and Adult Education Centers* function in both Tulsa and Oklahoma City. Many Indian people have migrated to Tulsa and Oklahoma City from rural areas where the agency they were most accustomed to dealing with is the Bureau of Indian Affairs. Upon coming to the city many are ill-equipped to cope with the confusion of urban life and the maze of agencies that are supposed to give service to the poor. Through these centers OIO tries to help people get services and at the same time learn how to deal with public and private agencies set up to help them. Also, courses in consumer education, credit buying, etc., are available through these centers.

Oklahomans for Indian Opportunity has also promoted a number of regional training seminars for Indian people who are interested in learning ways of getting on school boards, boards of Community Action Agencies, running for public office and other forms of community involvement.

These are some of the programs that Oklahomans for Indian Opportunity has developed in the first 3 years of its existence. We believe that they all have long range significance for the development of the economic independence of Indian communities. Since this paper should more properly address itself to the economic conditions of Oklahoma Indians and since OIO has itself, in the last several months, begun an economic development program for Indians in eastern Oklahoma, the rest of this paper will deal with the OIO Economic Development Program now in progress.

In the fall of 1968, Oklahomans for Indian Opportunity received a grant from the Division of Research and Demonstration community action program, Office of Economic Opportunity. The purpose of the grant is to show that Indian communities and individuals can successfully plan, develop, own, control and operate their own economic enterprises. The initial target area covers a 10 county area of eastern Oklahoma which lies against the Arkansas border.

This area is the home of two of the so-called Five Civilized Tribes, these two being the Choctaw and Cherokee Tribes. Originally inhabitants of the southeastern United States, they were among the first Indians to come into contact with the European colonists on the eastern seaboard. Even before this time they had developed successful farming and other enterprises and had a well-knit and sophisticated social and political organization. After the purchase of the Louisiana Territory these people were forced, under escort of the U.S. Army, to undergo a long march with shocking loss of life to Oklahoma, the designated area for unwanted Indians. Treaties were signed promising them ownership and control of the land in eastern Oklahoma, and that their land never would be included within the borders of any State or territory of the United States. Between the years of settlement and the outbreak of the Civil War, Cherokees and Choctaws were allowed to live relatively undisturbed, and they established a complex system of schools, legislative bodies, and courts. Moreover, they prospered economically. All progress virtually ended when various factions in the two tribes allied themselves with the Confederacy. After the war, the Federal Government used this as an excuse to suspend all previous treaties, and Oklahoma became a State in 1907, over the strong objections of the Indians. Settlers came to Oklahoma in droves and the Indians ceased to play a dominant role in the affairs of Oklahoma. Unaccustomed to private ownership of land, they lost approximately 96 percent of the land they once owned. At this time the five civilized tribes together held over 19 million acres of land in eastern Oklahoma. Today, less than 700,000 acres remain in restricted status.

Over the past 60 years the Indians of the area have been so systematically exploited that today they have no voice at all in the economic decisionmaking of the area. In the entire 10-county area there are less than 15 Indian-owned business enterprises.

In a 1964 survey of nearly 2,000 Cherokee families, *not one* had a total family income of more than $2,999. In a similar study of 2,384 Choctaw families, over 86 percent had total incomes of less than $3,000. In both of these tribal groups the largest percentile fell below $1,000 total family income annually.

Understandably, the apathy and discouragement among Indians in eastern Oklahoma is extreme. Oklahomans for Indian Opportunity believes that if Indian communities are to survive in the nonreservation situation of Oklahoma—then Indian people must have the opportunity to gain control of the economic situations that most vitally affect their daily existence. That is they must have the opportunity to work in a business owned by themselves or by other Indians, they must be able to buy the goods they need in stores owned by Indians if they so choose, they ought to be able to borrow from an institution controlled by other Indian people, whether it be a bank, loan company, or credit union, they ought to be able to live together—to preserve what they think is worth preserving—to discard what is not—they ought to be able to live in any way they please. But there must be an economic base for such freedom. And really one cannot talk about freedom to be different in our society unless one recognizes the need for economic security of minority groups.

As U.S. Senator Fred R. Harris has pointed out, America does not mean the melting pot, it means the right to be different—that is American pluralism. Pluralism should include the concept that certain racial, cultural, or religious groups have a right to a certain recognition in our national social, legal, and political makeup. The American Indian, as the first American and in return for the forfeiture of the North American Continent and thousands of broken treaties certainly has a right to *special recognition* and *special treatment* from the national government *over* and *above* every other racial and ethnic group, without diminishing in any way the force of basic civil rights legislation in the land.

The Oklahomans for Indian Opportunity program attempts to do what few Indian programs have tried—to put Indian people in control of the basic situations that dominate their lives.

There have been many Federal programs to improve the lot of Indian people in Oklahoma. There is a widespread belief that Indians have inherent gifts of manual dexterity and innate abilities in hand-eye coordination—thus it is that some Bureau of Indian Affairs and even some tribal publications echo this racist nonsense. The main results of such misguided propaganda is to promote the belief that Indians are only capable of menial or physical tasks that do not require any brainpower. As has been stated above, tragically many Indians have the same attitudes about themselves.

The Bureau of Indian Affairs has a very powerful effect upon Indian people in Oklahoma. Many informed persons believe this has resulted in a general situation of dependency on Bureau of Indian Affairs' services and lack of initiative both on the part of the Bureau of Indian Affairs and Indian people. It would seem that there is a direct correlation between Bureau of Indian Affairs ineptitude and Indian lassitude.

Let us take for example the BIA industrial development program. There is a great deal of publicity about various industrial enterprises that have been lured to eastern Oklahoma through BIA auspices—no doubt the BIA has been, on occasion, extremely helpful in providing incentives for industry to relocate in an Indian area, however, this does not mean that the BIA effort has been even largely helpful to Indian workers. One of the most effective BIA lures for industry is the training supplement whereby up to one-half of the Federal minimum wage is paid for as long as 1½ years. This committee has already received evidence which indicates that training supplements for such long lengths of time are largely unwarranted. Indeed, the evidence seems to indicate that the average Indian trainee in eastern Oklahoma gains proficiency in a manufacturing skill in one or two weeks of training—not in 1 or 1½ years as the subsidies seem to indicate.

We think that the main inference from this is that BIA-OJT training subsidies are in reality interest free capital grants to lure industries to Indian areas. Considering the fact that industry relocates in eastern Oklahoma mainly to find a cheaper labor supply, this type of investment on the part of the Federal Government is not in the long run favorable to Indian people. Indeed, one might say that the effect of such programs is to maintain the exploitation of Indian people! Why else would the Bureau fund as many enterprises that provide bare minimum wage subsistence to Indian people.

It is our belief that such programs should be restructured so that they are geared to train Indian people to work in Indian owned and controlled enterprises. This is very simple—BIA money should not go to the enrichment of white people at the expense of Indian labor or ownership—Period!

Similarly, important economic development programs such as SBA, FHA, and EDA should be reformed in such a way that a certain minimum of loan or investment funds available must be devoted to authentic Indian projects. None of these Federal programs has a particularly sparkling record in these areas. At the same time it must be emphasized that Federal funds should not be all allocated to projects that tend to be literally "Human Zoos" for Indian people (projects in which Indian culture is prostituted with feathers and beads and snakes and curios and fake Indian art and craft, to be viewed by believing tourists). Any project financed with Federal funds which results in white people coming to look at Indian people is obviously an outrageous waste of taxpayer funds.

Federal funds (if directed toward Indian ownership rather than Indian employment) can make a significant change in the economic status of Indians in Oklahoma.

Federal funds are also used extensively for various types of vocational training for Indians. We do not feel that these programs have been too beneficial for Indians—not because vocational training is not needed but because of poor quality training and because too often the training is for a job that does not exist or is not needed. How many thousands of Indians have been trained—or even still are being trained as welders or heavy equipment operators—as if there were no other occupation for which training would be useful? It would seem that vocational training programs are set up by persons who are only concerned with the present needs of industry and not with the long-range employment needs of Indian people.

Without diminishing the need for quality vocational training we believe that the main emphasis should be placed on a vastly expanded educational grant program through the BIA. Thousands of Indian young people of high aspirations are being denied or discouraged from higher education because of the lack of sufficient funds for this worthy program. Moreover, this grant program should be expanded to cover the needs of Indian college graduates for advanced studies.

This then, is how Oklahomans for Indian Opportunity feels about Federal programs as they affect Indians in Oklahoma. The remainder of this statement will detail the OIO economic development program as it has unfolded over the past 6 months.

The initial target area for the program includes the following counties: Delaware, Mayes, Cherokee, Adair, Sequoyah, Haskell, Latimer, LeFlore, Pushmataha, and McCurtain. The area was chosen because of its high concentration of Indian people and its great potential for economic development.

The administrative offices of the program are located at the University of Oklahoma, Norman. The staff working out of Norman includes the director, deputy director, specialists in agriculture and animal husbandry, a business economist, a finance and accounting specialist, an attorney, a marketing expert and the secretarial staff. The field staff consists of five field representatives and 10 neighborhood workers. Each field representative supervises two counties in the project. A neighborhood worker is located in each of the 10 counties. Both field representatives and neighborhood workers live in the project area. Neighborhood workers were residents of the counties where they serve prior to being employed by OIO and are able to speak either Cherokee or Choctaw.

The rural development program is responsible to the OIO board of directors and works closely with the special advisory committee to the project. The involvement of OIO board members and the area's Indian people with the ideas and talents of low-income residents of the area is necessary for project success.

Regular training sessions are held for all staff members. Emphasis is placed on techniques for locating individuals and groups with business ideas, identifying needs and providing or locating services. Information on other OIO programs is provided in order to assure close coordination in the overall effort.

The first year of the project has been devoted to developing demonstration projects and establishing small businesses and cooperatives. Buying clubs in communities such as Wright City, Talihina, Little Kansas, and Briggs not only provide opportunities for economy in food purchases but are effective organizational vehicles for all types of community activity.

Regular meetings are being held in over 20 rural communities to plan community involvement in the project. The field staff also is working with OIO youth councils in the 10-county area.

All types of businesses and cooperatives are considered for project participation. Examples of project developed enterprises are the Cherokee Graphic Arts Co., Tahlequah; Bob Lee Dry's Service Station & Auto Repair, Salina; Steen's Grocery & Service Station, Grove; and Cherokee Floats, Inc., Briggs. The Cherokee Float operation is particularly interesting since it will provide summer employment for a large number of Indian high school students. The Lost City and Bell Feeder Pig Cooperative involves over 20 families in the specialized feeder pig industry with the assistance of the OIO animal husbandry specialist.

Over 30 other projects are currently under development or consideration. Projects under consideration are as diversified as fiber glass manufacturing, rough fish processing, fish farming, franchising operations, and laundry facilities.

Technical assistance is provided to existing businesses and cooperatives such as the Bull Hollow Arts and Crafts Cooperative with 30 member families. The project is actively participating in the development of the proposed Northeastern Oklahoma Community Development Corp. The NOCDC is a 15-county demonstration of the Community Self-Determination Act designed to stimulate community owned industry and enterprise. OIO will work with Indian people involved in the program.

Working relationships have been established with local businessmen, banks, tribal groups, Federal Housing Administration, Bureau of Indian Affairs, OSU agricultural extension, Small Business Administration, economic development districts, the State OEO office, and community action agencies.

As these small OIO sponsored businesses and organizations grow, they will serve as building blocks for a larger organization—an organization composed of residents of the area, truly representative of the Indian people of the entire area and concerned with improving the economic and social conditions of the Indian people of the area. By building a regional economic development organization dominated by Indian people OIO hopes that Indian people can continue to develop their own enterprises under their own control in the years to come.

This basically is what we are trying to do. We have a strong commitment to help develop Indian-owned enterprises. Most of these projects will be small and involve only a few people at first. Ultimately, however, we feel that larger more successful and visible operations can be developed with the help of other private and public agencies.

Finally, because the problems and situations mentioned in this paper are not unique to our 10-county project area I am including an addenda of historical and statistical material on the economic, social, and educational status of Indians throughout the various areas of the State of Oklahoma.

FIVE CIVILIZED TRIBES

The Cherokee, Chickasaw, Choctaw, Creek, and Seminole Tribes are known as the "Five Civilized Tribes." These tribes were conspicuous at first, at the time the white settlers (English, French, and Spanish) colonized southeastern United States, as a warlike people, and later for their cultural and economic development. When they realized they could not prevent the whites from settling, they began to enter into competition with them on their own terms. Within about a century, long before the tribes were forced to move west of the Mississippi, the Five Civilized Tribes made rapid strides in civilization according to the European patterns.

The injustices and the hardships of their forced removal, between 1829 and 1846, arrested all progress they were making. After a decade of strife, when they were once again emerging into harmony and progress, their development was again disrupted by the Civil War.

After the hatreds and cruelties of the Civil War had somewhat subsided, progress among members of the tribes was again revived and continued with little interruption for the next half century. However, around 1890, white settlers once again overran the areas inhabited by the Five Tribes. This caused the Indians again to withdraw from society. Despite a treaty obligation to keep whites out, at statehood the entire Indian territory contained five times as many whites as Indians and the tribes were in a completely demoralized state.

To compound the problem, a series of legislative acts, from 1902 to 1959, had the effect of permitting Indian lands to pass from tribal ownership to individual Indians. From 1902 to the present time, approximately 19 million acres were turned over to individual Indians by means of deeds. While some owners benefited from their allotments, others sold out for a fraction of the land's value. Only 700,000 acres remain in restricted status. However, very few of these restricted tracts are of sufficient size or in a location to justify their consolidation for economic purposes.

Many of the members of the tribes have been able to ride the crest of white aggressiveness and hold their own. Accordingly, the social status of the tribes ranges from those who are highly educated and fully acculturated to those who are illiterate and living in the depths of poverty. Some of the most prominent doctors, attorneys, educators, bankers, and businessmen of Oklahoma are of Indian descent. On the other hand, many tribal members have little or no education, very low incomes, and are experiencing great difficulty in maintaining an existence. The economic and social status of the tribes is perhaps lower today than it was a half century ago.

A serious problem of economic necessity faces the Indian people in Oklahoma today. There is an urgent need for jobs that furnish permanent employment. The State of Oklahoma also realizes that it has moved beyond its ability to maintain its population and economy based upon agriculture and the oil industry. Therefore, it appears logical that the Indian and non-Indian people alike within the State face a common economic problem.

The development of an industrial and commercial recreation economy seems to be the common solution. Before substantial advances can be made, however, members need to have an appreciation for adequate housing and sanitation, better understanding of government from the community to the national level and a greater concern for general health and welfare. It will also be necessary for many members of the Five Tribes to be motivated to progress more rapidly than in the past to keep up with the country's technological advancement.

Statistical Data of the Five Civilized Tribes

As shown in table I, the Indian population of the Five Civilized Tribes has been steadily increasing since 1950. The population increased from 36,318 in 1950 to 38,503 in 1960, or 6 percent. By comparison, the total population of Oklahoma increased only 4.3 percent during the same period. The rate of population growth of Indians in Oklahoma is greater than the total Oklahoma population because migration to other States is less frequent among the Indian people than among the non-Indian. The lack of marketable skills discourages migration on the part of the Indians.

TABLE I.—*Population increase of the Five Civilized Tribes within the 40-county jurisdiction*

Year:	Population
1950	36, 318
1960	38, 503
1962	40, 042

Source: Bureau of Indian Affairs.

The age distribution of the members of the Five Civilized Tribes is shown in table II. Fifty percent of the population is less than 20 years of age. As is true of Indian tribes throughout the United States, the Five Civilized Tribes have a younger population than that of the general U.S. population.

TABLE II.—COMPOSITION. OF MEMBERSHIP BY AGE, JUNE 1962

Age	Population	Percent
1 to 19	19, 914	50
20 to 39	9, 618	24
40 to 59	7, 914	20
60 and up	2, 596	6
Total	40, 042	100

Source: Bureau of Indian Affairs.

The school enrollment figures shown in table III includes all the Indian children of the members of the Five Civilized Tribes who maintain permanent residence in the jurisdictions. The Bureau is encouraging all children to finish high school and secure college or vocational training following high school graduation. Such attainment will be important in stimulating economic and social growth.

TABLE III.—PERMANENT RESIDENTS OF JURISDICTION ATTENDING PUBLIC AND PRIVATE SCHOOLS, JUNE 1965

School	Boys	Girls	Total	Percent
Public	8, 000	9, 702	17, 702	90
Federal	733	724	1, 457	7
University	237	200	437	3
Total	8, 970	10, 626	19, 596	100

Source: Bureau of Indian Affairs.

Table IV provides a breakdown of the family income of the Five Civilized Tribes. About 90 percent of the families receive incomes of less than $3,000. The unskilled members of the tribes, who are in the majority and who depend on irregular farm labor and timber work, have few opportunities to earn more money. Continued emphasis by Bureau, State, and local agencies on vocational training, employment assistance, as well as industrial and commercial recreational development will provide means for employment and thereby increase the income level of the tribal members.

TABLE IV.—FAMILY INCOME OF MEMBERS OF THE FIVE CIVILIZED TRIBES, 1964

Income	Chickasaw	Creek	Cherokee	Choctaw	Seminole	Total	Percent
Unknown	0	146	0	109	1	256	2.6
Under $1,000	102	731	1,196	1,070	318	3,417	35.4
$1,000 to $1,999	479	1,170	498	500	597	3,244	33.6
$2,000 to $2,999	336	409	298	390	278	1,702	17.6
$3,000 to $4,999	41	292	0	260	80	673	7.0
$5,000 to $9,999	51	147	0	45	49	292	3.1
$10,000 and over	10	29	0	20	4	63	0.7
Total	1,019	2,924	1,993	2,384	1,327	9,647	100.0

Source: Bureau of Indian Affairs.

Table V presents information on the labor force and employment status of the group.

TABLE V.—LABOR FORCE, EMPLOYMENT AND UNEMPLOYMENT WITHIN THE FIVE CIVILIZED TRIBES AGENCY JURISDICTION, MARCH 1966

	Total	Male	Female
Labor force (14 years and over)	17,480	10,637	6,843
Employed, total	12,510	8,400	4,110
Permanent (more than 12 months)	8,042	5,571	2,471
Temporary (including persons away on seasonal work)	4,468	2,829	1,639
Unemployed	4,970	2,237	2,733
Percent unemployed	28.4	21.0	39.9
Not in labor force (14 years and over)	10,894	3,269	7,625
Students (14 years and over, including those away at school)	3,795	1,851	1,944
Men (all reasons)	1,418	1,418	
Women for whom no child-care substitutes are available	3,735		3,735
Women (all other reasons)	1,946		1,946

Source: Bureau of Indian Affairs semiannual report of Labor Force, Employment and Unemployment (March 1966).

The Indian-owned land of eastern Oklahoma is dispersed among that owned by non-Indians and is mostly hilly timberland. Because of this, large-scale farming is not usually possible in the Five Civilized Tribes area. As shown in table VI, only 15 percent of the Indian-owned land is used for farming, while 48 percent is used for open grazing.

In eastern Oklahoma, the trend has been away from a cash-crop type of farming to a grass-cattle economy. Accordingly, the principal Bureau activities in the field of land operations have been the development of improved pastures to increase cattle production which can produce incomes comparable with most of the cash-crop farms in the area.

TABLE VI.—LAND INVENTORY, DECEMBER 1964

| | Indian operated | | Non-Indian operated | | | | |
	Individual	Tribal	Individual	Tribal	Idle	Total	Percent
Dry farming	29,489	3,079	79,650	1,200	6,898	120,316	15
Open grazing	115,752	12,352	173,077	5,111	53,779	360,071	48
Noncommercial included	164,868	10,481	90,543	4,875		270,767	35
Nonagricultural uses			5,154			5,154	2
Total	310,109	25,912	348,424	11,186	60,677	756,308	100

INDIAN TRIBES RESIDING IN NORTH CENTRAL OKLAHOMA

HISTORICAL BACKGROUND

This report covers all or parts of 11 counties in north central Oklahoma, where 14 Indian tribes reside. The tribes are the Osage, Eastern Shawnee, Miami, Quapaw, Seneca-Cayuga, Kaw, Otoc-Missouria, Pawnee, Ponca, Iowa, Mexican Kickapoo, Pottawatomi, Sac and Fox, and Absentee Shawnee. The counties are Osage, Pottawatomie, Key, Pawnee, Delaware, Ottawa, Noble, Logan, Payne, Lincoln, and Cleveland. The jurisdiction of the Bureau of Indian Affairs is represented in the Osage, Miami, Pawnee, and Shawnee Agencies.

Osage Agency

The Osage Reservation, now Osage County, comprises 1,470,559 acres and is located in northern Oklahoma. Since the reservation was purchased pursuant to treaty, the Osage were excluded from the provisions of the General Allotment Act and their lands were not allotted until they agreed in 1906. The Act of June 28, 1906 (34 Stat. 559) entitled "An Act for the division of the lands and funds of the Osage Indians in Oklahoma Territory and for other purposes," known as the Osage Allotment Act, is the organic law governing the administration of current Osage affairs and marks the beginning of special legislation enacted by the Congress for the exclusive benefit of the Osage Tribe.

There were 2,229 Osage (of which 926 were full-blood and 1,303 were mixed-blood or adopted) enrolled under the provisions of the 1906 Act. These enrollees constitute the legal membership of the tribe and are referred to locally as "allotted" members. Each allottee received approximately 658 acres of land, a $3,819.76 credit on the books of the United States Treasury representing segregation of the balance of proceeds from the sale of Osage Kansas lands, and the right to a pro rata share of the income, distributed quarterly, from such trust funds and net tribal mineral income. These shares are known as headrights. The income is derived from Osage minerals and business activities related to these minerals.

Rapid assimilation with non-Indians took place in early years in the Osage Tribe. Those members of the tribe of one-fourth Indian blood almost without exception fully identify themselves with the non-Indian social and economic life of the communities in which they reside. Because of this rapid assimilation and the lack of adequate resources and opportunities on the reservation, a large percentage of the Osage people have relocated in other areas, the greatest segment outside of Oklahoma being located in California. Many are now gainfully employed and some have attained recognition and success in the arts, the professions, and in businesses.

A large number of Osage Indians, many of whom have one-half degree of Indian blood or more, still reside in Osage County. Many of them do not receive income from the headrights. Social integration of this group has been impeded by numerous factors. One major factor is the community attitude created by the Osage mineral trust, which is difficult to overcome. First of all, the community in general is envious of the headright owners, and every effort is made to separate them from their income or headrights. Secondly, because of the independent income from headrights, the individual Osage is somewhat separate from the general community and does not really consider himself a part of it. As a result, two distinct community divisions are attempting to exist in the same area. There is no longer a cohesive Osage culture, nor is the Osage able to live by the culture of the general non-Indian community. The greatest needs of the Osage Tribe are assistance and guidance for those 2,700 Osage residing in the county. Assistance is needed for everyday existence and in fostering social integration that will lead to their full acceptance by the community.

Miami Agency

The Eastern Shawnee, Miami, Quapaw, Seneca-Cayuga, and Wyandette Tribes, as well as Modoc, Ottawa, and Peoria Terminated Tribes. reside in northeastern Oklahoma under the jurisdiction of the Miami Agency. The jurisdiction covers all or parts of seven counties, with the agency headquarters in Miami, Ottawa County, Oklahoma. The reservations under the Miami jurisdiction originally comprised about three-quarters of Ottawa County, Oklahoma.

The tribes were descendants of midwestern Algonquian and Iroquoian Bands that roamed the areas from Lake Erie to Kansas. They were located in Oklahoma during the nineteenth century.

In the early 1800's all of the area, now under the jurisdiction of the Miami Agency, was known as Quapaw Country, although some Senecas and Shawnees lived there also. In 1867, the Quapows ceded a large portion of their reservation for settlement by other tribes, which tract was subdivided into small reservations for various tribes settling there.

The groups have been integrating into the social life of Oklahoma since the 1900's. Today, they are, for all practical purposes, assimilated. They do not call upon the Bureau for help, although Bureau services are legally available.

As of June 1, 1964, there were only 20,604 acres of restricted Indian lands; 90 percent of these agricultural lands are presently under lease with an effort being directed toward assisting the owners to use better economic practices on the land.

Pawnee Agency

Four tribes, Otee-Miscouria, Ponca, Kaw, and Pawnee, are situated within the jurisdictional area of the Pawnee Agency. Within this area, 86,823 acres of Indian-owned land are held in trust by the Federal Government; of this total only 7,515 acres are operated by Indians themselves. The total land is estimated to represent approximately $11 million in value. The lands are in trust, multiple, and tribal ownerships. A legal land survey is a serious need.

Of the 2,784 Indians that live in this area, fewer than 40 percent were gainfully employed in full or part-time jobs in 1962. The average income is below that for the adjacent area and consists mostly of agricultural rentals, oil and gas leases on trust land, pensions, part-time labor, and welfare.

The Indians in this area and in Oklahoma generally were allotted separate tracts of land. Then the interspersed areas were opened to setlement by homesteaders through the various acts of Congress, starting in 1887, either by run or lottery.

This area, along with many others in Oklahoma, is one of severe rural poverty. The situation will not improve until the economy is diversified and industrial or commercial enterprises are induced to locate in the area to provide job opportunities for wage seekers. Permanent local employment would not only aid Indians of this jurisdiction but also the entire north central part of the State.

Shawnee Agency

The jurisdiction of the Shawnee Agency covers all or parts of each of six countries in central Oklahoma. The agency is responsible for the Bureau affairs of five tribes, the Iowa, Sac and Fox, Mexican Kickapoo, Citizens Potawatomi, and Absentee Shawnee.

The tribes were originally indigenous to the Great Lakes area and were encountered by traders, colonial troops, and white settlers in the 18th century. During the 19th century, through various agreements with the U.S. Government, the tribes were eventually assigned lands in Kansas and later in Oklahoma.

At the present time there are approximately 2,400 Indians living within or adjacent to this agency jurisdiction. There are approximately 48,000 acres of trust land within the six counties.

Culturally the tribes range from the Mexican Kickapoo, who cling closely to the old religion and seldom marry outside the tribe, to the Citizens Potawatomi, who themselves have practically terminated their special statue because of the extent to which they have intermarried with the non-Indian and become submerged in the greater community.

This Indian population, like many in the Anadarko area, is unique in that a significant number live in "subcommunities" or "population clusters" located within boundaries of lands originally assigned to the tribe. The individuals usually reside on land in which they have a small, undivided, inherited interest or which belongs to a relative. They usually occupy an inadequate, deteriorated dwelling that was built by the allottee and which is often shared by other heirs. There are a few whose income from earnings approaches the average national level and yet who choose to live in the most primitive and dilapidated dwellings. Aside from land sales proceeds, supervised by this agency, the individual amounts spent for maintenance or improvements on these dwellings is negligible.

There is still present among the tribes residual cultural characteristics or traits that act as deterrents to the development and economic adjustment of both individuals and families. In addition, many still try to cling to the practice of securing their living from the land and refuse to leave the area for employment or to recognize the necessity for formal education or vocational training.

There is still much need to stimulate interest and to involve the Indian population of this area in activities of the greater non-Indian community. This will contribute to strengthening self-esteem and improving the public image of the tribes. There is also a need to assist families to remain together as units and to encourage children to finish high school and to secure college or vocational training.

GENERAL POPULATION, SOCIAL AND ECONOMIC CHARACTERISTICS

Population

As shown in table I, the Indian population of the Oklahoma tribes residing in north central Oklahoma has been increasing since 1950. The population increased from 8,640 in 1950 to 9,033 in 1960, or by 4.6 percent. This increase slightly exceeded that of the total Oklahoma population, which amounted to 4.3 percent between 1950 and 1960.

TABLE I.—*Population increase of Oklahoma Tribes residing in north central Oklahoma*

Year:	Population
1950	8,640
1960	9,033
1962	10,530

Source: Bureau of Indian Affairs.

Population of tribes in 1962 and principal county of residence

A breakdown by agency and tribe indicating population of the tribes in 1962 and principal county residence of tribal members is shown in table II.

TABLE II

Agency and Tribe	Population, 1962	Principal county residence of tribal members
Osage Agency	2,872	Osage, Potawatomi, Kay, Cherokee, Pawnee, Comanche, Delaware, Rogers, Mayes, Tulsa, and Washington.
Miami area field office	2,474	Ottawa and Delaware.
Eastern Shawnee	299	
Miami	299	
Quapaw	1,144	
Seneca-Cayuga	732	
Pawnee Indian Agency	2,784	Kay, Noble, and Pawnee.
Kaw	248	
Otoe-Missouria	973	
Pawnee	687	
Ponca	876	
Shawnee Indian Agency	2,400	Lincoln, Logan, Payne, Oklahoma, Pottawatomie, Cleveland, and Johnston.
Iowa	258	
Mexican Kicapoo	416	
Potawatomi	318	
Sac and Fox	656	
Absentee Shawnee	752	

Source: County locations of Federal Indian eservations and other land units, June 30, 1961, Bureau of Indian Affairs.

Composition by age

The age distribution in 1962 of the members of the tribes of north central Oklahoma is shown in table III. The tribal membership rolls of the Eastern Shawnee and Absentee Shawnee as of August 20, 1964, were used as the population documents from which samples were drawn. The average percent by age categories was computed from these two rolls and these percentage figures were applied to the 1962 population figure of 50,530 to compute the figures shown in the table. More than 50 percent of the total members were less than 20 years of age. As is true of Indian tribes generally throughout the United States, these tribes have a younger population than that of the general U.S. population. Only 39 percent of the U.S. population was under 20 years of age in 1960.

TABLE III.—COMPOSITION OF MEMBERSHIP, BY AGE, JUNE 1962

Age	Population	Percent
1 to 19	5,300	50
20 to 39	2,950	28
40 to 59	1,680	16
60 and up	600	6
Total	10,530	100

Source: Bureau of Indian Affairs.

Educational characteristics

The school enrollment figures shown in table IV includes all the Indian children of families who maintain permanent residence in the jurisdiction. In Oklahoma schools in general, 60 percent of the children entering the first grade never complete high school. In the jurisdiction of these tribes, the dropout figure is approximately 75 percent. Of all students graduating from high school in Oklahoma, 46 percent continue into higher education. For Indian graduates of high school, only 30 percent continue into higher education. The Bureau is encouraging all children to finish high school and secure college or vocational training following high school graduation.

TABLE IV.— PERMANENT RESIDENCE OF JURISDICTION ATTENDING PUBLIC AND PRIVATE SCHOOLS, JUNE 1965

School	Boys	Girls	Total	Percent
Public	2,493	2,471	4,964	92
Federal	133	133	266	5
University	91	66	157	3
Total	2,717	2,670	5,387	100

Source: Annual School Census Report of Indian Children, 1965, Branch of Education; Bureau of Indian Affairs.

TABLE V.—LABOR FORCE, EMPLOYMENT, AND UNEMPLOYMENT, MARCH 1966

	Total	Male	Female
Labor force (14 years and over)	4,728	2,516	2,212
Employed, total	2,744	1,696	1,048
Permanent (more than 12 months)	1,180	711	649
Temporary (including persons away on seasonal work)	1,564	985	579
Unemployed	1,984	820	1,164
Percent unemployed	41	32	52
Not in labor force (14 years and over)	2,445	1,092	1,353
Students (14 years and over including those away at school)	1,061	548	513
Men (all reasons)	544	544	
Women for whom no child-care substitutes are available	565		565
Women (all other reasons)	275		275

Source: Bureau of Indian Affairs Semiannual Report of Labor Force, Employment, and Unemployment (March 1966).

HISTORICAL BACKGROUND

The Cheyenne and Arapaho Tribes are members of the Algonquian speaking family. Around 1835 a portion of the migrating tribes separated itself from the main body, settling along the Arkansas River in Colorado to become known as the Southern Cheyenne and Arapaho. It is this group that was finally resettled on reservation land at Darlington, Indian Territory, in 1869, on what is today western Oklahoma. In 1877 they were joined by a group of more than 900 Northern Cheyenne who had been driven south from their lands at the headwaters of the North Platte and Yellowstone Rivers. About 350 of the Northern Cheyenne fled Oklahoma, and after several heroic skirmishes with U.S. Federal troops, were eventually settled on the Tongue River in southern Montana.

The original Cheyenne and Arapaho Reservation had an area of 4,294,459.59 acres. Under the act of February 8, 1887 (24 Stat. 338), as amended by the act of March 31, 1891 (26 Stat. 989), 3,331 Indians of the Cheyenne and Arapaho tribes were allotted 528,789 acres out of the original reservation. Approximately three and one-half million acres were opened to settlement and the balance set aside in reserves for miscellaneous school, agency, military, mission and other purposes. At the present time, there are approximately 110,000 acres of allotted land held in trust for the Cheyenne and Arapaho Indians. There are also approximately 10,000 acres of tribal land of which 5,873 are held in trust while fee patents have been issued on 3,889 acres. The grand total of tribal and allotted land is approximately 120,000 acres.

The former reservation of the Cheyenne-Arapaho Tribes of Oklahoma consists of all the counties of Blaine, Custer, Dewey, Washita, and parts of the counties of Beckham, Canadian, Kingfisher and Roger Mills. Approximately 54 percent of the total enrolled members reside in this area.

The principal resource of this area of western Oklahoma is its agricultural lands. The major portion of the income derived from these lands is being received by the non-Indian owners or leasees. The main farming non-Indian enterprises are cattle ranching and raising grain by dry farming.

The checkerboarding of Indian lands through sales and inheritance of allotments and the limited agricultural skills of the Cheyenne-Arapaho lead to leasing their agricultural land. As a consequence the tribal members receive little income from this resource. Of 1,148 separate land use units in Indian ownership, 1,121 are being utilized by non-Indian operators.

The Cheyenne-Arapaho area has good prospects for the development of the oil and gas industry in this area of Oklahoma. The area also has a potential for the development of small industries such as woodworking and textile plants close to Indian communities. Small industries would create new jobs and increase economic opportunities for Cheyenne-Arapaho tribal members. The completion of U.S. Highway 66, which crosses Cheyenne-Arapaho land, as a four-lane highway, will benefit this development.

The record reveals that the Cheyenne-Arapaho people were enjoying a stable society and lived peacefully in prereservation history. The impact of American civilization caused the loss of their native economy and extensive social disorganization. The sales and disposition of allotted lands have barred development of the Indian agricultural economy. The lack of any viable economy has resulted in the loss of status and self-confidence essential to the progress of any people.

STATISTICAL DATA OF THE CHEYENNE AND ARAPAHO TRIBES

POPULATION CHARACTERISTICS

There has been a steady increase of the population of the Cheyenne and Arapaho people during the past 18 years.

The available population data of the Bureau of Indian Affairs shows that the population within the area and adjacent thereto increased from 2,604 in 1944 to 3,640 in 1962. Table I shows this increase from 1944 to 1962.

TABLE I.—*Population increase of Cheyenne-Arapaho Tribal members within reservation area and adjacent thereto*

Year:

1944	2,604
1945	2,752
1950	3,019
1960	3,500
1962	3,640

GENERAL POPULATION, SOCIAL AND ECONOMIC CHARACTERISTICS : JUNE 1962
TRIBAL MEMBERSHIP

A research committee from the staff of the Concho Area Field Office at Concho, Okla., conducted a recent study of the enrolled members of the Tribes in an effort to learn where the tribal membership lives, and to obtain data regarding income, employment and educational achievements. This committee was selected from staff members who had a broad knowledge of the Cheyenne-Arapaho people and who had received training in conducting a research project. The tribal membership roll, which was prepared and issued by the business committee of the tribes on June 25, 1962, consisting of 4,671 persons, was used as a document from which information was drawn. The tribes are in the process of compiling a current roll and indications are that there are presently about 5,000 enrolled members to date.

Tables II to VI represent a concise summary of the findings of this committee and observations made regarding the tribal membership of this 1962 roll.

Place of residence of tribal membership

The findings indicate that 54 percent of the membership of the tribes continue to reside on former Cheyenne and Arapaho Reservation land in Oklahoma. It can be reasonably assumed that, since official inquiries did not reveal their place of residence, the 12 percent with an address unknown reside off the former reservation.

TABLE II.—LOCATION OF ENROLLED MEMBERS OF THE CHEYENNE AND ARAPAHO TRIBES OF OKLAHOMA BY PLACE OF RESIDENCE, JUNE 1962

Place of residence	Number	Percent
On former reservation in Oklahoma	2,522	54
Off former reservation in Oklahoma	654	14
In States other than Oklahoma	934	20
Address unknown	561	12
Total	4,671	100

Age and sex

The composition of the Tribes by age and sex as determined from the 1962 roll is shown in table III.

TABLE III.—COMPOSITION OF MEMBERSHIP—AGE AND SEX, JUNE 1962

Age groups (years)	Males	Percent	Females	Percent	Total	Percent
0 to 20	1,071	46	1,318	57	2,389	51
21 to 40	730	31	680	29	1,410	31
41 to 60	438	19	242	10	680	14
61 to 100	96	4	96	4	192	4
Total	2,335	100	2,336	100	4,671	100

Composition of membership by degree of blood

Table IV reflects that there are 2,466 (or approximately 53 percent) of the 4,671 members of the Cheyenne and Arapaho Tribes on the June 1962 roll who are full-blood Cheyenne and Arapaho.

TABLE IV.—COMPOSITION OF MEMBERSHIP BY DEGREE OF CHEYENNE-ARAPAHO BLOOD, JUNE 1962

Degree	Number	Percent
¾	2,466	53
¾ up to ¾	609	13
½ up to ¾	973	21
¼ up to ½	488	10
Less than ¼	135	3
Total	4,671	100

Economic and educational characteristics of 1962 enrolled members

(The following statistical information was compiled from a sample of the 1,870 persons on the tribal roll in age group 21–55.)

Income statistics

From the sample, it was found that the median annual income per family from all sources amounted to approximately $962 or a per capita mean income per person of $362. Table V below shows an analysis of this income data by number of families. The total family income ranges from $139 to $9,143 and the size of the family units from 1 to 17 members.

TABLE V.—TOTAL FAMILY INCOME FROM ALL SOURCES FROM A SAMPLE OF 26 FAMILIES WITH A MEMBER IN THE AGE GROUP 21 THROUGH 55 RESIDING ON THE FORMER CHEYENNE AND ARAPAHO RESERVATION IN OKLAHOMA, JUNE 1962

Income	Number of families	Percent
0 to $500	5	19
$501 to $1,000	8	31
$1,001 to $1,500	9	35
$1,501 to $2,000	1	4
Over $2,000	3	11
Total	26	100

Education characteristics

The educational level of the Cheyenne and Arapaho is below that of the non-Indian of western Oklahoma. This places the Indian at a disadvantage when competing for employment. A review of the school attendance records presents a very discouraging picture. The educational achievements of the tribal members from the sample are indicated in table VI below:

TABLE VI.—EDUCATIONAL ACHIEVEMENTS OF TRIBAL MEMBERS, AGES 21–55, JUNE 1962

Grades completed	Number	Percent
4 to 6	144	8
7 to 9	862	46
10 to 12	720	38
13 to 15	144	8
Total	1,870	100

LAND OWNERSHIP

The problem of fractionated land holdings is becoming more acute with time. Table VII below shows a breakdown of land holdings according to the number of owners. The land income received by individual Indians is, in most cases, insignificant. There is a tendency for many of the Indian people to rely on this and other unearned income for their livelihood rather than to obtain wage work. The belief of many Indians that the land is a great asset is out of proportion to its actual benefit.

TABLE VII.—*Ownership in tracts under the supervision of the Concho Agency*

Number of owners:	Number of tracts owned
1	430
2	128
3	73
4 to 6	154
7 to 10	105
11 to 20	118
21 to 50	64
Over 50	12

TABLE VIII.—LABOR FORCE, EMPLOYMENT AND UNEMPLOYMENT
CHEYENNE AND ARAPAHO TRIBES, MARCH 1965

	Total	Male	Female
Labor force (14 years and over)	1,504	662	842
Employed, total	555	245	310
Permanent (more than 12 months)	155	69	86
Temporary (including persons away on seasonal work)	400	176	224
Unemployed	949	417	532
Percent unemployed	63	63	63
Not in labor force (14 years and over)	740	326	414
Students (14 years and over, including those away at school)	500	220	280
Men (all reasons)	60	60	
Women for whom no child-care substitutes are available	75		75
Women (all other reasons)	105		105

Source: Bureau of Indian Affairs Semiannual Report of Labor Force, Employment and Unemployment (March 1965).

HISTORICAL BACKGROUND

Members of the Kiowa, Comanche, Apache, Fort Sill Apache, Wichita, Caddo, and Delaware Tribes reside in southwestern Oklahoma under the jurisdiction of the Anadarko Agency. The jurisdiction covers all or parts of 10 counties, and the agency headquarters are located in Anadarko, which is the county seat of Caddo County. Caddo County has the largest concentration of Indian population of any county within the jurisdiction.

The Kiowa, Comanche, and Apache Tribes are descendants of wandering plains tribesmen, who less than a century ago were primarily hunters, constantly on the move and warring with other tribes for possession of buffalo herds. Under the Medicine Lodge Treaty of October 21, 1867, they were assigned a reservation in southwestern Oklahoma, located between the Washita River on the north and the Red River on the south.

The Wichita, Caddo, and Delaware Tribes have had joint interests from the time they were affiliated in 1867. The reservation assigned to them was also in an area of what is today southwestern Oklahoma. Their agency headquarters were established in 1866 near what is now the town of Anadarko. Their land joined the Kiowa, Comanche, and Apache Reservation land on the north and was later consolidated with the Kiowa-Comanche-Apache Agency.

The reservations of these tribes are no longer in existence. In 1887, after allotting land to individual Indian owners, the remaining land was opened up to settlement. While many owners retained and benefited from their allotments, others sold out for a fraction of the land's value. As of June 1, 1964, there was a total of 330,350 acres remaining in trust or restricted status. There are, in addition, 5,353 acres of tribal land and 3,175 acres of Government land.

The "checkerboarding" of Indian lands through sales and inheritance of allotments and the limited extent of the agricultural skills of Indians of these tribes lead them to lease their agricultural lands. As a consequence, the tribal members receive little income from this source. In addition, the land base is gradually being reduced and the population is increasing, so that income from these resources is becoming more inadequate as time goes by.

Over the past few years, the economic situation has been improved somewhat due to the large number of oil and gas leases and to land sales. During fiscal year 1964, a total of $2,060,000 was derived from farming and grazing leases, oil and gas leases, permits and royalties on this land. This averages $493 a year per landholder. Exploration for other oil and gas resources in this area is currently underway, and income from oil and gas, affecting a comparatively small number of tribal members, appears likely to increase.

The area has a potential for small industries, which would create new jobs and increase economic opportunities for the Indians of southwestern Oklahoma. The establishment of the Sequoyah Mills at Anadarko is a good example of a small industry that has done much to give the Indians of southwestern Oklahoma a chance to improve their living and economic conditions. This mill, which manufactures tufted carpets, provides 90 Indians of this area with a living wage and has given them the first real chance to help themselves.

Some members of the western tribes, by reason of their customs and experience, have been disadvantaged in their ability to adjust to the requirements and demands of the society that surrounds them. Areas exist in western Oklahoma that may accurately be described as "pockets of poverty", where Indian Americans are living in isolation and segregation, separated from the larger community, rarely a part of it. These Indian people are desperately deprived. But absence of resources is not the most devastating aspect of Indian poverty. Rather it is the inability of many Indians to understand and accept the opportunities of American society that are open to them.

GENERAL POPULATION, SOCIAL AND ECONOMIC CHARACTERISTICS

Population

The Indian population of this jurisdiction has been steadily increasing since 1950. Table I shows that the population within the jurisdiction has increased from 5,574 in 1950 to 7,500 in 1962. The rate of annual population growth between 1950 and 1960 was 1.9 percent. By comparison, the annual rate of growth of U.S. population for this 10-year period was 1.7 percent.

TABLE I.—*Population Increase of Tribes Residing in Anadarko Agency Jurisdiction*

Year:	Population
1950	5,574
1960	6,727
1962	7,500

Source : Bureau of Indian Affairs.

Composition by age and sex

The composition of the tribes by age and sex is shown in table II. As shown in this table, 42 percent of the Indian population of the area is under 18 years of age and approximately 50 percent is less than 20 years of age. In contrast only 39 percent of the U.S. population was under 20 years of age in 1960.

TABLE II.—AGE AND SEX DISTRIBUTION, JUNE 1962

Age	Kiowa, Apache, Comanche	Wichita, Caddo, Delaware	Fort Sill Apache	Total	Percent	Cumulative percent
Under 13	1,826	604	30	2,460	33	33
14 to 17	539	178	9	726	9	42
18 to 54	2,204	730	37	2,971	40	82
55 to 64	441	146	7	594	8	90
Over 65	556	184	9	749	10	100
Total	5,566	1,842	92	7,500	100	100
Male	2,369	669	43	3,081		
Female	3,197	1,173	49	4,419		
Total	5,566	1,842	92	7,500		

Source: Bureau of Indian Affairs.

Educational characteristics

(The following statistical information was taken from the annual school census of Indian children of Oklahoma compiled by our branch of education. The data are for fiscal year 1965 and cover all the Indian children of the seven tribes of southwestern Oklahoma who have a permanent residence in the State and who are enrolled in school.)

It can be seen from table III that a large percentage (approximately 91 percent of the Indian children of these tribes attend public and private schools. However, the educational attainment of the Indian students of this area is lower than their white classmates. This educational disparity increases with the grade level. This places the Indian student at a disadvantage when competing with white students in higher grades and in college. Of 3,440 enrolled in school, only 146 are enrolled as undergraduate or postgraduate students.

TABLE III.—EDUCATIONAL DATA COVERING INDIAN CHILDREN PERMANENTLY RESIDING IN OKLAHOMA AND ENROLLED IN SCHOOL, JULY 1965

Classification of children	Apache, Kiowa, Comanche	Delaware, Caddo Wichita	Fort Sill Apache	Total
1. Total number enrolled in all schools	2,794	627	19	3,440
Living within the agency jurisdiction area	2,410	478	19	2,907
Living outside the agency jurisdiction area	307	142	0	449
Residence unknown	77	7	0	84
2. Total number enrolled in all schools	2,794	627	19	3,440
Public schools	2,523	561	16	3,100
All Federal schools	129	27	0	156
Mission and private schools	33	5	0	38
Colleges and universities	109	34	3	146

Land resources

The principal resource of this area is agricultural farming. However, the Indian people receive little benefit from the income accruing from agricultural activities. From table IV below, it can be seen that of a total of 161,316 acres of Indian land that is being utilized for dry farming, only 10,750 acres are being operated by Indian people. Similarly of a total of 132,205 acres being utilized for open grazing for cattle ranching, only 11,640 acres are under the management of Indians. Most of the agricultural income of Indian people of this area comes from seasonable farm labor but modern agricultural machinery is reducing the number of these seasonal agricultural jobs.

TABLE IV.—LAND INVENTORY, JUNE 30, 1964

	Dry farmed	Irrigated	Open grazing	Timber-land	Nonagri-culture uses	Total	Percent
Indian operated:							
Individual	10,610	320	11,630	2,441	570	25,571	7.6
Tribal	140		10		20	170	.1
Subtotal	10,750	320	11,640	2,441	590	25,741	7.7
Non-Indian operated:							
Individual	148,696	1,490	117,915	26,979	9,705	304,785	90.7
Tribal	1,870		2,650	590	70	5,180	1.6
Subtotal	150,566	1,490	120,565	27,569	9,775	309,965	92.3
Total	161,316	1,810	132,205	30,010	10,365	335,706	100.0

TABLE V.—LABOR FORCE, EMPLOYMENT AND UNEMPLOYMENT WITHIN ANADARKO AGENCY JURISDICTION, MARCH 1966

	Total	Male	Female
Labor force (14 years and over)	1,327	1,172	155
Employed, total	1,138	1,017	121
Permanent (more than 12 months)	828	762	66
Temporary (including persons away on seasonal work)	310	255	55
Unemployed	189	155	34
Percent unemployed	14	13	22
Not in labor force (14 years and over)	3,187	900	2,287
Students (14 years and over including those away at school)	820	405	415
Men (all reasons)	495	495	-----------
Women for whom no child care substitutes are available	194	-----------	194
Women (all other reasons)	1,678	-----------	1,678

Source: Bureau of Indian Affairs Semi-annual Report of Labor Force, Employment and Unemployment (March 1966).

POSITION WITH RESPECT TO THE NATIVE LAND CLAIMS ISSUE

By Emil Notti*

FOREWORD

Title to most of the land in Alaska remains under dispute. Prompt and equitable settlement of the land claims issue is fundamental to economic development in that State and to the full participation of the Alaskan natives in this development. The Alaska Federation of Natives has proposed four elements which should be included in a settlement of Native claims: granting of clear Native title to village land which they have historically used and occupied; payment of compensation to the Natives of $500 million plus a 2-percent royalty as compensation for lands previously taken and lands relinquished as part of a settlement; recognition of Native corporations as management agents for the land and funds; creation of an Alaska Native Commission to assist in the administration of the settlement act.

Introduction

The Board of Directors of the Alaska Federation of Natives ("AFN") has been asked its position on the settlement with the Federal Government of the one hundred year problem of Native Land Claims.** AFN feels that a settlement of native claims to land in Alaska should include:

A. Confirmation of title to land in the Native villages which has been used and occupied by the Native people from time immemorial. AFN proposes that said confirmation of lands should be in the amount of 40 million acres.

B. A payment of $500 million and an overriding royalty of 2 percent of the revenue derived from the lands as compensation for lands previously taken, and as compensation for the extinguishment of any and all claims against the United States, based upon aboriginal right, title, use and occupancy of lands in Alaska by any Native or Native group.

C. Recognition of a statewide Native corporation, and not more than 12 regional corporations as the management group for the land and funds.

D. Creation of an Alaska Native Commission to assist in the administration of the Settlement Act.

Each of these concepts (confirmation of title to a specific amount of land, payment of compensation and provisions for the administration of the settlement) have been included in prior bills introduced in Congress.

---

*President, Alaska Federation of Natives.
**AFN will attempt to achieve a separate settlement with the State of Alaska. Because of statements made by Governor Miller during the recent hearing of the Senate Interior Committee AFN is hopeful that it will be able to reach a final settlement with the State.

I. Confirmation of Title to Lands

The Natives of Alaska have watched the tremendous growth in their State without having had a full opportunity to participate in that growth. The historical use and occupancy of the lands by the Natives for many centuries is indisputable. AFN proposes that the title of land heretofore used and occupied by the Natives be confirmed to them in the total amount of 40 million acres in the manner specified below.

1. Each recognized Native village should have confirmed, subject to valid existing rights, a total of four townships, or 92,160 acres. Lands that have been tentatively approved for selection by the State of Alaska are to be included in the lands to be withdrawn on behalf of the Natives. All public lands withdrawn and subsequently conveyed shall be contiguous, except as separated by bodies of water, and shall be in units of not less than 1,280 acres. As provided in S. 1830, each of the villages should be named in the legislation, and the land withdrawals should be made by the legislation. Since the population of the villages varies, and because regional differences exist, an additional grant to the larger villages based on the number of Natives on the village rolls should be made. The additional grant should be calculated on the basis of 500 acres per person, less the grant of four townships, or 92,160 acres. The additional grants of land should be limited to the "claim area" of the regional association in which the community is now located, as shown on the Bureau of Land Management's "Native Protest Map", but need not be contiguous.

2. Regional corporations should be established by the legislation. Each of these corporations should operate in an area roughly analogous to the area now covered by one of the following regional associations:[1]

(a) Arctic Slope Native Association (Barrow, Point Hope).

(b) Bering Straits Association (Kotzebue, Seward Peninsula, Unalakleet, St. Lawrence Island).

(c) Association of Village Council Presidents (southwest coast, all villages in the Bethel area, including all villages on the lower Yukon River and the Lower Kuskokwin River).

(d) Tanana Chief's Conference (Koyukuk, Middle and Upper Yukon Rivers, Upper Kuskokowin, Tanana River).

(e) Cook Inlet Association (Kenai, Tyonek, Eklutna, Iliamna).

(f) Bristol Bay Native Association (Dillingham, Upper Alaska Peninsula).

(g) Aleut League (Aleutian Islands, Pribilof Islands, and that part of the Alaska Peninsula which is in the Aleut League).

(h) Chugach Native Association (Cordova, Tatitlek, Port Graham, English Bay, Valdez and Seward).

(i) Tlingit-Haida Central Council (southeastern Alaska).

(j) Kodiak Area Native Association (all villages on and around Kodiak Island).

---

[1] After further study of this matter, various changes may be made concerning the area covered by particular regional corporations.

(*k*) Copper River Native Association (Copper Center, Glennallen, Chitina, Mentasta).

A map showing the areas of jurisdiction of the proposed regional corporations, and a list of the villages which are entitled to have land withdrawn will be supplied.

3. After withdrawal of the lands in accordance with the proposed legislation, conveyance of those lands in fee simple should be made by the Secretary of Interior to the recognized Native village. The village, at its option, should be able to convey title to the regional corporation in whose area it is located, or to the statewide corporation with the consent of the regional corporation. Appropriate restrictions prohibiting conveyance to others should be included. AFN anticipates that most villages would convey the lands to their regional corporation.

The villages should have the right to manage the surface of the lands, if the right had not previously been granted to the regional or statewide corporation. All mineral interests [2] should be granted to the regional corporation in whose area the minerals are found, and any revenues received by a regional corporation from those interests should be divided in the following ratio: 50 percent to the regional corporation in whose area the mineral is found, and 50 percent to be divided among all of the other regional corporations on a population basis.

4. The lands withdrawn and conveyed to the villages may be located in National Parks, National Wildlife Refuges, National Forests, unimproved portions of Military Reservations, and various animal or bird sanctuaries. AFN respectfully submits that such withdrawals were made without any consideration to the Native occupants and that, equitably, the land in those withdrawals should be restored to the occupants.

5. All Indian Reorganization Act reserves, Executive order reserves, and administrative reserves (pp. 444 and 445 of "Alaska Natives and The Land", prepared by the Federal Field Committee for Development Planning in Alaska), which have been set aside for Native use or for the administration of Native affairs, should be granted subject to valid existing rights, to the villages using or occupying the land at the time of the passage of the legislation. These grants should include all mineral interests therein, and those interests should be managed as provided in paragraph 3 above. To the extent that any reserve is smaller than the area that could have been granted to the village under the terms of paragraph 1 above, additional lands should be granted to the village by the Secretary under the terms expressed in paragraph 1 above.

6. AFN believes that the lands not granted by the legislation should be subject to the protection of subsistence resources by appropriate provisions permitting the Secretary to declare any area closed to hunting, fishing or trapping by persons other than the residents of the area. As to any vacant public domain in Alaska, the Natives should have appropriate provisions in the legislation which will protect game, fish, berries, fuel and other products of the land required for subsistence purposes.

---

[2] As used in this paper the term "mineral" includes, without limitation, oil, gas, gold, copper, and all other leasable and non-leasable minerals.

7. Natives residing in urban areas shall be entitled to receive a patent to the surface of 160 acres of land as permitted in section 10(h) of S. 1830.

8. Natives shall be granted the land used by them for the harvest of fish, wildlife, berries, fuel or other products of the land. The nature and extent of such grants shall be as provided in section 10(d) of S. 1830.

9. Public Land Order 4582, which created the current land freeze should be revoked with the passage of the proposed act and the granting and conveyance of lands as provided herein.

II. Payment of Compensation

1. AFN proposes a payment of $500 million and an overriding gross royalty of 2 percent of all proceeds from any State and Federal lands as compensation for lands previously taken, and as compensation for the extinguishment of any and all claims against the United States, based upon aboriginal rights to all of the lands in Alaska. Sums should be apportioned 75 percent to the villages, 20 percent to the regional corporations, and 5 percent to the statewide corporation after native enrollment is completed. The apportionment should be on the basis of population.

The above distribution of compensation will be limited as to two particular groups:

(a) The Tlingit-Haida Indians, who were granted a judgment in the Court of Claims docket No. 47,900;

(b) Those villages who have claims pending before the Indian Claims Commission that may be reduced to judgment before the legislation passes.

As to those two groups, the amount of any judgments, after deducting the payment of attorneys' fees and costs, should be withheld and reapportioned among the other Native groups on a population basis. When the compensation due those two groups is equal to the amount of money that has been offset, they should be permitted to share in accordance with the above ratios. Separate provisions are also required to deal with distribution to the Tyoneks.

2. AFN proposes that the $500 million be appropriated and deposited to the credit of the Natives by granting $100 million in the first year and $50 million each succeeding year for a period of 8 years. Interest at the prevailing Federal rate should be paid against unpaid balances.

3. Direct per capita distribution of any funds in excess of 20 percent of the amount received by any village or corporation should be prohibited. Each village, regional corporation and the statewide corporation should be authorized to expend, invest or distribute its funds to promote the advancement of the Native people in Alaska, subject to authorization by the appropriate governing body and approval by the Alaska Native Commission.

4. AFN proposes, in place of the provisions in S. 1830, which included terms that the Native people share in the revenues derived from certain sources, an overriding gross royalty of 2 percent of all proceeds from all State or Federal land not patented to the Native people. Such payments should be paid into a special fund and distributed in accordance with paragraph 1 of this section; namely, 75 percent to

the villages, 20 percent to the regional corporations, and 5 percent to the statewide corporation. There should be no time limitation on the term of the overriding royalty and it should effectively grant the Native people a perpetual interest in the lands which have been theirs for thousands of years. The Native people should participate in future royalties and benefits derived from the land, and those funds could be utilized toward the improvement of conditions in the villages.

III. STATEWIDE NATIVE CORPORATION AND REGIONAL NATIVE CORPORATIONS

Historically, dependence and reliance on Federal and State programs has effectively denied the principle of self-determination to the aboriginal people of the United States. The Alaska Natives want to govern themselves within the limitations of the law. Control of their destinies must therefore be transferred to the Native people. Meaningful progress toward that end can be taken in the settlement legislation. AFN therefore proposes the creation of (a) a statewide Native corporation and (b) up to 12 regional corporations as described above. A stateside organization, as a federation of regional associations, presently exists. The Native people strongly believe that the regional corporations would provide a maximum of local self-determination without impairing efficiency. As is apparent from the proposed distribution of funds, AFN wants to build strong regional corporations. AFN believes that there is capable regional leadership to manage the lands and money granted in the legislation.

The regional corporations should have maximum flexibility and the power to engage in any commercial or eleemosynary activities, either individually or in groups. In order to make maximum use of their resources, the regional corporations should be empowered to merge, engage in joint ventures, employ common managerial services, or collectively take whatever steps are deemed appropriate to their boards of directors.

The Native people would be stockholders and owners in the village regional and statewide organizations.

ALASKA NATIVE COMMISSION

To assist the Secretary in the administration of the Native Claims Settlement Act, an Alaska Native Commission should be appointed as an independent agency of the United States. It should be composed of five members appointed by the President, and at least three members should be Alaska Natives. The Commission should have the power to review the budgets of the village, regional, and statewide organizations, and perform such other duties as may be prescribed in the legislation. The commission should be in existence for a period of 10 years after the effective date of the act.

EXTINGUISHMENT OF ALL CLAIMS

The legislation should be a full and final settlement of any and all claims against the United States based upon aboriginal right, title, use, or occupancy of public lands in Alaska by any Native or Native group, arising under the act of May 17, 1884 (23 Stat. 24), or the act of June 6, 1900 (31 Stat. 321), or any other act of Congress, including land claims pending before the Indian Claims Commission on the effective date of the act. An appropriation of funds should be made to the Secretary of the Interior to pay all reasonable expenses and attorneys' fees that have been actually incurred by those claimants in connection with cases that are dismissed as a result of the settlement legislation.

ADDITIONAL CONSIDERATIONS

1. *Enrollment.*—AFN advocates a single enrollment of the Natives of Alaska, which would include all Natives of one-quarter or more Native blood, and any individual as defined in section 2(c) of S. 3859 (90th Cong., second sess.). Each Native should be enrolled regardless of present residence. The enrollment of the regional corporation shall consist of the rolls of all the villages within the region of the corporation. The regional corporation enrollments shall constitute the rolls of the statewide Native corporation. Distribution of funds to the various regional corporations and villages should be made based on a temporary enrollment. A sufficient amount of funds should be reserved to adjust the distribution if the final enrollment differs from the preliminary enrollment.

AFN advocates an immediate enrollment of all the Native people in Alaska and proposes that the enrollment be conducted by AFN under contract from BIA.

2. *Native Allotment Act.*—No provision of the Settlement Act should affect the rights of the Natives as citizens to acquire public lands of the United States under the Native Allotment Act of May 17, 1906, as amended, or the provisions of other statutes giving land rights to Natives.

3. *Attorneys' fees.*—The bill shall contain provisions for the payment of all reasonable attorneys' fees or expenses actually incurred by any Native group, village, association, or federation in connection with legislation pertaining to the settlement of the lands issue.

4. *Appropriations.*—Sufficient funds should be appropriated to the Secretary of the Interior to carry out the duties required of him under the Settlement Act.

CONCLUSION

Because of the past failures to settle Native land claims in Alaska, almost all of the State's 365 million acres are in controversy. The Native people have asserted their rights under aboriginal title to almost all of the land. However, the Native people recognize their duties as citizens and urge the Congress to provide a prompt and just settlement. A final resolution of all the claims will be of substantial benefit to the Natives, the State of Alaska, and to the United States.

AFN believes that the proposals submitted above constitute an appropriate formula for settlement. The essential ingredients of land grants, compensation, and shares in future revenues may perhaps be mixed in different proportions if the overall result is substantially the same. In AFN's judgment, the above formula represents the best solution. If the State of Alaska, and the Native people who are its citizens, are to advance, an effective solution must be promptly found by the Congress.

Part III: THE RESOURCE BASE

Part III: THE RESOURCE BASE

INDIAN TRUST FUNDS

By ALAN L. SORKIN*

FOREWORD

Many Indian tribes have acquired substantial financial assets in recent years as the result of awards by the Indian Claims Commission. Earnings from the leasing of mineral rights are also significant. Alan Sorkin points out that while these funds are unevenly distributed among the tribes, some tribes are presented with an excellent opportunity to invest in their own economic development. To date, most tribal income has either been distributed in the form of per capita payments or has been left in trust with the Bureau of Indian Affairs. Possibilities for utilizing tribal income and trust funds for reservation development remain largely unexplored. The Bureau of Indian Affairs has not prohibited such uses of these funds, but neither has it actively encouraged such programs.

Introduction

Although about three-fourths of all reservation Indian families live in poverty,[1] many tribes have substantial deposits in the Federal Treasury or commercial banks in the form of tribal trust funds. This paper will examine various policy issues relating to these funds which total over $300 million, such as Bureau of Indian Affairs investment policy, the role of the Secretary of the Interior as guardian or trustee, and the part the funds could play in the economic development of the reservations. The sources of these funds, as well as their past and likely future growth will be discussed.

SOURCES OF TRIBAL TRUST FUNDS

In the early treaties with the Indian tribes the consideration was generally in the form of lump cash payment, an annuity in money or goods for a definite term or in perpetuity, or a combination of cash payments and annuities. The treaty with the Cherokees of February 27, 1819, was the first to create a trust fund to be held by the United States for the benefit of the tribe.[2]

During the remainder of the 19th century tribal trust funds were created for a variety of reasons. Sometimes the Government forced Indians to move from their native lands to selected reservations, obligating itself for a specific sum in consideration of their compliance. In other cases, the Government bought part of the lands outright, and deposited the purchase price in the treasury to the credit of the tribe.

---

*The author is a Research Associate at the Brookings Institution.

[1] U.S. Bureau of Indian Affairs, "Indian Housing, Needs, Priorities, Alternatives, and Program Recommendations," unpublished, 1966.
[2] Lawrence F. Schmeckebier, *The Office of Indian Affairs, Its History, Activities and Organization* (Institute for Government Research, the John Hopkins Press, 1927), p. 190.

Sometimes the Government simply took over the lands, and sold them for the benefit of the Indians who resided there, and deposited the proceeds in the treasury.[3]

Between 1840 and 1926 Indian trust funds increased from $4.5 million to $23.5 million. Since World War II, tribal trust funds have grown more rapidly from $28.5 million in 1947 to over $300 million in 1967. (See table I.) However, trust funds are very unequally distributed among tribes. Thus, five tribes have over $5 million in trust funds while over half have less than $100,000. (See table II.)

The rapid growth in tribal funds in recent years is due to two principal income sources. The first is income received from the settlement of Indian claims before the Indian Claims Commission. The second is the earnings received from deposits of oil, gas, and other minerals which have been found on Indian reservations.

Between 1950 and 1968 there were 247 cases heard before the Indian Claims Commission. Of these 247 cases, 136 were dismissed and 101 were decided in favor of the Indian tribes.[4] Between 1950 and 1967 almost one quarter of a billion dollars was awarded to Indian tribes as settlement for claims. In 1966–67 about $44 million was awarded.

The size of the awards varies greatly. For example, in 1966, the Cheyenne-Arapaho received $15 million while the Poncha of Oklahoma received $2,458.

Not all of the funds received by the tribes as settlement for claims became a part of the tribal trust funds. In fact, a large portion is never invested, but is distributed in per capita payments.

Per capita payments are usually distributed so that each member of the tribe receives an equal share of the proceeds. Thus, if $1 million is awarded a tribe with 2,000 members, each tribal member would receive $500. Of $102 million awarded by the Indian Claims Commission between 1951–64, approximately $42 million was distributed in per capita payments.[5]

TABLE I.—GROWTH OF INDIAN TRIBAL TRUST FUNDS, 1840–1967

	Tribal trust funds [1]	Interest account [2]
Fiscal year:[1]		
1840	$4,477,322	
1850	7,525,060	
1860	3,396,242	
1870	4,608,367	
1880	15,675,140	
1890	23,760,413	
1900	34,317,955	
1925	32,544,972	
1947	28,497,080	1,112,453
1950	42,224,129	3,335,822
1955	84,949,383	2,933,818
1960	157,757,238	2,875,978
1965	268,470,447	2,921,327
1966	257,657,379	4,212,686
1967	[3] 162,764,965	4,379,933

[1] Tribal funds in Treasury only. From 1840–1966, this was the only location of tribal trust funds. In 1967, $157,000,000 was in banks.
[2] Data for 1840–1925 not available.
[3] $167,000,000 on deposit in banks and Treasury securities.

Source: Data for 1840–1925 from Laurence F. Schmeckebier, The Office of Indian Affairs, Its History Activities and Organization (Institute for Government Research, The Johns Hopkins University, 1927), p. 191. Data for 1947–67 from combined statement of receipts, expenditures and balances of the U.S. Government for the fiscal year ended June 30 1947–67.

---

[3] Frances E. Leupp, *The Indian and His Problem* (Charles Scribner's Sons, 1910), p. 174.
[4] U.S. Department of the Interior, Bureau of Indian Affairs, Branch of Tribal Operations, Robert Pennington, "Summary of Indian Claims Commission Dockets," unpublished memorandum, January 1968, p. 2.
[5] Computed from Robert Pennington, *op. cit.* statement No. 5, pp. 1–3. It should be noted that Congressional legislation is necessary to finalize most of the awards of the Indian Claims Commission.

TABLE II.—DISTRIBUTION OF TREASURY DEPOSITS BY TRIBE, OCTOBER 1967

Amount	Number of tribes	Percent of tribes	Percent of tribal funds
Less than $10,000	64	36	0.24
$10,000 to $99,999	41	23	1.64
$100,000 to $999,999	47	27	10.50
$1,000,000 to $4,999,999	20	11	29.90
$5,000,000 or more	5	3	57.72

Source: Calculated from Bureau of Indian Affairs, "Statement of Trust Funds," unpublished tabulation, Oct. 1, 1967.

(The policy implications of per capita payments vis-a-vis economic development will be discussed in a later section of this paper.)

A second major income source for trust funds is from the earnings received due to the location of mineral deposits on Indian lands. Between 1949 and 1966, Indian tribes received $542,727,159 in income from oil and gas and $27,628,357 from other minerals.[6] As in the case of Indian Claims Commission Awards, much of the income (60 to 70 percent) accruing from mineral deposits on Indian lands is distributed in the form of per capita payments.[7]

The Navajo tribe has benefited substantially from reserves of oil and gas on reservation lands. More than $80 million obtained from these minerals has been placed in tribal trust funds. Another Indian group which has placed most of their mineral income in trust funds is the Tyonek Band of the Tlingit and Haida Tribes. In 1966 and 1967 this band received $14.4 million in mineral royalties and "bonus bids."

INVESTMENT OF INDIAN TRIBAL TRUST FUNDS

An act of January 9, 1837, provided that the Secretary of War should invest all money on which the United States had obligated itself to pay interest to the Indians. When the Department of the Interior was created in 1849, the control of Indian funds was transferred to the head of that Department. Owing to the lack of money in the Treasury, the capital of all funds was not invested for some years, Congress making an annual appropriation for the payment of the interest, but apparently by the late 1850's, money was available to invest the principal.[8]

In general, the funds were invested in United States or State bonds and railroad securities. By the act of June 10, 1876, the custody of the bonds was transferred to the Treasurer of the United States, who was authorized to make all purchases and sales of bonds and stocks, but the control of the investment remained with the Secretary of the Interior. In 1880, the practice of retaining the money in the Treasury was begun, a permanent indefinite appropriation being made to pay the interest prescribed by treaty or statute. As the bonds became due

[6] Calculated from Henry W. Hough, *Development of Indian Resources* (World Press, 1967), p. 118.
[7] The Osage Tribe in Oklahoma has distributed approximately $120,000,000 from mineral income in per capita payments during 1949–66. For further information see Hough, *Development of Indian Resources*, *op. cit.*, p. 120, and *The Osage People and Their Trust Property*, a Field Report of Bureau of Indian Affairs, Anadarko Area Office, Osage Agency, April 1953.
[8] Schmeckebier, *op. cit.*, p. 191.

the proceeds were deposited in the Treasury and by June 30, 1898, the last had been disposed of.[9]

Since 1818, the tribal trust funds deposited in the Treasury have drawn 4 percent simple interest, which is placed in a separate interest account. (See table I.)

Beginning in July 1966, the Bureau of Indian Affairs, in consultation with the tribes initiated a program for increasing the rate of return by channeling tribal trust funds into improved investments, in Government securities and commercial bank certificates of deposit which are secured by bond or commercial collateral, approved by the Treasury Department. The rate of return on these investments has been 5 to 6 percent (see table III) thus increasing by over $2 million the earnings for participating tribes.

In September 1968, Indian tribes had $157 million in tribal funds on deposit in various banks, plus an additional $10 million in Treasury securities. Since tribal funds totaled about $300 million in 1968, this indicates that slightly less than one-half the tribal funds remained on deposit in the Treasury.

TABLE III.—APPROVED INVESTMENTS, SELECTED TRIBES

Name of tribe	Type of investment	Amount invested	Rate of return (percent)[1]
Tlingit and Haida	Certificates of deposit	$5,500,000	6.25
Do	Treasury bills	1,051,000	5.55
Navajo	Certificates of deposit	39,987,832	5.90
Do	Treasury notes	8,067,500	5.50
Do	Treasury bonds	181,500	4.00
California Indians	Certificates of deposit	27,897,501	5.50
Ute Mountain	do	10,000,000	6.25
Do	Treasury bonds	197,000	4.00
Mescalero Apache	Certificate of deposit	5,933,016	5.70
Creeks	do	4,772,916	5.70
Utes (Utah)	do	6,925,000	5.65

[1] Weighted average of several certificates of deposit, Treasury bills, notes, and bonds.

Source: U.S. Bureau of Indian Affairs, "Investments as of Sept. 30, 1968," unpublished tabulation provided by Assistant Commissioner of Indian Affairs Norwood, November 1968.

Indian tribes do not always purchase certificates of deposit from banks which pay the highest interest rate. For example, one tribe in Montana purchased certificates of deposit paying 5 percent interest at a local bank although out-of-State banks were willing to pay as much as 6¼ percent. The tribal leaders preferred the local bank because they felt that a substantial deposit would make the bank more amenable to extending loans to individual tribal members.

OTHER INVESTMENTS

Several Indian tribes, with the supervision of the Bureau of Indian Affairs, and in consultation with private financial analysts, have begun to invest some of the funds, which were previously deposited in the

---

[9] During the period in which the funds were invested, the Government lost a considerable sum through the embezzlement of bonds valued at $890,000 from the Interior Department in the early part of 1861, and through the default in payment of interest on others amounting to $1,247,666. Practically all of the bonds in default were those of States which seceded in 1861, although Arkansas had never paid interest on a refunding issue of 1842 for the amount due at that time for principal and interest. In 1862, an appropriation was made to place $600,412 to the credit of certain tribes in lieu of the bonds that had been stolen. In 1894, the investment account was finally closed by reimbursements of $83,000 on account of stolen bonds and of $1,247,666 on account of bonds not paying interest. In addition to the principal sums mentioned above, enough money was appropriated each year to pay the interest.

Treasury, into common stocks and mutual funds.[10] Although there are little data available on the magnitude of these investments, the Navajo tribe has been the most active. The tribe has recently established a $10 million educational fund with money invested in common stocks and mutual funds.[11]

It is likely that investments of this type will increase over time. Not only is the Bureau of Indian Affairs more flexible regarding the kinds of income earning assets which may be purchased, but the increasing financial sophistication of some tribal leaders is creating a desire that these tribal funds earn the highest rate of return possible.

Some Policy Implications

The existence of several hundred million dollars in tribal trust funds under the guardianship of the Bureau of Indian Affairs (via the Secretary of the Interior) raises some important questions concerning Federal Indian policy. First, is the Bureau, as legal guardian of these funds, following a prudent course regarding investment of tribal moneys? Second, should the Federal Government be in the position of guardian (in effect telling the Indians what to do with their money?)[12] Third, what use is being made of these funds to assist the economic development of the tribes?

It would appear that in recent years the Bureau of Indian Affairs has made a determined effort to secure the highest rate of return possible on tribal trust funds that is consistent with a policy of low risk of capital loss. Moreover, the Bureau is increasingly willing to allow tribes to invest funds in stocks and mutual funds utilizing the advice of private investment consultants.[13]

Thus, given the fact that the Bureau of Indian Affairs seems to be doing a competent job regarding financial management of the Indian trust funds, is it in fact serving the long term interests of the tribes by continuing in this role?

There are several arguments which can be made in favor of continuing the guardianship role of the Bureau of Indian Affairs vis-a-vis Indian trust funds. First, because of the low level of schooling of most reservation Indians, including tribal officials, it is likely that they would lack the financial sophistication to make wise investments. Moreover, without Federal supervision, unscrupulous investment consultants would be able to take advantage of the tribal leaders. It is likely that this argument was quite valid in earlier years when illiteracy was high among reservation Indians, and relatively few spoke English. With the rapid increase which has taken place in the level of education of reservation Indians since 1940, the argument clearly has less weight than previously.

A second reason for continuing guardianship is that most tribal leaders prefer this arrangement since it frees them from the respon-

---

[10] The Bureau of Indian Affairs does *not* recommend which stocks to buy or in which mutual funds the tribes should invest their funds. However, the Bureau does determine whether or not the financial advisors utilized by the tribe are capable. Moreover, the Bureau does hold a veto power over whether the monies can be transferred from one type of earning asset into common stocks or mutual funds; or if the income has just been realized, whether or not it can be invested in stocks or mutual funds.

[11] Interview with Assistant Commissioner of Indian Affairs Norwood, November 1968.

[12] Not only must all investments of trust funds be approved by the Bureau of Indian Affairs (in practice most tribes leave it to the Bureau to invest the money for them), but major expenditures of monies from the trust funds must be approved by the Secretary of the Interior.

[13] One could not expect the Bureau of Indian Affairs to purchase stocks or mutual funds for the tribes since this would put the Government in the position of seeming to believe that some companies are better investment prospects than others.

sibility of having to worry about developing an adequate investment program. While the argument may be correct, it could be used to support a system of *voluntary* guardianship instead of *compulsory* guardianship. That is, those tribes who wish to have the Bureau of Indian Affairs manage their funds could continue to do so, while those who wish to manage their own funds could sever the present relationship.[14]

Perhaps the most important argument which can be made against the present arrangement is that the money is the property of the Indians and, as such, they should be able to control its consumption or investment. Thus, if a tribe through a special referendum or through elected officials decided to invest the money in a project which Government officials felt had little chance of returning the original investment, the decision should still remain with the tribe. On the other hand, the trust fund is the principal asset of many tribes, and the dissolution of this property as a result of bad investments would leave the tribe destitute.[15] Since this is a possibility, it can be maintained that the financial disaster which could befall Indian tribes if bad investments were made is a mistake which the Government in good conscience cannot allow the tribes to make.

On the whole, the Bureau of Indian affairs is maintaining a paternalistic role in regard to management of tribal trust funds. By continuing to serve as the master banker for the Indian tribes, it is perpetuating a system of indefinite dependence by the tribes on the BIA. Since one of the goals of the present Commissioner of Indian Affairs is to increase the self-sufficiency of the Indian tribes, it is clear that this objective cannot be fully accomplished by permitting the Bureau to continue as guardian of the tribal trust funds. This point, while certainly valid in theory, does not have to be as valid in practice. If the Bureau of Indian Affairs allowed those tribes, which desired to do so, to work out their own investment and expenditure plans (as they are doing with the Navajos), using private consultants with little or no interference from the Bureau, then it could be maintained that for those tribes the Federal government vis-a-vis the tribal funds would be guardian in same only.[16]

A final point which must be made in consideration of Federal policy regarding Indian trust funds is that they must be seriously considered in any future discussion of possible termination of the Indian tribes. If it is felt that a tribe cannot do an effective job of managing its trust funds, the Government, *for that reason alone*, would be committing a serious policy error if it went ahead with termination proceedings without attempting to secure competent nongovernmental investment counseling for the tribe.[17]

---

[14] Not all tribes wish to have the Bureau continue their role as guardian of the trust funds. The author interviewed several Indian leaders who expressed resentment at the present state of affairs

[15] Many tribes with little or no current income have received settlements from the Indian Claims Commission. These settlements are used to create the tribal trust fund. Other tribes have substantial current income so that possible business losses could be replaced.

[16] While it is true that paternalism is minimized if the Bureau of Indian Affairs authority is used actively, discretionary limitations of power can often be temporary, particularly if there is a frequent change in the Commissioner of Indian Affairs.

[17] The Menominee's of Wisconsin and the Klamath's of Oregon. two tribes that were terminated in the 1950's, suffered severe depletion of individual and tribal assets after Bureau supervision was ended.

Trust Funds and Economic Development

During 1966, the Indian tribes invested $58 million of their own funds in economic development projects, including $12 million in reservation industry.[18] However, a major portion of Indian financial resources, including current income, is either distributed in per capita payments or deposited in banks or the Treasury. Thus, many tribes have declined to commit a significant portion of their financial resources to economic and industrial development. There are several reasons for this. First, the majority of tribal leaders are relatively untrained in matters of business and finance and are understandably reluctant to commit funds to tribal enterprises which would likely have to be managed and operated by non-Indians.[19] Very few Indians have had any experience operating a business especially a large scale one.

Second, on some reservations, Indians have divided themselves into factions with respect to the distribution of tribal income or the allocation of trust funds. One group may insist on dividing the income among members of the tribe by means of a per capita payment. This is especially true among older Indians who may not be interested in possible long-term gains which could perhaps be realized by investing the money in industrial development.[20]

Another group may wish to spend the money on improvement of human resources through expenditures for higher education and through investment in employment-creating and income-earning projects. Often no action is taken and the money remains on deposit in the Treasury or in banks.[21] This is because tribal leaders prefer to reach a consensus of opinion before a decision is made. If a consensus cannot be attained, the decision is postponed.

A third reason that a larger fraction of tribal funds is not committed to economic development is that it is not clear whether the rate of return from business or industrial development projects would be greater than the rate of return from investment in Treasury certificates or time deposits. This position receives some support from the various industrial feasibility studies undertaken by the Area Redevelopment Administration and the Bureau of Indian Affairs which indicate that in most cases the expected rate of return would be low.

However, this approach can be criticized as short-sighted. The biggest problem on an Indian reservation is unemployment; there is a great need to put people to work. Thus, for tribes with several million dollars in trust or bank deposits, investment in economic development

---

[18] U.S. Bureau of Indian Affairs, "Indian Affairs, 1966, A Progress Report from the Commissioner of Indian Affairs" (Washington, D.C., 1966).

[19] Most of the industrial feasibility studies done on Indian reservations in the 1960's recommended that management initially be non-Indian.

[20] Moreover, if annual incomes are extremely low, pressure for per capita payments will also come from younger members of the tribe.

[21] A Northwest tribe recently received a $600,000 award for a claim before the Indian Claims Commission. However, because of internal strife between tribal members as to the disposition of this award (many insist on per capita payments), it may be years before a decision is reached.

projects with low rates of return would be preferable to the mental and physical degeneration which results from prolonged unemployment. [22] Long run human resource development is superior to the short run interest earnings being derived at the present time.

It is not clear what portion of the blame BIA deserves for the fact that so small a portion of the tribal trust funds have been used for economic development. If the tribes wish to retain their funds in banks or the Treasury, it might appear that the Bureau, as guardian, has no business trying to convince the tribe otherwise. However, if the tribes desired to withdraw substantial amounts from the trust funds and were prevented from doing so because of opposition by the Bureau to the project, then it would appear that the latter could be shortsighted. There is no evidence that the Bureau has ever prevented a tribe from using its trust funds for development; in fact, several tribes such as the Navajo have used tribal funds for such purposes. However, there is no evidence that the Bureau has ever *Encouraged* the tribes to use their funds for development. It appears that the Bureau has taken a narrow view of its guardianship role concerning tribal funds; that is, to obtain the highest rate of return with a minimum of risk. Since development projects may deviate from this objective, they are not encouraged.

Those tribes with several million dollars in tribal trust funds should be encouraged to use some of these funds for development purposes (25 tribes have over $1 million in tribal trust funds with five tribes having over $5 million) in projects planned jointly by the tribe and the Bureau of Indian Affairs (or by the tribes exclusively). If the tribes fail to show interest, then the Government would at least have the satisfaction of knowing that it was not the latter's shortsightedness which was the stumbling block to development.

Because of the unequal distribution of trust funds among the tribes, there is great variation in their ability to finance development by utilizing these funds as a source of capital. For example, the Navajo with $80 million in tribal funds, have aided reservation development by construction of water and sewer lines through electrification (at tribal expense) of the more remote parts of the reservation, by subsidization of industry, and through the operation of tribal enterprises, including a forest products industry and tourist facilities.

However, the Pine Ridge Sioux, with 12,000 members is wholly dependent on outside financing. The tribe has only $58,000 in trust funds. Geological surveys indicate that the reservation may be favorably situated regarding oil and gas potential. If commercial exploitation were undertaken, the tribe would be able to utilize the accrued revenue for development.

Economic Development and Per Capita Payments

It was pointed out above that the bulk of the income derived from reservation mineral wealth and a large fraction of the awards from the Indian Claims Commission have been distributed in the form of per capita payments. There are several reasons why this policy is questionable.

---

[22] Thus, the Navajo Indian Tribe has invested millions of dollars in public works project and additional funds in tribal enterprises with low rates of return because without these expenditures, jobs on some parts of the reservation would be nonexistent. However, if the *Government* were willing to make reasonable outlays to develop a reservation infrastructure, including public works projects, then it would not be as necessary for the tribes to utilize their trust funds for this purpose.

First, distribution of tribal assets in the form of per capita payments eliminates the opportunity to utilize the money for long-term reservation development. Since incomes of individual tribal members are frequently very low, personal saving can make little or no contribution to reservation development. Thus, the "exogenous" sources of income (minerals or awards by the Indian Claims Commission) are frequently the only possible sources of development capital.

Second, many Indians, who are unable to find suitable employment on the reservation, are nevertheless reluctant to leave because they do not want to miss a per capita payment.[23] From an economic standpoint this is irrational. Not only do many tribes give per capita payments to those who have left the reservation, but even if this were not the case, the economic sacrifice of remaining on the reservation (in terms of income lost) could seldom be made up by a one-time per capita payment which rarely exceeds $3,000.

Finally, because of the traditional poverty of the reservation Indian and the concomitant low levels of schooling, many of these individuals do not know how to manage large sums of money effectively. This problem is made worse by the high pressure salesmanship of non-Indian merchants who flock to the Indians with their wares as soon as a large per capita distribution is made.[24]

On the other hand, since the money belongs to the various tribes, they should have the right to decide its allocation. Thus, if the majority of tribal members wish per capita payments, shouldn't this decision be a guide to policy? Congress has been especially sympathetic to this view and has usually permitted per capita distribution of Indian Claims Commission awards if the majority of tribal members favor them. Similarly, the Secretary of the Interior has permitted per capita payments from current mineral income.

While the poverty of the reservation Indian no doubt creates a strong desire to realize immediately through per capita payments the benefits of an Indian Claims Commission award or other income, many would argue that the claims of future generations should also be considered. Thus, the Government should be as concerned about succeeding generations of Indians as today's Indians. If this is true, then it may be a wise policy to only pay out a portion of an Indian Claims Commission award or mineral income in the form of per capita payments reserving the remainder for other purposes.

While from the viewpoint of economic development, a strong case can be made for discouraging or limiting per capita payments, it is most important in the long run to leave the decision regarding investment or consumption of trust funds or current tribal income to the tribes. Ideally, the Federal role shoud be restricted to informing the tribe of the consequences of alternative decisions. To insure that Indian leaders would be able to evaluate this advice effectively, courses in financial and business management should be made available to tribal leaders, either as part of an expanded adult education program or through universities located near the reservations. These

---

[23] Some tribes distribute per capita payments to all those individuals or the heirs of those individuals on the tribal roll as of a certain past date. Others, after the award of the Indian Claims Commission is finalized, draw up a tribal roll and distribute the money to those who are on the new roll.
[24] The best example of this is the Osage Indians in Oklahoma, some of whom bought new cars every time a per capita distribution was made (every 3 months). However, some of their per capita payments have been used for housing and education.

courses would not only permit the participants to evaluate advice (whether from private consultants or the BIA), but would give them the knowledge to plan, if they so desired, *their own development projects.*

THE CROW FAMILY PLAN

One of the more progressive distributions of an Indian Claims Commission award occurred in connection with the Crow Tribe in Montana. A total of $10,242,984 was awarded to the Crow Tribe in 1961. The amount remaining after deduction of attorney's fees was $9,238,500. The Crow Tribal Council, with the approval of the Secretary of the Interior, allocated the money as shown in table IV.

Under the plan each family received an average of $3,019.[25] The plan required that money could only be spent for capital goods, durable consumer goods or for personal improvement via, for example, expenditures on health and education. Each family was required to submit a detailed proposal for use of family plan funds to the Bureau of Indian Affairs, before moneys were released. Funds could not be used for automobiles, vacations, daily living expenses or to pay debts incurred prior to the approval of the family plan.

It appears that virtually all of the expenditures were restricted to goods which it was permissible to purchase. Thus, four-fifths of the funds were used for durable consumer goods such as additional rooms in homes or renovation of homes, household furnishings, and water and sanitation facilities. Occupancy decreased from an average of 2 persons per room to 1.2 persons, a reduction of 40 percent.[26] Most of the remaining outlay was for capital goods. These were mainly purchased by ranchers and included livestock, machinery, and equipment. A relatively small part of the funds were spent for education, health, medical and other personal improvement purposes. From all indications this program has worked well and could be emulated in those cases where there is strong pressure for per capita payments.[27]

TABLE IV.—FAMILY PLAN ALLOCATION OF FUNDS, CROW TRIBE

Type of allocation	Dollars	Percent
1. Per capita payment (winter relief measure)	1,193,500	12.9
2. Family plan, $1,000 to each enrolled Crow	4,336,000	46.9
3. Tribal land purchase plan	1,000,000	10.8
4. Expansion of tribal credit program	257,000	3.0
5. Competent lease loans	1,000,000	10.8
6. Economic development of Crow Tribe	1,000,000	10.8
7. Educational purposes	200,000	2.2
8. Law and order	100,000	1.1
9. Construction of tribal headquarters	120,000	1.3
10. Unobligated funds	14,000	.2
Total	9,220,500	100.0

Source: U.S. Department of the Interior, Bureau of Indian Affairs, Missouri River Basin investigations project, "Family Plan Program, Crow Reservation, Montana," May 1967, p 1 (mimeographed).

[25] U.S. Department of the Interior, Bureau of Indian Affairs Missouri River Basin Investigations Project, Billings, Mont., "Family Plan Program Crow Reservation Montana," May 1967, p. 2.
[26] Missouri River Basin investigations project, *op. cit.,* p. 3.
[27] There is some evidence that a few families evaded the intent of the family plan by first purchasing durable goods and then after a short period selling them and using the money for unapproved purposes.

FUTURE GROWTH OF INDIAN TRIBAL TRUST FUNDS

It seems likely that the moneys held in trust for Indians by the Bureau of Indian Affairs will continue to grow but at a slower pace than recently. The docket has closed on the filing of claims before the Indian Claims Commission, and the Commission expects to have all claims settled by 1973. Thus, an important source of trust funds will be gone. Income from oil and gas has declined slightly from the peak levels of the late 1950's, but there are indications that some tribes are favorably situated with regard to oil and gas possibilities, such as the Standing Rock Sioux, the Cheyenne River, Rosebud, Brule, Crow Creek, Yankton, Pine Ridge Sioux, and several tribes in the Puget Sound area of Washington State.[28]

There will probably be a continuing decline in trust fund deposits in the Treasury as more of the funds are deposited in common stocks or certificates of deposit. If the rate of return on these latter assets continues to be much higher than the Treasury rate of 4 percent, then it is quite conceivable that virtually no Indian trust funds will be on deposit in the Treasury by the early 1970's.

Generally speaking, the possibility of utilizing tribal income and trust funds for reservation development remains unexplored. To encourage the use of these funds as a source of development capital, the BIA could plan with each tribe a description of the tribe's long-term goals with respect to outmigration, political evolution, and economic and social development. Included with the description of tribal goals would be an indication of what assets are on hand, and what additional funds are needed to reach the goals in the intermediate future (25 to 30 years). This type of planning would permit assessment of the year-by-year accomplishments and needs of each tribe relative to its own goals as well as the required Federal contribution to accomplish this purpose.

---

[28] Hough, *Development of Indian Resources*, op. cit., pp. 128–129.

FEDERAL ENCROACHMENT ON INDIAN WATER RIGHTS AND THE IMPAIRMENT OF RESERVATION DEVELOPMENT

By WILLIAM H. VEEDER*

FOREWORD

In the arid and semiarid regions of the Western United States, adequate rights to the use of water resources are a particularly crucial element in economic development. The responsibility for protecting the water rights of American Indian reservations rests with the Interior and Justice Departments. William Veeder argues that the conflicting responsibilities of these Departments make it virtually impossible for them to adequately fulfill their responsibility to the Indian reservations. He recommends that the responsibility for protecting the Indian water rights should be placed in an agency independent from the Interior and Justice Departments, and that this agency should move promptly to inventory Indian water rights and to determine the highest and best uses to which these valuable rights can be put.

Summary

1. American Indian Reservations in the western United States contain invaluable natural resources. These include the land of which they are comprised, minerals, forests, lakes, streams and other sources of water which arise upon, border, traverse or underlie the Reservations.

2. Economic development of the western Reservations is inseparable from Indian rights to the use of water, which in turn are the most valuable of all natural resources in the arid and semiarid regions. Those rights are the catalyst for all economic development. Without them the Reservations are virtually uninhabitable, the soil remains untilled, the minerals remain in place, and poverty is pervasive.

3. Since time immemorial the Indians' water resources were inextricably a part of their way of life; indeed, a prime feature of their sustenance. Highly sophisticated irrigation systems were developed along the Gila River by the Pimas and Maricopas. Menominees harvested their wild rice, used the streams for travel, fishing and hunting. The Mohaves, Quechans and other Colorado River Indians depended on the stream's annual Nile-like floods to irrigate their crops. The Yakimas lived upon and traded salmon taken from the Columbia, as

---

*Water Conservation and Utilization Specialist, Bureau of Indian Affairs, Department of the Interior.

NOTE: The analysis and conclusions in this paper are those of the author, and do not necessarily represent the position of the Bureau of Indian Affairs or the Department of the Interior.

did the Northern Paiutes—the fisheaters—who took the famous Lahanton cutthroat trout from the Truckee River and Pyramid Lake— their species destroyed by the Bureau of Reclamation.

4. The Indian *Winters Doctrine Rights* to the use of water in the streams or lakes which arise upon, border, traverse or underlie their Reservations, have been accorded by the Supreme Court and other courts a prior, paramount and superior status on the streams for the present and future economic development of the Western Reservations.

5. By the Constitution of the United States there was created a relationship between the Nation and the American Indians of transcendent dignity. That relationship of great dignity had its genesis in the policies adhered to by the European sovereigns who colonized this Continent and it was firmly established during the harsh and bitter years of the Revolutionary War and the years which were to ensue prior to and including the adoption of the Constitution.

6. It has been declared that the relationship existing between the American Indians and the Nation "resembles that of a ward to his guardian"—a trust relationship with all of the express and implied obligations stemming from it. Only the uninformed ascribe to that trust a demeaning connotation in regard to the American Indians.

7. Great stress must be applied to the nature of the Indian trust property, including Indian rights to the use of water.

(a) It is *private property*, legal title to which is held by the United States in trust for the American Indians as beneficial holders of equitable title.

(b) Indian property is *not public property* as is the other property of the Nation.

8. Plenary power and responsibility under the Commerce Clause of the Constitution reside with the Congress to effectuate the trust relationship between the United States and the American Indians.

9. Congress is likewise invested by the Constitution with plenary power over the "public lands," all other lands, all rights to the use of water, title to which resides in the Nation. These lands and rights to the use of water are to be administered for the Nation as a whole. It is imperative that the nature of the right, title, interests and obligations of the Nation in regard to these properties held in trust for the Nation as a whole be sharply distinguished from the lands and rights to the use of water of the American Indians.

10. Congress in the exercise of its plenary power over the Nation's lands and rights to the use of water has invested the Department of the Interior with broad authority to administer, develop, sell, dispose of, and otherwise to take all required action respecting those lands and rights to the use of water. Agencies within the Department of the Interior carrying out the will of Congress in regard to those properties held for the public as a whole include but are not limited to: The Bureau of Reclamation, Bureau of Land Management, National Park Service, Bureau of Outdoor Recreation and the agencies generally responsible for the propagation and protection of fish and wildlife.

11. Administrators, engineers, scientists, within the Department of the Interior, all acting within the scope of the authority vested in the Secretary of the Interior, are:

(1) Charged with the responsibility of fulfilling the Nation's trust status in regard to the Indian lands and rights to the use of water which, as stated, are private in character, to be administered solely for the benefit of the Indians;

(2) Charged with the responsibility of administering lands and rights to the use of water claimed in connection with reclamation projects, administration of grazing districts, and other land uses requiring the exercise of rights to the use of water; fish and wildlife projects, recreational areas and other activities, all of which require rights in the streams.

12. (a) Lawyers in the Department of the Interior directly responsible to the Solicitor, in whom resides the obligation of performing the "legal" work for that Department; all of the agencies of it, including the Bureau of Indian Affairs, Indians and Indian Tribes, are constantly confronted with the sharp conflicts of interests between the Indian land and rights to the use of water, and the numerous other agencies referred to that likewise make claims to those waters and contest the rights and claims of the Indians to them;

(b) Lawyers in the Department of Justice directly responsible to the Attorney General, the Nation's chief law officer, have the responsibility:

(1) To defend, protect, preserve and have adjudicated, title to the lands of the Indians and their rights to the use of water, and otherwise to act as lawyers for the trustee obligated to perform with the fullest degree of loyalty to the Indians;

(2) To proceed as an adversary against the Indian claims for the seizure of their lands and rights to the use of water, seeking to limit or otherwise defeat the claims of the Indians predicated upon the laws which other attorneys of the Justice Department are required effectively to espouse and advocate on behalf of the Indians;

(3) To perform legal services in regard to lands and rights to the use of water in streams and other water sources where the Indian rights are in conflict with claims of other agencies of the United States.

13. Both the administrators of the Department of the Interior and the lawyers of both Interior and Justice owe the highest degree of ethical, moral, loyal and equitable performance of their trust obligations to the American Indians. They are charged, moreover—as professionals—with the highest degree of care, skill and diligence in executing their broad assignments for the protection, preservation, administration and legal duties respecting Indian trust properties including, but not limited to, the invaluable Indian *Winters Doctrine Rights* to the use of water.

14. Conflicting responsibilities, obligations, interests, claims, legal theories—indeed, philosophies—oftentimes prevent the Interior and Justice Department administrators, planners, engineers and lawyers from fulfilling the trust obligation [which the Nation owes] to the American Indians in regard to natural resources, particularly in the complex and contentious field of Indian rights to the use of water in the arid and semiarid regions of western United States. Failure by those Departments, agencies and personnel to fulfill the Nation's obligation to protect and preserve Indian rights to the use of water

includes, but most assuredly is not limited to: (a) Lack of knowledge of the existence, or the nature, measure and extent of those rights to the use of both surface and ground waters—refusal to recognize Indian rights are private rights to be administered separate, apart and independent of the "public rights" of the Nation as a whole in identically the same manner as other private rights are protected and preserved; (b) Lack of timely action to preserve, protect, conserve and administer those rights; (c) Inability or reluctance at the decisional level to insist upon recognition and preservation of Indian rights to the use of water when to do so would prevent the construction—and/or administration in the manner desired—of a reclamation or other project conflicting with the Indians for water, the supply of which is insufficient; (d) Attempted subordination, relinquishment, or conveyance of Indian rights to the use of water which are in conflict with other claims, Federal, State or local; (e) Failure to assert rights, interests and priorities of the Indians on a stream or project when to do so would limit the interests of non-Indians; (f) Opening Reservations to non-Indian occupancy with the seizure of Indian land and rights to the use of water, with or without the payment of just compensation; (g) The imposition of servitudes, easements, and illegal occupancy or use of Indian lands and rights to the use of water.

15. Economic development of the American Indian Reservations in western United States, due largely to conflicting interests within the Interior and Justice Departments, or vacillating policies—a natural consequence of conflicting interests, responsibilities, and obligations within the Federal Establishment—has been (a) prevented by the abridgment or loss of Indian rights to the use of water; (b) intentionally prevented in whole or in part, or deferred in whole or in part, by the refusal to permit development of Indian lands with rights to the use of water.

16. Irreparable damage to the American Indians in western United States has ensued by reason of the consequences flowing from the conflicts described above. The Indians have suffered from extreme poverty, with the attendant ills of malnutrition, high infant mortality rate, reduced life expectancy, disease, and the shattering loss of human dignity which stems from poverty and deprivation of the necessities of life.

Conclusion

Economic development of the American Indian Reservations in western United States will continue to be prevented or severely curtailed in the absence of drastic changes in the laws and policies which would eliminate conflicting rights, responsibilities and obligations which presently exist among the several agencies of the National Government, all as reviewed in the accompanying memorandum and the summary set forth above.

Recommendation

Congress should enact legislation which would place in an agency independent from the Department of the Interior and the Department of Justice the full responsibility for the protection, preservation, administration, development, adjudication, determination, and control, including but not limited to all legal services required in connection with them, of the lands and rights to the use of water of the American Indian Reservations in western United States.

In furtherance of economic development of the American Indian Reservations in western United States it is imperative that there be undertaken an inventory of all of the Indian rights to the use of water in the streams and other sources of water arising upon, bordering upon, traversing or underlying their lands. This inventory should be undertaken with the objective of ascertaining, to the extent possible, the existence, character and measure of the rights as they relate to the present and future development of the Reservations. It is equally important to determine the highest and best use which can be made of these invaluable rights to the use of water and to chronicle those rights as they relate to each water source, indicating the highest and best present use to which they may be applied. They should likewise be evaluated from the standpoint of their maximum potential in the future by reason of the fact that those rights must be exercised in perpetuity and in contemplation of the ever-changing environment of western United States with its increasing population and water demands.

There follows the memorandum on which the preceding summary, conclusion and recommendation are predicated:

*   *   *   *   *   *   *

FOREWORD

In the arid and semiarid western United States, where most Indian reservations are located, water is a critical catalyst for all economic development. Without it, soil remains untilled, minerals remain in place, and habitation itself is difficult. Suffice to say, without water reservation lands or any other lands are virtually without economic value.

The main thrust of this paper is that non-Indian demands on an already limited water supply have severely impaired the economic growth potential for many reservations. Moreover, non-Indian interests have made, and are making, claims on water which, it is believed, belongs to Indians. That non-Indian claims on such water are usually successful is due in large measure to the effectiveness with which such interests influence the workings of the Federal Government—which in fact is charged to protect Indian rights and to support and encourage Indian development.

To fully understand the abridgement or loss of Indian water rights requires an understanding of the legal aspects of:

1. the Nation's trust relationship with the Indians and Indian Tribes;
2. the character of Indian rights to use of water.

Because rights to water are inextricably related to reservation lands, Indian titles to land and the use of water are discussed together.

I. FEDERAL EXPRESSIONS OF INTENT CONCERNING INDIAN PROPERTIES AND NATURAL RESOURCES

On September 12, 1968, Senate Majority Leader Mansfield placed in the Congressional Record Concurrent Resolution No. 11 entitled

"National American Indian and Alaska Natives Policy Resolution," [1]
together with excerpts from Report No. 1535, explaining the purpose
of the resolution. The report [2] stated that: "The resolution would
assure our Indian citizens that Federal programs * * * will be concentrated where the problems are most acute—on the reservations,"
and further that it is the "sense of Congress that Indian and Alaska
native trust property continue to be protected; * * * that efforts be
continued to develop natural resources."

Explicitly, the Concurrent Resolution states that:

"American Indian and Alaska native property will be protected;
that Indian culture and identity will be respected; * * * that
continued efforts will be directed to maximum development of
natural resources."

This Resolution clearly attempts to establish Federal commitment
to, and recognition and protection of Indian and native Alaskan rights
to their natural resources.

During the presidential campaign of 1968 President Richard M.
Nixon stated:

"Historically, these Native Americans * * * have been deprived
of their ancestral lands and reduced by unfair federal policies
and demeaning paternalism to the status of powerless wards of a
confused 'great white father.' " [3]

To correct the injustices of the past, President Nixon continued,
"My administration will promote the economic development of the
reservation by offering economic incentives to private industry to
provide opportunities for Indian employment and training."

In announcing national goals for the American Indian, former
President Johnson said that our goal must be:

"Freedom of choice: An opportunity to remain in their homelands,
if they choose, without surrendering their dignity * * *." [4]

There is a long history of similar Congressional and Executive
declarations. More than a decade ago, in a case where Federal actions
contradicted such declarations, a U.S. circuit judge observed:

---

[1] *Cong. Rec.* (Sept. 12, 1968) S. p, 10634.

NATIONAL AMERICAN INDIAN AND ALASKA NATIVES POLICY RESOLUTION

The concurrent resolution (S. Con. Res. 11) National American Indian and Alaska natives policy resolution was considered, and agreed to, as follows:

* * * * * * *

Resolved by the Senate (the House of Representatives concurring), That it is the sense of the Congress that—

(1) the deplorable conditions of American Indians and Alaska natives can only be alleviated through a sustained, positive, and dynamic Indian policy with the necessary constructive programs and services directed to the governing bodies of these groups for application in their respective communities, offering self-determination and self-help features for the people involved; and that our Government's concern for its Indian citizens be formalized in a new national Indian policy so that beneficial effects may be continued until the day when the Nation's moral and legal obligations to its first citizens—the American Indians—are fulfilled;

* * * * * * *

(d) American Indian and Alaska native property will be protected; that Indian culture and identity will be respected; that the necessary technical guidance and assistance will be given to insure future economic independence; that continued efforts will be directed to maximum development of natural resources; * * *

[2] *Cong. Rec.* (Sept. 12, 1968) S. p. 10634.
[3] Statement by Richard M. Nixon on September 27, 1968.
[4] 114 *Cong. Rec.* No. 36 (March 6, 1968), pp. S. 2311-2316.

"The numerous sanctimonious expressions to be found in the acts of Congress, the statement of public officials, and the opinions of courts respecting 'the generous and protective spirit which the United States properly feels toward its Indian wards,' * * * and the 'high standards for fair dealing required of the United States in controlling Indian affairs,' are but demonstrations of a gross national hypocrisy." [5]

A primary objective of this study is to demonstrate how the expression of the highest ideals by the Congress and the Executive have fallen far short of accomplishment by reason of policies and conflicts between agencies and personnel of the Federal Government. To that end it is important to understand how those ideals developed and the constitutional basis for those concepts which lends substance to them. It should also be realized, however, that this Nation with its Old World background has failed to recognize that Indians and native Alaskans have values which all too often have been frustrated or totally suppressed.

I. Rapport of American Indians With Their Homeland Must Not Be Ignored in Economic Development of Reservations

A man's heart is where his treasure lies. Frequently the American Indians occupying Reservations view their natural resources as a treasure, and seek to avoid destructive exploitation. Failure to take cognizance of the Indians' concept of nature and their relationship with the lands they and their ancestors occupied is to ignore a crucial aspect of any development program and to impair potential economic development.

The rapport between the Indians and the land is difficult to understand, much less describe. In a materialistic society the affinity between the Indians and their mountains, lakes, and rivers has been all too frequently disregarded.

The Mission Range, its streams and beauty have a worth to the Flathead Tribes that cannot be measured. Mohave Indians have names for all parts of their valley and segments of the Colorado River which traverses it. A map recently prepared designating those areas in the valley and segments of the River with Mohave names, and interpretations, goes far in explaining the Indian attachment to it. History records the resolute rejection by most Mohaves to move them from their core homeland. Like the White Mountain Apaches who revere sections of their forests, the mountains surrounding Mohave Valley are frequently referred to by the Indians in spiritual terms. The great wilderness on the slopes of Mount Adams has a meaning to the Yakimas understood only in the Long House.

Law is reflective of the mentality which formulates it. Hence the law applied to the Indian lands and rights to the use of water does not embrace intangibles. However, economic development need not connote smoke stacks, filthy air and water. To the fullest extent possible economic development should take cognizance of the special identification of the American Indians with their lands, lakes, and

---

[5] Judge Pope in his first opinion in *United States* v. *Ahtanum Irrigation District*, 236 F. 2d 321, 338 (CA6, 1956); Appellees' cert. denied 352 U.S. 988 (1956); 330 F. 2d 897 (1965); 338 F. 2d 307; Cert. denied 381 U.S. 924 (1965).

streams. If economic development simply submerges Indians in the so-called main stream of society, the present efforts most assuredly will have failed.

III. THROUGHOUT THEIR HISTORY AMERICAN INDIANS HAVE USED THE WATERS OF THEIR RIVERS, LAKES AND STREAMS FOR SUSTE-NANCE AND SHAPED THEIR LIVES TO THE ENVIRONMENT

As reviewed above, the Concurrent Resolution 11 expresses the "sense of Congress that Indian and Alaska native trust property continue to be protected; * * * that efforts be continued to develop [their] natural resources."

The Executive pronouncements mentioned above fully recognize and would implement the means for the protection of trust property including the natural resources, thus aiding the economic development of the Indian Reservations. The meaning of the term trust property, the legal aspects of it, what gave rise to it, and the activities required in the administration of that trust property are crucial to this consideration. Antecedent to that phase of the consideration, brief reference will be made to Indian use of the waters of the rivers, lakes and streams and their adjustment to the frequently harsh environment in which they lived by reason of that use.

This Nation's history following the War of Independence, with the accession of huge land areas from France, Great Britain, Spain and Mexico, lends meaning to the "trust" to which Congress makes reference in Concurrent Resolution 11. Virtually all of the lands acquired by the Nation were occupied by Indians and Indian Tribes who in good conscience must be recognized as the original owners of the land. However, the character of that ownership differed widely from that which stringent Anglo-Saxon law would accord recognition. Most of the lands acquired by the United States west of the Mississippi River are arid and semiarid. Agriculture, at the time of acquisition and now, could be successful only through irrigation. Earliest history describes the use of water by the Indians. No single resource was more important to the Indians of the southwest in particular, and western Indians in general. It was, in fact, an ingredient without which life could not prevail. However, it was a great deal more than that.

When an indigenous people called the Hohokams occupied the lands in the Gila and Salt River Valleys over two thousand years ago, they diverted water by means of canals which even now are recognized as highly refined engineering accomplishments. They long ago demonstrated that water applied to the land was essential if communities were to be maintained and have more than a rudimentary culture. They demonstrated the need for economic development which they undertook as a means of survival.[6]

Arizona's former Senator Hayden devoted much time to the history of the Pima and Maricopa Indians.[7] In great detail he chronicles the use of Gila River water by the Pima and Maricopa Indians. The first description of the Indian diversion and use of water in modern times,

---

[6] *National Geographic Magazine*, May 1967, Vol. 131, No. 5, pp. 670 et seq.
[7] *A History of the Pima Indians and the San Carlos Irrigation Project*, 89th Congress, 1st Session; Document No. 11, first printed in 1924 reprinted in 1965.

he reports, came from Father Kino, a Jesuit Missionary who visited the Pimas in 1687. The Missionary refers to the "very great aqueduct" constructed by the Indians to conduct Gila River water across great distances to irrigate large acreages of their river bottom lands.

The Pima and Maricopa Indians in Arizona had been a flourishing community of great magnitude. The Spaniards described it as it existed near the end of the seventeenth century and marveled at the Indian economic development. They observed the adjustment made by the Indians to a desert environment which, without water, produced a most meager subsistence. A half-century later another Spanish Missionary was to report the Pima and Maricopa communities still undisturbed by non-Indian intrusion. He described results of their use of Gila River water: [8] "All these settlements on both banks of the river and on its islands have much green land. The Indians sow corn, beans, pumpkins, watermelons, cotton from which they make garments, * * *." Wheat was also raised, according to the report.

A hundred years later the industrious Pimas and Maricopas continued to amaze soldiers, travelers, trappers, and explorers with their agricultural practices, their use of water, and the produce that supplied not only Indians but many others taking the southern route west. A short half century was to elapse before the seizure of Indian land and water was well under way, and in another twenty-five years the wanton divestiture of the Indian land and water was far advanced.

Like the Arizona Indians, the Pueblos of the Rio Grande Valley adjusted to a desert environment by using water to promote agricultural development.

Mohaves, Yumas, and Chemehuevis likewise adapted their lives to the surrounding desert by occupying the lands on both sides of the Colorado River. In the "Great Colorado Valley," as early explorers referred to it, the Spanish soldiers and Missionaries first encountered these Indians. Later, Lieutenant Ives in his 1858 explorations on the Colorado River reported the Quechan Indians using water to raise their crops. Of the Mohaves, Ives said: "It is somewhat remarkable that these Indians should thrive so well upon the diet to which they are compelled to adhere. There is no game in the valley. The fish are scarce and of inferior quality. They subsist almost exclusively upon beans and corn, with occasional water-melons and pumpkins, and are probably as fine a race, physically, as there is in existence." [9] Those Mohave crops were raised by Indians who planted the lush river bottoms as soon as the perennial overflow had receded, thus using the natural irrigation furnished by the Colorado River.

Importance of the rivers to the indigenous cultures in western United States is not limited to agriculture. In the vast desert areas of the present State of Nevada the Northern Paiutes long prior to Fremont's discovery of Pyramid Lake in 1844 depended upon fish taken from the lake and the Truckee River as a primary source of sustenance.[10] Fisheries to the Indians of the Northwest "were not much less necessary to the existence of the Indians than the atmos-

8 Ibid. *A History of the Pima Indians * * *,* p. 9.
9 *Mohave Tribe of Indians * * ** v. *United States of America,* 7 Ind. Cl. Comm. 219, Finding 12(a), and sources relied upon.
10 *Popular Science Monthly,* Vol. 58, 1900–1901, pp. 505–514.

phere they breathed." [11] Salmon and other fish taken from the Columbia River were always an important item of trade among the Indians as reported by Lewis and Clark.[12]

It is significant when transition from their traditional way of life was forced upon the Western Indians, they relied upon their streams and rivers as a source of sustenance. The Yakimas, in their transition from a nation given largely to hunting and fishing, were the first in the State of Washington to undertake to irrigate their meager gardens. That change came about under the direction of missionaries who attempted to assist in the economic development of the lands to which the Yakimas were restricted.[13]

And, of course, rivers were not only the source of sustenance for the American Indians; they were the arteries of crude commerce and travel.

It is upon that background that the legal characteristics of Indian rights to the use of water will be discussed. From that background it should be clear that water was and is as necessary a part of Indian life as the land which they occupied.

IV. Legal Aspects of Indian Rights to the Use of Water

American Indians probably did not give thought to the nature of the right to divert and to use water or the right of fishery. Indeed, the concept of title to land and the bundle of rights which constitute it was wholly foreign to them. Under those circumstances it is not surprising that the history of the transactions between the United States Government and the Indians is infamous, often involving outright swindling of Indians out of properties of immense value. In entering into treaties and agreements, whatever means were used, the Indians were totally innocent of the principles of conveyancing the formulation of written conventions. As a consequence they had little knowledge, if any, of the terms under the law which would be required to protect their interests. From an examination of the complex documents which they were required to execute, it is manifest that the Indians did not and could not know the legal implications flowing from those treaties and agreements.

(a) *Indian Winters Doctrine Rights to the use of water:*

The *Winters Doctrine* as enunciated by the courts is based upon the law, equity, history and good conscience. Factually the decision giving rise to that doctrine is very simple.

The Fort Belknap Indian Reservation in the State of Montana is the meager residue of a vast area once guaranteed to the Indians by the 1855 Treaty with the Blackfeet.[14] In 1874 the original area established by the Treaty was sharply constricted.[15] By an agreement in 1888 the Indians were limited to a small semiarid acreage which could be made habitable only by means of irrigation. The north boundary of the Reservation was the center of the Milk River, a tributary of the Missouri.

---

[11] *United States* v. *Winans*, 198 U.S. 371, 381 (1904).
[12] See *Journals of Lewis and Clark*, Bernard DeVoto, pp. 250 et seq.
[13] "* * * Ahtanum [Creek] was the cradle and proving ground of irrigation in the State of Washington * * *." *Yakima Valley Catholic Centennial*, the Beginning of Irrigation in the State of Washington.
[14] 11 Stat. 657.
[15] For a full factual and procedural review refer to *Winters* v. *United States*, 143 Fed. 740, 741 (CA9, 1906); *Winters* v. *United States*, 148 Fed. 684 (CA9, 1906).

In 1889 water was diverted from the Milk River to irrigate lands within the Fort Belknap Reservation. Upstream from the Indian diversion Winters and other defendants, non-Indians, constructed dams, diversion works, and other structures which prevented the waters of the Milk River from flowing down to the Indian irrigation project. An action to restrain the Winters diversion was initiated in the federal district court, and an injunction ensued. From that injunction Winters appealed. In sustaining the injunction, the Court of Appeals for the Ninth Circuit declared:

> "In conclusion, we are of opinion that the court below did not err in holding that, "when the Indians made the treaty granting rights to the United States, they reserved the right to use the waters of Milk River" at least to the extent reasonably necessary to irrigate their lands. The right so reserved continues to exist against the United States and its grantees, as well as against the state and its grantees." [16]

Thus it was the Indians granting to the United States; it was the Indians reserving to themselves that which was not granted—the rights to the use of water of the Milk River to the extent required for their properties.

The concept that the Indians granted title to the United States, and not the converse, is important in regard to the nature of the title of the Indians. It is reflective of the rationale of the *Winans Decision* rendered by the Supreme Court two years earlier. There the Court had before it the fishery provisions of the Treaty of June 9, 1855, between the United States and the Confederated Tribes of Yakima Indians.[17] By that document the Indians retained the "exclusive right of taking fish in all the streams where running through or bordering" their Reservation; "also the right of taking fish at all usual and accustomed places" on and off the Reservation. Patents were issued by the United States to lands along the Columbia River from which the Yakimas had traditionally fished. Those patents did not include any reference to the Indian Treaty fishing rights and the owners of the land denied that the lands thus patented were subject to those rights of fishery. Moreover, the State of Washington had issued to the owners of the land licenses to operate fishing wheels which, it was asserted, "necessitates the exclusive possession of the space occupied by the wheels." [18]

Rejecting the contentions of the land owners that the Yakima fishing rights in the Columbia River had been abrogated by the issuance of the patents, the Court declared:

> "The right to resort to the fishing places in controversy was a part of larger rights possessed by the Indians * * * which were not much less necessary to the existence of the Indians than the atmosphere they breathed. New conditions came into existence. to which those rights had to be accommodated. Only a limitation of them, however, was necessary and intended, not a taking away."

[16] *Winters* v. *United States*, 143 Fed. 740, 749 (CA9, 1906).
[17] *United States* v. *Winans*, 198 U.S. 371 (1904).
[18] *Id.* at 380 (1904).

Having thus appraised the Yakima Treaty, the Court then pronounced the crux of the decision:

"* * * the treaty was not a grant of rights to the Indians, but a grant of rights from them [to the United States] a reservation of those not granted." [19]

The Court further observed that: "the right [of fishing] was intended to be continuing against the United States and its grantees as well as against the State and its grantees." [20]

Thus, the nature of the title of the Indians under the Treaties between them and the United States was cast in the correct light. Indian title does not stem from a *conveyance to them*. Rather, the title which resides in them to their lands, their rights to the use of water, their rights of fishery, their timber—all interests in real property and natural resources were *retained by them* when they granted away title to vast areas which had been theirs.

Those pronouncements by the Supreme Court declared in advance of the *Winters Decision* are fundamental precepts of the law, recognizing that rights of fishery are interests in real property subject to protection under the Constitution.[21]

Yet today, as they have for generations past, the Yakimas still struggle to maintain their rights of fishery. They are also seeking to revive salmon runs destroyed by power and other developments on the Columbia River.

On appeal, the *Winters* case presented two basic problems to the Supreme Court for resolution: (1) Were rights to the use of water in the Milk River reserved for the Fort Belknap Indian land, though no mention of those rights is contained in the Treaty of October 17, 1855, the Act of 1874, or the Agreement of 1888; (2) assuming those rights were reserved for the Indian lands, was there a divestiture of them upon the admission of Montana into the Union? [22]

In rendering its keystone opinion the Supreme Court analyzed with care the relationship between the United States and the Indians, together with the objectives of the Agreement of 1888, in which the Indians ceded away a vast tract of land, retaining for themselves only a vestige of that which they formerly occupied. The Court then addressed itself to the untenable position of the non-Indians:

"The lands [retained by the Indians] were arid and, without irrigation, were practically valueless. And yet, it is contended,

---

[19] *Ibid.* p. 381 (1904).

[20] *Ibid.* 381–382.

[21] In considering the legal aspects of the property interests of the American Indians in the rivers, streams and lakes, it is emphasized that of necessity there has been applied principles of law which differ radically from the Indians' aboriginal view in regard to natural resources. Apparently title to the right of fishery as this Nation's jurisprudence developed had no place in the Indians' concept of taking fish from the streams where and when they could. At a very early date in the evolution of Anglo-Saxon law the right of fishery—akin to rights to the use of water as that law was much later to evolve—was a right in real property, a part and parcel of the land abutting upon or traversed by a stream or lake.

In Thompson on Real Property, per. ed., vol. 1, sec. 250, this statement appears: "It is held that fishing rights are incorporeal hereditaments, since they issue out of, * * * or are annexed to things corporeal."

It is also stated in 22 Am. Jur., Fish and Fisheries, sec. 7: "The right to fish at a certain place is a property right constitutionally protected from confiscatory legislation, * * *. It is an interest in real estate in the nature of an incorporeal hereditament, * * *."

The nature of the right of fishery is recognized in California Code, Civil, sec. 801, which is in part: "The following land burdens, or servitudes upon land, may be attached to other land as incidents or appurtenances, and are then called easements: * * * (2) The right of fishing; * * *." That principle was likewise recognized by the Supreme Court of the State of Oregon in the case of *Hume* v. *Rogue River Packing Co.*, 51 Ore. 237, 92 Pac. 1065 (1907), where it is stated that the right of fishery is a right in real property and not a personal right.

[22] *Winters* v. *United States*, 207 U.S. 564, 575 et seq. (1907).

the means of irrigation were deliberately given up by the Indians and deliberately accepted by the Government. * * * The Indians had command of the lands and the waters—command of all their beneficial use, whether kept for hunting, "and grazing roving herds of stock," or turned to agriculture and the arts of civilization. Did they give up all this? Did they reduce the area of their occupation and give up the waters which made it valuable or adequate?"

Answering the question which it had propounded, the Court declared:

"If it were possible to believe affirmative answers, we might also believe that the Indians were awed by the power of the Government or deceived by its negotiators. Neither view is possible. The Government is asserting the rights of the Indians." [23]

The Court reiterated the basic tenents of the *Winans* case—that the Indians, not the United States, were the grantors. Cogently the Court inquired: Did the Indians grant and the United States accept all of the Indian rights to the use of water without which the lands were uninhabitable? It rejected that proposition out of hand as being without merit. Likewise significant was the Court's observation that as the owners of the land and waters the Indians could use them for hunting, grazing, or, in the words of the Court, for "agriculture and the arts of civilization." The Court found no words of limitation upon the uses to which the Indians could apply their water rights.

Turning to the part-legal, part-political question—of Montana's jurisdiction over the Indian rights to the use of water, the Supreme Court had this to say:

"The power of the Government to reserve the waters and exempt them from appropriation under the state laws is not denied, and could not be. *The United States* v. *The Rio Grande Ditch & Irrigation Co.*, 174 U.S. 690, 702; *United States* v. *Winans*, 198 U.S. 371. That the Government did reserve them we have decided, and for a use which would be necessarily continued through years. This was done May 1, 1888, and it would be extreme to believe that within a year Congress destroyed the reservation and took from the Indians the consideration of their *grant, leaving them a barren waste*—took from them the means of continuing their old habits, yet did not leave them the power to change to new ones." [24]

The crucial aspect of the character of the Indian title is thus clear: (1) By the Agreement of 1888 the Indians reserved to themselves the rights to the use of water in the Milk River although that Agreement made no mention of rights of that nature; (2) the Indian rights thus reserved were not open to appropriation under the laws of the State of Montana upon its admission into the Union, but rather were exempt from the operation of those laws. The full import of the *Winters* and *Winans* decisions are central to the discussion that follows.

(b) *Winters Doctrine Rights are part and parcel of the land itself— interests in real property:*

The decisions rendered by the Court of Appeals for the Ninth Circuit and the Supreme Court are based on the concept of a grant

---

[23] Ibid., 207 U.S. 564, 576 (1907).
[24] *Ibid.*, 207 U.S. 564, 577 (1907).

from the Indians *to* the national government. They chronicle the successive transactions pursuant to which Indian domains, once embracing large segments of the present State of Montana, were diminished to a small area made habitable only by the availability of water.

The Yakimas' rights of fishery under their Treaty of 1855 are, under the *Winans* holding, interests in real property—part and parcel of the land itself. In the *Ahtanum* cases,[25] the Court of Appeals, considering that Treaty, applied the same principles to the water rights in Ahtanum Creek which the northern boundary of the Yakima Reservation.

In the first *Ahtanum* decision, the Court of Appeals discussed the nature and characteristics of the Indian *Winters Doctrine Rights* in the following terms:

"That the Treaty of 1855 reserved rights in and to the waters of this stream for the Indians, is plain from the decision in *Winters* * * *. In the Winters case, as here, the reservation was created by treaty; the reserved lands were a part of a much larger tract which the Indians had the right to occupy; and the lands were arid and without irrigation practically valueless. * * * This court, in its decision (143 F. 740, 746), which the Supreme Court was affirming, had said: "We are of opinion that it was the intention of the treaty to reserve sufficient waters of Milk River, as was said by the court below, 'to insure to the Indians the means wherewith to irrigate their farms', and that it was so understood by the respective parties to the treaty at the time it was signed."[26]

Continuing to define and declare the extent of the *Winters Doctrine Rights*, the court states:

"* * * [i]t must be borne in mind, as the Supreme Court said of this very treaty, that 'the treaty was not a grant of rights to the Indians, but a grant of rights from them—a reservation of those not granted.' United States v. Winans, 198 U.S. 371, 381. Before the treaty the Indians had the right to the use not only of Ahtanum Creek but of all other streams in a vast area. The Indians did not surrender any part of their right to the use of Ahtanum Creek regardless of whether the Creek became the boundary or whether it flowed entirely within the reservation."[27]

Having reviewed in detail the manner in which the Yakimas had reserved their *Winters Doctrine Rights*, the court applied to them the principles governing interests in realty:

"This is a suit brought by the United States as trustee for the Yakima tribe of Indians to establish and quiet title to the Indians' right to the use of the waters of Ahtanum creek in the State of Washington, * * *."[28]

With further reference to the nature of the rights and the action brought to have them determined, the Court states:

"The suit [to protect the Yakima rights], like other proceedings designed to procure an adjudication of water rights, was in its purpose and effect one to quiet title to realty."[29]

---

[25] See footnote 5 above.
[26] *United States* v. *Ahtanum Irrigation District*, 236 F. 2d 321, 325 (CA9, 1956).
[27] Ibid., 236 F. 2d 321, 326.
[28] Ibid., 236 F. 2d 321, 323.
[29] *Ibid.*, 236 F. 2d 321, 339.

Those rulings in regard to the characteristics of the *Winters Doctrine Rights* to the use of water as being interests in real property, comport fully with the *Powers Decision* rendered by the Supreme Court respecting the *Winters Doctrine Rights* of the Crow Indians.[30] There are several aspects of the *Powers Decision* that are of importance to the Indians in addition to it being a precedent respecting the nature of the *Winters Doctrine Rights*. The decision arose from an attempt to enjoin the use of water by a non-Indian, who had succeeded to the title to land from an Indian allottee. The Court upheld the lower court's refusal to grant the injunction, specifically declaring—in keeping with sound principles of real estate conveyancing—that the non-Indian succeeded to "some portion of tribal waters," adding this most important caveat when consideration is given to the implications of the *Powers Decision*:

"We *do not* consider the extent or precise nature of respondents' [non-Indian] rights in the water. The present proceeding [being an action to enjoin, not, as in *Ahtanum*, to quiet title] is not properly framed to that end." [31]

It is elemental that rights to the use of water are interests in real property.[32] Likewise elemental is the principle that a right to the use of water is usufructuary and does not relate to the corpus of the water itself.[33] Those principles are, of course, applicable to the *Winters Doctrine Rights*.

As interests in real property *Winters Doctrine Rights* are entitled to be protected, and the obligation to protect them against abridgement and loss is identical with the obligations respecting the land itself. This concept goes far towards the elimination of the confusion which has on occasion arisen respecting the course which must be pursued in the exercise and protection of them.

(c) *The measure of Indian rights to the use of water for the present and future economic development of their Reservations:*

The success of any program in furtherance of development in the western United States is, of necessity, predicated not only upon a *present* firm supply of water but likewise upon a firm supply in the *future*. In the application of the *Winters Doctrine* the courts recognized that the Indians would of necessity need additional quantities of water to meet their future needs:

"What amount of water will be required for these purposes may not be determined with absolute accuracy at this time; but the policy of the Government to reserve whatever water of Birch Creek may be reasonably necessary, not only for present uses, but for future requirements, is clearly within the terms of the treaties as construed by the Supreme Court in the Winters Case." [34]

In keeping with the declaration that the Indians had rights in the

---

[30] *United States* v. *Powers*, 305 U.S. 527, 533 (1939).

[31] *Ibid.*, 305 U.S. 527, 533 (1939).

[32] Wiel, *Water Rights in the Western States*, 3d ed., vol. 1, sec. 18, pp. 20, 21; sec. 283, pp. 298–300; sec. 285, p. 301. *United States* v. *Chandler-Dunbar Water Power Co.*, 229 U.S. 53, 73 (1913). *Ashwander* v. *TVA*, 297 U.S. 288, 330 (1936).

[33] *Fuller* v. *Swan River Placer Mining Co.*, 12 Colo. 12, 17; 19 Pac. 836 (1898). *Wright* v. *Best*, 19 Cal. 2d 368; 121 P. 2d 702 (1942). *Sowards* v. *Meagher*, 37 Utah 212; 108 Pac. 1112 (1910). See also *Lindsey* v. *McClure*, 136 F. 2d 65, 70 (C.A. 10, 1943).

[34] *Conrad Investment Company* v. *United States*, 161 Fed. 829 (CA9, 1908).

stream to meet their present and future needs, the Court of Appeals approved the means provided in the decree entered by the lower court in these terms:

"It is further objected that the decree of the Circuit Court provides that, whenever the needs and requirements of the complainant for the use of the waters of Birch creek for irrigating and other useful purposes upon the reservation exceed the amount of water reserved by the decree for that purpose, the complainant may apply to the court for a modification of the decree. This is entirely in accord with complainant's rights as adjudged by the decree. Having determined that the Indians on the reservation have a paramount right to the waters of Birch Creek, it follows that the permission given to the defendant to have the excess over the amount of water specified in the decree should be subject to modification, should the conditions on the reservation at any time require such modification." [35]

The same principle was declared by the Supreme Court in *Arizona* v. *California*.[36] There the Court, relying upon the *Winters* decision, stated that the quantities of water reserved for the Indians were sufficient "to make those reservations livable." [37] In sustaining the Report of the Special Master, the Court said:

"* * * We also agree with the Master's conclusion as to the quantity of water intended to be reserved. He found that the water was intended to satisfy the future as well as the present needs of the Indian Reservations and ruled that enough water was reserved to irrigate all the practicably irrigable acreage on the reservations." [38]

It is important that the Supreme Court not only declared that the *Winters Doctrine* comprehends water for future needs to make "livable" the Reservations then under consideration which it described as being comprised of "hot, scorching sands", but also accepted those criteria as a means—though in no sense the exclusive means—of measuring the rights to the use of water which were in fact reserved: "We have concluded * * * that the only feasible way by which reserved water for the reservations can be measured is irrigable acreage." [39]

When the United States petitioned to intervene in *Arizona* v. *California*—thus eliminating the objection to jurisdiction for want of indispensable parties—the irrigable acreage criterion was tendered to the Court as the best measure of rights claimed for the particular Reservations involved.

The Supreme Court also adopted a different criterion from that used in connection with the Indian Reservations. It stated:

"* * * the United States intended to reserve water sufficient for the future requirements of the Lake Mead National Recreation Area, the Havasu Lake National Wildlife Refuge, the Imperial National Wildlife Refuge and the Gila National Forest." [40]

[35] *Conrad Investment Company* v. *United States*, 161 Fed. 829, 835 (CA9, 1908).
[36] 373 U.S. 546 (1962).
[37] Ibid., 373 U.S. 546, 599.
[38] *Arizona* v. *California*, United States Intervener, 373 U.S. 546, 600 (1962).
[39] Ibid., 373 U.S. 546, 601.
[40] Ibid., 373 U.S. 546, 601 (1962).

There are numerous Reservations, all of which according to the Supreme Court must be "livable" by the Indians who reside on them. These Reservations vary from those situated on Puget Sound to those in the desert areas of southwestern United States. The quantities of water required in the humid regions differ widely from the "hot, scorching sands" to which the Court made reference. Similarly the water requirements will differ dependent upon the use to which the waters are to be applied in the economic development of each Reservation.

(d) *Indian Winters Doctrine Rights, like the lands of which they are a part, may be used for any beneficial purpose:*

Potential for economic development of the Indian Reservations is inextricably related to the legal title to the right to divert and use water. Those Reservations were established in perpetuity as a "home and abiding place" for the Indians. In the words of the Supreme Court, "It can be said without overstatement that when the Indians were put on these reservations they were not considered to be located in the most desirable area of the Nation." [41] Most of them were established during times when this Nation was experiencing great changes economically and socially. Changes were anticipated and changes came about and the process of change continues. From a predominantly rural culture geared to the cultivation of the soil, this nation has developed into an urban and industrial country.

Changes have likewise come about concerning the American Indians' occupation of Reservations which were established by treaty and agreement between the Indians and the national government. Reservations were likewise established unilaterally by Executive Orders and congressional enactments. At the time of their establishment those Reservations were primarily suitable for farming and livestock raising. Coinciding with the shift of our national economy, the Reservations have changed. Some, including the Pueblos of New Mexico and the Salt River Indian Reservation in Arizona, are close to and are rapidly becoming a part of urban areas.

Concomitant with the changes in land uses are changes in water uses. With prescience the Supreme Court in *Winters,* in 1907, stated:
> "The Indians had command of the lands and the waters—command of all their beneficial use, whether kept for hunting, 'and grazing roving herds of stock,' or turned to agriculture and the arts of civilization." [42]

That conclusion is the key to economic development on the Reservations. Having retained the title to lands, they retained all incidents of that title, including but not limited to rights to the use of water. Title to those rights were free of limitations on the purposes to which they could be applied. In *Conrad Investment Company,* the court referred to the fact there was vested in the Indians the rights to use the streams to meet future developments "for irrigating and other useful purposes."

In the second *Ahtanum* decision the court reviewed the main precepts of the *Winters Doctrine* in these terms:

[41] Ibid., 373 U.S. 546, 598.
[42] *Winters v. United States,* 207 U.S. 564, 576 (1907).

"This court held that by reason of the rule laid down in Winters * * * and other decisions of this court applying the rule of the Winters case, including Conrad Inv. Co. * * *

> All of the waters of Ahtanum Creek, or so much thereof as could be *beneficially used* on the Indian Reservation were, by virtue of the treaty, reserved for use by the Indian tribe upon their lands." [43] (Emphasis supplied)

Adopting a practice seldom pursued, the Court of Appeals formulated the decree and directed its entry, which, based upon the facts, adjudged that "after the tenth day of July in each year, [the date when water becomes in short supply] *all* the waters of Ahtanum Creek shall be available to, and subject to diversion by, the plaintiff [United States of America] for use on Indian Reservation lands south of Ahtanum Creek, *to the extent that the said water can be put to a beneficial use*." [44] (Emphasis supplied.)

Pertinency must be attributed to the fact that in *Arizona* v. *California*, as reviewed above—rights were declared to have been reserved for the widely disparate present and "future requirements" of a National (1) recreation area; (2) wild life refuge; and (3) national forest.

Economic development of Indian Reservations, as stated above, must be geared to land and water use. Hence the authority to decide the uses becomes important. It is, of course, an elemental proposition of constitutional law that there resides with the Congress of the United States, pursuant to the Commerce Clause, the plenary power and authority to conduct Indian affairs.[45] At a relatively early date in the nation's history the Supreme Court observed that "This power must be considered as exclusively vested in Congress * * *." [46] A concomitant Constitutional proviso—that "The Congress shall have Power to dispose of and make all needful Rules and Regulations respecting the Territory or other Property belonging to the United States" must also be considered.[47] It is equally applicable to the Indian lands and rights to the use of water [48] as it is to lands the government holds for the benefit of the people as a whole.

It is pertinent at this juncture to set forth this caveat:

> Although the constitution is the source of authority for the administration of Indian lands and water rights, those property interests are private, not public in nature. The precepts of the law which govern their administration are thus vastly different from those which govern "public" lands administered by various other agencies of the federal government.

(e) *Application of the Winters Doctrine to Treaty, Executive Order and Congressional Act Reservations*

In the *Walker River* case [49] the federal court had before it Indian claims to the use of water, Neither a treaty nor an agreement between

---

[43] *United States* v. *Ahtanum Irrigation District*, 330 F. 2d 897, 899 (CA9, 1964).
[44] Ibid., 330 F. 2d 897. 15 (CA9, 1964).
[45] Constitution he United States, 1787, Article I, Sec. 8, Cl. 3: "Section 8: The Congress shall have Power: "To regulate Commerce with foreign nations, and among the several States, and with the Indian Tribes; * * *."
[46] *Worcester* v. *Georgia*, 31 U.S. 515, 559; 580-581 (1832).
[47] Constitution of the United States, 1787, Article IV, Section 3, Cl. 2.
[48] *Arizona* v. *California*, 373 U.S. 546, 597-598 (1962).
[49] *United States* v. *Walker River Irr. Dist.* 104 F.2d 334, 336 (CA9, 1939).

the government and the Indians was involved, for the Walker River Indian Reservation had been created in 1859 by departmental action subsequently approved by an Executive Order.

In *Walker River* the court alluded to the fact that in *Winters* the Treaty was emphasized.[50] That the Indians had not retained any rights to the use of water in the Walker River did not alter the court's decision. Rather it declared: "The power of the Government to reserve the waters to the Indians and thus exempt them from subsequent appropriation by others is beyond debate." [51] In rejecting the alleged difficulties the non-Indian claimants would experience if the rights of the Indians were recognized, the court states: "The settlers who took up lands in the valleys of the stream were not justified in closing their eyes to the obvious necessities of the Indians already occupying the reservation below." Thus the decree in favor of the Indians by the court below was sustained.

Adhering to the same principles of the powers of the National Government to reserve rights to the use of water for the Indians, as reviewed above, the Supreme Court declared:

"They [cases relating to the ownership of beds of navigable streams] do not determine the problem before us and cannot be accepted as limiting the broad powers of the United States to regulate navigable waters under the Commerce Clause and to regulate government lands under Art. IV, Sec. 3 of the Constitution. We have no doubt about the power of the United States under the clauses to reserve water rights for its reservations and its properties." [52]

From the legal standpoint there is a substantial difference between the rights, title to which resided in the Indians and which they retained by Treaty or agreement, from those, title to which was in the United States, but passed to the Indians when their Reservations were created by Congress or Executive Order. Indian rights to the use of water under Treaties are immemorial in character having always resided in the Indians. Where Congress or the Executive granted title to the Indians those titles are from the United States subject to any interests outstanding when title was conveyed to the Indians. That difference—immemorial Indian title or invested Indian title—does not, it is believed, have bearing upon the economic development of the Reservations.

From the standpoint of this consideration—the need for rights to the use of water if the Indian Reservations are to have economic growth and establish a viable community—the question of immemorial title retained by the Indians or title vested by the United States in the Indians, is not of too great importance. Comment is warranted, however, as to the capricious course of conduct which was adhered to in connection with the dealings with the Indians. It is, of course, manifest that the immemorial title is of greater value than the invested title from the United States because the latter title could be subject to other outstanding interests which is not true in regard to the treaty rights. An example of that capriciousness has had far-reaching effect upon the rights and interests of the Mohaves and the

[50] Ibid., 104 F.2d 334, 336.
[51] Ibid., 104 F.2d 334, 336.
[52] *Arizona* v. *California*, 373 U.S. 546, 598 (1962).

Colorado River Tribes of the Colorado River Indian Reservation.[53]
Colonel Poston, in 1865 a Member of Congress but formerly a Superintendent of Indian Affairs for the Arizona Territory, presented a
graphic description of the course which was adopted in regard to the
previously proud and self-sufficient Yumas, Mohaves, and other
Colorado River Indians. Quite obviously he gave no thought to the
legal implications flowing from his patronizing attitude towards those
Indians, however benign his approach to them may have been. Those
Indians had been reduced to begging for food by reason of the fact,
in the words of Colonel Poston, that they had "been robbed of their
lands and their means of subsistence * * *." [54] He recited that as a
representative of the United States "* * * I did not undertake to
make a written treaty" with them because "* * * I considered that
the Government was able and willing to treat them fairly and hon-
estly * * *." In their dire distress he pointed out that the Yumas,
Mohaves and other Indians "there assembled were willing, for a
small amount of beef and flour, to have signed any treaty which it
had been my pleasure to write." Because he would attempt to obtain
from a "magnanimous Government some relief from their desperate
circumstances," he asked those Indians to abandon "* * * all the one
hundred and twenty thousand square miles, full of mines and rich
enough to pay the public debt of the United States" and to "confine
themselves to the elbow of the Colorado River, not more than seventy-
five thousand acres." That action resulted in the extinguishment of
the Mohave title with the attendant loss of invaluable lands and rights
to the use of water and an ensuing history of contradictions, discrimi-
nations and travail.

(f) *Indian Winters Doctrine Rights as distinguished from riparian
rights*

Economic development on the Indian Reservations has been keyed
throughout this consideration to *Winters Doctrine* rights to the use of
water. The location of Indian Reservations and competition to meet
present and future requirements necessitates reference to the individual, corporation, municipal, and quasi-municipal rights under the
doctrine of prior appropriation. *Winters Doctrine* rights have been
referred to as immemorial in character, prior and paramount, or in
similar terms, according to the Indians preferential status on streams.
Indian rights, having been retained by the Indians or invested in
them antecedent to settlement of the lands in the Western United
States, demonstrate the coalescence of history and the law. Those
water rights were never opened by the Congress to private acquisition.

(1) *The doctrine of prior appropriation:*

Title to most of the Western United States—land, water rights,
minerals, timber and all natural resources originally resided in the
national government. Miners came to the harsh environment of the
West exploring for precious minerals. Then, as now, water was the

---

[53] See 7 *Ind. Cl. Comm. Finding* 25(a) et seq., how the Mohaves, Yumas and others were deprived of the
benefits of treaties, is as follows:
"25. (a) No treaty was ever made between the United States and the Mohave Tribe for the purpose of
extinguishing the Indian title in said tribe to the lands it exclusively used and occupied. The lands found
herein to have been exclusively used and occupied by the Mohave were located in what are now the States
of California, Nevada and Arizona."
[54] *Cong. Globe,* 38th Congress, 2d Sess., March 2, 1865, p. 1320.

key to economic development. Without it gold remained in the granite and in 'the gravel. As a consequence, water was diverted out of the streams to the mine locations, frequently long distances at great costs of money, time and effort. The mining and water diversion were accomplished with the knowledge and acquiescence of the Government of the United States.

Violence is very much a part of the history of water law in the West. As law and order came to the Old West, there grew up in the mining districts the precept that the "First in time" was "first in right" on the streams of the public domain.

In 1866 the Congress, considering the nation's western lands, took cognizance of the laws of the mining States, which by that time had come into the Union, and declared:

> "Whenever, by priority of possession, rights to the use of water for mining, agricultural, manufacturing, or other purposes, have vested and accrued, and the same are recognized and acknowledged by the local customs, laws, and the decisions of courts, the possessors and owners of such vested rights shall be maintained and protected in the same; * * *." [55]

In 1870 there was further Congressional recognition of the rights to the use of water exercised pursuant to State law by enactment of the following language:

> "All patents granted, or preemption or homesteads allowed, shall be subject to any vested and accrued water rights, or rights to ditches and reservoirs used in connection with such water rights, as may have been acquired under or recognized by this section." [56]

Thus the patentee took his title from the nation subject to privately acquired rights in the streams on the "public land." [57]

In the 1877 Desert Land Act, Congress, to foster economic development of the arid public land, having provided for diversion and use of water under specified conditions, declared that:

> "* * * all surplus water over and above such actual appropriation and use, together with the water of all lakes, rivers, and other sources of water supply upon the public lands and not navigable, shall remain and be held free for the appropriation and use of the public, for irrigation, mining, and manufacturing purposes subject to existing rights." [58]

In summarizing the legal consequences flowing from the Acts of 1866, 1870 and 1877, the Supreme Court declared:

> "As the owner of the public domain, the government possessed the power to dispose of land and water thereon together, or to dispose of them separately, (Howell v. Johnson, C.C. 89 Fed. 556, 558. The fair construction of [the Desert Land Act of 1877] is that Congress intended to establish the rule that for the future the land should be patented separately; and that all non-navigable

---

[55] Act of July 26, 1866, Ch. 262, Sec. 9, 14 Stat. 253.
[56] Act of July 9, 1870, Ch. 235, Sec. 17, 16 Stat. 218.
[57] Act of July 9, 1870, Ch. 235, Sec. 17, 16 Stat. 218. *Note:* The quotations are from 43 U.S.C. 661 in which the Acts of 1866 and 1870 are in part codified. See in regard to the preceding review: *Jennison* v. *Kirk*, 98 U.S. 453 (1878); *California-Oregon Power Co.* v. *Beaver Portland Cement Co.*, 295 U.S. 142 (1935); *Federal Power Comm.* v. *Oregon*, 349 U.S. 435 (1955).
[58] Act of March 3, 1877, Ch. 107, Sec. 1, 19 Stat. 377.

waters thereon should be reserved for the use of the public under the laws of the states and territories named." [59]

When the Supreme Court declared that the National Government as owner of the public lands had the power to dispose of those lands and water rights separately—as Congress did by the Acts of 1866, 1870 and 1877—it relied upon the decision of *Howell* v. *Johnson* involving water rights acquired in a stream in Wyoming which traversed public lands.

"The rights of plaintiff do not, therefore, rest upon the laws of Wyoming, but upon the laws of congress.

"The legislative enactment of Wyoming was only a condition which brought the law of congress into force. The national government is the proprietor and owner of all the land in Wyoming and Montana which it has not sold or granted to some one competent to take and hold the same. Being the owner of these lands, it [the United States] has the power to sell or dispose of any estate therein or any part thereof. The water in an innavigable stream flowing over the public domain is a part thereof, and the national government can sell or grant the same, or the use thereof, separate from the rest of the estate, under such conditions as may seem to it proper." [60]

The doctrine of prior appropriation has been well stated in these terms:

"* * * To appropriate water means to *take* and *divert* a specified quantity thereof and put it *to beneficial use* in accordance with the laws of the State where such water is found, and, by so doing, to acquire under such laws, a vested right to *take* and *divert* from the same source, and to use and consume the same quantity of water *annually forever, subject only to the right of prior appropriations.* * * * *the perfected vested right to appropriate water flowing* * * * *cannot be acquired without the performance of physical acts through which the water is and will in fact be diverted to beneficial use.*" [61] (Emphasis supplied.)

(II) *Indian Winters Doctrine Rights differ drastically from common law riparian rights:*

Unsuited to the semiarid regions of the west and incompatible with the monopolistic aspects of the doctrine of prior appropriation, the common law doctrine of riparian rights—a product of a more

---

[59] *California Oregon Power Co.* v. *Beaver Portland Cement Co.*, 295 U.S. 142, 163–64 (1935).

[60] *Howell* v. *Johnson*, 89 Fed. 556, 558 (D. Mont. 1898). State court decisions appear generally in accord with this pronouncement.

Smith v. *Denniff*, 24 Mont. 20, 21; 60 Pac. 398 (1900). See also *Story* v. *Woolverton*, 31 Mont. 346, 353–54; 78 Pac. 589, 590 (1904).

Benton v. *Johncox*, 17 Wash. 277, 289; 49 Pac. 495, 499 (1897): "The government, being the sole proprietor, had the right to permit the water to be taken and diverted from its riparian lands; * * *."

LeQuime v. *Chambers*, 15 Idaho 405; 98 Pac. 415 (1908).

Lux v. *Haggin*, 69 Cal. 255, 338; 10 Pac. 674, 721 (1886): "It has never been held that the right to appropriate waters on the public lands of the United States was derived directly from the state of California as the owner of innavigable streams and their beds; and, since the act of congress granting or recognizing a property in the waters actually diverted and usefully applied on the public lands of the United States, *such rights have always been claimed to be deraigned by private persons under the act of congress, from the recognition accorded by the act, or from the acquiescence of the general government in previous appropriations made with its presumed sanction and approval.*" (Emphasis supplied).

Morgan v. *Shaw*, 47 Ore. 333, 337; 83 Pac. 534, 535 (1906).

Hough v. *Porter*, 51 Ore. 318, 391; 95 Pac. 732; 98 Pac. 1083, 1092 (1908, 1909).

2 Kinney, *Irrigation and Water Rights*, 1118 (2d ed. 1912), reiterates that proposition. From this latter source, at 692–93, this statement is taken:

"The Government is still the owner of the surplus of the waters flowing upon the public domain. * * * It therefore follows, as the result of the ownership by the United States of the waters flowing upon the public domain, that any dedication by a State of all the waters flowing within its boundaries to the State or to the public amounts to but little, in the face of any claim which may be made by the Government, *at least* to all the surplus or unused waters within such State."

[61] *Arizona* v. *California*, 283 U.S. 423 (1931).

humid, less harsh environment than that of Western United States—
was rejected by the States of Arizona, Colorado, Idaho, Montana,
Nevada, New Mexicó, Utah, and Wyoming. Water law is generally
the outgrowth of experience, not logic, and where logic purported to
override experience, as in California, Oregon and other states, who
adhere to even greatly modified concepts of riparian principles together with the doctrine of prior appropriation, confusion has ensured.
In a recent California proceeding the principles of the *Winters Doctrine*
were applied to Indian and Federal rights to both surface and ground
waters. The principles of privately owned riparian rights were applied
to surface waters, principles respecting correlative privately owned
rights were likewise applied to ground waters, and the principles
respecting appropriative rights were applied to both surface and
ground waters.[62]

This case suggests the difficult but imperative, immediate need of
enforcing the *Winters Doctrine* rights of the American Indians if
economic development on their Reservations is not to be totally
stifled in areas comparable to Southern California.

A riparian right is held and exercised correlatively with all other
riparian owners as "a tenancy in common and not a separate or sever-
able estate." [63] Obviously the concept of the "reserved right" in the
Indians is wholly at variance with the limitations which are present
in a tenancy in common. Further, "a riparian owner has no right to
any mathematical or specific amount of the waters of a stream as
against other like owners." [64] That aspect of the riparian right results
from the fact that those rights are held correlatively with all other
riparians. As a consequence the quantity of water riparian owners
may use must be "reasonable" in the light of the claims of all other
riparians. Reasonableness is, of course, a variant depending upon
the supply of water, the demands which differ from day to day, and
a multitude of other factors.[65]

Equally at odds with the concept of *Winters Doctrine* rights is the
limitation upon the exercise of rights riparian in character: " 'Land
which is not within the watershed of the river is not riparian thereto,
and is not entitled, as riparian land, to the use or benefit of the water
from the river, although it may be part of an entire tract which does
extend to the river * * *.' " [66] There is, of course, no legal basis for any
limitation of *Winters Doctrine* rights to the watershed in which the
Indian land is situated. Moreover, State law could not thus restrict the
power of Congress over the properties of the nation.[67]

It is pertinent at this phase of the consideration to turn to the state
law governing water rights of private persons and briefly to discuss the
exemption of Indian water rights from those laws.

[62] *United States* v. *Fallbrook Public Utility District*, 101 F. Supp. 298 (S.D. Cal. 1951); 108 F. Supp. 72 (1952); 109 F. Supp. 28 (1952); 110 F. Supp. 767 (1953); 202 F. 2d 942 (9th Cir. 1953); 165 F. Supp. 806 (1958); 193 F. Supp. 342 (1961); Reversed in part and affirmed in part, 347 F. 2d 48 (9th Cir. 1965). Noteworthy is the fact that on May 8, 1963, a final judgment was entered decreeing, in effect, every right and interest of Fallbrook Public Utility District subject and subordinate to the prior rights of the United States.
[63] *Seneca Consolidated Gold Mines Co.* v. *Great Western Power Co. of California*, 209 Cal. 206; 287 Pac. 93, 98 (1930).
[64] *Prather* v. *Hoberg*, 24 Cal. 2d 549; 150 P. 2d 405, 410 (1944).
[65] Hutchins, *The California Law of Water Rights* 218 (1956).
[66] Ibid., page 202.
[67] *United States* v. *San Francisco*, 310 U.S. 16 (1940).

483

(g) Federal-State relationship and economic development of Indian lands:

Judicial recognition of Indian *Winters Doctrine* rights is as broad as the Western United States and it has been applied to a vast variety of circumstances. It is of prime importance to the economic development of American Indian Reservations.[68] Equally important is the fact that the American Indian Reservations are at the headwaters of, border upon, or are traversed by the major interstate stream systems in the West. For a variety of reasons, moreover, Indian water rights have remained unexrecised to a very large extent. Sharp competition exists now—and will be accentuated with expanded economic development on the Reservations—between the vested Indian rights to the use of water and those claimed by individuals or corporations, public or private, asserted under State law.

Based upon sound logic, legal precedent, and expressed language upon which the States were admitted to the Union, the states and those claiming under them may not interfere with the rights of the American Indians. In practice the converse has prevailed.

Immunity of Indian *Winters Doctrine* rights from state interference or seizure has been guaranteed in a variety of ways. The State of Washington's Enabling Act and Constitution specifically provide that: "Indian lands shall remain under the absolute jurisdiction and control of the Congress of the United States * * *." [69] Concerning identical provisions in the Montana Enabling Act and Constitution, the Court of Appeals for the Ninth Circuit has unequivocally declared that the state laws respecting the appropriation of water rights would have no application to the Flathead Indian Reservation.[70] That same court later specifically rules as follows on the subject:

> "Rights reserved by treaties such as this are not subject to appropriation under state law, nor has the state power to dispose of them." [71]

In regard to water rights for lands withdrawn by the United States, the Supreme Court has declared: "the Acts of July 26, 1866, July 9, 1870, and the Desert Land Act of 1877" opening surplus rights to the use of water to appropriation "* * * are not applicable to the reserved lands and waters here involved." [72] Having thus ruled, the Supreme Court then proceeded to set forth the legal distinction between Indian lands and withdrawn lands, upon which the Pelton Project for the generation of electricity was to be located, and "public lands" to which the Desert Land Act of 1877 is applicable, by stating that the former "are not unqualifiedly subject to sale and disposition * * *." [73]

---

[68] *Winters* v. *United States*, 207 U.S. 564 (1907), affirming the Court of Appeals for the Ninth Circuit, 143 Fed. 740; 148 Fed. 684. *United States* v. *Powers*, 305 U.S. 527 (1939), affirming 94 F. 2d 783. *Arizona* v. *California*, United States, Intervener, 373 U.S. 546 (1962). *United States* v. *Walker River Irrigation District, et al.*, 104 F. 2d 334 (CA9, 1939). *Conrad Investment Co.* v. *United States*, 161 Fed. 829 (CA9, 1908). *United States* v. *McIntyre*, 101 F. 2d 650 (CA9, 1939.) *Skeem* v. *United States*, 273 Fed. 93 (CA9, 1921). *United States* v. *Ahtanum Irrigation District*, 236 F. 2d 321, (CA9, 1956); Appellees' cert. denied 352 U.S. 988 (1956); 330 F. 2d 897 (1965); 338 F. 2d 307; Cert. denied 381 U.S. 924 (1965).
[69] Enabling Act, Sec. 4, second subdivision; Constitution of the State of Washington, Article XXIV, second subdivision.
[70] *United States* v. *McIntire*, 101 F. 2d 650 (CA9, 1939).
[71] *United States* v. *Ahtanum Irrigation District* 236 F. 2d 321, 328 (CA9, 1956).
[72] *Federal Power Commission* v. *Oregon*, 349 U.S. 435, 445 (1955).
[73] Ibid, 349 U.S. 435, 448.

It will be recalled that the Court in *Winters* declared emphatically that the power of the nation under the Constitution "* * * to reserve the waters and exempt them from appropriation under the state laws is not denied and could not be * * *." [74]

Title to water rights, although stemming from the Constitution itself and fully recognized by the courts, does not in any sense guarantee to the American Indians that those rights cannot be taken from them. Far from humorous is the description of State permits to appropriate rights to the use of water as "hunting licenses." A permit to appropriate, for example, in California "* * * is * * * no assurance of a water supply * * *." [75]

However, "surplus" waters in a stream frequently are diverted and used, and economies are built upon those waters quite aside from the fact that the "surplus" is actually water the rights to which reside in the Indians. Constitutional law, ethics, and good conscience become mere technicalities to be avoided or ignored under the circumstances. To the holder of the permit from the State to appropriate water rights—although it is subject to vested rights—the existence of a surplus, though it may be momentary, allows him to expend money to develop its use with the hope that time will come to his aid as a barrier to the Indians recovering the waters to which they are justly entitled. As a consequence of actual practice, as distinguished from legal niceties, the American Indians' rights to the use of water are being rapidly eroded away by those claiming under the guise of compliance with State law. They eloquently prove a Western truism about water, however harsh and cynical it may be—"use it or lose it."

ECONOMIC DEVELOPMENT OF AMERICAN INDIAN RESERVATIONS MUST BE EFFECTUATED WITHIN THE PURVIEW OF THE CONSTITUTIONAL RELATIONSHIP BETWEEN THE NATION AND THE INDIANS

(a) *American history as it relates to the American Indians and the economic development of their Reservations:*

When the European culture encountered indigenous inhabitants of the Americas it is difficult to perceive the disparity which existed between them. From the outset the then great Continental powers, though desirous of occupying the lands loosely held by the Indians, did not deny that the Indians had rights to those lands. Rather, Spain acknowledged their ownership of the lands that they occupied and refused to enslave them. The Dutch and early colonists respected the Indian rights, treating with them as the owners of their lands.[76] It is, of course, a historical fact that William Penn took cognizance of the rights of the Indians and paid them for their properties.

It is clear that the European and Indian mores did not preclude efforts to resolve amicably the differences between the invaders of the land and its occupants. The English generally entered into treaties with the Indians in the territory which they occupied. As the Supreme Court observed of Britain's historical policy with the Indians: "This was the settled state of things when the war of our revolution commenced." [77]

---

[74] See supra, p. 14, footnote 15 et seq., particularly pp. 20–21 footnote 24.
[75] California's "*Rules and Regulations*" governing appropriation of rights to the use of water.
[76] *Federal Indian Law*, page 164.
[77] *Worcester* v. *Georgia*, 31 I.S. 515, 548 (1832).

History also records that the Colonies, in their rebellion against Great Britain desired most assiduously to avoid conflict with the Indians and conducted negotiations with them with that end in mind. Thus the original relationship between the former Colonies in revolt and the Indians was not that of a superior power enforcing its will upon the Indians. The basic objective was to placate a war-like people which might very well measure the difference between success and failure, victory or defeat. During the Revolutionary War the United States entered into numerous treaties with the Indians, among them being the "Articles of Agreement and Confederation with the Delaware Nation." [78] One objective of and need for the treaty was declared in the treaty itself:

"And whereas the United States are engaged in a just and necessary war, in defence and support of life, liberty and independence, against the King of England and his adherents, * * * " [79]

Continuing, the treaty recites that the "said King" was maintaining posts and forts throughout the lands of the Delawares and the United States was in need of access across the lands of the Delaware Nation. Provision was also made in the document pursuant to which the Delawares were to assist the struggling nation in its war against Great Britain and "to join the troops of the United States aforesaid, with such a number of their best and most expeart warriors as they can spare, consistent with their own safety, and act in concert with them, * * *." [80]

In consideration of the very valuable assistance accorded to it, the United States covenanted to—

"guarantee to the aforesaid nation of Delawares, and their heirs, all their teritoreal rights in the fullest and most ample manner, as it hath been bounded by former treaties, as long as they the said Delaware nation shall abide by, and hold fast the chain of friendship now entered into." [81]

Casting the arrangement in its proper perspective, this nation and the Indians referred to themselves in the treaty as "the contracting parties." No guardian and ward relationship there; rather a covenant for mutual assistance and recognition.

Similar treaties were entered into during the period when the Articles of Confederation were in force and effect.[82] After the adoption of the Constitution of the United States in 1787 numerous other treaties were entered into with the Indians, many of them involving lands in Western United States. A review of those treaties, many of which were contemporaneous with the adoption of the Constitution, is instructive as to the relationship between the nation and the Indians at the time and provides the correct perspective of that relationship. Frequently the arrangement between the United States and the Indians was denominated "A Treaty of Peace and Friendship" as with the "Creek Nation." [83]

---

[78] 7 Stat. 13 et seq.
[79] Article III.
[80] Article III.
[81] Article VI.
[82] Schmeckebier, The Office of Indian Affairs—U.S. Government Service Monograph No. 48; page 14 Fort Stanwix, with the Six Nations (7 Stat. L., 15) Fort McIntosh, with the Delawares, Wyandots, Chippewas, and Ottawas (7 Stat. L., 16); Hopewell, with the Cherokees (7 Stat. L., 18); Hopewell, with the Choctaws (7 Stat. L., 21); Hopewell, with the Chickasaws (7 Stat. L., 24); Mouth of the Great Miami, with the Shawnees (7 Stat. L., 26); Fort Harmar, with the Wyandots, Delawares, Ottawas, Chippewas, Potawatomi, Sauk, and Six Nations (7 Stat. L., 18, 33).
[83] 7 Stat. 35 et seq.

Violations of the treaties by the United States does not detract from the nature of the covenants when they were effectuated by the parties to them. Those violations caused consternation to President Washington during his incumbency.[84] For almost one hundred years the government and the Indian Tribes were to negotiate and attempt to resolve their differences by mutual agreements.

From those treaties, some of which are cited above, it is evident that the economic development of the United States and of the Indians were the expressed objectives. It is clear beyond question that the National policy was to create a continuing obligation to the Indians in consideration of their relinquishment of vast areas of invaluable land, water rights, forests, and other natural resources which contributed so abundantly to the affluence of the United States.

It was on that background that the Nation formulated its policy with the American Indians. Altruism undoubtedly was an ingredient giving rise to that policy. However, peace and trade with the Indians—need for domestic tranquillity—far outweighed the benign attitude toward the Indians which is frequently attributed to the Nation's founding fathers—in a word, they were practical in their efforts to survive during the formative period.

(b) *It is the Constitution which established the Nation's relationship with the Indians—the courts have interpreted it as constituting the Nation a guardian and the Indians the wards under a trust responsibility:*

Under the Articles of Confederation the provision was made that
"The United States in Congress assembled shall also have the sole and exclusive right and power of regulating * * * the trade and managing all affairs with the Indians, not members of any of the States, provided that the legislative right of any State within its own limits be not infringed or violated * * *."[85]
James Madison in the *Federalist* pointed out the anomaly created by the last quoted vague and uncertain provision, in urging the adoption of the New Constitution.[86]

---

[84] Schmeckebier, *The Office of Indian Affairs—U.S. Government Service Monograph No. 48*, pages 20–21:
"Serious and earnest comments on Indian affairs appear in all of Washington's messages; some relate to aggressions of the Indians, but more are devoted to the necessity of legislation to curb the unlawful practices of the whites. In the annual address of November 6, 1792, after referring to the war in the region north of the Ohio and to Cherokee depredations on the Tennessee, the President referred to the frontier situation as follows:
"'I cannot dismiss the subject of Indian affairs without again recommending to your consideration the expediency of more adequate provision for giving energy to the laws throughout our interior frontier and for restraining the commission of outrages upon the Indians, without which all pacific plans must prove nugatory. To enable, by competent rewards, the employment of qualified and trusty persons to reside among them as agents would also contribute to the preservation of peace and good neighborhood. If in addition to these expedients an eligible plan could be devised for promoting civilization among the friendly tribes and for carrying on trade with them upon a scale equal to their wants and under regulations calculated to protect them from imposition and extortion, its influence in cementing their interest with ours could not but be considerable.'
"In the annual address of December 3, 1793, another plea was made for the regulation of trade 'conducted without fraud, without extortion, with constant and plentiful supplies, with a ready market for the commodities of the Indians and a stated price for what they give in payment and receive in exchange.'"
[85] Articles of Confederation, 1777, Article IX.
[86] *Federalist and Other Constitutional Papers*, Scott, page 236:
"The regulation of commerce with the Indian tribes, is very properly unfettered from two limitations in the Articles of Confederation, which render the provision obscure and contradictory. The power is there restrained to Indians, not members of any of the States, and is not to violate or infringe the Legislative right of any State within its own limits. What description of Indians are to be deemed members of a State, is not yet settled; and has been a question of frequent perplexity and contention in the Federal councils. And how the trade with Indians, though not members of a State, yet residing within its Legislative jurisdiction, can be regulated by an external authority without so far intruding on the internal rights of legislation, is absolutely incomprehensible. This is not the only case, in which the Articles of Confederation have inconsiderately endeavored to accomplish impossibilities; to reconcile a partial sovereignty in the Union, with complete sovereignty in the States; to subvert a mathematical axiom, by taking away a part, and letting the whole remain."

In lieu of the wholly objectionable language of the Articles of onfederation, this provision was adopted as a part of the Constiution of the United States of America: "Section 8: The Congress hall have Power: "To regulate Commerce with foreign nations, and among the several States, and with the Indian Tribes; * * *."[87] All doubts as to the plenary power of the nation in regard to its relationship with the Indians are swept away by that clause.

Also contemporaneous with that delegation by the states to the new nation of all power and authority in Indian matters, is this reflection of federal policy as enunciated in the "Ordinance of 1787: The Northwest Territorial Government":

"* * * The utmost good faith shall always be observed towards the Indians; their lands and property shall never be taken from them without their consent; and in their property, rights, and liberty they never shall be invaded or disturbed, unless in just and lawful wars authorized by Congress; but laws founded in justice and humanity shall, from time to time, be made, for preventing wrongs being done to them, and for preserving peace and friendship with them." [88]

From the shaky first steps of sovereignty the nation was to progress and to become stronger. It was no longer seeking, as it did with the Delawares, a propitious arrangement which was of mutual assistance to the "contracting" parties. Force rather than diplomacy became the method with which to transact business with the indigenous "savages". It became increasingly clear that the reciprocity between the nation and the Indians was no longer of paramount importance. Nevertheless, until relatively recent times it was propitious for the nation to come to terms with embattled Indian Tribes and in return for the lands seized from them to guarantee economic development in regard to the vestige of lands left to them.

A half century after the adoption of the Constitution Chief Justice Marshall labored greatly in an effort to analyze what he termed the "anomalous * * * character * * *," of the Nation's relationship with the Indians. He determined that an Indian Tribe was neither a state nor a foreign nation when the Cherokees sought to invoke against Georgia the Court's jurisdiction.[89] On the subject of that relationship

"The condition of the Indians in relation to the United States is, perhaps, unlike that of any other two people in existence. In general, nations not owning a common allegiance, are foreign to each other. The term *foreign* nation is, with strict propriety, applicable by either to the other. But the relation of the Indians to the United States is marked by peculiar and cardinal distinctions which exist nowhere else."

He then summarized as follows:

"* * * *their relation to the United States resembles that of a ward to his guardian.*" [90] (Emphasis supplied.)

he stated:

Repeatedly the Supreme Court would express the thought:

"The relation of the Indian tribes living within the borders of the United States, both *before* and *since* the Revolution, to the

---

[87] Constitution of the United States of America, 1787, Article I, Sec. 8, Cl. 3.
[88] See Article III.
[89] *Cherokee Nation* v. *Georgia*, 30 U.S. 1, 15 (1831).
[90] Ibid., 30 U.S. 1, 17 (1831).

people of the United States *has always* been an anomalous one and of a complex character." [91] (Emphasis supplied.)

More recently Mr. Justice Murphy, speaking for the Supreme Court, said:

"'* * * this Court has recognized the distinctive obligation of trust incumbent upon the Government in its dealings with these dependent and sometimes exploited people.'" [92]

The Constitutional obligation here involved has also been referred to as "the generous and protective spirit which the United States properly feels towards its Indian wards." [93] In keeping with that platitude the Court has alluded to the "high standards for fair dealing required of the United States in controlling Indian affairs." [94]

Failure of the United States to fulfill its obligation as a trustee is one of the gravest difficulties in regard to the economic development of the American Indian Reservations. Through the dissipation of the remaining assets of the Indians by the failure of the nation to fulfill that obligation the hope of economic development becomes increasingly remote.

"'From the very beginnings of this nation, the chief issue around which federal Indian policy has revolved has been, not how to assimilate the Indian nations whose lands we usurped, but how best to transfer Indian lands and resources to non-Indians.'" [95]

(c) *Standard of diligence required of the United States in administering Indian rights to the use of water in furtherance of economic development of Indian Reservations:*

Performance in the fulfillment of the nation's trust responsibility to the Indians is, of course, the crux of the matter. In this section the criteria in establishing the care, diligence and skill to be required of the nation, its agencies and personnel in protecting, preserving and administering Indian lands and rights to the use of water will be briefly reviewed.

It is basic that:

"The trustee [guardian] is under a duty to the beneficiary [ward] in administering the trust to exercise such care and skill as a man of ordinary prudence would exercise in dealing with his own property; and if the trustee has greater skill—[here engineers, hydrologists, soil scientists, contract negotiators, administrators, lawyers]—than that of a man of ordinary prudence, he is under a duty to exercise such skill as he has." [96]

An important concomitant proposition is that, *the guardian is under a duty to the ward affirmatively "to take and keep control of the trust property."* [97] He is, moreover, to the extent of his capacities "* * * under a duty to the beneficiary to use reasonable care and skill to preserve the trust peoperty." [98] It is instructive to turn to the timber blowdown *Menominee Case* in Wisconsin. There Congress in its consent that the National Government could be sued, declared, among other things:

[91] *United States* v. *Kagama*, 118 U.S. 381 (1886).
[92] *Seminole Nation* v. *United States*, 316 U.S. 286 (1942).
[93] *Oklahoma Tax Commission* v. *United States*, 319 U.S. 598, 607 (1943).
[94] *United States* v. *Tillamooks*, 329 U.S. 40, 47 (1946).
[95] *United States* v. *Ahtanum Irrigation District*, 236 F. 2d 321, 337 and footnote 23 (CA9, 1956).
[96] American Law Institute, *Restatement, Trusts*, Section 174.
[97] Ibid. Section 175.
[98] American Law Institute, *Restatement, Trusts*, Section 176.

"At the trial of said suit the court shall apply as respects the United States the same principles of law as would be applied to an ordinary fiduciary and shall settle and determine the rights thereon both legal and equitable of said Menominee Tribe against the United States notwithstanding lapse of time or statute of limitations." [99]

From the findings, conclusions and the judgment in that decision it is evident that the broad precepts of the law reviewed above were applied to the United States of America.

In a companion case, the court observed as to the performance of the trust responsibility owing by the United States to the Indians:

"We further think that the provision of Section 3 of the jurisdictional act concerning the principles applicable to an 'ordinary fiduciary' add little to the settled doctrine that the United States, as regards its dealings with the property of the Indians, is a trustee." [100]

Moreover,

"Where discretion is conferred upon the trustee with respect to the exercise of a power, its exercise is not subject to control by the court, except to prevent an abuse by the trustee of his discretion." [101]

From that same source are taken the criteria set forth below, which determine whether the trustee has fulfilled his obligation.[102] Full consideration of those principles goes far in establishing the nature of the nation's obligations to the Indians.

Concerning exercise of administrative discretion, one scholar wrote:

"To the extent to which the trustee has discretion, the court will not control his exercise of it as long as he does not exceed the limits of the discretion conferred upon him. The court will not substitute its own judgment for his." [103]

It is important to observe that the courts are explicit in the manner in which the trustee must perform:

"Even where the trustee has discretion, however, the court will not permit him to abuse the discretion. This [exercise of discretion] ordinarily means that so long as he acts not only in good faith and from proper motives, but also within the bounds of a reasonable judgment, the court will not interfere; but the court will interfere when he acts outside the bounds of a reasonable judgment." [104]

Perhaps the most basic concept of the trust obligation of the National Government to the American Indians is that it must exercise the highest degree of fidelity to them. It has been declared in regard to the loyalty of the guardian to the ward that, "The trustee is under

---

[99] *The Menominee Tribe of Indians* v. *The United States*, 101 Ct. Cls. 22, 23 (1944).
[100] Ibid., 101 Ct. Cls. 10, 19 (1944).
[101] American Law Institute, *Trusts*, Section 187, page 479.
[102] "In determining the question whether the trustee is guilty of an abuse of discretion in exercising or failing to exercise a power, the following circumstances may be relevant: (1) the extent of the discretion intended to be conferred upon the trustee by the terms of the trust; (2) the purposes of the trust; (3) the nature of the power; (4) the existence or nonexistence, the definiteness or indefiniteness, of an external standard by which the reasonableness of the trustee's conduct can oe judged; (5) the motives of the trustee in exercising or refraining from exercising the power, (6) the existence or nonexistence of an interest in the trustee conflicting with that of the beneficiaries." (American Law Institute, Trusts, Section 187, pp. 480–481.)
[103] III Scott on *Trusts*, 3d ed., Section 187, p. 1501.
[104] III Scott on *Trusts*, 3d ed., Section 187, p. 1501.

a duty to the beneficiary to administer the trust solely in the interest of the beneficiary." [105] Recently one court declared that the United States owed "the most exacting fiduciary standards" with respect to the Indians, even if it should prefer to pursue other interests.[106] Under no circumstances can the United States in furtherance of its other obligations, act in competition with the Indians or in derogation of their rights.[107]

Freedom in the exercise of discretion is the key for the care, skill and diligence required for the proper performance by the United States, Trustee, in regard to the administration of lands and rights to the use of water for the economic development of the Indian Reservations. Sharp constriction of that freedom of discretion by reason of laws now in force gravely impairs the activities of the officials and agencies charged with the obligation of fulfilling the trust responsibilities to the Indians. That constraining influence upon the economic development of Indian Reservations is considered below.

CONFLICTING RESPONSIBILITIES UNDER THE LAW GRAVELY IMPAIR THE PRESERVATION, PROTECTION, ADJUDICATION AND ADMINISTRATION OF INDIAN LANDS AND WATER RIGHTS BY THE SECRETARY OF THE INTERIOR AND THE ATTORNEY GENERAL

(a) *Economic development of Indian lands and water rights within the purview of the Constitution:*

The trust responsibility of the United States to the Indians must be fulfilled within the purview of the Constitution. Though in theord the plenary power over Indian *Winters Doctrine* rights was delegateg to the Nation, in actuality the authority of the states or those claiming rights to the use of water under them have a very real and far-reachiny impact upon Indian rights.[108]

Inherent, though not explicitly declared in the Constitution, is the doctrine of the separation of powers among the three great branches of the Federal Government, the Executive, the Legislative and the Judicial. The checks and balances stemming from that separation of powers in the field of water resources are very real.

(i) *Congress has invested the Secretary of the Interior and the Commissioner of Indian Affairs with the power and obligation to exercise the functions of the Executive Branch of the Government in fulfilling the trust relationship of the Nation with the Indians:*

Executive power to administer the trusteeship discussed above is vested almost exclusively with the Secretary of the Interior. There resides in the Secretary of the Interior broad powers of administration, including but not limited to, the authority to issue required regulations, to direct the officers and agents of the Department in fulfillment of legal responsibilities and otherwise to carry out the will of Congress.[109] Congress has, moreover, "charged" the Secretary of the

---

[105] American Law Institute, *Trusts*, Section 170.
[106] *Navajo Tribe of Indians* v. *United States*, 364 F. 2d 320, 322 (Ct. Cls. 1966).
[107] American Law Institute, *Trusts*, Section 170, p. 431 et seq.
[108] See Indian *Winters Doctrine Rights* as distinguished from riparian rights above, page 37.
[109] 5 U.S.C. 22.

Interior "with the supervision of public business relating to the following subjects: * * * 10. Indians * * *." [110] Congress has likewise provided that: "The Commissioner of Indian Affairs shall, under the direction of the Secretary of the Interior, and agreeably to such regulations as the President may prescribe, have the management of all Indian affairs and of all matters arising out of Indian relations." [111]

Sweeping nature of the powers of the Secretary of the Interior and the Commissioner of Indian Affairs is evidenced by the rules and regulations which have been promulgated, now are in force and effect.[112]

Economic development of American Indian Reservations in western United States through the exercise of Indian rights to the use of water is provided for in detail in those rules and regulations.[113] Those rights are presently exercised in connection with irrigation, fishing,[114] power development,[115] recreation, and numerous other uses.

    (ii) *Congress has invested the Secretary of the Interior and the Commissioner of Reclamation with the power and authority to construct and administer reclamation projects to irrigate arid and semiarid lands in western United States, and other purposes:*

In furtherance of making habitable the arid and semiarid "public land" in western United States, the Congress in 1902 adopted the Reclamation Act.[116] Pursuant to that Act "The Secretary of the Interior is authorized to perform any and all acts and to make such rules and regulations as may be necessary and proper for the purpose of carrying out the provisions" of the Reclamation Act. Congress likewise, under that Act established the office of the Commissioner of Reclamation.[117] Numerous acts amendatory of the original Reclamation Act and supplementary to it have been passed by the Congress. For example, in 1939 the Secretary was authorized to build projects "to furnish water for municipal water supply" and other purposes, including but not limited to industrial uses.[118]

Broad authorization for the construction of projects of great magnitude has been granted to the Secretary of the Interior, including the Missouri River, Colorado River, Columbia River, and Rio Grande Basins. In each of those vast drainage areas are located numerous American Indian Reservations, the economic development of which is geared to the availability of water for agriculture, industry, recreation, and all other uses.

    (iii) *Solicitor's Office: Lawyer for Bureau of Indian Affairs; Bureau of Reclamation; other Bureaus administered by the Secretary of the Interior:*

Congress has declared that: "The legal work of the Department of the Interior shall be performed under the supervision and direction of the Solicitor of the Department of the Interior, who shall be ap-

---

[110] 5 U.S.C. 485.
[111] 25 U.S.C. 2; See also 25 U.S.C. 1, 1A.
[112] Title 25 Code of Federal Regulations; Indians.
[113] 25 C.F.R. 191.1 et seq.
[114] 25 C.F.R. 89.1.
[115] 25 C.F.R. 231.1 et seq.
[116] See 43 U.S.C. 371 et seq.
[117] 43 U.S.C. 373a: "General authority of the Secretary of the Interior * * * * * * Commissioner of Reclamation; appointment.
"Under the supervision and direction of the Secretary of the Interior, the reclamation of arid lands, under the Act of June 17, 1902 and Acts amendatory thereof and supplementary thereto, shall be administered by a Commissioner of Reclamation who shall be appointed by the President."
[118] See 43 U.S.C. 485 et seq.

pointed by the President with the advice and consent of the Senate." [119]
Associate Solicitors for the Bureau of Indian Affairs, the Bureau of
Reclamation, Bureau of Land Management, and others, are under the
immediate direction and responsible to the Solicitor of the Department of the Interior.

(b) *Congress has constituted the Attorney General as the chief law
officer of the United States to protect Indian rights on the one hand and
defend the U.S. against Indian claims on the other.*

The Attorney General, and more precisely, members of the Justice
Department Lands Division, represent the American Indians in
actions to preserve, protect, and adjudicate their rights to the use
of water. Moreover, the Attorney General, through the Department's
Lands Division, represents the United States against the Indians
in their actions for compensation before the Indian Claims Commission,[120] and before the Court of Claims or in the United States
District Courts.

(c) *Antipodal positions which Interior must take in administering
streams in which Indian rights conflict with Reclamation and other
projects:*

There are no major interstate stream systems—indeed, there are
few tributaries of major streams—where there are not agencies in
the Interior Department competing with Indians for a supply of
water which is inadequate to meet all present and future demands.
Because of the magnitude of its projects, the Bureau of Reclamation
is the chief competitor with the Indians for that insufficient supply.
Politically oriented and powerfully backed, the Bureau of Reclamation has taken and continues to take from the American Indians
throughout western United States rights to the use of water for the
projects which it builds. Satellite agencies of Reclamation join forces
with it in this uneven struggle with the Indians.[121]

The confrontation of the agencies competing for the always short
supply of water is far-reaching and gives rise to results which frequently are disastrous to the Indians. A legal impasse is created by
efforts to fully support the *Winters Doctrine Rights* of the Indians as
enunciated by the courts. The Bureau of Reclamation could not
countenance it. To force payment to the Indians for the rights which
have been seized for Reclamation Projects goes far beyond the power
of the Solictor—indeed, the tenuous basis of project financial feasibility might well collapse. It is in a milieu of contradictions in law,
policies, and administration that the Solicitor and his staff undertake to represent the American Indians. In their struggle to protect
the last vestige of their heritage in the streams of western United
States, the American Indians are confronted with a coalescence
of forces far beyond the control of those who are charged with the
legal responsibilities for protecting their interests. It is not an overstatement to declare that the Solicitor's representative are frequently
professional victims of a system ill suited to protect much less advocate
the Indian interests.

---

[119] 43 U.S.C. 1455.
[120] 25 U.S.C. 70; 25 U.S.C. 70 w.
[121] Numerous agencies, Fish and Wild Life, Recreation, National Parks, Bureau of Land Management
all participate in the developments undertaken on the stream systems by the Bureau of Reclamation.

(d) *Conflicts within Justice Department respecting the American Indian rights to the use of water comparable to those within Interior:*

In fulfilling the responsibilities and exercising the powers conferred by Congress upon it concerning the American Indian rights to the use of water, the conflicts confronting the Department of Justice are similar—sometimes more severe—than those confronting the Department of the Interior. Charged with the obligation of prosecuting suits to protect and have Indian rights declared, that agency is likewise charged with the obligation of representing the United States when Indians seek restitution for seizure of their rights by other agencies of the government. Thus attorneys in the Department of Justice have actually been engaged in preparing to defend against claims asserted by the Indians simultaneously with another group of attorneys in the same division preparing to try suits to protect those Indian rights. As a consequence the attorneys acting on behalf of the fiduciary are confronted in the same office with the attorneys defending against the claims, thus presenting the irreconcilable conflict which could never prevail in a private law office.

When Indian rights to the use of water are being adjudicated on streams upon which the Bureau of Reclamation likewise is asserting claims, the Justice Department attorneys are confronted with perplexing, if not impossible circumstances, in representing the Indians and at the same moment representing the chief opponents of those Indian claims. Loss to the Indians, either actually through the form of the decree or subsequently the interpretation of it, starkly outlines the impossible situation in which the American Indians seek to have their rights preserved.

In the light of the preceding review there is a grave question whether the trust responsibility owing to the American Indians in regard to the economic development of their Reservations can be fulfilled by the Nation under the existing laws and administration.

ANALYSIS OF FEDERAL PERFORMANCE OF ITS TRUST RESPONSIBILITY TO INDIANS REGARDING WATER RIGHTS

Throughout this phase of the consideration an effort has been made to select and review representative areas throughout western United States to demonstrate the problem of protecting and preserving Indian *Winters Doctrine* rights. Without water in the arid and semiarid regions any program of economic development on the Indian Reservations must fail. Characteristic examples of the problem, which is widespread throughout the country, will be briefly discussed as they relate to the subject.

I. YAKIMAS' STRUGGLE TO PRESERVE THEIR RIGHTS TO THE USE OF WATER IN AHTANUM CREEK

(a) *Yakimas' immemorial rights:*

Few cases are better documented than that involving the struggle of the Yakimas and the Bureau of Indian Affairs to protect and preserve the rights of the Indians in Ahtanum Creek. The Ahtanum Creek is often considered the cradle of irrigation in the State of Washington.[122] There the Yakimas first irrigated their gardens in the late 1840's.

---

[122] See above, footnote 13.

In 1855 the Yakimas entered into their Treaty with the United States and Ahtanum Creek was constituted the northern boundary of their Reservation. In the early 1860's lands north of the Creek were patented and early settlers occupied them. Without water neither the lands of the Indians south of the stream nor the non-Indian lands north of it could be successfully cultivated.

By the turn of the century the Indians had, by their own efforts, constructed several small ditches irrigating approximately 1,200 acres; the non-Indians by innumerable small diversions, irrigated an estimated 4,800 acres. Conflicts among the non-Indians over their respective rights in Ahtanum Creek gave rise to adjudications among themselves—not with the Indians.[123] Serious conflicts between the Yakimas and the non-Indians developed shortly after 1900.

The first record of a request to the Justice Department to protect the Yakimas' rights was August 23, 1906.[124] Almost a half century was to elapse before any action was taken. It is a history replete with evasions of responsibilities stemming from conflicts within the Federal Government, and with politically powerful non-Indian land owners.[125] During this period invaluable land of the Yakimas was to lie idle or only partially cultivated due to the diversion of water by non-Indians.

(b) *Conflicts within Interior between Bureau of Indian Affairs and Bureau of Reclamation in regard to claims of the Yakimas*

In 1906 the Bureau of Reclamation undertook the construction of the Yakima Reclamation Project. Ahtanum Creek is a tributary of the Yakima River from which the Reclamation Project was to receive its water supply. Reclamation officials were gravely concerned over the conflict between the Indians and non-Indians because it might interfere with the project they wished to build.[126] Chief among Reclamation's concerns were the principles of law the Bureau of Indian Affairs desired to rely upon to defend the Indian claims. Reflective of the agonizing impasse between contesting Bureaus within the Interior Department not only as to the rights to the use of water but as to the theory of law which would obtain, in this statement:

"The Reclamation Service is endeavoring to build up the theory of appropriative rights as the most safe and most equitable guide for its operations, * * * It is understood that the Indian Bureau proposes to defend its water rights on Ahtanum Creek on the common law doctrine of riparian rights. *For one department of the Government to thus assume a position directly antagonistic to that assumed by another department of Government, it seems to me must prove embarrassing, particularly in view of the fact that the Reclamation Service is appealing to the various state legislatures to adopt an irrigation code based upon the doctrine of appropriation.*" [127] (Emphasis supplied)

That statement evidences the grave character of the conflict between two Bureaus functioning within the Department of the Interior. Rationale of that statement sixty years later is repeated and

---

[123] *Benton* v. *Johncox,* 17 Wash. 277; 49 Pac. 495 (1897); In re Ahtanum Creek, 139 Wash. 84; 245 Pac. 758 1926.

[124] Letter from Acting Secretary of the Interior to the Attorney General.

[125] For review of the documentation in regard to the procrastination and the reasons for it, a chronicle of the documents on the subject is set forth in 236 F. 2d 321, 328 et seq.

[126] Letter October 7, 1907 to the Secretary of the Interior from Indian Service Engineer Code.

[127] Letter October 1, 1907 from Reclamation District Engineer to Supervising Engineer.

reaffirmed today as the Bureau of Indian Affairs and the Indians themselves seek to protect their interests against the steady encroachment upon the Indians' rights by the Bureau of Reclamation.

(c) *Winters Doctrine enunciated and applied by the Judiciary; circumvented by the Executive Departments:*

In 1907 the Supreme Court enunciated the *Winters Doctrine*.[128] In 1908 the Court of Appeals for the Ninth Circuit in the case of *Conrad Investment Company* v. *United States*, in applying the *Winters Doctrine*, declared that the Indian rights to the use of water could be exercised "* * * not only for present uses, but for future requirements" on the Reservations, insuring economic development to meet increased needs.[129]

Consternation flowed from the pronouncement of the *Winters Doctrine* and its application in *Conrad*. That consternation was expressed, oddly enough, [130] by the Chief Engineer of the then Indian Service in carrying out an investigation which he was directed to undertake by the Secretary of the Interior. Having referred to the fact that the United States Attorney, as directed by "Washington" had postponed the litigation which was intended to protect the Indian rights in the stream, he recommended a settlement of the dispute, stating among other things:

"The Reclamation Engineers in charge of the Yakima Project are very anxious that litigation may be avoided on the Ahtanum, fearing that * * * litigation * * * might stop all Reclamation work." [131]

He added that the *Winters Doctrine* might make a settlement difficult "in view of the recent Montana decisions, especially that of the United States vs Conrad Investment Co. * * *"". Continuing, this investigator for the Secretary declared:

"To a layman, it seems that, as between the early white settler, who has made prior and beneficial use of the waters of a boundary stream, and the Government, which, as guardian of the Indians' water rights, had *not* done ·so, the latter would be the party to make restitution to the Indians."

Code's letter to the Secretary of the Interior is reflective of the gravity of the situation facing the American Indians. As an employee of the Department of the Interior he was requested to investigate a conflict between the Indians and non-Indians. Recognizing the failure of the Department of the Interior to fulfill its trust responsibility to the Indians and to protect their rights, he recommended an abandonment of those rights to the non-Indians. He, moreover, concurred in the postponement of the initiation of proceedings by the Justice Department. Code's course of conduct was but one phase of an unconscionable course of conduct by two major Departments of the Federal Government which failed to protect the Indian interests in clear violation of their obligations.

---

[128] See above, footnote 22, et seq.

[129] See above, footnote 34, et seq.

[130] It is of interest that Chief Engineer Code in regard to the Salt River Indian Reservation and Camp McDowell Indian Reservation, similarly was a party to seeking to deprive the Indians of the benefits of the Winters Doctrine. The infamous *Kent Decree* on the Salt River entered in 1910 is a part of Code's failure properly to assert the Indian rights. His activities have also been found in various other areas. His is but an example of employees in the Department of the Interior who totally ignore the fact that the Indians are entitled to protection in their claimed rights.

[131] Letter dated October 17, 1907, from Chief Engineer Code to the Secretary of the Interior.

(d) *The Interior Department attempts to give 75% of Indian Ahtanum Creek water to non-Indians and retain 25% for the Yakimas:*

Confronted with conflicts between the Indians and the non-Indians, obviously fearful that the Indian interests might prevail, pressured by the Bureau of Reclamation, and indeed, guided by the Chief Engineer of the Indian Service, the Secretary of the Interior by an agreement dated May 8, 1908, purported to grant to the non-Indians 75% of the Ahtanum Creek waters and to retain 25% for the Indians. Years were to pass before the Indians were informed of the greeement.

Repeated efforts were made by the Yakimas and the Bureau of Indian Affairs to seek redress for the great wrong thus perpetrated against the Indians. In 1915 the United States constructed the Ahtanum Indian Irrigation Project. Its benefits to the Indians were minimal due to the fact that after approximately July 10 of each year the non-Indians under the 1908 agreement received virtually all of the usable water in the stream.

Stunted crops, poverty, and bitterness on the part of the Yakimas whose lands were entitled to water from Ahtanum Creek were, of course, results of the 1908 agreement. Hostility between the Indians and the non-Indians was all-pervasive, becoming open struggles each irrigation season, accentuated when the yield of Ahtanum Creek was reduced by reason of a light snow pack in the mountains where it had its source.

When the Yakimas brought an action against the United States to protect their rights, Justice successfully moved to have the case dismissed for want of jurisdiction—for want of the legal capacity of the Indians to proceed against it for their own protection—notwithstanding the fact it adamantly refused to act for them.[132]

Politics always prevailed and no action was taken to restore to the Yakimas the invaluable water to which they were entitled under their Treaty. Those conditions continued for two generations with the attendant damage to the Indians.

(e) *Forty-one years after first request to Justice it filed action to quiet title to Yakima rights in Ahtanum Creek; fifty-eight years later the Yakimas recovered their rights; Yakimas forced to act to prevent loss of the rights which they had decreed to them:*

After repeated delays over a period in excess of forty years the Justice Department initiated an action to quiet the title to the rights of the Yakimas in Ahtanum Creek. In excess of fifty-five years after the matter was referred to that Department for action the Court of Appeals for the Ninth Circuit directed the entry of a decree awarding to the Yakimas each year: (1) all of the water of Ahtanum Creek after July 10, the commencement of the short water period;[133] (2) a right of reversion to the quantity of water strictly limited to irrigation the non-Indians are permitted to use during the period of high runoff, as those irrigation uses are reduced.[134] The non-Indians are permitted prior to July 10 of each year to divert up to 47 cubic feet per second of the flow of the stream, strictly limited to the purpose mentioned.[135]

---

[132] See *Totus* v. *United States* in the United States District Court for the Eastern District of Washington.

[133] 330 F. 2d 897, 913, 915 et seq.

[134] 330 F. 2d 897, 913; the reversionary clause enunciated by the court is as follows: "when the needs of those parties, [i.e. these particular individuals] were such as to require less * * * then their rights to the use of the water was correspondingly reduced, and those of the Indians, in like measure, greater."

[135] NOTE: In addition the Court of Appeals recognized the Indian right to recover compensation for the severe losses they had experienced by the 1908 agreement. A claim previously filed by the Yakimas for the monetary loss was dismissed based upon the decree entered in their favor at the direction of the appellate court, all as reviewed above. C.f.s. is measurement of flowing water. The number of cubic feet of water flowing past a given point each second of time.

After the decree was entered in their favor as directed by the Court of Appeals, an effort was made to force upon the Yakimas a "settlement." When the Yakima Tribal Council was advised that Justice was contemplating a settlement, they came to Washington, informed the officials that they would reject any effort of that nature again to invade their rights. Had the Tribal Council failed to act promptly and vigorously they would undoubtedly have been subjected to another chapter of their history since 1906.

(f) *Economic development of Yakima lands curtailed by acts of Justice and Interior; effects of that conduct continues; threat of loss remains:*

Flagrant breach by the United States of the trust responsibility to the Yakimas most severely curtailed, for two generations' the economic development of the Indian land entitled to water from Ahtanum Creek. Yakima Valley is one of the world's great produce areas, especially for apples, cherries, pears, and similar fruit. Hops are an important crop. All require late water. Indian lands are some of the finest orchard acreage in the entire country. However, because of the agreement purporting to give to the non-Indians 75% of the water, fruit could not be successfully raised. Accordingly, the Indian lands only produced short-water crops, for example, grain and less than two full cuttings of alfalfa.

In the brief time since the decree was entered in their favor, alfalfa production has greatly increased. No longer are the lands limited to the short-water crops. Orchards are now being planted on a large scale, though production from them is, of course, years away. Income from the lands in question has risen by hundreds of thousands of dollars a year. Yet it is too clear for question that the Yakimas were gravely injured from the standpoint of economic development and that damage of necessity is continuing in character because of the retardation imposed by the unconscionable 1908 deal made without their knowledge.

Threats against the Yakimas' rights continue. The Bureau of Reclamation has attempted to secure their agreement to the construction of a reclamation project on Ahtanum Creek. Now well experienced, the Indians peremptorily reject that Bureau's activities. Yet the Bureau continues projects along the Yakima River and it is reasonable to expect that the Indians will be presented with further threats of seizure or invasion of their rights.

Another cause celebre involving the stifling of economic development of Indian lands by seizure of their water will now be considered.

II. DESTRUCTION OF PYRAMID LAKE

(a) *Pyramid Lake not only an Indian, but a National asset of incalculable value:*

One hundred and twenty-five years ago General Fremont had this to say of Pyramid Lake which he discovered in 1844:

"Beyond, a defile between the mountains descended rapidly about 2,000 feet; and filling all the lower space was a sheet of green water some twenty miles broad. It broke upon our eyes like the ocean. The waves were curling in the breeze and their green color showed it to be a body of deep water. For a long time we sat enjoying the view. It was like a gem in the mountains which from our position seemed to enclose it almost entirely." [136] Interior's Bureau of Outdoor Recreation, in 1969, reiterated Fremont's glowing description of Pyramid Lake:

"Pyramid Lake by virtue of its leviathan proportions, year-round water-oriented recreation season, outstanding sport fishery potential, and wealth of aesthetic, geological, ecological, archeological and historical phenoma is presently a recreation resource of national significance.

"Pyramid Lake offers greater undeveloped potential for supporting high-quality water-based recreation opportunities for a large number of users than any other lake in northern Nevada and California." [137]

Not mentioned by the last report is the potential destruction of Pyramid Lake if present plans of the Bureau of Reclamation are not changed. [138]

The history of Pyramid Lake is a reflection of the callous disregard of Indian property, their rights and interests. Moreover, it is a prime example of the disdain of unchecked political power exercised against a woefully weak minority deprived of any means of preserving the most elemental features of human dignity. [139]

(b) *1859–the establishment of the Pyramid Lake Indian Reservation*:

The Northern Paiute Indians were the victims of the westward movement of "civilization." In the late 1840's gold and silver brought miners to Nevada. Shortly thereafter the ranchers and farmers arrived. These lands so attractive to the miners and ranchers had been the home and abiding place of the Northern Paiute Indians who had adjusted to the desert environment and survived the rigors of it. To a marked degree the Paiutes gained their sustenance from fish taken from the Truckee River and Pyramid Lake. The Truckee River rises on the California side of Lake Tahoe, proceeds down the precipitous eastern slopes of the High Sierras, crosses the common boundary separating California and Nevada, and terminates in Pyramid Lake, which has no outlet.

"* * * Captain John C. Fremont * * * reported: 'the [Pyramid] lake [in 1844] was found to be teeming with untold millions of brilliantly colored giant cut-throat trout. Indians came from as far away as the Great Salt Lake to obtain them for food.' " [140]

Forty-one years after this succinct statement by Fremont, the United States Geological Survey stated in 1885 that, "The [Pyramid] Lake is abundantly supplied with splendid trout, Salmo purpuratus Henshavi * * * " [141]

As an Interior Department Task Force observed: "The Paiute Indians of the Pyramid Lake were and are a fish-eating people. Their primary natural resource for many generations has been the Lake and its fish." [142] Because of conflicts between the settlers and the Northern

[136] Harold W. Fairbanks, Ph. D., Berkeley, Cal., U.S. Geological Survey Library March 5, 1901 *The Popular Science Monthly*, 505, 507.

[137] 1969 *Report of Bureau of Outdoor Recreation*, page 14.

[138] See House Document No. 181, 84th Congress, 1st Session, Washoe Project, Nevada-California Letter from the Assistant Secretary of the Interior transmitting a report and findings on the Washoe Project, Nevada and California, pursuant to section 9(a) of the Reclamation Project Act of 1939 (53 Stat. 1187).

[139] See in this regard the articles in *The New Yorker*, January 1 through January 22, 1955.

[140] Action Program for Resource Development, Truckee and Carson River Basins, California-Nevada, 1964, p. 20.

[141] United States Geological Survey, *Geological History of Lake Lahontan*, Israel Cook Russel, 1885, page 62.

[142] *Action Program For Resource Development Truckee and Carson River Basins California-Nevada*, 1964, page 20.

Paiute Indians, the Pyramid Lake Indian Reservation was established in 1859. It is comprised of a limited land area which completely surrounds Pyramid Lake and embraces a segment of the Truckee River. From that date the Indians resided on the Reservation with the fishery constituting a source of subsistence and income.

In 1895, the National Geographic reported on the "abundant fish life" in both Pyramid and the then existing Winnemucca Lakes.[143] Immediately after the turn of the century there is reported the fact that Lake Pyramid" * * * is well supplied with large trout, as well as several other kinds of fish." [144]

Yet the task force in 1964 reported to the Secretary that:

"The once famous cutthroat-trout fishery of Pyramid Lake and the lower Truckee River ceased to exist about 1938, largely because recession of the lake has made the lower river all but inaccessible to spawning fish. A trout fishery has been partially restored by natural and artificial means since 1950." [145]

(c) The Newlands Federal Reclamation Project:

In 1902 Congress enacted the Reclamation Act,[146] the objective of which, as reviewed above, was to make habitable the arid and semi-arid public lands, thus attracting settlers. Nevada's then Senator Newlands was a prime advocate of the Act. As a consequence the Newlands Reclamation Project was one of the first to be constructed.

Geography, history, and politics coalesce in regard to the Newlands Project and have spelled disaster to the Northern Paiutes. South of the Truckee River Basin—and entirely separate from it—is the Carson River Basin. That river, like the Truckee, rises in California and enters Nevada. Early settlers in Nevada diverted water from the Carson River to irrigate their lands. Like all western snow-fed streams, it is highly erratic, producing an abundance of water in the early spring and declining rapidly in flow as the snow melts away. The need to impound water for late season use was a necessity. Lahontan Reservoir on the Carson River was built to impound water from both that source and the Truckee River.

To the reclamation planners the yield of the Carson River was insufficient. They desired to provide additional water for the Newlands Project by the construction of the Truckee Canal to divert Truckee River water out of the Truckee River Basin away from Pyramid Lake for use in the Carson River Basin. That Canal was completed in 1906.

Grandiose plans for the Newlands Reclamation Project failed. Poor soil, a short growing season, poor drainage, and bad engineering contributed to that failure. Of a huge reclamation area originally planned to embrace 287,000 acres of irrigated land, the average annual irrigated area within the project, after sixty years of operation, has been estimated at slightly in excess of 50,000 acres.

Financial failure of the Newlands Project was, of course, the result of its physical failure. Write-offs of almost half of the interest-free Federal investment were made. Massive subsidies in addition to write-offs came from the sale of electricity and collection of grazing

---

[143] National Geographic Society, *Physiography of United States, Present and Extinct Lakes of Nevada*, V. 1: 1896, pp. 101, 114, 115.
[144] *Popular Science Monthly*, Vol. 58, 1900–01, pp. 509.
[145] *Action Program for Resource Development*, etc. pages 26–27.
[146] See above, footnote 116, et seq.

fees; other sources of income having no relationship to agricultural production from the irrigated lands, have kept this grossly submarginal project in existence.

(d) *Seizure of Indian Truckee River water without payment of compensation, for diversion out of the Truckee Basin for the Newlands Project and unconscionable waste of that water on the project, cause disastrous decline of Pyramid Lake and destruction of invaluable Indian fishery:*

From 1859 to 1910 there had been substantial irrigation development using Truckee River water in the Reno-Sparks area. Those diversions all within the Truckee River Basin did not seriously affect Pyramid Lake and Winnemucca Lake situated nearby, which actually fed from overflow from Pyramid Lake. A large part of the diversions after irrigation returned to the river and flowed into Pyramid Lake.

Diversions out of the Truckee River Basin to irrigate Carson Valley lands in the Newlands Reclamation Project, either directly or from impoundment in Lahontan Reservoir, drastically reduced the quantities of water entering Pyramid Lake.

Under a 1926 contract between the Secretary of the Interior and the Truckee-Carson Irrigation District, a Nevada public corporation, the District assumed the responsibility of administering the Newlands Project, including but not limited to the diversion of Truckee River water away from Pyramid Lake, with the disastrous consequences to that Lake which have been described.

For over forty years the District had practiced uncontrolled diversion of Truckee River water away from Pyramid Lake. In anticipation of the need to secure sufficient water for the Washoe Reclamation Project now under construction, changes were required in the diversions by the Irrigation District from the Truckee River. Even with those changes Indian water is grossly wasted by the District.

Seizure of the Indian rights to the use of water has been done without compensation to the Indians. If Congress authorized the condemnation of the rights of the Pyramid Lake Tribe—that matter has never been resolved—then there are two prime factors which have been totally ignored: (1) the Indians are entitled to payment for those rights which have actually legally been condemned; [147] (2) Indian rights, if in fact condemned, could not be taken for wasteful purposes because under the Reclamation Act, the basis, the measure, and the limit of any right on Reclamation Projects is beneficial use.[148]

Compensation for the Indian right of fishery, so wantonly destroyed, has not been paid. Yet, as reviewed above, that right of fishery, like the right to the use of water, is an interest in real property having the dignity of a freehold estate.[149] The injustice in the seizure of Indian rights without just compensation is underscored by this description of the Newlands Reclamation Project by a hydrologic engineer:

"Of special interest to this study are the relatively large areas of non-agricultural land that consume river water either directly or indirectly. The survey shows 19,225 acres of permanent water surface and some 44,172 acres of dense and very dense phreatophytes. Thus, there are nearly 64,000 acres of heavy water con-

---

[147] *United States* v. *Gerlach Live Stock Company,* 339 U.S. 725 (1949).
[148] 43 U.S.C. 372; 383 et seq.
[149] See above, footnote 21, et seq.

suming nonagricultural lands or nearly as much area as was covered by agricultural crops in 1967. Although these lands are used for wildlife purposes, they have relatively little, if any, value for cattle grazing purposes." [150]

This report refers to the "extremely low efficiency of water use"—a kindly way of charging waste—on the Newlands Reclamation Project. It concludes in substance that even with an efficiency of 34%—roughly a waste of 66%—100,000 acre-feet of water annually could be saved for Pyramid Lake.

While Pyramid Lake was precipitously declining with an ever-increasing saline content—assuring the ultimate death of this great natural resource—the politically powerful forces in Nevada ignored the plight and poverty of the Northern Paiute Indians. The Bureau of Outdoor Recreation reported earlier this year the effects of diversions to the Newlands Reclamation Project, with its great waste.

"Since 1910, however, the lake level has gradually been receding with the exception of a few brief periods when heavy runoff years once again revived the failing lake. Pyramid Lake is currently 82 feet below the lake level recorded 58 years ago and 72 feet below the lake level which Fremont saw in 1844.

"The white man's tampering with related natural resources in the Truckee and neighboring Carson River basins has greatly accelerated the decline of the lake. Between 1888 and 1890, sawdust from upstream mills clogged the Truckee River channel just north of the lake and the river waters were diverted through Mud Lake Slough into the nearby and now dry Winnemucca Lake. The Indians dammed the Slough in 1890 and diverted waters back through their normal channel into Pyramid Lake. Later the Federal government, through the Bureau of Reclamation, began diverting water out of the Truckee River Basin into the Carson River Basin to supply irrigation waters for one of the first irrigation projects in the Southwest—the Newlands Project at Fallon, Nevada. These diversions began when Derby Dam on the Truckee River was completed in 1905 and have greatly accelerated the decline in the level of Pyramid Lake. An average of 250,000 acre feet is diverted annually out of the Truckee River Basin for irrigation uses on the Truckee Bench and the Newlands Project." [151]

(e) *Stifling of economic development on Pyramid Lake Indian Reservation by reason of rapidly declining water surface of Pyramid Lake:*

Reference has already been made to Pyramid Lake's great potential for recreation. Yet there has been nothing but the most meager development. Investors could not expend funds of any magnitude because of the imminent destruction of the Lake by Federal Reclamation Projects both existing and abuilding.

Poverty among the Pyramid Lake Tribe of Indians—despair and travail for generations—is the lot of these people by reason of the construction and operation of the Newlands Reclamation Project— a submarginal wasteful project—maintained with Federal funds.

---

[150] *Report on Lower Truckee-Carson River Hydrology Studies*, by Clyde-Criddle-Woodward, Inc. Consulting Engineers, Salt Lake City, Utah April 1968.
[151] *1969 Report of Bureau of Outdoor Recreation*, pages 43–44.

(f) *Economic ·development of immense value to the Northern· Paiute Indians and the Nation, if Reclamation Projects are prevented from destroying Pyramid Lake:*

If Pyramid Lake is not intentionally destroyed, economic development would be very feasible with high financial returns for the Pyramid Lake Tribe of Indians. As the Bureau of Outdoor Recreation states:

"A properly developed Pyramid Lake will help meet the·water-based recreation needs of a combined day-use and weekend/vacation-use (includes the San Francisco Bay Area) zone population of 13,814,243 in the year 2000. Visitation to Pyramid Lake in that year should total 2,375,000.

"If Pyramid Lake's recreation resources are properly developed, significant tangible and intangible benefits will accrue to the U.S., Nevada, Washoe County, the Reno-Sparks complex, local interests and the Pyramid Lake Indian Tribe. The direct tangible economic benefits from recreation at Pyramid Lake could total $1,425,000 in general admission fees, $15,482,625 in visitor expenditures at the lake and over one-half million dollars in jobs annually by the year 2000. In the 32-year interim between today and the turn of the century, a total gross income from the admission fees and visitor expenditures generated by a developed Pyramid Lake would accumulate to an impressive $202,380,000. A developed Pyramid Lake will also generate additional annual expenditures in the millions of dollars by visitors outside of the recreation area for sporting equipment, car services, food, lodging, and gaming, etc." [152]

(g) *Final coup to Pyramid Lake—The Washoe Federal Reclamation Project:*

Demise of the "gem in the mountains," as Fremont described Pyramid Lake, is assured if the Washoe Reclamation Project now under construction is completed. Again, the interagency clash between the Bureaus of Reclamation and Indian Affairs, with the Indians victimized, has become intensified. In explicit terms the plans to build the Washoe Reclamation Project have been set forth; in explicit terms the Project can be constructed only by the seizure of the last vestige of the Indian rights in the Truckee River. Concomitantly the destruction of Pyramid Lake, for all practical purposes, is planned.

(i) *Stampede Dam on the Truckee River:*

The Stampede Dam is now being built on the Truckee River. It is a major component of the Washoe Project. Capacity for it is now planned at 225,000 acre-feet. If used as proposed under the Washoe Project it will take from Pyramid Lake the water required ultimately to stabilize it as a viable body of water, accentuate the decline of the lake, greatly increase the salinity of it, leaving it a dead sea.

(ii) *Watasheamu Reservoir on the Upper Carson River:*

Another major component of the Washoe Project is Watasheamu Reservoir on the Carson River. Substantial quantities of the waters which would flow down to the Newlands Reclamation Project, will be impounded in that reservoir for use in the Carson Valley above the Newlands Project Lahontan Reservoir.

---

[152] Ibid. pages 15–16.

(h) *Seizure of Indian water to provide a supply of water for Washoe Project:*

When Carson River water is impounded at the proposed Watasheamu Reservoir, thereafter to be used above the Newlands Project, an equivalent amount of Indian water will be diverted from the Truckee River away from Pyramid Lake to compensate for it. That seizure of Indian water will, of course, accelerate the lake's already precipitous decline. Flood waters of the Truckee which historically could not be diverted through the Truckee Canal and away from Pyramid Lake have been the only source of the meager supply reaching Pyramid Lake. When Stampede Dam on the Truckee and Watasheamu Dam on the Carson River, with their planned appurtenant works, are in operation, the destruction of this great natural resource will be consummated; the Northern Paiutes will have suffered the final seizure of their property; the final indignity will have been heaped upon them, because they are without means to withstand the monolithic forces which have conspired against them.

(i) *Resolution of conflicts over contesting claims between the Newlands Reclamation Project and the Washoe Reclamation Project:*

Prodigal waste of water by the Newlands Reclamation Project could not be tolerated if the Washoe Reclamation Project was to become feasible. With the ingenuity of prime planners, using their immensely capable engineering staff, and with judicious use of their vast powers, the Bureau of Reclamation developed a plan.[153]

For example, no longer would the Truckee-Carson Irrigation District divert Truckee River "winter water"—not required for irrigation—for the generation and sale of electricity, with attendant income so profitable to it in the past. That water would have to be stored in Stampede Dam to meet the Washoe Project water requirements. A reduction would have to be made in the quantities of Carson and Truckee River waters wasted down the Carson River to maintain swamps for ducks. This would impinge to a degree upon Interior's Stillwater Wild Life Refuge—a fringe beneficiary of the excessive diversions of Indian Truckee River water to the Newlands Reclamation Project. Carson River water entering Lahontan Reservoir and there impounded for use on the Newlands Project would be drastically reduced by impoundments in the Watasheamu Reservoir for use in the Upper Carson Valley and above Lahontan Reservoir. To compensate for the reduction of Carson River water previously available, Truckee River water impounded in Stampede Dam would be diverted out of the Truckee River Basin in addition to that previously diverted away from Pyramid Lake.

Simply stated: All increased quantities of water required for the Washoe Reclamation Project would be taken away from Pyramid Lake to the further injury of the Northern Paiutes.

(j) *Pyramid Lake Indians object to Washoe Reclamation Project— they were momentarily appeased, then recognized the need to renew their opposition:*

Opposition to the Washoe Reclamation Project was interposed by the Pyramid Lake Tribe of Indians. Assurances were given by the

---

[153] House Document No. 181, 84th Congress, 1st Session, Washoe Project, Nevada-California.

Department of the Interior that their interests would be preserved and, indeed, enhanced. They withdrew their opposition momentarily. There is thus presented a prime obstacle to preserving and protecting Indian assets within a single Department having as disparate and conflicting interests as the Reclamation Bureau and the Northern Paiutes. At all costs—invariably Indian costs—a consensus must be reached. Yet the elemental precepts of trust law reviewed above necessarily reject all acts of the trustee who bargains against the beneficiary for himself or any third party. Very properly the trustee is required that he have a single loyalty to the beneficiary. Yet the Department of the Interior was forced to weigh conflicting interests, the Indians with no political power against the powerful Bureau of Reclamation.

The substance of the assurances to the Indians was that in the administration of the conjunctive use of the waters of the two rivers, efforts would be made to maximize the use of the Carson River waters and to minimize the use of the Truckee River for the Newlands Project so that Pyramid Lake would be benefited. In actuality the Indians found that: (1) they would be deprived of the quantity of Truckee River water required to resolve the conflict between the two reclamation projects; (2) they would be stripped of the last vestige of the rights they claimed for Pyramid Lake to make the Washoe Project physically feasible.

When the light of those facts shone through, the Bureau of Indian Affairs withdrew its approval of the Departmental Task Force Report;[154] the Indians in effect joined the Bureau in its action.

(k) *Secretarial rules and regulations on the Truckee-Carson Rivers:*

Impossibility of fulfilling splintered and irreconcilable conflicts within the Department of the Interior is often glossed over by the issuance of rules and regulations which are a composite of vagaries enmeshed in contradictions. That course was pursued in regard to conflicting interests on the Truckee-Carson River Systems. The impossible objective was to stretch insufficient supplies to provide water for: (1) the Newlands Reclamation Project; (2) the Truckee Storage Project; (3) the Washoe Reclamation Project; (4) migratory birds; and (5) Pyramid Lake Indian Reservation.

Those rules and regulations were primarily to obtain sufficient water for the Washoe Reclamation Project, through further diversions of water away from Pyramid Lake and the limitation upon the grossly wasteful practices of the Newlands Reclamation Project, thus providing Washoe with water previously wasted by Newlands.[155] To placate the Paiute Indians—but never to recognize that the Indians had rights to maintain Pyramid Lake as a permanent viable body of water—the rules and regulations provided for the conjunctive use of the available supplies from those two streams, and that:

"* * * coordinated operation and control of the Truckee and Carson Rivers in regard to the exercise of water rights of the United States * * * to (1) comply with all of the terms and provisions of the Truckee River Decree and the Carson River

---

[154] Memorandum of July 14, 1966, from the Commissioner of Indian Affairs to the Chairman of the Task Force.

[155] Any doubt that the objective of the rules and regulations is to provide water for the Washoe Reclamation Project is removed when consideration is given to the above cited Washoe Project, Nevada-California, House Document No. 181, 84th Congress, First Session, and the plans now progressing to complete that project.

Decree; and (2) maximize the use of the flows of the Carson River in satisfaction of Truckee-Carson Irrigation District's water entitlement and minimize the diversion of flows of the Truckee River for District use in order to *make available to Pyramid Lake as much water as possible.*" (Emphasis supplied)

The "as much water as possible" for Pyramid Lake is, of course, gratuitous and is not intended to be a recognition of the Indian rights to maintain the Lake.

Provision is also made in the rules and regulations that the Newlands Reclamation Project would receive an annual supply of 406,000 acre-feet of water. The rules and regulations provide that the 406,000 acre-feet of water annually "may be reduced." That concession came about only after bitter inter-agency struggles. Both the Indian Bureau and the Indians were well aware that the 406,000 acre-feet annual water allowance was tantamount to a guarantee to the Truckee-Carson Irrigation District that Indian Truckee River water would be wasted, as the quantity far exceeded that required for reasonable beneficial use on that project. Hence, the term "may be reduced" held out hope that the dissipation of Truckee River water with the attendant adverse effect on Pyramid Lake might be controlled.

As will be seen, the hope for better times for the Indians under the rules and regulations became a shadow with the substance passing to the Reclamation Bureau and its satellites.

(1) *The "nine-point package agreement":*

Limitation upon the Newlands Reclamation Project—administered by the politically powerful Truckee-Carson Irrigation District—was neither undertaken lightly nor accomplished with ease. Without restrictions on the historic waste of that ill-starred project there would be insufficient water for the Washoe Reclamation Project, even with the seizure of all of the Indian water in the Truckee River that could be economically diverted away from Pyramid Lake for Washoe.

There emerged the "nine-point package agreement"—thus named by its sponsors. It is important here primarily because it resuscitated the then expiring Washoe Reclamation Project which, as stated, is the terminal catastrophe to the Northern Paiutes. Principally from the standpoint of the Indians the "package" provides for an increase of acreage above the historic 51,000 acres annually irrigated on the Newlands Project, to 74,500 acres and for an assured firm annual supply of 406,000 acre-feet of water. No reduction in the 406,000 acre-feet would be permitted as provided for in the much publicized but largely vacuous rules and regulations, except that "The Department [of the Interior] would reserve the right to commence suit to challenge the correctness of" the 406,000 acre-feet allocation for the Newlands Reclamation Project. Conveniently left open were the type of action which would be brought, the issues that would be tried, by whom, against whom, when and in what court. Indeed, the Secretary of the Interior might well be one of the prime parties against whom the Indians would proceed.[156]

Ultimately, the Northern Paiutes were again left with an illusion and the Washoe Reclamation Project moved nearer to completion when peace was purchased from the Truckee-Carson Irrigation

[156] See exchange of correspondence respecting "nine-point package agreement" dated July 13, 1967, August 10, 1967, related documents, between Department of the Interior and the Truckee-Carson Irrigation District.

District—purchased, let it be emphasized, with water desperately needed by the Northern Paiutes to maintain Pyramid Lake.

(m) *Decrees unenforced—need to "settle" Alpine Case to assure Carson River water for Watasheamu Reservoir—Indian Truckee River water would be seized to compensate Newlands Reclamation Project for loss of Carson River water:*

A Temporary Restraining Order was entered in March 1950 which is a preliminary adjudication of rights on the Carson River including those of the United States required for the Newlands Reclamation Project.[157] That Order is based largely upon the evidence introduced by the Justice Department in support of the direct flow and storage rights asserted for the Newlands Project. The decree has never been enforced. Had that decree been strictly enforced with Carson River water being diverted only for beneficial purposes in the Upper Basin of the Carson River, based upon priority and limited to the acreage set forth in the decree, and had the beneficial use requirements been enforced against the Newlands Reclamation Project, it would have greatly reduced the quantity of water to be diverted out of the Truckee River for that project. The Indians and Pyramid Lake would have benefited greatly for every acre-foot of water from the Carson River diverted without right under the decree, or wasted, must be replaced with Truckee River water. Failure to enforce the March 1950 decree and reducing the need for Truckee River water in the Carson Valley, is demonstrative of the need for policy changes and the elimination of conflicts between agencies of the Department of the Interior.

Economic development of Pyramid Lake has been retarded not by a single act or omission by the federal establishment, but rather by a composite of seemingly disparate events—failure, for example, to enforce the decree in the *Alpine Case.* Yet upon examination of all of the facts, it is evident that this omission to fulfill the trust obligation to the Indians stems directly from the conflict among federal agencies for the waters of the Carson and Truckee Rivers.

(n) *Enforcement of the rights and priorities in the Alpine Decree would prevent construction of Reclamation's Watasheamu Dam, a major component of the Washoe Project:*

The broad plan for the Washoe Project involved taking Carson River water from the Newlands Reclamation Project and compensating Newlands with increased diversions of Indian Truckee River water away from Pyramid Lake. That exchange of Newlands Carson River water constitutes the use of trust property for the benefit of the trustee to the irreparable damage of the beneficiary of the trust.

To use Newlands Carson River water at Watasheamu Reservoir and its appurtenances requires the abandonment by the United States of its invaluable priorities on Newlands which are set forth with specificity in the Alpine 1950 decree. Enforce those priorities and there would be no Watasheamu Reservoir and Reclamation's plans would be thwarted. The Criddle Report summarizes the need to abandon the Federal Newlands rights to accomplish Reclamation's plans for Watasheamu:

"Studies by the Carson River Hydrology Task Force indicate that if prior rights are respected [those of the United States for

[157] *United States* v. *Alpine Land & Reservoir Company, et al.,* Defendants, in the United States District Court for the District of Nevada, Equity No. D-183.

the Newlands Project, and all others], little water would be available for Watasheamu and that under the above Secretarial policy, it seems mandatory that rights be respected if such action affects the demand on Truckee River." [158]

(o) *Northern Paiutes forced to expend their meager resources to prevent "settlement" by Justice of Alpine Case; Justice opposes Indians:*

Repeatedly the Federal Establishment has attempted to secure a settlement of the *Alpine Case* with the politically powerful landowners in the Upper Carson River Valley. Those owners will not tolerate interference with their historically wasteful practices of diverting Carson River water without controls of any kind, including headgates, measuring devices, or any other means of administration usually applied in western United States, all in violation of the decree Justice had entered in March 1950.

A settlement which would please those powerful landowners in the Upper Carson by freeing enough Carson River water from the Newlands Project to make feasible the Watasheamu Reservoir was the objective of the innumerable meetings between Interior, Justice, and the lawyers representing the Upper Carson landowners. As the negotiations progressed the Northern Paiutes and the Bureau of Indian Affairs were frustrated in every attempt to prevent the arrangement with the attendant increased call for water from the Truckee River.

Confronted with sure disaster if the "settlement" was consummated, the Northern Paiutes, through their attorneys, filed a petition to intervene in the *Alpine Case*. In their petition to intervene the Indians alleged the failure of the United States properly to perform its functions as their trustee, the irreparable damage they suffered from the waste of water, and the failure of the United States to enforce the March 1950 decree. To that and other allegations of the failure of the trustee, Justice responded as follows:

"The United States admits a reluctance to insist upon enforcement of the [1950] temporary decree insofar as it differs from the Report of the Special Master.

[The Report which, if approved by the court, would be clearly at variance with the evidence introduced by Justice, particularly in regard to the strict enforcement of priorities, beneficial use and related restrictions upon upstream water users, with the attendant increase in demands for Truckee River water.] If this is construed by this Court as a failure of the fiduciary duty of the United States to the Applicant, then the United States herein immediately requests complete enforcement of the temporary decree whether or not Applicant is allowed to intervene."

Because Justice had declared that the Indians' effort to intervene and thus assist themselves in the protection of their rights constitutes an adversary proceeding, it refused to supply the Indians with the exchange of correspondence and related data between the Department of the Interior and Justice. Justice, moreover, succeeded in having the court deny the Northern Paiutes their day in court. An appeal has been filed by them to the Court of Appeals for the Ninth Circuit and is now pending.

---

[158] *Report on Lower Truckee-Carson River Hydrology Studies* * * * by Clyde-Criddle-Woodward, Inc. Consulting Engineers, Salt Lake City, Utah April 1968.

Caught between the monolothic Departments with their conflicting responsibilities, the Northern Paiutes–poverty-stricken, destitute–are expending their meager funds to defend themselves against the Federal agencies, including their lawyers within the agencies.

Intervention by the Northern Paiutes in the *Alpine Case* has been fruitful. They stopped the settlement so disastrous to them. However, they had the power of their opponents brought forcefully to their attention. Incredibly the long-disputed California-Nevada Compact was revised to include the main thrust of the "settlement." Nevada's legislature has approved it. California's legislature adjourned without approving the compact.

(p) *Discriminatory interpretation of Orr Water Ditch Decree against the Northern Paiute Indians—thwarted economic development of Pyramid Lake:*

Provisions in the *Orr Water Ditch* decree adjudicating the rights to the use of waters of the Truckee River, primarily for purposes of irrigation, have been used to discriminate against the Pyramid Lake Tribe of Indians, sometimes in this consideration referred to as the Northern Paiutes.

An all-important element in the ownership of the water rights is the ability to change the place of use and purpose of them. Similarly the right to sell, transfer, or exchange water rights is a primary ingredient, as in the title of any property. Indeed, freedom from restraints against the alienation, use, sale, or disposition of property in the absence of injury to others is a basic precept of the law. However, the decree entered pursuant to the consent of Interior and Justice Departments, adjudicating Indian irrigation rights to the use of water, was declared to impose upon those Indians' rights the most severe limitations.

On May 5, 1955, the Solicitor ruled as follows:

"This is in response to an inquiry you have received whether water available for the irrigation of Pyramid Lake Indian lands may be allowed to flow into Pyramid Lake in aid of the fish resources of the Reservation.

* * *

"The Truckee River decree is specific as to the use of water under the rights adjudicated to the Indians and other parties under the decree. In these circumstances, it is my opinion that the Indians do not have the right to divert the use of the water adjudicated to them by the said decree to the propagation of fish resources in Pyramid Lake." [159]

---

[159] No. M–36282, May 5, 1955, from Associate Solicitor, Indian Affairs to Commissioner of Indian Affairs. The portion of this ruling omitted in the text reads as follows:

"The Pyramid Lake Reservation was created before Nevada statehood by the withdrawal of lands by the Department November 29, 1859, later confirmed and approved by Executive Order of President Grant dated March 23, 1874. The area was a part of the land acquired by the United States in a cession from Mexico in 1848. The Lake is approximately 30 miles in length and 10 miles wide at its broadest point and is entirely within the Reservation.

"The Indians have adjudicated water rights in Truckee River which flows through a portion of the Reservation and empties into the Lake. These water rights were awarded by final decree entered September 8, 1944, by the United States District Court, District of Nevada equity—Docket No. A3, in the case of *United States of America* v. *Orr Water Ditch Company, et al.* Under the decree the Indians are entitled to a maximum of approximately 30,000 acre-feet of water per year for irrigation and domestic uses.

"It is fundamental in irrigation law that there can be no ownership of the corpus of water flowing in a stream prior to its being diverted from the stream into canals, ditches or reservoirs of the party entitled to use the water (Kinney on Water Rights, Vol. 2, 2nd ed., p. 1340). 'Neither sovereign nor subject can have any greater than a usufructuary right in running water.' (Kinney on Water Rights, Vol. 1, 2nd ed., pp. 548–549 and cases there cited). It is also a familiar rule that water adjudicated for irrigation purposes if not utilized for that purpose must be allowed to flow downstream for the benefit of other water users with later rights in the stream."

Those severe limitations imposed by the *Orr Water Ditch* decree upon the Indians' rights is contrasted in regard to the non-Indians' rights under that decree:

"Persons whose rights are adjudicated hereby, their successors or assigns, shall be entitled to change, in the manner provided by law the point of diversion and the place, means, manner or purpose of use of the waters to which they are so entitled or of any part thereof, so far as they may do so without injury to the rights of other persons whose rights are fixed by this decree."

Ridiculous though the Solicitor's opinion may be—inept; unprofessional; failing to mention much less consider the legal issues involved in the change of place of use or purpose of rights to the use of water— no mention is made that the water for the purposes of the fishery could injure no one, the Indians being the last users on the stream, no mention is made of the unconscionable limitations consented to by Interior and Justice which the decree imposes upon the Indian rights and no mention is made of the surplus waters in the Truckee River which the Bureau of Reclamation was to attempt to seize for the Washoe Project and to which the Indians obviously are legally entitled. That opinion, nevertheless, had this very salient, destructive effect upon the Indians: It became the law of the Department of the Interior to the irreparable damage of the Northern Paiute Indians, constituting a barrier to the economic development of the vast potential of Pyramid Lake and the Truckee River for the benefit of the Indians. It was, indeed, the party line upon which the Washoe Reclamation Project was to proceed in the attempt, not yet consummated, to seize the last of the Indian Truckee River water.

Nine years after this Solicitor's opinion, in October 1964, the Secretary of the Interior approved and adopted a report entitled, "Action Program for Resource Development Truckee and Carson River Basins, California-Nevada." No effort was made to preserve Pyramid Lake. Rather the decline and ultimate destruction of the Lake by the Newlands Reclamation Project and the Washoe Reclamation Project was prognosticated. Recommendation No. VI of the Report did provide that Justice would be requested to seek an amendment to the *Orr Water Ditch* decree permitting the Indians to use the meager quantity of water allowed to them for irrigation—30,000 acre-feet annual maximum—for purposes of fishery.[160]

By a letter dated November 2, 1964, the Department of the Interior requested Justice to bring an action because "The Indians want to use part of their decreed water for reestablishing the fishery at Pyramid Lake." No effort was to be made to preserve the Lake, planned out of existence by the Bureau of Reclamation.

Legalisms, never researched, but only vaguely formulated among the Interior and Justice lawyers, caused the request of November 2, 1964, to amend the *Orr Water Ditch* decree, to languish and no action to this date has ever been taken in regard to it.

(q) *Successful demands to reconsider Interior's legal and policy decisions made by Bureau of Indian Affairs and by the Indians:*

Freeing the Indians from the restrictions imposed upon them entailed months of disengaging action. By 1966 the Bureau of Indian

---

[160] *Note:* The vast proportion of the decreed rights could never be used by the Indians for purposes of irrigation by reason of the Nation's failure to build a project which could use it, and the dilapidated condition of the small project now in existence.

510

Affairs and the Indians were able to demonstrate the needless disaster being imposed upon them through the planned destruction of Pyramid Lake.[161] In July 1966, the Commissioner of Indian Affairs withdrew the Bureau's approval of the October 1964 Action Program Report. The press came to recognize the plight of the Indians and the news media brought forcefully to the attention of the public the manner in which the great Indian and national asset was being destroyed. Ultimately the struggle to preserve the Lake with its vast potential was being recognized.

(r) *California-Nevada Compact—A grave peril to the Indians and to Pyramid Lake:*

In keeping with the concept of the Bureau of Reclamation and the Truckee-Carson Irrigation District that the Indian Truckee River rights to the use of water could be seized without compensation (destruction of the famous fishery, indeed, the destruction of Pyramid Lake itself with poverty-in-perpetuity for the Indians, would be countenanced without a struggle), the California-Nevada Compact purporting to divide between the States the waters of the Truckee, Carson and Walker Rivers was prepared. The Compact, so clearly violative of the Constitution of the United States, so flagrantly an invasion of the Nation's rights, powers and obligations to the Indians, was rejected out of hand by the Federal Government.[162]

A revised 1968 Compact was adopted by the California and Nevada Commissioners. It had all the objectionable features of the earlier compact with this addition: It set forth the "settlement" which the Interior-Justice-Upper Carson River water users had failed to consummate by reason of the intervention in the *Alpine Case* by the Northern Paiutes. Seldom has such power politics been used to strike down Indian claims. Failing to succeed when the Indians intervened in *Alpine*, the Nevada Compact Commissioners cooperated by writing the substance of the unconscionable "settlement" into a compact and received approval of it by the Nevada legislature. Again strenuous objection was interposed to the compact by the Federal Government and the Indians.[163]

Losing in their own State of Nevada in their struggle against the destruction of Pyramid Lake, the Northern Paiutes received gracious treatment by California's legislature. Secretary Hickel's letter of March 18, 1969, strongly opposed the Compact. The Indians and their lawyers were heard by the California representatives. On March 20, 1969, the Indians received a reprieve from destruction by the California-Nevada Compact—at least momentarily—by reason of an amendment California has proposed, exempting the Indian rights from the operation of the Compact.

(s) *Ambivalence within the Department of the Interior respecting Indians exemplified by Pyramid Lake struggle:*

Ambivalence is the hallmark of Interior in regard to its trust responsibility towards the American Indians. Practical politics—the

---

[161] Pyramid Lake in Nevada is not only a Home, Abiding Place and a Source of Livelihood for Northern Paiute Indians—it is a National Asset: of Great Scenic Beauty; with Vast Potential for Recreation; of Historic Import; of Scientific significance—It Must Be Preserved.
[162] See letter April 22, 1966, Assistant Secretary Anderson to Bureau of the Budget. Also Analysis of *California-Nevada Interstate Compact concerning waters of Lake Tahoe, Truckee River, Carson River and Walker River Basins* dated January 20, 1966.
[163] See letter January 14, 1969, Secretary of the Interior to Bureau of the Budget.

lifeblood of the Bureau of Reclamation—are daily confronted with good conscience and the need to fulfill the trust responsibility to the Indians. Erosion of Indian title to rights to the use of water is the consequence. Congressional enactments and reclamation project approval clash with obligations owed by Interior's Secretary to the Indians. Agonizing appraisals and reappraisals are made; reports are written and speeches given. Yet none of them produce sufficient water—indeed, any water—to provide for the Indians and the *plans* of Reclamation for its projects.

Life or death of Pyramid Lake is the perfect example of Interior's agonizing, for:

1. Destruction of Pyramid Lake is assured if the Washoe Reclamation Project is constructed. The United States cannot have Pyramid Lake and the Washoe Project; there is simply insufficient water in the Carson and Truckee Rivers for the Lake and the Project.

2. Destruction of Pyramid Lake is assured if the contract now approved by Interior is authorized by Congress, increasing the Newlands Reclamation Project from its historic average irrigated acreage of 51,000 acres to 74,500 acres, guaranteeing a firm supply of water to the Newlands Project of 406,000 acre-feet annually.

Interior proceeds with the construction of the Washoe Reclamation Project.

Papers are written in regard to Pyramid Lake and its vast potential for public benefit—witness the 1969 report of the Bureau of Outdoor Recreation alluded to above.

Promises are made of litigation to protect the Indian rights in the Truckee River and Pyramid Lake. Currently the Solicitor's Office refers to a letter to Justice requesting that court action.

Contracts are signed to assure 406,000 acre-feet of water annually to Newlands Reclamation Project and increased water right acreage to 74,500 acres.

The harsh fact is this: Reclamation obtains action—results of practical politics; the Indians receive words—results of good conscience being placated.

Water required for the Washoe Reclamation Project is to be obtained through prohibiting Newlands grossest waste, nevertheless gravely wasteful practices still continue on Newlands. When occasional momentarily available quantities of water enter Pyramid Lake, they are loudly trumpted as being evidence of Indian protection.

When Nature supplies a huge snow pack in the high Sierras—at widely spaced intervals over the years—and the existing Reclamation facilities cannot carry the volume of runoff, some of the water must enter Pyramid Lake. This is not looked upon by Reclamation as an Act of God, but a spiritual rapport between conflicting agencies. But this vanishes when another Act of God results in a light snow pack and short water supply; or more practically when Recalmation has completed Stampede Reservoir on the Tuckee; Watasheamu on the Carson.

(t) *Congress alone can preserve Pyramid Lake:*

This is not a new story in Indian history. It is no different today than when President Andrew Jackson nullified the Supreme Court's decision by simply refusing to permit its implementation by Executive action and a grave stain never to be removed, was indelibly written on a Nation's conscience.[164] Nor is it different than when Congress passed the Act of August 1, 1914, to restore *Winters Doctrine Rights* to the Yakima Indians who, Congress said, "have been unjustly deprived of the portion of the natural flow of the Yakima River to which they are equitably entitled."

What is being done to the Northern Paiutes today differs not at all from what Jackson did to the Cherokees; only the dates and the names are changed, with one exception—the Northern Paiutes have no place to go.

Congress can stop the inhumanity being perpetrated on the Northern Paiutes. It can:

1. Refuse to appropriate funds for the Washoe Reclamation project or vitiate Congressional approval of the project;

2. Refuse to appropriate funds to carry out the contracts which would enlarge the Newlands Reclamation Project beyond its historic irrigated acreage and limit the project to beneficial use of all waters diverted to it, thus striking down the firm supply of 406,000 acre-feet of water which the contracts in question would guarantee;

3. Refuse to approve the California-Nevada Compact if it fails to protect, preserve and guarantee the Indian Truckee River rights and their right to maintain Pyramid Lake as a permanent viable body of water.

4. Direct Justice to fulfill its responsibilities in regard to the protection of the rights of the Northern Paiutes in the Truckee River and Pyramid Lake, to desist from opposing the Indian efforts to protect themselves by intervening in the *Alpine Case*, but rather to assist them in it, and to have the principles of beneficial use of water enforced under the *Orr Water Ditch* decree on the Truckee River and the *March 1950 Decree* on the Carson River.

Finally, if Congress were to declare that Pyramid Lake should be preserved for the benefit of the Indians and the nation and that the fisheries destroyed by diversions to the Newlands Reclamation Project should be restored, a long step would be taken in correcting one phase of innumerable, sometimes ghastly, wrongs perpetrated on the Northern Paiutes.

III. POLICIES PAST, PRESENT AND FUTURE IN REGARD TO THE INDIAN RIGHTS TO THE USE OF WATER IN LOWER COLORADO RIVER VALLEY—A CRUCIBLE

Politics and water readily mix creating an unstable, volatile combination. Only the strong prevail when confronting the combination. That is, of course, the Indian problem in general, and most particularly in the Lower Colorado River Valley. Economic development of Indian lands has long been retarded by reason of politics in and out of the Interior Department.

(i) *Arizona v. California, United States, Intervener:*

Arizona had failed in the Supreme Court because in early cases the United States had been declared an indispensable party, which was immune from suit and had failed to evidence an inclination to become a party to a suit to have adjudicated the rights to the use of water

---

[164] Schmekebier, The Office of Indian Affairs, page 35.

of the Colorado River. That stream drains 244,000 square miles in seven States, with every square mile and drop of water an intemperate political issue.[165]

By the end of the 1940's and the early years of 1950, population pressures in the Southwest—particularly the California and Arizona area—forced the National Government to reconsider its historical reluctance to become a party to the gruelling struggle among the sister States of the Colorado River Basin. Conversations within Justice were undertaken and the matter fully reviewed with Interior. At the first meeting after it was agreed the suit would be initiated, this strong caveat was given: Play down the Indian rights! To that caveat the response was made that there probably would not be a justiciable issue in the case if the Indian rights were played down.

On November 2, 1953, the "Petition of Intervention on Behalf of the United States of America" was filed in *Arizona* v. *California*. Among other things, the petition alleged the United States of America was the trustee for the Indians and Indian Tribes and asserted

"that the rights to the use of water claimed on behalf of the Indians and Indian Tribes as set forth in this Petition are prior and superior to the rights to the use of water claimed by the parties to this cause in the Colorado River and its tributaries in the Lower Basin of that stream." [166]

Immediately an all-out attack was launched against the Attorney General. The powerful politicians and their political attorneys from the Lower Basin States would not tolerate the assertion that Indian claims were "prior and superior" to the claims of the States. Yet the petition with the required copies had been filed. No real problem, said the powerful ones—withdraw the petition, strike the offending passage pleaded on behalf of the Indians, and refile it. That was done. The truncated version reads as follows:

"XXVII

"The United States of America, as trustee for the Indians and Indian Tribes, claims in the aggregate on their behalf rights to the use of water from the Colorado River and its tributaries in the Lower Basin of that stream in the States of Arizona and California as set forth in Appendix IIA of this Petition." [167]

Thus the odd-looking page 23 of the present petition, with its wide spaces between the lines, is explained. It suffered from power failure by those inclined towards the Indians.

---

[165] *Arizona* v. *California*, 298 U.S. 558 (1936).

[166] Petition of Intervention, *Arizona* v. *California*, No. 10 Original, filed November 2, 1953, Paragraph XXVII, page 23.

[167] The two provisions are set forth here in full: From first Petition filed November 2, 1953:

"XXVII

"The United States of America, as trustee for the Indians and Indian Tribes, claims in the aggregate on their behalf rights to the use of water from the Colorado River and its tributaries in the Lower Basin of that stream in the States of Arizona and California as set forth in Appendix IIA of this Petition. The United States of America asserts that the rights to the use of water claimed on behalf of the Indians and Indian Tribes as set forth in this Petition are prior and superior to the rights to the use of water claimed by the parties to this cause in the Colorado River and its tributaries in the Lower Basin of that stream."

From Petition filed December 1953:

"XXVII

"The United States of America, as trustee for the Indians and Indian Tribes, claims in the aggregate on their behalf rights to the use of water from the Colorado River and its tributaries in the Lower Basin of that stream in the States of Arizona and California as set forth in Appendix IIA of this Petition."

The Supreme Court in *Arizona* v. *California*, applied the principles of *Winters, Conrad Investment Company, Walker River, Ahtanum*, declaring the basic concepts of those cases to be applicable to reserved lands of the United States. [168] However, there are aspects which require most careful consideration.

(ii) *State apportionment threat to economic development of the Indian Reservations under Arizona v. California:*

Politics smothered the rights of the Indians to assert their claims against the entire Colorado River System. Those rights are properly against the river—not political subdivisions, but the Upper Basin States (Wyoming, Colorado and Utah) where most of the water rises, had the political power to stay out of the case. As was pointed out in regard to the *Winters Doctrine Rights*, they are against the stream system:

"The suggestion that much of the water of the Ahtanum Creek originates off the reservation is likewise of no significance. The same thing was true of the Milk River in Montana; and it would be a novel rule of water law to limit either the riparian proprietor or the appropriator to waters which originated upon his lands or within the area of appropriation. Most streams in this portion of the country originate in the mountains and far from the lands to which their waters ultimately become appurtenant." [169]

In sharp contrast to the principles enunciated—invariably applied— the Supreme Court in *Arizona* v. *California*, drastically limited the Indian rights:

"* * * we note our agreement with the Master that all uses of mainstream water within a State are to be charged against that State's apportionment, which of course includes uses by the United States." [170]

As a consequence the Indians are at the mercy of the wheeling and dealing by the states as they attempt to obtain projects and water. A most ominous threat to the Colorado River Valley Indians is the fact that the Colorado River has been outrageously overappropriated. Where the water for the Central Arizona Project, in the light of guarantees to California, must come from should be clear warning to the Indians. The same powerful people who forced the Attorney General to change the Petition in *Arizona* v. *California* are exercising those powers—powers that can strip from the Indians the rights which originally were to be "played down." Economic development has thus been thwarted on all Indian Reservations in the Colorado River Valley.

(iii) *"Giveaway" of 1,500 acres of Mohave Indian land:*

Without notice to the Fort Mohave Tribe of Indians or to the Bureau of Indian Affairs, the Solicitor's Office conducted a proceeding initiated by California in the Bureau of Land Management. 1,500 acres of invaluable Indian land was awarded to California by a decision dated March 15, 1967, allegedly as coming within the Swamp

---

[168] See above, *Winters Doctrine*, footnote 22, et seq.
[169] *United States* v. *Ahtanum Irrigation District*, 236 F. 2d 321, 325.
[170] 373 U.S. 546, 601.

and Overflow Act. Only by chance when the matter was then on appeal did it come to the attention of the Bureau and the Indians.

Efforts by the Bureau of Indian Affairs to intervene were denied— the Solicitor, it was said, perhaps facetiously but none the less officially, was representing the Bureau, although the Bureau was given no notice or opportunity to be heard. Under most severe restrictions the Indians were allowed drastically limited intervention. An astounding fact was forcefully brought to the Indians' attention: The Solicitor's position was not the lawyer for the Trustee, the United States; rather he emphasized, he was Judge and in fact owed a trust obligation to California. Anomalous? Not at all; that's the law as enunciated by the Solicitor. The matter is now before the Secretary of the Interior for reconsideration. It is but a single example of outrageous conduct by conflicting agencies within the Interior Department, perpetrated against the Mohaves in regard to their lands which are inseparable from their rights to the use of water.

(iv) *Conflicts within Interior—Failure to protect and define boundaries, rights to the use of water:*

Grave damage to the economic development of the Colorado River Indian Reservation has occurred and is occurring, due to the failure of conflicting federal agencies to resolve basic differences. Lands have been separated from the Reservation and Indian occupancy lost for periods up to half a century.

A boundary dispute lasting virtually one hundred years, recently brought out an irrational opinion which declared: The boundary was the unknown high-water line in 1876, but for "administrative convenience" another line could be used. This opinion has created administrative and jurisdictional problems which cause economic chaos, not development. Moreover, even more damaging to the Indians is the loss of between 2,000 and 4,000 acres of invaluable lands and rights to the use of water in the Colorado River.

Loss of land and rights to the use of water on the Colorado River Indian Reservation reflect only part of the damage. In an area where recreation, year-round, is rapidly growing, the loss of access to the Colorado River has prejudiced and will continue to gravely prejudice economic development for these Indians.

(v) *Fort Yuma Indian Reservation:*

This tormented Indian Reservation has suffered more than most. In 1893 the Indians had an agreement imposed upon them by force. All facts point to fraud, diverse and general culpability on the part of officials of the national government. Those who refused to sign for the Indians were whipped into submission. Others, it is reported, were held in jail for months without charge.

Purportedly the Yumas—Quechans as they are known—were to retain some of their irrigable lands. Other lands were to be sold and payment made to the Indians. They were not sold. Title remains in the United States. Today the Bureau of Land Management is leasing land taken forceably from the Yumas. Those lands are being irrigated and rental for irrigated lands is collected by the last named Federal agency. The question is raised, How can these lands be declared non-irrigable—as they have been—when they are in fact irrigated?

Simple enough, the Bureau of Reclamation states they are non-irrigable! By that fiat the Indians are deprived of their lands and the economic development of the Reservation delivered a smashing blow.

IV. MISSOURI RIVER BASIN—A VAST AREA WHERE ECONOMIC DEVELOPMENT HAS BEEN DEFEATED BY FEDERAL AGENCIES, LAWS AND POLICIES

(i) *Seizure by the Bureau of Reclamation of Fort Peck Indian water supply:*

The Fort Peck Indians owned invaluable *Winters Doctrine Rights* in the Milk River. The Bureau of Reclamation built the Milk River Reclamation Project. It seized the Indian water without compensation and is using it on the Reclamation Project. As a consequence the economic development of the Fort Peck Indian Reservation was gravely retarded. Confronted with the Bureau of Reclamation, water was sought from another source and at great cost the Indian project was reconstructed.

(ii) *Seizure without right or compensation of Indian rights to the use of water at Yellowtail Dam on the Crow Indian Reservation and elsewhere in the Missouri River Basin:*

One of the most flagrant examples of the Bureau of Reclamation's disregard of Indian water rights will be found at Yellowtail Dam and Reservoir in Montana's Crow Indian Reservation. There the Bureau of Reclamation not only did not pay the Crows for their *Winters Doctrine Rights* in the Bighorn River, but is selling the Indian water, depositing the proceeds to a non-Indian account, and seeking to charge coal developers on the Reservation for Indian water, thus driving down the payment the Indians will receive for their coal.

Detailed reviews of the principles of the *Winters Doctrine Rights* have been made including the Crow Indian Yellowtail Dam matter.[171] Time and space do not permit a review of all damage done to Indian rights to the use of water throughout the Missouri River Basin, and its effect upon the economic development of the many Reservations in the Valley. That damage is high and is continuing.

V. CALIFORNIA'S INDIANS ROBBED OF THEIR RIGHTS TO THE USE OF WATER; FAILURE OF THE UNITED STATES TO FULFILL ITS OBLIGATIONS; GRAVE CONFLICTS WITHIN FEDERAL ESTABLISHMENT DEPRIVES CALIFORNIA'S INDIANS OF ADEQUATE REPRESENTATION

Failure of the United States to protect Indian rights to the use of water to which the California Indians are entitled has defeated all hope of economic development of some Reservations. Economic development—Indian or non-Indian—in Southern California is geared to the availability of water to a degree unsurpassed on this Continent. It explains the devastation brought to the Mission Indians—the La-Jollas, Rincons, Palas. Their rights have been seized without compensation. Their efforts to defend themselves have been defeated. Others, unless the seizure of these rights is prevented, will experience the same

---

[171] See memorandum dated October 13, 1965, entitled *Winters Doctrine Rights in the Missouri River Basin*. Also memorandum dated December 5, 1967, entitled *Analysis of Opinion November 16, 1967*, to the extent that it relates to the rights of the Crow Indians in the Bighorn River.

grave damage. So widespread, so all-encompassing is this failure of the Nation to fulfill its obligations to the Indians it is impossible to chronicle here the magnitude of the damage done to them, particularly those Indians in Southern California.

Shaken by this failure of the Nation to fulfill its obligations, the California Indian Legal Services has become actively engaged and is rendering legal assistance to the Indians. There are conflicts within the federal establishment which have caused it to fail these Indians in a most serious way. Recently a brief in opposition to the claims of certain of the Mission Indians and others demonstrates the impossibility of Justice Department to protect adequately Indian rights to the use of water. In that brief there is a failure fully to cite an authority repeatedly relied upon; fully to review the results of the litigation giving rise to the decision relied upon, or correctly to interpret the decision in its present status in view of decisions not cited by Justice.[172]

That effort to sustain a proposition which, if successful, would defeat a claim of the Indians for compensation is diametrically opposed to the position taken by Justice in support of Indian claims.[173] Indeed, the brief referred to above applies principles seeking to defeat the Indian claims, which have not been applied against non-Indians seeking restitution for the alleged taking of rights to the use of water.[174] This matter and related disparities in regard to conflicts within Justice and Interior is the subject of present intensive investigation. California's Indians are aroused over the loss of their rights due to the conflicts in question and are greatly in need of legal assistance if they are to avoid further seizure of their rights.

VI. Economic Development Gravely Retarded by Purported Seizure of Indian Land and Rights to the Use of Water on Other Indian Reservations

(i) Flathead Indian Reservation:

Magnitude of disasters inflicted upon the Salish and Kootenai Tribes by the opening of the Flathead Indian Reservation to non-Indians and later to other developments, has never been determined. That opening took place in the early 1900's. There has been a continuous disregard of the Indian rights, a claim by the Solicitor that all of those Flathead rights had been preempted by the United States for the largely non-Indian project, and a failure to take cognizance of priority accorded to Indian rights in the administration of the irrigation project.[175]

Every effort to institute an action to protect or have determined the rights of the Salish and Kootenai Tribes has been denied by the Solicitor's Office. A full investigation of the matter is now under way to

---

[172] See brief filed August 1968 before the Indian Claims Commission, Docket No. 80-A, Baron Long (El Capitan), Campo, Inaja, La Jolla, et al., v. United States of America, defendant; Defendants requested findings of fact, objections to petitioners' proposed findings of fact, and brief, pages 28, 29.

[173] This is not new—see memorandum dated June 19, 1956, captioned Water Rights on Indian Reservations (filed under Gila River Pima-Maricopa Indian Community, et al., v. United States, Docket No. 236, before Indian Claims Commission).

[174] In effect the brief before the Indian Claims Commission declares that the Indians are not entitled to compensation without a general adjudication. That position is, of course, wholly incorrect—see United States v. Gerlach Lire Stock Co., 339 U.S. 725 (1949).

[175] See memorandum prepared at request of Solicitor dated April 28, 1967, "Memorandum relative to the titles to rights to the use of water and the authority to control and administer them on the Flathead Indian Reservation."

the end that those rights will be inventoried and, it is hoped, in some manner protected against further encroachment by the non-Indians permitted to occupy the Fathead Indian Reservation.

(ii) *Gila River Indian Reservation—Pima Maricopa Community; economic development greatly impeded by attempted seizure of immemorial rights of Indians in the Gila River:*

The San Carlos Indian Irrigation Project was undertaken [176] purportedly for the benefit of the Pima Indians who had from time immemorial irrigated their lands. What occurred has been a violation of the nation's trust responsibility to the Indians—an attempted illegal seizure of most of the rights of the Indians. Moreover, the broad *Winters Doctrine Rights* for future development of the Indian Reservation have been systematically denied.

It is infrequent that a court decree—here with the consent of Justice and Interior—sets forth a violation of the Indians' *Winters Doctrine Rights*. [177] In the cited paragraphs of the decree and elsewhere in it the prior immemorial rights of the Indians are recognized and then are specifically subordinated to the junior rights.

This course of conduct, among others, in connection with the project in question reflects innumerable violations of the surface and ground water rights of the Indians. A full investigation must be undertaken in regard to this outrageous circumstance. It will reveal the extent of the damage to economic development that the Indians have experienced.

AN ATTEMPT TO RECTIFY ANCIENT WRONGS IN REGARD TO INDIAN LANDS AND RIGHTS TO THE USE OF WATER

The Commissioner of Indian Affairs has authorized and directed a program, strenuously prosecuted to recover for the Indians, lands and water rights of which they are wrongfully deprived. Progress is being made. Yet the lack of legal assistance or outright opposition within the government and without has created grave problems in connection with the program. Should that program be stopped or retarded, the economic development of the American Indian Reservations may very well be precluded for all time because of the rapidity with which their lands and rights to the use of water are being eroded away by the failure properly to protect them.

---

[176] See *A History of the Pima Indians and the San Carlos Irrigation Project,* Senate Document No. 11, 89th Congress, 1st Session.

[177] See Decree entered June 29, 1935, Globe Equity No. 59, *The United States of America* v. *Gila Valley Irrigation District,* et al.

THE HEIRSHIP LAND PROBLEM AND ITS EFFECT ON THE INDIAN, THE TRIBE, AND EFFECTIVE UTILIZATION

By Stephen A. Langone*

FOREWORD

Joint land ownership by multiple heirs of the original owner creates a serious administrative burden for the Bureau of Indian Affairs, which holds this land in trust for the Indian owners, and, more importantly, prevents efficient economic use of much of this land. Ownership of the heirship lands has by now become so fractionalized that few of the present owners receive any significant income or other benefit from their lands. A substantial amount of land is not put to any use whatsoever due to the difficulties created by multiple ownership. Stephen Langone describes the history of this Indian land problem, showing how the present complicated situation was allowed to develop. He points out that unless prompt action is taken, the situation will grow increasingly complicated as the number of heirs continues to multiply. He then suggests a number of steps which could be taken to simplify the problem and reduce it to more manageable proportions. Among Langone's recommendations are limitations on future inheritance rights, a program of land consolidation and exchange, and the granting of full title in fee simple to individual landowners where the owner is competent to manage his own affairs and where removal from trust status would not be detrimental to effective utilization of surrounding lands.

Introduction

The "heirship," or as it is sometimes called "fractionated" Indian land problem is basically that tracts of Indian land are owned by more than one individual and the Federal Government holds title in trust for them. While the land originally was in the name of one Indian, upon his death, and the death of subsequent heirs, the probate action has been taken by the Federal Government and the land divided—on paper—among succeeding heirs. The resulting group ownership of a tract of land, along with restrictive Federal regulations, has denied the owners any opportunity for maximum utilization of the land or of its money value. There has also been a direct effect on actual and potential tribal land consolidation programs and on the Federal Government in terms of ever-increasing administrative overhead. Since the land held in the name of individual Indians constitutes almost one quarter of the total Indian land base it is obviously a problem of serious consequences.

To discuss the problem in terms of the situation "today" is not possible statistically, due to the complexity of the situation, and lack of recent statistics. However, the nature of the problem is such that until a solution is found the situation will continue to become worse rather than better. So, the lack of current statistics to rely on is not a serious handicap since the problem is surely greater than it is

---

*Analyst, American Indian Affairs, Government and General Research Division, Legislative Reference Service, Library of Congress.

presented here. There are three major sources of information concerning the heirship problem that are available, though outdated, at this time. The three studies referred to are those by the Senate Interior and Insular Affairs Committee,[1] the House Interior and Insular Affairs Committee,[2] and a report by the Comptroller General.[3] Together the three represent the most comprehensive study of a specific Indian problem that has ever been undertaken. In this paper the author has leaned heavily on these studies for the background material presented.**

What does land mean today to the American Indian? Land is the Indian past, present, and future. Whatever economic opportunities lie in the future for the American Indian tribes will be directly related to their land base, and for many individual Indians their own future is in their land. For those Indians who have moved, or intend, or hope, to move away from the reservation into the general society— or "mainstream" as the popular term goes—their land represents money value that they cannot see or spend although it does belong to them.

What is Indian land to the Federal Government? To the Federal Government Indian land represents the areas where Indians reside; where the Government has jurisdiction over an ethnic group; where the administrative problems are all encompassing and time consuming, where the complexities have reached a stage of almost complete hopelessness. Indian land is where tribes that might be able to improve their economic future cannot do so due to a land shortage. The land is there but owned by individual tribal members. Individuals—if all their land interests were consolidated—might have a sufficient area for self-support or a homestead, but because they have divided interests in scattered tracts of land they may not even have a place to live or raise a subsistence crop. The State may refuse welfare aid to an Indian because he owns land, yet he cannot sell, lease, or live on it, due to the fractionated ownership and consent required from all other coowners.

Heirship land is, to the writer, a keystone in the field of Indian affairs, a keystone that binds together and continues other related Indian problems. Probably no other area of the relationship between the individual Indian and the Federal Government presents such a breeding ground for antagonism, discouragement, hopelessness, and general despair as evidenced by the heirs who expressed their opinions in answer to the questionnaire of the House Interior Committee. As a high Government official testified before a congressional committee[4] the problem "is capable of becoming a monster that will consume the usefulness of the land and, in the long run, deprive the Indian owner of productive real estate."

To state the problem, in its depth and diversity, is the purpose of this paper. The fact has been kept in mind that any analysis of the

---

** The author participated in both congressional studies.

[1] U.S. 86th Congress, second sess. Senate. Committee on Interior and Insular Affairs. *Indian Heirship Land Survey.* Committee print. Two parts. 1,183 pp. Dec. 1, 1960.
[2] U.S. 86th Congress, second sess. House. Committee on Interior and Insular Affairs. *Indian Heirship Land Study.* Committee print No. 27. 2 vols. (vol. 1, 555 pp.; vol. II, 1,010 pp.). Dec. 31, 1960.
[3] U.S. Comptroller General of the United States. Audit Report to the Congress of the United States. *Administration of Indian Lands by Bureau of Indian Affairs, Department of Interior.* January 1956. 53 pp.
[4] Commissioner of Indian Affairs Philleo Nash, testimony before the Senate Interior and Insular Affairs Committee on S. 2899 "A Bill Relating to the Indian Heirship Land Problem". 87th Congress, second sess. Hearings, part 2; April 2, 3, 1962. P. 207.

Indian heirship land program requires a constant awareness of the danger represented by getting too deeply involved in statistics. In this paper the author has attempted to skirt this pitfall, including only those statistics necessary to establish a general picture, and hitting the highlights as they have been established through the studies referred to.

THE GENERAL ALLOTMENT ACT[5]

Before getting into the legislative origins of heirship land it is useful to consider the historical attitude of the Indians toward real property as compared to the attitudes of the non-Indian. Within the Indian culture, land was owned by the tribe and held for the use of all tribal members as a group. This practice probably came about because most tribal cultures were primarily those of the hunter and one man could not go hungry waiting for a deer to set foot on his property. Although in some tribes there was a semblance of recognition—or we might say assignment—to individuals for a specific tract of land, the tribes usually held the land for common usage. On the other hand the non-Indian culture was one of the individual owning land marked by fences, walls, markers, and so forth, to show to all others that "this belongs to me." It might be said, however, that in both cultures land was and is the binding force within.

While the Indian and non-Indian cultures differed in their attitudes toward ownership of land by individuals there were certain areas of similarity in attitudes toward land in general. Both cultures were geared to the desire for more and more land and both cultures "took title by conquest." The history of both cultures is replete with battles over land with the vanquished moving away and the conquerors moving in. The legal title in many cases—throughout the history of both cultures—was the power to take and hold the land.

When the two cultures met, a process of treaty-making fortunately emerged that continued until the late 19th century. Usually such treaties, when referring to the remaining or new tracts of land given to the Indians, recognized title as resting in the tribe rather than the individual member. This approach came about through recognition of the Indian culture and attitudes toward land ownership along with the non-Indian's desire to obtain a "clear" title to protect him against claims of other non-Indians. There was also—as previously stated— the feeling that an Indian tribe was some sort of "sovereign body" (not clearly defined) and when two "sovereigns" negotiate for land title is not in the name of individuals.

One of the first departures from tribal title in a U.S. treaty was that with the Choctaw on November 16, 1805 (7 Stat.: 98). In article I there is a specific designation of land for two individuals with the Federal Government confirming title. In the year 1839 the Federal Government negotiated a treaty with the Brothertown Indians (5 Stat.: 349) in the Territory of Wisconsin and under the terms of that treaty the land was "partitioned and divided among the different individuals composing said tribe of Brothertown Indians, and may be held by them separately and severally in fee simple * * *". In this treaty, the word "allotted" was used for the first time, a word that in future years would signify a major change in U.S. Indian policy

---

[5] An excellent study entitled *History of the Allotment Policy* by D. S. Otis, appears in: *Readjustment of Indian Affairs.* Hearings before the Committee on Indian Affairs, House of Representatives, 73d Cong., second sess. on H.R. 7902. Pp. 428–489. LC E93 U66272.

and a major change for the Indian culture. The allotment policy would provide—near the end of the century—the general basis for the "heirship land problem."

During later years many treaties carried provisions for allotment of lands to individual Indians and it became more and more frequent to provide for division of tribal lands among the members of the tribe. The Commissioner of Indian Affairs' annual report for the year 1885 [6] contains a table of the allotment statistics up to September of that year. Included are over 12,000 allotments made through 88 separate treaties with Indian tribes. As allotment of land became more and more common, the stage was set for the General Allotment Act which would apply to all tribes.

The beginnings of consideration of a general allotment policy can be seen threading its way through various Government pronouncements years before the action was taken. In his report for 1870 Commissioner of Indian Affairs E. S. Parker, in referring to the Indians of Michigan, Wisconsin, Minnesota and Kansas stated: [7]

Another indication of progress in this direction is that many [Indians] are asking for the survey of their reservation, where it is held in common, and for allotments in severalty, of tracts of 80 or more acres to each, and in some cases the work of surveying is being effected with this object in view. The policy of giving to every Indian a home that he can call his own is a wise one, as it induces a strong incentive to him to labor and make every effort in his power to better his condition. By the adoption, generally, of this plan on the part of the Government, the Indians would be more rapidly advanced in civilization than they would if the policy of allowing them to hold their land in common were continued.

Again in 1871 [8] Commissioner Parker spoke of allotting lands to individual Indians and said:

The true policy of their preservation from utter extinction, before many years pass, it is generally admitted, is to prepare them as rapidly as possible to assume the relation of citizenship by granting them increased facilities for the education of the young; by habituating them to industrial pursuits, and by the incentive to labor incited by a sense of ownership in property, which an allotment of their lands in severalty would afford, and by the benign and elevating influences of Christian teachings.

A later Commissioner, Edward P. Smith, [9] came to the same general conclusion and pointed out that there were "certain difficulties which lie in the way of progress" for the Indian. In a discussion of the subject Commissioner Smith stated:

A fundamental difference between barbarians and a civilized people is the difference between a herd and an individual. All barbarous customs tend to destroy individuality. Where everything is held in common, thrift and enterprise have no stimulus of reward, and thus individual progress is rendered very improbable, if not impossible. The starting—point of individualism for an Indian is the personal possession of his portion of the reservation. Give him a house within a tract of land, whose corner—stakes are plainly recognized by himself and his neighbors

[6] U.S. Office of Indian Affairs. Annual Report of the Commissioner of Indian Affairs. 1885. Pp. 320–1. LC E93.U71.
[7] U.S. Bureau of Indian Affairs. Annual Report of the Commissioner of Indian Affairs. 1870. P. 9.
[8] U.S. Bureau of Indian Affairs. Annual Report of the Commissioner of Indian Affairs. 1871. P. 5.
[9] ——— 1873. P. 4.

and let whatever can be produced out of this landed estate be considered property in his own name, and the first principle of industry and thrift is recognized. In order to [sic] this first step, the survey and allotment in severalty of the lands belonging to the Indians must be provided for by congressional legislation.

The general idea of allotting tribal lands to individual Indians ran through the minds of Government officials and interested private parties even to the point of *forcing such allotment*, as indicated by Commissioner J. Q. Smith in 1876,[10] when he stated rather forcefully:

It is doubtful whether any high degree of civilization is possible without individual ownership of land. The records of the past and the experience of the present testify that the soil should be made secure to the individual by all the guarantees which law can devise, and that nothing less will induce men to put forth their best exertions. No general law exists which provides that Indians shall select allotments in severalty, and it seems to me a matter of great moment that provisions should be made not only permitting, but requiring, the head of each Indian family, to accept the allotment of a reasonable amount of land, to be the property of himself and his lawful heirs, in lieu of any interest in any common tribal possession. Such allotments should be inalienable for at least 20, perhaps 50 years, and if situated in a permanent Indian reservation, should be transferable only among Indians.

I am not unaware that this proposition will meet with strenuous opposition from the Indian themselves. Like the whites, they have ambitious men, who will resist to the utmost of their power any change tending to reduce the authority which they have acquired by personal effort or by inheritance; but it is essential that these men and their claims should be pushed aside and that each individual should feel that his home is his own; that he owes no allegiance to any great man or to any faction; that he has a direct personal interest in the soil on which he lives, and that that interest will be faithfully protected for him and for his children by the Government.

Congress was considering the transfer the of Bureau of Indian Affairs to the War Department—during the year 1879—and appointed a joint committee to survey the subject and make recommendations. In the final report of that committee [11] the recommendation was made that "The Indian should have his land allotted and the permanent title thereto given, with the precaution provided that he is not despoiled of his rights; and in addition to this, a law should be enacted which will virtually prevent the Indians from selling or disposing of their lands and houses to sharp and designing persons for not less than 25 years." This same idea was expressed that year by Secretary of the Interior Schurz [12] when he listed as one of the objectives of the Interior Department: "To allot parcels of land to Indians in severalty and to give them individual title to their farms in fee, inalienable for a certain period, thus to foster the pride of individual ownership of property instead of their former dependence upon the tribe, with its territory held in common."

---

[10] ———— 1876. P. IX.
[11] U.S. 45th Cong., third sess. H. Rept. No. 93. *Report of the Joint Committee Appointed to Consider the Expediency of Transferring the Indian Bureau to the War Department*, 1879, p. 18.
[12] U.S. Secretary of the Interior. Annual Report, 1879, p. 5. LC J 84 .A5.

From this stage on various bills were considered in the Congress. Suggestions for such a program came from different sources (both in and out of Government) and resulted in passage of the General Allotment Act of February 8, 1887 (24 Stat. 388). While there were differences of opinion at that time, as evidenced by the debates on the floor of Congress, the prevailing opinion was that by dividing up the tribal property and allotting parcels to individual Indians they would be on their way to becoming full-fledged members of this society.

A brief summary of the act [12a] follows:

Section 1 of the act authorized the President to allot tribal lands in designated quantities to reservation Indians. See 25 U.S.C. 331. Section 2 provided that the Indian allottee shall, so far as practical, make their selections of land so as to embrace improvements already made. 25 U.S.C. 332. Section 3 provided that allotments should be made by agents, regular or special. 25 U.S.C. 333. Section 4 allowed "any Indian not residing upon a reservation, or for whose tribe no reservation has been provided" to secure an allotment upon the public domain. 25 U.S.C. 334.

Section 5 sets forth a limitation on the alienability of land by preventing an Indian allottee from making a binding contract in respect to land which the United States holds for him as a trustee. It provided that title in trust to allotments should be held by the United States for twenty-five (25) years, or longer if the President deemed an extension desirable. During this trust period encumbrances or conveyances were to be void. In general, the laws of descent and partition in the State or Territory were to apply after patents had been executed and delivered. If any surplus lands remained after the allotments had been made, the Secretary was authorized to negotiate with the tribe for the purchase of such land by the United States, purchase money to be held in trust for the sole use of the Tribes to whom the reservation belonged but subject to appropriation by Congress for the education and civilization of such tribe or its members. This section also contained an important provision for the preference of Indians in employment in the Federal Government. 25 U.S.C. 348.

Section 6 of the act set forth the nonpecuniary benefits which the Indians were to receive in view of the distribution of tribal property and termination of tribal existence. 25 U.S.C. 349.

Section 7 of the legislation provided the basic law upon which water rights to allotments were measured. 25 U.S.C. 381.

The remainder of the act contained sections which exempted from the allotment legislation various tribes of the Indian Territory, the reservations of the Seneca Nation in New York, and an Executive order reservation in the State of Nebraska, and which authorized appropriations for surveys. In addition, the act contained various saving clauses for the maintenance of then existing congressional and administrative powers.

Nearly 5½ million acres of land were allotted in severalty by the turn of the century with the allotment program reaching its peak during the first decade of the 20th century. While decreasing in scope,

[12a] Library of Congress. Legislative Reference Service. American Law Division, *The General Allotment Act of 1887 and the Potential of Current Application*, June 21, 1966.

the allotment program was carried on until 1934 when the enactment of the Indian Reorganization Act (48 Stat: 984), in effect, put a stop to the allotment process. Through the period of allotment there had been a total of 246,569 made accounting for 40,848,172 acres. Although originally the Allotment Act provided for title to be held in trust for a period of 25 years there were extensions made from time to time continuing the trust period for millions of acres.

This is the general background of the Government policy to allot parcels of land to individual Indians with the idea in mind that the road to "civilization" for the Indian led through private rather than communal ownership of land. With such good intentions why are we now faced with such a problem as that of heirship land?

Since the General Allotment Act provided that title would be held in trust by the Federal Government for 25 years—and this period was continued by congressional and presidential action—the death of an Indian owning such a tract required that, as his estate, it be divided among his heirs. Obviously, since the title was held in trust—and the heirs were considered "incompetent" to handle their own affairs—there could be no physical partition but only a division of interests on paper. For the non-Indian the same situation would be met by sale of the land and a division of the proceeds or by physically dividing the land among the heirs, each parcel thereafter being a separate estate. But the Federal Government, in attempting to protect the Indian, brought about the Indian heirship land problem we are facing today. Through the 80-odd years since the General Allotment Act the same tract of land may have been divided several times—on paper—and the number of heirs to one tract of land, in many cases, exceeds 100. Consider also that when an Indian husband died the wife may have inherited part or all of his interests in addition to those of her mother and father, etc. On her death these "parts of parts" were further divided among her heirs with tremendous complication resulting in heirs owning many small interests in many scattered tracts of land. The problem has snowballed to the extent that it is overwhelming in its complexity today.

The Emergence of Heirship Land as a Problem

While there has been much written about the heirship problem and fractionated land, few accurate historical statistics are available. The problem itself was emphasized in 1935 by the National Resources Board [13] in a report that stated:

A very large area of land now in Indian possession is practically sterilized by the complexities of title and ownership arising out of the inheritance process. Some 6 million acres are now comprised in inherited Indian estates, and a large portion of this area produces neither crops nor income for the Indian heirs. . . . Since the partitioning of relatively small parcels of land among numerous heirs and title to fractions of various sizes proved impracticable, and since the sale of these parcels to white bidders has ceased, leasing of the inherited lands became the practical necessity * * *. These leasing operations were enlarged, with in-

---

[13] U.S. National Resources Board, Land Planning Committee, *Indian Land Tenure, Economic Status and Population Trends*, pt. X of the Supplementary Report of the Land Planning Committee to the National Resources Board, 1935, p. 3. LC HD 183 .N3 .A5.

creasing complications, as larger areas of allotted land passed into the heirship status. As a result of these conditions, the Office of Indian Affairs has for 30 years been doing an enormous real estate business, selling and leasing the lands of its wards— *with the income from the operations constantly decreasing while the cost of the real estate transactions multiplied. [italic ours].*

The situation as seen at that time was of such extensive proportions that the general feeling was that action was long overdue. This was the condition in existence approximately 24 years ago.

Three years later, the Bureau of Indian Affairs held a conference on Indian land problems at Glacier Park, Mont.[14] Participants at the conference included John Collier, Commissioner of Indian Affairs, William Zimmerman, Jr., Assistant Commissioner, Felix Cohen, Assistant Solicitor of the Interior Department, and other high-level staff. In addition, the Attorney General sent one of his special assistants and the Department of Agriculture sent a representative. During this conference the heirship land problem was a primary consideration. Commissioner Collier, in his opening statement, referred to the beginnings of the problem—the General Allotment Act—and pointed out that at that time in our history "one finds, as he reads the literature and the annual reports of the seventies and eighties and the debates in Congress, substantially no contradiction of the doctrine that individual ownership in fee simple was the inevitable and only way." Commissioner Collier went on to point out just how serious a problem heirship land had become by citing specific facts, as follows:

Sixty percent of the Agency [Sisseton] costs, or $30,000 a year goes to allotted land business, chiefly heirship. To keep the work reasonably current, overtime, year in and year out, is required, and vacations are rarely allowed.

However, the picture is much more than this. The 40 percent of the Agency business *not* put on allotment adjustments is constructive effort defeated by the land situation.

Due to this situation, the Indians have become just a band of wandering and bewildered gypsies.

There is not a single factor at this Agency that is peculiar to it. We only represent a somewhat advanced point in the operation of money waste, administrative defeat, defeat of professional ambitions, demoralization of the Indians, and creeping paralysis of the whole system of Indian affairs.

Commissioner Collier also pointed out that "Before this administration, the hopelessness of the situation had been faced," and that his administration took over with the intention to give an allottee the choice of taking the land in fee or exchanging it for some equivalent value from the tribe. However, the idea "was completely destroyed by opposition that arose at once. Allotted Indians did not want it; to them it meant confiscation." Since that time, according to the Commissioner, "We have simply gone on and on, wondering from time to time what to do."

During the course of the conference many suggestions were made and discussions held concerning various actions that could be taken to solve the problem. The general feeling seemed to be that of all

---

[14] *Resume of Proceedings; Conference on Indian Allotted and Heirship-Land Problem.* Aug. 14–17, 1938. Glacier Park, Mont., 57 p. Unpublished. In: Department of Interior Central Library files. File No. 38496.

Indian problems this one had such serious effect on the entire Indian program, and was increasing at such a rapid rate, that immediate action was necessary. Some of the suggestions made included: (1) Using the 1910 act that empowers the Secretary of the Interior to sell heirship lands which cannot be divided into economic units to "bring into line the unwilling minority, or those whose whereabouts are unknown," and transfer the land to the tribe for consolidation purposes under a deferred payment plan; (2) using the 1910 law to sell economically unfeasible units to Indians or Indian groups; (3) having the Indian heirs carry on their own administrative work concerned with leasing, and so forth, of fractionated land; (4) purchasing through the Government single ownership lands before they become fractionated; (5) applying a one-half or one-quarter Indian blood rule for inheritance purposes; (6) purchasing fractionated or single owner tracts with tribal moneys; (7) buying heirship lands with the downpayment being made with Federal funds and the balance paid from income; and (8) converting fractionated interests to an appropriate number of shares in a corporation which would handle leasing of the land.

One of the recommendations respecting Indian land policy was that "Indian land policy shall seek the most rapid possible reduction of uneconomic and nonproductive administrative expenditures, particularly in connection with the management of heirship lands." During the conference a committee had been instructed to consider changes in Indian probate procedures. The committee report points out that:

Under existing law it is the duty of the Secretary of the Interior to determine the heirs of deceased Indians in accordance with the laws of succession of the respective States in which the lands are situated. Under this situation the allotted lands are fast passing into undivided fractional interests so small as to deprive them of all economic value, to the detriment of the Indian and the added and useless expense of management and administration by the Government. Your committee therefore presents the following suggestions and recommendations, to be made effective either by legislation or modification of existing regulations as may be determined feasible.

The recommendations made were (1) alienation would be restricted to the heirs at law or to a person who is a member of the tribe having jurisdiction over the land, or to a tribe; (2) heirs would be limited to lineal descendants, collateral heirs being excluded, with the land reverting to the tribe should there be no heirs; (3) a devise would be limited to an heir (as defined in the second recommendation) or to a member of the tribe, but no devise should be approved unless the land is an economic unit; (4) limit the inheritance rights of nonmember surviving spouse to a life use of a designated interest to be terminated upon remarriage; (5) surviving spouse would hold a life interest terminating on remarriage; (6) limit the right of inheritance when the individual already has an economic unit; (7) limit the right of inheritance when it would comprise less than an economic unit; and (8) limit inheritance to persons of one-half or more Indian blood.

The recommendations were considered by the full group and were acted on as follows: 1, 3, 4, 5, and 7 were agreed to. No. 2 was "agreed upon in principle." On No. 6, "It was agreed that this item should be given further consideration." No. 8 was "not approved."

Another recommendation, respecting Indian land policy, was agreed to as follows: "Indian land policy shall seek the most rapid possible reduction of uneconomic and nonproductive administrative expenditures, particularly in connection with the management of heirship lands." In his concluding statement Commissioner Collier pointed out that "we have been attacking here that part of the Indian problem which is the most fatally important part, and which has been regarded heretofore as hopeless. If we can get anywhere at all on it, we shall have made an advance." However the specific recommendations on inheritance were not put into effect and the problem continued.

In 1956 the Comptroller General issued an audit report [15] to the Congress concerning the administration of Indian lands by the Bureau of Indian Affairs. A section of that report was devoted to the difficulties experienced by the Indians and the Federal Government as a result of fractionated landownership. The comptroller emphasized the difference in settling fractionated landownership by Indians, as compared to non-Indians:

> Although there appears to be no clear authority in Federal statutes for the sale or partition of undivided owners, the right of any owner of an undivided interest in land to force a partition or sale of land not under Federal jurisdiction is well settled by the courts. In this connection, section 27 of the title, "Partition," volume 40 of the American Jurisprudence, states that "whenever persons interested in land as owners and cotenants cannot, by consent and agreement among themselves, a division thereof, that is, have a voluntary partition by judicial proceedings—a compulsory partition—which takes place without regard to the wishes of one or more of the owners." Section 83 of the same title states that "the manifest hardship arising from the division of property of an impartable nature has been almost universally avoided by statutory provisions which give to a person entitled to partition the right to have the premises sold, if they are so situated that partition cannot be made. . . .

Some of the factors pointed out as creating the continuing complication of the heirship problem were that Indian heirs usually do not have cash or credit to settle estates when they cannot be physically partitioned; the responsibility and cost of administration of their land is handled by the Federal Government so there is no incentive for the heir to take any action to simplify the problem; and that Indian family relations are more complicated than those of non-Indians although in some States marriage and divorce follow State law.

ACREAGES INVOLVED

Prior to writing this paper the Bureau of Indian Affairs was contacted to determine if there were, at this time, up-to-date statistics on heirship lands. It seems, however, that the most accurate and comprehensive information available is still the analysis and report made by the Senate Interior Committee in 1960.

The only additional information available that would be of any value to this paper were the following:

Comparison of gain of loss—Tribal and Individually Owned Lands,[16] (*compared to the figures of 1967*)

Tribal	39, 585, 518. 37+153, 625. 23
Individual	10, 893, 635. 19−125, 579. 57

---

[15] See footnote 3.
[16] Department of the Interior. Bureau of Indian Affairs, dated Feb. 27, 1969.

The following statistical breakdown of ownership statistics is dated September 27, 1965, and included only to indicate the multiplication of the problem. These figures are for 52 reservations and the memo[17] pointed out that:

It is interesting to note that the number of single ownerships in the 1952 report is $52\frac{1}{2}$ percent of the total, while the attached figures are now down to $39\frac{3}{4}$ percent. Further the percentages for the 2–5 owner group of tracts has increased from 27 percent to 31 percent, and the balance, (being those tracts with 6 or more owners) has increased from $20\frac{1}{2}$ percent to $29\frac{1}{4}$ percent.

Area	Number of reservations	Total tracts	Single owner	2 to 5 owners	6 to 10 owners	11 or more owners
Gallup	2	346	244	30	31	41
California	4	342	256	70	11	5
Anadarko	2	3,443	1,321	1,044	457	621
Aberdeen	3	11,043	4,753	2,862	1,338	2,090
Portland	28	18,162	7,255	4,958	2,467	3,482
Phoenix	2	5,835	2,030	1,683	936	1,186
Billings	11	22,607	8,580	8,530	2,256	3,241
Total	52	61,778	24,439	19,177	7,496	10,666

While the statistics in the Senate report are admittedly 10 years old they still reflect the extent of the problem since Indian land has—in the ensuing years—moved into and out of heirship status. During the period studied by the committee there were 6,466,548 acres of land in heirship and 6,449,327 acres still in single ownership.

From the beginning of allotment through the year 1959 there had been a total of 241,972 allotments made covering a total acreage of 23,951,550. Of this number, 76,721 allotments representing a total of 12,915,875 acres remained in individual ownership. The Bureau of Indian Affairs has administrative subdivisions in the field called area offices, with specific geographic responsibilities. The following table presents the overall picture with a breakdown by area office.

*TABLE 3.—INDIVIDUAL ALLOTMENTS (BY NUMBER AND ACREAGE) STILL IN TRUST STATUS, TOTAL, ALL AREAS

Area Office	All allotments [1]		Allotments in heirship status	
	Number	Acreage	Number	Acreage
Aberdeen	22,128	4,405,020	11,898	2,457,376
Anadarko	7,951	972,388	3,963	432,335
Billings	14,567	3,921,604	6,860	1,699,903
Gallup	5,033	791,693	2,143	340,380
Minneapolis	2,573	169,816	1,855	130,784
Muskegee	259	855,712	[2] 192	337,236
Phoenix	9,849	326,384	5,803	222,115
Portland	12,444	1,409,549	7,085	809,641
Sacramento	1,917	63,709	988	36,778
Total	76,721	12,915,875	40,787	[3] 6,466,548

[1] Now in trust.
[2] Five Civilized Tribes is not included under "number" but is under "acreage." See table on p. 863 for explanation.
[3] See table on p. 866 for a more firm figure.
*The tables in this report, unless otherwise noted, are taken from the Senate Interior and Insular Affairs Committee study, Indian Heirship Land Survey of the 86th Cong., 1st sess.

[17] Department of the Interior. Bureau of Indian Affairs. Memo to Chief Title Examiner, Land Records Improvement Program on Ownership Statistics, dated Sept. 27, 1965.

It must be kept in mind that although these statistics were collected directly from the Indian agencies involved they can only be considered as "fairly accurate" since, for example, many of the subtotals add up to less than the totals provided by the same agency and in one case the officer in charge reported that he did not know how many acres were in allotted status.

To place these statistics into a more understandable form, insofar as specific reservations are concerned, and to show how general and widespread a problem this is, the following compilation indicated the heirship problem in relation to the specific reservations involved.

INDIAN HEIRSHIP LAND SURVEY

TABLE 7.—*Total acreage of Indian land in "heirship status," total, all areas*

Area office	Acreage
Aberdeen	2, 286, 736
Anadarko	432, 335
Billings	1, 688, 902
Gallup	309, 236
Minneapolis	130, 784
Muskogee	329, 148
Phoenix	222, 115
Portland	786, 719
Sacramento	36, 779
Total	6, 222, 754

TABLE 8.—*Total acreage of Indian land in "heirship status," by areas*

Agency	Acreage in heirship status
Aberdeen area:	
Cheyenne River	96, 160
Fort Berthold	187, 423
Pierre	101, 157
Pine Ridge	[1] 849, 714
Rosebud	405, 607
Sisseton	91, 025
Standing Rock	449, 480
Turtle Mountain	53, 015
Winnebago	[2] 53, 155
Total	2, 286, 736
Anadarko area:	
Cheyenne-Arapaho	84, 943
Kiowa	193, 090
Osage	44, 852
Pawnee	52, 686
Potawatomi	18, 711
Shawnee	38, 053
Total	432, 335

[1] Total acreage in heirship status at Pine Ridge agency was given as 1,020,314. However, by adding that acreage owned by two to five heirs with the acreage owned by six or more, the total arrived at was 849,714, a difference of 170,600. Further study established that 170,600 acres of Indian land is owned by individual Indians (other than original allottee) and therefore should not have been included.

[2] Total acreage in heirship status at Winnebago agency was given as 52,835. However by adding acreage owned by two to five heirs with the acreage owned by six or more, the total arrived at was 53,155. No explanation was found for this and the 53,155 figure seemed more firm so it is used in this tabulation.

TABLE S.—*Total acreage of Indian land in "heirship status," by areas—Continued*

Agency	Acreage in heirship status
Billings area:	
Blackfeet	449, 364
Crow	[3] 546, 667
Flathead	[4] 36, 473
Fort Belknap	148, 864
Fort Peck	295, 902
Northern Cheyenne	120, 624
Wind River	91, 008
Total	1, 688, 902
Gallup area:	
Consolidated Ute	7, 920
Jicarilla	322
Navajo	[5] 276, 080
United Pueblo	11, 174
Zuni	13, 740
Total	309, 236
Minneapolis area:	
Great Lakes	80, 148
Minnesota	50, 636
Total	130, 784
Muskogee area:	
Five Civilized Tribes	[6] 318, 000
Quapaw	[7] 11, 148
Total	320, 148
Phoenix area:	
Colorado River	8, 717
Nevada	64, 148
Papago	33, 116
Pima	69, 969
San Carlos	960
Umtah and Ouray	45, 205
Total	222, 115

[3] Total acreage in heirship status at Crow agency was given as 554,667. However by adding that acreage owned by two to five heirs to that owned by six or more, the total arrived at was 546,667, a difference of 8,000 acres. No explanation was found for this and the 546,667 figure seemed more solid so it is used in this tabulation.

[4] Total acreage in heirship status at Flathead agency was given as 39,474. However by adding that acreage owned by two to five heirs to that owned by six or more, the total arrived at was 36,473, a difference of 3,001 sites. No explanation was found for this and the 36,473 figure seemed more solid so it is used in this tabulation.

[5] Total acreage in heirship status at Navajo agency was given as 307,224. However by adding that acreage owned by two to five heirs to that owned by six or more, the total arrived at was 276,080, a difference of 31,144 acres. A check of the return reveals that the 31,144 acres in question are owned by individual Indians (not original allottees) and therefore should not have been included.

[6] The report from the Five Civilized Tribes Agency states that the total acreage in heirship land is "unknown" and no estimate is given. However, a report from the same agency to this committee in 1958 printed in " Land Transactions,"(p. 482) gives 318,000 acres as being in heirship status at that time. Since an entry for this agency would throw off the statistics completely, we are using the 1958 figure which should (bring us closer to an accurate total.

[7] Refers only to Quapaw Tribe.

TABLE S.—*Total acreage of Indian land in "heirship status," by areas—Continued*

Agency	Acreage in heirship status
Portland area:	
Colville	143, 155
Fort Hall	157, 047
Northern Idaho	91, 572
Warm Springs	[8] 70, 643
Western Washington	[9] 118, 462
Yakima	205, 840
Total	786, 719
Sacramento area:	
California	20, 456
Hoopa	10, 204
Riverside	6, 119
Total	36, 779

[8] In the return from Warm Springs, 5-percent estimates were given in answer to the question dividing ownership of heirship land into two categories (two to five owners and six or more), therefore they could not be checked against this figure.

[9] Total acreage in heirship status of Western Washington Agency was given as 93,565. However, by adding that acreage owned by two to five heirs to that owned by six or more, the total arrived at was only 70,643, a difference of 22,922 acres. No explanation was found for this and the 70,643 figure seemed more solid, so it is used in this tabulation.

CLASSIFICATION, VALUE, USE, AND NONUSE OF HEIRSHIP LANDS

Is the Federal Government simply acting as a land corporation, and handling the management of Indian lands by leasing to non-Indians? An understanding of the type of land—irrigated, dry farm, grazing, forest, its value, and the extent of use by Indians and non-Indians, is necessary to an overall understanding of the problem. This type of information was obtained directly from the reservation superintendents and compiled on a total basis for all returns.

TABLE 12.—INDIAN HEIRSHIP LAND, TOTAL, ALL AREAS (BY USE CLASSIFICATION AND VALUE)

Classification	Used by Indians (acres)	Used by non-Indians (acres)	Not used (acres)	Total [1] (acres)	Value per acre	Total value
Irrigated	34, 157	107, 512	69, 675	211, 344	$220.62	$34, 658, 988. 04
Dry farm	79, 187	725, 044	60, 208	869, 037	119. 58	46, 271, 605. 00
Grazing	1, 688, 461	2, 548, 385	150, 245	4, 381, 109	20. 47	74, 235, 081. 94
Forest	210, 922	111, 067	127, 871	405, 312	42. 48	20, 261, 626. 27
Other	40, 994	137, 844	133, 306	309, 225	587. 66	3, 955, 332. 02
Total	2, 053, 721	3, 629, 852	541, 305	6, 176, 027	198. 16	179, 382, 636. 00

[1] This total does not agree necessarily with a total for the 1st 3 columns. In some agencies this was brought to our attention when they explained that some tracts are partly one type of land and partly another, e.g., forestry and grazing.

TABLE 13.—INDIAN HEIRSHIP LAND, BY AREA (BY USE CLASSIFICATION AND VALUE)

ABERDEEN AREA OFFICE

Classification	Used by Indians (acres)	Used by non-Indians (acres)	Not used (acres)	Total (acres)	Average value per acre [1]	Total estimated value
Irrigated	None	None	None	None	None	None
Dry farm	19, 244	282, 432	9, 710	311, 389	$15. 63	$17, 696, 618. 96
Grazing	741, 942	1, 571, 007	20, 135	2, 332, 095	20. 07	43, 160, 772. 31
Forest	182, 244	640	14, 430	197, 314	18. 33	[2] 4, 783, 093. 24
Other	36, 513	4, 028	15, 465	56, 066	([3 4])	([5])
Total	979, 943	1, 858, 107	59, 740	2, 896, 894		65, 640, 484. 51

See footnotes at end of table, p. 534.

TABLE 13.—INDIAN HEIRSHIP LAND, BY AREA (BY USE CLASSIFICATION AND VALUE)—Continued

ANADARKO AREA OFFICE

Classification	Used by Indians (acres)	Used by non-Indians (acres)	Not used (acres)	Total (acres)	Average value per acre [1]	Total estimated value
Irrigated	125	1,220	None	1,345	[6] $262.00	$150,650.00
Dry farm	17,450	214,617	9,582	241,241	99.84	[7] 2,000,652.38
Grazing	15,202	187,824	2,214	205,244	38.48	7,625,725.54
Forest	None	None	None	None	None	None
Other	None	2	None	2	None	None
Total	32,777	403,661	11,796	447,830	-----------	9,777,027.92

BILLINGS AREA OFFICE

Classification	Used by Indians (acres)	Used by non-Indians (acres)	Not used (acres)	Total (acres)	Average value per acre [1]	Total estimated value
Irrigated	12,900	27,702	12,950	53,730	$68.14	[3] $3,805,890.50
Dry farm	20,190	108,781	35,938	169,918	42.50	[9] 8,080,927.00
Grazing	355,829	500,085	89,132	938,047	12.60	[10] 11,632,481.00
Forest	None	320	None	329	([5] [11])	([5])
Other	None	970	746	970	([5] [11])	([5])
Total	387,018	637,957	138,766	1,162,904	-----------	23,490,298.50

GALLUP AREA OFFICE

Classification	Used by Indians (acres)	Used by non-Indians (acres)	Not used (acres)	Total (acres)	Average value per acre [1]	Total estimated value
Irrigated	1,793	360	400	2,553	$80.00	$204,240.00
Dry farm	400	-----------	40	440	10.16	[13] 5,125.00
Grazing	327,646	-----------	1,344	328,900	3.82	[14] 1,163,248.50
Forest	8,265	29	-----------	8,394	23.00	[12] 185,365.00
Other	-----------	112.788	-----------	112,788	None	[16] None
Total	338,204	113,177	1,784	453,165	-----------	1,557,968.50

MINNEAPOLIS AREA OFFICE

Classification	Used by Indians (acres)	Used by non-Indians (acres)	Not used (acres)	Total (acres)	Average value per acre [1]	Total estimated value
Irrigated				None	-----------	
Dry farm	130	450	325	905	$200.00	[17] $181,000
Grazing						
Forest	160	1,600	100,943	[18] 102,893	[19] 2.50	257,232
Other	3,052	84	2,150	5,286	([5] [20])	-----------
Total	3,342	2,050	103,418	109,084	-----------	438,232

MUSKOGEE AREA OFFICE [1] [21]

Classification	Used by Indians (acres)	Used by non-Indians (acres)	Not used (acres)	Total (acres)	Average value per acre [1]	Total estimated value
Irrigated						
Dry farm	1,396	4,993	-----------	6,389	$27.00	$199,145.00
Grazing	1,310	3,526	-----------	4,837	11.20	66,785.00
Forest				None	-----------	
Other			158	158	[22] 5.00	790.00
Total	2,706	8,519	158	11,384	-----------	266,720.00

PHOENIX AREA OFFICE

Classification	Used by Indians (acres)	Used by non-Indians (acres)	Not used (acres)	Total (acres)	Average value per acre [1]	Total estimated value
Irrigated	12,888	24,578	43,510	80,978	$225.00	[23] $13,124,300.00
Dry farm		151	-----------	151	None	([24])
Grazing	48,620	51,893	5,721	106,234	30.33	[25] 6,291,786.00
Forest				None	-----------	
Other	-----------	6,935	-----------	6,935	250.00	[26] 1,733,700.00
Total	61,508	83,557	49,231	104,298	-----------	21,149,800.00

PORTLAND AREA OFFICE

Classification	Used by Indians (acres)	Used by non-Indians (acres)	Not used (acres)	Total (acres)	Average value per acre [1]	Total estimated value
Irrigated	6,281	53,542	12,685	72,508	$188.62	[27] $17,258,857.00
Dry farm	20,368	113,034	3,614	137,020	83.58	[28] 17,724,337.00
Grazing	199,164	224,505	17,865	441,534	8.85	[29] 3,859,040.25
Forest	20,153	108,469	12,493	96,382	126.12	[30] 15,035,256.00
Other	136	12,689	112,641	126,166	458.00	[31] 229,150.00
Total	246,102	512,239	159,303	873,010	-----------	54,107,330.75

See footnotes at end of table, p. 534.

TABLE 13.—INDIAN HEIRSHIP LAND, BY AREA (BY USE CLASSIFICATION AND VALUE)—Continued

SACRAMENTO AREA OFFICE

Classification	Used by Indians (acres)	Used by non-Indians (acres)	Not used (acres)	Total (acres)	Average value per acre [1]	Total estimated value
Irrigated	80	20	130	230	$500.00	$115,000.00
Dry farm		586	999	1,584	242.00	403,800.00
Grazing	748	9,545	13,834	24,128	20.40	435,213.04
Forest				None		
Other	1,293	358	2,146	924	1,055.00	1,725,712.00
Total	2,121	10,509	17,109	26,866		1,679,755.00

[1] This is an average of values for the entire area and no weight has been given to the number of acres valued at each figure. The total value column however represents acres at each agency multiplied times value for those specific acres. Where the returns did not state a value, the average for the area was used.

[2] At Turtle Mountain Agency there were 8,028 acres of forest land listed but no value per acre was given. The average value figure ($18.33) was, therefore, used to compute total value for that agency of forest land.

[3] "Other" land includes wastelands, coulees, etc., and, therefore, a value per acre is difficult to set.

[4] Not applicable.

[5] Unknown.

[6] Kiowa area field office divided irrigated land into 2 categories, bottom land and upland. Bottom land value was given as between $300 and $400 while upland value was given as between $120 and $200. In addition, the only other agency in the area reporting irrigated land (Cheyenne and Arapahoe) answered the question concerning value by entering "none." We have split the difference between the low and high figures given at Kiowa and consequently used $262 as an average value.

[7] At Kiowa area field office dry farm is divided into upland and bottom land and categories with ranges from $50 to $130 for upland and $150 to $250 for bottom land. We have used $145 as an average to compute the value.

[8] Flathead Agency reported a range of $75 to $100 and Fort Belknap $35 to $70. For Flathead a figure of $87 was used and for Fort Belknap $52.50 was used.

[9] Flathead Agency reported a range of $25 to $40 and Fort Belknap $35 to $40. For Flathead $32.50 was used and for Fort Belknap $37.50 was used.

[10] Crow reported a $12 to $25 range, Flathead $12.50 to $15, Fort Belknap $6 to $10. For Crow $18.50 was used, for Flathead $13.75 and for Fort Belknap $8.

[11] This land is on Crow Agency but instead of giving a value per acre the return simply stated "timber only, $10 per thousand board feet measure".

[12] This land includes roadways, ditches, homesites, etc., and no value per acre is given.

[13] Zuni dry farm land ranged from $7 to $10 per acre, we therefore used the figure of $8.50.

[14] Consolidated Ute was valued from $1 to $5, Navajo from $3 to $4, Zuni from $3 to $5 and Ramah Navajo from $3 to $4. We have used $2 for Consolidated Ute (based on the number of acres valued at $1 and the number valued at $5), $3.50 for Navajo, $4 for Zuni and $3.50 for Ramah Navajo.

[15] Navajo forest land was valued at from $10 to $50 per acre, we used $30 as a median.

[16] No value was given for this land (it was all at Navajo) but the return stated it was under oil and gas lease.

[17] Minnesota Agency did not state a value per acre for dry farm land so the Great Lakes value ($200) was used.

[18] There is 200 acres difference between the total acres and the acres by category for Great Lakes Agency.

[19] No figure was given for Great Lakes Agency and the Minnesota Agency listed $2.50 plus timber. Therefore the $2.50 figure was used for both with the understanding it did not include timber.

[20] This land is recreational, lake frontage and homesites. Great Lakes return stated the lake frontage value was $4 a foot but this could not be used to estimate total value.

[21] The Five Civilized Tribes Agency return did not list the total acreage in heirship status or the value. There are somewhere in the neighborhood of 318,000 acres of heirship land in that jurisdiction that are not included in this list.

[22] This is described as rocky, hilly, etc.

[23] Fallon and Walker River Reservations did not list an acreage value so the average was used.

[24] No value was listed for dry farm.

[25] Carson City and Pima did not estimate value of grazing land so the average value was used.

[26] This land was described as "nonproject irrigated."

[27] Fort Hall value ranged from $125 to $300 ($212.00 was used). Warm Springs ranged from $40 to $75 ($57.50 was used).

[28] Fort Hall ranged from $35 to $80 ($57.50 was used). Warm Springs ranged from $18 to $30 ($24 was used).

[29] Fort Hall ranged from $7.50 to $15 ($10 75 was used). Warm Springs ranged from $6 to $10 ($8 was used).

[30] In the Yakima return a certain number of acres (forest) had been included in grazing lands. We have placed them in their proper category and based the value on estimates for forest land. Western Washington did not include the value of standing timber. Fort Hall ranged from $65 to $100, we used $82.50.

[31] These land values ranged from $50 to $1,000 with 2 agencies not answering the question. It was therefore not considered feasible to use the average value to compute the value of 125,061 acres not included. Use of these lands ranged from business leases to sand and gravel.

TABLE 14.—AMOUNT OF HEIRSHIP LAND NOT BEING USED FOR INCOME-PRODUCING PURPOSES AS A DIRECT RESULT OF ITS HEIRSHIP STATUS, AREAS COMPARED

Area office jurisdiction	Number tracts	Number of acres	Area office jurisdiction	Number tracts	Number of acres
Aberdeen	503	77,684	Phoenix	42	479
Anadarko	88	7,288	Portland	3,360	257,821
Billings	488	54,661	Sacramento	30	1,020
Gallup	12	1,784			
Minneapolis	1,156	72,700	Total for all areas	5,679	473,437
Muskogee					

TABLE 15.—AMOUNT OF HEIRSHIP LAND NOT BEING USED FOR INCOME-PRODUCING PURPOSES AS DIRECT RESULT OF ITS HEIRSHIP STATUS, BY AREA

PHOENIX AREA

Jurisdiction	Number of tracts	Number of acres
Colorado river	None	None
Yuma subagency	20	200
Fort Apache	None	None
Hopi	None	None
Nevada	None	None
Papago	22	279
Pima	(1)	(1)
San Carlos	None	None
Uintah and Ouray	None	None
Area total	42	479

PORTLAND AREA

Colville	None	None
Fort Hall	349	10,626
Northern Idaho	4	350
Warm Springs	400	50,000
Western Washington	2,579	192,865
Yakima	28	3,980
Area total	3,360	257,821

SACRAMENTO AREA

California agency	(2)	(2)
Hoopa area field office	30	1,020
Riverside area field office	(1)	(1)
Area total	30	1,020
Grand total all areas	5,679	473,437

1 No statistics.
2 No answer.
3 275–350.

TABLE 16.—USE OF HEIRSHIP LANDS

	Used by tribe (acres)		Used by heirs (not leased) (acres)		Used by other Indians (individuals) (acres)	
	Leased	Other arrangements 1	As home	For income-producing purposes	Leased	Other arrangements 2
Irrigated	None	None	8,081	16,423	11,736	
Dry farm	None	None	21,506	47,048	75,094	
Grazing	45,565	None	332,069	444,838	660,201	
Forest	None	None	17,735	19,835	20,678	
Other (specify)	None	None	4,709	1,741	4,238	
Total	45,565		384,100	529,000	771,857	

1 The information in the table is the data analyzed by the committee staff.
2 Explain whether "other arrangements" are with the permission of heirs and what type of arrangements they are. Also state whether these arrangements are made between the user and the heirs, tribe, or Bureau officials.

Table 12 reveals that more than half of the heirship land is used by non-Indians and that 541,305 acres are not used at all. The figures for acreage not used are important because such lands—if put into use—might yield an additional income to the Indian owners. Table 14 is a compilation indicating those tracts of land not being used for income producing purposes *as a direct result of its heirship status.* This land, 473,437 acres, could be producing sorely needed income or be used as homesteads, if the titles were not so confused.

The Senate committee study provides the best available information on the scope of the administrative problem imposed on the Federal Government by the heirship land problem. Questionnaires were circulated to all levels of administration from the central office of the Bureau of Indian Affairs down through the area offices, reservations, and tribal governing bodies. One of the problems faced was the "great difficulty in using the statistics presented by the field offices * * * in some cases the statistics were contradictory and in others either incomplete or omitted entirely." [18] There were conflicts found, for example, concerning the leasing of heirship land. A reservation superintendent pointed out to the committee that heirship land could not, under present regulations, be leased without the signatures of all heirs. The central office of the Bureau of Indian Affairs, however, stated that such land could be, and implied it was, leased without all signatures. This points up some of the confusion within the Bureau itself concerning this problem of multiple ownership. Some of the administrative problems pointed out were (1) an increase in the number of recordings required in maintaining official land records; (2) increase in the number of probate proceedings to be examined in determining current title status; (3) complicated computations of large common denominators have reached 54 trillion, billions are not uncommon and millions are commonplace; and (4) increased work involved in answering inquiries concerning family histories in connection with the ownership of undivided interests in land.

Many of the agencies reported a tremendous workload in leasing, selling, and preparing data for probate of estates. At the time of the study it was found that 112 employees (at a cost of $675 387) were devoting their entire time to the heirship problem and that it was estimated the Indians themselves were losing approximately $417,000 a year income, due to the fractionation problem making a total of well over a million dollars as the annual cost to the Federal Government and the individual Indian. This figure was qualified as minimal "due to the complexities of the subject and the other Government agencies involved" and that the Bureau of Indian Affairs had stated—in reporting on S. 311 (83d Congress)—"Thousands of such (heirship) allotments are subject to so many undivided interests that they cannot be effectively utilized by the Indian owners, and an enormous amount of Federal money is expended in the cumbersome mechanism required for the administration of these lands."

The findings of the committee are very important to any consideration of the subject matter since they are based on such an exhaustive and complete study of the problem.

Heirship land is a major problem for our Indian population. Resulting ramifications create other problems of administration and use that are themselves approaching the point of becoming insoluble.

(1) Approximately 6 million acres of land are now in heirship status and another 6 million acres will become heirship land in the near future unless prompt action is taken.

---

[18] Senate report, p. X.

(2) The heirship problem is not only present in surface ownership of land but also in mineral ownership.

(3) Requiring all heirs to sign lease or sale papers is one of the foremost obstacles to the American Indian in utilizing his heirship land, and to the Federal Government in administering it.

(4) The heirs themselves have expressed an active interest in the problem as evidenced by the 38,871 requests for various actions made to Bureau of Indian Affairs officials during fiscal year 1958.

(5) Most local jurisdictions of the Bureau feel that present authority is inadequate to solve the problem and are almost unanimous in recommending corrective legislation.

(6) Some tribal councils have evidenced an interest in this problem as it relates to consolidation of the tribal land base.

(7) Continuing to hold allotted Indian lands in trust or restricted status without any consideration given to the individual's ability to manage his own land without supervision is serving to intensify the heirship problem.

The following case illustrates how complicated the problems of administration can be. One of the cases cited by the Comptroller concerned a tract of heirship land owned by 66 heirs and within 1 year—through death and probate—was owned by 90, an increase of 24 heirs. Another example given concerns a lease of 40 acres of heirship land where the annual rental income is $20 and the Federal Government must divide this among 75 heirs. "Only one of the 75 heirs receives more than $1 of the annual rental and 66 heirs receives a share of 25 cents or less which is entirely absorbed by the lessor fee charged to cover the cost of handling the collection. It is probable, that during the 5-year term of the lease, the distribution of the income may have to be recomputed, possibly each year, as a result of deaths among the present heirs which will further reduce the lease income to individual Indians from the land originally allotted." An example of the complications of probate actions to divide an estate was given for a specific allotment and probate action.

The estate of allotment No. 144, valued at $240, had 71 heirs at time of probate. Forty-three heirs received more than a $1 share in the estate, and of the remaining 28 heirs, 14 received shares valued at less than 10 cents. The fractional shares ranged from 837/4,515,840 to 263,655/4,515,840.

One Indian shared in nine estates through her second husband and also in two other estates. The total value of her share of these 11 estates was $703, with six of the estates being valued at less than $15. Her nine children and seven of her grandchildren shared in these estates at her death. Consequently, the interest in the 11 estates was divided into 176 shares ranging in amount from 3 cents to $30.

Each such probate case requires the Federal Government to compute the interest of each individual and their share of the probate costs. Such procedures usually result in man days spent to compute and collect moneys that amount to less than the cost of computation. The following is a worksheet of just such a computation.

Number of heirs:	Pro rate share of fee	Total	Number of heirs—Continued	Pro rate share of fee	Total
2	$0.02	$0.04	1	.25	.25
7	.05	.35	1	.31	.31
13	.08	1.04	2	.47	.94
3	.14	.42	3	.94	2.82
1	.20	.20	1	7.50	7.50
1	.21	.21			
4	.23	.92	39		15.00

In the words of the Comptroller General: "The worksheet for this distribution was prepared by three employees in 2 man-days. The cost of calculating the distribution was greater than the probate fee."

Some idea of the work required by the Bureau of Indian Affairs and the examiners of inheritance in the probate process are indicated by the following workload tables:

TABLE 21.—NUMBER OF HEIRSHIP CASES, EMPLOYEES, AND COSTS, BY FISCAL YEARS, BUREAU OF INDIAN AFFAIRS[1]

	Fiscal years						
	1953	1954	1955	1956	1957	1958	1970
On hand 1st of year	1,601	1,533	1,956	2,978	1,845	1,880	1,820
Forwarded during year	1,768	1,538	1,916	3,151	2,042	2,246	2,014
Pending at close of year	1,253	1,399	2,330	1,448	1,584	1,213	1,363
Employees responsible for compiling such information (number)	51	52	55	59	61	69	66
Total cost of handling heirship cases (estimate) [2]	$176,691	$189,685	$214,851	$249,536	$268,114	$311,237	$446,785
Total costs for such services connected with probate of cases [3]	58,414	59,439	73,678	88,124	99,154	109,166	136,044

[1] Basis for this estimate would be at present staff levels, and projected workload.
[2] This is for Bureau personnel only and includes leasing, distribution of income, salaries, etc. All phases of handling heirship lands (at this jurisdiction only) from date of heirship status to final settlement.
[3] This estimate is for actions directly concerned with settlement of heirship cases and does not include leasing, distribution of lease income, of any actions by other than BIA employees of this jurisdiction.

TABLE 34.—HEIRSHIP PROBATE CASES BY FISCAL YEARS HANDLED BY EXAMINERS OF INHERITANCE

	Fiscal years—						
	1953	1954	1955	1956	1957	1958	1970[1]
On hand, 1st of year	1,378	1,602	1,964	1,910	1,264	1,118	1,026
New cases received during year	742	599	944	1,210	1,560	1,356	1,353
Settled during year	519	763	970	1,966	1,758	1,303	1,519
Pending at close of year	1,602	1,649	1,634	1,167	1,118	1,198	889
Employees responsible for handling such cases	8	8	19	24	24	24	23
Total cost for handling heirship cases [2]	$47,801	$48,901	$101,801	$129,185	$137,920	$144,087	$146,882

[1] Basis for projection changes from 1953 to 1958. Statistics for 1970 would be estimated on the basis of keeping the workload current at that time.
[2] Through final settlement.

In attempting to sell their interests heirs run into other complications that compound the administrative work of the Government. On the Winnebago Reservation there was a request for sale of one allotment and for a period of 3 years the agency attempted to get the written consent to sell from all heirs. However, only 78 percent of the signatures were obtained. In this particular case the heirs of one decedent "a non-Indian who owned a 7/2016 interest in this estate, will probably never be determined." This man left no children and the Bureau found the relatives uninterested in the small amount involved.

Another case concerned an Indian who owned a half interest in 120 acres and because he had reached the age of 82 wanted the cash to use. "The application for sale was denied because one of the eight individuals having a one twenty-fourth interest in the land refused to consent to the sale. All the other owners had given their consent." These are just a few examples representing hundreds and thousands of such cases.

What Do We Know About the Heirs as People?

A general picture of the Indian heir was developed in the study of the heirship land problem by the House committee. The average heir is in the 41- to 50-year-of-age category; is a full blood; does not live on the reservation or on trust land; has an annual income between $1,000 and $2,000 (it is interesting to note here that there was a direct relationship shown between income and degree of Indian blood with the income increasing as the Indian blood quantum decreased, probably indicating a level of acculturation); and received from $50 to $100 a year from his fractionated land interests. More than half want all their heirship interests sold, 13 percent some sold, and 32 percent do not want any sold. Another interesting fact developed during the study was that many heirs owned other lands of their own in a fee simple status. The percentage of fee land ownership varies by area office with a high of 32.4 percent in Sacramento to a low of 10.4 percent in Phoenix (an average of 22.2 percent for all). Many of the heirs reported attempts to sell some of their heirship interests with varying degrees of success ranging from 69.8 percent in the Muskogee area to 27.7 percent at Gallup.

The occupation of the heirs is of interest. Are they skilled workers, unskilled, semiskilled, and so forth? In referring to the subject the committee report states that: "Among the heirs there are persons with occupations ranging from corporation president to college professor, to sheepherder and medicine man." A reading of the occupations is revealing. For example, the U.S. Government is retaining control of land interests and making the necessary decisions for three real estate brokers, licensed by their State to carry out real estate transactions for other citizens and to manage the property of other citizens in their State.

Interests in More Than One Heirship Tract

One facet of the Indian heirship land problem that must be kept in mind is that an heir is not necessarily heir to only one undivided interest but may well own undivided interests in several widely scattered tracts of land. Of those heirs surveyed it was established that 5,751 owned undivided interests in 19,856 tracts of land making the average number of undivided interests 3.4 per heir.

Welfare assistance was being received by 1,927 heirs, the majority of this group residing on reservations. The majority of heirs in the Aberdeen, Gallup, Minneapolis and Portland area offices reported receiving welfare assistance. Of those heirs living on their land interests (1,318), 357 ranch or farm the land. It is interesting to note that of those living on heirship land (1,318), 1072 are full bloods, and 401 of this number received welfare assistance. Remembering that annual income, as reported, relates directly to blood quantum, and comparing the figures concerning heirs residing on the land, it would seem reasonable to assume that neither the land nor income from it can provide an adequate living for the heirs, but only supplemental income.

OPINIONS OF THE HEIRS

The Indian heirs were given the opportunity, not only to answer specific questions, but to tell the Congress in their own words how they felt about the problem and what they would like to have done. The heirs indicated that such lands has caused bitter dissension in the family, hard feelings toward the tribe and the Federal Government, and a general feeling of hopelessness about the whole situation. Some of the most interesting and thought provoking statements on the subject came from the heirs themselves, providing a look at the problem from their point of view. In some cases the heirs did not know they had inherited any land interests and in others they had no idea where the land was, how much there was of it, or for that matter, anything else about it. In an effort to show some of the feelings and emotions involved, the following are direct quotes from the heirs themselves:

"What little money I do get and what I don't—surely don't help me any. I pay the same taxes the white people pay, I would never move back to the reservation, so why should I want to own land on the reservation: I think I have invested my money wisely. Why can't I do the same with my share of the heirship lands?"

_____

"I know many people like myself who own shares in many pieces of land. This land is nearly impossible to do anything with, such as sale, or lease because of the amount of heirs involved.

_____

"I have received the amount of rental (72 cents) due to me which cost the Government more and more to cash the check."

_____

"I remember those heirship land I have interest in ever since I was a little boy, over 50 years ago, it seems the settlement of these lands were dragging along year after year even at that time. To tell the truth I have never entertained any thoughts of ever realizing anything from them."

_____

"The office [Bureau of Indian Affairs] leases my heirship land to people I don't want to have it even if I won't sign the lease and I want another person to have it."

_____

"Where is our land located? How much land do we have? How many heirs are there to this?"

". . . [I] was requested to sign a 'consent to sale' I signed and my share was 31/777600 and 31/129600 and 31/388800. I have received three big checks now—one for 4 cents, another for 2 cents and the last one was for 2 cents and 10 cents worth of postage stamps plus administration."

"I only get $6.95 a year from inherited lands . . . I don't know where it is and no one else seems to know. I never sign a lease."

"I have an undivided interest, 51030/10886400 in * * * 10 acres. There are quite a few heirs and I think it would be advisable to sell. I spoke to someone at the * * * Agency about it who informed me that there were too many heirs to contact in order to sell. As the years go on more heirs are added. I assure you my share of land is so small you probably could cover it with a postage stamp."

"Yes. How did I acquire the above land? Of which nets me an income of $1.40 or $1.80 a year. Who on earth could make a living on 3,500/11,975,040 percent of 80 acres of Indian land? I would like to sell my cup of Indian soil."

"My water charge on one tract was $9.00 and my lease money [income] was $4.60."

"I am getting old and I am completely dependent on my lone living child, I feel that I am a burden to my child.—The land is no use to me—if I could sell it or lease it, it could help me to be independent for the rest of my life."

THE GENERAL SITUATION TODAY AND POSSIBILITIES OF SOLUTION

Approximately 24 percent (12 million acres) of the Indian land base (50 million acres) is owned by individual Indians. The acreage in individual ownership is about equally divided between single ownership and those tracts in heirship status already. A discussion of whether or not the General Allotment Act was a wise move on the part of the Federal Government would be of little value today. The fact is that the individual owner, the tribe, and the Federal Government are faced with a pressing problem of almost unimaginable complexity. It should be kept in mind that the heirship problem today is only half the problem it will be if the other 6 million acres, now in single ownership, move into the heirship category. So, complex as the problem is today, it may be worse in the future.

As has been stated there are tracts owned by more than 100 heirs and calculating the fractional interests requires using common denominators as high as trillionths. It is possible with computer technology to go on keeping track of these small interests but this would be a victory for the machines, not for the Indian people involved. Our goal should not be up-dated recordkeeping but up-dated economic assistance to the Indians and the tribes.

The question concerning the costs of management of many small interests and the necessity to obtain the consent of Indian owners bears heavily on the problem. A former Commissioner of Indian Affairs pointed out that the "signature" problem in leasing such tracts brings reduced rental income to the heirs.[19] One of the major factors that must be faced is that the problem—through inheritance alone—will increase in geometric proportions. The Examiners of Inheritance— who carry out probate actions—have indicated by rough estimates that the average number of heirs, in a probate case, is seven. Multiplying the present number of heirs (over 50,000) by seven gives a rough indication of the future fractionation of such interests.

At the heart of the Indian heirship land problem is the economic loss to the Indian, either through the loss of rentals, or the nonuse of land due to the complicated title. Actual income considered "lost" as a result of the fractionation problem amounted to $417,868 in 1958. This figure, although it may appear to be somewhat insignificant in the light of other expenditures today, may be a very real problem to the Indians involved. Considering the low income of heirs, as reported, any additional income would be of help to them. In addition to the loss of income there is another very significant problem when we consider that many heirs—if all their fractionated interests were combined—might well have a unit large enough for subsistence farming or for homesteading.

Of what actual value, to the heirs, are these fractionated land interests at this time. It has been established that the average annual income—from the land interests—is less than $100, certainly an amount insufficient to support a family, and that only 1,318 are reported as living on heirship land and only 357 ranch or farm the land. Many of the heirs have indicated a desire to sell and others have indicated an interest in consolidating their holdings.

The tribes on the other hand are concerned that heirship land, if removed from trust status, will—in some cases—be detrimental to present or planned tribal land consolidation programs and future income possibilities for the tribes. Where this is the case it is of understandable concern to the tribe and through the tribe, to the individual. Since an individual Indian is on the one hand an Indian owner and on the other, usually, a member of the tribe, he is affected in both ways.

The Federal Government, as represented by the Interior Department, would like to solve the problem not only to remove itself from the arena of an extremely difficult and emotional problem, but also to get back to the work at hand, namely, assisting the Indians—tribes and individuals—in becoming acculturated to the general society.

A beginning step, in terms of correcting the problem, is to attempt to find an area of general agreement among all parties concerned. This, of necessity, requires steering clear of the more emotional and controversial areas and the too technical approach that may bog the problem down.

[19] 85th Cong., second sess. Senate. *Indian Land Transactions.* Committee on Interior and Insular Affairs. Dec. 1, 1958.

The following are offered as possible general areas of agreement that could be used as a springboard into areas of effective action.

1. There is no easy simple solution to the problem.

2. No solution will meet with the complete approval of all parties concerned.

3. A solution to the problem cannot be reached without expenditure of money on the part of those concerned.

4. The problem, as it is now constituted, is unmanageable, increasing in scope, and requires solution.

5. Fractionation is an economic problem for the individual Indian owner, the tribe, and the Federal Government.

6. The Indian owners are of primary concern in any attempt to solve the problem, with the tribe being of secondary concern and the Federal Government, third.

7. The present administrative and personnel cost to the Federal Government could be more effectively used by other Indian assistance programs.

8. Possible remedies to reduce or solve the problem include: inheritance restrictions, exhange, sale, partition, escheat, and fee title.

9. Whatever approach is taken, reservation of minerals in trust, the holding of cash estates in trust, etc., will continue—to some extent—the fractionation, inheritance, and recordkeeping problem.

With these factors in mind we can go on to suggestions for possible solution of the problem. The suggestions that follow are related to: (1) inheritance of fractionated land interests; (2) administrative costs; (3) heirship land consolidation; (4) mineral rights; (5) fee title; (6) competency; and (7) key tracts.

(1) *Inheritance of fractionated land interests should be limited to the surviving mate and then lineal descendants in joint tenancy.*

One of the first steps that could be taken by the Federal Government to limit the expansion of the heirship land program would be legislation providing that inheritance of individual trust lands will be to the surviving mate—if any—and then by lineal descent in joint tenancy. Such legislation applied to both the 6 million acres of land now in heirship status and the 6 million still in single ownership would have several advantages. The two most important are: (a) the land will remain in the same family, and (b) there will be an initial probate when an owner passes away and no further probates until the last heir passes away. As a death occurs, among the heirs, the shares of remaining heirs would simply be recomputed, the land gradually returning to single ownership. At the death of the last remaining heir there would be a probate action and the cycle would begin again. As applied to the tracts now owned by one individual this approach would prevent such tracts from ever becoming as badly fractionated as those tracts now in heirship status. Such an approach could be taken regardless of any other overall legislative solutions since it would work to contain the problem indefinitely.

(2) *The actual cost of administration should be charged to the heirs. When the administrative cost exceeds annual income from the interests the heir should be given the choice of paying the cost, forfeiting the income, or taking the cash value for the interest.*

Should the heir decide to forfeit the income it could be used to buy out other small shares of heirship land on the reservation. If the heir chooses the cash value, the Federal Government could buy him out, allow any other heir to purchase that interest or divide it into the remaining interests. This approach would have various benefits, among them: (a) Allowing the heir to divest himself of uneconomic small interests; (b) allowing heirs to purchase other interests in a tract they might want to consolidate; (c) reimbursing the Federal Government for the cost of administration and the time involved, leaving that time or money for other more effective use; and (d) reducing the number of very small interests.

(3) *An individual Indian land consolidation program could be established in conjunction with a tribal land consolidation program and used as the basis for an exchange program among heirs and among heirs and the tribe, providing opportunities to consolidate land holdings.*

In this day of computers it would seem possible to carry out an exchange program on a "one-shot" basis by setting aside an area as an "individual land consolidation area" and using this in conjunction with any tribal land consolidation program to exchange interests among heirs and the tribes resulting in a reasonable consolidation of interests for both.

The first step would be to contact all heirs to determine whether they wanted their fractionated interests consolidated or if they would rather have cash value for their interests. In such cases as minors, heirs that cannot be located, unprobated estates, and so forth, the Secretary of the Interior would act for the party. For each tract of land a simple majority of owners answering would be sufficient to place that tract in the exchange program. For those owners wanting to sell their interests the Government would purchase at fair market value. During this process of exchange the Government could trade with the tribe for areas that would help both in their consolidation efforts. Once the tribal and individual land trades were made the Government could then divide up the individual consolidation area and assign each heir one consolidated tract reflecting the total of his previous land interests. Of major consideration in such an action would be the heir living on a tract in which he owns an interest, since he should have his land consolidated in such a way that moving is not necessary.

The income from sale of interests owned by heirs that cannot be located would be held for a 5-year period and then—unless claimed—be turned over to the tribe for use in tribal land consolidation programs. The reasoning behind this approach is that some heirs haven't been heard from in over 20 years and disbursing the money back to the tribe is one means of benefiting all the Indians on the reservation. It is recognized that such a program is not simple in its application and that many problems will have to be worked out. However, combined with the recommendation on inheritance it could simplify the heirship land titles and consolidate the tracts into more reasonable units and result in more effective utilization in the future.

(4) *Surface and mineral rights of individual Indian Trust Land should not be separated unless the owner reserves the mineral rights in fee simple.*

One of the findings of the Senate study was that "The heirship problem is not only present in surface ownership of land but also in mineral ownership." In the study published by the House the same problem was pointed out: "In some returns the heirs have requested the land be sold but that mineral rights be retained by them. If this were done (and the title held in trust) an equally difficult heirship minerals problem would doubtlessly arise."

With the retention of mineral rights in trust the problem continues, since at the death of each owner there must still be a probate to divide the mineral interests. And what is the probate situation? Back in 1958 the Gallup area director reported that "With the present staff of the examiner of Inheritance, some 15 to 20 years will be required to dispose of this backlog."

What is the affect of mineral reservations in trust on the record-keeping problem of the Bureau of Indian Affairs? It would seem that whether the leases are for minerals or grazing, the problems of collection, disbursement, and recordkeeping are the same. We can recognize however, that many mineral reservations will not be leased and there would consequently be a decrease in recordkeeping. It would seem at this time though that unless any mineral reservations are taken in fee simple that the specter of another heirship problem will be haunting us. Another factor of great importance is that we could create a situation of *doubling the probates* since we could at one time be probating an estate for surface ownership of a tract and an entirely separate probate for mineral ownership of the same tract.

5. Any Indian who is sole owner of a tract of trust land can request title in fee simple and it will be issued if he is competent and if the land is not a "key tract" that—by removal from trust status—would be detrimental to the maximum utilization of other Indian land in the area.

Any legislation, concerned with the solution of the heirship land problem, must come face to face with one of the most emotional areas in the subject field, individual Indians taking fee title to their tract of land. There are two major factors involved in consideration of this approach (a) when is an Indian "competent" to take title in fee; and (b) what is a "key tract."

The discussion on the subject of "competency" has gone on for years within the Federal Government and tribal structures without any specific right of the individual Indian to *declare himself competent.* As the Federal Agency with direct responsibility for Indians, the Bureau of Indian Affairs has defined competent as being a "synonym for capable" but then we are faced with a definition of "capable" as it applies to Indians. A few selections from the occupations of heirs— FBI agent, aeronautical engineer, analytical chemist, apartment houseowner, aquatic biologist, attorney, college professor, real estate broker, corporation president—indicates that many Indian heirs are more than competent or capable however we define the words. But must an Indian be a lawyer or real estate broker before we consider him capable of handling his own property? Obviously the answer is "No," so we must look for something more reasonable and yet not so loosely defined as to create a situation where Indians would lose their land without any benefit to them as opposed to an Indian that might sell his land and use the money constructively.

The Anadarko area officer some years back referred to competency of Indians as follows:

There are many adult Indians today who own tax-exempt trust lands, both original allotments and heirship interests, who have had schooling at level equal to or above that of the national average, have adequate financial status and the proven ability to provide for themselves, are reasonably well adjusted in their respective communities or are capable of so becoming, and in general are on a par with other citizens of the community.

This officer of the Federal Government working directly with the Indians recommended that such Indians be issued a "certificate of capability" and full title in fee simple to all his property, real and personal.

The Secretary of Interior's task force stated that: "* * * the task force believes that eligibility for special Federal services should be withdrawn from Indians with substantial incomes and superior educational experience, who are as competent as most non-Indians to look after their own affairs." In discussing what the objectives of the Bureau of Indian Affairs should be the task force recommendations were along the lines followed by this recommendation:

"1. Maximum Indian economic self-sufficiency

"2. Full participation of Indians in American life

"3. Equal citizenship privileges and responsibilities for Indians."

Taking all the factors into consideration a reasonable approach would be:

Any Indian with an educational background and annual income equal to, or exceeding, the average for all citizens of his State can declare himself competent.

Such individuals making competency declaration and requesting title to their land should receive title within 90 days providing that the land concerned is not held to be a "key tract." A "key tract" is one that controls the water supply for the surrounding area, or a shipping point, access to other land, or in more general terms one that if removed from trust status—and thereby Federal Government control—would adversely affect other Indian trust lands. Where the land is considered as a "key tract" the Government could assist the individual in negotiating a sale to the tribe or another Indian, if his purpose was to sell. Otherwise the land would continue in trust status.

One of the problems to be avoided is that, without a specific definition, each agency might well interpret "key tract" differently. The writer encountered such a problem while analyzing material for a congressional study.[20] At that time a questionnaire had been circulated to agency officials and part II was devoted to the problem of "key tracts." In referring to the problem that sale of "key tracts" would have on other Indian lands, Commissioner Emmons stated:

As for the effect which the fee patenting may have on other Indian lands, the Bureau's policy and position are quite clear. While the Bureau recognized the competent Indian's undeniable right to ask for and receive a fee patent, it also keeps in mind in continuing trust responsibilities to the tribal group and to

[20] 85th Cong., second sess. Senate. *Indian Land Transactions.* Committee on Interior and Insular Affairs. Dec. 1, 1958.

other Indian landowners whose holdings may be affected. Consequently, if there is any real possibility that *the disposal of a particular allotment might adversely affect other Indian lands in trust* [underlining ours] the Bureau will take the initiative in consulting with the Indians concerned and will give them every possible assistance in working out a satisfactory solution to the problem. In some cases this will involve purchase of the patented allotments by the tribal group, in other cases it will involve other various types of arrangements. The Bureau believes that all such problems can be fairly and equitably resolved in one way or another.

Examples of various interpretations by officials in the field are evidenced by the following statements concerning the existence of "key tracts" on the reservation:

"The tribal council considers all land within the reservation as 'key lands.'

"The * * * acreage was not recognized by Bureau officials as being key tracts * * * the sale of these tracts *has interfered* [underlining ours] with the best use of the tribal grazing land adjoining these tracts, which were excluded by fencing.

"Two tracts of fee land have been purchased in connection with moving of homes * * * from a location that floods frequently due to melting snows, to a location where the flooding problem is eliminated.

"There are several definitions of 'key tracts.'

"It must be borne in mind that personalities and policy of succeeding council members differ with respect to criteria for 'key tracts.' "

It is obvious from the foregoing that a specific definition of "key tract" must be given to agency officials and possibly a procedure should be instituted for tribal and individual appeal whenever there is a difference of opinion concerning whether the land in question fits the definition of "key tract."

The recommendation above is an attempt to find a reasonable middle ground that provides an Indian individual—sole owner of a land tract in trust status—the right to take fee title if he so desires, and is capable, and in addition provide necessary protection for other Indians and the tribes when their holdings may be adversely affected by such action. In recommending that income and educational attainment be related to the average for the State, it was felt such a procedure would make it relatively easy for the Indian to prove he has reached that level and the Interior Department would not have to go through any involved process before issuing a fee title. As envisioned it would simply require the heir to show proof of his income and educational background which could then be compared to the latest information published by either the State or the Federal Government (Bureau of the Census). The tribe would then be notified by the agency with the agency declaring whether they considered the land as a "key tract." If the agency and the tribe decided it was not, the title in fee would be issued. Otherwise an appeal process to the Interior Department could be instituted, by any one of the three.

Summary Conclusion

The writer has attempted to state the highlights of the problem without getting into too much detail and, as requested, come up with some recommendations for action that could be taken to solve the problem. It is realized that the recommendations made are not complete in all the necessary detail but they are presented as general approaches to the problem with the understanding that in actual application they would have to be broadened and detailed. Again credit is to be given to the Senate and House Interior Committee studies which are to date the most extensive collection of data available and on which the writer depended heavily.

FRAMEWORK FOR DECISION*

By ESTHER C. WUNNICKE, ROBERT D. ARNOLD, and
DAVID M. HICKOK

FOREWORD

The majority of Alaskan Natives—Eskimos, Indians, and Aleuts—currently live in extreme poverty. The nature of the settlement arrived at in the Alaskan land claims dispute will profoundly affect the economic future of these Native groups. In this excerpt from the Report of the Federal Field Committee for Development Planning in Alaska, Ester Wunnicke, Robert Arnold, and David Hickok describe the possible elements which might go into a land claims settlement and the economic consequences which different aspects of the settlement would have for the Native groups. The major types of settlement available are the grant of land titles, the provision of compensation, and the establishment of organizations to manage land and revenues. Among the crucial developmental factors will be insuring that compensatory payments are effectively put to use in economic development projects and that the management arrangements are of a type which will permit the Alaskan Natives to eventually assume full control over their own affairs.

ELEMENTS OF THE PROBLEM

An examination of the elements of the Native land claims problem reveals the varying, and sometimes conflicting, objectives of the Nation, the State, and the Native people to be resolved in its solution.

THE NATIVE PEOPLE

About three-fourths of Alaska's 53,000 Eskimos, Indians, and Aleuts live in 178 predominantly Native communities, most of which are at locations remote from the road system of the State. The median size of these places is 155 persons. In these villages, the few, permanent, full-time jobs at highest rates of pay are typically held by non-Natives. Low cash income and high prices, even though supplemented by free health and educational services, and food-gathering activities, have resulted in exceedingly low standards of living for villagers: dilapidated housing, absence of sewer and water facilities, and electric power. State public assistance programs provide income to almost one of four households in villages; temporary relief programs provide income to about the same proportion, but usually for 3 months or less. Most village adults have less than an elementary school education, and large numbers have no formal education at all; for village adults speaking English, it is a second language. Nearly all Native communities have schools, but educational opportunity ends at the eighth grade in most places. Owing largely to socioeconomic conditions and the difficulty of providing health services to remote

*Chapter VII, from Alaska Natives and the Land, Report of the Federal Field Committee for Development & Planning in Alaska, Anchorage, 1968.

villages, the health status of Alaska Natives is inferior to that of other Alaskans.

About one-fourth of Alaska's Natives are residents of predominantly non-Native communities where job opportunities exist. Because adult Natives are often less well educated than other adults and lack marketable skills, their rate of joblessness in these communities is higher than among other groups, and those who are jobholders are typically in lower-paying positions. Migrants from villages to urban areas are frequently ill equipped, by cultural as well as educational background, to make an easy transition to new patterns of life and work, but few communities have begun to provide assistance to them; and the consequences for too many are severe stresses resulting in alcohol problems and other personality disorders.

Alaska Natives are eligible for a wide range of Federal services offered by the Bureau of Indian Affairs and the Division of Indian Health of the Public Health Service, but such eligibility does not necessarily assure that a service will be afforded them owing to inadequate funding or the difficulty of providing such services. Although Alaska Natives may be employees of these agencies, and with increasing frequency are acting in an advisory way to them, they are not really involved in the planning and implementation of the programs.

Among Alaska Natives today there is an ever increasing ability as well as a desire to more fully participate in decisions affecting their lives. Fifty-eight villages are chartered under the Indian Reorganization Act and have constitutions, by-laws, and charters under which they may provide services and engage in business. Twenty of these places also are organized under State law as fourth, second or first class cities. Another 21 villages are organized only as cities under State law. The remaining villages are organized only on a traditional basis.

Most villages are affiliated with regional associations and with the statewide federation of Natives, and their delegates participate in deliberations and decisions of these organizations. There are today 14 such regional groups. In addition, there are seven Native organizations organized on a community basis in Anchorage, Fairbanks, and other places. It is through these organizations that protests to the transfer of lands by the Federal Government to others have been filed. They rely in their protests upon possessory rights earned by continuous aboriginal use of the land.

USE AND OWNERSHIP OF LANDS

Aboriginal Alaska Natives made use of all the biological resources of the land, interior and contiguous waters in general balance with its sustained human carrying capacity. This use was only limited in scope and amount by technology. In their use of the biological community for livelihood the Native people "occupied" the land in the sense of being on and over virtually all of it in pursuit of their subsistence, but they did not "occupy" the land in an agrarian or legal sense as understood in Anglo-American jurisprudence.

Native settlement patterns have been very substantially affected by natural physical and biological forces and, in more recent time, by the decisions and actions of church, government, and industry.

Such forces continue to influence settlement patterns today. Thirty-seven Native places existing in 1950 had declined to one or two families or had been abandoned by 1967, but 21 additional places had become established as villages by 1967. Eighty percent of the 178 villages are larger than they were in 1950.

Aboriginal group or "tribal" territoriality with definable bounds did exist in Alaska. Most Native groups also recognized individual and family or group "property rights"—particularly in the usufruct sense—to harvest the products of the land, and the amount of land used and occupied by peoples in Alaska to support their livelihood varied greatly in amount among ethnic groups dependent upon diverse environments. Such variety continues to be the pattern today. And while not all villages or villagers depend upon resources of the land and waters for subsistence to the same extent, reliance upon gathering activities is generally characteristic of most of the predominantly Native communities where about three-fourths of Alaska's Eskimos, Indians, and Aleuts live.

Alaska Natives who claim two-thirds of the State own in fee simple less than 500 acres and hold in restricted title only an additional 15,000 acres. Some 900 Native families share the use of 4 million acres of land in 23 reserves established for their use and administered by the Bureau of Indian Affairs. All other rural Native families live on the public domain. And reindeer reserves account for 1¼ million of the 4 million acres of reserved lands. Without Government permit, these reindeer lands may only be used for reindeer husbandry and subsistence purposes.

Specific land legislation passed for Alaska Natives—the Alaska Native Allotment Act of 1906 and the Townsite Act of 1926—has failed to meet the land needs of the Native people. In the 62 years since passage of the Native Allotment Act only slightly more than 15,000 acres of land have been deeded, by restricted deed, to 175 Native allottees. And in the 42 years since the passage of the Townsite Act, only 28 Native villages have been surveyed with deeds issued to their inhabitants; and title in fee simple to less than 500 acres has been conveyed.

Of the 272 million acres in the public domain, Natives claim 250 million acres; of the 85 million acres of land reserved by the Federal Government for specific purposes, they claim 75 million acres; of the 12 million acres thus far in process of selection by the State under the terms of the Statehood Act, they claim all but 100,000 acres; and of the 6 million acres already patented to the State or to private individuals, they claim 3 million acres.

Aboriginal possessory rights, based upon continuous aboriginal use, are valid against all but the sovereign—in this case the Federal Government—and are compensable rights once permission to bring an action for their loss is granted by the sovereign.

Any lands granted as compensation for rights in land lost must be from lands still within the control of the Federal Government; and although the State may elect to assist in the settlement by granting shares in future revenues to Alaska Natives, the claim for money compensation, like land compensation, is against the Federal Government.

Unappropriated lands presently under Federal control total over 250 million acres. But these lands are not uncommitted. On the contrary, in the Statehood Act for Alaska passed 10 years ago, the State was given the right to select nearly 103 million acres—and 85 million acres of this commitment remain to be selected. In addition to the public domain lands there are 85 million acres of federally withdrawn lands which the State sees as the source of grants under the settlement, or as a reimbursement to the State for other lands used in the settlement to which the State might be entitled. The legislative history of the Statehood Act reveals a strong statement of the willingness of Congress to reexamine Federal withdrawals in Alaska, and a detailed study is now being conducted by the Public Land Law Review Commission. Far-reaching decisions as to the merits of particular withdrawals may be left to congressional determination in the light of this study, with full awareness that as large acreage grants reduce the amount of desirable land available for State selection. the pressures to release existing Federal withdrawals will increase. However, adequate information on existing Federal withdrawals in Alaska is available to the Congress to make specific findings should they be required in the settlement of the claims.

National policy with respect to the public lands is one of multiple-use management which recognizes disposal under certain circumstances, access requirements for commercial development of resources, and the support of other national objectives. The withdrawal of lands for specific purposes has been the method of meeting some of those national objectives in the past. For example, Alaska is an area of military significance; and those lands presently withdrawn, or those lands to be withdrawn in the future for defense purposes, are particular sites to which top priority is to be assigned. Also, as the last and most extensive wilderness area in the United States and an area of unparalleled grandeur, the development of national wildlife ranges and refuges and national parks in Alaska is also of high priority. A broad range of public purposes is also met by the management of the two large national forests in the State.

Although some of the Federal withdrawals have the management of a particular resource as their purpose, other important resources of the State are located on, or under, the public domain, or lands or waters belonging to the State.

USE AND MANAGEMENT OF RESOURCES

Alaska's wildlife resources which are of national significance are afforded habitat preservation and management by the Federal Government. While Alaska Native populations depend in whole or in part upon biotic resources in order to sustain life and while many of Alaska's wildlife resources are of national significance, there is little conflict between the national wildlife objectives and Native subsistence requirements, with the possible exception of some migratory bird nesting populations. Increasing conflict between the sport or commercial harvest of wildlife resources and the subsistence harvest of these same resources by the Native people is, however, developing.

Legislative jurisdiction for all wildlife resources, except for migratory birds, is vested in the State of Alaska. On the other hand, proprietary jurisdiction of most of Alaska, the habitat of wildlife, is vested, at this point in time, primarily in the Federal Government which has the right to prescribe who, where, and in what manner persons may enter, travel across, and conduct activities upon land within its jurisdiction.

As in the case of wildlife resources, the Native "property right" in the fishery resource was "taken" when legislative jurisdiction over fish and wildlife resources passed to the State by virtue of the Statehood Act. Alaska's Native people rely heavily upon the fisheries, but they share in these resources only as members of the general public.

The fishery resource is a natural resource which offers immediate direct promise for major economic participation; one in which Natives can compete as wage earners with moderate outlays of capital. It is a renewable resource with which Natives are familiar.

The general development and allocation of Alaska water resources is essential to economic growth and community welfare in Alaska. Furthermore, Alaska is a region of water surplus and is considered as a future potential continental water source for water-deficient areas in the Western United States and Canada. While the largest possible use for Alaska water resources is hydroelectric power development, this, with the exception of a few sites, does not exhibit favorable cost-benefit ratios. The Federal withdrawal of many hydroelectric power-sites which have no foreseeable reservoir areas, however, prevents a conflict with potential landownership to many Native groups and villages.

Many Alaska aboriginal groups recognized a "user right" to individuals or families for a net, wire, or other fish-catching place on a river or lake; no such exclusive "right" now exists on navigable waters because the Statehood Act extinguished any personal proprietorship and vested general ownership of lands beneath navigable waters in the State.

There is need to provide watershed protection to water source supplies for Alaska's cities, towns, and villages. Depending upon location and physiography, community watersheds may have to be of considerable size in order to provide for safe and adequate supplies in the future. There is need also to provide land for public flood plain zoning in many regions of Alaska as economic and community growth increases.

Alaska possesses 16 percent of all U.S. forest resources. Nearly all forest resources of Alaska are subject to Federal jurisdiction. The important commercial forests of the coastal zone are administered by the U.S. Forest Service within the Chugach and Tongass National Forests. Interior forests on the public domain, comprising 32 percent of the total land area of Alaska, 21 percent of which is commercial timber, are administered by the Bureau of Land Management. These interior forests are subject to State selection and also offer a possible resource to Native claimants.

Almost all available cropland in Alaska has been selected by the state or patented to private interests. The undeveloped agricultural resource significant to Native claimants and non-Natives alike, however, is grazing land—particularly on the Alaska Peninsula, Kodiak Island, and the Aleutian Islands. With improved transportation and changing economic feasibility, livestock production (cattle and sheep) is a potential expandable use for the grasslands of western

Alaska. However, conflict with wildlife use of the same lands is probable; and at the present time, wildlife is the more economically valuable resource. A particularly important grazing land use occurs on lands of the Seward Peninsula, St. Lawrence Island, and Nunivak Island and a few other small areas of western Alaska where Native reindeer husbandry is practiced.

Although present areas of intensive recreational use cover less than one-sixth of Alaska—chiefly in areas adjoining the major communities—the recreational resources of the State are one of the most potentially valuable economic assets of the Nation, State, and Natives in the years ahead. Estimates are that by 1980 nearly three-quarters of a million tourists will have visited Alaska, adding thereby $225 million to the Alaskan economy in the 15 years following 1964.

The potential wealth of Alaska mineral and oil and gas resources is not known, although it is estimated to be many billions of dollars. So little of the State's geology is understood—many regions of the State being virtually unexplored—that it is impossible to pattern a rational distribution of land based upon mineral wealth. Nevertheless, sufficient knowledge exists to say that geologic distribution of known deposits is extremely unequal and variable.

ELEMENTS OF THE SETTLEMENT

The major elements of settlement available for a solution of the problems presented by Alaska Native land claims can be treated in three broad categories:

(1) The grant or protection of lands and land rights now used by Alaska Natives for townsites, hunting and fishing camps, and subsistence hunting, fishing, and other food and fuel gathering areas;

(2) The provision of compensation, either in lands or revenues, for those possessory rights to land taken in the past or to be taken as a result of this legislation; and

(3) The establishment of organizations for the management and administration of lands and revenues and the adjudication of conflict.

LAND FOR USE

Village sites and camp sites

That is the expressed policy of the Nation to protect the Alaska Native people in their present occupancy of lands is stated in the President's message to Congress of March 6, 1968, in which specific attention was paid to Alaska Native land claims and in Senate Concurrent Resolution 11, passed by the Senate of the 90th Congress on September 12, 1968, pledging support for policies which meet the moral and legal obligations of the Nation toward American Indians and Alaska Natives—specifically in the protection of their lands.

No economic ill-effect or detriment to public land management can be seen in the granting of village sites. On the contrary, villagers can anticipate real economic gains; and Government will be relieved of a burdensome and expensive managerial responsibility.

Even under the most strict interpretation of possessory rights, there is no alternative to the granting of title to village sites and fishing and hunting camps.

Most of the proposals before Congress contemplate transfers of village sites to villages with subsequent transfers of parcels to individuals. Because townsite surveying is a time-consuming process, it is desirable that the Secretary of the Interior withdraw land by projected least civil divisions. A minimum of one township for each existing village is necessary to protect such lands as are used and as may be needed for expansion until the internal townsite surveys can be completed. Once townsite surveys are completed, the Department would transfer the parcels to the individuals occupying them; and the remaining lots would be transferred to the village government.

The transfer of township units for villages, either separate or in close juxtaposition, is desirable to provide room for relocation due to natural problems that arise affecting village location. Where villages are in close proximity, the number of villages times the township unit could be the total amount surrounding the entire group of villages. For example, in the Bethel area where there are nine villages in close proximity, the grant of a minimum of nine townships for village sites would be desirable. Such grants would total a little more than 4 million acres for all presently existing villages. Finally, so that individual land ownership not be too long delayed, legislation should include funding and authorization for an acceleration of the current program of townsite surveys.

Grants of fishing, hunting, and food-gathering sites may be made to individuals now using them or to Native groups for later transfer to the individuals in possession. Since agencies do not have knowledge of the locations of all such camps nor their users, the most practical approach is to have Government teams meet with villages in the field to obtain applications from villagers for the sites they use. Even residents of the largest villages continue to use historic sites for hunting, fishing, and trapping—sometimes for longer periods than they reside in what may be called their home villages.

Congress might impose a maximum number of subsistence-use sites and a maximum acreage that might be embraced by all applications from each head of a household or other adult, but in so doing it should be remembered that the number of subsistence sites required for each family in their subsistence quest varies throughout the State.

While the 160-acre limitation of the Alaska Native Allotment Act might be adequate, the limitation to only four parcels would not cover the number of sites now in use by many families. Because identification and transfer of these subsistence-use sites might take as long as 5 years, written nominations of land by villages to cover these uses should be the cause for immediate withdrawals by the Secretary to protect such sites until village hearings and formal applications are received. It is estimated that about 1.5 million acres would meet minimum needs for these sites.

While it is doubtful that a case can be made against granting of village or subsistence use sites on most Federal withdrawals, the location of some villages in Alaska's two national forests does raise a question. Of the Native villages in the forests, only two remain unsurveyed; and surveys there and subsequent grant of titles should be promptly made. The question is: Would the allocation of lands for hunting and fishing camps in the national forests unduly affect public managerial responsibilities of the Forest Service, not only for timber harvest, but also for watershed protection, wildlife management, and recreational purposes? If the answer to this question favors the allocation of hunting and fishing sites in the forests, a second question is whether such grants should be made to villagers in southeast Alaska where lands included in the Tongass National Forest have been included in the Tlingit-Haida judgment. Despite the judgment, Congress might take the opportunity to treat all groups equitably by transferring lands, which the court of claims could not do, and granting subsistence sites to the Natives of southeastern Alaska.

Since there may be several hundred Alaska Natives who live outside of Native villages and who are living on public lands, the legislation also might provide for confirmation of title to lands in their possession. Complicated procedures followed under the Alaska Native Allotment Act have resulted in virtually no Native allotments being issued in present rural areas. So, if the act is considered as a means of granting title to these rural nonvillagers, amendment to simplify procedures may be necessary.

Lands for subsistence use

There is no dispute that the right of Alaska Natives to go upon Federal lands for the purpose of taking fish and game should continue. Although all of the proposals before the Congress provide for the granting of the right, the authority to regulate the taking of fish and game on all but certain federally withdrawn lands belongs to the State of Alaska.

Even the grant of surface title to lands used for subsistence purposes would not eliminate the authority of the State to regulate the taking of fish and game on those lands. It would, however, enable the owners of the land to prohibit the entry of sportsmen or commercial interests for the harvest of fish and game as well as non-Native subsistence use. Should the granting of surface title be the means of assuring the Natives use of the lands for subsistence, it would require a grant in varying amounts according to geographic location and biotic carrying capacity, totaling at least 60 million acres.

Although the Federal Government cannot regulate the taking of fish and game, and the State under the terms of its Constitution cannot grant exclusive hunting and fishing rights, Congress in effect could grant exclusive hunting and fishing rights by granting an easement to Natives only to enter the public domain for these purposes. Present proposals enable the Secretary of the Interior to grant such exclusive easements as a discretionary power. While a grant of exclusive easements across all public lands would not be wise public policy, because it would undermine the pattern of subsistence use by non-Natives, limit recreational attractions of the State, and encourage racial divisiveness, permitting the Secretary to protect threatened subsistence resources by this technique is probably good policy.

An alternative means of protecting subsistence resources is to grant exclusive rights to go upon the public lands within certain well-defined ranges adjacent to particular villages to the occupants of those villages—Natives or non-Natives. If there is doubt that entrance to subsistence use areas of Alaska may be unduly limited by disposal of the lands before subsistence uses cease, it would be possible to provide for such access on a nonexclusive basis as a condition of transfers of the land from Federal ownership.

Generally, the State's management of fish and wildlife resources is excellent. However, there are important instances of conflict of Native subsistence needs, recreational needs, and commercial exploitation of fish and game. The Congress may well wish to secure the definitive position of the State relative to its approach to the management of these resources in conflict.

The granting of lands for village sites, camp sites, and subsistence use—or the protection of subsistence use by other means—will resolve the uncertainty of right to land and protect the present livelihood of Alaska Natives. Other grants of land, particularly those which include subsurface rights, may be considered a form of compensation for aboriginal rights lost. In addition, they may be the means by which Alaska Natives participate in the future economic growth of Alaska.

COMPENSATION

Compensable claims by Alaska Natives are based upon past withdrawals by the Federal Government and upon the failure of Government to protect them in the possession of their aboriginal lands from the takings of others. Similar claims have been honored for other American aborigines by the Congress and by the courts. The additional dimension of the Alaska Native land claims is that a settlement itself— by exchanging some lands for others and some land rights for others— may constitute the greatest taking of all.

When all compensable takings are considered, the problems of determining compensation are twofold: to determine the amount of compensation based upon the amount of land rights taken, the time of taking, and their market value at that time; and to determine the form and distribution of the compensation.

Amount of compensation

This basic determination may be made by decisions in two broad categories:

(1) *Time of taking.*—The dates of lands lost by specific federal withdrawals can be determined with accuracy as can the dates of lands lost by State selection. The loss of usufruct hunting and fishing rights, as well as the loss of rights in any tideland and inland waters, can be tied to the date of statehood. The loss of other claimed lands not confirmed in Native ownership can be said to have been taken on the date and by the terms of this settlement.

(2) *Market value.*—Market value of lands at the time of the Federal withdrawals, at the time of statehood, and at present can be broadly determined. Although merely a possessory right of use and occupancy, it is recognized that the market value of the "Indian title," under which Alaska Natives claim, is to be computed as though the lands were owned in fee. Thus, the market value of the land would include the value of its known mineral content although not its speculative value. Each year of delay, as the resources of Alaska are developed, results in increased land values for which compensation is sought.

Form of compensation

Money, in installments, or a lump sum, is not the sole form of compensation. Land, and interests in land, as well as participation in future revenues from land or resources may also be used alone or in combination with other compensation forms.

(1) *Grants of land as compensation*

Proposals before the Congress provide for confirming title of both surface and mineral estates of the presently existing reserves together with land grants to other Native groups. Total proposed grants for use and compensation range from no more than 20 million acres in the bill presented by the Department of the Interior to no less than 40 million acres in the bill presented by the Alaska Federation of Natives. But, as previously stated, if grants to meet subsistence needs are to be made which recognize varied subsistence ratios between people and acres of land, then a minimum of 60 million acres would be required. If land grant provisions of the settlement are computed in terms of a static, acre-per-person formula, this crucial question is overlooked. The question is not how much land per capita but rather how much land in relationship to the number of people the land will support. Similarly, if grants are to be made to provide a future economic base for Native groups, then a computation in terms of acres per person overlooks regional variation in resource endowment.

Accenting this problem are proposals calling for enrollment procedures which allow Natives away from their own villages, even in urban places, to elect enrollment in a village in which they no longer live, indeed in a village which no longer exists. Enrollments of urban Natives that inflate village populations would appear to serve no good end for the urban Native unless enormous mineral wealth exists in the land and a share is distributed to him. Enrollment of persons at now abandoned village sites or at other places they were born, such as summer fish camps, would have the unfortunate consequence of increasing the number of villages to which grants would be made, and if resettlement occurred, to which public services would have to be extended. It is conceivable, based upon the historic record that 200 to 400 old village sites could be reoccupied thereby tripling the number of rural Native places in Alaska.

Given the conflicts and complexities of grants of land as compensation a decision to make such grants should be accompanied by a consideration of making the grants to groups of villages or regional associations.

Land grants for compensation in excess of confirmation of title to village and subsistence-use sites, should be made only with recognition of intervening public and private purposes and recognition of the likely consequences of such grants.

Intervening public and private purposes include:

(a) *Lands within Federal withdrawals.*—It is likely that some of the 85 million acres now federally withdrawn may be released following review by the Public Land Law Review Commission of Federal land policy in Alaska, but at this time—unless Congress acts respecting those withdrawals—they are unavailable to the settlement.

(b) *Lands subject to State selection.*—If the State should choose only one-half the acreage to which it is entitled under the Statehood Act, its selections, if given priority, would inevitably remove most of the best lands that might otherwise go to native claimants. The 18 million acres selected thus far have already encompassed many village and subsistence-use sites, particularly those of the Tanana and Tanaina Indians of the Fairbanks and Cook Inlet regions, respectively.

(c) *Lands open to public uses.*—Finally, increasing demands of American citizens generally for outdoor recreation focus attention upon the wilderness of Alaska.

Another problem whose dimensions are not fully known is that grants as small as 50,000 acres per village would pose numerous conflicts, particularly in southwest Alaska, as to what lands would go to one of several villages in close proximity.

Great disparities appear when proposals to grant 50,000 acres, or a township, or the multiple of 500 acres per person are compared with the confirmation of title to a reserve such as the Chandalar Native Reserve of over 1 million acres. Although the most recent proposal supports grants of title to all existing reserves, earlier proposals provide for such grants only to villages organized under the Indian Reorganization Act.

Given the variations in size of Alaska Native reserves, the addition of mineral title commensurate with surface boundaries only increases inequities. It should be noted, however, that any decision against conveying mineral rights in lands granted, if existing reserves are included, would result in the loss of the only mineral rights now producing revenues for Alaska Natives—those revenues accruing to the villagers of Tyonek on the Moquawkie Reserve.

A reasonable alternative to denying or granting mineral rights in all land conveyed across the board might be one which gives the option to Native groups of accepting the mineral rights in the lands conveyed them or in sharing pro rata in future revenues from a general acreage.

Another possible consequence of granting land as compensation to Alaska Natives may be that the compensation realized will be empty of real meaning for their future. While such grants would give the fullest protection to present subsistence use, in some areas the scarcity of commercial resources would promise little prospect for modern economic growth, would provide a disincentive to move to areas of economic activity, and, in all likelihood, would diminish the amount and kind of compensation that might otherwise be awarded.

Alaska is now a viable, dynamic frontier. Its society is integrated in the best sense of that word. Should grants of blocks of land result in the kind of isolation experienced by some American Indian groups on reservations, tragic social and economic consequences to Nation, State and Alaska Natives could be expected to follow.

There are other methods of awarding compensation in the form of estates in land aside from granting lands that surround village townsite grants.

(2) *Percentage of future revenues*

One alternative is the granting of a percentage of the revenues derived from public lands. As Alaska prospers because of the wealth of its now largely undeveloped resources, the Natives of Alaska desire to share in that prosperity.

A grant of a percentage of future revenues has the advantage of retaining management of the lands in Government and avoiding the socioeconomic problems usually associated with reservations *qua* reservations.

Such revenue sharing has a precedent in State action affecting the claims. While the 5-percent grant of revenues from State lands to be selected in the future is not being made owing to its being conditioned upon a lifting of the "land freeze," it does indicate the State's willingness to consider revenue sharing.

The concept also has ample precedent in other Federal legislation. For example:

Ninety percent of the revenues from leasable minerals on Federal lands go to the State;

Twenty-five percent of the revenues from the sale of surface resources on the national forests and national wildlife refuges go to the State or its boroughs;

Seventy percent of revenues from the Pribilof Islands fur seal harvest go to the State; and

Five percent of surface resource and land sales from the public domain go to the State.

In considering the grant of a share in future revenues, the question is not only the amount of the percentage of revenues but also from whose present share of revenues—the State or Federal Government—the percentage is to be taken.

Other alternative forms of participation in future revenues include:

(*a*) Assigning revenues from mineral estates, if such estates in land are granted, on a pro rata basis to all the Natives of Alaska; this alternative would avoid the creation of "have" and "have not" villages;

(*b*) Assigning a percentage of mineral revenues from a particular source such as the Outer Continental Shelf; and

(*c*) Earmarking of a specified percentage of revenues from national forests, fish and wildlife lands, and the public domain by amending existing formulas for sharing of such revenues.

(3) *Revenues from specific lands*

An alternative form of granting land as compensation might be designation of township units on a checkerboard basis as "Native lands" and the granting of revenues realized from the sale or lease of such lands and their resources to Alaska Natives. Management and control of the lands might remain in the Federal or State government.

(4) *Land grants to towns and boroughs*

Not all of the Natives of Alaska live in rural villages. One-fourth of them live in towns and cities having populations of more than 1,000. Although their need for land may be less and different from the need for land of the rural Natives, land also may be used as a portion of the settlement for nonrural Natives.

Based upon the resident Native population of a town or village, or of an organized borough, grants of land to the governing body of the town or borough could be used for transfer to Natives of the community upon application by them, much as a veterans' preference is given in other laws. This might further facilitate grants of land for community expansion contemplated in the Statehood Act but which have not come to pass. After a designated time any lands remaining might be retained by the community for any public purpose.

(5) *Grants of money as compensation*

The most flexible form of compensation which may be used to meet the need and satisfy the claims of rural and urban Natives alike is money. Questions raised on money compensation are the method of payment and its distribution. It may be paid in lump sum or installments over a period of time. It may be distributed to individuals, Native villages or groups, or regional or statewide organizations. Present proposals call for installment payments. However, Congress may make a lump sum payment after determination of the budgetary limitations of the Federal Government and examination of the question of whether a lump sum payment would be in the best interests of the Native people. Given the pressures on the Federal Government at the moment, it is doubtful that adequate compensation can be achieved for Native rights lost by lump sum payment. The more important question than the method of payment is to whom payments are to be made.

Beneficiaries of compensation

Essential to the determination of how compensation is to be distributed is a determination of its beneficiaries.

All Alaska Natives in Alaska and other places, with but few exceptions, are slated to be beneficiaries of proposed legislation. Alaska Natives are descendants of Tlingit-Haida Indians of southeast Alaska, the Athapascans of the interior, and the Eskimos and Aleuts whose ancestors established aboriginal claim to Alaska before the purchase from Russia. Many have intermarried with non-Natives, and two principal Federal agencies providing services to Alaska Natives—the Bureau of Indian Affairs and the Public Health Service—afford such services to persons who claim to be one-quarter or more Eskimo, Indian, or Aleut. Most legislative proposals follow this definition, but one also defines a Native as one who is so regarded. Because of the difficulty of establishing blood quantum, the latter approach is probably preferable because it will allow government to deal with the Natives of Alaska on the basis of need as well as right.

Excluded from a share in compensation until the $7.5 million judgment granted them by the Court of Claims has been matched by their proportionate part of this settlement are the Tlingit-Haidas. The Tlingit-Haidas judgment is for lands taken before 1935. They also have claims pending before the Indian Claims Commission for other lands taken between 1935 and 1946. As a consequence of the land settlement, a fair compensation for these lands should be computed as a part of this settlement, and the Tlingit-Haidas should be allowed to share in that portion of the compensation without offset of the Court of Claims judgment. In addition, if equity of treatment of all aboriginal groups of Alaska is to be the rule of the Congress, there is another consideration. Indian title was confirmed by the Court of Claims in the Tlingit-Haidas of 2.6 million acres of land in southeastern Alaska which has not yet been taken. If these lands are taken as a part of the land claim settlement, compensation for them also should be a part of the settlement in which Tlingit-Haidas would share.

Not excluded from present proposals are the beneficiaries of substantial revenues, the Tanaina Natives of the village of Tyonek. Oil and gas bonuses and royalties paid them for lease of their present reserve have totaled $15 million. Whether their case warrants special treatment in the legislation is a matter for determination.

A problem area is in the matter of claims pending before the Indian Claims Commission. The sense of current land claim settlement proposals is to require the dismissal of these claims. Since decisions by Native groups themselves are to be preferred, the option should be given them to pursue their claims before the Indian Claims Commission or take under the terms of the general land claims settlement. Not all of the Alaska claims pending before the Indian Claims Commission are for possessory land rights lost. Some of them are for other damages to lives and property.

A final subject for consideration here is compensation for urban Natives. Keeping in mind that increasing numbers of Natives are moving into urban areas, that problems confronting them are often different from those of villagers and that they may not be declared as sharers in land grants made to villages and villagers, Congress may well want to give particular attention to the problems of these Natives in economic and social transition. A deficiency in all legislation thus far proposed is the lack of specific provisions to meet needs of urban Natives. Often undereducated, jobless, or in low-paying jobs, and sometimes culturally ill equipped for city life, they need, among other things, increased opportunities for education and training, extensive supportive services, and the ability to obtain housing so that they do not find themselves in ghettos. Congress might award compensation that would result in a program that would, for instance, embrace the establishment of acculturation and training centers and provide for low-interest mortgage money for housing and small business enterprises.

As computation of land grants on acres-per-person ratios may not recognize variations in needs and resources, a similar mathematical computation of money compensation on a per capita basis may not recognize urban-rural, reserve-no reserve, and other disparities.

Settlement provisions concerning the distribution of compensation and its use may provide the opportunity to resolve inequities as well as assure the realization of maximum benefits from the compensation granted.

Distribution and uses of compensation

Immediate beneficiaries of compensation awarded might be individuals, villages or other groups, regional groups or associations, or a statewide organization. All of these have been proposed in varying combinations in pending legislation. Closely related to these issues is the matter of whether, or to what extent, Congress should determine to what uses compensation could be put.

Although the ultimate beneficiaries of compensation are individuals, making them immediate recipients of per capita payments is also a possibility. Such funds would enable recipients to purchase equipment so they might compete more effectively in the harvest of resources for commercial and subsistence use, enable them to improve their dwellings, and purchase clothing for children and provide other family necessities. Although Congress has usually ruled out the use of *all* funds received in land claim settlements for per capita grants, the poverty and enormous unmet needs of Alaska Natives argue for settling at least a portion of the compensation immediately upon them as individuals.

Distribution of funds to villages is suggested because most villages lack community facilities—sewer and water, electricity, community centers, fire protection, police protection—and all the other facilities and services which most Americans take for granted. While only 29 villages presently levy taxes and spend the funds as communities, village councils are increasingly playing responsible roles in seeking community planning and improvements. Unless grants of land or money to villages were of substantial size, however, single villages would be unable to employ professional consultants to plan for and capitalize community improvements.

In order to realize the fullest benefits of grants intended for village advancement, compensation might be awarded to groups of villages formed for this purpose. The granting of compensation to groups of villages would also enable them, in some areas, to invest in or capitalize commercial resource development and to provide local jobs and a sustained economic base. Groups of urban Natives could likewise use funds awarded to help meet their many needs.

Compensation awarded a State organization of Eskimos, Indians, and Aleuts would enable it to employ skilled professionals who could be assigned to assist regional groups or villages in planning and implementation of projects and programs for general economic betterment and provide a more powerful voice for Alaska Natives. The question before the Congress might be whether it should grant compensation directly to a statewide organization or whether the decision to support such an organization should be left to regional groups or villages obtaining compensation under the act.

Although no bills before the Congress at the present time describe the uses to which compensation must be put, Congress may wish to earmark parts of the settlement for specific purposes. For instance, since present funds made available from the Congress for post-high school education always fall short of meeting the increasing needs of Alaska Natives, an educational scholarship fund might be established. Such a fund might be used, not only for college students, but for high schoolers who are unable to attend secondary schools appropriate to their needs and wants and for high school graduates who wish to attend trade schools or college preparatory schools. In none of these areas is Government now providing adequate opportunity for Alaska Natives.

Earmarking by Congress should be done only with an awareness that it is substituting its judgment for the judgment of a group of people whose rights are being compensated for and whose ability at decision making is increasingly responsible. Because Government cannot know fully all the needs, wants and aspirations of any group of people, particularly those with a different cultural heritage, Government must allow—indeed, encourage—them to be active shapers of their own future.

While present Native organizations have addressed themselves to important policy questions, they have, for the most part, not possessed budgets that would permit a wide scope of action. Two Eskimo associations in the west, however, are expected to receive a Federal grant for local economic development efforts; and the Alaska Federation of Natives has a staff of seven for a number of programs. The federation is administrator of nearly a third of a million dollar grant from the Department of Labor for the contracting of on-the-job training for 200 persons. It is also the recipient of a Foundation grant that is to be used to conduct education and training courses for village leaders.

There are many on-going programs of health, education, and welfare designed for the benefit of the Alaska Native which will not be reduced in any way by the settlement of the land claims. They may be supplemented and made more effective by the settlement, however; and the settlement will contribute to the improvement of Native circumstance and life so as to better equip them to fully share in the design and implementation of these programs.

The transition away from dependence upon special programs to full control over their own affairs is desirable. Proposals before Congress endorsed by Alaska Natives indicate they wish the path to be carefully charted in legislation rather than left to future determination by government. To devise adequate organizations and machinery to accomplish this objective is no small task.

ORGANIZATION

Three organizational functions to be considered are adjudication, administration, and management of lands and revenues. While these elements are always of importance, they are of especial importance in the proposed land claims settlement in order that the land claims settlement is not simply compensation for rights taken, but that it also makes a maximum contribution to the solution of the economic problems of Native peoples. So that the settlement bill becomes the vehicle for giving Alaska Natives an opportunity to live in full social and economic equality with other Alaskans, decisions affecting these functions become of even greater significance.

Adjudication

Many determinations which are necessary cannot be made in any proposed legislative settlement, but will have to be adjudicated by an organization designated in the legislation: the determination of eligibility of beneficiaries and the resolution of conflict between beneficiaries such as between individuals for specific hunting and fishing sites, between villages as to the bounds of village territory, and between ethnic groups as to broader territorial boundaries. If a grant of village lands were to be based on a formula of acreage per person, rather than historic use and occupancy or present need, it would give rise to a number of conflicts requiring adjudication.

The task of adjudication might be assigned to a group within the Department of the Interior, or it might be assigned to an independent commission. Both alternatives are contained in pending proposals. Of the two, an independent commission is more desirable. Due to real and imagined conflicts, the commission should not be located within the Department of the Interior since adjudication, by its very nature, requires an independence from existing institutions, particularly those that have an historic relation with the land and the people involved. Similarly, proposals which require the appointment of Alaska Natives to such a commission violate the proposition that an adjudicatory body be composed of persons without vested interests in the problem at hand. Appointments of Natives to such a commission should be neither required nor prohibited. The main office of the commission and its staff should be in Alaska. Finally, the quasi-judicial process thus established will require authority for final judicial review in the courts.

Administration

The principal administrative functions of surveying and conveying granted lands, transmitting appropriated funds, and establishing procedures for the crediting of apportioned revenues are functions now exercised by the Department of the Interior as a part of its charge to administer the public lands of the United States. These tasks, such as determining the location of village sites, hunting and fishing camp sites, and individual town lots, and the identification of Federal withdrawals or other land boundaries, are an area of expertise associated with the Bureau of Land Management. It has the technical knowledge and skilled personnel to perform the work efficiently and at a minimum cost to the Government. It is proper that this Department exercise this function with regard to any Alaska Native land claim settlement. Unlike revenues accruing from public lands which would be administered by the Bureau of Land Management, appropriations for lump sum or installment compensation could be handled directly by the Treasury Department.

Another important administrative function is that of enrollment of beneficiaries. Two alternatives for the conduct of this administrative duty are the Bureau of Indian Affairs in the Department of the Interior, and the Bureau of the Census in the Department of Commerce. No agency has fuller specific knowledge of Alaska Natives, by name and location in Alaska in 1968 than the Bureau of Indian Affairs, but the Bureau has little knowledge of Alaska Natives who have moved to other States. The coincidence of timing in this land claim settlement will probably result, however, in the Bureau of the Census having the fullest specific knowledge of Alaska Natives by name in Alaska and in other States, by the end of 1970, particularly if this task of enrollment is assigned to the Bureau of the Census as it carries out its decennial census.

Management of assets granted

The grant of assets to Native beneficiaries will require management of land and money, including the distribution of funds, capital investment, planning and project development, and reporting and auditing.

There are two basic approaches: one grants assets to beneficiaries directly and relies upon their management of their assets; the second grants assets in trust to the Secretary of the Interior for the benefit of Alaska Natives. One seeks to protect Native assets by adding another layer of decision making; the other seeks to assign full and final responsibility to the beneficiaries for the management of their assets. While the Native leadership prefers the management responsibility to be given to the people rather than to the Department of the Interior, they are also fully cognizant of the varying abilities of villages to make final management decisions respecting large expenditures of money.

Native leaders, in legislative proposals, have advocated organizations of beneficiaries for the management of assets at three levels: at the village level; in regional associations; and in a Statewide organization. They recognize that some villages have the expertise to accomplish community betterments as well as make capital investments while others do not. Further, Native leaders believe that all villages are capable of an appraisal of their own abilities, and their proposals rely upon the villages themselves to decide whether or not to invest their money in local businesses and local improvements, or to seek assistance and advice from broader regional and Statewide organizations.

One aspect of the latest legislative proposal with regard to organizations of beneficiaries offers some difficulty in that limitation is placed upon the number of associations. Additional testimony from Native groups may help determine those existing Native groups or associations to be recognized as the overall beneficiaries for their member participants. Some isolated villages, such as Inalik on Little Diomede Island, or Anaktuvuk Pass, may prefer to act independently.

Although a trust arrangement is not supported by the Native leadership, it appears they do wish the Congress to spell out the mechanisms of corporate or organizational structure for asset management which will protect both their own and the public interest.

Involved in the decisions respecting organizations for the management of assets is a search for a balanced approach which encourages independence and responsibility, but at the same time, prevents exploitation. If the perfect balance cannot be struck, it is preferable that the imbalance be in favor of Native management of their own assets and determination of their own destiny.

Auditing and reporting, as well as other functions of administration of a settlement are analyzed in the supplement to "Alaska Natives and the Land" which compares specific provisions of legislative proposals for the settlement of the claims.

A Concluding Note

It is recognized that this framework cannot respond fully to the whole range of complex questions confronting the Congress. It is hoped, however, that it succeeds in providing a useful perspective and assists in identifying key issues and considerations for future hearings and deliberations of the Congress in its resolution of the claims to land of Alaska Eskimo, Indian, and Aleut people.

O